CRUISING GUIDE TO
EASTERN FLORIDA

Sailing on Indian River

CRUISING GUIDE TO
EASTERN FLORIDA

FIFTH EDITION

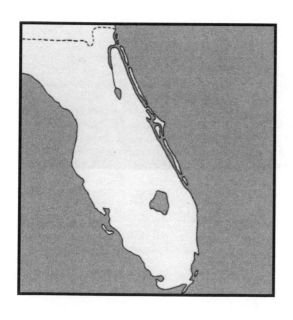

By Claiborne S. Young

PELICAN PUBLISHING COMPANY
GRETNA 2005

First edition, 1987
Second edition, 1990
Third edition, 1996
Fourth edition, 2000
Fifth edition, 2005

Maps by Virginia Ingram
All photographs by the author or Karen Ann Young

Library of Congress Cataloging-in-Publication Data

Young, Claiborne S. (Claiborne Sellars), 1951-
    Cruising guide to eastern Florida / by Claiborne S. Young.— 5th ed.
        p. cm.
    Includes bibliographical references and index.
    ISBN 9781589802551 (pbk. : alk. paper)
    1. Boats and boating—Florida—Guidebooks. 2. Marinas—Florida—Guidebooks. 3.
Florida—Guidebooks. I. Title.

    GV776.F6Y68 2004
    797.1'09759—dc22

                                                        2004011352

> Please note that channel conditions, depths, aids to navigation, and almost all on-the-water navigational data are subject to change at any time, without notice. While the author has been careful to verify first-hand all navigational information, on-the-water conditions may be quite different by the time of your cruise. Failure to follow current on-the-water reality, even when it differs from the instructions contained in this guide, can result in expensive and dangerous accidents. There are potential hazards in any cruising situation for which captains, navigators, and crew are solely responsible. Information in this guidebook is based on authoritative data available at the time of printing. Prices and hours of operation of businesses listed are subject to change without notice. Readers are asked to take this into account when consulting this guide.
>
> Neither Pelican Publishing Company nor the author make any guarantee as to the accuracy or reliability of the information contained within this guidebook and will not accept any liability for injuries or damages caused to the reader by following this data.

Printed in the United States of America
Published by Pelican Publishing Company, Inc.
1000 Burmaster Street, Gretna, Louisiana 70053

This book is dedicated

to the memory

of my father,

CLAIBORNE CLARK YOUNG

His love

for the waters

of eastern Florida

lives on!

Just as this fifth edition of *Cruising Guide to Eastern Florida* was set to be printed, Hurricanes Frances and Jeanne roared ashore within a few weeks of each other near the community of Melbourne. A number of marinas south of Titusville to Palm Beach were damaged, some severely.

After a telephone survey, we discovered that actually fewer marinas than we thought had suffered damage severe enough to completely close their fuel and/or transient docks. In many instances, even those reporting such damage were well on their way to recovery, and there was and is every reason to believe that they will be back in full operation by the time this guidebook finds its way into your hands.

Of course, there are some exceptions to this happy rule. For this reason, we *strongly* suggest that you contact your intended marina destination well ahead of time to be certain it is offering the services you and your vessel will need.

Contents

Acknowledgments

First and foremost I want to thank my first-rate, first mate Karen Ann Young, without whose help as an experienced navigator, research assistant, photographer, and partner this book would not have been possible. I would also like to extend a warm thanks to my mother for all the help with the stories of Florida in the good old days and for all the great memories.

A very special thanks goes to my tireless research assistants, Bob Horne, Bud Williams, and Kerry Horne, with whom I have been traveling the back roads and back waters of eastern Florida for many years now. We will be retelling the tales of these journeys for the rest of our lives.

I am especially grateful to my aunt, Mrs. George Young; my late uncle, Mr. George Young; and my cousin (and virtual "sister"), Ms. Dolly Young, for their long-suffering efforts to acquire research material and for many days and nights of fondly remembered lodging and fellowship.

A very warm thanks goes to Ms. Carolyn Sakowski, Ms. Virginia Ingram, Ms. Marcia Harmon, and Ms. Virginia Hege for all their assistance and encouragement in helping to realize the original dream of *Cruising Guide to Eastern Florida*.

I gratefully acknowledge the invaluable aid of the May Memorial Library of Burlington, North Carolina, in acquiring the seemingly endless list of research volumes I needed from the Florida State Library in Tallahassee. Cheryl Gilliam and Suzanne Lankford were particularly instrumental in assisting with this project.

A very special acknowledgment is gratefully paid to Mr. Larry Dennis, former boating editor of the *Florida Times-Union* in Jacksonville, Florida, for his selfless efforts to help this writer exhaustively update cruising conditions in the Jacksonville-St. Johns region. For many years now, this guide has been far the better for Larry's invaluable contributions.

Special acknowledgment should also be made to Ms. Valaire Jones and Mr. Ted Guy, both of Stuart, Florida, for keeping me up to date in regards to marinas, boatyards, and navigational conditions on the Okeechobee Waterway and the waters lying about the city of Stuart.

And, of course, there is my faithful, hardworking, super-efficient assistant, Ms. Carol Meyer, to thank. Without her invaluable aid with the day-to-day chores of this crazy business, I would have given up long ago.

Finally, I would like to thank Dr. Milburn Calhoun, Ms. Nancy Calhoun, Ms. Kathleen Calhoun Nettleton, Ms. Nina Kooij, Ms. Cynthia Williams, and all the rest of the "Pelican Bunch." It has been a genuine pleasure to work hand in hand once again with the finest publisher in the United States.

Introduction

The waters of eastern Florida are, without a doubt, the most diverse of any state's coastline in all of America. Where else can you find cruising grounds as dissimilar as the broad, unrestrained path of St. Johns River, the backwater, almost secret streams of the Okeechobee Waterway, and the passages through the awesome "condo caverns" of Hollywood and Miami? In between are many other bodies of water that offer even more diverse cruising conditions. Consider for a moment the vast, challenging reaches of Indian River, the historic waters of St. Augustine, and the swamplike rivers lying about Fernandina Beach. Captains and crew who become bored while cruising eastern Florida may as well give up the sport.

Cruising visitors to the Sunshine State's eastern coast will find many attributes to recommend the region. Dozens of protected anchorages are available to the mariner who prefers to drop the hook in the solitude of her own overnight haven rather than visit the sometimes-crowded piers of a marina. Some overnight stops, particularly in northern Florida, are found far from any trace of civilization, while others to the south may be set amidst high-rise condos and dense residential development.

Unfortunately overnight anchorage anywhere near urbanized regions in Florida now often carries the additional burden of local regulation. With the state's skyrocketing development over the past several decades, more and more cruisers have been taking to the waters of the Sunshine State. Along the way a few less-than-responsible skippers have blocked canals and channels on Florida's heavily populated waterways. Others of this ilk have beached their dinghies in residents' backyards without so much as a please or thank-you. In a classic case of governmental overreaction, overnight anchorage rules have often been adopted that this writer would prefer to describe in far saltier terms than gentility permits here. Between Jacksonville and Miami, cruisers will now find that, more often than not, overnight stops swinging on the hook are locally restricted to a seventy-two-hour period and sometimes even to forty-eight or twenty-four hours. In the body of this work, I have endeavored to point out all these restrictions, but, be advised, Florida anchorage regulations are inconsistent, in flux, and undergoing a strong challenge by local boating groups.

Florida's east coast can boast more marina facilities than any other state on the eastern seaboard. Most of these establishments are well managed and offer a variety of useful services. A surprising number are so-called "supermarinas," offering extensive dockage with full repair, refueling, and dining facilities. Many other marinas are smaller, well-run operations that depend on overnighters for their profit. Transient vessels invariably receive a warm welcome at these facilities. Finally, there are those low-key enterprises that seem to be run by someone not really interested in making a profit. Nights spent in these facilities are best soon forgotten. Fortunately, such lower-quality marinas are now seen less and less in eastern Florida.

Cruising mariners should be aware of the

high cost of transient dockage in eastern Florida. Some years ago, the state of Florida began to charge marinas a bottomland leasehold fee for the waters over which their docks are located. Coupled with high overhead and prodigious construction costs, it's not too hard to understand why dockage fees often carry a premium price, particularly in southeastern Florida.

In the past, this writer has always shied away from any listing of overnight, transient dockage rates for marinas. These sorts of charges change at such dizzying speeds that any such tabulation would be long out of date by the time the ink in this book was dry on the paper. *However,* for the first time in this new edition, we *are* going to institute a very simple transient-dockage fee-rating system. All marinas that provide overnight transient berths will be rated "above average," "average," or "below average." Hopefully, this simple system will give you at least some idea of what to expect when it comes time to pony up your overnight dockage bill.

And, while we are on the subject of new features, this 2004 edition of *Cruising Guide to Eastern Florida* introduces an element that will eventually become part of all this writer's guidebooks. Near the beginning of each chapter, we will now provide an "Anchorage Summary" and "Marina and Yacht-Club Summary." We hope this feature will allow you, gentle reader, to take a quick synopsis of what anchorages and pleasure-craft facilities are available within a particular region. If you spy an anchorage or marina that looks interesting, the summary will direct you to the appropriate pages where you will find an in-depth account of this point of interest.

The "Anchorage Summary" presents the location of the potential haven, its minimum depth, and the page numbers where you will discover our detailed description. Similarly, the "Marina and Yacht-Club Summary" lists the facility's telephone number, its location, the availability of transient dockage, the availability of gasoline and/or diesel fuel, the minimum depth of the water, and the page numbers where the marina or yacht club in question is discussed in detail. In the case of marinas and yacht clubs, it will sometimes be possible, by asking the appropriate dockmaster for a deep-water slip, to discover better soundings than the minimum depths we list in the summary.

Please note that depths given in our two summaries are minimum depths if, and only if, you keep to the channel, whether marked or otherwise. The soundings given in our summaries do not imply that shallower water is not present in the area. Cruisers who wander into nearby shoals can still run aground or worse!

Besides the watery ribbon of the Intracoastal Waterway (ICW) stretching from Fernandina Beach to Miami, the St. Johns River and the Okeechobee Waterway offer many miles of cruising off the beaten path. The St. Johns' cruisable waters stretch for some 148 nautical miles from the river's inlet at Mayport to the city of Sanford on Lake Monroe. This magnificent body of water is perhaps this coastline's greatest single find for visiting cruisers.

Offering reliable access to Florida's Gulf Coast, the Okeechobee Waterway borders on some of the least settled lands in all of Florida. A trip across this magnificent passage is surely one of the most extraordinary cruising experiences in the state.

Eastern Florida offers a number of inlets for those cruisers planning to put to sea. While some of these seaward cuts are subject to constant shoaling and strong currents, others are stable enough for strangers to use safely. The St. Johns, St. Augustine, Canaveral Barge Canal, Fort Pierce, Lake Worth, Port Everglades, and Miami Government cuts can all be used by visiting navigators with no more than the usual inlet-running problems.

Cruisers can enjoy a wide variety of shoreside attractions on the Sunshine State's east coast. Eastern Florida is justly famous for its fine beaches. Many have sand that resembles spun sugar. Year after year, thousands of tourists make the trek to Daytona, Palm Beach, Fort Lauderdale, and Miami to soak up a few rays. Pleasure-craft mariners have the opportunity to visit these popular sun-worshippers' meccas as well as more isolated shores accessible only by water.

Cruising captains traversing the Florida ICW for the first time will be impressed by the wide variety of restaurants convenient for dockside dining. Many have their own piers to which patrons are free to tie, while others are only a short walk from a local marina. While beef, chicken, and sandwiches are served by many dining establishments (and served well), fresh seafood is clearly the most popular offering in eastern Florida's restaurants. Frankly, with some exceptions noted throughout this guide, this writer and his mate often find the quality of seafood dishes in eastern Florida restaurants to be a bit inferior to that in western Florida, the Gulf states, and the Carolinas. Clearly, however, our opinion must be in the minority judging from the popularity of eastern Florida's seafood dining spots.

Disney World, the fabulous theme park near Orlando, is accessible by regular bus tour from many towns along the east coast ICW. Titusville and Melbourne are the closest ports of call, but bus service is available from as far north as St. Augustine. There is very little I can say to enhance the incredible variety of exhibits and rides Disney World and its various offsprings use to titillate the senses. Suffice it to say, those who miss this once-in-a-lifetime attraction have not really seen eastern Florida.

Another popular attraction in eastern Florida is the "Spaceport, USA" exhibit at the Kennedy Space Center. Visitors are treated to a tour of the complex's various launching ramps and the huge Vehicle Assembly Building, now used to set up the various components of the "Space" Shuttle. NASA also presents two spectacular, large-screen movies. One dramatically documents the early Space Shuttle voyages before the Challenger disaster and the other focuses on mankind's impact on the earth's environment.

When Space Shuttle flights are in the offing, cruisers have the opportunity to anchor within five miles of the launch pad for a spectacular view of the liftoffs. If you happen to be in this region when a mission is scheduled, don't miss this opportunity to witness one of America's great achievements.

Leaping back several hundred years in character, the historic communities of St. Augustine and Fernandina Beach continue to attract increasing numbers of both waterborne and landlubber tourists every year. St. Augustine enjoys a particularly rich heritage. Its story stretches back to the earliest European settlement of North America. The nearby Castillo de San Marcos is the oldest surviving military structure on the American continent from the North Pole to Mexico.

Fernandina was instrumental in the struggle to bring Spanish Florida into the American fold. Several abortive revolutions were launched from this once-lawless community.

Today, Fernandina has beautifully restored its downtown section with a turn-of-the-century theme. Visitors may delight in fond reminiscences of an earlier day.

Eastern Florida's geography is just as varied as its coastal waters. To the north, large tracts of undeveloped land border the ICW and St. Johns River. First-time visitors could be readily excused for thinking they are in the vast, swamp-filled regions of coastal Georgia and the South Carolina Low Country.

Twenty-two nautical miles south of Fernandina, the ICW crosses the easterly reaches of the mighty St. Johns River. This mammoth stream offers diverse cruising conditions of its own. Initially, the river is a tidal stream with an active seagoing fleet regularly plying the channel to Jacksonville. South of this historic city, the St. Johns broadens out into a mighty river averaging several miles in width. At Palatka, the river begins to narrow, until it becomes an almost swampy stream south of Lake George. The river's banks are absolutely beautiful. Some of the most magnificent scenery I have seen in all my travels through eastern Florida lies along the banks of the St. Johns River.

Farther south, the ICW knifes between the mainland shore and barrier islands of varying width to the east. Shoreside conditions run the gamut from land completely in its natural state to heavy residential and commercial development. Jacksonville Beach, St. Augustine, Daytona Beach, and New Smyrna Beach are significant ports of call in this region.

South of New Smyrna, the coastline begins to undergo a radical change. First the Waterway runs through the broad but shallow reaches of appropriately named Mosquito Lagoon. Then a short cruise through Haulover Canal introduces visiting cruisers to the vast reaches of Indian River. Stretching for more than one hundred nautical miles from Titusville to St. Lucie Inlet, Indian River is eastern Florida's largest single body of water, excepting the mighty St. Johns.

As Indian River meanders south, the land to the east also undergoes a transformation. The narrow barrier islands to the north strike east and become a major body of land in their own right. This region has become famous as Cape Canaveral, home of the Kennedy Space Center.

Finally, Indian River gives way to a narrow, mostly man-made passage south of St. Lucie Inlet near the coastal city of Stuart. The trans-Florida Okeechobee Waterway intersects the ICW via St. Lucie River at Stuart. This reliable passage to Florida's Gulf Coast carries the fortunate cruiser to some of the most wide open, little developed lands in the state. While much of the surrounding scenery is obscured by high dikes, there are enough gaps for one to catch glimpses of the adjoining tabletop-flat lands, teeming with cattle and sugarcane, that are so typical of central Florida.

Huge Lake Okeechobee sits astride the midpoint of the waterway bearing its name. As the second-largest freshwater lake in the nation, it is an awe-inspiring sight for first-time visitors.

Returning now to the path of the Atlantic ICW, after passing historic Jupiter Inlet Lighthouse, the Waterway flows into Lake Worth and the world-famous resort community of Palm Beach. The lake itself is visually less than exciting, but a stroll down Worth Avenue or a spin along Palm Beach's ocean-front drive is one of the most sumptuous experiences for any visitor to the Sunshine State.

The majority of the passage south from Palm Beach consists of a watery ribbon flowing through heavy residential, condominium, and commercial development. This is the famous "Gold Coast," land of the "condo caverns." Skippers cruising the Waterway between Palm Beach and Miami could be readily excused for imagining they are in a deep canyon surrounded by walls of concrete, steel, and glass.

The yachting city of Fort Lauderdale guards the northern approaches to Hollywood and Miami. Boasting the most extensive pleasure-craft services in the entire state, this fascinating community stands ready to greet visiting cruisers with a mind-boggling array of attractions. Your biggest problem may be deciding where to eat, where to berth, and what to do next.

The passage down Florida's east coast ends at Miami. Miami is clearly a city in the process of trying to pull itself up by its collective bootstraps. The city acquired a rough reputation only a few years ago, but its far-sighted community leaders have already done much to clean up Miami's waters and shoreline, though Miami's financial problems certainly continue unabated.

Even though Florida is known as the Sunshine State, more than a few clouds appear in the sky from time to time and the wind has also been known to blow. Winter is the ideal season for cruising the state's waters. While cold snaps may occasionally lower nighttime temperatures to the forties (with occasional freezes), most days are warm, bright, and shining. There is usually just enough breeze for a good sail, though stronger winds blow from time to time. Of course, an occasional shower or cold, low-pressure front, known locally as a "norther," can mar this pattern of good weather for several days, but in general a winter cruise of eastern Florida's waters is almost sure to be a delight.

Spring is also a good time to visit eastern Florida. Although temperatures and humidity are on the rise by the end of April and thundershowers occur frequently, usually these sometimes-heavy downpours last only thirty minutes or less and are followed by bright sunshine. Winds vary from almost calm to twenty-five-knot blows, but there are few major storms during the spring months.

From May through September, the summer doldrums descend on Florida. The heat and humidity are usually oppressive, to say the least. Frequent, sometimes violent, thunderstorms occur regularly during summer afternoons, accompanied by high winds and jagged lightning. Even without thunderstorms, winds can exceed fifteen knots. If you must cruise the coast of eastern Florida during the summer, my best advice is to get under way early in the morning, cruise late into the evening, and take a long siesta during the afternoon.

Fall is the most changeable season in eastern Florida. Some days seem to be born in paradise, with bright sunshine and balmy breezes. On the other hand, the months between August and November are the hurricane season. During the past several years, a goodly number of these tropical storms has developed in the waters southeast of Miami and made their way north along the eastern seaboard. No matter what the know-it-alls say, a hurricane is nothing to muck about with. If your weather radio says that one of these great storms is coming your way, head for the safest harbor you can find and don't stick your nose out until NOAA gives the all-clear!

In this guide I have endeavored to include all the information waterborne visitors may need to take full advantage of eastern Florida's tremendous cruising potential, from the Georgia state line to Miami. I have paid particular attention to anchorages, marina facilities, and danger areas. All the navigational information necessary for a successful cruise has been included. These data have been set apart in their own subsections and screened in gray for ready identification.

Each body of water has been personally visited and sounded for the latest depth information. However, remember that bottom configurations do change. Dockside depths at marinas seem to be particularly subject to rapid variation. The cruising navigator should always be equipped with the latest charts and "Notice to Mariners" before leaving the dock.

This guide is not a navigational primer and it assumes that you have a working knowledge of piloting and coastal navigation. If you don't, you should acquire these skills before tackling the coastal waters.

Generally speaking, successful navigation of eastern Florida's waterways is simply a matter of faithfully following deep, well-marked channels. This is not a coastline that requires a great deal of exotic navigation. There are many daybeacons, buoys, and other aids to help you on your voyage. These numerous navigational markings are even present on the farthest reaches of the St. Johns River and Okeechobee Waterway.

Eastern Florida skippers will find it most advantageous to keep the current chart and a pair of good binoculars in the cockpit or on the flybridge at all times. With these aids on hand, problems can be quickly resolved before you have a close encounter of the grounding kind.

The modern miracle of satellite-controlled GPS (Global Positioning System), particularly when interfaced with a laptop computer loaded with the latest digitized nautical charts, is yet another powerful navigational aid.

While GPS is not as important on the waters of Eastern Florida as it is on the western coastline of the Sunshine State, it is still an awfully nice advantage.

Since we have been talking about electronic navigation, this would seem a good time to announce a new feature in this guide. Approximate latitude and longitude positions of marinas and many anchorages have now been included within the body of this volume. All of these lat/lon positions are presented strictly for informational purposes; they must not be used as GPS or Loran way points!

Please also note that lat/lon positions for anchorages in this guide are given to help generally locate an overnight haven. With very few exceptions, mariners need not drop the hook at the exact location given. Within most creeks, bays, and other sheltered bodies of water appropriate for anchorage, there will likely be many places where you can rest comfortably and safely for the evening, swinging tranquilly on the hook.

With the phenomenal increase in popularity of computerized navigational software, we thought it important to begin providing this lat/lon information. For instance, this data can be plugged into Nobeltec's "Navigational Suite" or the "Cap'n" software, and the program will immediately place an icon on the digitized image of the appropriate nautical chart, almost exactly where the marina or anchorage you are making for is located. That's a real, on-the-water advantage, but to be repetitive, please don't use this data as simple way points.

There are several reasons why. Loran C and GPS readings give mariners a straight-line distance or bearing to the intended way-point destination. Straight-line tracks do not take into account such vagaries as shoals you will need to avoid, peninsulas you will be unable to cross, or islands that just seem to get in the way.

There are several other aspects of eastern Florida cruising that call for special caution. Much of the Waterway between Fernandina Beach and Miami is tidal (the upper Indian River and Okeechobee Waterway are two major exceptions to this fact). The tides are cause for concern not so much because of their range but because of the swiftness of the resulting currents. Unwary skippers can see their vessels quickly set outside of marked channels by these swift-moving waters. It is important to watch not only your course ahead, but also your stern in order to note quickly any leeway slippage. By following this wise practice, you can make corrections in your course before grounding depths are reached.

Eastern Florida's strong currents can cause numerous problems when coupled with the coast's many restricted bridges. While some older bridges have now been thankfully replaced by fixed, high-rise spans, there are still a host of lower clearance bridges with regulated openings between Fernandina and Miami.

Pleasure craft waiting for a bridge opening may be swept into other nearby vessels or even into the bridge's pilings or fenders by tidal currents. Traffic jams often occur near well-traveled, low-level regulated spans. Such unintended gatherings often cause rude collisions. Low-power craft should exercise extreme caution when approaching bridges in tidal sections, and all boats should be on the alert.

Additionally, several bridges along the coast have shallow depths immediately adjacent to their approach channels. Cruisers waiting for the scheduled hour may be eased onto a shoal by the strong currents without their pilots ever knowing that anything is amiss. My best advice is to stay alert, keep a watch on the sounder, and study the movements of your fellow vessels whenever you are waiting for a regulated bridge to open.

Fortunately, a move is now underway by the state of Florida to replace all bridges crossing the ICW with 65-foot, fixed, high-rise spans. While it will take many years before this ambitious goal is fully realized, more and more swing and bascule bridges are disappearing. Check out our bridge listing at the beginning of each chapter to see what new high-rises are already in place. Passing cruisers should also be ready to avoid a considerable collection of construction barges and equipment wherever new bridge construction is underway. And, for the next several years at least, the list of these building projects will be anything but short.

As if the Waterway's numerous bridge restrictions were not cause enough for delay, cruisers must also contend with official "no wake" zones. As development in eastern Florida has reached ever-higher peaks, many homes have been built along the banks of the ICW. Some of these palatial houses have their own private docks. In order to prevent having their boats rocked and their lawns sprayed with salt water by each passing vessel, residents have petitioned for and been granted "minimum wake" and "no wake" speed restrictions in ever increasing numbers during the last several years. I have tried to detail the major "no wake" areas, but be warned: new regulations are being put into effect constantly, and you can just about bet the old homeplace there will be many more by the time you read this account than there were during my research.

During the last several years, other slow-speed zones have sprung up along Florida's various coastlines for a very different reason. The fascinating, gentle sea cow known as the manatee was threatened by injuries from high-speed props as the boating population of the region rose dramatically. Numerous idle-speed zones were established in the frequent habitats of these docile creatures. Some restrictions are in effect only from November 1 to March 31, while others are year round. Please observe all manatee signs.

Since the last edition of this guide appeared, the number and length of manatee no-wake and idle-speed zones has multiplied exponentially. Many stretch along the most traveled portions of the eastern Florida ICW. Power cruisers should now include extra time in their cruising itineraries for these slow-speed sections. Frankly, with this increase, even those power captains sympathetic to the plight of the manatee may be a bit frustrated. You can only grin and bear it—slow-speed manatee zones are now part and parcel of cruising all of the Floridian coastline.

Just so you are clear on the meaning of the different types of manatee slow-speed zones in Florida, here are the official definitions according to the Florida Marine Patrol. A manatee idle-speed zone is "a zone in which boats are not permitted to go any faster than necessary to be steered." A manatee slow-speed zone is "a minimum wake zone where boats must not be on a plane and must be level in the water."

There are those in the cruising community who would argue that the danger to manatees is now past, and the proliferation of manatee no-wake zones is no longer justified. We will not take a definitive stand on that issue within these pages, but I would enthusiastically refer the reader to the Web site of Standing Watch (http://www.StandingWatch.org). These good folks have rendered great assistance by representing the cruiser's interest in the Florida state legislature (and elsewhere) and, at least in this writer's opinion, have done all of us who take to the water a great service!

All navigators should have a well-functioning depth sounder on board before leaving the dock. This is one of the most basic safety instruments in any navigator's arsenal of aids. The cruiser who does not take this elementary precaution is asking for trouble. An accurate knotmeter/log is another instrument that will prove quite useful. It is often just as important to know how far you have gone as to know what course you are following.

In this guide, lighted daybeacons are always called "flashing daybeacons." I believe this is a more descriptive term than the officially correct designation, "light," or the more colloquial expression "flasher." Also, to avoid confusion, daybeacons without lights are always referred to as "unlighted daybeacons." Similarly, lighted buoys are called "flashing buoys."

Things Change

If there is one constant in the world of cruising guides, it's that things change, sometimes before the ink is dry on the paper. We encourage our fellow cruisers to send us information about what comes to light as being new and different during their time on the waters of Eastern Florida. Have you discovered a new marina? We want to hear about it. Has there been a recent change in aids to navigation? Please let us hear from you. Are the regulations in a particular anchorage different from those we quote in the guide? Send this data our way.

Perhaps, the easiest way to send this info is via e-mail. I can be reached at the following address:

opcom@cruisingguide.com

Possibly most important of all, we also publish an extensive, on-line, quarterly newsletter,

The Salty Southeast, which allows fellow cruisers to exchange information and also helps to keep our readers updated on recent changes, modifications, and additions to the waters we cover in our guidebooks. This is a free service. All you need do to subscribe is send an e-mail containing the word, "subscribe" to opcom@cruisingguide.com.

May we also extend an invitation to visit our Web site at http://www.CruisingGuide.com. Here you will find not only information about our guidebooks, but also several photo galleries and a set of annotated links to every marina and yacht club from North Carolina to New Orleans that has a Web site. Please check us out!

And Finally

I hope you, my fellow cruisers, will find all the information you need within this guide to enjoy fully your cruise of eastern Florida's diverse waters. It is my opinion that no other coastline in America offers so many different types of cruising. Bathed in tropical sunshine and washed by the Gulf Stream's warm waters, the Sunshine State's east coast beckons. Good luck and good cruising!

CRUISING GUIDE TO
EASTERN FLORIDA

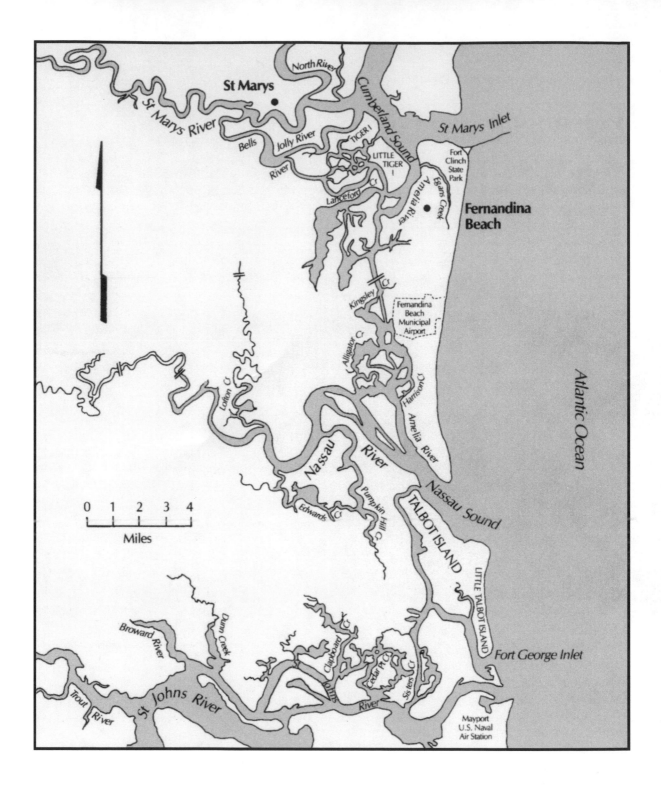

From Georgia to St. Johns River

Crossing into northernmost Florida on St. Marys River, cruising visitors encounter one of the many faces of eastern Florida's waters. Captains and crew are soon reminded of the swampy streams and winding creeks of Georgia and the South Carolina Low Country rather than the swaying palms and high-rise condos of postcard Florida. Indeed this so-called "First Coast" region of eastern Florida is quite different from the state's modern image. Don't be fooled into making a quick exit! This region is full of history and can provide rewarding cruising grounds for mariners who are willing to take the time to explore the area's many possibilities.

Eastern Florida's northernmost waters consist of the St. Marys, Amelia, Nassau, and Fort George rivers, augmented by Cumberland Sound and a host of lesser streams. These diverse water bodies are connected by the north-south route of the ICW, which provides ready access to the local rivers and creeks. Several of these streams provide reliable cruising grounds far from the beaten path and multiple anchorage possibilities.

Only two towns are to be found along this stretch. The northernmost, historic St. Marys village, sits perched on the northern shore of the river bearing the town's name. While officially a part of Georgia, the settlement has figured prominently in the history of northern Florida. Passing cruisers will be happy to learn that St. Marys boasts adequate facilities for transient craft.

The storied community of Fernandina Beach guards the intersection of Amelia and Bells rivers. The ICW tracks its way south directly abeam of the town's waterfront. Passing pleasure craft have made this charming town a port of call for many years. Fernandina is certainly one of the most historic cities in all of Florida. Its past is peppered with colorful and mysterious figures. For me, Fernandina is clearly eastern Florida's star cruising attraction on the ICW north of St. Augustine.

Anchorages abound on most of the nearby streams. Skippers can pick from a wide range, varying from small, isolated creeks to a well-known anchorage abeam of Fernandina. Marinas in the vicinity are adequate, with St. Marys, Fernandina, and Amelia Island all boasting facilities that cater to the passing cruiser. All these marinas are worthy of your attention, and two offer easy foot access to adjacent historic districts.

Bent on reaching the "condo caverns" of southern Florida, all too many cruisers lay on the throttle or crank out the jib a bit more, and pass through these northern waters with scarcely a thought. Little do they suspect that in doing so they have bypassed some of the most interesting and anchorage-rich cruising grounds on Florida's entire east coast.

Charts You will need two charts, possibly three, for complete navigational coverage of the waters between Cumberland Sound and St. Johns River:

11489—ICW chart that covers the Waterway from Georgia to a point well south of this chapter's scope. It also details the St. Marys,

Jolly, North, and Bells rivers, along with their associated creeks
11503—large-scale chart showing St. Marys Inlet and an expanded view of the region's rivers and creeks

11502—small-scale, large-format chart useful for approaching St. Marys Inlet from the ocean, showing the easternmost aid to navigation in the inlet omitted by 11503; otherwise, 11503 would better serve those navigating the inlet

Bridges

Cruisers need only concern themselves with three bridges crossing the ICW between the St. Marys and St. Johns rivers. Fortunately, the two lower-level spans open on demand.
Kingsley Creek Railway Bridge—crosses ICW at Standard Mile 721, south of unlighted daybeacon #13—Bascule—5 feet (closed)—usually open unless a train is due

but expect to wait 15-30 minutes if a train is coming
Twin Highway Amelia Island Railway Bridges—cross ICW at Standard Mile 721—Fixed—64 feet
Sisters Creek Bridge—crosses ICW at Standard Mile 740, southwest of flashing daybeacon #85—Bascule—24 feet (closed)—opens on demand

Chapter 1 Anchorage Summary

(Anchorages are listed in geographic order, moving north to south.)
St. Marys River Anchorage—located near 30 42.427 North/081 32.274 West, southwest of flashing daybeacon #10, off the southern banks of St. Marys River—8-foot depths—reviewed on pages 24, 49-50
St. Marys Village Waterfront Anchorage—located near 30 43.172 North/081 32.881 West, immediately south of the St. Marys village waterfront—10-foot depths—reviewed on pages 24-50
Jolly River Anchorage (Standard Mile 712.5)—located near 30 42.598 North/081 30.588 West, in the midwidth of the Jolly River, west of this stream's first turn to the west—10-foot depths—reviewed on pages 24, 49
North River Anchorages—located near 30 43.940 North/081 31.357 West and 30 44.334 North/081 32.380 West, on the course of the North River, which makes into the St. Marys River, north of flashing daybeacon #3—

8-foot depths—reviewed on pages 24-25, 50
Fernandina Beach Waterfront Anchorage (Standard Mile 716.5)—located near 30 40.204 North/081 28.147 West, just off the Fernandina Beach waterfront and hard by flashing daybeacon #12—6-foot depths—reviewed on pages 33-34
Bells River Anchorages (Standard Mile 716.5)—various lats/lons—located along the splintered course of Bells River—this stream intersects the ICW abeam of the Fernandina Beach waterfront, hard by flashing buoy #10—7-foot depths in the unmarked channel—reviewed on pages 40, 51-52
Waterway Anchorage (Standard Mile 718.5)—located near 30 39.623 North/081 29.160 West, south of flashing daybeacon #1, just off the western shoreline of the combined track of the Amelia River and the ICW—6-foot depths—reviewed on pages 41, 52
Jackson Creek Anchorage (Standard Mile 719.5)—near 30 38.700 North/081 29.014 West, off the ICW's eastern banks just south of

flashing daybeacon #3—6-foot depths along the northern portion of the stream's entrance only—reviewed on pages 41-42, 52-53

Upper Amelia River Anchorage (Standard Mile 720)—located near 30 38.367 North/081 29.697 West, on the waters of upper Amelia River, which intersects the ICW southwest of flashing daybeacon #7—7-foot depths—reviewed on pages 42, 53

Alligator Creek Anchorage (Standard Mile 726)—various lats/lons—entrance lies north-northeast of the ICW's unlighted daybeacon #36—6½-foot depths—reviewed on pages 43-44, 54

Nassau Sound Auxiliary Channel Anchorage (Standard Mile 730.5)—located near 30 30.709 North/081 27.658 West—westerly entrance to this stream lies east of the ICW's flashing daybeacon #48—4½-foot depths (navigationally *difficult* channel)—reviewed on pages 45, 56

Fort George River Anchorage (Standard Mile 735)—located near 30 26.460 North/081 26.285 West, just west of unlighted daybeacon #5—the westerly entrance to Fort George River, from the ICW, lies east-southeast of flashing daybeacon #72—6-foot depths in the channel—reviewed on pages 46, 56-57

Chapter 1 Marina and Yacht-Club Summary (Please note that marinas and yacht clubs are listed in geographic order, moving north to south.)

Lang's Marina—(912) 882-4452—located near 30 43.189 North/081 32.796 West, along the St. Marys village waterfront—transient dockage available—gasoline and diesel fuel available (east-side basin only)—12-foot minimum depths—reviewed on pages 25-26, 50

Fernandina Harbour Marina (Standard Mile 716.5)—(904) 491-2090—located near 30 40.209 North/081 27.968 West, along the Fernandina Beach waterfront, east of flashing daybeacon #12—transient dockage available—gasoline and diesel fuel available—5-foot minimum depths, westernmost dock *only*—reviewed on pages 31-33, 52

Amelia Island Yacht Basin (Standard Mile 720.5)—(904) 277-4615—located near 30 37.882 North/081 28.646 West—entrance to the marina's approach canal lies along the ICW's easterly banks, south of unlighted daybeacon #13, and just north of the Kingsley Creek Railway Bridge—transient dockage available—gasoline and diesel fuel available—3½-foot minimum depths—reviewed on pages 42-43

Cumberland Sound

Broad Cumberland Sound flows south from Georgia and intersects the St. Marys and Jolly rivers near the Florida border at flashing buoy #29. The sound itself is wide and unprotected, with no facilities. Winds over 15 knots can make for a dusty crossing, but on days of light breezes, the Cumberland makes a pleasant introduction to Floridian waters. The sound is traversed by a well-marked channel that splits between flashing buoys #31 and #29. The ICW continues on to the south while the eastward passage leads to St. Marys Inlet.

St. Marys River (Standard Mile 712.5) (Various Lats/Lons—see below)

The mouth of St. Marys River lies just west

of flashing buoy #29. This impressive stream serves as Florida's northern boundary. It originates in the great Okefenokee Swamp in Georgia, long a source of mystery and romance. The river is deep and easily navigable as far west as the village of St. Marys. It is reasonably well marked and has only a few shoals to trouble visitors. Cruising craft of almost any size and draft can explore the eastern portion of St. Marys River with confidence.

The St. Marys shoreline remains delightfully undeveloped saltwater marsh, except for the St. Marys village waterfront. Another exception, and an unfortunate one, is the large pulp-processing mill just north of flashing daybeacon #3. This plant is one of several in the region. When the wind is from the wrong quarter, the smell of progress is not so sweet.

The only marina on the river is located along the St. Marys village waterfront. This facility, detailed a bit later in this chapter, is anxious to attract passing cruisers and offers twin dockage basins.

Along with its two principal auxiliary waters, North and Jolly rivers, St. Marys River offers several protected overnight anchorages. The broad section of the river east of flashing daybeacon #3 is too open and too well traveled for anchorage consideration. Cruisers will do far better to consider the more sheltered spot just off the river's southerly banks, west of flashing daybeacon #10 (near 30 42.427 North/081 32.274 West). Depths run 8 feet or better, but, even here, the surrounding marsh-grass shores do not provide adequate protection in heavy weather. Be sure to anchor south of the main channel, and don't forget to show an anchor light.

Another possibility is to anchor abeam of St. Marys village (near 30 43.172 North/08132.881 West) in 10 to 20 feet of water. Protection is particularly good from northern blows, and it is a quick dinghy trip to the village. Tie your dinghy to the small pier at the public launching ramp in the midsection of the waterfront.

Jolly River Anchorage (Standard Mile 712.5) (30 42.598 North/081 30.588 West)

The northern entrance to Jolly River lies along the southerly banks of the St. Marys River, near this latter stream's meeting with the waters of Cumberland Sound. The Jolly's mouth cuts the southerly shoreline southwest of flashing daybeacon #2, itself east of Point Peter. Minimum depths of 10 feet can be carried upstream to the charted marsh island in the river's second jog to the south, located northwest of Tiger Basin. While there are a few unmarked shoals along the way, basic navigational skills should see most cruising craft safely to the waters north of the marsh island. However, because of the river's lack of markings, it is not recommended for boats over 40 feet long.

Jolly River is much larger than a quick inspection of chart 11489 might lead you to believe. Thanks to the marsh-grass shoreline, high winds can make for an uncomfortable evening swinging on the hook. However, in light or moderate breezes, Jolly River can be a delightful place to rest from your travels.

The northernmost section of the river is a bit open and should probably be bypassed in favor of the more sheltered waters upstream. A good spot to drop the hook is found in the midwidth of the stream's first cut to the west (near 30 42.598 North/081 30.588 West). Here, you can anchor in some 10 to 16 feet of water with fair protection.

North River Anchorages—Various Lats/ Lons—see below

North River makes into the northern shore of

St. Marys River opposite flashing daybeacon #3. This stream offers a sheltered place to anchor. Unfortunately, the pulp mill mentioned earlier overlooks the river's western bank at its second bend to the north. With eastern or southern winds, the plant is not too much of a problem, but in a northern blow, you might want to seek shelter elsewhere. Except for the pulp mill, North River's banks are mostly undeveloped. Marsh grass alternates with higher ground, providing an eye-pleasing mix.

Minimum depths of 8 feet can be expected along North River's centerline until you reach the charted patch of shallower water north of the pulp mill. Farther upstream, shoaling not noted on the latest edition of chart 11489 has occurred, and there are depths of 4 feet or less. Be sure to discontinue your exploration before reaching these shallows.

One of the best anchorages for visiting vessels is found in the body of North River's first bend to the north, near 30 43.940 North/081 31.357 West. Boats up to 40 feet long can

drop the hook here in some 9 to 25 feet of water with fair protection. High ground to the east gives good protection in easterly breezes.

Yet another possibility are the waters just east of the large waste-wood hill shown as a rough circle on chart 11489 (near 30 44.334 North/081 32.380 West). This high ground affords good protection in westerly winds, and depths run to about 25 feet. Owing to the large amount of anchor scope necessitated by the deep water, only boats up to 36 feet long will find adequate swinging room in this spot.

St. Marys and Associated Facilities (30 43.189 North/081 32.796 West)

St. Marys village (http://www.stmaryswelcome.com/) is one of the quaintest and most easygoing ports of call along the Georgia-Florida coastline. This writer highly recommends a stroll along its shaded streets, lined by restored historic homes.

St. Marys boasts good facilities for visiting cruisers. Lang's Marina offers two dockage basins flanking the principal St. Marys waterfront to the east and west. Overnight transients are usually accommodated at the easterly set of piers (near 30 43.189 North/081 32.796 West), which consist of modern concrete floating docks, complemented by the latest in power and fresh-water connections. Neither dockage complex offers enough shelter for really nasty weather, but at all other times, visiting cruisers can moor in either basin with reasonable confidence.

Lang's Marina does not employ a regular dockmaster. Wise mariners will call ahead and arrange for someone to meet them, particularly if their cruising itineraries call for arrival after 5 P.M. Otherwise, seek out the offices of Lang's Seafood Company, just a short hop west of the east-side dockage basin on St. Marys Street.

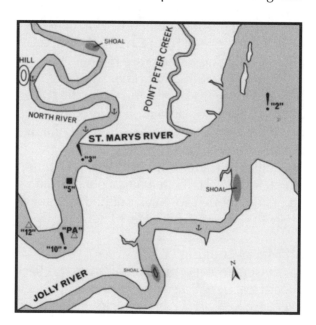

The office manager can usually help you during regular business hours.

Soundings alongside the eastern docks run 15+ feet, with at least 13 feet of water at the westerly piers. Obviously, depths are not a problem at Lang's. Gasoline and diesel fuel are available for dockside purchase at the east-side facility only. Shoreside showers are found at both locations.

The owners of Lang's Marina also operate a restaurant just behind the west-side docks. This dining attraction is reviewed below. All in all, we have always found a welcoming attitude at Lang's Marina. Of course, it would be ever-so-much nicer with a dockmaster in attendance, but this facility nevertheless allows for good, secure dockage within an easy step of St. Marys' fascinating historical district. We suggest that you coil your lines here for an evening or two and let the village's calm seep into your bones. Your cruise will be a richer experience for this side trip.

Lang's Marina (912) 882-4452

Approach depths—12+ feet
Dockside depths—15+ feet (easterly basin),
13+ feet (westerly docks)
Accepts transients—yes
Transient dockage rate—below average
Floating concrete piers—yes
Dockside power connections—30 and
    50 amps (easterly basin), 30 amps
    (westerly docks)
Dockside water connections—yes
Showers—yes (both locations)
Gasoline—yes (easterly basin only)
Diesel fuel—yes (easterly basin only)
Restaurant—many nearby

St. Marys Dining

Ever since this writer has had the good fortune to begin visiting St. Marys village, it has always been apparent that volunteers and the local business people have contributed greatly to the renovation, restoration, and revitalization of the downtown business district. There are places to shop, dreamlike historic homes to view, and excellent restaurants to enjoy while you take a break from your life on the water.

If you arrive in downtown St. Marys with a good appetite, then, as the saying goes, you've come to the right place. Let's start off with some good old down-South-style seafood. As mentioned earlier, the good folks who own and operate Lang's Marina (and, perhaps more importantly in this instance, Lang's Seafood Company) also maintain Lang's Marina Restaurant (912-882-4432), located just behind the west-side dockage complex on St. Marys Street. Several years ago, we were lucky enough to arrive on all-you-can-eat shrimp night. It tasted as if the shrimp had just been unloaded from the boat. Bob Horne, my ace research assistant, was equally taken with his blackened grouper. Lang's Marina Restaurant is highly recommended by this writer.

If you prefer something a little elegant, or even dining outside under an arbor, then consider Pauly's Cafe (102 Osborne Street, 912-882-3944). Lunches here are memorable.

Another good local choice is the Colonial Dinner House (711 Osborne Street, 912-882-2003). This dining attraction merged with the old Whispers Coffee House & Café after a disastrous fire.

Seagle's Restaurant (105 West Osborne Street, 912-882-4187) remains a popular dining attraction, though we have not had the opportunity to review the bill of fare lately.

St. Marys Lodging

Cruisers looking for a break from the live-aboard regime will also find much to pique their interest in St. Marys. We would first recommend the Spencer House Inn Bed and Breakfast, guarding the corner of Osborne and Bryant streets (200 Osborne Street, 912-882-1872, http://www.spencerhouseinn.com). This massive three-story structure features some of the most delightful rooms that this writer has had the good fortune to occupy. They boast period antiques, and there are also white porches with cypress rockers that overlook Osborne Street. This is a great spot to relax with an afternoon or evening cocktail. The breakfast is all that a hearty appetite could ask for, and there is even a resident ghost! The 1872 edifice served as a hotel in its previous life. After a stint as an office building, it was magnificently restored into the handsome inn that greets modern-day visitors. It was further renovated by the present owners in 1995, and this superfriendly husband-and-wife innkeeper duo is definitely in the right business. They will be glad to pick up and deliver cruising guests to and from Lang's Marina.

The Goodbread House (912-882-7490) is found just across Osborne Street from Spencer House. This Victorian-era bed-and-breakfast inn prides itself on being the county's first modern inn of this genre. Built in 1870, the old homeplace features seven fireplaces (two in bathrooms) and wide pine floors. The warmth of the welcome is all one could ask for.

The Riverview Hotel (912-882-3242) is located atop Seagle's Restaurant at the corner of Osborne and St. Marys streets, only a short walk east of Lang's Marina docks. Built in 1916 and renovated in 1976, the hotel offers 18 second-story guest rooms and a large veranda.

Downtown St. Marys

There is much for visiting cruisers to see and do in the St. Marys historic business district.

There are any number of fine gift and antique shops, including the Blue Goose (126 Osborne Street, 912-673-6828). Anyone interested in coastal Georgia literature will want to visit Once Upon a Bookstore, just south of Spencer House (110 Osborne Street, 912-882-7350).

Sightseers and history buffs will want to acquaint themselves with the Orange Hall Museum House (912-576-3644) and the St. Marys Welcome Center (406 Osborne Street, 912-882-4000). Simply walk north on Osborne Street and watch to your left for impressive Orange Hall. This magnificent homeplace, circa 1820, is a wonderful example of Greek Revival architecture. Notice the huge Doric columns and wide front veranda with steps leading up to the second-floor main entrance. The welcome center is just across the street from Orange Hall.

The Orange Hall Museum House is open Monday through Saturday, 9 A.M. to 5 P.M., and Sunday, 1 to 5 P.M. Guided tours are available during these hours.

Construction is now complete on a new National Park Service-sponsored museum (912-882-4336) devoted to the fascinating history of nearby Cumberland Island. This attraction is located on Osborne Street in downtown St. Marys, diagonally across from Spencer House Inn. It is open to the public all year (except Christmas day), 1:00 P.M. to 4:30 P.M. daily.

Visitors should also note that a National Park Service boat leaves regularly from the St. Marys Waterfront to visit fascinating Cumberland Island National Park (888-817-3421, http://www.nps.gov/cuis/). This most noteworthy attraction is covered in detail within this writer's *Cruising Guide to Coastal South Carolina and Georgia*.

Mariners interested in learning more about their underwater counterparts will want to make a call at the Submarine Museum (102 West St. Marys Street, 912-882-ASUB, http://stmaryssubmuseum.com/). Sponsored by submariner veterans who once served at the nearby Kings Bay Submarine Base, this small facility is fascinating. It is open Tuesday through Saturday, 10 A.M. to 4 P.M., and Sunday, 1 to 5 P.M.

Clearly, St. Marys has much to offer considering its small size. Every single cruiser is urged to take advantage of the village's considerable charms and abundant attractions before heading south into the waters of the Sunshine State.

St. Marys History The town of St. Marys stands perched upon a bluff that was once the site of an Indian village. An old legend relates that the tribe was ruled by a queen who was reputed to be the most beautiful Native American in the thirteen original colonies.

The lands lying about St. Marys were part of the so-called debatable land, which was contended for by both England and Spain until the Georgia line was extended south to St. Marys River following the Revolution.

In 1787, a group of citizens purchased property on St. Marys River for the express purpose of founding a port. The town's original industry consisted of cutting and exporting lumber. Its population was swelled by the arrival of French-speaking Acadians and refugees from Santo Domingo.

One of the most prominent early citizens of St. Marys was Maj. Archibald Clark. He moved to the new port in 1802 and opened a law office. Aaron Burr was entertained in Clark's home when he visited St. Marys in 1804. Clark established a host of sawmills in and around the young community. His industry and enterprise went a long way toward ensuring the port's early prosperity.

During the War of 1812, a fort was established at St. Marys. This military depot was overwhelmed by invading English forces in 1815. Strangely enough, the war had already ended at that point, but the word had not reached either the invaders or the defenders. During the occupation, Major Clark was taken prisoner because of his refusal to disclose the town treasury's hiding place. When it became known that the war was at a negotiated end, Clark was released and became even more of a local hero.

St. Marys grew ever more prosperous in the antebellum period. Early accounts note that cotton, rice, sugarcane, corn, peaches, oranges, lemons, and figs were some of the town's exports. By the 1820s, St. Marys had become the business and cultural center of southeastern Georgia. In 1828, the old Union Church was reorganized as Independent Presbyterian Church. This stately white structure survives to this day (just across Conyers Street from present-day Orange Hall). By 1829, the church members had built a parsonage, which became known as Orange Hall. This classic Greek Revival structure is now a house museum and open to the public (see above). Carved over the fireplace in Orange Hall are words that embody the special tranquility of this peaceful community:

> Happy is the home that shelters a friend.
> O turn thy rudder thitherward awhile,
> Here may the storm-beat vessel safely ryde!
> This is the port of rest from troublous toyle,
> The World's sweet Inn from pain and
>   wearisome turmoyle.

By the late 1840s, Georgia's new railroads

Fort Clinch, St. Marys Inlet

were stealing much of the commercial traffic from St. Marys' waterfront. The town was abandoned with the arrival of Union forces during the Civil War. The invaders stabled horses in the Independent Presbyterian Church, but fortunately most of the historic buildings in the village survived the war.

With her commercial prosperity gone, St. Marys became a sleepy little fishing village. The arrival of the Gilman Paper Company in 1945 breathed some new life into the local economy, even if it did little good for the citizens' breathing.

Modern visitors to downtown St. Marys will find a beautiful village still blessed with many historic buildings. Notice the now-dead hulk of the old oak tree in the middle of Osborne Street. It is called the "Washington Oak," and according to tradition, it was planted in 1799 to commemorate our first president's death.

Whether you stop only for a night or tarry for a week, there are few places where you could spend your time more profitably than tranquil St. Marys.

St. Marys Inlet (Standard Mile 714)

Well marked and mostly reliable, St. Marys Inlet is eastern Florida's northernmost seaward cut. A short jog east of flashing buoy #25, the ICW takes a sharp turn to the south. Cruisers can abandon the Waterway and continue east-southeast past #25 into the well-outlined inlet channel.

The inlet's mouth is guarded by twin stone jetties to the north and south, which have apparently succeeded in stabilizing the channel. Aids to navigation are charted on chart 11503 and 11502, a clear indication of stable bottom strata. No other reliable seaward passage is to be found north of the St. Johns, so if you are planning to set your course toward the briny blue, the St. Marys Inlet would be a good bet.

Fort Clinch

Fort Clinch is readily visible along St.

Florida Petroleum Company, Fernandina Beach

Marys Inlet's southerly banks, south of flashing buoy #22. Fort Clinch was built by the federal government in 1847 to guard this seaward cut. As far as this writer has been able to determine, the fort never fired a shot in anger until it was seized by Florida state troops in 1861 at the beginning of the War Between the States. In March 1862, with the approach of a superior Union force, the Confederates abandoned Fort Clinch and it was subsequently occupied by Northern forces. A federal garrison was maintained at the fort until 1869, when it was withdrawn.

Until 1926, when the fort was sold, eventually to become a state park, the old fortification was used for a variety of purposes ranging from a marine hospital to barracks for troops involved in the Spanish-American war. Today the American flag still waves proudly from Fort Clinch Park, a monument to a military installation that was rarely used or needed.

Florida Petroleum Company (Standard Mile 716)

The first facility visiting cruisers will encounter on Floridian waters is Florida Petroleum Company (904-261-3291). Located along the Waterway's eastern shore, nearly abeam of flashing buoy #10, this facility is primarily a diesel refueling stop. While many commercial craft make use of this fuel pier, pleasure craft are welcomed as well. No other services for cruising craft are offered.

The docks at Florida Petroleum Company are rather high, and the pilings, particularly at low water, present a barnacle-encrusted face. Added to these difficulties are the incredibly swift tidal currents that plague the entire Fernandina Beach waterfront. Obviously you should approach the Florida Petroleum Company docks with caution.

Fernandina Beach (Standard Mile 716.5) (http://www.aifby.com)

After turning south from Cumberland Sound and the westerly reaches of St. Marys Inlet, the ICW soon approaches the Fernandina Beach waterfront near flashing buoy #10. Along the way you will pass one of the town's two pulp mills and a containerized-cargo-ship loading wharf, southeast of flashing buoy #8. If you're lucky, the wind won't be blowing from the east as you pass the paper mill!

The town of Fernandina Beach is quite simply one of the most charming and historically interesting communities in all of Florida. Whether your taste runs to good dining, interesting shops, or even historic bed-and-breakfast inns, Fernandina will not be a disappointment. Be sure to leave sufficient time in your cruising plans to take full advantage of this community's many attractions.

Fernandina Harbour Marina (30 40.209 North/081 27.968 West)

Fernandina Harbour Marina, found just east of flashing daybeacon #12, is downtown Fernandina Beach's only facility offering dockage for cruising craft. It sits square in the village's exciting historic district. Fernandina Harbour has gone through some difficult times since the 1980s. Then, the entire harbor was rebuilt in a first-class fashion with all-new, floating-concrete-decked piers and a completely dredged basin. An impressive on-the-water restaurant and shopping complex were added as well, and the new marina seemed bent on a successful future.

Unfortunately, it was not long before the swiftly moving tidal currents began to reassert themselves, and the marina's inner slips shoaled badly. During any number of visits, we have watched sadly from the windows of adjacent Brett's Waterway Cafe as every boat in the harbor sat in the mud at low tide.

Happily, the long, outer-face dock still maintains 15+ on its western side and 5- to 10-foot depths on its inner (eastern) face. Transients are readily accepted on this outer dock (both sides), and every berth features full power and water connections. Take the swiftly moving waters into account as you approach the dock, and have your largest fenders ready for action.

The on-site showers and Laundromat are in good shape and located in a separate building bordering the southeastern portion of the harbor. Fernandina Harbour features full fueling services and a tiny ship's store doubling as the dockmaster's office. On-line mariners can also hook up their portable computers here to download e-mail. The harbormaster can sometimes arrange for mechanical repairs through independent local contractors. A few basic food supplies and some absolutely top-notch fresh seafood can be purchased at the Atlantic Seafood and Fish Market (904-261-4302) in the southeastern corner of the complex. Taxi service is readily available (Benjamin's Taxi, 904-261-7278) to transport visiting cruisers to several supermarkets a few miles from the downtown district.

The on-site Bretts Waterway Cafe (904-261-2660) is absolutely superb. Often we find large restaurants located amidst marinas to be of mediocre quality, at best, but Bretts is a fortunate exception. Recently, this writer was absolutely captivated by his fresh, broiled-grouper sandwich, as was his first-rate first

Fernandina Harbour Marina

mate with her shrimp salad. The portions were ample and the service was all that one could ask. We found the outside tables overlooking the harbor to be delightful in fair weather. In short, this writer highly recommends Bretts for cruisers willing to foot a moderate (but not trivial) bill for dining ashore. After dinner, be sure to check out the adjacent Front and Centre gift shop.

Longtime Atlantic ICW veterans will remember Fernandina Harbour Marina as the one-time site of the (then) only on-the-water welcome station along the eastern seaboard. Every year Waterway cruisers looked for the teepee-shaped brick building as they passed. Visitors could expect a glass of cold, fresh Florida orange juice and a warm welcome. Unfortunately, this happy structure was displaced by the new marina and is now only a distant memory. North Carolina can now lay claim to the only on-the-water welcome center along the path of the Atlantic Intracoastal Waterway.

Fernandina Harbour Marina (904) 491-2090

Approach depths—12+ feet (western face
   of outer dock)
5-10 feet (eastern face of outer dock)
Dockside depths—15+ feet (western face
   of outer dock)
5-10 feet (eastern face of outer dock)
1-2 feet (inner slips)
Accepts transients—yes
Transient dockage fee—average
Floating concrete piers—yes
Dockside power connections—30 and 50 amp
Dockside water connections—yes
Showers—yes
Laundromat—yes
Gasoline—yes
Diesel fuel—yes
Mechanical repairs—yes (independent
   contractors)
Ship's store—yes (small)
Restaurant—on site and many others nearby

Fernandina Beach Anchorage and Dinghy Dockage (30 40.204 North/081 28.147 West)

Cruisers often anchor hard by Fernandina Harbour Marina in the deep water around flashing daybeacon #12. For those who enjoy anchoring out, this spot delightfully combines the privacy of swinging on the hook with the convenience of having downtown Fernandina only a short dinghy ride away. You can anchor in some 6 to 15 feet of water with good holding ground, but be sure to set your hook so as to swing well clear of the Waterway channel. We have always noticed a bit of "rock and roll" when anchored on these waters, but usually not enough to mar a good overnight stay.

Mariners dropping the hook here have access to a most convenient dinghy dock at adjacent Fernandina Harbour Marina. For a

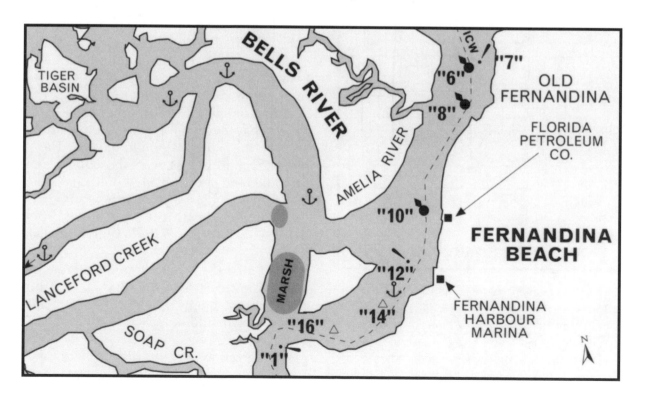

modest fee of $5 per day, those swinging at anchor can make use of the marina facilities including showers, trash disposal, and the on-site Laundromat. Visitors not paying the daily fee can tie up for a maximum of six hours. With the nearby dinghy dock, this anchorage can boast some truly unusual amenities for a very moderate charge. While protection is not adequate against heavy winds, particularly from the north and west, the town's high ground gives fair protection from easterly breezes.

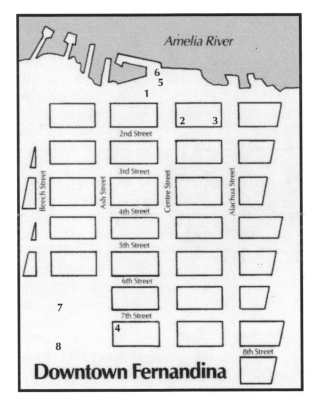

1 Chamber of Commerce
2 The Palace
3 Crab Trap
4 Bailey House Inn
5 Bretts Waterway Cafe
6 Fernandina Harbour Marina
7 Fairbanks House
8 Beech Street Grill

Downtown Fernandina Beach

Downtown Fernandina, just east of the marina docks, has been lovingly restored over the past several decades. Aluminum and ceramic panels have been removed to reveal the facades of a bygone era. Centre Street (the main street) cannot help but remind visitors of a 1900 community in its heyday. The fifty-block downtown area is now on the National Register of Historic Places.

If you arrive during business hours, consider beginning your visit to Fernandina Beach with a stop at the Chamber of Commerce (904-261-3248) in the renovated railway depot on Centre Street, just east of the marina docks. This structure once served as the depot for the first cross-Florida railway system. The staff are eager to greet visitors and will provide you with any information you may need including a brochure outlining a fascinating walking tour of the historic district.

Moving farther east on Centre Street and its various tributaries, visitors will find downtown Fernandina's renovated buildings to contain a delightful collection of restaurants and shops—everything from sedate bookstores to the oldest saloon in Florida. Those interested in local history, or those just wanting something new to read, should check out The Book Loft (214 Centre Street, 904-261-8991), Books Plus (215 Centre Street, 904-261-0303), and The Sailor's Wife (310 Ash Street, 904-261-5845).

Don't miss the Amelia Island Coffee Cafe at 207 Centre Street (904-321-2111). This shop features yummy pastries, ice cream, and sandwiches in addition to great coffee, cappuccino, and espresso.

Another attraction of note in downtown Fernandina is the Amelia Island History

Fernandina Beach Chamber of Commerce, downtown Fernandina Beach

Museum (233 South Third Street, 904-261-7378). This worthwhile point of interest is lodged in an old brick building at the intersection of Third and Cedar streets, four blocks from Centre Street. Here, you can view some of the memorabilia from Fernandina and Amelia Island's fascinating history, recounted in this guide. Tours of both the self-guided and hosted variety can be arranged. The museum is well worth your time. Ask at the Chamber of Commerce for directions.

Cruising visitors should also take into account Fernandina Beach's several annual festivals. Probably the largest of these celebrations is the Isle of Eight Flags Shrimp Festival, usually held the first weekend in May. June brings on the annual Kingfish tournament and there is also a "Heritage Festival" in November celebrating the village's rich history. If you can time your arrival to coincide with any of these events, your cruise will be far richer for the effort.

Fernandina Beach Restaurants

Dining will never, ever become dull in downtown Fernandina Beach. In addition to Bretts Waterway Cafe (described above) there are more places to slake a healthy appetite in downtown Fernandina than you can imagine. Some of this writer's personal favorites are listed below.

Any discussion of fine dining in Fernandina Beach must begin with a mention of Beech Street Grill (801 Beech Street, 904-277-3662). This outstanding restaurant, housed in a historic, restored "conch house," has a varied and imaginative menu. Many seafood dishes are seasoned with fresh-cut herbs, sauces special to this restaurant, and heavenly chutneys. The atmosphere is surprisingly easygoing but the prices could not be described as anything approaching inexpensive. Nevertheless, you'll find this writer sampling the fare at Beech Street Grill during each and every visit to Fernandina. Ahhh, my mouth is watering now.

The Marina Restaurant, just a few steps from Fernandina Harbour, at 101 Centre Street (904-261-5310), was once one of the places to avoid if you wanted a good meal. Happily, new management took over some years ago, and this dining spot has since been awarded a five-star rating by the *Florida Times-Union*.

Among all the other dining choices in downtown Fernandina, there are two veterans that still demand attention. The Crab Trap is found in a converted warehouse at 31 North Second Street (904-261-4749), just three blocks from the marina docks. Of the many seafood restaurants that I have reviewed, the Crab Trap clearly serves some of the best fried catch of the day that it has been my pleasure to enjoy. The interior decor features bare brick walls and a long bar, which sweeps across the left wall. With its usual warm and convivial crowd, the Crab Trap is sure to be a hit with any passing cruiser.

Downtown Fernandina Beach

The Palace Saloon, at 117 Centre Street (904-491-3332), claims to be the oldest saloon in Florida. Built in 1878, this highly interesting restaurant features a handcarved bar, original mural paintings, and antique furniture.

Fernandina Beach Lodging

For those cruisers who wish to take a break from the live-aboard routine, the Fernandina Beach historic district has (at least) two choices for shoreside lodging that can only be described with that often overused but in this case completely appropriate word, "fantastic." The Fairbanks House (227 South Seventh Street, Fernandina Beach, Florida 32034, 904-277-0500) is, quite simply, one of the most impressive bed-and-breakfast inns that this writer has ever reviewed. When we are not cruising, my first-rate first mate and I are "inn hoppers." Believe you me, we've seen and lodged at some wonderful inns, but few if any have matched the Fairbanks House for its sheer magnificence.

Palace Saloon, downtown Fernandina Beach

Housed in a historic home originally built in 1885 by architect Robert Schuyler, the structure has had a long and interesting history. Today, in its incarnation as a hostelry, the inn boasts a rich harmony that few can match. The foyer features intricately carved woodwork leading to the sweeping staircase, while the dining room boasts a fireplace tiled with scenes from Shakespeare's works and Aesop's fables. The rooms are all impeccably furnished with four-poster, canopied beds. Some feature oversized bathrooms with large, sunken tubs and all have cable television, telephones, and air conditioning. A European-style breakfast is included in the price of each room. Guests can dine either in the formal dining room or, during fair weather, on one of the inn's four piazzas. If by now you have detected a certain rampant enthusiasm on this writer's part for the Fairbanks House, then you are on the right track. Even if you normally reside aboard, give this inn a try. You won't be sorry for the extra effort.

The charming Bailey House Bed and Breakfast at 28 South Seventh Street (904-261-5390) is found within an easy walk from the town marina. This inn is just the ticket for those who want to slip back to an earlier, simpler era. Housed in a restored Victorian home and delightfully furnished with period antiques, Bailey House is informal and relaxed. Each visitor is treated to a sumptuous breakfast.

For those with more mainstream lodging tastes, a Hampton Inn and Suites is now located in downtown Fernandina Beach, immediately behind the chamber of commerce. This member of the well-thought-of hotel chain is extremely convenient for cruisers berthing at Fernandina Harbour Marina.

Fernandina History   Without a doubt, Fernandina Beach is one of the most historic communities in all of Florida. Colorful figures and events that helped to shape Florida's destiny fill Fernandina's story like grains of sand in an hourglass. With present-day Fernandina's respect for its history, a visit to this wonderful

The Fairbanks House, Fernandina Beach

city is like taking a trip into eastern Florida's past.

Fernandina was not clearly defined as a separate community until the early nineteenth century, so the early history of the region is tied to that of Amelia Island. Amelia was visited by the French explorer and colonist Jean Ribault in 1562, but it was not until the Spanish established St. Augustine in 1565 that any attempt at permanent settlement was made.

In 1811, under instructions from Spanish governor Enrique, Surveyor Gen. George Clarke laid out the original town of Fernandina, which was located in the section marked as "Old Fernandina" on chart 11489. Fernandina was to know its greatest political prominence during the next fifty years.

Even before the town's official birth, the Jefferson embargo of 1807 had brought new life to the region. With its excellent harbor, Fernandina became a natural base for smuggling slaves and other contraband north into the young United States.

Spanish rule following the Revolutionary War was never very strong, and Florida became a popular destination for vagrants, runaway slaves, and pirates. Partly to suppress these undesirables and partly because of land hunger, Pres. James Madison schemed with the so-called Florida patriots to bring about Spanish cession of Florida. Failing peaceful means, the patriots were ready to take the territory by force. None of these eastern Florida revolutions was successful, and most ended in tragedy.

One such attempt was hatched by Gen. George Matthews, special emissary of President Madison and his secretary of state, James Monroe. Matthews gathered supporters in nearby St. Marys and recruited popular John Houston McIntosh as a nineteenth-century version of a "front man." On March 13, 1811, a force of some seventy Georgians and nine Floridians moved into Florida and raised the flag of the Florida patriots. Fernandina was established as the temporary capital of eastern Florida, and McIntosh was elected governor of the territory. Matthews' forces next moved against St. Augustine but were stopped short by the fortifications in the old capital city. Shortly thereafter Matthews died and the revolution seemed to take a downhill slide.

A combination of Spanish soldiers and loyal Indians defeated the patriot forces on all fronts, and Madison was forced to disavow the revolution. He dispatched several more special commissioners, but they served little purpose except to prolong the incident. Finally, in March 1812, prompted by congressional fears of English intervention, the patriots withdrew from Fernandina to the northern shores of the St.

Marys River; the East Florida Rebellion was over.

There followed a period of limbo in which Fernandina was only nominally governed by the weak Spanish rule in St. Augustine. It was during this time that two of the most colorful figures in Fernandina's history put in their appearance.

In June 1817 Gregor McGregor, pirate, freebooter, and rascal, landed in Fernandina and raised the Green Cross of Florida in yet another attempt to secure Florida from Spain. McGregor advanced on Fernandina with such bravado that the small Spanish garrison surrendered without resistance. With only a few troops under his command, he declared the east coast of Florida blockaded from Fernandina to the Perdido River. When the hoped-for support from the north did not materialize, McGregor apparently lost heart and quietly slipped away.

Two days later Luis Aury, another pirate and brigand, arrived, raised the flag of the Republic of Mexico, and took over the local government with little pretense of legality. Soon pirates, privateers, and slave traders were making unrestricted use of Fernandina's harbor.

The young United States government soon had enough of Aury. In November 1817 an American naval squadron landed 200 troops on Amelia Island. Like McGregor, Aury hauled down his flag and slunk away in the night. American troops occupied Amelia Island in a state of so-called protective custody until Florida came under direct American rule.

Eventually, in 1821, Spain did cede Florida to the United States. During the early years of American rule, rice and Sea Island cotton were grown successfully on Amelia Island. In spite of these agricultural efforts, however, the economy of Fernandina entered a troubled period. The emerging prominence of Jacksonville as a major shipping port robbed Fernandina of most waterborne commerce, so that by 1840 it was reported that barely one ship a year was making use of Amelia's fine harbor.

The economy was boosted in the 1850s, when the town was moved to its present site after the terminus of Florida's first cross-state railroad was established on Amelia island.

Had the Civil War not interrupted the town's growth, Fernandina might have become a major port on the northern Florida coast. By January 1861 Fernandina was suffering under a Federal blockade, and Confederates feared an invasion by Northern forces. Despite all the talk of mounting a defense, very little preparation was actually undertaken, and when Union forces did arrive in March of the same year, the Southern troops left without a shot having been fired.

Fernandina entered a new era beginning in 1875, when wealthy tourists from the north discovered Florida. Visitors flocked to Fernandina. Two elegant hotels welcomed guests, and the local economy boomed with the influx of capital.

Fernandina's boom ended as Henry Flagler established rail service to southern Florida during the early 1900s. Eastern Florida's "First Coast" was temporarily abandoned by the tourists, and it seemed as if Fernandina would become a quiet village again.

Several events in the twentieth century, however, served to spur Fernandina into a new era of progress. Early in the century the modern shrimp industry was pioneered in Fernandina by Mike Salvador, Salvatore Versaggi, and Antonio Poli. These three enterprising individuals invented the boom-net shrimping assembly that is still seen on trawlers all along the eastern seaboard. In the 1930s two pulp mills were established near Fernandina. These two plants brought much-needed local employment to the island, even if they have lent their particular odor to the region ever since. Finally, with the crowding of southern Florida since the 1970s, tourists have begun to discover anew the delights of the "First Coast." Helped by the delightful renovation of Fernandina's historic district, the town is today quickly becoming one of the most prized stops on the entire Florida ICW.

It would be an easy task to continue listing Fernandina's many attractions, but it's time to continue our southward trek down the ICW. Perhaps by now you have acquired the idea that Fernandina is indeed a port of call that cruisers bypass at their considerable loss. If so, you have the right impression.

Bells River Anchorage (Standard Mile 716.5) (Various Lats/Lons—see below)

Bells River makes into the western shores of Amelia River, west of flashing buoy #10, abeam of the Fernandina waterfront. Though the stream's all-natural, marshy shores lack any facilities, they provide the best overnight anchorage in the region. Minimum depths of 8 feet can be held well upstream short of Tiger Basin. Craft less than 45 feet long can cruise the river with confidence. There are a few unmarked shoals to avoid, but careful navigators should be able to bypass these hazards successfully. Be sure to read the navigational section on Bells River later in this chapter before attempting first-time entry.

The river's shores are composed almost exclusively of saltwater marsh, which gives only minimal protection in heavy weather. In light to moderate airs, however, Bells River is an ideal spot to spend an evening.

Some visiting cruisers have been known to anchor just north of the Bells River-Lanceford Creek junction, near 30 40.700 North/081 28.777 West. While craft up to 45 feet can drop the hook here amidst depths of 8 to 15 feet, they will find better protection on the waters just short of the stream's first sharp bend to the west, near 30 41.366 North/081 29.084 West. Boats up to 42 feet will have plenty of swinging room in this second haven, and the higher ground of Little Tiger Island to the north gives some protection from northerly blows. Depths run an impressive 20+ feet, so it will take a lot of anchor rode to maintain a good 6 to 1 scope.

Craft under 38 feet, drawing 5 feet or less, may also consider anchoring in the river's northern fork short of the first charted northwesterly offshoot (near 30 41.316 North/081 29.583 West). The stream narrows a bit at this point, and protection from inclement weather improves correspondingly. Depths on this portion of the river are considerably shallower than the soundings shown on chart 11489. Still, you can pretty much count on finding at least 7 to 8 feet of water.

Adventurous captains who pilot boats under 38 feet that draw 5 feet or less might consider following the main southerly branch of Bells River to the west for some 3 nautical miles until coming abeam of the high ground near the charted village of Chester (near 30 41.135 North/081 32.239 West). Here you can drop the hook in some 9 feet of water in about as secure a spot as you are likely to find. The heavily wooded southern banks and the high ground of Martins Island to the northeast afford excellent protection from all but strong easterly blows.

Lanceford Creek

Lanceford Creek intersects Bells River on

its western bank near the larger stream's easterly reaches. For many years now, this writer has recommended that captains piloting craft drawing more than 2½ feet not attempt entry into this stream. The mouth has shoaled considerably and is quite shallow at low or even midtide. All cruisers would do far better to stick with the deeper waters of Bells River.

Waterway Anchorage (Standard Mile 718.5) (30 39.623 North/081 29.160 West)

Back on the southerly path of the ICW, some boats anchor in the deep water abutting the Waterway's western shoreline, south of flashing daybeacon #1. Minimum 6-foot depths run to within 50 yards of the low-tide waterline on the westerly banks. While there is certainly sufficient swinging room for almost any size craft, you will be exposed to the wake of all passing vessels, and a southerly blow can make your evening downright uncomfortable

Jackson Creek Anchorage (Standard Mile 719.5) (30 38.700 North/081 29.014 West)

Jackson Creek breaks off from the Waterway's eastern banks just south of flashing daybeacon #3. Minimum depths of 6 feet can be carried at the creek's entrance by successfully avoiding the considerable shoal lying along the southern shore. These shallows seem to be building to the north, and have even further reduced the available deepwater swinging room during the past several years.

If you enter Jackson Creek at high tide, it is quite easy to overestimate the swinging room you will have. At low water the shallows on the southern banks bare completely, and you are left in a considerably smaller body of water

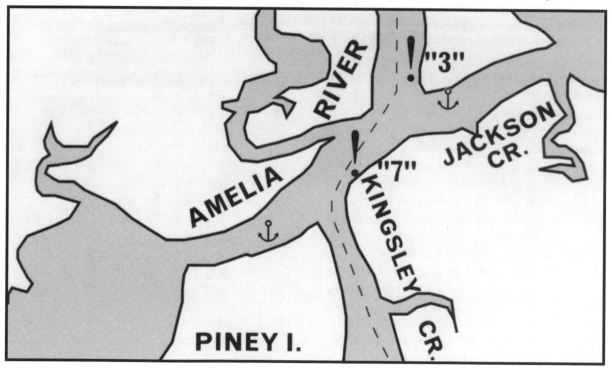

than you might at first have thought. Given these limitations, only craft as large as 34 feet can drop the hook safely. Your best bet would be the waters just inside the creek's westerly mouth. A Bahamian mooring would be a good safety precaution. Be sure to read the Jackson Creek navigation information before making use of the stream.

Upper Amelia River Anchorage (Standard Mile 720) (30 38.367 North/081 29.697 West)

Southwest of flashing daybeacon #7, the ICW takes a sharp swing to the south and leaves Amelia River behind as it begins to wend its way down Kingsley Creek. The upper portion of Amelia River, abandoned by the ICW, strikes out to the west between #7 and unlighted daybeacon #9. There are two unmarked shoals at the entrance that must be avoided, but otherwise this stream affords fairly good overnight anchorage for boats up to 38 feet, in all but heavy weather. Minimum depths of 7 feet (considerably shallower than indicated on chart 11489) hold upstream as far as the first small creek that intersects the Amelia's southern banks west of Piney Island. West of this point, shoaling has occurred that is not noted on the latest edition of chart 11489 at the time of this writing. Depths of 3 to 4 feet are all too quickly encountered thereafter.

The surrounding shores are mostly composed of undeveloped marsh, and do not give adequate protection in a really hard blow. The higher ground of Piney Island to the south does give some lee from southerly breezes.

Your best bet for a snug overnight stay is to watch for a large, private dock on the southerly banks after entering the stream. Drop the hook some 75 to 100 yards short (east) of this pier. Low-water depths here run

8 to 10 feet and there should be enough room for vessels as large as 38 feet.

Sailing on Amelia River

Amelia Island Yacht Basin (Standard Mile 720.5) (30 37.882 North/081 28.646 West)

Amelia Island can boast a second pleasure-craft facility in addition to the downtown Fernandina docks. Amelia Island Yacht Basin lies along the easterly terminus of the small, charted stream making into the Waterway's easterly flank, south of unlighted daybeacon #13. This facility offers full service and a very friendly welcome. Unfortunately, entrance depths on the canal that connects the dockage basin to the ICW now run a meager 3½ to 4 feet (over a "soft mud" bottom) at low water. Even to maintain that depth, visiting craft must stick very strictly to the stream's midwidth. Captains piloting boats that draw 4 feet or more must coincide their entry and egress with high water or at least midtide. Deep-draft vessels should call the marina prior to their arrival to check on the latest channel conditions.

The dockage basin itself boasts depths alongside of around 6-7 feet and is completely surrounded by a concrete seawall. It is well protected from all weather short of a hurricane.

While transients are still eagerly accepted at Amelia Island, the dockmaster has informed this writer that his facility has "exploded with resident craft." Wise captains will make advance dockage reservations rather than risk disappointment.

Shoreside, visiting cruisers will find beautifully manicured landscaping, two nonclimate-controlled sets of showers, a Laundromat, dry-stack storage for smaller power craft, and a cruiser's lounge immediately adjacent to the dockmaster's office. A small paperback exchange library is found in the lounge as well. Both gasoline and diesel are available at the fuel dock. Still not enough for you? Well, how about full mechanical repairs and haul-outs courtesy of a 35-ton travelift? Those wanting to visit the nearby Fernandina Beach historic district will be heartened to learn that the marina has a courtesy van. There is also an on-site ship's store, and a few snacks plus cold drinks can be purchased in the cruiser's lounge/dockmaster's office building. While Sonny's Barbecue Restaurant is within walking distance, this writer suggests that you take advantage of the marina's courtesy vehicle and visit one of the outstanding dining spots in downtown Fernandina, described above. With all these many positive attributes, coupled with a true can-do attitude, Amelia Island Yacht Basin is a great find for any passing cruiser whose vessel can stand the thin entrance soundings.

Amelia Island Yacht Basin
 (904) 277-4615 (marina)
277-2484 (repair yard)
http://www.ameliayacht.com

Approach depths—3½ feet
 minimum (low water)
Dockside depths—6 feet
Accepts transients—yes
Transient dockage rate—average
Floating concrete piers—yes
Dockside power connections—30 and 50 amp
Dockside water connections—yes
Showers—yes
Laundromat—yes
Waste pump-out—yes
Gasoline—yes
Diesel fuel—yes
Below-waterline repairs—yes
Mechanical repairs—yes
Ship's store—yes
Variety store—small
Restaurant—one within a long walk,
 others accessible by courtesy vehicle

Alligator Creek Anchorage (Standard Mile 726) (Various Lats/Lons—see below)

South of the ICW's passage through Kingsley Creek the Waterway meets up with another overnight anchorage as it flows into South Amelia River. North of unlighted daybeacon #36 a side channel wanders to the north-northeast off the ICW behind a marsh-grass island. The stream eventually leads to an intersection with Alligator Creek and then continues on toward Amelia City and a more northerly section of the Waterway. Minimum depths of 6½ feet are held in the side channel for at least 200 yards north-northeast of the intersection with westward-running Alligator Creek. Typical soundings run in the 7- to 12-foot range.

Do not attempt to enter this stream by way of its northerly entrance, southeast of flashing daybeacon #28. The channel is squeezed between large, unmarked shallows at this point.

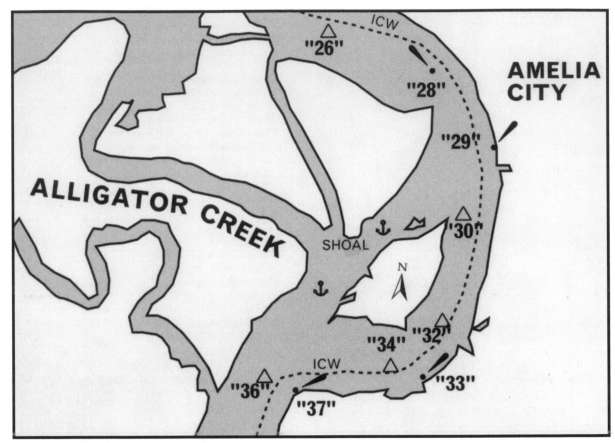

In our experience, the best spot to anchor is found on the waters just south of the intersection with Alligator Creek, near 30 34.493 North/081 28.288 West. There is plenty of swinging room for a 45 footer, and fair protection courtesy of the marshy shores to the east and west. Strong blows from the south could make for a bumpy evening.

We have also observed any number of Waterway craft anchored north of the Alligator Creek intersection near 30 34.692 North/081 28.127 West. While 8- to 9-foot depths hold for several hundred yards north of the juncture, unmarked shoals begin to impinge upon the channel's edge. Of course, cruising carefully along with an eagle eye on the sounder,

you may well avoid these shallows, but farther to the south, this potential problem is minimized.

We do not recommend entrance into Alligator Creek itself. Over the past several years, some large shoals have built out into both flanks of this stream's entrance. While local navigators, with their day-to-day outlook on the nearby waters, will undoubtedly make good a safe entrance into this creek, visitors are advised to leave Alligator Creek to those with truly local knowledge.

Nassau Sound and River (Standard Mile 729)

The ICW enters the open waters of Nassau

Sound southeast of flashing daybeacon #45. Nassau Sound is perhaps the most changeable and shoal-prone section of the entire northeastern Florida ICW. Be ready for new and different markers from those pictured on chart 11489, or even from the configuration of aids to navigation discussed in the next section of this chapter. These would be excellent waters on which to try out your new GPS chart plotter or a GPS interfaced with a laptop computer.

Your introduction to broad Nassau Sound is likely to be a choppy one unless you arrive on a day of light airs. Nassau Sound is noted for its dusty crossings. In southeasterly blows the wind has more than enough fetch to raise very uncomfortable seas in the ICW channel. Even if the wind is blowing from another quarter, you can usually expect more than a few jolts.

The southeastern portion of Nassau Sound, abandoned by the ICW, leads through a shallow and virtually impassable inlet to the open sea. A fixed bridge now crosses this inlet. The older, swinging span, still the only bridge pictured on chart 11489, has been left in place just north of the new span to serve as a very popular fishing platform. We strongly recommend that you do not attempt to approach either of these bridges and bypass entirely the waters of eastern Nassau Sound.

Nassau River cuts west and northwest from the northwesterly reaches of Nassau Sound. In spite of Nassau River's deep soundings noted on chart 11489, cruising captains are strictly advised to avoid these waters as well. Due to the presence of many unmarked and, in some cases, uncharted shoals, Nassau River is a body of water where exploration, even by aggressive skippers, is far more likely to result in a hard grounding than successful gunkholing.

Nassau Sound Auxiliary Channel Anchorage (Standard Mile 730.5) (30 30.709 North/081 27.658 West)

After leaving the often-choppy waters of Nassau Sound behind, the ICW follows a sheltered passage along the reaches of Sawpit Creek to the south-southwest. Chart 11489 shows several sidewaters between the passage across Nassau Sound and Fort George River that might, at first, seem to be overnight anchorage possibilities. However, on-site research reveals that all but two of these potential havens have shoaled dangerously.

One highly questionable anchorage, for truly wild-eyed captains (only) whose craft draw 3½ feet or (preferably) less, is found east of flashing daybeacon #48. Here cruisers will discover an alternate channel that meanders back northeast to Nassau Sound. The entrance is downright treacherous and tidal currents run swiftly indeed, but if (and only if) you can find the channel, minimum depths of 4 to 5 feet can be carried into the deeper interior portions of the stream.

Once you are past the tricky entrance, good depths of 6 to 8 feet or more spread out almost from shore to shore. A good spot to drop the hook lies in the first bend to the north (near 30 30.709 North/081 27.658 West), well short of the fixed bridge at the Nassau Sound entrance. Here boats up to 40 feet long can anchor in some 8 to 16 feet of water, with good protection provided by the high southeastern banks. There is some light development along this shoreline.

Talbot Island Stream (Standard Mile 732)

East of unlighted daybeacon #55, a small offshoot makes into the Waterway's eastern shore. Over the past several years, depths on this sidewater have declined markedly. At the time of this writing, contrary to the soundings shown on chart 11489, vessels attempting entry into the creek's mouth will soon hit depths of 3 to 4 feet or less. The southwesterly banks are particularly shoal. We once observed a beautiful 40-foot Hinckley sailcraft aground amidst these shallows during our research. Fortunately, the rising tide soon freed our friends, and they quickly cruised down the Waterway to a far better anchorage on Fort George River (see below).

We no longer recommend that captains attempt to anchor on this offshoot or even along its approach from the Waterway, no matter what size and draft their vessels might be. Trust me, keep tooling south to the Fort George River. You'll be glad you did!

Fort George River Anchorage (Standard Mile 735) (30 26.460 North/081 26.285 West)

Attractive Fort George River splits off from the ICW to the east and southeast at flashing daybeacon #72. The reasonably well-marked channel has minimum depths of 6 feet until falling off to 5 feet or less just west of unlighted daybeacon #7. Shoaling immediately adjacent to the marked passage has increased over the last several years, so it is now more important than ever to carefully take heed of all the various daybeacons. Nevertheless, craft 40 feet or less in overall length, with drafts less than 6 feet, can visit the river's waters west of #7 and probably come out unscathed.

While you can set the hook almost anywhere west of #7, unquestionably the best spot is found as the higher ground of Fort George Island comes abeam to the south. Look to the south as you come abeam of unlighted daybeacon #5 and you will quickly sight Kingsley Plantation. Anchoring in the shadow of this historic plantation can make for an evening that will be long remembered. For maximum swinging room, it is now best to drop the hook a touch west of the plantation house.

If you happen to arrive abeam of Kingsley Plantation between 8 A.M. and 5 P.M. break out the dinghy and go ashore for an inexpensive tour of the house. The entire plantation is now a historic state park and the tour is well worth your time. If you go ashore at Kingsley Plantation, be sure to secure your dinghy carefully along the shoreline as no dock is available. Otherwise, the rising tide might leave you swimming for your anchored craft.

Except for the plantation house, development along the southern shore in the navigable portion of Fort George River is light and the northern banks are marsh. If your cruising plans call for anchoring anywhere in the general vicinity of Fort George River, this is the spot. You won't regret the decision.

Fort George Island and Kingsley Plantation History

There are many nineteenth-century plantations along the coastlines of the Carolinas, Georgia, and Florida that can lay claim to a historic figure or two. How many, though, can boast of three occupants who have figured prominently in the history of their respective states? This is the case with Kingsley Plantation on Fort George Island, site of the oldest plantation house in Florida.

Even before the advent of Kingsley Plantation, Fort George Island itself has more than one historic tale to tell. By 1674 the Franciscan mission, San Juan del Puerto, had been established on the island. In 1733 Gen. James Oglethorpe, the founder of the Georgia colony, established a fort on the island as part of his campaign against Spanish St. Augustine.

Fort George was soon abandoned, but its name stuck to the island.

In 1787 a Spanish census showed only one family of six living on Fort George Island, but things were soon to change. It was not long, 1791 in fact, before the romantically splendid rascal John McQueen put in an appearance at Fort George. Obtaining a land grant from the king of Spain, "Don Juan," as he was known to his friends, soon took up residence and built the rear portion of present-day Kingsley Plantation.

John McQueen was an interesting character who led a varied life. He resided on a Georgian plantation until 1776, but as the Revolution overtook his adopted state, McQueen took up the patriot banner. As the war progressed, he became a valued confidant of George Washington himself. Washington subsequently dispatched his friend on delicate diplomatic missions abroad to seek aid for the patriot cause.

Following the war, McQueen returned to his Georgian plantation only to suffer bankruptcy owing to unwise and prodigious land investment. Preferring the hospitality of Florida to his angry creditors, our hero left his entire family behind and fled south. Arriving in Florida, McQueen quickly began to employ his considerable diplomatic talents. He became a close friend of the Spanish governor in St. Augustine and even converted to Catholicism. Later studies of his private letters suggest his conversion was more a matter of political convenience than religious conviction.

Somehow, McQueen secured an appointment as "commander of the St. Johns River." Of course, there was not too much commanding to do, but the job was a good source of income and apparently ingratiated McQueen to the Spanish king enough to net his land grant on Fort George Island.

When not engaged in "commanding" the St. Johns River, McQueen is reputed to have given his attention to no small number of amorous affairs, a pastime that earned him the nickname of Don Juan.

McQueen had only one problem: he wished his family to join him from Georgia. Unfortunately, the authorities in Georgia would not allow his children to emigrate until his debts there were settled. McQueen therefore obtained an unlimited license to practice "wrecking" along Florida's east coast. Wreckers were those infamous crews who were supposed to salvage any useful cargo from vessels that had foundered on the coastal shoals. It is often whispered that the wreckers or conchs, as they were sometimes called, moved buoys and erected false lights to supplement the bounty provided by nature's storms and inept navigation. Whether McQueen would have engaged in these shady practices will never be known, for just as he was poised to begin his wrecking career, he died of a heart attack.

Following McQueen's demise, the plantation was acquired by John Houston McIntosh in 1804 before his exploits in the East Florida Revolution, which have already been related. In 1817 McIntosh sold the land to its most famous owner, Zephaniah Kingsley.

We know little of Kingsley's early years save that he immigrated to America with his father from Scotland before the Revolution. The Kingsleys took a loyalist stand during the war and were apparently forced to flee to Florida.

By 1817 Kingsley had established several plantations on St. Johns River at Orange Park and Drayton Island. With the collapse of the East Florida Rebellion and subsequently of John McIntosh's finances, Kingsley was able to buy his plantation on Fort George Island at a bargain price. He moved his entire household to the island and lived there till the end of his days.

Kingsley enlarged the plantation grounds and built most of the house, which still stands. Cotton and rice were grown on Kingsley's plantation, but these staple crops were not his primary source of income, for Kingsley was one of the most successful slave traders in Florida's history. Reportedly a learned man, he believed that slavery was the only humane treatment for the Negro and the only recipe for Southern agricultural success. With the abolition of slave importation in the United States, Kingsley began to buy large numbers of black slaves. While advocating lenient treatment for all slaves, he was relentless in their training. It is said that a slave trained by Kingsley brought several hundred dollars more at market than a newly arrived black.

Strangely enough, Kingsley was married to a black woman. Anna Madegigine Jai Kingsley was descended from a long line of African kings. Just how she and Kingsley came to be married is not recorded. State law did not allow the husband and wife of different races to live under the same roof, so Kingsley installed her in the old McIntosh homeplace and built the new addition for his residence. It is said that he always treated his wife with the greatest respect and carefully legitimized all their offspring. Truly, Kingsley's point of view is hard for the modern mind to grasp. If you are interested in learning more of the seeming enigma that was Zephaniah Kingsley, I suggest reading Branch Cabell and A. J. Hanna's *The St. Johns—A Parade of Diversities*.

Sisters Creek (Standard Mile 739)

Veteran Waterway cruisers will remember the old location of Sisters Creek Marina, which once overlooked the Waterway's northwesterly banks, a short hop southwest of flashing daybeacon #85 (hard by the Sisters Creek bascule bridge). After languishing in obscurity for several years, this site has been redeveloped as a joint project by the city of Jacksonville and the Jacksonville Kingfish Tournament. No services seem to be currently available for passing cruisers.

GEORGIA TO ST. JOHNS RIVER NAVIGATION

The waters of northernmost Eastern Florida are generally deep and mostly forgiving. However, navigators need to know that recently all the markers on Nassau Sound and St. Marys Inlet have been renumbered. Be sure to have the **latest** editions of chart 11503 and 11489 aboard!

One special cause of concern in this section is the 6- to 7-foot tidal range. Imagine cruising confidently into a creek at high water with the sounder showing a full 6 feet of water under your keel, only to find yourself high and dry at low tide. With this phenomenon in mind I have leaned toward the conservative with the soundings given in this chapter.

Along with the prodigious tidal range come swift tidal currents. We once towed a sailcraft for a considerable distance north of the Kingsley Creek Railway Bridge because it was not able to make any headway against the tide with its Seagull outboard auxiliary.

Low-powered craft should try to plan their passage to correspond with the appropriate tide. Also, all skippers should be on guard against the considerable lateral leeway often caused by the swift current. Proceed with the usual caution and you should enjoy your passage through these most northeasterly of Floridian waters. Be too lax, and you might spend an afternoon contemplating the values of good coastal navigation from a sandbar.

Florida Bound   As you approach Floridian waters, simply follow the well-marked ICW channel south down Cumberland Sound from Georgia. For much of this passage, the Waterway follows the large-ship's channel running north from St. Marys Inlet. The inlet channel takes precedence over the usual ICW markings, and southbound captains should now take all red, even-numbered aids to navigation on their (the cruisers') port sides and green markers to starboard. This configuration holds until the ICW departs the large-ship's channel, just east of flashing buoy #25. South of #25, markers resume their typical ICW pattern with southbound craft once again passing green beacons to their (the cruisers') port sides and red aids taken to starboard.

As you near the intersection with St. Marys River, south of flashing buoy #30, the waters will often become rougher. In stiff easterly and southerly winds, the Waterway's passage through Cumberland Sound can rattle more than a few fillings.

St. Marys River   If you choose to visit St. Marys River and the charming village of the same name, break off from the ICW's track at flashing buoy #29 and set course due west into the midwidth of the river. Successful navigation of St. Marys River is an elementary matter of following a few navigational beacons until coming abeam of St. Marys village on the northern shore. These beacons mark the few shoals adjoining the river's eastern reaches. Simply pass each on the appropriate side, and don't approach them closely. Afterwards, you can take a break from your depth-sounder vigil while on St. Marys River.

Jolly River   Jolly River breaks off to the south near St. Marys River's eastern entrance. The mouth of the Jolly is flanked by a large shoal on its western shore. To avoid this considerable hazard, favor the eastern banks when entering. As the river begins to swing to the west, cruise back to the midwidth. Between this point and the stream's next bend to the south is a good place to drop the hook.

If you choose to proceed farther, begin favoring the northern shore heavily as you approach the turn to the south. There is some shallow water abutting the turn's southern point. Once through the bend, cruise back to the centerline. Remember to discontinue your cruise before coming abeam of the charted marsh island that bisects the river. Past this point, the winding channel is much too uncertain for larger cruising craft.

On the St. Marys   Continue cruising west along the midwidth of St. Marys River until you approach the streams's first aid to navigation, flashing daybeacon #3. Squeeze to the north and northwest a little bit as you round #3 and follow a sharp southward turn in the river. As correctly forecast on chart 11489, shoal water shelves out from the southerly bank just east of #3.

As you come abeam of flashing daybeacon #3, the mouth of North River will lie to the (what else?) north.

North River   Enter North River by favoring the western shore slightly. Once on the stream's interior, cruise back to the mid-width until the river swings almost due west as it begins to approach the large pulp mill. Chart 11489 correctly shows a shallow patch along the northern shore in this section. Favor the southern banks until the stream begins to swing back to the north, then reenter the centerline and continue along the middle until reaching the charted shallows north of the mill. Continued passage upstream is not recommended without specific local knowledge.

On to St. Marys Village   After passing flashing daybeacon #3, be sure to come abeam and pass unlighted daybeacon #5 by at least 75 yards to its westerly quarter. Once #5 is in your wake, set course to pass some 25 yards (at least) east of unlighted daybeacons #6 and #8. These aids mark a long patch of shoal water making out from the westerly banks. As we are now going upstream, anyone who remembers the old "red, right, returning" will immediately understand this configuration of aids to navigation.

South of #8, the St. Marys follows a turn to the west and then northwest. Round this bend by passing flashing daybeacon #10 to its southerly side. Shoal water lies north of #10.

Set a new northwesterly course and point to come abeam and pass unlighted daybeacon #12, by at least 25 yards to its southwesterly side. Continue on the same track, passing flashing daybeacon #13 by about the same distance to its northeasterly quarter. Do not approach #13 closely; the charted shoal seems to be building to the east and northeast from the southwesterly banks.

Past #13, the river bends yet again, this time to the west. Favor the northerly shores slightly, and you will soon come abeam of the St. Marys (village) waterfront along the northern banks.

St. Marys Waterfront   The St. Marys waterfront will be sighted along the northern shores of the like-named river, northwest of flashing daybeacon #13. First up will be the docks of Lang's Marina's easterly dockage basin. This facility will be followed by some commercial piers and a public launching ramp. A bit farther to the west, Lang's Marina's west-side docks will also be spied. Do not attempt to follow St. Marys River west of St. Marys village into its uncharted upper reaches. Unmarked shoals are far too prolific for cruising-size craft.

South on the ICW   South of flashing buoy #29, the combined large-ship's and ICW channel begins slanting to the southeast. Pass between the various pairs of buoys until coming between flashing buoys #25 and #24. Once between these aids, the inlet lies to the east-southeast, while the ICW cuts south.

St. Marys Inlet   Navigation of the St. Marys Inlet channel is a simple matter of following a well-marked track. Continue east-southeast by passing between flashing buoys #23 and #22. Soon the inlet channel takes a more easterly heading.

Point for the broad, deep passage between flashing buoys #E and #F. From this point, the channel tracks generally east between twin jetties. Simply pass between the charted pairs of buoys and you should not have any undue difficulty.

On the ICW   The ICW splits off from the St. Marys Inlet channel east of flashing buoy #25. Continue on course to the east for some 100 yards after passing #25 and then turn 90 degrees to the south. Set course to pass between the two aids west of Fort Clinch, flashing buoys #1 and #2. As mentioned above, the normal color configuration of the Waterway's aids to navigation resumes at this point. Southbound navigators should now return to taking all red, even-numbered markers to their (the cruisers') starboard sides, and pass green beacons to port.

As you are cruising toward the gap between flashing buoys #1 and #2, the charted, unnumbered light will be passed west of your course. This aid to navigation is actually perched atop three pilings and rears its head 26 feet above the water. Obviously, you would almost need to be blind to miss it. This marker serves as a good point of reference for those following the Waterway south.

As you go south on the Waterway, watch the eastern shore and you will soon spy a large, abandoned fish-processing plant, followed by the northernmost of Fernandina's pulp mills. Before long the Fernandina waterfront will come abeam to the east and Bells River to the west. A containerized-ship loading facility overlooks the eastern banks near flashing buoy #8.

South of flashing buoy #10, no-wake restrictions protect the Fernandina Beach waterfront. Be sure to proceed strictly at idle speed while cruising by.

Bells River   Enter Bells River on its midwidth and continue on the center section as the stream turns sharply to the north. Guard against any slippage to the south as you enter this stream. A long shoal runs east from Bells River's southerly entrance point.

At high tide the easterly reaches of Bells River can be confusing. The marsh area to the south, marked on chart 11489 as "Bares at MLLW," is covered with some 5 to 6 feet of water at high tide. When this region is covered, it is all too easy to wander into the shallows rather than following the main track of Bells River. Slow down if necessary and study the waters carefully before proceeding forward. Bells River will be the northernmost of the three streams before you. We have often discovered that this is a great spot to make use of our GPS and laptop computer to avoid confusion.

After following Bells River through its northerly bend, begin favoring the eastern banks to avoid the charted shallows around a marked rock and extensive oyster banks. Eventually, the stream will begin to turn to the west and split into two branches.

Some cruisers may choose to follow the midline of this secondary northern arm for a short distance and anchor. Depths in this region are much shallower than shown on chart 11489, typically 7 to 8 feet. Discontinue your exploration of this northerly section of Bells River before coming abeam of the first offshoot to the north.

The primary southerly branch of Bells River remains consistently deep along its centerline width until the stream turns to the north, just west of the charted high ground at Chester. In spite of soundings noted on chart 11489, 3- and 4-foot readings amidst numerous oyster beds are encountered past this point.

Lanceford Creek   Entry into Lanceford Creek is strictly not recommended by this writer for any but small, very shallow draft power craft. Be sure not to mistake the mouth of Lanceford Creek for Bells River. The river is the northern- and easternmost of the streams described above.

Fernandina Harbour Marina   The long, outer-face dock and fuel pier at Fernandina Harbour Marina will be readily spotted to the east of flashing daybeacon #12. Except for the swift tidal currents that plague this entire portion of the ICW, dockage on the outside (western) face of the outer pier at Fernandina Harbour Marina is relatively simple. However, should you be assigned a space on the inner (eastern) side of this dock, a bit more caution is in order.

Curl around the southern side of the long face pier, passing fairly close to the southerly tip of this structure. As you work your way back to the north toward your slip, pass as close to the long pier (and any boats already moored to this structure) as possible. Avoid any slippage to the east. Depths in the remainder of the harbor (to the east) are quite shallow.

On the ICW   South of unlighted daybeacon # 14, the Waterway follows a sharp jog to the west, then turns back south just as abruptly near flashing daybeacon #1. Be sure to pass west of #1. Shallow water lies east of this aid to navigation.

Waterway Anchorage   South of flashing daybeacon #1, some cruisers (in fair weather only) may choose to anchor in the deeper water running out from the westerly shoreline. Don't approach to within less than 50 yards of the westerly banks for best depths.

On the ICW   South of #1, it is a long, markerless run before coming abeam of flashing daybeacon #3 to its westerly quarter. The entrance to Jackson Creek lies along the ICW's easterly flank, a short hop south of #3.

Jackson Creek   Cruisers entering Jackson Creek should heavily favor the northern shore upon entering the stream's mouth. This maneuver will help to avoid the considerable shallows to the south that cover completely at high water. Discontinue your explorations before cruising more than 50 yards upstream. Farther to the east, the already skinny channel becomes even narrower and hugs the northern shore tightly. Even by heavily favoring this shoreline, you will encounter 3- and 4-foot readings long before chart 11489 would lead you to expect them.

Those anchoring in Jackson Creek should probably drop the hook just inside the stream's westerly mouth. These waters boast the maximum swinging room. Farther to the east, the channel narrows considerably between the northerly banks and the substantial mud shoal to the south.

Take care to set the hook so as not to

swing into the southerly shoals. This can be a tricky proposition in any sort of wind. Agile crews might consider a Bahamian-style mooring to minimize swinging room.

On the ICW Once abeam of flashing daybeacon #3, the ICW takes a run to the southwest. Point to pass unlighted daybeacon #5 and flashing daybeacon #7 to their northwesterly sides. After leaving #7 behind, the Waterway soon bends back to the south. Point to pass unlighted daybeacon #9 to its westerly side as you pass through this turn. Before reaching #9, the upper reaches of Amelia River, abandoned by the ICW, are accessible to the west.

Upper Amelia River Enter the upper reaches of Amelia River by favoring the southerly shores as you pass through the stream's mouth, west of unlighted daybeacon #9. However, don't approach this shoreline too closely either. Chart 11489 correctly shows a patch of very shallow water on the northern tier of the entrance. Keep a weather eye on the sounder as you cruise through the entrance for an early warning that you might be encroaching on these shallows.

Once on the stream's interior, cruise back to the midwidth. Stop before coming abeam of the river's first small offshoot on the southern banks. In spite of depths shown on the chart, 3- to 4-foot readings are consistently found farther upstream.

Probably the best spot to anchor is found some 75 to 100 yards short of the large, private pier that will be spied on the port shore. Anchor along the centerline and be sure to show an anchor light.

On the ICW South of unlighted daybeacon #13 the Waterway quickly flows to meet the Kingsley Creek twin bridges. The northern span is a railroad bridge with a closed vertical clearance of only 5 feet, but it is usually open unless a train is due. However, be warned that the trains hauling wood to the Fernandina pulp mills can be quite long. If you happen to be unfortunate enough to catch one of these lengthy railway delays, be on guard against the extremely swift tidal currents that plague the waters lying about the bridge. Slow-moving craft should stop to wait well short of the spans or risk the tidal current pushing them into the bridge pilings before course corrections are possible.

The second span is a fixed, high-rise highway bridge with an official vertical clearance of 65 feet. However, on several of our passages we have observed high-tide clearances of as little as 64 feet courtesy of the bridge's tidal gauge. Skippers of tall sailcraft should take this reading into account and make their approach at low water if necessary.

While passing under the high-rise highway bridge, you may catch sight of the Down Under Restaurant and a small wooden pier associated with this dining spot to the west. Due to the strong currents, and less than ideal position of this dock, we do not suggest that cruising craft attempt to make use of this facility.

South of the twin spans, the Waterway enters a region that you may well find quite different from what might be expected from a study of chart 11489. The large mud flats shown on the chart between flashing daybeacon #14 and Amelia City are covered at high water. The careless navigator can suddenly find herself or himself in a wide body of water just when he or she expects a protected passage. This considerable width can give strong winds more than enough fetch to raise an uncomfortable chop. As if that were not enough, you must be very careful to keep strictly to the marked ICW channel. The waters outside the ditch are usually only a few inches deep. In short, this is one of those problem stretches that occasionally plague the ICW and that require more than their share of caution. Watch your stern carefully for leeway, keep a sharp watch on the sounder, observe all ICW markers scrupulously, and you should come through with nothing worse than a pair of white knuckles.

Be particularly careful to pass unlighted daybeacon #21 to its western side, pass between unlighted daybeacon #23 and flashing daybeacon #24, and take unlighted daybeacon #25 to its southern quarter. These aids mark a huge shoal to the east and northeast.

Cruisers passing flashing daybeacon #28 will catch sight of the charted high ground around Amelia City on the eastern shore. Only a few houses are evident but they certainly are welcome after the treacherous mud flats.

Remember not to attempt entry into the northerly mouth of the channel leading south to Alligator Creek, west of Amelia City. Use the southerly entrance only as described below.

Alligator Creek and Its Approaches Cruise north-northeast from unlighted daybeacon #36 and enter the midwidth of the channel striking north to Alligator Creek. For maximum swinging room, anchor before coming abeam of the intersection with Alligator Creek.

Be sure to discontinue your northerly cruising well before reaching a position abeam of unlighted daybeacon #30, well to the east. Farther to the north-northeast the channel becomes much too tricky for larger cruising craft.

Please remember, we no longer recommend that cruising-size craft attempt to enter Alligator Creek itself. The charted 3-foot shoal flanking this stream's northerly entrance point has built considerably to the south, and at low water it is covered by a mere 18 inches of water.

The ICW through Nassau Sound   South of Amelia City, the ICW follows shoal-plagued South Amelia River to Nassau Sound. This is not a section of the Waterway that passing cruisers can take casually. At last check, all the major trouble spots were well marked, but woe to mariners who miss an aid to navigation. You could well spend the evening contemplating your repair bill for damaged underwater hardware.

Watch carefully for new and different markers along the course of the Waterway's run through South Amelia River. It doesn't require much imagination to divine that the Corps of Engineers makes frequent shifts and additions to aids to navigation to follow the ever-shifting shoals.

Similarly, pass at least 35 yards west of flashing daybeacon #37 and unlighted daybeacon #39. Shallows run between these two aids to navigation and lie along the Waterway's easterly flank.

Be sure to pass well east of unlighted daybeacon #42. Shoal water is found west and north of #42.

Once #42 is in your wake, expect an increase in chop as Nassau Sound is approached. Point eventually to pass between unlighted daybeacon #43 and flashing daybeacon #44. Continue out into the sound's widening waters by coming abeam of and passing flashing daybeacon #45 to its southwesterly side.

It's now time to stop for a moment and contemplate the problem of successfully navigating the Waterway's passage across lower Nassau Sound. For at least the last decade, markers have come and gone, been moved, and sometimes mysteriously disappeared overnight along this problem stretch of the Waterway. In 2003, the most important Nassau Sound ICW marker was twice run down during the night by commercial tows. Thanks to a timely tip-off by fellow cruisers, we were able to get a message off to everyone on our *Salty Southeast* mailing list immediately (just another reason to take out a free subscription—see this guide's introduction for details).

But, as often happens, I digress. All navigators should proceed out into Nassau Sound with binoculars in hand, slow down, and access the current configuration of aids to navigation (or lack thereof). Be ready to discover very different markings than those we describe below. If you do spot different aids to navigation, respect them, and follow their course. Otherwise, it could lead to an encounter of the rocky kind, and I don't mean Balboa!

At least for the moment, from #45, it is critically important for you to set course to come abeam of flashing daybeacon #46 well to its northeasterly and eastern side. This aid is set well out into the open waters of Nassau Sound. Continue on the same course, pointing to pass just northeast of unlighted daybeacon #46A. This aid (#46A), in particular, may or may not be here when you arrive. If it is present, curl around #46A and point to the mouth of Sawpit Creek to the southwest. Set course to pass between unlighted daybeacon #46B and flashing daybeacon #47. It's then a straight shot into Sawpit Creek

Before moving our discussion into Sawpit Creek, it should be noted that there seems to be a tendency to shortcut #46 and #46A. We watched during an earlier on-the-water research as a large power craft came very close to finding the bottom west of #46. Fortunately, our waving and calls on the VHF warned the captain off.

OK, with that last warning out of the way, let's move into Sawpit Creek. Soon after entering this stream begin watching for unlighted daybeacon #47A. Pass #47A to its fairly immediate northwesterly side.

Eventually, you will spy flashing daybeacon #48 marking the westerly side of the ICW channel. Pass #48 to its easterly side.

Upper Nassau River and Nassau Sound Inlet Visiting cruisers are strictly advised to bypass explorations on the upper reaches of Nassau River and its tributaries to the west and northwest. The numerous "Shoaling Reported" notations on chart 11489 should be enough to warn you away, but if they should fail, you might consider a look at my bent prop if you still have any doubts.

Similarly, the Nassau Sound inlet is now virtually impassable, even for small power craft. As mentioned earlier in this chapter, the inlet channel is now crossed by both the charted 15-foot bascule bridge and a new, uncharted fixed span. Do yourself a big favor and confine your explorations to the waters well west of both bridges.

Nassau Sound Auxiliary Channel Anchorage A quick study of chart 11489 might lead mariners to expect a number of good anchorages on Sawpit Creek. However, our on-site research revealed only two that are suitable for cruising-size craft.

The first of these is found on the unnamed stream cutting east from flashing daybeacon #48. This passage eventually leads to Nassau Sound. It has a very difficult entrance, but it does offer good anchorage for those who successfully reach its interior sections. Only the adventurous need apply to this stream, and, even then, it's certainly possible to find the bottom.

Those who choose to take the chance should set a course to parallel the southern banks some 60 feet from the shoreline. Proceed at idle speed and don't take your eye off the sounder. Continue on this course until you are some 100 yards short of the first small offshoot on the southern shore. Begin cruising back to the midline at this point. As the stream slowly turns to the north, good depths open out almost from shore to shore, though there is still a small patch of shallows abutting the western banks. Discontinue your cruise well before reaching the bridge blocking farther progress toward Nassau Sound.

On the ICW The Waterway's passage through the remainder of Sawpit Creek is fairly straightforward and well marked. Again, though, this is not the place to go exploring outside of the buoyed cut. The charted shoals along both banks are for real. Hold to the centerline of the Waterway channel and you should come through without undue difficulty.

The long loop cutting into the Waterway's western shore between flashing daybeacons #51 and #53 has shoaled badly. The northern entrance has a sandbar across much of its width and even the channel along the westerly shore has some low-tide depths of 3 feet. The southerly entrance is even worse; low-tide depths of 2 feet are prevalent.

Talbot Island Stream Please remember that we no longer recommend anchorage on the stream that runs southeast from unlighted daybeacon #55. Even the approaches to this creek from the Waterway have shoaled. Keep on trucking to Fort George River.

On the ICW Moving south, the ICW channel enters Gunnison Cut on its way to Sisters Creek near flashing daybeacon #61. The loop charted as having deep water along the western banks between flashing daybeacon #67 and unlighted daybeacon #71 exhibits low-tide depths of 3 to 4 feet, making it inaccessible to larger craft.

Fort George River The Fort George River channel is reasonably well marked by a series of unlighted daybeacons. As you approach unlighted daybeacon #7, the channel narrows and depths become uncertain. Larger craft are strictly advised to discontinue their cruise of the river before reaching this point.

Enter Fort George River by leaving the ICW some 25 yards south (no more) of flashing daybeacon #72. Avoid the mouth of charted Garden Creek to the south as you enter the river. Shoals seem to be building north from this errant stream.

Point to pass unlighted daybeacon #2 to its immediate northeasterly side and come abeam of unlighted daybeacon #3 to its fairly immediate southwesterly side. Don't ask me to make sense out of this color scheme of the Fort George River's aids to navigation. The passage just outlined would seem to be just the opposite of "red, right, returning."

Continue favoring the southerly shore as you track your way upstream. Very shoal water lines the north side of the channel between #3 and #5. If you should enter at high tide, this shoal will not be evident, but believe me, it's there.

Eventually you should come abeam of unlighted daybeacon #5 to its southerly side. As you approach #5, you will sight Kingsley Plantation on the northern shores of Fort George Island. This is a great spot to drop the hook. To maximize swinging room, anchor just a touch west of the plantation house. Be sure to show an anchor light as the river is often frequented by small fishing vessels.

Between #5 and unlighted daybeacon #7, the channel is squeezed by a long, sandy shoal to the north and the mainland

of Fort George Island to the south. As you approach #7, depths drop off to some 5 to 6 feet. All but small, shallow-draft power craft should cease their forward progress well before reaching #7.

On the ICW   South of Fort George River the Waterway follows Sisters Creek to the St. Johns River. Don't attempt the small offshoot on the eastern banks near flashing daybeacon #82. In spite of the depths shown on chart 11489, this small stream has shoaled to create low-tide depths of 2 feet or less.

South of flashing daybeacon #83, no-wake restrictions are in effect all the way to the St. Johns River. These strictures are apparently designed to protect the Jacksonville-owned Sisters Creek Marina, overlooking the Waterway's northwesterly banks immediately northeast of the bascule bridge, and the public launching ramps lining the westerly shore, just south of the span.

Southwest of flashing daybeacon #85, the Waterway flows under the Sisters Creek swing bridge. This span has a closed vertical clearance of 24 feet and opens on demand.

Once through the bridge, set course to pass east of flashing daybeacons #86 and #88. Shallows seem to be building out from the westerly banks. Favor the easterly shores slightly to avoid this hazard.

South of #88, the ICW soon passes out into the wide and swiftly moving waters of the St. Johns River. Continued Waterway coverage resumes in chapter 3.

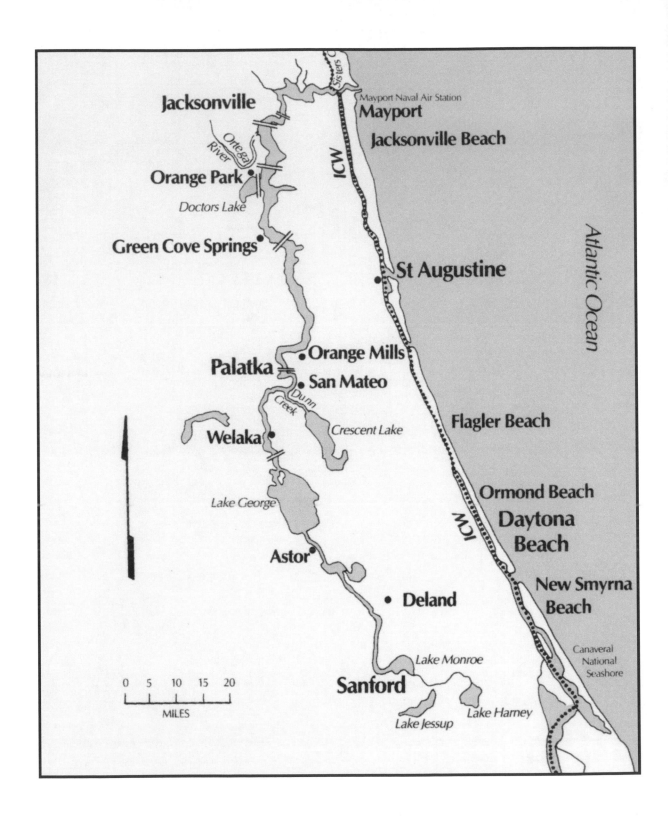

Jacksonville

Mayport Naval Air Station

Mayport

Jacksonville Beach

Ortega River

Orange Park

Doctors Lake

ICW

Atlantic Ocean

Green Cove Springs

St Augustine

Orange Mills

Palatka

San Mateo

Dunn Creek

Crescent Lake

Flagler Beach

Welaka

Lake George

Ormond Beach

Daytona Beach

ICW

Astor

New Smyrna Beach

Deland

Canaveral National Seashore

Lake Monroe

Sanford

Lake Harney

Lake Jessup

0 5 10 15 20

MILES

CHAPTER 2

The St. Johns River

What though Welaka's name this changing world has lost?
I'll sing of thee, St. Johns, and of thy glories boast . . .
Thy current moves, like Time, with long imprisoned souls
Who mark how much their life, like thine, has tides and shoals;
And though procrastination is of Time the thief,
But well we know, to those thus bound, Time brings relief . . .
And that is why, St. Johns, I sing of thee,
Calling to friends up north, "Come down and see!"

SOLON ROBINSON
The Glories of the St. Johns

The warm, golden light of a late afternoon sun slatted across the small whitecaps on the surface of the St. Johns as my ace research assistant, Bud Williams, and I headed back to Palatka after a long day of research. It had been yet another in a series of remarkable days spent exploring this storied river. We had watched the wide, saltwater shorelines recede to cypress swamps as the river narrowed to a smaller stream. Earlier, we had anchored our boat in a little cove as we ate lunch. The swampy growth that led up from the shoreline was the richest I had ever seen, undisturbed by man, seemingly from the very beginning.

It is my hope that you will have the opportunity to gain the same sense of this mighty river that held us in its sway on that golden spring afternoon so many years ago.

The St. Johns River

The poet William Cullen Bryant once observed that the St. Johns River is "one of the noblest streams of the country." Noble it is, not only in its character but also in its length and breadth. Stretching almost 270 miles from its source to the Atlantic Ocean, the St. Johns is one of a handful of northward flowing streams in America. The river cuts through the heart of Florida and has been described as the liquid backbone of the region.

For cruising purposes, mariners can consider the 148 nautical miles between the St. Johns Inlet at Mayport and Lake Monroe prime ground for exploration and gunkholing. South of Lake Monroe, the river becomes a winding, splintered stream that is not really suited for large craft, though many a black bass has been taken from small skiffs in the region.

The St. Johns' ever-changing nature lends a special fascination to cruising this remarkable river, which can be roughly divided into four regions. First comes the purely tidal portion of the river, stretching for some 19 nautical miles from its inlet to Jacksonville. Here the river is usually less than a mile wide and is bounded by a continually changing display of salt marsh and higher ground. Tidal current is very much in evidence. Incidentally, visiting explorers may well share their passage to Jacksonville with one or more large oceangoing ships.

From Jacksonville to Palatka (about 50 nautical miles), the St. Johns becomes a vast inland river whose waters become fresher as one moves farther south. Often more than 3 nautical miles wide, this portion of the St. Johns exhibits higher, well-wooded banks, frequently indented by coves, creeks, and bays that offer good overnight anchorage.

As you move south for 79 nautical miles from Palatka to the city of Sanford on Lake Monroe, the St. Johns narrows perceptibly and completes its transformation to a fresh, almost swampy stream. Mighty cypress trees line the river's shores, and the visitor cannot escape the impression that he is journeying into a great wilderness. Of course, from time to time, pleasant communities and isolated houses appear along the stream's course to remind him that he is in the twenty-first century. There is even one state park of notable interest. The blend of wilderness and development is a pleasant one, and, frankly, this is my favorite portion of the St. Johns.

South of Lake Monroe, the St. Johns River is a true wilderness stream, and exploration is pretty much limited to small craft. Numerous lakes intercept the river, which is often splintered into many alternate passages. While fascinating, this portion of the river will not be covered in this guide since it is unsuitable for larger cruising vessels.

Several major communities line the St. Johns at various points along its route. Jacksonville, the most important city in northern Florida, guards the river's sharp swing to the south. Long a major commercial port, Jacksonville has a rich history that is still remembered in these days of rapid progress.

Palatka is an increasingly busy community that has always looked to the commerce and bounty of the St. Johns River for its livelihood. Today, Palatka presents a peaceful image to the river and beckons the passing cruiser to stop at its facilities and spend a day or two exploring its charms.

The progressive community of Sanford sits perched on the southern shores of Lake Monroe. Boasting excellent facilities for the visiting cruiser, Sanford is quickly becoming a major pleasure-boating center.

Successful navigation of the St. Johns is generally a matter of following the well-marked channel. Numerous daybeacons and buoys are found all the way to Lake Monroe, and most are placed exactly where they should be to warn of obstructions. The few exceptions will be noted in the body of this chapter.

With a vertical clearance of 45 feet, the fixed Shands Bridge spanning the St. Johns at the small village of Green Cove Springs sets the height limit for the upper portion of the river. Sailcraft that cannot clear this height must have their mast unstepped to reach Palatka.

Facilities along the course of the St. Johns River are fairly numerous, though long stretches of open water often separate the various marinas. Most marinas accept transients and enjoy excellent reputations. Happily, these numerous facilities are not found just along the river's northerly portion but stretch all the way to Lake Monroe. Cruising skippers can explore the St. Johns River confidently, with the knowledge that marina facilities are within a few hours' run at most.

During recent years, diesel fuel has become a scarce commodity along the course of the upper St. Johns River. South of Jacksonville to Lake Monroe, there are currently only three facilities offering diesel (and one of these marinas has only a 4- to 5-foot entrance channel). Craft powered with these trusty engines should be very sure their tanks are topped off before tacking the upper St. Johns south of Jacksonville.

Diverse anchorages abound along the St. Johns. They range from small, secluded creeks with undeveloped banks to more open bays and coves along the river's main track. Cruisers can choose from a vast array of good spots to drop the hook.

Due to this chapter's length, we will present sectional marina and anchorage summaries, rather than have two summaries that cover the entire chapter. I feel this will enhance the summaries' usefulness, rather than forcing cruisers to sort through literally dozens and dozens of marinas and anchorages mentioned in a single instance.

Far too many visiting cruisers simply cross the St. Johns on the ICW's track and give the river only a brief glance on their way to the "condo caverns" of southeastern Florida. What a mistake! There is perhaps no other single river on the entire east coast of the United States that can lay claim to so many cruising opportunities. Those who take the time to make the St. Johns' acquaintance will undoubtedly come away with some of the richest cruising experiences of their lives.

Charts You will need three charts to cover the River from its seaward inlet to Sanford, while a fourth details just the ICW across the river:
11489—follows the ICW across the St. Johns River. This chart is of minimal aid in navigating the river itself
11491—details the St. Johns River from its inlet to Jacksonville

11492—covers from Jacksonville to Racy Point
11487—details the waters from Racy Point to Dunns Creek
11495—covers from Dunns Creek to Lake Dexter
11498—details from Lake Dexter to Lake Monroe and the city of Sanford

Bridges
Dames Point Bridge—crosses the St. Johns west of flashing daybeacon #45—Fixed—169 feet
Trout River/Highway 17 Bridge—crosses Trout River west of Pier 68 Marina—Fixed—29 feet
Trout River Railway Bridge—crosses Trout River immediately west of Trout River/Highway 17 Bridge—Swing bridge—2 feet (closed)—opens on demand 6 A.M. to 10 P.M., unless a train is due—during nighttime hours, opens only with 12 hours' notice
Matthews Point Bridge—crosses the St. Johns south of flashing buoy #78—Fixed—152 feet
Hart-Commodore Point Bridge—crosses the St. Johns west of flashing buoy #79—Fixed—135 feet
Main Street Bridge—crosses the St. Johns near downtown Jacksonville, west of unlighted nun buoy #82—Lift bridge—40 feet (closed)—does not open 7:30 A.M. to 9:00 A.M. and 4:30 P.M. to 6:00 P.M.—opens on demand 9:00 A.M. to 4:00 P.M. and during the evening and nighttime hours
Acosta Bridge—crosses the St. Johns in downtown Jacksonville hard by charted

Hendricks Point—Fixed—75 feet

Florida East Coast Railway Bridge—crosses the St. Johns immediately west of the Acosta Bridge—5 feet (closed)—usually open unless a train is due—delays before, during, and after a train passes can be lengthy

Fuller Warren/I-95 Bridge—crosses the St. Johns River in downtown Jacksonville near the charted location of San Marco—Fixed—65+ feet

Ortega River/Sadler Point Bridge—crosses the mouth of Ortega River southwest of Sadler Point and flashing daybeacon #1—Bascule—9 feet (closed)—opens on demand

Ortega River/Highway 17 Twin Bridges—crosses Ortega River southwest of Sadler Point Marina—Fixed—45 feet

Ortega River/CSX Roosevelt Railway Bridge—crosses Ortega River immediately southwest of the Highway 17 span—2 feet (closed)—usually open unless a train is due

Three Mile/I-295 Bridge—crosses the St. Johns south of Beauclerc Bluff and unlighted daybeacon #9—Fixed—63 feet (officially listed as 65 feet)

Doctors Inlet/Highway 17 Bridge—crosses the entrance to Doctors Inlet and Doctors Lake at Orange Point—Fixed—37 feet

Julington Creek Bridge—crosses Julington Creek east of Mandarin Holiday Marina—Fixed—15 feet

Black Creek/Highway 17 Bridge—crosses the entrance to Black Creek west of Wilkies Point—Fixed—30 feet

Shands/Green Cove Springs Bridge—crosses the St. Johns southeast of the village of Green Cove Springs and flashing daybeacon #20—Fixed—45 feet (sets the height limit for cruising the St. Johns south of Green Cove Springs)

Trout Creek/Highway 13 Bridge—crosses Trout Creek north of Palmo Cove—Fixed—14 feet (local reports place the clearance at 17 feet but we could not verify this during our on-site research)

Rice Creek Railway Bridge—crosses Rice Creek west of unlighted daybeacon #13—Swing bridge—2 feet (closed)—usually open unless a train is due—if closed, try blowing your horn and/or calling the bridge on VHF channel 9

Rice Creek/Highway 17 Bridge—crosses Rice Creek a short hop west of the railway span reviewed above—Fixed—45 feet

Palatka/Highway 17 Bridge—crosses the St. Johns south of flashing daybeacon #48—Fixed—65 feet

Buffalo Bluff Railway Bridge—crosses the St. Johns at Buffalo Bluff, near unlighted daybeacon #27—Bascule—7 feet (closed)—usually open unless a train is due but it can be closed for up to 40 minutes both before and after a train's passage

Astor Highway Bridge—crosses the St. Johns at the village of Astor, south of flashing daybeacon #28—Bascule—20 feet (closed)—opens on demand

De Land/Whitehair Bridge—crosses the St. Johns south of flashing daybeacon #39—Bascule—15 feet (closed)—opens on demand

Port of Sanford Railway Bridge—crosses the St. Johns immediately northwest of the juncture with Lake Monroe—Bascule—7 feet (closed)—usually open unless a train is due

Lake Monroe/Highway 17 Bridge—crosses the St. Johns immediately northwest of the juncture with Lake Monroe—Fixed—45 feet

Lake Monroe/I-4 Bridge—crosses the St. Johns immediately northwest of the juncture with Lake Monroe—Fixed—45 feet.

St. Johns Inlet to Jacksonville

The lower reaches of the St. Johns River run west for 19 nautical miles from the stream's inlet to Jacksonville. This stretch of the river is certainly not the largest or most exciting portion of the St. Johns; however, it does run past two significant historical sites, and Jacksonville's impressive shoreline awaits you at the end of your upriver trek.

Large oceangoing commercial and naval craft regularly ply the waters of the lower St. Johns upriver to Jacksonville. You may well meet one or more of these impressive vessels during your upstream voyage. If so, take a good look, but remember to keep clear. These large craft have limited maneuverability in the river channel.

This portion of the St. Johns River averages less than a mile in width, but strong winds from the east or west can still raise an unwelcome chop. Swift tidal currents can also be a problem for trawlers and sailcraft from time to time. Except for these hazards, navigation upstream to Jacksonville is a delight. With the river's large volume of commercial traffic, the channel is well maintained and carefully marked. One would almost have to be asleep at the helm to run aground here, but stranger things have happened, so stay alert.

Marina facilities are relatively few east of Jacksonville. One marina at Mayport accepts transients and two facilities are perched on the shores of Trout River, just a stone's throw from downtown Jacksonville. Jacksonville itself boasts a privately managed city marina with a good restaurant and ample services. A host of other full-service marinas are found just to the west on Ortega River.

The lower portion of the St. Johns River offers several excellent overnight anchorages. Some are sheltered enough to use in a heavy blow, while others are more open and should only be considered in light airs.

The lower St. Johns shoreline alternates between the usual saltwater marsh and higher ground. In addition to the natural scenery, you will observe several large commercial and military docks. Often large craft are moored here for loading and refitting. The presence of these seagoing giants can certainly make for an interesting cruise.

While perhaps not as exciting as the upper reaches of the St. Johns, the river's lower section can still make for a pleasant trip upstream with several opportunities to drop the hook along the way. Jacksonville is a most impressive sight from the water and its marinas are the perfect place to rest and refuel before tackling the next stretch. Take your time, keep alert, and enjoy the sights.

St. Johns Inlet to Jacksonville Anchorage Summary (Anchorages are listed in geographic order, moving downstream to upstream.)
St. Johns Anchorage—located near 30 23.442 North/081 29.186 West, along the southerly banks of the St. Johns River, southwest of flashing buoy #27—10-foot depths—reviewed on pages 67-68, 88
St. Johns Bluff Anchorage—located near 30 23.272 North/081 29.654 West, along the southern banks of the St. Johns River, hard by the charted location of St. Johns Bluff and between flashing daybeacons #31 and #33—12-foot depths—reviewed on pages 68, 88

Clapboard Creek Anchorage—located on the waters of Clapboard Creek, upstream of the 12-foot fixed bridge, near 30 25.325 North/081 30.155 West—7-foot depths in channel—note that entry into this anchorage is greatly restricted by the 12-foot bridge—reviewed on pages 70-71, 89

Cedar Point Creek Anchorage—located near 30 24.604 North/081 30.068 West, along the centerline of Cedar Point Creek, which flows off Clapboard Creek (see just above)—9-foot depths, but it is easy to wander into 1-foot soundings—this is a navigationally difficult anchorage, and you must fit under the 12-foot fixed bridge described above—reviewed on pages 71, 89

Mill Cove Anchorage—located near 30 23.001 North/081 32.323 West, on the waters of the broad stream stretching from the St. Johns to Mill Cove, west of flashing buoy #43—8-foot depths—reviewed on pages 71, 90

Trout River Anchorage—located near 30 23.616 North/081 38.579 West, on the mid-width of Trout River between Seafarers Marina and Pier 68 Marina—6½-foot depths—reviewed on pages 74, 90-91

Exchange Island Anchorage—northern anchorage located near 30 19.715 North/081 36.789 West—southern anchorage located near 30 19.569 North/081 36.797 West—both anchorages are found on the broad ribbon of water running between Exchange Island and the mainland community of "Arlington," south and east of flashing buoy #75—7-foot depths, though some shoals surround the approach to the southerly anchorage—reviewed on pages 75-76, 91-92

Ortega River Anchorage—located near 30 16.690 North/081 42.662 West, off the northwestern side of the Ortega River channel and northeast of Ortega River Boat Yard—5-foot depths—reviewed on pages 82, 93-94

St. Johns Inlet to Jacksonville Marina and Yacht-Club Summary (Please note that marinas and yacht clubs are listed in geographic order, moving downstream to upstream.)

Mayport Marine—(904) 246-8929—located near 30 23.820 North/081 25.735 West, northeast of the charted ferry dock on the Mayport waterfront—transient dockage available—gasoline and diesel fuel available—15+ feet on outer dock, 5 feet on inner slips—reviewed on pages 66-67, 87

Clapboard Creek Marina—located near 30 24.345 North/081 30.604 West, on the southwesterly entrance point of Clapboard Creek, where this stream intersects the Blount Island Channel—reviewed on pages 70, 89

Seafarers Marina—(904) 765-8152—located near 30 23.420 North/081 38.546 West, on the southwesterly shores of Trout River—transient dockage sometimes available—7-foot minimum depths—reviewed on pages 73-74, 90-91

River City Marina—(904) 398-7918—located near 30 19.234 North/081 39.652 West, on the southerly banks of the St. Johns River between the Main Street lift bridge and the fixed, high-rise Acosta Bridge—transient dockage available—gasoline and diesel fuel available—10-foot minimum depths—reviewed on pages 78-80, 93

Ortega River Boat Yard—(904) 387-5538—located near 30 16.646 North/081 42.774 West, along the northwesterly banks of the Ortega River—transient dockage available—gasoline and diesel fuel available—6-foot minimum depths—reviewed on pages 82-83, 93-94

Ortega Yacht Club Marina—(904) 389-1199—located near 30 16.562 North/081

Freighter on the St. Johns River

42.937 West, guarding the northwestern banks of Ortega River—transient dockage available—gasoline and diesel fuel available—6-foot minimum depths—reviewed on pages 83-84, 93-94

Lambs Yacht Center—(904) 384-5577—located near 30 16.289 North/081 43.168 West, also along the northwestern banks of the Ortega River, just southwest of the charted 45-foot fixed bridge—transient dockage available—gasoline and diesel fuel available—6-foot minimum depths—reviewed on pages 85-86, 93-94

St. Johns Inlet

The twin-jettied St. Johns Inlet is one of the most reliable seaward passages in all of Florida. The channel is used regularly by a wide variety of large commercial and naval craft. The numerous flashing buoys marking the channel are carefully maintained and clearly charted. If your plans call for an offshore voyage, this is the inlet to use for your seaward passage.

Mayport Naval Air Station

Cruisers passing through the water of St. Johns Inlet cannot help but notice the large naval air station in Mayport Basin on the seaward channel's southern banks. Naval craft ranging from destroyers to missile frigates are usually very much in evidence. You may be lucky enough to witness a search and rescue exercise involving several navy helicopters.

While you are, of course, free to enjoy the

sights and even take photographs from the St. Johns, don't attempt to enter the channel leading to the naval basin at flashing buoy #1, north of St. Johns Point. This entire area is off-limits to pleasure craft except in an extreme emergency.

Mayport and Mayport Marine (30 23.820 North/081 25.735 West)

The bustling community of Mayport is found on the St. Johns' southeastern shoreline northeast of flashing buoy #17. Mayport boasts two principal attractions for visitors. First, a large, active charter fishing fleet makes regular trips from the village's waterfront to offshore waters in search of any catch from billfish to king mackerel. If you would like to try your luck at saltwater angling in northern

Florida, Mayport may well be your best bet. Second, for those of us who are more interested in eating seafood than catching it, Mayport plays host to an unusually large number of seafood restaurants. Leaning toward the down-home in both atmosphere and cuisine, Mayport's restaurants have long since acquired a reputation up and down the Waterway for some of the finest fried seafood to be enjoyed anywhere.

While cruising past the Mayport waterfront, watch to the east and you may catch sight of the red brick Mayport Lighthouse. This old sentinel is now abandoned, though it still appears to be in mint condition.

Mayport boasts one marina catering to the needs of visiting cruisers. Mayport Marine is

Mayport Marine

found just downstream (northeast) from the charted ferry dock on the Mayport waterfront (near 30 23.820 North/081 25.735 West). Its location is noted as facility designation #7 on chart 11491. While Mayport Marine's primary concern is the dry-stack storage of smaller power craft, the marina does maintain a limited number of wet slips fronting directly onto the St. Johns. Transients are accepted for overnight or temporary dockage at these floating, concrete-decked piers. Depths on the outer docks are an impressive 15 feet or better, while you will find 5-foot low-water soundings on the innermost slips. The harbor is wide open to wind and wave, and as usual on this section of the St. Johns, the tidal currents can be prodigious.

Full power and water connections are on hand, as are gasoline, diesel fuel, waste pump-out service, and new, climate-controlled showers. Mechanical repairs are available for gasoline engines (particularly outboards and I/Os), and independent technicians can be called in for diesel work. The marina maintains a ship's store on the premises.

When it comes time to slake a healthy appetite, acquired after a long day on the water, virtually all the Mayport restaurants are within walking distance. We suggest that you give Singleton's Seafood Shack (4728 Ocean Street, 904-246-4442) a try. It may not be much to look at from the outside, but the seafood is simply wonderful. See you there for lunch!

Mayport Marine (904) 246-8929
   http://www.mayportmarine.com

Approach depths—15+ feet
Dockside depths—15+ feet (outer docks)
   5 feet (minimum—inner docks)
Accepts transients—yes
Transient dockage rate—above average
Floating concrete piers—yes
Dockside power connections
   —30 and 50 amps
Dockside water connections—yes
Showers—yes
Waste pump-out—yes
Gasoline—yes
Diesel fuel—yes
Mechanical repairs—yes
   (diesel—independent contractors)
Ship's store—yes
Restaurant—several nearby

Sand Dollar Restaurant

The Sand Dollar Restaurant (904-251-2449) and adjacent marina overlook the St. Johns' northwesterly shoreline, opposite the Mayport waterfront, some 100 yards northeast of the charted ferry terminal. This dining spot reportedly features reasonably good seafood, coupled with several concrete decked floating docks just south of the restaurant. Unfortunately, depths in the harbor have shoaled to 4 feet or even less at low water. It's even possible to run aground while cruising to the inner slips. Happily the southeastern face of the outermost pier carries at least 8 feet of water. This dock is not in the very best of repair, and it was completely occupied by local vessels during our last visit. The marina itself seems to be a pretty low-key operation, with the adjacent ship's store and dockmaster's office now long closed. For all their promise, the docks at Sand Dollar are probably best left to local cruisers or, at most, a quick call at the outer dock (assuming you can find space there) while dining ashore.

St. Johns Anchorage (30 23.442 North/081 29.186 West)

The large bubble of deep water that extends to the southwest from flashing buoy #27 toward the river's southern banks can offer anchorage in light to lower-moderate airs. Depths of 10 to 19 feet run in fairly close to shore. Protection from the high banks is good in a southerly breeze, but there is little shelter for winds from any other direction. You will also be exposed to the wake of all passing traffic. Since the 1980s, this shoreline has become host to some moderate residential development. While all-natural shores would be nice, the pleasant homes overlooking the water are certainly not objectionable.

St. Johns Bluff Anchorage (30 23.272 North/081 29.654 West)

St. Johns Bluff is a large mass of very high ground overlooking the river's southern banks between flashing daybeacons #31 and #33. The bluff is readily recognizable from the water by its considerable elevation. This high promontory is overlooked by a modest collection of tasteful homes.

Good depths of 12 feet or better run to within 50 yards of shore between #31 and #33. In southerly winds or moderate easterly blows, there is sufficient protection on these waters for overnight anchorage with enough swinging room for the Queen Mary. With even moderate winds in the offing from the north, or particularly the west, better try another overnight strategy.

Fort Caroline Park is perched atop St. Johns Bluff, but, unfortunately, nothing of the park's structures or grounds are visible from the water. Not only are there not any landing facilities, but if you should make the attempt by dinghy, it is likely that you would find yourself on private property. The historic importance of this site certainly makes it worth a visit, but landside transportation will be necessary to access the park.

St. Johns Bluff History   The earliest account of the St. Johns by a European describes the region as "the fairest, fruit-fullest and pleasantest" land. These are the words of Jean Ribault, a French seaman who sailed into the St. Johns in 1562 in search of a refuge in the New World for himself and his fellow French Huguenots. Spanish sailors had explored Florida long before this. Spain had even sponsored several colonization attempts, which had all ended in miserable failure. However, the first semipermanent settlement of Florida's east coast was constructed under the gaily waving fleur de lis of France, rather than under the flag of King Philip.

Two years after Ribault's visit, the French returned under the command of Rene Boulaine de Laudonniere, one of Ribault's lieutenants from the earlier voyage. (Ribault himself was temporarily imprisoned in England.) The French chose a bluff rising some 90 feet above the river as the site of a colony. The settlers dubbed it Fort Caroline in honor of their young king.

Trouble soon arose at Fort Caroline. Food ran short and the colonists took to begging or stealing supplies from the local Indians. When an English trader, Sir John Hawkins, called at the struggling settlement, the French traded gunpowder and cannon for one of Sir Johns' ships. The whole colony prepared to return to France. By August of 1565 all preparations had been completed for departure when quite unexpectedly newly freed Adm. Jean Ribault dropped anchor off Fort Caroline with a fleet of seven ships. On board were more than 600 new settlers.

Strangely enough, the same day, the Spanish conquistador Don Pedro Menendez de Aviles arrived at the "River of Dolphins," which he renamed St. Augustine for the feast of San Augustin. Menendez was under orders from his king to remove every vestige of French settlement from Florida's shores. Within a month he had fulfilled his commission so thoroughly that historians still argue about whether Menendez was just unusually loyal and efficient or truly bloodthirsty. We shall hear more about Menendez and St. Augustine in the next chapter, but for the purposes of this account, we need only note that the Spanish general soon sailed north with a goodly portion of his 800-man force, expecting to overwhelm the upstart French colony easily.

Menendez was surprised to find four of Ribault's ships anchored off the St. Johns inlet bar. After hastily disengaging, the Spanish force hurried back to its new settlement and prepared for the attack that was sure to follow by the superior French fleet.

Ribault did put to sea a few days later, intent on the destruction of the Spanish forces to the south, but a violent storm scattered the French fleet and shipwrecked most of the expedition south of Matanzas Inlet. We shall hear the sad story of these shipwrecked soldiers later.

Meanwhile, not knowing the French fleet's fate, Menendez boldly prepared to attack Fort Caroline overland. After a forced march of four days through swamps and hostile terrain, the Spanish took the French completely by surprise. In the attack 138 French were killed and many more made prisoner. Only a handful, including Laudonniere, were able to escape on two small ships that Ribault had left behind. Menendez renamed the former French fortification Fort San Mateo and left a small garrison behind as he beat a hasty retreat to deal with the expected French attack, which, of course, never came.

As bloody as Menendez's victory had been, it was not to be the last chapter in the grim history of St. Johns Bluff. In 1567 a French fleet under the command of Dominique de Gorgues appeared on the St. Johns. Bolstered by Indian allies, the French attacked Fort San Mateo just as the Spanish were having their evening meal. Their surprise was complete, and the fort was overwhelmed with only token opposition.

Some historians claim that Gorgues had all his bound captives assembled in a group beside the river. He addressed the captives in their native language, supposedly telling them that they had acted properly in annihilating the Protestant heretics of Fort Caroline. (Gorgues, of course, was Catholic, as were both his entire war party and the Spanish prisoners.)

At this point, tradition tells us that Gorgues called for a drink of water. Certainly the Spanish prisoners must have felt relieved, but, alas, their good feelings were to be short-lived. Gorgues went on to tell his prisoners that in spite of their right-minded actions, those whom they had killed were, after all, citizens of his beloved France and it was his duty, however painful, to avenge their deaths. Having completed his speech, Gorgues proceeded to hang all 200 prisoners, 10 by 10. So intent was Gorgues on avoiding any misconception that he is supposed to have attached a sign to each corpse stating that the Spanish had been hanged not on religious grounds but merely as murderers.

Blount Island Channel

Blount Island Channel is actually a large loop of the St. Johns that splits off from the river's primary track abeam of flashing buoy #35. Both the entrance to the north of #35 and its westerly counterpart just east of the high-rise Dames Point Bridge are easily entered from the St. Johns. Excellent depths of 10 to 35 feet are consistently held in the channel's midwidth, but there is some shallow water abutting Blount Island's eastern shoreline. The loop is blocked near the northern tip of Blount Island by twin fixed bridges with only 8 feet of vertical clearance. The mainland shores on the easterly portion of the channel are lined with private homes, but there is heavy commercial development on most of the other mainland banks. Blount Island itself hosts a large and varied industrial complex, which is readily seen from the water.

Because of the stream's considerable width and frequent commercial waterborne traffic, anchorage in the Blount Island Channel is not a practical consideration. However, there is one sidewater that offers a sheltered haven for smaller power craft.

Back River

Veteran St. Johns cruisers who have not visited the river for several years will find big changes in the body of water known as Back River. This artificial stream strikes northwest from flashing daybeacon #38 into the body of Blount Island.

For many years these waters played host to a huge crane that was quite visible from the main body of the St. Johns River. As far as this writer has been able to determine, the crane was used on but a single occasion to unload the main unit of a nuclear reactor.

The seldom-employed crane is gone and Back River is now the site of a whole collection of active commercial-shipping docks and wharves. There is certainly no room for anchorage by pleasure craft, but if you are

of a mind, exploration (at idle speed) can be interesting.

Clapboard Creek Marina and Anchorages (Various Lats/Lons—see below)

Clapboard Creek makes into the northeasterly banks of Blount Island Channel as the easterly arm of the loop begins its turn to the northwest. A fixed bridge with only 12 feet of vertical clearance spans the entrance to Clapboard Creek and limits entry to low-lying craft. If by some lucky chance you can clear the span, the creek offers several anchorages. Minimum depths of 7 feet are held well upstream, with most readings being in the 9- to 15-foot range.

Clapboard Creek Marina (near 30 24.345 North/081 30.604 West) is a tiny facility located on the northwest point of Clapboard Creek's entrance (short of the low-level bridge). Chart 11491 notes a "Jetty" just west of the marina's single, fixed, wooden piers. This small facility caters mostly to local craft, but an on-site travelift can also serve pleasure cruisers' haul-out needs. Some mechanical repairs are also available for gasoline-powered power plants.

Once through the Clapboard Creek bridge, you can drop the hook almost anywhere you choose. The lower section of the stream is bordered exclusively by saltwater marsh, which would give only minimal protection in a heavy blow. Better sheltered is the section some distance upstream, where the high ground of Pelotes Island abuts the western shore (near 30 25.325 North/081 30.155 West). There is some light residential development along the island's shoreline on this portion of the stream. Surprisingly strong tidal currents plague both Clapboard Creek and Cedar Creek (see below). Be sure

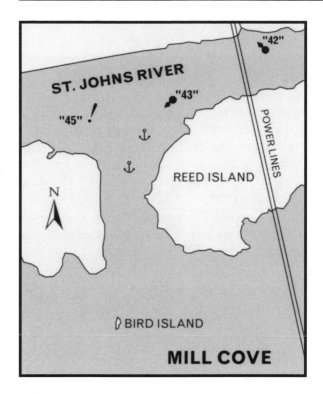

the hook is well set before abandoning your anchor watch.

Cedar Point Creek Anchorage (30 24.604 North/081 30.068 West)

A branch of Cedar Point Creek intersects Clapboard Creek's eastern banks just north of the larger stream's bridge. While minimum depths of 9 feet are carried in Cedar Creek's channel for quite a distance upstream, and overnight anchorage is a possibility, the stream's entrance is surrounded by unmarked shoals and is quite tricky. Adventurous skippers (who can clear the Clapboard Creek 12-foot bridge) in craft drawing 3½ feet or preferably less might give this stream a try, but must be sure to feel their way carefully along at idle speed with a weather eye on the sounder.

Should you successfully enter Cedar Creek, consider dropping the hook just before coming abeam of the first offshoot on the northern shore. Depths range from 10 to 15 feet here, and the holding ground seems to be thick mud.

Mill Cove Anchorage (30 23.001 North/081 32.323 West)

A deep, wide creek cuts south from the St. Johns, just west of flashing buoy #43, to mostly shallow Mill Cove. This approach stream carries minimum 8-foot depths north of the privately maintained markers to the south, and provides good anchorage without leaving the main body of the St. Johns too far behind. As usual, there is plenty of current, so check the anchor carefully before heading below for that first well-earned toddy.

North of Mill Cove, a series of uncharted, privately maintained markers carries local, shallow-draft craft between the twin arms of a submerged breakwater, possibly the remnants of an old bridge. Depths in this marked cut hold at 7-foot levels or better, but the waters beyond are shallow. Cruising captains are strongly advised to anchor well north of the markers. Depths in these waters run from 8 to 30 feet, and there is ample swinging room for the largest pleasure craft. The surrounding shores are mostly undeveloped, though you will have a good view of the commercial wharves to the north, on the opposite side of the St. Johns River. This anchorage offers superb shelter to the east and west, and the underwater jetties and shallows give some lee to the south. Strong winds over 25 knots from the north could make you imitate a Mexican jumping bean. When blows of this ilk are in the offing, better seek shelter elsewhere.

Dames Point Bridge

Just west of the St. Johns-Blount Island Channel (western arm) intersection, the Dames Point Bridge proudly spans the mighty river. This most impressive structure is the longest suspension bridge in the United States, surpassing even the more famous Golden Gate. As you cruise through, take a moment to admire this engineering marvel. It is an awesome sight from the water.

Just downstream from the high-rise span, a large collection of containerized-ship loading wharves overlooks the northern banks. The large ships usually docked here make for interesting viewing. During an earlier cruise on these waters, we observed a large, incredibly ugly automobile transport vessel.

Broward River

The southeasterly mouth of Broward River makes into the St. Johns well northwest of flashing buoy #57. While quite wide, the Broward is consistently shallow. The one deepwater channel into the river has been cut off by a large fuel dock on the entrance's northeastern flank. Cruising craft are strictly advised to bypass Broward River.

Dames Point Bridge, St. Johns River

Trout River Marinas and Anchorage (Various Lats/Lons—see below)

Trout River boasts the best facilities on the St. Johns River east of Jacksonville. It's not too bad for overnight anchorage either. A marked channel leads west-northwest into the main body of the stream from flashing buoy #66. Holding minimum depths of 7 feet on its centerline, the river eventually leads to two marinas and a series of bridges guarding its upper reaches.

Both Trout River marinas lie on the southwestern shoreline about midway between the St. Johns intersection and the upstream bridges. These facilities are open to a considerable chop in strong easterly breezes but are fairly well sheltered from other winds.

The easternmost of the two is Seafarers Marina (near 30 23.420 North/081 38.546 West). This true mom-and-pop operation is very popular with live-aboards. The marina motto is "Once at Seafarers, always at Seafarers." While transients are gratefully accepted at the fixed, wooden piers, most of the available slips seem to be filled by local craft. Be sure to call ahead of time to check on berth availability.

All of Seafarers' slips feature water and 30- and 50-amp power connections. Depths alongside range from as much as 11 feet at the outer berths to 7½ feet close to shore. Nice showers and washer and dryer are available just behind the piers. Some mechanical repairs can be arranged through local, independent technicians. The dockmaster has a few marine items in her office, but there is really not a true ship's store on site. Jackie's Seafood Restaurant (904-764-0120) is within walking distance and reportedly serves a wonderful "catch of the day."

Both a grocery store and pharmacy are within a six-block walk of Seafarers' docks.

Courtesy transportation is sometimes available through the marina. Check with dockmaster (and owner) Barbara Bowman.

All in all, we found Seafarers to be a friendly facility that will appeal to live-aboards and those cruising on a budget. As the owner put it to this writer, "Yachtsy people don't like us, but true cruisers come back time and time again." That just about says it all.

Seafarers Marina (904) 765-8152

Approach depths—7 feet (minimum)
Dockside depths—7½-11 feet

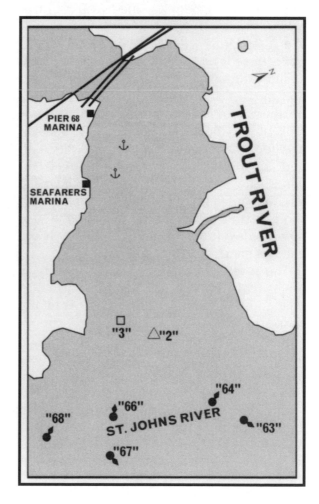

Accepts transients—yes
Transient dockage rate—below average
Fixed wooden piers—yes
Dockside power connections —30
  and 50 amps
Dockside water connections—yes
Showers—yes
Laundromat—yes
Mechanical repairs—yes
  (independent contractors)
Restaurant—nearby

During our many visits to Trout River research we have often observed a host of anchored and moored vessels ensconced on the waters lying between the two Trout River marinas (near 30 23.616 North/081 38.579 West). As far as we have been able to determine, there is no restriction to anchoring here besides the usual strictures of proper waste and garbage disposal. Please don't try to pick up any of the private mooring buoys.

Depths in the anchorage run 6½ to 8 feet at low tide. There is good protection to the south and fair shelter from northern and westerly winds. Strong blows from the east could make for a very uncomfortable stay. The surrounding shores feature moderate, but not unsightly, residential development, and both marinas are within sight of the anchorage.

The westernmost Trout River facility is once again known as Pier 68 Marina. A change in management and focus is taking shape here just as this account is being tapped out on the keyboard. For some years now, a Travis Boating Center has been making its residence at this location, but by the time this account finds its way into your hands, the facility will once again be known as Pier 68 Marina. In keeping with this writer's longstanding policy of not commenting on marina or repair-yard facilities until they can be reviewed in person, we will say

nothing else of the new incarnation of Pier 68 until the next edition of this guide. Watch our Salty Southeast on-line newsletter to learn more sooner.

Farther to the west, a series of bridges crosses Trout River. The first is the Highway 17 fixed span with 29 feet of vertical clearance. Past the U.S. 17 bridge, an old highway bridge has been left in place with the central span removed. Finally, a low-level railroad crosses the river. This span opens on demand from 6:00 A.M. to 10:00 P.M. unless a train is due. Twelve hours' notice is required for the bridge to open during the nighttime hours.

The upstream section of Trout River is very attractive, with light to moderate residential development on the mostly high-ground shoreline. Minimum depths of 7 feet are held on the midsection until readings begin to fall off to the north of Ribault River.

Trout River has several sidewaters but none with adequate depths for larger craft. The most promising, Ribault River, has shallower depths at its entrance than those shown on the latest edition of chart 11491 at the time of this writing. Currently, 4- to 5-foot low-tide depths can be expected at the Ribault's northern mouth.

Depths fall off markedly near the Trout River shoreline. If you choose to drop the hook in the river, you will only be able to get within several hundred yards of a lee shore. Because of this and the Trout's large size, the river can only be recommended as an anchorage in light to lower-moderate airs.

Jacksonville Port Terminal

The large port facility at Jacksonville becomes increasingly evident on the western and southwestern shores upstream of flashing buoy #71. From this point until you reach the first of the St. Johns' high-rise bridges past flashing buoy # 78, you will be able to observe an interesting and varied collection of large ships, tankers, and barges berthed at the extensive wharves. Loading and unloading are often in progress and make for fascinating sightseeing as you cruise along. If you proceed at idle speed, you are permitted to cruise quite close to the big ships. However, be sure to stay clear of any that might be entering or leaving the port.

Exchange Island Anchorage Various Lat/Lons—see below

A deepwater channel borders the St. Johns' easterly shoreline, east and south of flashing buoy #75. This cut eventually runs between the mainland to the east and charted Exchange Island to the west. While some navigational care must be exercised to successfully round the shoals lying between the main river channel and this side passage, prudent mariners should be able to carry minimum 8-foot depths.

The channel behind Exchange Island is spanned by a low-level section of the Matthews Point Bridge. Most larger craft will not be able to clear this fixed bridge, but it is a simple matter to enter the deep waters from either the northern or the southern point of Exchange Island. The waters to the north and south of the Matthews span provide opportune anchorage just where you would least expect to find a sheltered haven.

There is even one small facility adjoining these waters. Arlington Marina (904-743-2628) overlooks the easterly banks immediately north of the charted cove labeled as "Surfaced Ramps" on chart 11491. This is a dry-stack

storage facility, and no services other than gasoline sales are available for cruising craft. Depths alongside range from 5 to 11 feet.

Just south of Arlington Marina, a huge commercial marine railway indents the easterly shoreline. We have often observed several large tugboats hauled up as we pass.

After leaving the tug railway behind, typical soundings of 8 to 14 feet stretch south to the Matthews fixed bridge. This would be a super spot to anchor with enough swinging room for even the largest cruising craft (near 30 19.715 North/081 36.789 West). Protection is nearly perfect for winds blowing from the east or west, and it's not too shabby for southerly winds either. Only northerly breezes of 20 knots or better are likely to raise an uncomfortable chop. The mainland shores exhibit moderate residential development but Exchange Island is completely in its natural state.

After dropping the hook, notice the small wooden building perched on a pier just short of the bridge. With the use of your binoculars you'll be able to read the designation "Jones College" on the building's side. Conversations with local cruisers reveal that a local sculling team operates out of this small structure. If you happen by during a practice session, it can certainly make for some interesting ogling through the binoculars.

It is also possible to work your way around the southern tip of Exchange Island into the deep waters south of the fixed bridge. Here you can drop the hook in 7 to 12 feet of water under conditions very similar to those described above (near 30 19.569 North/081 36.797 West). Unmarked shoals are far more prolific on this passage than its counterpart to the north. Nevertheless, we have followed the channel successfully on any number of occasions. For those who want to be sure of navigational simplicity, the northerly cut is recommended over these waters.

Jacksonville

By the time you pass under the high-rise Matthews Point fixed bridge on the main St. Johns River channel, the teeming city of Jacksonville will be more than obvious along both shorelines. The corporate limits of Jacksonville encompass more land than any other city in the United States. Without a doubt, Jacksonville is the most commercially important community in northern Florida. The city's active port facilities are the largest between Savannah and Miami. Perhaps these data (and they do not even begin to tell the whole story) will begin to clue you to Jacksonville's boisterous progressivism. This is truly a city on the move, and it is refreshing to note that its rapid progress has not taken place at the expense of the community's appearance, particularly from the water.

In fact, Jacksonville has been engaged in a vigorous waterfront redevelopment project on both shores of the river since the mid-1980s. Cruisers will be particularly impressed with the Riverwalk project, a series of docks, piers, and attractive wooden walking ramps stretching across much of the city's waterfront on both sides of the river. Judging from the attractive shoreline and the impressive number of pedestrians we have observed making use of the Riverwalk, this project would seem to be a rousing success.

As you can well imagine, it is a very special experience for cruisers to observe the Jacksonville skyline from the water. The mammoth skyscrapers, interspersed with attractive riverside parks fairly bursting with flowers, present a photographic opportunity that is all too rare, even for cruising-guide authors. The captain who bypasses the chance to cruise through this very special city is missing one of the great boating treats in all of Florida.

Numbers to know in Jacksonville:
Gator City Taxi—904-355-8294
Budget Car Rental—904-296-8058
Avis Rent A Car—904-741-2327
West Marine—904-388-7510
Boat/U.S. Marine Center—904-642-6505
Boater's World—904-724-3601

Jacksonville Facilities and Waterside Attractions

As recently as 1986, the only marina facilities available in Jacksonville were located well west of the downtown district on Ortega River. With the addition of River City Marina and the Jacksonville Landing shopping (and dining) complex in the 1990s, downtown Jacksonville now has much to offer visiting cruisers. Additionally, there are several other restaurants with docks that demand attention, assuming your craft can handle the sometimes thin water at these piers.

After passing under the Hart-Commodore Point fixed bridge and leaving flashing buoy #81 and unlighted nun buoy #82 in your wake, you will sight what will appear to be a marina along the northerly banks. These piers are associated with the city of Jacksonville's Metropolitan Park. Depths alongside range from 8 to 10½ feet. This park has been a popular concert site for many years, as well as the setting for numerous festivals and shows.

The Gator Bowl football stadium sits just behind the park. The Jacksonville Jaguars National Football League team has been playing home games in the Gator Bowl for several

Downtown Jacksonville, St. Johns River

years now. Metropolitan Park has taken on even more importance with the addition of this very popular sports attraction.

For years there has been discussion about what to do with the docks at Metropolitan Park. Various plans to establish a second city marina at this site have gone nowhere. Now, with the Jaguars in residence, there is renewed discussion of revitalizing the docks as a full-fledged marina with various conveyances to the Gator Bowl during football games. All of this is still very indefinite at the time of this writing and, in the absence of any firm information to the contrary, cruisers should not count on finding any overnight dockage at this facility.

A bit farther to the west (upstream), on the southern shore, the Chart House restaurant (904-398-3353) makes for a striking sight from the water with its large, plate-glass windows. Diners may be assured of really first-class food

Jacksonville Landing, Jacksonville

at the northernmost representative of this notable restaurant chain. Currently, the Chart House is open only for the evening meal.

Cruising patrons of the Chart House may also berth at the adjacent Riverwalk docks, with low-water depths alongside of some 5 feet. Obviously, you should only make use of these berths if your craft draws less than 5 feet.

Jacksonville boasts its own marina within the downtown district. This facility flanks the St. Johns' southerly shores between the Main Street lift bridge and the fixed, high-rise Acosta Bridge (near 30 19.234 North/081 39.652 West). The marina has gone through more than its share of growing pains over the last decade and a half. First opened as a privately managed complex with a large, adjacent restaurant, this firm went out of business after scarcely a year. The city then reluctantly ran the marina until 1994.

Since that time this marine and dining complex has once again been taken over by a private entity. Renamed River City Marina, and managed by River City Brewing Company, the marina and adjacent restaurant have both been revitalized. Transient space is somewhat reduced at River City Marina than it has been in years past, due to an influx of resident craft. There are still usually five to eight slips open for overnighters at any given time. All berths at this facility feature floating, wooden-decked piers, sporting full power, water, telephone, and satellite-television connections. The impressive dockside soundings range from 10

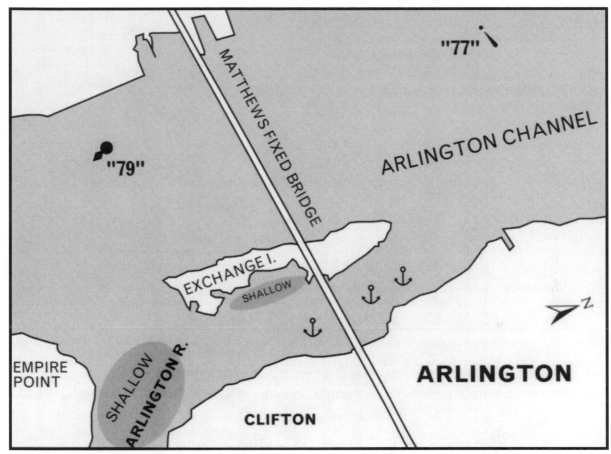

to as much as 17 feet. A considerable tidal current does run through the dockage basin, so be ready for this rapid water movement as you approach the docks.

Shoreside, you will find fair showers and a Laundromat. The bathroom/shower facilities are shared with the outside patrons of the adjoining restaurant. This is not what we would call an ideal arrangement. Gasoline and diesel fuel can be purchased, and some repairs can usually be arranged through independent contractors.

The on-site River City Brewing Company restaurant is known for its "hand crafted" beers. They are all brewed on the premises in one of the increasingly popular microbreweries. We felt compelled to sample several varieties and found them to be uniformly superb. The food we enjoyed on two occasions was fair to good, with the fresh, broiled seafood a particularly noteworthy choice. The rates of fare were not inexpensive, however. All in all, we recommend a meal (or two) at this dining spot, assuming your wallet can stand the strain.

River City Marina (904) 398-7918

Approach depths—12+ feet
Dockside depths—10-17 feet
Accepts transients—yes
Transient dockage rate—average
Floating wooden piers—yes
Dockside power connections—30 and 50 amp

Dockside water connections—yes
Showers—yes
Laundromat—yes
Gasoline—yes
Diesel fuel—yes
Mechanical repairs—yes
    (independent contractors)
Restaurant—on site

The Jacksonville Riverwalk boasts several interesting attractions located just behind River City Marina. The Museum of Science and History (904-396-6674) and the Jacksonville Maritime Museum (904-398-9011) are worth your time and attention. Just next door to these points of interest, visitors will discover Friendship Park. This park is centered around an absolutely mammoth fountain that is incredibly impressive when operational.

Another waterside development of interest to visiting cruisers is Jacksonville Landing, "a riverfront shopping mall," located directly across the St. Johns from River City Marina. This attractive, popular complex contains some seventy-five specialty shops and restaurants. It is the creation of the Rouse Company, already famous for similar projects in

River City Marina, Jacksonville

Baltimore and New York.

Jacksonville Landing maintains a 180-foot floating public dock fronting directly onto the St. Johns River. Parts of the Jacksonville Landing pier are concrete decked while the center portion features a wooden platform. Patrons of Jacksonville Landing are encouraged to dock here while ashore, but no overnight stays are allowed. The pier can become quite crowded on weekends. Depths run better than 15 feet alongside, so any size craft should be able to dock safely. Again, however, be on guard against swift tidal currents. Mariners docking at River City Marina can reach Jacksonville Landing via a very long walk across the Main Street Bridge or by taking a water taxi directly from the marina.

In addition to all these nautical points of interest, the many piers and docks lining the impressive Riverwalk project can sometimes provide additional berths during special events. Be warned, however: depths near many of these public piers run as shallow as 3 to 4 feet. Fortunately, some of the docks display signs clearly showing the dockside depths. If you do choose to berth at any of these piers during one of the many festivals centered around the Riverwalk, approach with caution and keep a wary eye on the depth sounder.

Jacksonville History   Long before the first Europeans touched the shores of the St. Johns River, Native Americans had found a convenient place to cross the mighty stream near its sharp turn to the south. They called this ford Wacca Pilatka or Cow Ford.

The Spanish census of 1787 found 126 persons living near Cow Ford. In late 1816 Lewis Hogans and his wife built a log cabin at the ford. They are usually considered the first permanent residents of the region. By 1821 it was time to bring order to the new settlement and Abram Bellamy, a civil engineer, laid out the town plan.

During this early period, Cow Ford was helped by the presence of the nearby "King's Road," which led from New Smyrna and St. Augustine to points north. Cow Ford was a natural spot to found a ferry, and one John Brady, who had run a tavern in the small village since 1818, did so in 1821.

In 1822 the grateful citizens of Cow Ford renamed their small town Jacksonville, in honor of Gen. Andrew Jackson. The future president was instrumental in bringing Florida into the American fold, and most of the local citizens had looked forward to this conversion for many years.

Isaac Hart built the village's first hotel in 1830, and the town received its charter two years later. Hart is considered the "father of Jacksonville." His hostelry was the beginning of a lively tourist business that brought early prosperity to the town. Travelers stopped over on their journeys north or south, and the luxurious yachts of wealthy tourists dotted the river.

By 1840 Jacksonville could count 600 citizens in its ever-widening civic sphere. Three hundred lumber ships cleared the port city in 1853 in addition to other commerce on the water. If the Civil War had not intervened, Jacksonville might have progressed to a position of economic dominance in northern Florida long before it actually achieved that status.

As it was, however, the War Between the States brought destruction and ruin to Jacksonville. The city was invaded and abandoned by Federal troops on four separate occasions. After the third invasion, in March 1863, when the Northern forces left, a fire broke out. It has never been established whether the retreating Northern troops or Southern sympathizers started the blaze, but if General Finegan's nearby Confederate forces had not acted promptly, the whole city might have burned.

In February 1864 Union troops again moved into Jacksonville on their way west to the Battle of Olustee. Northern forces were completely routed in the engagement by a far smaller Confederate force. The Battle of Olustee ranks as the most serious defeat in Florida suffered by either force during the Civil War.

Like all the South, Jacksonville suffered through the Reconstruction era, but by 1888 the city could number some forty hotels that entertained upwards of seventy-five thousand customers a year. The St. James Hotel opened in 1869 and became known as the "the Fifth Avenue Hotel of Florida."

Again, however, the city suffered a setback when in 1888 one of the worst yellow fever epidemics on record was centered in Jacksonville. Working in total ignorance of the disease's real cause, local citizens burned pine and tar to "clear the air," applied lime and disinfectant to tree trunks and fence posts, and even fired fifty rounds of heavy shells, hoping to drive away the bad vapors. Between deaths and evacuees, the city's population fell from 17,201 to 13,757 in the space of a few months.

The epidemic was followed by the great fire of 1901. One hundred and forty-eight blocks of the city were consumed in the great conflagration, and the light from the flames was observed from Savannah. Smoke from the fire was reported as far north as Raleigh, North Carolina.

In spite of these calamities, Jacksonville steadily progressed during the twentieth century. The city quickly recovered from the fire. By the following year, building permits covering more than half the burned area had been issued.

Jacksonville's port facilities became an increasingly important part of the city's economy, and during the relatively brief period that World War I affected America, more than twenty-five ships were built and launched in Jacksonville as part of the war effort. Today, the city combines tourism and corporate business with its active port to fashion the most successful municipal economy in northern Florida.

Ortega River (Various Lats/Lons—see below)

Ortega River enters the St. Johns west-southwest of Jacksonville, well west-southwest of flashing daybeacon #2. This stream really belongs to the next section of this chapter, but because it houses a very impressive collection of marine facilities within striking distance of Jacksonville, it will be reviewed here.

Entry into Ortega River can be a tricky process. Even if you follow the channel exactly, you may encounter some 5½- to 6-foot depths. Be sure to read the Ortega River navigation section below before attempting first-time entry into the river.

The various Ortega River facilities are found along the stream's northwestern shore, southwest of the charted 9-foot (closed vertical clearance) bascule bridge. There is also a local anchorage to consider.

All of the Ortega River marinas are within walking distance of the huge Roosevelt Shopping Mall. Nautical visitors will be interested to learn that the Jacksonville branch of the ultrapopular West Marine retail stores fronts the shopping center (904-388-7510). Hard by West Marine, you will also discover great sandwiches at Tom & Betty's restaurant (904-387-3311), amidst an interesting "old automobile" theme. There is also an Eckerd Drugs in the mall.

A Publix supermarket is located at Roosevelt Mall as well. Not only can you restock your galley larders, but this Publix has an extensive deli with their own cafe.

Two other nearby restaurants are well worth your consideration, though they are too far for access by foot. A taxi (see above) will get you there in a jiffy. Harpoon Louie's (4070 Herschel Street, 904-389-5631) is a combination restaurant and bar that has gallons of ultracold "liquid sunshine" on tap, not to mention some super cheeseburgers and fish sandwiches. Visiting cruisers will quickly discover that this is where the local sailing crowd hangs out. On weekends, the wait for a table can be lengthy, so come early.

If you're up for the best breakfast (and a mighty good lunch) in Jacksonville, spare no effort to find your way to the Fox Restaurant (3580 St. Johns Avenue, 904-387-2669). You need only look once at the line of customers waiting for breakfast to know that this is "the" best place to break your nightly fast.

Moving upstream from the bascule bridge, watch for a collection of anchored and moored boats off the northwestern side of the channel, short of the first Ortega River marina (near 30 16.690 North/081 42.662 West). Here you can drop the hook amidst low-water depths of 5 to 7 feet with superb protection from all but gale-force northeasterlies. Don't approach the northwesterly shoreline too closely, as these banks are shoal.

Southwest of the anchorage, Ortega River Boat Yard is the first facility to come up on the river's northwestern banks, near 30 16.646 North/081 42.774 West. This firm's extensive piers, some of which are covered, will be more than obvious from the water. Ortega River Boat Yard is glad to accept transients at its fixed, wooden piers featuring water and 30- and 50-amp power connections. The marina maintains one rank of covered slips, but the rest are open and suitable for sailcraft. Many berths boast 7 to 8 feet of water at low tide.

Three tiled showers and a complete Laundromat are available on the marina grounds. Gasoline, diesel fuel, and waste pump-out services are offered at the marina fuel dock. Hard-to-find block ice can also be purchased at this facility.

As its name implies, Ortega River Boat Yard offers full service repairs. Service work is available for both gasoline and diesel engines. A 25-ton travelift facilitates haul-outs and below-waterline repairs. Additionally Millers Marine Service (904-388-3690), Pat Robey's Sail Repair shop (904-389-1001), and the yard's own ship's and boat-sales store are also located on the premises. How's that for an impressive lineup of repair capabilities?

Ortega River Boat Yard (904) 387-5538
http://www.ortegariverboatyard.com

Approach depths—7-8 feet
Dockside depths—6-8 feet
Accepts transients—yes
Transient dockage rate—below average
Fixed wooden piers—yes
Dockside power connections—30
  and 50 amps
Dockside water connections—yes
Showers—yes
Laundromat—yes
Waste pump-out—yes
Gasoline—yes
Diesel fuel—yes
Below-waterline repairs—yes (extensive)
Mechanical repairs—yes (extensive)
Ship's store—yes
Restaurant—several nearby

Just upstream from Ortega River Boat Yard, the extensive piers of impressive Ortega Yacht Club Marina guard the northwestern banks near 30 16.562 North/081 42.937 West. In spite of its name, this facility is a privately owned marina open to the public. It seems to be quite popular with visiting and resident mariners alike. Transients are accommodated at modern, floating concrete docks. Low-water depths at the piers run around 6 to 7 feet. No slips are specifically set aside for transients, but the friendly dockmaster has informed this writer that space is almost always available for visitors. Just to be on the safe side, consider calling ahead and making advance arrangements.

All berths feature full power and water connections, and gasoline and diesel fuel can be purchased dockside. Excellent, climate-controlled showers and a full Laundromat (with a tiny paperback exchange library) are found in the support building overlooking the dock's connecting link with the mainland. Just beside this building, visiting cruisers will discover an attractively landscaped picnic and cookout area. Again, the restaurants at the Roosevelt Mall are within walking distance, and many other choices are available via taxi. Ortega Yacht Club

Ortega River Boat Yard

Marina is a first-rate facility that has always impressed me as being unusually helpful.

Ortega Yacht Club Marina (904) 389-1199
   http://www.oycm.com
Approach depths—7-8 feet
Dockside depths—6-7 feet (minimum)
Accepts transients—yes
Transient dockage rate—below average
Floating concrete piers—yes
Dockside power connections—30
   and 50 amps
Dockside water connections—yes
Showers—yes
Laundromat—yes

Gasoline—yes
Diesel fuel—yes
Restaurant—several nearby

Sadler Point Marina (904-384-1383) flanks the northwestern banks just short of the Ortega River twin bridges. Sadler Point usually rents out its somewhat limited wet-slip dockage on a strictly month to month basis. Full mechanical repairs are offered and the yard maintains a 25-ton travelift for haul-outs. Gasoline is also available dockside.

Cruisers visiting Ortega River will find one

Ortega River Yacht Club Marina

of the largest ship's and nautical stores in the country just behind Sadler Point Marina. The Ship's Locker-Pier 17 (904-387-4669) carries a mind-boggling array of nautical equipment including clothes, nautical publications, and a huge selection of parts and ground tackle. It's not going too far to say that if you don't find it here, you may as well give up the effort. Be sure to tell Grace or Cindy that we sent you.

The two remaining Ortega River facilities are located on the upstream side of the charted twin bridges. The railway span is usually open, but the fixed highway bridges have a vertical clearance of 45 feet. Sailcraft that can't clear this height are prevented from visiting Lamb's Yacht Center or Huckins Yacht Corporation.

Just southwest of the twin highway and railroad spans, the docks of Huckins Yacht Corporation (904-389-1125) will come abeam on the northwestern shore. Huckins specializes in building impressive sportsfishermen boats, but also offers all types of repair and modification to other brands of pleasure craft, including Awlgrip and Imron painting services.

After you leave the Huckins plant behind, one of the real class acts in the Jacksonville marine community comes up on the northwestern banks near 30 16.289 North/081 43.168 West. If you should miss the extensive covered and open slips of Lamb's Yacht Center, better make a very quick appointment with your eye doctor. There is a definite flavor of power boating at Lamb's Yacht Center, but my sailing brethren (who can clear the 45-foot fixed bridge) may well find much to interest them here as well. Quite simply, this is a huge complex that offers just about every imaginable service for pleasure craft.

Transient dockage, both covered and open, is extensive. Lamb's features both fixed wooden and fixed concrete piers. Thirty-amp electrical and water hookups are found at all slips, and some have 50-amp connections as well. Showers (in fair condition) are readily available, and both gasoline and diesel fuel are sold at the fuel dock fronting directly onto Ortega River. Waste pump-out service is available as well.

Lamb's also features an extensive, on-site ship's store with an extensive collection of both parts and marine supplies, in very attractive surroundings. Give it a look.

Copious dry-stack storage is also on hand immediately adjacent to the marina dockage basin. This service is carried forward under the auspices of Surface's Marine (904-384-6447).

To say that repair facilities at Lamb's Yacht Center are extensive might be somewhat akin to claiming that Cate Blanchett has been a moderately successful movie actor of late. To be succinct, if you can't get it fixed here, better find out how the new boating market has been doing lately. Full mechanical, electrical, and carpentry services are all readily available. Need to be hauled? Well, choose from three marine railways or two travelifts rated at 30 and 40 tons.

Lamb's Yacht Center specializes in a friendly, can-do attitude for all its patrons. Few will come away from this facility with anything less than total satisfaction.

Lamb's Yacht Center (904) 384-5577
http://www.lambsyachtcenter.com

Approach depths—6-8 feet
Dockside depths—6 feet (minimum)
Accepts transients—yes
Transient dockage rate—below average
Fixed wooden piers—yes
Fixed concrete piers—yes
Dockside power connections —30 amps
  (all slips), 50 amps (some slips)
Dockside water connections—yes
Showers—yes
Waste pump-out—yes
Gasoline—yes

Sadler Point Marina, Ortega River

Lamb's Yacht Center, Ortega River

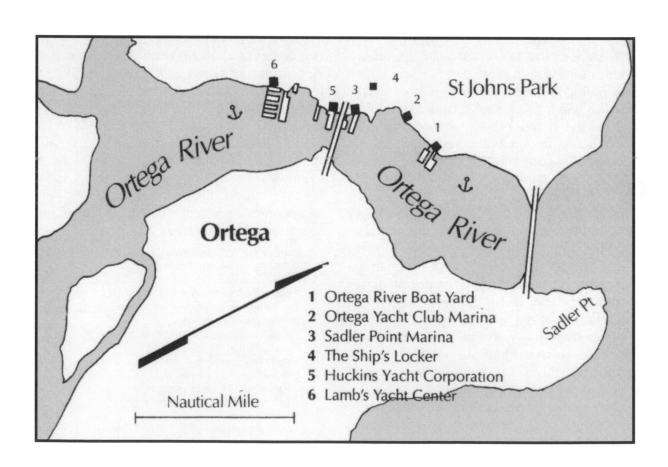

1 Ortega River Boat Yard
2 Ortega Yacht Club Marina
3 Sadler Point Marina
4 The Ship's Locker
5 Huckins Yacht Corporation
6 Lamb's Yacht Center

Nautical Mile

Diesel fuel—yes
Below-waterline repairs—yes (extensive)
Mechanical repairs—yes (extensive)
Ship's store—yes
Restaurant—several nearby

In addition to the anchorage found on the waters adjacent to Ortega River Boat Yard, reviewed above, cruising skippers might also consider dropping the hook southwest of Lamb's Yacht Center, in the correctly charted tongue of 7-foot soundings, near 30 16.179 North/081 43.202 West. Depths of 5 to 6 feet continue for a short distance farther upstream. It should be possible for boats up to 40 feet to drop the hook in the river's midline, provided heavy weather is not imminent.

ST. JOHNS INLET TO JACKSONVILLE NAVIGATION

The St. Johns River channel from its inlet to Jacksonville is extremely well marked and carefully maintained. Most aids to navigation are flashing buoys, though a few daybeacons are sighted from time to time. For the most part, cruising skippers can take a break from their vigil over the sounder on this portion of the St. Johns. However, tidal currents run very swiftly in this section of the river, particularly around Mayport. If you happen to ride the Mayport ferry, you will see a graphic example of the current's effect. The ferryboat seems to make as much lateral progress with the tide as it does forward with its engines. If you pilot a slow-moving trawler or a sailcraft, be alert for the side-setting effect of the tidal currents. Even though the river's broad channel makes the possibility of a mishap rather remote, it still pays to be safe rather than sorry.

St. Johns Inlet   The St. Johns River inlet is considered one of the safest in Southeastern United States. You should not encounter any other than the usual inlet running problems unless the weather is stormy. Simply follow the well-outlined channel on chart 11491, watch for excessive leeway, and you should come through with nothing worse than a little spray.

On the St. Johns   From its seaward passage to Sisters Creek, the St. Johns River channel continues to be wide and easily followed. A study of chart 11491 reveals several ranges along the way. You may certainly make use of these, but most pleasure-craft navigators will be able to tick off their progress easily by following the various buoys.

Don't attempt to enter the channel running to the west-southwest, upstream of flashing buoy #7. This cut leads to the U.S. Naval wharves in Mayport Basin. As you might well imagine, these waters are off-limits to pleasure craft.

After leaving flashing buoy #11 behind, the St. Johns flows through a lazy turn to the southwest. Immediately after passing through this turn, Mayport Marine will come abeam to the southeast, while Sand Dollar Restaurant and Marina will be spied along the northwestern banks.

Should you choose to enter Sand Dollar Marina's shallow inner harbor, favor the starboard side of the channel on the way in. We ran aground in a small power craft by going up the middle. Also please note that we once spotted a manatee in the Sand Dollar dockage basin. Power craft should proceed with caution.

Auto ferries still cross the St. Johns at Mayport. The northside docks are found just upstream of Sand Dollar Restaurant while the southerly terminal is perched immediately southwest of Mayport Marine. If the ferry is in operation as you pass, be sure to stay clear. These clumsy craft are all but at the mercy of the swift tidal currents during the ebb and flow.

Upstream of the auto ferry terminal, you will sight the colorful Mayport shrimp fleet along the easterly shoreline. Large power craft should reduce their wakes while passing the docks.

Northwest of flashing buoy #24, mariners bound upriver on the St. Johns will cruise northwest, perpendicular to the north to south ICW passage across the river from Sisters Creek to the more sheltered route leading south to Jacksonville Beach. This important channel will be covered in the next chapter.

For those bound upriver to Jacksonville, set course from flashing buoy #24 to eventually come between flashing daybeacon #26 and flashing buoy #25. This run is charted on 11491 as "Training Wall Reach." Ignore the ICW markers to the south (beginning with flashing daybeacon #1) and the aids to navigation on Sisters Creek to the north.

Don't approach flashing daybeacon #26 closely. This aid is founded in shallow water. Instead, come abeam of #26 by several hundred yards to its southwesterly quarter.

Upstream of #25 and #26, the St. Johns' channel follows "Short Cut Turn" to flashing buoy #27. Southwest of #27, the first opportunity for anchorage on the St. Johns River will come abeam.

St. Johns and St. Johns Bluff Anchorages
To enter the open anchorage to the southwest of flashing buoy #27, come abeam of #27 to its northerly side. Turn to the southwest and work your way carefully in toward the southern banks. If depths rise to 6 feet or less, you are encroaching on the shallower water to the east. Retrace your steps a bit to the west before setting the hook.

You might also choose to anchor in the lee of charted St. Johns Bluff between flashing daybeacons #31 and #33. Don't approach to within less than 75 yards of the southerly banks for best depths. Please remember that most of the St. Johns Bluff shoreline is private property. Dinghy landing would be a most unwise practice.

Blount Island Channel   The eastern entrance to the Blount Island Channel is marked by an unnumbered flashing daybeacon on its easterly reaches and by flashing daybeacon #36 to the west.

Enter the channel by passing between the two aids, favoring the western shores slightly. Begin cruising back to the midwidth as you approach a position abeam of Clapboard Creek to the northeast. As chart 11491 clearly shows, shallows abut the Blount Island shoreline above Clapboard Creek. Be on the watch for numerous crab pots lining the channel in this area as well. Nighttime entry calls for particular caution and liberal use of the searchlight. Remember, you must discontinue your cruise of this portion of the channel at the northern tip of Blount Island unless you can clear the twin fixed bridges with 8 feet of vertical clearance.

Craft that can't clear the 8-foot bridge can visit the western section of the Blount Island Channel via the stream's westerly entrance. To enter this portion of the channel, break off from the St. Johns several hundreds yards east of the high-rise Dames Point suspension bridge. Cut to the north and point to pass flashing daybeacon #1 by some 100 yards to its easterly side. Avoid the stream's southeasterly entrance point. A small shoal seems to be building to the south from this point of land.

Continue upstream past #1 along the centerline as far as the low-level fixed bridges. At this point, most all pleasure craft will have to retrace their steps back to the St. Johns.

Clapboard Creek   Enter Clapboard Creek on its centerline. Soon you will have to pass under the 12-foot fixed bridge. Craft that cannot clear this low span must forego a cruise on Clapboard and Cedar creeks.

Once past the bridge, continue cruising up the stream's midline until you are just short of the Cedar Creek entrance to the east. Begin favoring the western banks slightly as you come abeam of this stream. Chart 11491 correctly forecasts a large shoal protruding into Clapboard Creek from the northern Cedar Creek entrance point.

Good depths continue on the midwidth of Clapboard Creek until the high ground of Pelotes Island comes abeam to the west. Farther upstream the unmarked

channel is encroached upon by numerous shoals. Continued exploration is not recommended for cruising craft.

Cedar Point Creek   If you choose to enter treacherous Cedar Creek, feel your way along and keep a sharp watch on the sounder. Favor the southern banks heavily at the entrance. As the first shallow sidewater on the southern shore comes abeam, be on guard against the charted finger of 3-foot water extending into the southern tier of the creek's channel. Once past the southern sidewater, cruise back to the midsection. Remember to discontinue your exploration well before reaching the charted marsh island that bisects the stream.

On the St. Johns   Skippers continuing up the main body of the St. Johns River past Clapboard Creek and Back River should follow the St. Johns' turn to the west upstream of flashing buoy #35. Keep to the middle, passing flashing buoy #37 well south of your course.

Look to the north as you pass #37 and you will sight Back River and its commercial facilities. The entrance to this stream is marked by flashing daybeacon #38 on its western tier.

West of #37, there is a long markerless run up the Dames Point-Fulton Cutoff Reach to a point well south of flashing buoy #42. West of #42 the channel crosses under an extensive set of power lines with a charted clearance of 175 feet.

Soon after leaving the power lines behind, you will pass well north of flashing buoy #43. Immediately west of #43, one of the lower St. Johns best anchorages comes abeam to the south.

Mill Cove Anchorage   Simply enter the wide channel leading to Mill Cove on its midwidth and drop the hook almost anywhere near the middle of the stream. Stay at least 150 yards north of the small, unlighted daybeacons leading south to Mill Cove for best depths. The privately marked channel leading south past the submerged twin stone breakwaters into Mill Cove is not recommended for strangers.

This stream exhibits fairly swiftly moving waters. Be sure your anchor is well set before heading below.

Power skippers should know that this entire stream is an official manatee no-wake zone. Cruise into the cove and leave at idle speed.

On to Trout River   West of flashing daybeacon #45 and the Mill Cove stream, you will begin your approach to the impressive Dames Point suspension bridge. Trust me, you won't have any trouble spotting it while on the water.

Short of the bridge, the river's northern, Blount Island, shoreline is honeycombed by a series of containerized loading wharves. These docks are usually busy and can make for a fascinating view from the river.

The Dames Point Bridge has a vertical clearance of 169 feet. Anyone have a mast taller than that?

As you come abeam of flashing buoy #53, look to the north and you may catch sight of two monstrous naval vessels that are often moored in the charted deep water just southeast of Dunn Creek. They are an impressive sight from the water and can certainly serve to humble us captains who pilot a mere 35 footer.

Upstream of flashing buoy #55, the St. Johns passes through a long but sharp turn to the west-southwest. Both Dunn Creek, lying northeast of #55, and Broward River, northwest of flashing buoy #57, are shallow and impassable to pleasure craft.

The charted spoil island to the southeast of flashing buoy #61 is much more substantial than a cursory study of chart 11491 might lead you to believe. It currently boasts several trees and fairly high banks. Don't be confused by this seemingly permanent landmass where you expected to sight nothing but marsh grass.

Soon you will begin tracking your way south on Trout River Cut Reach. Between flashing buoys #64 and #66, the entrance to Trout River will come abeam to the west-northwest.

Trout River   Successful entry into Trout River is a simple matter of cruising between the two charted beacons. Come abeam and pass unlighted daybeacon #2 well to its southerly side and unlighted daybeacon #3 well to its northerly quarter. Past #3, hold to the midsection until the two Trout River marinas come abeam on the southern banks.

If you choose to anchor, select a spot between the various anchored and moored vessels that you will most likely spy between the two marinas. Don't approach the southerly banks too closely. Shoal water shelves out from this shoreline for some 75 to 100 yards.

If you continue exploring Trout River past the two marinas, remember that you must be able to clear a 29-foot fixed bridge. Begin favoring the southern banks slightly as you approach the bridges. Chart 11491 correctly identifies a large patch of shallows abutting the northern shoreline.

The first bridge is the 29-foot fixed structure, followed immediately by an older span whose center section has been removed. Then, almost on the heels of this second span, you must pass through a railroad bridge with only 2 feet of closed vertical clearance. Fortunately, this bridge is usually open unless a train is due.

Once through the tri-bridges, good depths continue on the midwidth of Trout River through the second fixed bridge (with 29 feet of vertical clearance) until charted Ribault River comes abeam to the southwest. Upstream of this point, the unmarked channel begins to wander, and captains are advised to discontinue exploration.

Exchange Island Anchorage East and south of flashing buoy #75, an alternate deepwater channel cuts in toward the river's eastern banks. This broad but unmarked passage leads to the northerly portion of the Exchange Island anchorage and Arlington Marina.

To make good your entry into these sheltered waters, leave the main channel just north of #75 and begin slowly working toward the eastern shore. Once you are about .2 nautical miles from the banks, turn south and follow the midwidth of the broad channel until you pass between the mainland to the east and the Exchange Island shoreline to the west. Do not approach the eastern banks too closely during this run. As chart 11491 shows,

there is some very shallow water abutting a portion of the mainland shoreline along the way.

As you begin your approach to the waters behind Exchange island, Arlington Marina will come abeam to the east, followed by a tugboat marine railway. Consider anchoring about halfway between the island's northerly tip and the fixed bridge. Here you will have maximum swinging room and shelter,

Chart 11491 does not give a clearance for the section of the Matthews Point Bridge that crosses the waters east of Exchange Island. However, to our eyes, the vertical clearance was no more than 10 to 14 feet. If you should be able to clear this span anyway, you might also choose to anchor in the charted deep waters between the bridge and Exchange Island's southerly tip.

The only problem with this anchor-down spot is that successful passage to the south and west back to the main St. Johns River channel is complicated by numerous unmarked shoals lying to the east around the mouth of Arlington River. Of course, those of you who are able to pass safely under the bridge can always retrace your steps to the north, but if your craft is too tall for this strategy, the only approach to the southerly Exchange Island anchorage is past the Arlington River shoals.

Assuming you can't clear the bridge, but would still like to visit the southern anchorage, continue cruising upstream on the St. Johns main "Terminal Channel" under the Matthews Point fixed bridge (vertical clearance 152 feet). Come abeam of flashing buoy #79 to its westerly side. You can then leave the main channel and turn east and southeast, tracking your way carefully around the southerly tip of Exchange Island. Keep at least 75 yards off the island's southerly point and be very mindful of the Arlington River shoals to the east and southeast. Work your way around to the north, passing into the center of the broad patch of deep water between the mainland and the easterly shores of Exchange Island. Favor the eastern (mainland) shores slightly. As shown on chart 11491, some shallow water flanks the Exchange Island banks along this stretch. To rejoin the St. Johns, retrace your steps to the south and west.

On to Jacksonville   South of flashing buoy #78 and flashing daybeacon #77, the main St. Johns "Terminal Channel" passes under the Matthews Point fixed bridge. With a clearance of 152 feet, no pleasure skipper need have any concern.

Upstream of flashing buoy #79, the river takes a sharp turn to the west. As you pass through this bend you will cruise under the Hart-Commodore Point fixed, high-rise bridge. This span also boasts an impressive vertical clearance of 135 feet.

After leaving the Hart bridge behind, point to come abeam and pass flashing buoy #80 to its southerly side. From #80, set course to pass between flashing buoy #81 and unlighted nun buoy #82. Once past #81 and #82, the docks of Metropolitan Park will be sighted to the north. The Gator Bowl-NFL Jaguar stadium should also be readily visible a bit farther inland to the north.

Farther upstream, the docks of the Chart House restaurant will be sighted along the southerly banks.

West of #81 and #82, cruising skippers will begin their passage through the downtown Jacksonville district. Have the camera ready—this is one of the most visually impressive on-the-water sojourns in Florida.

Jacksonville   Successful navigation of the St. Johns River through most of downtown Jacksonville is the usual straightforward task of following a well-marked channel. However, past the Main Street bridge the numerous aids cease for a while. The river remains quite deep, however. For best depths, favor the northern and western shores until you pass through the Fuller Warren/I-95 Bridge.

Four bridges span the St. Johns as the river passes through the heart of downtown Jacksonville. While all but the railway span have sufficient vertical clearance for power cruisers to traverse without problem, sailors must take the bridges' height and restricted opening hours into their cruising plans.

Moving upstream from flashing buoy #81 and unlighted nun #82, you will first encounter the blue-colored Main Street bridge with 40 feet of closed vertical clearance. This span opens on demand between 9:00 A.M. and 4:00 P.M. (and during the evening and nighttime hours). It does not open at all during the peak automobile traffic hours of 7:30 A.M. to 9:00 A.M. and 4:30 P.M. to 6:00 P.M. Recently (as of March 2004), repairs on the Main Street span have relegated it to hourly openings from 9:00 A.M. to 4:00 P.M. However, hopefully, these restrictions will be a thing of the past by the time this account finds its way into your hands.

No-wake regulations are now in effect between the Main Street and Fuller Warren/I-95 bridges. Power craft should cruise along at slow speed rather than risk an unhappy meeting with the Florida Marine Patrol or local law-enforcement officials.

After you pass under the Main Street span, Jacksonville Landing will be prominent to the north while the docks of River City Marina will be spotted to the south. Remember to watch for swift tidal currents when attempting to dock at either facility.

Next up is the Acosta fixed bridge. Vertical clearance is a generous 75 feet. Strangely enough, this bridge's pass through is not on its tallest center section as you might guess, but rather it leans toward the northern banks, just as chart 11491 indicates.

Immediately beyond is the low-level railroad bridge with a bare closed vertical clearance of 5 feet. Fortunately, it is usually open unless a train is due. Skippers should watch for a flashing sign on the fender of this span that warns that the bridge is about to close. Be warned also that some of the trains crossing this bridge can be long and slooow. You might try giving the operator a call on VHF channel 13 if the bridge is closed upon your arrival to see how long a wait you have in front of you.

Once through the railway bridge, favor the northwestern shores slightly for best depths. This strategy will also shorten your passage to the pass-through of the last downtown Jacksonville span, the Fuller Warren/I-95 Bridge.

Construction is now complete on the new, fixed, high-rise version of the Fuller Warren Bridge, and the old, 45-foot, bascule span has been removed. Chart 11491 still shows the bascule bridge, but it's not there anymore. While I have been unable to find a published vertical clearance for the new span, it's a safe bet that it's 65+ feet.

On to Ortega River   To the south of the Fuller Warren/I-95 span, the St. Johns opens out into a very large and impressive body of water. Navigational aids are scarce on this section of the river.

Set your course from the central pass through of the I-95 bridge to follow the deep water as it flows south around Winter Point. Be on guard against the charted twin patches of very shallow water to the east and west.

As Winter Point comes abeam to the west, set a new course to the south, for the midwidth of the broad passage between flashing daybeacon #1 and flashing daybeacon #2. Cruisers continuing upstream should point to pass flashing daybeacon #3 well to its western side.

On a hazy or rainy day, all these aids to navigation can be difficult to spot. If necessary, use your binoculars to pick out the beacons. From this point, the main body of the St. Johns River beckons to the south and southeast while the entrance to Ortega River is found to the west.

Ortega River   To enter Ortega River, continue on course upstream until you are about .3 nautical miles south of flashing daybeacon #2. Break off from the upriver channel, and set a careful course for flashing daybeacon #1, marking Ortega River's entrance.

Be sure to pass well south of the "Warning Shoal" marker west of the St. Johns' flashing daybeacon #2 as you make your run to Ortega River's flashing daybeacon #1.

Point to come abeam and pass flashing daybeacon #1 by some 25 yards (at least) to its northwesterly side. Be warned that #1 can be difficult to spot. The aid seems to blend in with the land on St. Johns Park to the west. For this reason, it is essential to run a careful compass (or GPS) course as you make your way towards #1.

As you make your approach to flashing daybeacon #1, be on guard against any slippage to the south or southeast. Shallow water juts out into the mouth of Ortega River for a surprising distance from charted Sadler Point.

After putting flashing daybeacon #1 in your wake, point for the central pass through of the Ortega River bascule bridge. This span, which has a closed vertical clearance of 9 feet, opens on demand, and the operator seems to be prompt. Be on guard against some fairly swift currents as you pass through this span.

Past the bridge, stick to the river's center section until the first facility comes abeam to the northwest. If you continue farther upstream, hold to the stream's middle. You will eventually pass through the Highway 17 twin fixed bridges and a single bascule railway bridge. Vertical clearance on the fixed highway spans is set at 45 feet while the railway bridge has a bare closed vertical clearance of 2 feet. Fortunately, this latter structure is usually open unless a train is due. Tidal currents are even more in evidence at these bridges. Be ready for some strong currents.

Begin slightly favoring the northwestern banks after passing through the triple spans. Once you are abeam of Lamb's Yacht Center, deep water continues for only a short distance upstream. If you cruise no farther than .1 of a nautical mile past Lamb's, 5- to 7-foot depths should be maintained. Past this point readings drop off to 4 feet or less.

St. Johns River from Jacksonville to Palatka

From Jacksonville to Palatka (about 50 nautical miles), the route leading south up the St. Johns can only be described as an open run. Averaging more than 2 nautical miles in width, this section of the river can foster a very healthy chop when winds exceed 15 knots. In general, power craft under 20 feet and sailboats under 25 feet should be sure to consult the latest weather forecast before tackling this portion of the St. Johns. Even larger craft would do well to check if a strong blow or severe thunderstorms are forecast. However, if you keep a careful ear toward the NOAA weather channel, your cruise to Palatka can be a genuine delight.

Good markings on the St. Johns resume south of Ortega River and continue to Palatka. Excellent depths open out from shore to shore for the most part in this section. Just keep chart 11492 handy, follow compass/GPS courses between the beacons that are located more than 1 nautical mile apart, and you should not encounter any undue navigational difficulty.

There are no major cities bordering the St. Johns River between Jacksonville and Palatka. The largest town is Green Cove Springs, but after your cruise through Jacksonville, Green Cove is bound to seem little more than a pleasant village.

Green Cove Springs is also home to the notorious Shands Bridge. With its fixed vertical clearance of 45 feet, many sailcraft skippers are barred from the most interesting upstream reaches of the St. Johns River.

The riverbanks north of Palatka are generally higher than those leading from Jacksonville to the open sea and are mostly well wooded. Attractive residential development along much of the shore makes for interesting sightseeing.

The shoreline south of Jacksonville is

Old house on the St. Johns River

indented at regular intervals with large coves. Some of these lead to deepwater creeks, but many of these sidewaters are too shallow for larger craft.

Several of the coves along this stretch of the St. Johns offer safe anchorage for the evening except in heavy weather. By carefully studying chart 11492 and the information presented in this chapter, visiting skippers can track their way to a variety of peaceful havens. In really heavy blows, a few of the creeks north of Palatka provide enough shelter to safely ride out almost any storm.

Facilities are fairly numerous, and several accept transients readily. Only one marina between Ortega River and Palatka, however, offers diesel fuel. If your craft is piloted by a trusty diesel, be sure your tanks are topped up before beginning your cruise.

Jacksonville to Palatka Anchorage Summary (Please note that anchorages are listed in geographic order, moving downstream to upstream.)

Pirates Cove Anchorage—located near 30 15.243 North/081 41.595 West, on the waters of Pirates Cove, west and north of the Florida Yacht Club—4-foot depths—reviewed on pages 98-99, 119

Plummers Cove Anchorage—located near 30 11.565 North/081 38.221 West, southeast of unlighted daybeacon #9 and just north of the Interstate 295 bridge—5-foot depths—reviewed on pages 99, 120

Doctors Lake Anchorages—various lats/lons (see detailed account)—located on the waters of Mill Cove, Swimming Pen Creek, and Sugarhouse Cove—4½-foot depths, but many soundings in the 5½- to 6-foot range—reviewed on pages 103-4, 121

Julington Creek Anchorage—located near 30 07.755 North/081 38.068 West, on the centerline of Julington Creek, west of the charted 15-foot fixed bridge—5-foot depths—reviewed on pages 105, 122

Cunningham Creek Cove Anchorage—located near 30 05.664 North/081 38.446 West, west of the entrance to Cunningham Creek, and well east of the St. John's flashing daybeacon #15—6-foot depths—reviewed on pages 105, 122

Black Creek Anchorages—located well west of the St. John's flashing daybeacon #17A—many possible anchorages, but one good spot is found near 30 03.219 North/081 43.305 West—12-foot depths—reviewed on pages 106-7, 122-23

Florence Cove Anchorage—located near 29 59.139 North/081 35.076 West, southeast of the Shands/Green Cove Springs Bridge and well east of flashing daybeacon #22—5-foot depths—reviewed on pages 108-9, 129

Colee Cove Anchorages—various lats/lons (see detailed account)—Colee Cove lies well east of flashing daybeacon #24—6-foot depths—reviewed on pages 110, 124

Rice Creek Anchorage—located near 29 41.991 North/081 39.938 West, on the waters of Rice Creek, west of the charted 45-foot fixed bridge, and north of the small, charted island that bisects the stream—6-foot depths—reviewed on pages 111-12, 125-26

Cow Creek Anchorage—located near 29 40.458 North/081 37.540 West, off the easterly banks of the St. Johns River, north of unlighted daybeacon #43—8-foot depths—reviewed on pages 112-13, 126

Carman Cove Anchorage—located near 29 39.185 North/081 36.702 West, on the centerline of Carman Cove, east-northeast of flashing daybeacon #48—5-foot depths—reviewed on pages 113, 126

Jacksonville to Palatka Marina and Yacht-Club Summary (Please note that marinas and yacht clubs are listed in geographic order, moving downstream to upstream.)

Florida Yacht Club—(904) 387-1653—located near 30 15.113 North/081 41.348 West, well west of flashing daybeacon #5—guest dockage available for members of other yacht clubs with appropriate reciprocal privileges—5½-foot minimum depths—reviewed on pages 98, 119

Whitney's Marine—(904) 269-0027—located near 30 08.778 North/081 41.979 West, hard by the southern shores of Doctors Inlet, well west-southwest of the St. Johns' flashing daybeacon #11—transient dockage available—6½-foot minimum depths—reviewed on pages 101-2, 121

Doctors Lake Marina—(904) 264-0505—located near 30 08.776 North/081 42.092 West, along the southerly banks, just west of the 37-foot Doctors Inlet Bridge—some transient dockage available—gasoline available—minimum 3½-foot depths, though many slips have deeper soundings—reviewed on pages 102-3, 121

Mandarin Holiday Marina—(904) 268-1036—located near 30 07.997 North/081 37.891 West, on the northern shores of Julington Creek, just west of the charted 15-foot fixed bridge—limited transient dockage available—gasoline available—minimum 4-foot depths—reviewed on pages 104, 122

Julington Creek Marina—(904) 268-5117—located near 30 08.030 North/081 37.811 West, overlooking the northerly banks of Julington Creek, just east of the charted 15-foot fixed bridge—limited transient dockage available—gasoline available—5-foot minimum depths—reviewed on pages 104-5, 122

Amity Anchorage (marina)—(904) 287-0931—located near 30 05.720 North/081 38.294 West, just off the southern shores of Cunningham Creek's westerly entrance, well west of the St. John's flashing daybeacon #15—limited transient dockage available—3-foot minimum depths, though many berths have 5 to 6 feet of water—reviewed on pages 105-6, 122

Green Cove Springs Marina—(904) 284-1811—located near 29 59.035 North/081 38.940 West, southeast of flashing daybeacon #20—transient dockage available—5-foot minimum depths—reviewed on pages 107-8, 123

Pacetti's Marina—(904-284-5356)—located near 29 59.141 North/081 33.931 West, on the western shores of Trout Creek, north of Palmo Cove—5-foot minimum depths in a tricky entrance channel—reviewed on pages 109-10, 124

Crystal Cove Marina—(386) 328-4000—located near 29 40.693 North/081 39.058 West, along the westerly banks of the St. Johns River, well west-northwest of unlighted daybeacon #43—transient dockage available—gasoline and diesel fuel available—minimum 4-foot depths—reviewed on pages 112, 126

Palatka Holiday Inn Docks—(386) 328-3481—located near 29 38.839 North/081 37.615 West, along the westerly banks of the St. Johns River, a short hop north of the 65-foot Palatka Bridge—transient dockage available—7-foot minimum depths—reviewed on pages 113-14, 127

Palatka City Docks—(386) 329-0100—located near 29 38.595 North/081 37.797 West, west of flashing daybeacon #1—transient dockage available—5-foot minimum depths—reviewed on pages 114-15, 127

Boathouse Marina—(386) 328-2944—located near 29 38.554 North/081 37.894 West, west-southwest of flashing daybeacon #1—transient dockage available—6-foot minimum depths—reviewed on pages 115-16, 127

Florida Yacht Club, St. Johns River

Florida Yacht Club and Pirates Cove Anchorage (Various Lats/Lons—see below)

The breakwater-enclosed harbor of venerable Florida Yacht Club occupies the southerly point, flanking the easterly shores of charted Pirates Cove, well west of flashing daybeacon #5, near 30 15.113 North/081 41.348 West. The site is designated as "Clubhouse" on chart 11492. This large, obviously affluent yacht club (a charter member of the Florida Council of Yacht Clubs—FCYC) accepts members of other clubs with appropriate reciprocal arrangements. The dockmaster is on duty Tuesday through Sunday, 11:00 A.M. to 7:00 P.M. Advance reservations are all but mandatory.

Berths are provided at fixed, concrete piers with modern water and 30-amp (plus some 50-amp) power connections. Depths in the harbor run 5½ to 6 feet, with at least 7 feet of water in the approach channel. The already-mentioned breakwater affords good protection from all winds.

Shoreside the club features showers, a large swimming pool, and numerous tennis courts. Lunch is served daily, and dinner is available Tuesday through Sunday. A coat and tie are required in the main dining room after 6:00 P.M.

Florida Yacht Club (904) 387-1653
  http://www.thefloridayachtclub.org

Approach depths—7 feet (minimum)
Dockside depths—5½-6 feet (minimum)
Accepts transients—members of other yacht
  clubs with appropriate reciprocal
  arrangements
Fixed concrete piers—yes
Dockside power connections—30
  and 50 amps
Dockside water connections—yes
Showers—yes
Restaurant—on site

Study chart 11492 for a moment and notice the waters west of Florida Yacht Club, leading northwest into the bay called Pirates Cove. The 4-foot sounding noted on chart 11492 at the southerly entrance to this cove was verified by our on-site research. However, if your craft draws less than 4 feet, you might anchor on the waters to the northwest, near 30 15.243 North/081 41.595 West. By stopping well

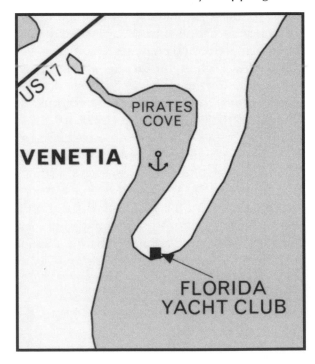

short of the correctly charted 2- and 3-foot waters bounding the extreme northern and northwestern shores of Pirates Cove, craft as large as 40 feet should find ample swinging room with 6- to 8-foot depths. Shelter is nearly perfect from all but strong southeasterly blows. We did find the bottom in Pirates Cove to be a bit on the silty side, however. Be sure your anchor is well set. In really foul weather you might even want to set an anchor watch.

The shores of Pirates Cove are overlooked by a close-packed collection of sumptuous homes. Pay particular attention to the private residence overlooking the point, just west of Florida Yacht Club. Knob Hill has come to Florida.

Goodbys Creek

The mouth of shallow Goodbys Creek cuts into the eastern banks of the St. Johns east of flashing daybeacon #7. The mouth of the stream's entrance channel is denoted by flashing daybeacon #1 and a series of somewhat-confusing, white PVC pipes. In years past, Goodbys Creek played host to a small, boat dealer and minimal marina along its northern shore, just west of the charted 11-foot fixed bridge. This facility seems to be nonoperational at the time of this writing, but there is a good chance things may have started up again by the time of your arrival.

Goodbys Creek itself is bordered by attractive private homes, many with their own docks. Eventually the stream is spanned by two fixed bridges east of Mandarin Marine with 11 feet of vertical clearance.

Boats under 32 feet that can clear the fixed bridges and can stand consistent 4-foot soundings might consider dropping the hook just east of the span. However, swinging room is minimal, and the relatively shallow depths are a genuine cause for concern.

Plummers Cove Anchorage (30 11.565 North/081 38.221 West)

Plummers Cove cuts deeply into the St. Johns' eastern shoreline south of Beauclerc Bluff and unlighted daybeacon #9. The cove's attractive shoreline exhibits moderate residential development. Minimum 5- to 6-foot depths are held to within 100 to 150 yards of the easterly banks. With lower to moderate winds from any quarter except the west and southwest, this would be a reasonably secure haven for almost any size pleasure craft to anchor. The waters are too broad to be a comfortable foul-weather hidey-hole.

On a still night some automobile noise and headlight flashes could be a problem courtesy of the Interstate 295 bridge just to the south. We have never found this to be too much of a concern, however.

Rudder Club of Jacksonville (30 11.510 North/081 41.454 West)

Opposite Plummers Cove, the single pier of the Rudder Club of Jacksonville (904-264-4094, http://www.rudderclub.com) strikes out from the St. Johns' westerly banks, immediately north of the I-295 bridge. This is a very active sailing club that sponsors the famous "Mug Race" (see below). Unfortunately, no guest dockage is available due to the limited number of slips.

Villas Continental and Yacht Club (30 09.654 North/081 41.668 West)

A well-defined channel leads west from flashing daybeacon #10 (south of charted Orange Park) to the Villas Continental and Yacht Club (904-264-2467). This facility is enclosed in a concrete breakwater that protects it from easterly breezes. It is associated with a huge condo and hotel complex that stretches back for some distance from the water.

During the last several years the harbor and

entrance channel have shoaled. Approach depths at low water are now only some 4½ to 5 feet, with 3½ to 4½ feet of water dockside. Long-legged craft should exercise caution when making use of this facility.

Dockage is at fixed, wooden piers with fresh-water and 30-amp power connections. With advance arrangements, there is ample shoreside lodging on the grounds, and the on-site English-pub-style restaurant is truly elegant. A supermarket is found within a walk of three to four blocks.

While some local yacht clubs occasionally make this facility a port of call through special arrangements with the management, normal transient visitors are no longer allowed to spend the night aboard. This prohibition will certainly limit Villas Continental and Yacht Club's appeal to most cruisers.

Mandarin History   Almost due east from flashing daybeacon #11, Mandarin Point guards the eastern flank of the St. Johns. The nearby village of Mandarin dates back to the eighteenth century. While many interesting historical characters are associated with the community, it perhaps never received a more curious visitor than the small, strong-willed woman who arrived in March 1867.

Following the Civil War, Harriet Beecher Stowe, author of Uncle Tom's Cabin and various other novels purporting to describe the South prior to the war, decided to live in the region she had once so despised. Arriving at the village of Mandarin after a voyage up the St. Johns from Jacksonville, she was enchanted to discover a small cottage for sale. Mrs. Stowe lost no time in purchasing this haven.

In a burst of energy she decided to help establish a chain of churches along the St. Johns for the religious edification of the river's black population. When not involved with the church work, she devoted her time to writing. She seems to have been unworried about having written so many damaging books about a region that she never even bothered to visit until after the war that she had done so much to perpetrate.

Doctors Lake (Various Lats/Lons—see below)

Intriguing Doctors Lake is located due west of Mandarin Point. Of the many sidewaters that we have explored on the St. Johns, none is more attractive or has more to offer than Doctors Lake. Marinas, good anchorages, excellent depths, attractive shorelines with just enough development—this water body has it all! Craft of almost any size (that can clear the 37-foot fixed bridge) drawing 6 feet or less can cruise the lake. If you are anywhere in the region and want to stop for the night, or if you have some extra time and want to take a small side trip, don't pass up Doctors Lake.

The entrance channel leading from the St. Johns to the lake is known appropriately as Doctors Inlet. This channel is crossed by a fixed bridge with 37 feet of vertical clearance. Sadly, sailcraft that cannot clear this span must forego the considerable charms of Doctors Lake.

There is one other caveat to anchoring on Doctors Lake. Several years ago, during a heavy blow, we had a bit of trouble getting our Danforth anchor to hold. Nothing serious, but it was enough to make us study the bottom strata more closely. What we discovered was a far siltier bottom than we had previously suspected. While this problem is certainly not serious enough to deter cruisers from using this otherwise wonderful anchorage, it does suggest that an anchor watch might be appropriate in really foul weather.

Two marinas are located along the southern banks of the inlet. Whitney's Marine (30 08.778 North/081 41.979 West) is the easternmost of the two, and it bears the distinct advantage of being on the St. Johns side of the fixed bridge. Whitney's remains a very good, sailing-craft-oriented marina. Carol Ellis and the entire staff at Whitney's Marine are to be congratulated on a job well done.

Whitney's features both an inner and outer harbor with separate channels to each (see our navigational discussion of Whitney's Marine in the next section of this chapter). The outer dockage basin is partially protected by the outermost dock, which serves as a partial breakwater, while the inner harbor is well sheltered by a concrete barrier. Maneuvering room inside the inner basin is a bit on the tight side.

Transients are eagerly accepted at fixed, wooden, finger piers stretching out from a concrete seawall on the inner harbor, and at ultra-modern, concrete-decked floating piers in the outer basin. Fresh-water and 30-amp power connections are on hand at every berth, save for a very few slips set aside for smaller craft. Waste pump-out service is sometimes available.

Approach depths run around 6½ to 7 feet, with 7 to 8 feet of water dockside. Shoreside you will find fully climate-controlled showers and a good ship's store. A Laundromat and drugstore are located less than a one-mile walk to the north on Highway 17.

Whitney's grounds were newly landscaped some four years ago, and the results are quite attractive. Take a moment to contemplate the beautiful waters of the St. Johns from the on-site gazebo, and you may just conclude that this is what cruising is really all about.

Still not enough for you? Well, consider the adjacent eight-mile biking and jogging trail that runs from a position abeam of Whitney's all the way south to the Black Creek Bridge. All you runners, and those cruisers voyaging with bicycles aboard, will want to make the acquaintance of this outstanding public attraction.

As we mentioned above, a Laundromat and drugstore can be found less than one mile north of the marina, on the western side of Highway 17. A short hop to the north, visitors will discover Sarnelli's Restaurant (open for the evening meal only) next to a Dunkin' Donuts and Baskin Robbins. Two miles south of the marina is a Papa John's Pizza, and one mile farther brings you to a Publix supermarket plus several fast-food restaurants. Construction has begun at this same location for a Wal-Mart, Winn-Dixie supermarket, and drugstore.

Haul-outs are accomplished through the use of Whitney's on-site 20-ton travelift, and servicing for diesel engines (mostly sailcraft auxiliary power plants) is readily available through an independent contractor. We were very impressed with the number of sailcraft hauled out of the water and sitting on cradles during our last visit. Obviously, this facility is serious about service.

We continue to recommend Whitney's Marine for an evening, a few days, or even a week. It is a great spot to rest from your sojourns. Tell them we sent you!

Whitney's Marine (904) 269-0027
http://www.whitneysmarine.com

Approach depths—6½-7 feet
Dockside depths—7-8 feet
Accepts transients—yes
Transient dockage rate—below average
Floating concrete piers—yes
Fixed wooden piers—yes
Dockside power connections—30 amps
Dockside water connections—yes
Showers—yes
Waste pump-out—yes (sometimes)

Below-waterline repairs—yes
Mechanical repairs—yes
   (independent contractors)
Ship's store—yes
Restaurant—¾-mile walk away

Just to the west of the Doctors Inlet bridge, Doctors Lake Marina waits to greet boats that can clear this 37-foot span near 30 08.776 North/081 42.092 West. Several years ago, this facility changed hands, and it was considerably updated at that time. The results have been enjoyed by visiting and resident cruisers alike.

Visiting pleasure craft will find good-quality, fixed, wooden piers with full power and water connections. Some slips are covered, while others are open to accommodate sailcraft. Dockside depths range widely from 5 to 6 feet at the outer slips, 4½ feet at the midberths, and 3½ feet at the innermost slips. Visitors are reminded of the ¾-mile hike up Highway 17 to reach the nearest restaurant.

Whitney's Marine, St. Johns River

Gasoline but no diesel fuel is available at a fuel pier on the eastern side of the dockage basin. Be advised that low-water depths at the fuel dock are only 3½ feet, and maneuvering room in this portion of the marina is a bit skimpy. Waste pump-out service is in place as well.

Doctors Lake Marina (904) 264-0505

Approach depths—6 feet
Dockside depths—5-6 feet (outer berths)
  4½ feet (middle berths)
  3½ feet (fuel dock and inner berths)
Accepts transients—yes
Transient dockage rate—below average
Fixed wooden piers—yes (some covered)
Dockside power connections—30
  and 50 amps
Dockside water connections—yes
Waste pump-out—yes
Gasoline—yes
Restaurant—¾-mile walk away

On Doctors Lake itself, there are at least three prime places to drop the hook. As you move up the lake, the first is Mill Cove, along

1 Villas Continental and Yacht Club
2 Whitney's Marina
3 Doctors Lake Marina

the southeastern shoreline. Minimum 4½- to 5-foot depths are carried almost into the extreme southeastern point of the cove. Depths shown on chart 11492 are incorrect near the cove's eastern edge. Boats under 35 feet, drawing less than 4 feet, can cruise carefully past the charted pilings and drop the hook within 100 yards of shore in some 4½ to 5 feet of water near 30 07.449 North/081 43.184 West. Larger craft drawing 4 feet or better should anchor northwest of the pilings. Depths in this outer haven run from 7 to 10 feet. This is a particularly attractive cove, even for generally attractive Doctors Lake, and we recommend it heartily.

Possibly the most sheltered Doctors Lake anchorage is found on the waters of Swimming Pen Creek. This relatively small, protected stream makes into the eastern flank of the lake's southwestern limits. Again, depths shown on chart 11492 are incorrect. Extensive soundings taken during on-site research showed that minimum soundings of 5 to 5½ feet (with many 6- to 7-foot readings along the way) are carried from the lake into the creek as far as the stream's first low-level fixed bridge, which bars passage for all but small craft. Boats up to 37 feet will find plenty of swinging room and enough shelter for even heavy weather short of the bridge near 30 06.040 North/081 44.813 West. The creek's western banks exhibit light residential development, but much of the eastern shore is still in its natural state.

Whitney's Fish Camp Restaurant (904-269-4198) overlooks the stream's easterly banks of Swimming Pen Creek, just short of the fixed bridge. While no dockage is available for cruising-sized craft, it should be a snap to dinghy ashore. We have not had a chance to sample the fare here yet. If you give it a try, let us know what you think! E-mail us at opcom@cruisingguide.com.

Sugarhouse Cove cuts into the northwestern shore of Doctors Lake north of Peoria Point. While a bit more open than the anchorages mentioned above, this cove would make an ideal spot to drop the hook in northern or northwesterly winds. Several attractive homes overlook the cove, but the development still leaves plenty of natural scenery. Minimum depths of 6 feet are held to within some 75 yards of the western and northwesterly banks near 30 07.533 North/081 45.534 West. Craft of almost any size can swing easily on the hook here if the fickle wind is blowing from the right quarter.

Julington Creek (Various Lats/Lons—see below)

Old Bull Bay leads into Julington Creek on the eastern shore of the St. Johns River, east of flashing daybeacon #12 and unlighted daybeacon #13. Minimum depths of 5 to 6 feet are carried as far as, and for a very short distance upstream of, the 15-foot fixed bridge that spans the creek about .7 nautical miles east of its mouth. Julington Creek is the home of two marinas, both of which have only limited space for transients.

Mandarin Holiday Marina (30 07.997 North/081 37.891 West) guards Julington Creek's northern banks immediately west of the charted, fixed bridge. This firm is very popular with resident sailors. Transient dockage is offered on a strictly space-available basis. It would be best to call ahead of time and check on slip availability before committing to a stay at this facility. Dockage is provided at fixed wooden piers with water and 30-amp power connections. Dockside depths range from 5½ to 9 feet at most slips. A few of the innermost berths display soundings as skinny as 4 feet.

Gasoline can be purchased dockside and the marina maintains a well-stocked ship's and variety store. Mechanical repairs for gasoline power plants are offered, and haul-outs are available courtesy of a 15-ton travelift. At the present time, there is no restaurant within walking distance.

Mandarin Holiday Marina (904) 268-1036

Approach depths—6-7 feet
Dockside depths—4-9 feet
Accepts transients—limited
  (when space is available)
Transient dockage rate—below average
Fixed wooden piers—yes
Dockside power connections—30 amps
Dockside water connections—yes
Gasoline—yes
Below-waterline repairs—yes
Mechanical repairs—yes
  (gasoline engines only)
Ship's and variety store—yes

Just east of the 15-foot fixed span, Julington Creek Marina overlooks the northerly banks near 30 08.030 North/081 37.811 West. This is a well-managed, power-craft-oriented marina facility that can be used with confidence by all craft that can clear the bridge's 15-foot restrictive height. In addition to wet-slip dockage (both covered and uncovered), there is a large, state-of-the-art dry-stack storage building on site.

Limited transient dockage is afforded on a space-available basis. Again, it would be best to call ahead rather than risk disappointment. Wet berths are provided at fixed wooden piers with most soundings ranging from 5 to 6 feet. About two-thirds of the slips are covered and one-third open to the weather. Fresh-water and 30-amp power connections are available all along the dock. Gasoline but no diesel fuel can be purchased at the adjacent fuel pier. A tiny ship's store overlooks the docks, and some limited mechanical repairs for power craft are offered as well.

As with Mandarin Holiday Marina, just to the west, there are currently no restaurants within walking distance. Bring your own supplies.

Julington Creek Marina (904) 268-5117

Approach depths—6 feet
Dockside depths—5-6 feet
Accepts transients—limited
  (when space is available)
Transient dockage rate—below average
Fixed wooden piers—yes (some covered)
Dockside power connections—30 amps
Dockside water connections—yes
Gasoline—yes
Mechanical repairs—yes (gasoline only)
Ship's store—limited

East of the fixed bridge, depths on Julington Creek begin to drop off to 4 feet or less. Passage farther upstream for larger craft is not recommended.

However, anchorage west of the 15-foot fixed bridge is a possibility for most any size pleasure craft in fair weather. Try dropping the hook near 30 07.755 North/081 38.068 West. Clearly this is not the sort of haven fit for a heavy blow. Depths can run to as little as 5 feet. Captains of deep-draft vessels should keep an eagle eye on the sounder. For maximum swinging room and depth, anchor within 25 to 50 yards of the midwidth, and be sure to show a bright anchor light.

Cunningham Creek Cove and Amity Anchorage (Various Lats/Lons—see below)

Shallow Cunningham Creek makes into the St. Johns' eastern shores almost due east of flashing daybeacon #15. While the creek itself should not be entered by any but small outboard craft, the cove leading to the stream can be used as an anchorage in light winds or moderate east-

erly blows. Minimum depths of 6 feet or more are held to within 200 yards of the creek's mouth. The jutting banks to the north and south give some lee when winds are blowing from either of these quarters. The shoreline exhibits light residential development. For a small fee, you can dinghy ashore at Amity Anchorage (see below) and make use of the clubhouse and other shoreside facilities. Try anchoring near 30 05.664 North/081 38.446 West.

One of the more "funky" marine facilities on the St. Johns River flanks the easterly tip of Cunningham Cove, south of Cunningham Creek, near 30 05.720 North/081 38.294 West. Amity Anchorage is sort of a combination dock, marina, swimming pool, and clubhouse. Its one and only long, fixed wooden pier stretches out for a considerable distance into the midline of the cove. You will almost certainly spot it by the wealth of local sailcraft docked along its length.

During any number of earlier visits to Amity Anchorage (marina), most of the available slips have always been filled with resident vessels. Transients are accepted on a space-available basis. Give owner and dockmaster Barbara Williams a call ahead of time. She is a real sailor and friend to all cruisers.

All slips feature fresh-water and 30-amp power connections. Depths at dockside run from a minimum of 5 feet on the outer slips to 4 feet at the midberths. Closer to shore, soundings can rise to 3 feet. The dock is wide open to winds blowing across the St. Johns from the west, northwest, or southwest. There is good shelter via the mainland to the east, and the cove's points to the north and south give some protection from these directions.

Shoreside, visiting cruisers will find an attractive but informal clubhouse with swimming pool and paperback exchange library.

There are also pool and Ping-Pong tables, as well as a 50-inch, color television. Excellent showers are available on the grounds, but there are no Laundromat facilities. The dockmaster maintains a small ship's store just beside her office. While there are some kitchen facilities in the clubhouse, and the management sometimes operates a snack bar, there is no full-service restaurant on site or within walking distance.

So, if the fickle wind cooperates, and you want to try something truly different in the way of marinas, give Amity Anchorage a visit. It's not for everyone, but it just might be what you've been looking for.

Amity Anchorage (904) 287-0931

Approach depths—6 feet (minimum)
Dockside depths—3-5 feet (minimum)
Accepts transients—limited
  (when space is available)
Transient dockage rate—below average
Fixed wooden pier—yes
Dockside power connections—30 amps
Dockside water connections—yes
Showers—yes
Ship's store—yes (small)

Hibernia

Hibernia Point, just west of unlighted daybeacon # 16, recalls the former presence of a great St. Johns plantation. During the period of British rule following the conclusion of the French and Indian War, many large plantations were established in northeastern Florida by well-to-do immigrants from the thirteen colonies to the north.

Newly married George Fleming was one of these settlers. The island north of Black Creek still bears his name. Fleming's father-in-law, Francis Fatio, owned a large plantation almost directly across the St. Johns from Hibernia at New Switzerland. Fleming and

his bride received thirty-two slaves as a wedding present from Fatio. The settler lost no time in beginning the arduous process of clearing land about the point. His two sons, Lewis and George, Jr., are said to have spent their entire lives enlarging the family holdings. Before the vast farm was broken up after the Civil War, its tilled acres covered the vast majority of Fleming Island. It is fitting that the name of this large landmass recalls the hard work and dedication of the two generations of Flemings who struggled to build an agricultural empire out of the wilderness.

Black Creek (Various Lats/Lons—see below)

After exploring Doctors Lake, any cruiser would be excused for thinking that it might be a long time before he or she comes upon another body of water that offers such a pristine setting. However, Black Creek, some 6.5 nautical miles upstream from (south of) Doctors Lake, is almost as delightful a cruising find. Of course, you must be able to clear the correctly charted 30-foot fixed bridge at the creek's entrance to access all the good upstream cruising.

Stretching for some 18 nautical miles from its intersection with the St. Johns' westerly banks, south of Hibernia Point (well to the southwest of flashing daybeacon #17A), to the old river village of Middleburg, the creek is exceptionally deep and consistently pleasing to the eye. The lower banks are well wooded and almost totally undeveloped. Farther upstream there is some light residential development, particularly on the port shores. Several houses sit atop high earthen cliffs and look down through a leafy maze to the creek.

Minimum depths of 7 feet can be expected on Black Creek's midwidth all the way to

Middleburg. While some points have shoaled a bit, the creek is deep almost from shore to shore. Craft up to 45 feet that can clear the 30-foot fixed bridge spanning the entrance and the 20-foot railroad and highway bridges farther upstream can cruise the entire stream with few navigational worries.

The generally high banks of Black Creek provide excellent protection for anchorage even in the heaviest weather. About the only problem you might encounter in dropping the hook stems from the stream's unusually deep water. With depths of as much as 40 feet, it may take a lot of anchor rode for a proper 6 to 1 scope. Consequently, craft over 35 feet long should consider anchoring in the creek's wider, lower reaches southeast of the charted power lines that cross the stream northeast of Russell village, perhaps near 30 03.219 North/081 43.305 West. A Bahamian mooring might also be a good idea. Smaller boats can anchor almost anywhere they choose.

Peters Creek makes into the southern banks of Black Creek about .6 nautical miles upstream of the bridge spanning the larger stream's entrance. While this small creek is quite deep, it is too narrow for anchorage by any but small craft. Boats over 28 feet should avoid entering the creek for any reason as they may not find sufficient room to swing around.

The old river community of Middleburg marks the practical upstream cruising limits of Black Creek. The town's history stretches far back into the first Spanish era, but unfortunately only a few historical structures have survived.

Cruisers entering Black Creek will spot a single, fixed wooden pier and a public launching ramp on the southerly banks before passing under the fixed, 30-foot highway bridge.

Black Creek History From 1820 to the 1830s, Florida's new capital, Tallahassee, became the center of a rich cotton-growing region. Unfortunately, the long, expensive, and often dangerous ship's voyage south around Key West to bring the precious fibers to markets in the northeast ate up a good portion of the planter's profits.

Black Creek was to provide the solution to this vexing problem. Cotton was transported overland to Middleburg, the creek's old port town, and then shipped down its winding course to the St. Johns River. The barges then made their way to Jacksonville, where the cotton was loaded on freighters for delivery to England, Europe, or the northeastern states.

As early as 1826, Black Creek was surveyed as a possible link for a canal connecting the east and west coasts of Florida. There was much support for this idea at the time, and enthusiasm for the project continued after the Civil War. Recalling the struggles of early coastal North Carolina for a ready outlet of commerce, Floridians of the nineteenth century believed that canals were the only effective means of establishing communication between the two coasts. In spite of its popular support, the dream of a trans-Florida waterway was not to be realized until the 1930s with the building of the Okeechobee Waterway.

Green Cove Springs Marina (29 59.035 North/081 38.940 West)

Dating from the mid-nineteenth century, the village of Green Cove Springs sits perched on the St. Johns' western shores, southwest of flashing daybeacon #19. This small community's waterfront is quite shoal. Don't attempt to approach Governors Creek or the waters to the south around Green Cove Point.

Fortunately, there is another, safe approach. Study chart 11492 for a moment and notice

Green Cove Springs Marina

the series of large, charted piers southeast of Green Cove Springs. This was once the site of an active naval base, but those days have now faded far into the past. All is not lost, however. The southeasternmost pier and its adjacent bulkhead now serve as the headquarters for Green Cove Springs Marina.

We have always been somewhat reluctant to recommend this facility to our fellow cruisers. Once upon a day, the marina and adjacent yard were in sad shape indeed. Several years ago a new dockmaster took over the operation, and while one could still not accurately assert that Green Cove Springs Marina is in pristine shape, things certainly are far better than once they were. Besides the addition (several years ago) of new slips along the inner harbor bulkhead, one of the marina's biggest improvements is the addition of first-class, climate-controlled showers and a Laundromat.

Transients are accepted at either the long, face pier or the new, inner floating slips. If you dock at the long pier, expect a long climb up from your decks to the dock's surface. All slips feature fresh-water and 30-amp power hookups. Depths alongside run an impressive 6 to 11 feet with one notable exception.

Past visitors to this facility will remember a small, semisunken tramp freighter occupying the outer portion of the dock's northwesterly face. Silting around this old derelict has raised depths in the marina's entrance channel to 5-foot levels.

Green Cove Springs Marina has gained a strong reputation among the do-it-yourself crowd. The yard's 37-ton travelift will haul your craft, place it on stand-offs, and allow you to do all the work yourself. In fact, this is the only way bottom work is available at this establishment. Mechanical repairs for gasoline engines (only) can also be arranged.

The on-site seafood restaurant burnt many years ago. There is no longer any dining spot on site or within walking distance. A supermarket is a long, long hike from the docks. Few will want to try this journey on foot. Ask the friendly dockmaster for help with transportation.

Green Cove Springs Marina (904) 284-1811

Approach depths—5-10 feet
Dockside depths—6-11 feet
Accepts transients—yes
Transient dockage rate—below average
Fixed concrete pier—yes
Floating wooden piers—yes
Dockside power connections—30 amps
Dockside water connections—yes
Showers—yes
Laundromat—yes
Below-waterline repairs—yes
Mechanical repairs—yes (gasoline only)

Florence Cove Anchorage (29 59.139 North/081 35.076 West)

Florence Cove cuts into the northeastern banks of the St. Johns River northwest of Jack Wright Island. Minimum depths of 5

GOVERNORS CR.

SHALLOW

GREEN COVE POINT

GREEN COVE
SPRINGS

SHALLOW

SHALLOW

"20"

GREEN COVE
SPRINGS MARINA

feet are held to within 150 yards of the cove's northeastern banks. However, very shallow water adjoins the cove's northwestern and southeastern shores. Take extra care when entering.

This cove makes an excellent overnight stop with enough protection against strong winds from any quarter except the southwest. The attractive shoreline exhibits alternating patches of natural terrain and light residential development.

This is one of our favorite anchorages between the Shands/Green Cove Springs Bridge and Palatka. Just watch out for those surrounding shoals!

Pacetti's Marina (29 59.141 North/081 33.931 West)

Pacetti's Marina (904-284-5356) is a small, somewhat-dingy facility located on the western shores of Trout Creek, east of Jack Wright Island. Pacetti's encompasses a campground, variety store, and tiny marina catering almost exclusively to small power craft. Entrance depths into Trout Creek from Palmo Cove run from 5 to 6 feet in a poorly marked, somewhat tricky channel. To reach the marina you must be able to clear a 14-foot fixed bridge. While the facility is friendly to local fishermen and small power boats, cruising craft will find little to interest them here.

Colee Cove Anchorages (Various Lats/Lons—see below)

Colee Cove carves a deep hollow in the St. Johns' eastern shore, south of Pacetti Point and well east of flashing daybeacon #24. Minimum 6-foot depths are held to within 100 yards of the eastern banks. Moderate residential development rings the water body. While a bit open for snug anchorage in high winds, Colee Cove can serve as a delightful overnight stop in light to moderate airs.

If winds are wafting from the east or northeast, try anchoring on the waters at the rear of the cove, near 29 56.250 North/081 34.435 West. If fresh breezes are blowing from the north or northeast, try anchoring behind Pacetti Point, near 29 56.772 North/081 34.904 West.

Picolata

Today the small village of Picolata is a barely noticed community on the St. Johns' eastern shores, near flashing daybeacon #25. Strangely enough, however, this small village played a critical role in the cultural history of the mighty river, a role that would, through English literature, ultimately bring the St. Johns River before the world.

The history of Picolata stretches back into the first Spanish era of colonization. A large Catholic mission was established here from which priestly expeditions departed for the river's western shores. Much later, in 1884, the English composer Frederick Delius was banished by his father to an old plantation at Picolata, known as Solano Grove. One cannot but speculate whether some of his music was inspired by the hauntingly lovely banks of the St. Johns.

Whatever Picolata's other claims to renown, undoubtedly its greatest contribution to the fame of Florida came through a young, destitute poet. William Bartram was the son of an English botanist who had established one of the first botanical gardens in the New World near Philadelphia. Having failed at business and farming on numerous occasions, in 1766 William decided to settle on the banks of the St. Johns. There he planned to live a hermit's life as a lonely, romantic poet.

Within a few months of taking up residence here, however, William found himself in dire need. He had allowed his small house to lapse into disrepair, even though his generous father had provided several slaves to help him with the day-to-day tasks.

Fortunately for William, Dr. John Fothergill, a correspondent of William's father in London, employed him to record observations about various flora and animal life in the southern United States. Having left Florida by this time, William journeyed through the Carolinas, Georgia, and Florida, recording his observations in the most colorful and minute detail. As Cabell and Hanna comment, "The man, just somehow, had been born with that talent for noticing sharply, and for remembering sharply what he had noticed, which, in a world of mostly muggy minded persons, is a born writer's uncompromising chief assistant."

William Bartram's *Travels through North and South Carolina, Georgia, East and West Florida* was published in 1791 and was soon being printed throughout England and the European continent. The Romantic poets Coleridge, Wordsworth, Southey, and Thomas Campbell took Bartram's descriptions to heart, and it was not many months before the St. Johns River began to make its appearance in contemporary poetry.

Perhaps the most famous picture of the river is in Coleridge's "Kubla Khan." The story goes that as the poet lay in a drug-induced stupor, he had a vision and that upon awakening, he began to write down the haunting, immortal verses that he called "Kubla Khan." Just before falling into his drugged sleep, Coleridge is said to have been reading Bartram's account of the St. Johns River. It is only natural, therefore, that some people have been able to discern that river in the poem:

So twice five miles of fertile ground
With walls and towers were girdled round:
And here were gardens bright with sinuous rills
Where blossomed many an incense-bearing tree;
And here were forests ancient as the hills,
Enfolding sunny spots of greenery.
But oh! that deep romantic chasm which slanted
Down the green hill athwart a cedarn cover!
A savage place! as holy and enchanted
As e'er beneath a waning moon was haunted
By woman wailing for her demon-lover!

As if the *Travels* themselves were not enough, Bartram went on to write an early account of the Seminole Indians, who were just then migrating south into Florida. Romantic as it may be, this cultural history still stands as one of the most complete accounts of the Seminoles' lifestyle.

William Bartram's great contribution to the St. Johns will always be his *Travels*, and the ensuing worldwide prominence he gave to this mighty river. Pause in your own travels and reflect on the inspiration that Bartram must have received as he paddled along in his small boat, often wholly alone, to create this timeless account.

Orange Mills

Look south of Murphys Cove (itself south of flashing daybeacon #40) on chart 11487 and you will note the old river village of Orange Mills. In the 1870s, Col. Robert Cole had a fruit plantation bordering the river at this point. Cole's plantation was rather typical of the many St. Johns orange plantations of this period. It was thought that the moist river breezes combined with the fertile soil to give the fruit a naturally sweet flavor.

In addition to his orange trees, Colonel Cole raised another fruit on his plantation that was thought to be an oddity. This strange citrus fruit was larger than an orange and it grew in clusters. Those who tasted it could not decide whether it was bitter or sweet or both. There was no ready demand for this strange foodstuff, so Cole simply grew it to confound his visitors. If only the colonel had known what a large market grapefruit would one day command, he might have given this fruit's cultivation a bit more attention.

Rice Creek (29 41.991 North/081 39.938 West)

The marked channel leading to deep Rice Creek intersects the main St. Johns River channel west of Forrester Point. Rice Creek eventually leads to a large pulp and paper mill, which serves as one of the principal employers for nearby Palatka. The stream is used regularly by barges transporting wood to the mill, and its channel is carefully maintained. The mostly undeveloped shores are quite attractive and look as if they might harbor more than a few black bass. One fixed highway bridge with 45 feet of vertical clearance and a railway span that is usually open unless a train is due cross the creek between its entrance and the pulp mill. Apart from these obstacles, you are unlikely to meet any navigational difficulty on the stream.

Due to the prevalent barge traffic, we do not recommend anchoring anywhere on the main body of Rice Creek. Fortunately, there is an alternative. West of the highway bridge, the creek's channel is bisected by a small island. The main route continues up the southerly branch, but the northerly arm has minimum depths of 6 feet (with most readings being much deeper) on its midwidth and enough swinging room for boats up to 34 feet to drop the hook. This would be a great spot to ride out heavy weather. Protection is excellent from all winds and the undeveloped shores are inviting. In short, you would have to look far to find a better place to spend the evening, unless, of course, the wind happens to be blowing from the pulp mill.

Crystal Cove Marina (29 40.693 North/081 39.058 West)

South of Forrester Point and the Rice Creek channel, the St. Johns turns again sharply to the south. On a clear day, you will soon spy a line of tall power poles to the south marching across the river west to east. Short of these shocking obstructions, a marked and charted cut runs west to Crystal Cove Marina at the charted location of Log Landing. This is a small but friendly marina associated with a large motel and restaurant complex.

Transients are welcomed at a single, fixed, wooden pier. Depths in the entrance channel run 5 to 6 feet with 4 to 5 feet of water dockside. Obviously, this is a not a marina suited to deep-draft vessels. On the other hand, if you can stand the depths, our experience suggests that you will find a warm welcome. Berths feature good, fresh-water and 20- and 30-amp power connections. Shoreside you will find a covered cookout area, showers, and an expanded combination ship's, variety store, and gift shop. Gasoline and diesel fuel are for sale dockside. Crystal Cove is one of only two locations on the upper St. Johns that offer diesel

fuel. Mechanical repairs for both gasoline and diesel engines can now be arranged.

If you want to take a break from the live-aboard routine, the adjacent Crystal Cove Motel (386-325-1055) is extremely convenient. There is also an overnight-dockage price break for those who also take a room at this hostelry.

The on-site Corky Bell's Restaurant (386-325-1094) seems to be very popular, though we have never had the opportunity to sample its fare. Judging from the number of cars that always seem to be in the parking lot around mealtime, we should perhaps repair this oversight as soon as possible.

Crystal Cove Marina (386) 328-4000

Approach depths—5-6 feet
Dockside depths—4-5 feet
Accepts transients—yes
Transient dockage rate—average
Fixed wooden pier—yes
Dockside power connections—20
    and 30 amps
Dockside water connections—yes
Showers—yes
Gasoline—yes
Diesel fuel—yes
Mechanical repairs—gasoline
    and diesel engines
Ship's and variety store—yes
Restaurant—on site

Cow Creek Anchorage (29 40.458 North/081 37.540 West)

With light airs in the offing or moderate breezes from the east, you might try dropping the hook within 150 yards or so of the St. Johns' easterly banks between Cow Creek and the overhead power lines (north-northeast of unlighted daybeacon #43). For best depths, anchor some 100 yards north of the overhead cables and their poles. The adjoining shoreline is only modestly developed and makes a good backdrop for the evening. Of course, if an evening thunderstorm comes ploughing through, you may be wondering just why you picked this spot, but, in fair weather, it should be snug enough.

Carman Cove Anchorage (29 39.185 North/081 36.702 West)

Boats drawing 4 feet or less might consider spending the evening on Carman Cove, just north of Palatka. This large body of water indents the eastern coastline, southeast of flashing daybeacon #47, and just north of the high-rise Palatka bridge. Depths of 5 feet or better are held to within 200 yards of the eastern banks. Protection is not adequate for anything approaching heavy weather, but there is good shelter to the east, and a fair lee to the northeast courtesy of the cove's northerly entrance point. The shoreline is peppered with handsome homes peeping out amidst tall trees. Could you ask for more?

Palatka

The old river town known as Palatka sits serenely on the west banks of the St. Johns River, south of flashing daybeacon #47. Palatka is a community something between a quiet river village and a bustling city, retaining elements of both. Palatka is a very convenient stopover for those cruising this section of the St. Johns. Its marinas, riverside parks, and abundant shoreside lodging all have appeal for visiting cruisers.

To be brutally honest, however, this writer finds present-day Palatka somewhat less appealing than it was just a few years ago. One of the best restaurants convenient to the local marinas has now been closed for several years, and cheap, strip, shopping-center-type development seems to be reaching an ever greater crescendo along Highway 17. Added to these unfortunate developments is a seemingly faster pace of life than I seem to remember from my earlier visits. So, while there is still much to warrant recommending a stop in Palatka, cruisers who have not visited here for several years may find their stay to be a bit different from their last stopover.

Palatka Facilities (Various Lats/Lons— see below)

As you arrive from the north, the Palatka Holiday Inn Docks are the first facility you will come across. The single, wooden pier will be spied along the western banks, south of flashing daybeacon #48, just north of the 65-foot fixed Palatka bridge (near 29 38.839 North/081 37.615 West).

Transients are gratefully accepted for overnight or temporary dockage at this facility's single, fixed wooden pier. Surprising depths of 7 to 13 feet are discovered dockside. Fresh-water and 30 amp power connections are available at most berths. The adjacent swimming pool is a most refreshing attraction after a summer's cruise. Showers and a Laundromat are provided for transients, and you do not have to be a guest in the motel to use these services.

The Holiday Inn has its own somewhat less-than-spectacular restaurant, or you may choose to walk to Angel's Diner (see below). While no grocery stores are within walking distance, it's only a quick taxi ride (Diamond T Taxi Service—386-328-2653) to and from one of the local supermarkets, drugstores, or liquor stores.

The Holiday Inn also can boast of being the closest marina to the North Palatka Historic District, including the Bronson-Mulholland House and St. Marks Episcopal Church. These attractions are covered in detail below.

Palatka Holiday Inn Docks (386) 328-3481

Approach depths—10+ feet
Dockside depths—7-13 feet
Accepts transients—yes
Transient dockage rate—below average
Fixed wooden pier—yes
Dockside power connections—30 amps
Dockside water connections—yes
Showers—-yes
Laundromat—yes
Restaurant—on site and another nearby

South of the high-rise bridge, you will quickly spy an attractive park overlooking the western banks. Sharp-eyed cruisers will be able to pick out the community outdoor amphitheater. Soon the Palatka town docks will come abeam amidst this same riverside park, near 29 38.595 North/081 37.797 West. This pier now consists of a solidly built, fixed, wooden dock with several slips adequate for vessels as large as 40 feet. Soundings in the various berths range from 5 to 9 feet, with most slips having at least 6 feet of water. There are a few, very low key, 20-amp power and fresh-water connections. The entire dockage complex is a bit open, particularly with strong easterly breezes in the offing. In most weather, however, the docks should be reasonably secure.

There is no regular dockmaster on duty at the Palatka City Dock. After tying up, call the city hall at (386) 329-0100, or if you arrive after hours, the local police department at (386) 329-0111. Someone will come by later to collect the $25 per night dockage fee. A maximum stay of three nights is enforced.

Behind the pier, visitors can stroll Palatka's attractive riverfront park. Here you will find

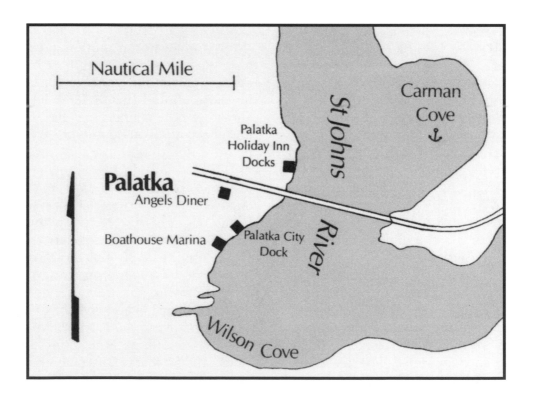

cookout facilities, bathrooms (but no showers), and telephones. It's a quick walk to Angel's Diner, the downtown business district, and the South Palatka Historic District (see below). Again, you will most likely need a taxi (Diamond T Taxi Service—386-328-2653) to facilitate a visit to one of the local supermarkets.

Palatka City Dock (386) 329-0100

Approach depths—10+ feet
Dockside depths—5-9 feet
Accepts transients—yes
   (3-night maximum stay)
Transient dockage rate—below average
Fixed wooden pier—yes
Dockside power connections—a few, minimal, 20-amp connections
Dockside water connections—limited
Restaurant—nearby

A short jog south of the Palatka town docks, Boathouse Marina also guards the westerly shoreline near 29 38.554 North/081 37.894 West. This marina, which has gotten a bit shabbier during the past several years, does accommodate transient visitors, and berths are provided at both fixed concrete and fixed wooden piers with water and 30-amp (mostly) power connections. Depths are good, with most slips showing 6 to 8 feet of water. Ashore, cruisers will find barely adequate showers and a washer and dryer. A ship's store stocked mostly with old junk adds to the marina's offerings, but mechanical servicing is no longer available.

Again, all the local restaurants are within walking distance, and the marina borders on the heart of the South Palatka Historic District. Taxi service (Diamond T Taxi Service—386-328-2653) will again be necessary for groceries and most supplies.

Boathouse Marina (386) 328-2944

Approach depths—10+ feet
Dockside depths—6-8 feet (minimum)

Palatka City Dock

Accepts transients—yes
Transient dockage rate—below average
Fixed wooden piers—yes
Fixed concrete piers—yes
Dockside power connections—30
    amps (one slip with 50 amps)
Dockside water connections—yes
Showers—yes
Laundromat—yes
Ship's store—yes
Restaurant—nearby

Palatka Restaurants

In addition to the Holiday Inn Restaurant, there is at least one other dining establishment worthy of any Palatka visitor's interest. Angel's Diner (386-325-3927), located at 209 Reid Street (Highway 17), is within a three-block walk of all the town dockage facilities. Angel's is one of the last real railway dining car type restaurants in America. It has been in continuous operation since 1936, and it looks every inch the part of vanishing small-town America. Angel's is open for all three meals of the day, and the food is surprisingly good, even if a bit on the fatty side. We wouldn't miss breakfast at Angel's whenever our travels take us to Palatka. Besides the superb hot cakes and omelets, there is always a crowd of loyal locals in attendance, and those who listen carefully can usually discover what's been going on lately in town.

Palatka Attractions

Palatka features two historic districts. The southern district, fronting River Street, is found directly behind Boathouse Marina and within a one-block walk of the city docks. A row of almost dreamlike Victorian and old Florida Conch houses overlooks the street and stretches for several blocks to the southwest. Chief among these attractions is the restored 1884 Tilghman House, headquarters of the Palatka Art League.

Art classes are held here regularly and there is a small gallery open to the public during the winter months, Thursday through Saturday 11 A.M. to 2 P.M. and Sunday 1 to 4 P.M.

The north historic district is found (you guessed it) north of Reid Street (Highway 17), bordering on the St. Johns River. The district is within a one-block walk of the Holiday Inn Docks, while a stroll of some five blocks from the city pier and Boathouse Marina is required to visit the area. Be sure to drop by the magnificent Bronson-Mulholland House (100 Madison Street, 386-329-0140) and the adjacent Putnam Historical Museum. The Bronson-Mulholland House was built by Judge Isaac Bronson in 1854. Bronson, a native New Yorker, proposed Florida's statehood while a member of the U.S. Congress. Later he was commissioned as a federal judge for the Eastern District of Florida, and eventually moved to Palatka. Once ensconced in his new position, the judge wasted no time in drafting and sponsoring his new hometown's city charter in the Florida legislature.

The homeplace was sturdily built of native cypress planks that were most likely floated down the Oklawaha River to Palatka. A steam sawmill on the shores of the St. Johns River in Palatka then prepared the fine boards.

Following Judge Bronson's death, his widow continued to live in their magnificent home until the Civil War, at which time she moved back to New York. During the initial years of the great war, the Bronson-Mulholland House remained empty except for a few Confederate soldiers who tradition claims used the attic windows as a lookout. Later the venerable structure served as barracks for Union troops.

In 1866, Charlotte J. Henry of New York, a friend of the Bronson family, opened a school for freed slaves in the house. She married

Bronson-Mulholland House, Palatka

Nathanial P. White and together they made extensive alterations. Following Mrs. White's death in 1904, a loyal nurse, Mary Mulholland, inherited the house. During both world wars, the house served as the center of Red Cross activities.

After going through a succession of owners the Bronson-Mulholland House was purchased by the city of Palatka in 1965. Following extensive renovations and restoration of many original furnishings, it was opened to the public in November of 1977.

The adjacent Putnam Historical Museum is housed in the oldest surviving structure in Palatka. Constructed in 1838, the homelike building was originally used as an officers' quarters for nearby Fort Shannon. This military fortification was active during the Second Seminole War. The museum contains an extensive collection of items from the various periods of Putnam County history.

Both the Bronson-Mulholland House and the Putnam Historical Museum are open Tuesday, Thursday, and Sunday from 2 to 5 P.M.

Walk a few blocks farther to the west and look for the 1854 St. Marks Episcopal Church at the corner of Main Street and North Second Street. During the War Between the States, this building was used as a hospital for wounded Union soldiers. After the conflict, the church served as a missionary center for the Episcopal church in the St. Johns valley. Today, the original building is still in use, though it has been altered a bit over the years.

You might also want to visit nearby (Azalea) Ravine State Gardens. A one-mile walk southwest down River Street from Boathouse Marina will bring you to this public facility. Begun as a FERA and Civil Works Administration (WPA) project in 1934, Ravine State Gardens now encompasses better than 180 acres. Hiking and nature trails wind among the many ravines that give the park its name. Depending on the timing of your visit, you can wander amidst a profusion of flowers and other flora. There is also a public golf course within a half-mile of the park.

Mug Race

Palatka serves as the starting point for one of the largest and certainly one of the funkiest inland sailboat races in the U.S. The Mug Race is named for the huge mug kept in the sponsoring Rudder Club's headquarters on which the winner's name is inscribed every year. This is an informal, family-oriented event where virtually everyone is out for a good time rather than blood-and-guts racing. According to my good friend, Doran Cushing, former publisher of Southwinds magazine, perhaps as many as 50 percent of the participants do not enter any other racing event all year other than the Mug. There were some 200 participating sailcraft of all sizes, shapes, and configurations in the 1999 Mug.

The Mug Race begins in Palatka and moves north to Jacksonville. It is usually held in May. While there are two starts (one for multihulls and another for monohulls), and several classes in each start, the one and only requirement for entering the race is that your mast must be able to clear the Shands/Green Cove Springs Bridge. If you happen to be cruising the St. Johns during the month of May, ask any local sailor for details on the current Mug Race. It's always fun to watch, and even more of a blast to participate.

Palatka History   Palatka was established as a trading post on the St. Johns River by James Marver in about 1820. Eventually this post became part of the Patton and Leslie Trading Company. This firm maintained a virtual monopoly on the lucrative Indian trade from the end of the Revolution through the second period of Spanish rule.

More by virtue of its location than any other asset, Palatka continued to prosper slowly until the first of the Seminole Indian wars. The village was an important river crossing and commerce moving from St. Augustine to the river's western banks tended to pass through the small settlement.

The Seminole Indian War of 1835-42 led to a general evacuation of the region. The federal government erected a short-lived fort at Palatka, where more soldiers died from disease than in battle.

After the Seminole War, Palatka began to grow quickly and was by all accounts a bustling little town until the Civil War.

During the early years of the war, cotton from the interior of Florida was ferried across the St. Johns at Palatka and then carted overland to New Smyrna. Swift blockade runners carried this precious cargo to England, where it was converted to much-needed cash. Eventually, however, the St. Johns was occupied by Federal gunboats, and one Union naval base was located just across the river from Palatka.

After the war, Palatka benefited from the growth of tourism in northern Florida. The poet and writer William Cullen Bryant visited Palatka in 1873 and reported the town was "still largely a forest." Apparently this was an exaggeration because in 1879 the sumptuous Putnam House Hotel opened in Palatka with a grand ball in honor of General Grant. By 1887 one account places the town's population at some four thousand citizens.

During the early twentieth century Henry Flagler's development of the east Florida railroad and the resort complexes at St. Augustine and Palm Beach began to take their toll on Palatka's tourism industry. The proud steamboats that had once plied the river were all gone by 1929. A boost was given the Palatka economy in 1931, when the International Paper Company opened a large pulp mill just north of the town. This facility has remained a mainstay of local employment to the present day.

JACKSONVILLE TO PALATKA NAVIGATION

Visiting cruisers must be mindful of good, sound coastal navigation on the open stretch of the St. Johns River between Jacksonville and Palatka. While the channel remains well marked and most trouble spots are clearly indicated, several nautical miles often separate the various daybeacons. Take the time to plot compass courses on chart 11492 or set up a series of GPS way points before beginning your run upriver. Follow your plotted courses carefully, watching for excessive lateral leeway. Even though this stretch of the St. Johns River is deep almost from bank to bank, it's easy to become disoriented on the broad waters. A little extra care with chart and compass can ensure an enjoyable voyage.

On the St. Johns   After passing between flashing daybeacons #1 and #2, west of Craig Creek, set course to come abeam of flashing daybeacon #3, lying west of charted Point La Vista, to its westerly side. Once abeam of #3, consider setting a bisected course to bring flashing daybeacon #5, west of Christopher Creek, eventually abeam well to its westerly side. Don't approach the charted shallows surrounding Point La Vista during this run. Set your original track to avoid the point; then once the point is abeam well to the east, alter your course to bring #5 abeam to its westerly quarter. Once abeam of #5, the headquarters of the Florida Yacht Club and the adjacent anchorage will come abeam on the western banks.

Florida Yacht Club and Pirates Cove Anchorage   To visit the Florida Yacht Club and Pirates Cove, set course from a position abeam of flashing daybeacon #5 for the waters just south of the point designated as "Clubhouse" on chart 11492. As you make your approach to this promontory, you will catch sight of the club's breakwater-enclosed harbor to starboard. The entrance is found on the southwestern corner of the basin.

To continue upstream into Pirates Cove, hold to the midline as the waters sweep around the point and flow to the northwest. Expect some low-water 4-foot soundings as you pass through this turn to the northwest. Eventually, the waters will open out and depths will improve to 6 to 8 feet. Drop the hook well short of the correctly charted 2- and 3-foot shallows to the north.

On the St. Johns   South of flashing daybeacon #5, follow the midwidth of the broad river as it curves toward the south-southwest. Soon Piney Point will come abeam on the western banks. A large industrial plant occupies the point. Interested mariners can cruise to within 100 yards of the western shoreline for a better look. Be sure to avoid the charted patch of submerged pilings northeast of Piney Point. The channel just south of the point is used by commercial traffic going to and from the industrial complex. Pleasure craft should stay clear.

Soon after you pass Piney Point, eagle-eye navigators will catch sight of flashing daybeacon #7, lying well to the east of charted Black Point. Come abeam and pass #7 to its western quarter. Goodbys Creek will come abeam to the east as you leave #7 in your wake.

Goodbys Creek   Remember that the Goodbys Creek channel holds only 4 feet or less at low water. To enter the stream, come abeam of flashing daybeacon #1 to its immediate southerly side. Look toward the creek's mouth and you will see a series of white PVC pipes rising vertically from the water's surface. These serve as somewhat confusing markers for the stream's entrance. Try to pass between and abeam of the various pipes, hoping that you guess the correct side on which to pass the single units. until you are on the interior portion of the creek, Take care not to drift to the south while entering Goodbys Creek. As chart 11492 clearly shows, many partially submerged pilings guard the entrance's southerly point.

Once past the creek's mouth, stick to the centerline for best depths. Even by following this procedure, you can expect some 3- to 4-foot depths, both at the entrance and on the western portion of the creek. Even shallow-draft vessels should discontinue their explorations shortly after passing through the stream's 11-foot, twin, fixed bridges.

On the St. Johns From a position abeam of Goodbys Creek, set your course for the central pass through of the large Three Mile/I-295 Bridge that spans the St. Johns at Plummers Point. Along the way you should pass well west of unlighted daybeacon #9. This aid to navigation marks a long, long tongue of shoal water stretching west from charted Beauclerc Bluff. Be sure to stay well west of #9.

Just before you reach the I-295 span, Plummers Cove will come abeam to the east.

Plummers Cove Enter Plummers Cove on its midsection. As you are cruising into the cove, look toward the southern banks and you will spy many old pilings. This area is marked "Ruins" on chart 11492. Apparently there was once a large barge pier here. Pleasure craft should strictly avoid these waters. An underwater piling could be waiting to spoil your entire day. Stay at least 200 yards from the eastern, southern, and northern shorelines

and you should be able to maintain minimum depths of 5½ to 6 feet.

On the St. Johns The Three Mile/I-295 Bridge has an official vertical clearance of 65 feet. Several local sailors have informed this writer that during times of high water, the actual height can drop to as little as 63 feet. Those with a mast height close to the limit should proceed with the greatest caution and be ready for a very quick reversal on the auxiliary.

South of the I-295 highway span, the St. Johns narrows briefly between Orange and Mandarin points. Some shallow water surrounds both points, particularly along the western banks. Flashing daybeacon #10 marks the shallows to the west, as does flashing daybeacon #11 to the east. Stick to the river's central waters and pass between these two aids. As #10 comes abeam to the west, the entrance to the Villas Continental and Yacht Club is accessible.

Villas Continental and Yacht Club The entrance to Villas Continental and Yacht Club is well marked but still requires caution. Come abeam of flashing daybeacon #10 to its immediate southerly side. Turn sharply to the west and point to pass unlighted daybeacon #1 to your port side and unlighted daybeacon #2 to starboard. Continue on course, passing between unlighted daybeacons #3 and #4. Once past these two aids, swing to starboard and enter the marina on the midwidth of the passage between the concrete breakwater to starboard and the rock island to port. You will spy a sign to port warning of an underwater rock breakwater near the little island.

Keep to the center of the channel to avoid this hazard.

Doctors Lake and Inlet   South of flashing daybeacon #11, cruisers have the option of turning west and visiting enchanting Doctors Lake, with its two marinas and many fine anchorages. Just remember that you must be able to clear the 37-foot fixed bridge to reach all but one of these attractions.

To enter, favor the northern shore slightly when cruising through Doctors Inlet to Doctors Lake. As chart 11492 clearly shows, a large bubble of shallow water extends north from the inlet's southern point. There are also some charted shallows shelving out from the entrance's northerly shores to worry with. Unlighted daybeacon #2 denotes the southeastern tip of these shoals. Be sure to pass well southeast and south of #2 to avoid this additional hazard.

After passing #2, the bridge spanning Doctors Inlet will be obvious dead ahead. Just short of this span, Whitney's Marine will come abeam to the south.

Whitney's has both an inner and outer harbor, which are served by separate entrance channels. To make good your entry into the more spacious outer dockage basin, turn sharply south and point for the harbor's entrance, which you should spy ahead. Along the way you should pass two unadorned wooden pilings to your port side.

To reach the inner harbor, turn due south just short of the Doctors Lake bridge. Point to pass unlighted daybeacon #1 to your port side. Continue on course by passing unlighted daybeacon #3 to port and then cruise between unlighted daybeacons #5 and #6. Favor the bridge side of the channel all the way between #1 and #6. After you pass between #5 and #6, the entrance to the marina's breakwater-enclosed, inner dockage basin will then be obvious.

Immediately after passing under the 37-foot fixed Doctors Inlet Bridge, Doctors Lake Marina will come abeam, also on the southern banks. For best depths, moor to the outer pier. Walk ashore to find the dockmaster.

The main body of Doctors Lake farther to the southwest is deep and easily navigated. There is one patch of 5-foot water west of Romeo Point, but this hazard is easily avoided by favoring the northwestern banks a bit in this section.

To enter Mill Cove on Doctors Lake, hold to the water body's centerline until you catch sight of several pilings at the cove's southeastern limit. Craft drawing more than 4 feet should discontinue their cruise northwest of the piles. However, boats that draw 3½ feet or (preferably) less may carefully explore east of the piles and expect 5-foot depths if they do not approach the shoreline too closely.

Swimming Pen Creek is easily entered on its midwidth. Remember, in spite of depths shown on chart 11492, you can expect minimum soundings of 5 to 7 feet in the creek and its entrance. Eventually, farther upstream, passage on Swimming Pen Creek is barred by a low-level, fixed bridge with only 6 feet of vertical clearance.

On the St. Johns   From a position abeam of Doctors Inlet on your westerly flank, set course to pass between flashing daybeacon #12, correctly charted east of Ragged Point, and unlighted daybeacon #13. Flashing daybeacon #12 is founded in shoal water while #13 is well out into the river's deeper section. Obviously you should favor #13 when passing between this pair of markers.

The St. Johns next sidewaters, Old Bull Bay and Julington Creek, are found almost due east of unlighted daybeacon #13.

Julington Creek   To enter Julington Creek, follow the midwaters of Old Bull Bay into the stream's westerly entrance. Continue on the middle until Mandarin Holiday Marina comes abeam on the northern banks, west of the Julington Creek Bridge, Julington Creek Marina is also located on the northern shore east of the span. Remember to discontinue your cruise soon after passing under the 15-foot, fixed Julington Creek Bridge. Farther upstream, depths deteriorate quickly.

On the St. Johns   Navigators bound upstream on the great river towards Palatka should next look for flashing daybeacon #15, lying well east of Peters Brook. Come abeam and pass #15 fairly close to its westerly side. There is actually good water both to the east and west of #15, but the nearest shallows lie well to the west and northwest, so, to be really cautious, a reasonably close encounter with #15 would seem to be a good idea.

Once you are abeam of #15, Cunningham Creek and Amity Anchorage come abeam well to the east.

Cunningham Creek Cove and Amity Anchorage   You may enter broad Cunningham Cove pretty much where you please. Simply stay at least 200 yards from the easterly banks for good depths.

The docks of Amity Anchorage will be spotted abutting the easterly shoreline, a short hop south of charted Cunningham Creek. The two flashing markers west of the pier mark the underwater terminus of a processed-waste disposal pipeline. Stay well clear.

Don't attempt to enter Cunningham Creek. Depths run to 2 feet and the bottom is foul with underwater stumps and other debris.

On the St. Johns   Moving south, the next set of aids to navigation on the St. Johns River are unlighted daybeacon #16 and flashing daybeacon #17, hard by New Switzerland Point. There is a very broad, fair water passage between these two markers, but be advised that #16 sits well within a large shoal striking east from Hibernia Point. Favor the easterly banks and #17 a bit to avoid this potential trouble spot.

Black Creek   Black Creek's entrance presents virtually the only navigational problem on the entire 18-mile passage upstream to Middleburg. Even here, elementary coastal navigation should see you through without any undue difficulty.

Favor the creek's southern shore east of the 30-foot fixed bridge spanning the entrance. Once through the bridge, immediately begin favoring the northern and northeastern banks to avoid the clearly charted shallows in the cove to the southwest. Abeam of the charted road leading northeast to Hibernia Point good depths open out almost from shore to shore.

Peters Creek makes into the southern banks of the main stream about .6 nautical miles from the Black Creek Bridge. While this small stream is quite deep, it is too narrow for anchorage by any but small craft. Boats over 28 feet should avoid entering the creek for any reason as they may not find sufficient room to swing around.

Some .3 nautical miles upstream past Peters Creek, a small island bisects the main stream. While both the eastern and western passages are quite deep, the easterly channel offers more swinging room.

After passing a small island abutting the northeasterly banks, Black Creek passes under a power line with 47 feet of vertical clearance. Sailors take note.

Eventually, you will spy a railroad bridge spanning the creek from north to south with 20 feet of closed vertical clearance. This span is usually open unless a train is due. It is now operated (apparently) automatically.

Soon after the railroad span, Black Creek leaves chart 11492. However, you may continue in safety by simply holding to the stream's centerline.

Several miles farther upstream you will pass under a second power line. Shortly thereafter the stream splits. Be sure to take the port-side branch when headed upstream. Finally, you will catch sight of a second highway bridge. While I could not find any official measurement of this span's vertical clearance, it was apparently no less than the 20-foot clearance of the railway span.

Intrepid cruisers who continue farther upstream will eventually spy the Middleburg scattered waterfront. Further upstream exploration on Black Creek is strictly not recommended as depths finally become uncertain.

On the St. Johns From a position abeam of Black Creek, consider setting course to pass between flashing daybeacon #19 and flashing daybeacon #18. Shoal water stretching out from Popo Point lies east of #19. Favor #18 and the western side of the channel when passing through.

Once #18 and #19 are in your wake, continue cruising upstream by pointing to eventually come abeam of flashing daybeacon #20 to its northeasterly side. Be on guard against the large, charted patch of shoal water extending south from Hallowes Cove when cruising between #18,#19, and #20. Along the way, you will pass the village of Green Cove Springs on the southwestern banks. Don't attempt to enter the cove bordering the town. Chart 11492 correctly identifies a large patch of shoal water adjoining the village's waterfront.

Once you are abeam of #20, the old naval piers and Green Cove Springs Marina lie just to the south.

Green Cove Springs Marina If you choose to visit Green Cove Springs Marina, cruise from #20 toward the last pier to the southeast. Turn in toward the southwestern banks on the dock's northwestern side. Watch your sounder. Soon after passing the dock's outermost tip, you will encounter the semisunken tramp freighter described earlier. Watch for a patch of 5-foot depths as you ease around this derelict. Closer to shore, water levels improve to 7 feet or better. The marina office is a quick hop to the northwest from the landward side of the tall pier. The newer floating docks flank the southwestern banks, just northwest of the tall dock.

On the St. Johns From flashing daybeacon #20, set course for the central pass through of the Shands/Green Cove Springs Bridge.

As noted earlier, this span's vertical clearance of 45 feet sets the height limit for the upper St. Johns. Sailcraft that can't clear this bridge must unfortunately forgo cruising the upper reaches of the river.

Continue on course upstream by coming abeam and passing flashing daybeacon #22 well to its easterly side. At #22, Florence Cove and Trout Creek on the northeastern banks beckon to be explored.

Florence Cove   Favor the northwestern banks slightly when entering Florence Cove. Very shallow water extends well out into the cove from the opposite shore. Stay at least 200 yards from the northeasterly and northwesterly shorelines, and you will hopefully maintain minimum depths of 5 feet.

Trout Creek   The entrance to Trout Creek is very tricky and only indifferently marked. Currently, the only aid is a single upright piling designated "Marker" on chart 11492.

Cruise into Palmo Cove heavily favoring the southern shore. A large patch of extremely shoal water extends south from Jack Wright Island for more than .2 nautical miles. Begin working your way carefully to the northeast until the upright piling comes abeam to port. Turn sharply to port, pass the piling on its immediate westerly side, and continue on course pointing to enter the midwidth of Trout Creek.

Keep a weather eye on the sounder from the time you enter Palmo Cove, and proceed at idle speed. If depths start to rise, stop and assess the situation before you reach grounding depths.

Once on the main body of Trout Creek, stick to the midsection. Depths improve markedly on the stream's interior, ranging up to 15 feet. After you pass under the charted 14-foot bridge (which local reports place at an actual clearance of 17 feet), Pacetti's Marina will come abeam on the western shore. Excellent depths continue upstream short of the charted log boom at Hardwood. However, the stream narrows markedly in this upper stretch, and these waters are not recommended for boats over 28 feet.

South on the St. Johns   From flashing daybeacon #22, the St. Johns remains well buoyed to the twin range markers west of Solano Point. Shoal waters are clearly indicated by the various daybeacons, except for a long tongue of 4-foot water extending well to the east from the unnamed point north of Clark Creek. Be sure to favor the eastern banks when passing this shoal.

Colee Cove   Colee Cove, lying well east of flashing daybeacon #24, is the only good sidewater for exploration or anchorage between #22 and the Solano Point range markers. Enter the cove on its midsection. There are some shoals abutting the southerly banks, but a broad band of deep water crosses most of the bay. You can approach to within 200 yards of the eastern banks and hold good depths.

On the St. Johns   As you begin your approach to Solano Cove and its like-named point to the south, be sure to pass well west of unlighted daybeacon #27. This aid to navigation marks a long shoal striking out from the easterly banks. At times, it can be hard to spot from the water.

At Solano Point a pair of lighted range

markers directs you through a long, improved channel to flashing daybeacon #33. Come abeam of #33 to its westerly side. Consistently deep water surrounds this cut on all sides, and while it is not really necessary for pleasure craft to stick to the marked channel, it's always the safest course of action.

South of #33, you can pick up another range immediately south of Racy Point, which leads you safely past the charted shoal at Ninemile Point. Favor the easterly side of the channel as Ninemile Point comes abeam to the west, and be sure to pass well east of flashing daybeacon #36.

Once past the point, set a new course to come abeam of flashing daybeacon #37 by some 75 yards to its westerly side. From #37, it is a quick run upstream to come abeam of flashing daybeacon #38 to its southeasterly side. Here you can follow yet another set of range markers till you are abeam of Whetstone Point to the northwest.

As you come abeam of the forward Whetstone Point range marker, the St. Johns takes a hard turn to the west. Pass just north of the forward range marker and set course almost due west. Eventually you will come abeam and pass flashing daybeacon #41 to its northerly side. As you make your approach to #41 look to the north and you will spy two large, funnel-shaped smokestacks. These are part of a large coal-fired power plant.

From #41, set course to come abeam of the forward range marker, well northwest of Forrester Point. You can follow this track south to another set of range markers, hard by the marked Rice Creek entrance channel.

Rice Creek   Rice Creek has a well-outlined entrance cut and excellent depths. To enter, pass between unlighted daybeacons #2 and #3 and point to come abeam of unlighted daybeacon #4 to its immediate southerly side. Be sure to stay south of #4. The waters north of this marker are foul with stumps and snags.

Between #3 and #4 you may spy several nondescript markers leading to the southwest. This channel serves a barge-loading dock along the river's western shoreline. Don't attempt to enter this commercial-oriented cut.

Once past #4, head straight toward the forward range marker near the western banks. Just before reaching this beacon, swing to starboard (the northwest) and point to pass unlighted daybeacon #6 to your starboard side and take unlighted daybeacon #7 to port. Continue on course passing flashing daybeacon #8 to starboard and flashing daybeacon #9 to port.

Farther upstream the marked channel continues, but good depths for pleasure craft open out almost from shore to shore. Shortly after passing unlighted daybeacon #13, you will encounter the Rice Creek railroad bridge (closed vertical clearance—2 feet).

You will soon pass under the fixed highway span, which has a vertical clearance of 45 feet. Just to the west, the stream is split by a small island. Captains cruising through or anchoring in the northerly passage should stick strictly to the arm's midwidth. A few shoals extend out for a short distance into the creek from the island.

If you decide to explore Rice Creek upstream to the large pulp and paper mill, continue on the centerline till you spot unlighted daybeacon #18. Follow the stream's southerly branch and you will soon spy the mill dead ahead. Be sure to leave yourself plenty of room to turn around before approaching the mill's wharves too closely.

On the St. Johns   South of the St. Johns-Rice Creek intersection, two more ranges lead you to the charted 60-foot power lines. Between the forward range markers and the power poles, a large patch of shoal water abuts the western banks. Guard against excessive leeway to the west as you are making this run.

Crystal Cove Marina   Short of the power lines, a marked and charted channel leads west to Crystal Cove Marina and its adjacent motel and restaurant. Remember that this cut holds minimum depths of only 5 feet, while you will find a scant 4 to 5 feet of depth dockside. If these soundings are not a problem for your vessel, you can make good your entry by simply cruising between the various markers, keeping red aids to navigation on your starboard side and green beacons to port. Be advised that the daymark portion of these aids to navigation are currently in poor shape, and the numbers are all but impossible to make out. Nighttime entry could be tricky indeed for first timers.

After coming abeam of the channel's westernmost marker, unlighted daybeacon #7, cruise straight in toward the head of the pier that you will sight along the shoreline.

Cow Creek Anchorage   The entrance to shallow Cow Creek lies east of the Crystal Cove Marina entry channel. To successfully enter the deep waters south of the creek,

abutting the St. Johns' easterly banks, abandon the main channel some 100 to 150 yards north of the charted power lines. Cruise carefully toward the eastern shoreline, keeping a close watch on the sounder. Do not attempt to approach to within less than 100 yards of the banks unless your craft can stand some 4-foot depths.

On the St. Johns   The charted power lines crossing the St. Johns have a clearance of 60 feet over most of their run, but this height is increased to 90 feet over the main channel. Two markers help you keep to the channel as you pass under the power lines. Unlighted daybeacon #43 lines the channel's easterly side just north of the lines, while flashing daybeacon #44 outlines the cut's western edge immediately south of the power poles. Pass #43 to its westerly side and #44 to its easterly quarter.

Once the power lines are in your wake, continue on the same course, pointing to come abeam eventually of flashing daybeacon #47, off Moritani Point, by some 50 yards (at least) to its western side. Immediately south of #47, boats drawing 4½ feet or less can anchor in Carman Cove.

Carman Cove Anchorage   Cruise into the midwaters of Carman Cove south of flashing daybeacon #47. Feel your way along carefully toward the eastern banks, limiting your approach to a position no closer than 200 yards of the easterly shoreline. You may encounter some 5-foot depths on this run, but most soundings hold at 6 feet.

On to Palatka   Once abeam of flashing

daybeacon #47, point your bow toward the Palatka bridge's central pass through. Between #47 and the Palatka bridge, watch the western shoreline carefully for the Palatka Holiday Inn Docks. They will come up suddenly from behind a large metal building. While searching for the docks, be sure to pass flashing daybeacon #48 to its easterly side. This aid marks a small patch of shoal water lying to the west.

The Palatka high-rise bridge has a vertical clearance of 65 feet. After leaving the span behind, point to pass flashing daybeacon #1 by some 50 yards (or more) to its western side. Between the bridge and #1, the principal Palatka waterfront will be obvious along the western shoreline.

Palatka   Most of the Palatka shoreline is quite deep and visiting craft can cruise to within 50 yards of the western shore for a good view of this charming community. The city docks lie along the town waterfront south of the bridge, and Boathouse Marina is just a bit farther upstream.

Don't attempt to cruise southwest of Boathouse Marina into Wilson Cove. While you may see a few local craft anchored near the marina, the waters farther inside the cove are suspect at best. A sawmill was once located on this cove's shores, and this operation has left behind a host of pilings (some submerged) and underwater debris. Much of the bottom is foul, and depths of 4 feet or less are all too common.

Palatka to Lake George

South of Palatka the St. Johns River narrows perceptibly and soon loses every trace of its tidal nature. The river's banks become a deep cypress swamp, broken here and there by residential development. The shoreside foliage is often lush and begs to be explored and fished by dinghy. Small but deep creeks intersect the river regularly all the way to Lake Monroe. Many offer safe haven for the night, but a few are blinds waiting to trap unwary navigators. All in all, this is perhaps the most interesting stretch of the St. Johns River for those who relish the feeling that every puff of wind or turn of the screw leads them farther from the madding crowd.

While the character of the St. Johns is fairly consistent between Palatka and Lake Monroe, we will first cover the stretch to Lake George, then the run to Sanford. The 79 nautical miles that separate these two cities are a bit much for a single section.

From Palatka to the southern shores of Lake George, facilities are few. One boatyard, a seedy trailer park, and one small but first-class marina are supplemented by numerous fishing camps. Most of these latter facilities, however, are strictly for small craft; cruising skippers will find little for their size vessel. On the other hand, anchorages abound. There is perhaps no other stretch on the river that offers so many secure places to rest.

The St. Johns is extremely well marked all the way to Sanford, but shoals do exist and are fairly numerous in some sections. Be sure to plan your route carefully ahead of time and have charts 11492 and 11495 at hand. Otherwise, simply observe all markers carefully, and you should have a most pleasant cruise south.

Palatka to Lake George Anchorage Summary (Please note that anchorages are listed in geographic order, moving downstream to upstream.)

Porters Cove Anchorage—located near 29 37.128 North/081 35.979 West, off the west banks of the St. Johns River, south-southwest of flashing daybeacon #11—8-foot depths—reviewed on pages 129, 140

Dunn Creek Anchorage—located near 29 34.904 North/081 37.664 West, on the centerline of Dunn Creek, abeam of its intersection with Murphy Creek—6-foot depths—reviewed on pages 130-31, 140-41

Crescent Lake—Weidernoch Point Anchorage—located near 29 28.270 North/081 31.508 West, on the western shores of Crescent Lake, south of Weidernoch Point—7-foot depths, but a difficult approach to the lake must be traversed through Dunn Creek—reviewed on pages 131, 141

Murphy Creek Anchorages—eastern mouth of Murphy Creek intersects Dunn Creek (see above) near the latter stream's northern mouth—various lats/lons (see detailed account)—5-foot depths if the adjoining shoals are avoided—reviewed on pages 131-32, 141

Browns Landing Anchorage—located near 29 35.689 North/081 38.263 West, off the northern banks of the St. Johns River, west-northwest of flashing daybeacon #16—8-foot depths—reviewed on pages 132, 141-42

Seven Sisters Anchorages—located south of Buffalo Bluff and southeast of flashing daybeacon #28—various lats/lons (see detailed account)—8-foot depths—reviewed on pages 132-33, 142-43

Stokes Island Loop Anchorage—located near 29 34.308 North/081 41.899 West, at the rear of the loop stream that enters the St. Johns near flashing daybeacon #31—7-foot depths—reviewed on pages 133, 143

Turkey Island Anchorages—sandwiched between the St. Johns' easterly banks and Turkey Island, south of flashing daybeacon #42—various lats/lons (see detailed account)—8-foot depths—reviewed on pages 135-36, 143-44

Beecher Point Anchorage—located near 29 27.855 North/081 40.934 West, east-northeast of flashing daybeacon #53—6-foot depths—reviewed on pages 134, 145

Buzzards Point Anchorage—located near 29 26.067 North/081 40.343 West, northeast of unlighted daybeacon #60—5+-foot depths—reviewed on pages 137, 145

Fruitland Cove Anchorage—located near 29 25.728 North/081 39.304 West, east and a bit south of flashing daybeacon #63—7-foot depths—reviewed on pages 137-38, 145-46

Black Point Anchorage—located near 29 23.405 North/081 39.750 West, west and a bit south of flashing daybeacon #68—5+-foot depths—reviewed on pages 138, 146

Palatka to Lake George Marina and Yacht-Club Summary (Please note that marinas and yacht clubs are listed in geographic order, moving downstream to upstream.)

Acosta Creek Harbor—(386) 467-2229—located near 29 30.482 North/081 40.677 West, east of unlighted daybeacon #42A—transient dockage available—7-foot minimum depths—reviewed on pages 134-35

Burger King Dock

Northeast of flashing daybeacon #6, overlook-ing the river's northerly banks, cruisers will find what must surely be one of the only fast-food restaurant docks in the United States. The local Burger King maintains a single pier to which mariners are welcome to tie while ordering their Whopper and fries (no overnight stays are allowed). Craft up to 40 feet in length should find enough space alongside for easy mooring. Depths immediately adjacent to the pier run in the 6½- to 7-foot range while, only a foot or two farther out into the river, soundings deepen to 9 and 10 feet. No dockside power, water, or other marine-oriented services are available.

After having a Whopper, cruisers in need of supplies can quickly walk across the street to a drugstore, grocery store, and several other retail businesses. Please don't abuse your docking privileges by visiting these firms without patronizing the Burger King.

Porters Cove Anchorage (29 37.128 North/081 35.979 West)

A few boats occasionally anchor in the correctly charted 8- to 10-foot waters of Porters Cove, north of flashing daybeacon #12. Good depths persist to within 75 yards of the well-wooded, all-natural westerly banks. There is just about enough swinging room for the Trump Princess. The opposite shoreline displays moderate development. With even moderate winds from the north, south, or east, you would do better to select one of the more sheltered anchorages farther upstream on the St. Johns. This spot is also fully exposed to the wake of all passing power vessels.

Gibson Dry Docks (29 36.701 North/081 35.449 West)

Gibson Dry Docks (386-325-5502) is a large, do-it-yourself repair yard on the river's east banks, east of flashing daybeacon #12. The yard is apparently quite popular with local cruisers, judging from the number of craft we

always find high and dry on its unpaved grounds. Gibson's travelift is rated at 20 tons. All bottom work is strictly do-it-yourself or arranged through independent contractors. The scant wet-slip dockage is reserved for service customers. Be advised that approach depths run in the 4½- to 5-foot range, with some 4-foot soundings immediately adjacent to the travelift.

Captains and crew patronizing Gibson Dry Docks should take the opportunity to walk up the entrance road toward the highway. This track leads through a lush forest with wavy swaths of grey moss streaming from tall cypress and oaks. The old Gibson homeplace is visible to the north, but the house is off-limits. This hike affords a glimpse of the old Florida that is now quickly vanishing into the past.

The Strange Plantation

Just east of Gibson Dry Docks is the village of San Mateo. In 1764, what must surely rank as the strangest plantation ever to grace the shores of the St. Johns River was established just north of the present-day town.

Denys Rolle, a London physician, somehow formulated the idea of gathering some "practicioners of the oldest profession," and transporting them to the New World. There, he thought they could be magically reformed by hard work on his plantation. Amazingly, Dr. Rolle was able to obtain a grant from the British Crown, and even more surprisingly he somehow persuaded forty destitute "ladies of the evening" to accompany him on the overseas crossing.

Trouble began almost immediately. Rolle insisted that his partially reformed charges construct a church on the new plantation before building a house to provide shelter. When they asked how they could earn any money for themselves, Rolle allowed them to sell half of the practically worthless palmetto roots they cut in clearing the fields.

The entire group eventually left the plantation and took refuge in nearby St. Augustine. The British governor, James Grant, was basically sympathetic to the prostitutes' plight, and he had a profound personal dislike for Dr. Rolle. Nevertheless, the doctor had come with a royal letter requesting the governor to lend all possible assistance, so reluctantly Grant gathered up all of Rolle's charges and sent them back to the plantation.

Of course, these thoroughly disgusted colonists were even less enthusiastic about working for Dr. Rolle than they had been before their escape. Finally, the master must have decided that he had done all that was humanly possible to reform his charges. Besides, he was not making a profit. Sorrowfully, he released them without money or means of transportation in a hostile land and left them to make out as best they could. He soon purchased black slaves to take their place, and—lo and behold!—the plantation did indeed begin to prosper.

Dunn Creek (29 34.904 North/081 37.664 West)

Dunn Creek flows north into the St. Johns' southern shore west of flashing daybeacon #15. This stream leads south to beautiful Crescent Lake but it is littered with shoals. The creek is spanned along its northerly reaches by a fixed, high-rise bridge with 45 feet of vertical clearance.

Wild-eyed skippers who pilot craft less than 35 feet long that can clear the bridge, and, most importantly, with a draft less than 4 feet, may choose to follow Dunn Creek to Crescent Lake. If you decide to make this risky side trip,

be sure to read the Dunn Creek navigation information below before entering this upper portion of the creek.

Cruisers who undertake the trek to Crescent Lake will be treated to some lovely, undeveloped banks to starboard, while portions of the port-side shores exhibit fairly heavy but nonetheless attractive residential development. There are no facilities either on the creek or in Crescent Lake.

North of the bridge, Dunn Creek is basically free of shallows, excepting the waters immediately adjacent to the easterly shoreline. This portion of the stream offers sheltered anchorage for boats up to 38 feet. The waters abeam of Murphy Creek offer maximum swinging room. Minimum depths in the broad channel between the entrance and the Murphy Creek intersection run around 6 feet with some

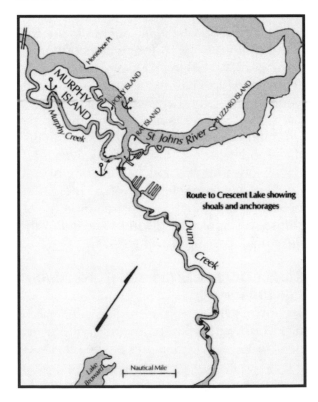

Route to Crescent Lake showing shoals and anchorages

soundings going up to 20 feet. About the only problem you might have in dropping the hook here comes from the considerable small-craft traffic on the creek (particularly on weekends). If you can put up with this inconvenience, don't hesitate to use this fine anchorage.

Crescent Lake

Crescent Lake is an absolutely magnificent body of water that stretches south for almost 10 nautical miles from the Dunn Creek entrance to Green Bay. Its average width is 2 nautical miles.

Apart from the Crescent City waterfront, most of the lake's shoreline is undeveloped. If you are fortunate enough to cruise the lake, you may observe many local anglers trying their luck along the cypress-crowded shores. According to one native, Crescent Lake is the bass capital of the world, a title that, incidentally, is often also used to describe all of the upper St. Johns.

Depths on Crescent Lake run from 5 to 13 feet, except for shallower soundings within 200 to 300 yards of the various shorelines. Most of the banks are shoal, with depths of less than 3 feet. There is also a large patch of shallow water surrounding and extending southeast of Bear Island. The northern entrance into the lake from Dunn Creek has some 5-foot shoals, and you must be careful when running the unmarked channel. Otherwise, boats drawing less than 4 feet should not encounter any navigational difficulty on the lake north of Hopkins Point.

Surprisingly, Crescent Lake offers only one secure anchorage. The lake is a near-perfect oval and has few coves along its shoreline. Boats up to 38 feet can anchor in the offshoot of deep water south of Weidernoch Point, near 29 28.270 North/081 31.508 West. Here min-

imum depths of 7 feet are held within 100 yards of the western banks. Don't approach the point too closely. As chart 11487 clearly shows, it is surrounded by shoal water.

Crescent City guards the lake's midline to the west. Unfortunately, there are no docking facilities for larger pleasure craft on the city waterfront (or anywhere else on the lake). There is a small park with an adjacent launching ramp. In fair weather, you could anchor off this park and dinghy ashore. A walk of four blocks or so will lead you up to the main street with a whole array of shoreside businesses, including grocery and drugstores.

Even with the scarcity of facilities and anchorages, not to mention its difficult approach from the St. Johns, Crescent Lake is attractive. The generally undeveloped character of the lake coupled with the feeling that few larger pleasure craft have come this way before contributes to a sense of excitement that is all too rare in modern cruising.

Murphy Creek (Various Lats/Lons—see below)

Murphy Creek cuts into the western shoreline of Dunn Creek near the latter stream's northerly mouth. The easterly reaches of undeveloped Murphy Creek are consistently deep and offer excellent anchorage for craft up to 40 feet. Protection is even sufficient for heavy weather in winds from any quarter. Minimum depths are 5 feet at the intersection with Dunn Creek but rise to 7-foot soundings on interior reaches of Murphy Creek, with an occasional 20+-foot sounding making an appearance.

Farther upstream, several unmarked shoals make navigation a bit tricky for boats over 38 feet. However, if you can clear these obstructions, the creek continues to offer near ideal anchorage until it rejoins the St.

Johns River south of flashing daybeacon #26.

The westerly entrance of Murphy Creek makes into the main river south of flashing daybeacon #26. This passage is not recommended for larger cruising craft. While there is a 7-foot channel leading out to the river, it is narrow and unmarked. The prudent navigator will retrace his steps to Dunn Creek to reenter the St. Johns.

Probably the best spot for large craft to anchor is found on the waters of the creek's first sharp bend to the north, southwest of its intersection with Dunn Creek, near 29 35.00 North/081 38.125 West. Here craft as large as 38 feet will find plenty of elbowroom set amidst depths of 10 to 20 feet and beautifully undeveloped shores.

Another good spot is discovered along the long, straight stretch of the creek, depicted just below the words Murphy Island on chart 11495 (near 29 35.058 North/081 39.526 West). Swinging room is sufficient for craft as large as 36 feet and depths along the midsection of the creek run 10 to 15 feet. Be advised that you must travel through a few somewhat shoally turns of the creek to reach this latter haven, but most mariners will be able to come through in fine fashion.

Browns Landing Anchorage (29 35.689 North/081 38.263 West)

West of the St. Johns-Dunns Creek intersection, the river follows a turn to the west-northwest. Between flashing daybeacon #16 and unlighted daybeacon #18, passing cruisers will find good depths of 8 feet or better to within 100 yards of the northerly banks. With winds blowing from the north, this is a secure haven. Shelter is fair to the south and east, but strong blows from the west or northwest call for another strategy. There is plenty of swinging

room for boats as large as 50 feet. Be sure to anchor well away from the main channel and show an anchor light.

Seven Sisters Anchorages (Various Lats/Lons—see below)

Southeast of flashing daybeacon #28 and the bascule railroad bridge, deep creeks running between the islands known as the Seven Sisters (on the St. Johns' eastern shore) offer excellent anchorage. While the islands themselves are undeveloped, the mainland shore abeam of the various anchorages exhibits moderate residential development.

The northernmost anchorage is entered by a

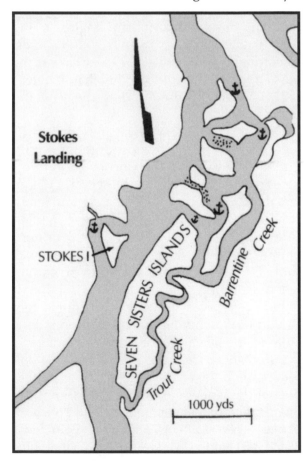

broad channel of deep water adjoining Buffalo Bluff. You can easily follow this stream to a point just short of the charted 2-foot shoal north of Barrentine Creek. Further exploration into the creek's entrance is strictly not recommended. North of the shoal water, boats up to 45 feet can drop the hook with plenty of swinging room, 8-foot minimum depths, and good protection from all winds. One of the best spots is found near 29 34.858 North/081 40.750 West.

Another deep creek northeast of flashing daybeacon #31 leads east into the southerly portion of the Seven Sisters chain. Good depths of 8 feet or better continue as the stream follows a hairpin turn to the north (though you must take great care to avoid the westerly banks on this portion of the creek) but quickly deteriorate after coming abeam of the charted sharp point of land on the northwestern tip of the oblong island bordering Barrentine Creek.

The easiest of the Seven Sisters anchorages is found along the initial section of this channel between the cut's intersection with the primary waters of the St. Johns River and the stream's first swing to the north, near 29 34.240 North/081 41.171 West. Craft up to 38 feet will be comfortable here, and there is good shelter from all but strong western and northwesterly winds.

Another spot to consider is located around the waters abutting the easterly banks, north of the above-described channel's first sharp cut to the north. Boats as large as 36 feet can anchor near 29 34.301 North/081 41.009 West with enough shelter for the heaviest weather.

Stokes Island Loop Anchorage (29 34.308 North/081 41.899 West)

A deep stream loops around Stokes Island south of flashing daybeacon #31 on the St.

Johns' western shore. While there are a few shallows to avoid, most of the creek carries minimum depths of 7 feet. Swinging room should be sufficient for boats up to 36 feet to anchor here.

Even if it's not time to set the hook for the evening, you may want to cruise through the Stokes loop. A large but now apparently defunct commercial ship manufacturing and repair facility is located in a small stream on the loop's extreme northwesterly corner. Several old derelicts both ashore and seemingly permanently installed on the waters abeam of this old facility make for interesting viewing.

Cross-Florida Barge Canal

The entrance to the never-completed Cross-Florida Barge Canal lies west of unlighted daybeacon #33A. This controversial channel leads west to a large lock. The canal on the far side flows into Lake Oklawaha. This fascinating body of water was created by a dam constructed on the old Oklawaha River as part of the initial construction of the barge canal. The lake is littered with hundreds of stumps, not all of which are above the waterline. In some places ghost forests of long-dead trees line the shore and are readily visible from the barely recognizable channel. The shoreline is generally undeveloped, though there are a few recreation areas and campsites along the banks.

While small fishing skiffs sometimes travel through the locks into Lake Oklawaha, cruising craft are strictly advised against this passage. The many underwater stumps and semisubmerged logs can bring even the careful mariner to grief.

Over the past several years, with the abandonment of plans for the canal, there has been some discussion about removing the dam and allowing the Oklawaha River to resume its old course. There have also been more than a few funding problems associated with the lock between the St. Johns River and Lake Oklawaha. The resolution of these discussions and problems remains unclear at the time of this writing.

Cross-Florida Barge Canal History During the New Deal administration of Franklin Delano Roosevelt, the idea arose, as it had before, of building a trans-Florida waterway from the St. Johns River to the Gulf Coast. Five million dollars was included in the 1935 federal budget for the construction of a trans-Florida canal, which would follow the course of the Oklawaha River. Even then, opposition on environmental grounds was strong. Concerned citizens and experts argued that the canal would allow salt water to penetrate the fresh-water region of central Florida, with disastrous ecological results. The opposition succeeded in halting the project, but only temporarily.

The issue arose again in 1943 and 1956, but it was not until 1964 that the long-awaited and long-feared project actually got under way. By the late 1960s, Oklawaha River had been dammed and a canal and lock had been completed to give access to the new Lake Oklawaha. However, there were major difficulties in obtaining the necessary rights-of-way to continue construction. After a negative economic feasibility study, President Nixon ordered construction halted permanently in 1971. No new construction has taken place since then, and the project now seems to be thoroughly dead.

Shell Harbor (29 31.268 North/081 40.715 West)
The long, fixed wooden face dock associated with Shell Harbor trailer camp (386-467-2330) will come abeam on the eastern banks

near flashing daybeacon #40A. Transients are sometimes accepted at this seedy establishment, and most berths have fresh-water and low-key 20- and 30-amp power connections. Depths at the pier range from 6 to 7 feet.

A set of steep wooden stairs leads up from the docks to a large campground and trailer park that is not in the best of repair. You'll most likely know what you're in for when you spot the first of several peacocks that are allowed to roam freely over the grounds. After a little while, their loud calls can be truly annoying. The nearby showers could not be described as clean, and the so-called Laundromat is virtually in the open air. A swimming pool is available and open to cruising transients.

Acosta Creek Harbor (29 30.482 North/081 40.677 West)
East of unlighted daybeacon #42A, the sturdy piers of Acosta Creek Harbor guard the eastern shoreline. Even after undergoing a change in ownership, this facility remains our favorite marina on the St. Johns between Palatka and De Land. Transients are eagerly accepted at two fixed wooden piers. The docks are in excellent condition, and all berths feature full 30- and 50-amp power and fresh-water connections. Typical depths alongside range from 7 to as much as 13 feet. Superclean showers (one climate controlled and one not) and a full Laundromat are located behind the main house. It's a bit of a walk from the docks to these facilities.

Mechanical repairs can almost certainly be arranged through independent contractors. Acosta Creek features a 30-ton marine travelift, and judging from the number of hauled craft that we observed during our last visit, Acosta's below-waterline services must be equally as impressive as the remainder of this first-class facility. Acosta Harbor boasts one of the best marine carpenters in this region of Florida.

A large, rambling, but somehow friendly homeplace sits atop a small knoll overlooking the Acosta Creek dockage complex. A wide swath of green lawn covers the broad grounds between the docks and the house. It makes for a very impressive sight from the water. While the old homeplace is no longer operated as a bed-and-breakfast inn, shoreside lodging is available in several cedar cabins, suites with king-size beds, and one cottage.

There is no on-site restaurant, but transportation to a nearby dining spot is sometimes available

Trust us on this one, fellow cruisers. If you are looking for a friendly, top-notch marina between Palatka and De Land, by all means give the nod to Acosta Creek Harbor.

Acosta Creek Harbor (386) 467-2229
http://www.acostacreek.com

Approach depths—10+ feet
Dockside depths—7-13 feet
Accepts transients—yes
Transient dockage rate—below average
Fixed wooden piers—yes
Dockside power connections—30
    and 50 amps
Dockside water connections—yes
Showers—yes
Laundromat—yes
Below-waterline repairs—yes
Mechanical repairs—yes
    (independent contractors)

Turkey Island Anchorages (Various Lats/Lons—see below)

South of flashing daybeacon #42, several deepwater channels around Turkey Island

Acosta Creek Harbor

offer good anchorage. Some moderate residential development lines the mainland shore, but Turkey Island itself is undeveloped. There are only four other acceptable anchorages between Turkey Island and Lake George. None of these havens offer as much protection as the waters lying about Turkey Island. If you are planning to drop the hook short of Lake George, this is the best spot.

Cruisers can break off from the main river channel at flashing daybeacon #42 and follow a deep channel with 8-foot minimum depths that hugs the eastern shoreline. Boats up to 36 feet will find plenty of room to anchor north of Turkey Island. This is a particularly convenient spot for southbound craft. Probably the best anchorage will be discovered where chart 11495 notes soundings of 17 and 18 feet, abeam of the several small but charted islands to the west (north of Turkey Island and near 29 30.099 North/081 40.690 West).

Careful navigators can continue south into another excellent anchorage on the 10+-foot waters south of Turkey Island (west of Welaka Springs and near 29 29.683 North/081 40.705 West). To successfully reach this second overnight stop from the northerly anchorage,

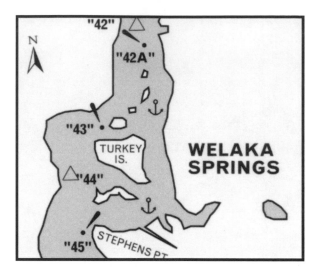

you must avoid the charted but unmarked 3-foot shoal east of Turkey Island. Alternately, cruisers might choose to enter the southerly anchorage via the broad channel sweeping east from the main body of the St. Johns, just north of flashing daybeacon #45.

While it is possible to anchor most anywhere on this broad, southerly anchorage (south of the 3-foot shoal), the spot with the best swinging room is found abeam of the unnamed, shallow creek cutting east-southeast to Welaka Springs. Boats up to 48 feet can anchor here with plenty of swinging room and superb protection from all winds.

Two channels lead back into the St. Johns from this southerly anchorage. The northern cut hugs the southern banks of Turkey Island, while the far broader and more easily followed southern channel passes west along Stephens Point and rejoins the St. Johns north of flashing daybeacon #45.

Welaka

The old river village of Welaka gazes over the St. Johns' eastern banks, south of flashing daybeacon #48, much as it has for the past two hundred years or so. A profusion of small fishing camps lines the town waterfront, but no facilities catering to larger pleasure craft are currently available. Several of the camps have restaurants associated with them, however. According to area natives, the seafood served in these small eateries ranges from unforgettable to meals they would just as soon forget. Ownership changes often so that it is difficult to suggest which restaurants are worth a visit from one season to the next. Although some of these establishments have their own docks, depths alongside are consistently less than those required for cruising-size craft. Hungry mariners in an experimental mood might try anchoring just off the main river channel and dinghying ashore. Take your best guess at a good restaurant. Good luck!

Welaka History   Welaka is another river town originally founded as a trading post during British rule. The village's name recalls the Native American name for the St. Johns River, Welaka, meaning "chain of lakes."

Welaka is associated with one of the most daring and colorful military officers in Floridian history. During the latter stages of the War Between the States, Capt. J. J. Dickinson led a band of legendary Confederate guerrilla cavalry in many daring raids along the shores of the St. Johns.

Perhaps his boldest exploit was a surprise counterattack launched on two Federal gunboats sent to capture him and his guerrillas. One, the Ottawa, sustained extensive damage but was able to limp away to the north. The captain of the other, the Columbine, unceremoniously loosed his moorings and hastened to the south. The next day, Dickinson and his troops ambushed the Federal ship, which was immediately disabled and eventually struck a sand bar. After the battle, it was learned that only 65 of the ship's complement of 148 crew members had survived the attack; many of these were seriously wounded. So complete was the Confederate victory that the Union infantry that had been on its way to help capture Dickinson withdrew.

The patriotic ladies of nearby Orange Springs were so grateful for Dickinson's defense of their homeland that they presented him with a pair of silver spurs. Until his death in 1902, the valiant Confederate captain was known as the "Knight of the Silver Spurs."

Oklawaha River

The remnants of Oklawaha River make into the St. Johns' western shore near flashing daybeacon #52. While this river was once an active avenue of commerce and tourism, the present-day dam at the foot of Lake Oklawaha has cut off most of the stream's drainage into the St. Johns. At this time, lily pads and shallows block the Oklawaha's easterly mouth, and even small craft will find it difficult to enter. Cruisers are strictly advised to stay away.

Oklawaha River History   From the late nineteenth to the early twentieth century, commodious river boats made their way up the twisting Oklawaha River to Silver Springs and the various lakes along the river. During northern Florida's tourist boom, the trip from Jacksonville or Palatka to Silver Springs was one of the most popular outings of the day.

During the 1880s, Capt. Hubbard L. Hart worked tirelessly to clear the Oklawaha's twisting channel and promote the river trip, traveling as far north as Georgia to do so. It was the southern poet Sidney Lanier, however, who established the Oklawaha securely in Floridian tradition when he featured the river

prominently in a guide book to Florida that the Atlantic Coast Railway Company commissioned him to write.

Beecher Point Anchorage (29 27.855 North/081 40.934 West)

In northerly blows the bubble of deep water south of the condo development at Beecher Point (east-northeast of flashing daybeacon #53) can serve as a good anchorage for almost any size craft. When winds are from the south or east, however, this would be a decidedly uncomfortable spot. Minimum depths of 6 feet are held short of the correctly charted shallows to the east.

Buzzards Point Anchorage (29 26.067 North/081 40.343 West)

One of our favorite anchorages along this section of the St. Johns is found on the deep waters south of Buzzards Point, east of flashing daybeacon #59. Good depths of 6 to 20 feet run to within 50 yards of the magnificently undeveloped northerly banks. There's tons of swinging room. With winds from the north or northeast, you could not pick a lovelier spot to spend the evening. Strong breezes from the west or particularly the south might well prompt you alternately to select one of the Turkey Island anchorages to the north.

The best and most sheltered spot is found north of the charted patch of 6-foot waters. We discovered some 5-foot soundings in this area during our on-site research. Nevertheless, this somewhat shallower water is easily avoided. The small cove to the north is idyllic.

Fruitland Cove Anchorage (29 25.728 North/081 39.304 West)

East of flashing daybeacon #63, depths of 7 feet or better parallel the northern banks of

Fruitland Cove for some 200 yards to the east of the main channel. If winds are blowing from the north and east, boats of almost any size can drop the hook here with good protection. Southerly or westerly breezes over 15 knots, on the other hand, may make you feel a bit like a Mexican jumping bean. The adjacent shoreline has moderate but attractive residential development.

Black Point Anchorage (29 23.405 North/081 39.750 West)

Chart 11495 shows a broad band of deep water extending for about .3 nautical miles to the west, south of Black Point and flashing daybeacon #68. Depths are currently not as deep as depicted on 11495. Cruisers entering this haven can expect some 5+-foot soundings.

You must take care not to encroach on the shallows to the south or to cruise too far to the west into the shoal waters of Muddy Cove. Otherwise, with winds wafting from the north, this is a good spot for boats up to 50 feet (drawing *less than* 5 feet) to anchor. Breezes of 15 knots or better from any other quarter would render this an inappropriate overnight stop.

Georgetown

The small river village of Georgetown is perched on the river's northeastern shore just short of the Lake George entrance. A small ferry crosses from Georgetown's waterfront to Drayton Island. As at Welaka, many fishing camps and small-craft dockage basins line the shoreline. Again, there are no provisions for larger boats. If you are cruising through these waters at dinnertime, you might consider dropping the hook and dinghying ashore to try your luck at one of the several restaurants associated with the various fishing camps.

Lake George

Lake George is a huge body of water that spans some 10.5 nautical miles from the north to the south and averages 5.5 nautical miles in width. Like Crescent Lake, it is known for its angling, and also like its smaller sister, Lake George is an almost-perfect oval, lacking any deep, protected coves along its shoreline. There are virtually no marina facilities anywhere directly on the lake's shoreline. On the other hand, there is one fascinating gunkhole opportunity for shallow-draft vessels only!

Silver Glen Spring Run

Study chart 11495 for a moment and note the small stream known as Silver Glen Spring Run lying along the great lake's westerly shores, west of unlighted daybeacon #9. The entrance makes into Lake George near 29 14.909 North/081 37.974 West.

Silver Glen is fed by a series of cold-water, underground springs, resulting in waters so clear that you can see straight down to the lush vegetation lining the stream's bottom. Those who go slowly will observe all sorts of aquatic life sporting along in these delightful waters. The shores have barely been touched by human development, and, except for a few structures, the banks shelve back up into some of the most verdant lands that this writer has ever witnessed.

Silver Glen Spring Run is, as you might expect, a favorite spot for houseboaters, snorkelers, and small powerboat gunkholers. If your craft can fit the rather stringent requirements outlined below, then by all means give this sidewater your most earnest attention. There are few more visual spots on the entire St. Johns River passage.

Now for the bad news. Approach and interior depths on Silver Glen Spring regularly run as thin as 3 feet. The haphazard channel markings are more than slightly confusing in places, and it's all too easy to find yourself in only 2 feet of water. Clearly, given these limitations, this delightful sidewater must be sadly consigned strictly to small craft drawing less than 3 feet. Larger, deeper-draft vessels might consider anchoring well east of the stream's entrance, and then dinghying in to the creek. Be advised, however, that it will be a long ride into the stream's mouth. As chart 11495 correctly depicts, shallow waters run east for a goodly distance from Spring Run's mouth.

Silver Glen Spring Run, Lake George

PALATKA TO LAKE GEORGE NAVIGATION

In marked contrast to the St. Johns' northerly reaches, the waters between Palatka and Lake George are peppered with shoals. The good news is that all but a few of these shallow patches are marked with daybeacons, and all (but one) are clearly charted on 11492, 11487 and 11495.

This is not the place to go charging ahead at full speed, following the markers by eye. Be sure to plan your trip carefully before venturing out on the water and keep a wary eye on the sounder at all times.

Leaving Palatka South of the 65-foot, Palatka fixed bridge, set course to come abeam of flashing daybeacon #1 to its westerly side. From #1, the channel takes a sharp turn first to the southeast and then almost due east. Come abeam of flashing daybeacon #2 to its northeasterly side. Adjust your course to the east and pass south of unlighted daybeacon #3 and north of flashing daybeacon #4. Be sure to stay northeast of #2. Farther to the southwest, the shallow, debris-filled waters of Wilson Cove wait to trap the unwary.

At flashing daybeacon #4, the channel turns again, this time to the northeast as it starts around a sharp, hairpin turn known as the Devil's Elbow. Flashing daybeacon #6 marks the southerly point of the elbow while flashing daybeacon #7 sits along the northern banks. This latter aid can be hard to spot. Be sure to pass #6 to its western and northern side. Shoal water lies south of this aid and flanks the western side of the point to the south.

As you come abeam of #6, the Burger King Dock will be spotted along the northerly banks. A large sign makes identification easy. A steep rank of steps leads up from the water to the fast-food restaurant's parking lot.

Upstream of #6, the river turns sharply to the south-southeast. Be sure to pass flashing daybeacon #8, unlighted daybeacon #8A, and flashing daybeacon # 10 to their easterly sides. Extensive shallows strike out from the westerly shoreline between #8 and #10. From the water, this shoal isn't obvious, and unwatchful navigators could be in for an unhappy meeting of keel and bottom.

After passing #10, swing a bit to the south-southwest and point to come abeam of flashing daybeacon #11 to its westerly quarter. Good water once again stretches out almost from shore to shore for some distance south of #11. Between #11 and the next upstream aid to navigation, flashing daybeacon 12, cruisers might choose to anchor along the western shoreline on the waters of Porters Cove.

Porters Cove Anchorage   Remember that an overnight stop on Porters Cove is not recommended in any save fair weather. Continue cruising south from flashing daybeacon #11 on the main river channel until you are some 300 to 400 yards south of the sharp, unnamed point of land along the eastern banks near charted Bray Creek. Turn west off the main cut and feel your way in with the sounder.

Gibson Dry Docks   The entrance channel to Gibson Dry Docks lies east of flashing daybeacon #12. The cut is marked by pairs of privately maintained stakes. Cruise between the various markers and enter the small creek paralleling the repair yard on its midwidth. Exercise extreme caution if you continue cruising up this stream. We unexpectedly come across an underwater stump off the southern banks on the creek's upper limits.

On the St. Johns   Favor the southeastern banks between flashing daybeacons #12 and #13. Shoal water shelves out around Buzzard Island to the northwest.

Southwest of #13, the St. Johns follows a long, lazy turn to the west. Pass flashing daybeacon #15 well to its northerly side.

Shallower water abuts the northerly shores of Rat Island, west of #15.

Don't attempt to enter Dunn Creek by way of the small stream cutting southwest from #15. This stream is shoal. Instead, continue following the river's midline to the west. The entrance to Dunn Creek will come up on the southern banks, short of flashing daybeacon #16.

Dunn Creek   Enter Dunn Creek at idle speed on its center section. Watch the sounder carefully. Shallow water flanks both the east and west points of the entrance. Once on the creek's interior, favor the western shore slightly. We have never found the charted piles on the stream's eastern shore during on-site research.

Continue favoring the western banks as your cruise past the mouth of Murphy Creek and approach the Dunn Creek fixed bridge. Cruise back to the midwidth as you approach this span.

Remember, only devil-may-care cruisers who pilot boats less than 35 feet and, most importantly, drawing less than 4 feet should attempt to follow Dunn Creek to Crescent Lake. The creek is peppered with unmarked shoals between the bridge and the lake. If you do make the attempt, feel your way along at idle speed and keep one eye glued to the sounder.

Southeast of the 45-foot fixed bridge, there is a long stretch of shoal-free water. The first tricky spot comes as the creek cuts sharply to the south after passing a series of canals to the northeast. You will encounter some 5-foot depths just before swinging back to the east. You can avoid the next charted 5-foot shoal by heavily favoring the northern banks just before the creek passes through a hairpin turn.

As you are cruising through the next sharp turn, favor the western banks heavily to avoid the charted shoal. At Sutherlands Still, you must heavily favor the southwestern banks in order to bypass the charted 2-foot shoal. Similarly, favor the western shore markedly to avoid a second charted 2-foot shoal just south of Sutherlands Still. This shallow patch will appear as a small grassy island on the creek's eastern side.

There are two other patches of 5-foot water between Sutherlands Still and Monroe Lodge, but if you draw less than 4 feet, you should be able to get through.

South of Monroe Lodge, there is a long stretch of shoal-free water. Then as you round the sharp bend at Piney Bluff Lodge, favor the northerly banks to avoid the charted shoal. As the creek begins to bend back to the south, begin heavily favoring the westerly shore to avoid the charted lily pad-island shoal.

Soon the creek turns yet again, this time back to the southeast. Favor the northeasterly shore in order to bypass the charted hazard. Finally, favor the southwestern banks to avoid the last charted 4-foot shoal.

Crescent Lake   As you enter the northern tip of Crescent Lake from Dunn Creek, set a southeasterly course to avoid the 3- and 4-foot depths in Willow Cove. Otherwise, as long as you don't approach any of the banks or Bear Island too closely, you should not encounter any difficulty north of Hopkins Point. Don't attempt to explore the lake's southerly reaches leading to Dead Lake. Depths in this region are much too uncertain for any boat drawing more than 3 feet.

If you choose to use the lake's one anchorage south of Weidernoch Point, feel your way in carefully toward the southwestern shore, southeast of the point. Do not cruise too near the point itself; it is surrounded by shoal water.

Murphy Creek   Murphy Creek should be entered from its eastern entrance emptying into Dunn Creek by all but small craft. The channel leading from the stream's westerly extremes back into the St. Johns, south of flashing daybeacon #26, is too narrow and tricky for larger boats.

Enter the creek on its centerline. Excellent depths continue on Murphy Creek just short of the western entrance, provided you stick scrupulously to the middle. As chart 11495 shows there are a few small shoals adjoining several of the creek's sharp bends, but judicious planning should see you by these hazards.

In particular, guard against the charted shallows on the hairpin turn south and west of the charted 7-foot sounding on chart 11495. To avoid this hazard, favor the eastern banks as you cruise into the turn and then favor the northerly shoreline after rounding the bend.

Browns Landing Anchorage   West of Dunn Creek's juncture with St. Johns River, you will soon come abeam of flashing daybeacon #16 to its southerly side. Between # 16 and the next upstream aid to navigation, unlighted daybeacon #18, 8-foot depths run to within 100 yards of the northern banks. On the other hand, shoals lie west and northwest of #18. To access the anchorage, leave the main channel about halfway between #16 and #18. Feel your way toward the northern shoreline with your sounder. Be sure to anchor before approaching to within less than 100 yards of the banks. Closer in, soundings rise dramatically.

On the St. Johns   West-northwest of unlighted daybeacon #18, one of the trickiest spots on the entire run from Palatka to Lake George presents itself. Study chart 11495 and notice the finger of 2½-foot waters southeast of flashing daybeacon #20. These shallows are for real! Thankfully, a new marker, flashing daybeacon #19, now warns of this obstruction. Set course from a position south of #18 to pass north of #19 and bring #20 abeam to its immediate southerly side.

From #20, point to pass south of flashing daybeacon #22. Shallower water lies east and northeast of this marker. After leaving #22, the channel cuts a bit to the northwest as it flows around Horseshoe Point. Come abeam of flashing daybeacon #23 to it northerly quarter.

To continue cruising upstream, turn southwest from #23, set course to pass unlighted daybeacon #25 to its northwesterly side, and come abeam of flashing daybeacon #26 by at least 25 yards to it southerly side. Be sure to stay northwest of #25. Shoal water of 2 feet or less lies in wait south and southwest of #25.

After coming abeam of #26, the shoals are left temporarily behind. The river now takes a sharp bend to the northwest and soon approaches the 7-foot (closed vertical clearance) railroad bridge at Buffalo Bluff in the elbow of a hairpin turn. This bridge comes up suddenly from behind the bend, and it can be a real surprise if you haven't been following your position on the chart. As you make your approach to the railway span, pass north of unlighted daybeacon #27. Shallows abut this aid to the south and west.

The 7-foot railway span is usually open, but it can be closed for as long as forty minutes both before and after a train is due. All we can suggest is that you admire the scenery while you wait.

Once through the railroad bridge, the hairpin turn continues with a sharp bend to the south. Point to pass flashing daybeacon #28 on its easterly side. Southeast of #28, the good anchorages off the Seven Sister islands are accessible.

Seven Sisters Anchorages   To enter the northerly Seven Sisters anchorage, split off from the main river route at flashing daybeacon #28 and follow the charted deep channel along the eastern shore. You can cruise as far south as the eastern tip of the second of the Seven Sisters islands and hold good depths. Farther upstream, toward Barrentine Creek, there are several uncharted shoals. These waters should not be entered without specific local knowledge.

It's a simple matter to drop anchor behind the lee of the first unnamed island that flanks this cut to the west, or you can easily continue to follow this stream to a point just short of the charted 2-foot shoal north of Barrentine Creek and set the hook here.

Bold cruisers can take a shortcut to rejoin the St. Johns from the northern Seven Sisters anchorage. As chart 11495 shows, a narrow but deep channel runs parallel to the southern banks of the northernmost Seven Sisters island. If you do make use of this passage, favor the northern island's shore heavily. A broad shelf of shoal water is found south of this cut, abutting the northerly banks of the second Seven Sister's island.

Enter the southern anchorages by holding to the midwidth of the passage between the northeastern point of Trout Island and the fifth (counting from north to south) Seven Sisters island. The initial portion of this channel is a good spot for larger craft to anchor. Cruisers who continue upstream should follow the creek as it turns sharply to the north. All captains must favor the eastern side of the stream as they come through the turn. Discontinue your cruise before coming abeam of the sharp point jutting west from the oblong Seven Sisters island that borders Barrentine Creek. For maximum swinging room, anchor south of this point of land.

Stokes Island Loop   Favor the starboard banks when entering the northern tier of the Stokes Island loop. Once abeam of the island's northern point, cruise back to the center section. Watch to the northwest for the commercial boatyard described previously. Continue on the centerline all the way through the southern exit into the St. Johns.

Cross-Florida Barge Canal   As the trip up the Cross-Florida Barge Canal to Lake Oklawaha is explicitly not recommended for pleasure craft over 20 feet, no navigational information about it will be presented here. Cruisers who choose to ignore this warning and enter the canal anyway are taking quite a chance.

On the St. Johns   Be sure to pass unlighted daybeacon #35, northeast of Horse Landing, well to its westerly side. This aid marks a small shoal that is a favorite fishing spot for local anglers.

Flashing daybeacon #37 denotes the beginning of an easterly bend in the St. Johns. Pass west of #37 and favor the southwestern banks slightly through the body of the turn. Shallows strike out from the eastern and northeastern banks. Point to eventually come abeam of flashing daybeacons #38 and #40 to their northerly sides. At #40, abeam of Possum Bluff, the river once again bends to the south.

South of flashing daybeacon #40, watch the eastern banks and you will spy several interesting homes in the small community of Saratoga.

After coming abeam of flashing daybeacon #40A (to its eastern side) near Grand View Grove, shoals again become a bit of a problem moving to the south. Set a careful course to come abeam of flashing daybeacon #41 to its westerly quarter. At this point, an improved channel cuts to the south-southeast. Follow this cut to a point abeam of unlighted daybeacon #42A on its easterly side. As you cruise between #41 and #42A, the docks of Acosta Creek Harbor will come up to the east.

From #42A, continue more or less on the same course until coming abeam of flashing daybeacon #42, also to its easterly side. From #42, cruisers have access to the northerly anchorage around Turkey Island.

Turkey Island Anchorage   To enter the deep passage running south along the easterly banks to Turkey Island, leave the main St.

Johns channel between unlighted daybeacon #42A and flashing daybeacon #42. Cruise quickly toward the eastern banks, and when you are about 30 to 50 yards from land, begin following the shoreline to the south. Be sure to avoid the shoal water striking east from the three small charted islets to the west.

Most cruising skippers will wisely choose to discontinue their exploration of this cut well north of the correctly charted 3-foot shoal off the eastern shores of Turkey Island. It is a far better plan to enter the southern Turkey island anchorage, north of Stephens Point, by way of the broad channel cutting east from the St. Johns, north of flashing daybeacon #45.

Should you attempt to cruise past the 3 foot shoal, be sure to stay within 25 yards of the easterly shore as Turkey Island comes abeam to the west. This maneuver may allow you to avoid the shallows off the Turkey Island shoreline.

To access the southerly anchorage, leave the main St. Johns channel some 100 yards north of flashing daybeacon #45. Cruise to the east and enter the midline of the broad passage between Stephens Point to the south and the two small, unnamed islands (south of Turkey Island) to the north. Don't approach the small islets. The shoal water around these petite landmasses seems to growing.

After coming abeam of the last islet's easterly tip, follow the channel through a long, slow bend to the north. For best depths set your anchor before coming abeam of Turkey Island's southeasterly tip. The 3-foot shoal discussed above lies just north of this point.

Two channels offer access back to the St. Johns from this south-side anchorage.

The first simply calls for retracing your steps back to the waters north of flashing daybeacon #45. The second, far-narrower, cut runs along the southerly shores of Turkey Island. This passage is recommended solely for the intrepid explorers among us. Should you make the attempt, cruise to the west, keeping some 25 to 35 yards off the southern banks of Turkey Island. Guard against any slippage to the south into the shallows around the two charted islets. Eventually, if you're lucky, the main river channel will be rejoined east of unlighted daybeacon #44.

On the St. Johns   The St. Johns channel between flashing daybeacons #42 and #45 is rather tricky, Come abeam of flashing daybeacon #42 to its fairly immediate easterly side. Turn to the southwest and carefully set course upriver to come abeam of flashing daybeacon #43 to its fairly immediate northwestern side.

As chart 11495 shows, the passage between #42 and #43 is pinched by two shoals to the east and west. Proceed at idle speed between the two beacons, with a weather eye on the sounder. If depths start to rise, assess the situation at once and make appropriate corrections before grounding depths are reached.

Once abeam of #43, adjust your course a bit to the south and point to come abeam of unlighted daybeacon #44 by some 25 yards (no closer) to its easterly quarter. Shallows wait to trap poor navigators north and west of #44. Turkey Island will be passed east of your course on the run from #43 to #44. From #44, point to come abeam of flashing daybeacon #45 to its westerly side. The wide entrance to the southern Turkey Island anchorage, reviewed above, will come abeam some 100 yards north of #45.

From flashing daybeacon #45 to flashing daybeacon #48, all the trouble spots are reasonably well marked. Between #48 and the next upstream aid to navigation, flashing daybeacon #50, caution is again called for. Notice the charted 4-foot shoal north of #50. To avoid this hazard, favor the easterly side of the channel as you make your approach to #50 and come abeam of this marker on its easterly quarter. Between flashing daybeacons #48 and #50, you will pass the Welaka waterfront to the east.

Beecher Point Anchorage   Enter the deep water south of Beecher Point by striking a course to the east-northeast from flashing daybeacon #53. Be sure to discontinue your progress before reaching the shallows in Mud Creek Cove.

On the St. Johns   South of Beecher Point, the main channel follows an improved cut across Little Lake George. Keep to the marked channel as depths outside of this passage are very uncertain. The dredged cut ends at unlighted daybeacon #57 and flashing daybeacon #58, but you're not yet through with surrounding shoals. From #57 and #58, the channel follows a lazy turn to the east. Be sure to come abeam of flashing daybeacon #59 to its southerly side. A 2-foot shoal is found just north and northeast of the run between #58 and #59. At #59, cruising captains have the option of anchoring off the southern shores of Buzzards Point.

Buzzards Point Anchorage   Abandon your upriver run on the St. Johns a little less than halfway between flashing daybeacon #59 and unlighted daybeacon #60. Cruise toward the northern banks, keeping at least 50 yards offshore.

To reach the most secluded spot, follow the shoreline to the east, keeping some 50 yards offshore. Eventually, this strategy will lead you past the charted 6-foot (5 feet in actuality) depths, south of your course. Drop the hook in the small cove that will come up along the northerly banks, still keeping at least 50 yards offshore. Settle back for an evening of peace and security.

On the St. Johns   Another improved channel spans the gap between unlighted daybeacon #60 and flashing daybeacon #61. Shoal water abuts the northern and southern sides of the channel. Come abeam of #60 to its immediate northerly side and set course to come abeam of and pass #61 to its immediate southerly side.

East of #61 the St. Johns is spanned by an overhead power cable with 65 feet of vertical clearance. A small, private ferry supposedly crosses the river at this point, but we have yet to see it.

During our last trip on St. Johns River, we were more than surprised to discover some 5-foot soundings immediately adjacent to unlighted daybeacon #62. Pass at least 25 yards north of #62 to avoid this building shoal.

Fruitland Cove Anchorage   Enter Fruitland Cove by setting a course to the east from flashing daybeacon #63 into the deepwater section of the cove. Stay about 50 to 100 yards off the northerly banks. Be sure to stop before cruising more than 300 yards from the main channel. Farther passage to the east will land you in the extensive shallows along the cove's eastern shores.

On the St. Johns Between flashing daybeacons #63 and #65, the principal channel is again squeezed between two shallows. Come abeam and pass unlighted daybeacon #64 to its immediate northeasterly side, and continue on the same course to come abeam of flashing daybeacon #65 to its westerly quarter in order to avoid these hazards.

Black Point Anchorage To enter the deep-water section of Muddy Cove, continue on the river channel for some 300 yards (at least) southeast of flashing daybeacon #68. Then curl back around to the west and parallel the Black Point banks to the north for as much as .2 nautical miles to the west. Keep at least 100 yards south of the northerly shoreline. In spite of charted soundings, expect some 5- to 6-foot depths as you enter this anchorage.

Be sure to stay away from Black Point itself. It is surrounded by very shoal water. Drop the hook before reaching the charted shallows to the west.

All the waters surrounding Black Point are an official, manatee slow-speed zone. Powercraft captains take note. Enter and leave this haven at idle speed.

Onto Lake George At flashing daybeacon #68, the channel turns hard to the east-southeast and begins its approach to Lake George. East-southeast of #70, a second private ferry crosses the river from Georgetown to Drayton Island.

After passing flashing daybeacon #72, the channel follows a slow turn to the south-southeast into the main body of Lake George. Point to pass fairly close by the western side of the forward, charted range marker, west of Lake George Point. From this position, the channel heads out into the main body of Lake George.

Lake George The passage across Lake George is arrow straight and marked by pairs of daybeacons. The various aids are spaced more than 2 nautical miles apart, and prudent mariners will want to run compass or GPS courses across the lake.

Except for the possible shallow-draft-vessel side trip outlined below, it would be a good idea to stay in the channel—depths outside of the cut are suspect and the lake's easterly waters are used as a U.S. Navy bombing range. There have also been reports of underwater rocks outside of the marked passage.

In strong winds, particularly from the north or south, Lake George can produce a vicious chop. Small craft should be alert to weather conditions before setting out on this passage.

As you approach the southern entrance to the upper St. Johns, the marked cut follows a dredged channel through the shallow Volusia Bar. Between flashing daybeacons #15 and #19, keep faithfully to the channel. Study chart 11495 ahead of time to familiarize yourself with this sometimes tricky passage.

As you make the run between #15 and #18, you will pass twin wooden hyacinth fences flanking both sides of the channel. Formerly, hyacinths were very much a problem in this area. However, a new, very effective control program has almost eliminated this problem.

This writer remembers the hyacinth fences for a very different reason. It was here that my father and I spent many an early-winter's day fishing for largemouth bass. Those were golden, far broader days, still fondly remembered.

Silver Glen Spring Run Please remember that cruising visitors to beautiful Silver Glen Spring Run should be piloting craft that draw 3 less than feet. If your vessel meets these requirements, depart the main Lake George channel once abeam of unlighted daybeacon #9. Set a careful compass or GPS course from #9 for the charted easterly mouth of Silver Glen Spring Run. It is a cruise of 2.3 nautical miles between #9 and the creek's entrance.

As you approach Silver Glen Spring Run, slow down. You will soon be cruising through 3- to 5-foot waters. Use your binoculars to pick out the charted can and nun buoy marking the run's easterly genesis. Cruise between these aids to navigation, keeping red nun #4 to your starboard side and green can #1 to port.

Shortly after entering the stream, you will come upon two (one red and one green) uncharted, spar-type markers. Again, anyone who remembers "red, right, returning" will know to pass the red marker to his or her (the cruiser's) starboard side and take the green marker to port.

Upstream of the spar markers, Silver Glen Spring Run is marked by a series of small, ultra-confusing buoys. At one point, the channel splits, and it's hard to tell just where you should be going. Adding to this confusion are the large numbers of houseboats and smaller power vessels that can usually be found exploring this clear-water stream, even on a summer's weekday. Take your time, and have a good look around. Just don't be too surprised to find yourself in 2 feet of water.

Lake George to Sanford

South of Lake George, the St. Johns continues to narrow and its shores become even swampier. These waters are very popular with the small-craft boating crowd, particularly on weekends. You will most likely be joined by a small armada of outboard and I/O vessels on Saturdays and Sundays.

Apart from a few trouble spots, successful navigation of the St. Johns south to Sanford is not an exacting process. The river is mostly deep from shore to shore and the trouble spots are well marked.

The shoreline along this upper portion of the St. Johns is a true delight. Deep cypress swamps are broken only occasionally by light residential development. Tall trees, often with garlands of grey moss, watch over the slow current of the St. Johns as they have for uncounted years. Sidewaters usually lead to virgin territory. If you are one of those people who enjoy leaving the trappings of civilization behind, this is the section of the St. Johns for you.

While several deep streams pierce the

upper St. Johns shoreline at regular intervals, anchorages for craft over 32 feet are surprisingly sparse north of Lake Monroe. Most of the regional streams are too narrow to afford sufficient swinging room for larger vessels.

Facilities north of Lake Monroe are adequate, though widely spaced. Numerous fishing camps and two low-key marinas are found at the river village of Astor. Another facility comes up just north of the De Land Bridge. South of the bridge, Pier 44 Marina offers the only diesel fuel short of Sanford and Lake Monroe. Two marinas will be discovered hard

by Hontoon Island State Park, but only one has any appreciable transient dockage. Lake Monroe and Sanford boast two large marinas that offer a friendly welcome and full services for cruising craft. Except for these facilities, the visiting cruiser is on his own while exploring the upper St. Johns.

The uppermost reaches of the St. Johns River are absolutely delightful. The generally undeveloped character, the numerous gunkholes, and the broad waters of Lake Monroe combine to offer cruising as good as any in eastern Florida.

Lake George to Sanford Anchorage Summary (Anchorages are listed in geographic order, moving downstream to upstream.)
Morrison Creek Anchorage—located near 29 10.832 North/081 32.393 West, east and a bit south of unlighted daybeacon #26—6-foot depths—reviewed on pages 149, 161-162
River Forest Anchorage—located near 29 01.173 North/081 23.757 West, southwest of unlighted daybeacon #36—6-foot depths—reviewed on pages 152, 163
Hontoon Dead River Anchorage—located near 28 57.295 North/081 21.789 West, on the northerly reach of the lagoon-like body of water where charted Snake Creek makes in from the east—5-foot depths—reviewed on pages 154, 164
Lake Beresford Anchorage—located near 28 59.356 North/081 20.821 West, on the center section of Lake Beresford, southeast of Lake Beresford Yacht Club—5-foot depths—reviewed on pages 155, 164
Starks Landing Cutoff Loop Anchorage—

located near 28 56.756 North/081 20.879 West, west-southwest of flashing daybeacon #69—6-foot depths—reviewed on pages 155-160, 165
Dutchmans Bend Anchorage—located near 28 55.227 North/081 21.114 West, south of flashing daybeacon #81—6-foot depths—reviewed on pages 156-157, 165
Emmanuel Bend Anchorage—located near 28 52.734 North/081 21.765 West, south of flashing daybeacon #93—6-foot depths—reviewed on pages 157, 165
Butchers Bend Anchorage—located along the St. Johns' northeasterly shores, north-northwest of unlighted daybeacon #110—various lats/lons (see detailed account)—5-foot depths—reviewed on pages 157, 165-166
Last Anchorage—located near 28 50.332 North/081 19.325 West, on the square-shaped cove making into the St. Johns' northeasterly banks, between the second and third bridges that cross the St. Johns River just before this stream enters Lake Monroe—5-foot depths—reviewed in pages 158-159, 166

Lake George to Sanford Marina and Yacht-Club Summary (Marinas and yacht clubs are listed in geographic order, moving downstream to upstream.)

Astor Bridge Marina—(386) 749-4407—located near 29 10.030 North/081 31.334 West, along the eastern banks of the St. Johns, just south of the Astor Bridge—transient dockage available—gasoline available—3½-foot minimum depths—reviewed on pages 150, 162

Boat Show Marina—(386) 736-6601—located near 29 00.586 North/081 22.992 West, a short hop north of the De Land/Whitehair Bridge, along the St. Johns' northeasterly banks—transient dockage available—gasoline available—minimum 6½-foot depths—reviewed on pages 152, 163

Pier 44 Marina—(352) 589-8370—located near 29 00.476 North/081 22.920 West, south of the De Land/Whitehair Bridge, along the St. Johns' westerly banks—transient dockage on a space-available basis—gasoline and diesel fuel available—minimum 5-foot depths—reviewed on pages 152-53, 163

Holly Bluff Marina—(386) 822-9992—located near 28 59.291 North/081 21.204 West, along the St. Johns' easterly banks between flashing daybeacons #47 and #49—transient dockage available—gasoline available—minimum 4-foot depths—reviewed on pages 153, 164

Hontoon Island State Park Docks—located near 28 58.492 North/081 21.502 West, east-southeast of flashing daybeacon #53 and the northeasterly mouth of Hontoon Dead River—one-day dockage available—minimum 3-foot depths—reviewed on pages 153-54, 164

Hontoon Landing Marina—(386) 734-2474—located near 28 58.569 North/081 21.496 West, just opposite the Hontoon Island State Park Docks (see above)—gasoline available—minimum 5-foot depths—reviewed on pages 154, 164

Lake Beresford Yacht Club—(386) 734-3854—located near 28 59.559 North/081 21.120 West along the Westerly bank of Lake Beresford—transient dockage available for members of other yacht clubs with appropriate reciprocal privileges—4-foot minimum depths—reviewed on pages 154-55, 164

Hidden Harbour Marina—(407) 322-1610—located near 28 50.128 North/081 19.696 West, in the charted "Port of Sanford" region, just northwest of the three bridges crossing the St. Johns River, just before this stream enters Lake Monroe—transient dockage available—gasoline available—5½-foot depths—reviewed on pages 157-58, 166

Monroe Harbour Marina—(407) 322-2910—located near 28 48.879 North/081 15.885 West, on the southern banks of Lake Monroe, in the heart of the charted Sanford waterfront—transient dockage on a space-available basis—gasoline available—large quantities of diesel fuel available—6-foot minimum depths—reviewed on pages 159-60, 167-68

Morrison Creek Anchorage (20 10.832 North/081 32.393 West)

The northern entrance to loop-shaped Morrison Creek divides the St. Johns' eastern banks near unlighted daybeacon #26. The stream holds minimum depths of 6 feet on its northerly section. Boats up to 38 feet can drop the hook near the creek's northwestern mouth and have plenty of swinging room with excellent protection.

The creek's southerly branch loops west back to the St. Johns at flashing daybeacon #28. Some 4-foot readings on this portion of the stream make navigation too risky for cruising-size vessels. All but the smallest craft should enter and exit by the northerly branch.

This anchorage offers a bonus for cruising craft equipped with a dinghy. Paramour's Fish Camp overlooks the creek's northeastern shores at the charted position of Morrison Bluff. We found that they were amenable to dinghy mooring for a short period of time. A small grocery store with an extensive meat counter is accessible within a two-block walk of the fishing camp.

Ask anyone on the dock for directions.

Astor (Various Lats/Lons—see below)

The charming river village of Astor straddles the St. Johns some 3 nautical miles south of Lake George. Marine facilities declined along the village waterfront during the 1990s. Transient dockage is limited, except for some temporary berths for patrons of one of the local restaurants.

Several "no wake" zones protect the Astor waterfront. The various signs should be carefully observed. The Florida Marine Patrol is famous for strict enforcement in this area.

Fishing camps line both shores in the Astor area. While most are oriented strictly to small craft, careful cruisers might be able to feel their way cautiously to one of the many docks for gasoline, ice, or possibly even a hot meal.

Just south of the Astor bascule bridge, Blackwater Inn (352-759-2802) will be quickly spied along the western shore. This delightful dining spot offers starved voyagers the freshest seafood. Locals and visitors alike have been enjoying this fine eatery's fare for many years. The restaurant is open for lunch Saturday and Sunday only, but dinner is served every evening except Monday.

Blackwater Inn features its own small, fixed wooden slips to which patrons are welcome to moor while dining. The berths are large enough for vessels up to 35 feet. Be sure to dock bow in for soundings of 4½ to 5 feet under your stern; closer to shore depths are almost nil. There is also one larger dock that sticks out into the river. A single 38 footer can probably tie up on the very outer end of this dock in 6 to 7 feet of water. However, don't try to berth on either the north or south side of this long pier, running back toward shore. Depths run to 3 feet.

Directly across the river from Blackwater Inn, the Astor Bridge Marina and Motel (formerly Hall's Lodge) will be spotted near 29 10.030 North/081 31.334 West. This facility has recently changed hands, and the shoreside buildings have all received a much-needed face-lift. Under the new regime, some transient dockage, gasoline, and waste pump-out are available. All slips (consisting of tiny, fixed, wooden, finger piers) are found in a basin behind the motel. While depths in this little lagoon are a respectable 8+ feet, the small canal leading in from the river only carries 3½ to 4 feet of water. Some berths feature 30-amp power hookups, while all have fresh-water connections.

The on-site, restaurant is no longer open for breakfast and currently only operates on the weekends. Of course, you can always take a quick stroll across the bridge to Blackwater Inn.

Astor Bridge Marina and Motel
(386) 749-4407
   http://www.astorbridgemarina.com

Approach depths—3½ to 4 feet
Dockside depths—8+ feet
Accepts transients—yes
Transient dockage rate—average
Fixed, wooden, finger piers—yes
Dockside power connections—some
   slips have 30 amps
Dockside water connections—yes
Gasoline—yes
Waste pump-out—yes
Restaurant—one on-site
   with limited hours and another nearby

Just south of Blackwater Inn, the docks of Midway Marine (352-759-3838) will come abeam on the western shore. This facility has no wet-slip dockage but it does offer gasoline, mechanical repairs for gasoline engines, a good ship's store, and haul-outs with a 30-ton travelift. Depths at the fuel pier run 6 feet or better.

Astor History   Astor still preserves the memory of the busy river traffic that once thrived south of Lake George. Many traders crossed the river to and from the old trading post at Volusia, just across the St. Johns from Astor. On the Astor side of the river a large store was built by the Patton and Leslie Trading Company during the late 1700s. Originally managed by Charles McLatchey, one of the most knowledgeable traders in all of Florida, the store grew into an important outlet for commerce along the Florida frontier.

Shortly before Florida became a part of the young United States, an interesting individual, Moses Levy, established a plantation near Volusia. Born in Morocco, the son of a grand vizier, Levy was descended from an important Portuguese Jewish family. Convinced that Florida would soon become a part of the United States and impressed by the religious freedom guaranteed by the U.S. Constitution, he decided to establish a Jewish refuge in Florida.

Levy purchased more than 50,000 acres along the banks of the St. Johns and then traveled to Europe, where he recruited French and German Jewish settlers. He also convinced several groups to immigrate from New Jersey and New York. As the years went by, Levy's Hope Hill Plantation along the St. Johns prospered with the willing work of many grateful hands. He also established the settlement of Pilgrimage near present-day Gainesville and settled many of the refugees there.

During the Civil War, the Astor-Volusia region was the setting for one of the final acts in the Confederate tragedy. Gen. John Cabell Breckenridge, Southern secretary of war, arrived at Astor on May 26, 1865, fleeing from almost certain capture by Union forces. Three of Captain Dickinson's guerrillas awaited Breckenridge in a small boat lying close by the Astor waterfront. Under darkness the fugitives slipped down the St. Johns. Living off the land, they arrived at Lake Harney several days later. Breckenridge continued by oxcart to the Atlantic, and eventually he was able to make his way to safety to England by way of Cuba.

Following the war, Astor slipped back into relative obscurity as a quiet fishing village, and it has continued pretty much in the same vein to the present day. Such a status is not to be sneezed at, however. Anglers in the know will tell you that Astor is the true bass capital of the world. I would not presume to settle the conflicting claims of Astor's anglers with their counterparts on Crescent Lake.

Lake Dexter

South of flashing daybeacon #8, the St. Johns River channel tracks its way through an improved cut across the westerly reaches of Lake Dexter. While local fishing skiffs travel the waters of this large lake day in and day out in search of largemouth bass, numerous unmarked shoals and many 4-foot soundings render this body of water off-limits to cruising-size craft.

Loop Creek

South of flashing daybeacon #30 an errant arm of the St. Johns loops around a small island and returns to the river via two channels. While this cut maintains minimum depths of 6 feet, there is only enough swinging room for anchorage by boats up to 25 feet. The loop does make an interesting side trip, however, for craft as large as 35 feet. The banks are completely undeveloped, lush, and swampy. Be sure to read the navigation information below before attempting to navigate the entire creek.

River Forest Anchorage (29 01.173 North/081 23.757 West)

Just north of the small village of River Forest, another bypassed loop makes off to the southwest at unlighted daybeacon #36. This cut boasts minimum 6-foot depths and has enough room on its southwesterly extreme for boats up to 36 feet to drop the hook. Protection is excellent from all winds, and the holding ground seems to consist of thick mud. Two houses near the anchorage break the otherwise undeveloped shoreline. This is one of the most reliable anchorages north of Lake Monroe. If you are ready to stop for the evening and your craft meets the size limitations, it would be advisable to anchor here.

Boat Show Marina (29 00.586 North/081 22.992 West)

South of flashing daybeacon #39, the St. Johns passes through a small elbow leading briefly to the west-southwest and then hurries toward the De Land/Whitehair Bridge. The docks of Boat Show Marina (formerly Crows Bluff) line the river's northeastern banks just short of the span.

Boat Show offers transient dockage and is fortunately situated about halfway between Astor and Sanford. The marina features both fixed and floating wooden docks on the river and some fixed and floating wooden piers on a protected harbor behind the ship's store and fuel dock. Most of these inside slips are covered. Transients are usually accommodated on the river. Depths on the St. Johns docks run 6½ to 10 feet, with 7 to 7½ feet of water in the inner dockage basin. Watch out for some fairly swift river currents as you approach the outer slips.

All berths offer full power and water connections. Gasoline can be purchased dockside, and showers are available as well. There is a ship's store and extensive mechanical-repairs department associated with this facility. Service work is available for outboards, I/Os, and gasoline inboards. Boats up to 66,000 pounds can be hauled with a 30-ton travelift. The marina features its own sandwich shop, bar, and lounge, open from 10:30 A.M. to 3:00 P.M. There are no other restaurants within walking distance.

Boat Show Marina (386) 736-6601

Approach depths—10+ feet
Dockside depths—6½-10 feet (outer docks)
　7-7½ feet (inner harbor)
Accepts transients—yes
Transient dockage rate—below average
Fixed and floating wooden piers
　—yes (some covered)
Dockside power connections—30
　and 50 amps
Dockside water connections—yes
Showers—yes
Gasoline—yes
Below-waterline repairs—yes
Mechanical repairs—yes (mostly gasoline)
Ship's store—yes
Restaurant—on site (open for lunch only)

Pier 44 Marina (29 00.476 North/081 22.920 West)

Just south of the 15-foot De Land bascule bridge, Pier 44 Marina (352-589-8370) lines the western shoreline. Occasionally, some very limited transient dockage is available strictly on a space-available basis, but the real news at Pier 44 is that both gasoline and diesel fuel can be purchased dockside. There is also a good, on-site ship's store on the premises. Resident berths feature 5-foot minimum depths and 30- and 50-amp power hookups and fresh-water connections. Extensive dry-stack storage is offered for smaller power craft. Mechanical repairs can be arranged for gasoline power plants.

Drigger Island Loop

East of flashing daybeacon #41, a small creek loops Drigger Island and returns to the St. Johns northeast of flashing daybeacon #42. While this cut maintains minimum depths of 6 feet, much of its course is constricted by hyacinths and lily pads. There is only enough swinging room for anchorage by craft up to 25 feet. Even though the undeveloped shoreline is lovely, larger cruising boats should probably bypass this side cut.

Holly Bluff Marina (28 59.291 North/081 21.404 West)

The dock of accommodating Holly Bluff Marina will be spied along the eastern banks between flashing daybeacons #47 and #49. This facility has a long, wooden pier fronting directly onto the St. Johns. Transients are accepted for overnight or temporary dockage at Holly Bluff at very affordable rates. Depths on the outer side of the pier run around 6 feet, with 4 to 5 feet of depth on the inner (eastern) slips. Deep-draft vessels should obviously request a berth on the outside face. Power connections of the 30- and 50-amp type, as well as water connections, are on hand, as are gasoline and a nice ship's/variety store. Showers and a Laundromat add to the marina's offerings.

Repairs for gasoline engines and haul-outs with a 30-ton travelift are also available at Holly Bluff. How's that for almost full service?

With the demise of most transient dockage at Hontoon Landing Marina, just to the south, Holly Bluff pretty much is the only game in town for visitors between Boat Show Marina and Lake Monroe. It is fortunate that the management seems so intent on making visiting craft welcome.

Holly Bluff Marina (386) 822-9992
http://www.hollybluff.com

Approach depths—10 feet
Dockside depths—6 feet
  (outside face of outer dock)
  4 feet (inner dock)
Accepts transients—yes
Transient dockage rate—well below average
Fixed wooden pier—yes
Dockside power connections—30
  and 50 amps
Dockside water connections—yes
Showers—yes
Laundromat—yes
Gasoline—yes
Below-waterline repairs—yes
Mechanical repairs—yes (gasoline only)
Ship's and variety store—yes

Hontoon Island State Park (28 58.492 North/081 21.502 West)

The Hontoon Island State Park docks flank the St. Johns' southern shore just short of flashing daybeacon #56. Mariners are welcome to tie temporarily or overnight to the park's wooden floating piers for a modest fee, but dockside depths of 3 to 4 feet limit their usefulness for most cruising craft. For

Holly Bluff Marina

shallow-draft vessels, power and water connections are available at dockside, but there are no fueling or repair facilities. Showers are available on the park grounds.

Craft requiring deeper water would be wise to anchor off temporarily and dinghy ashore. You might also consider docking at Holly Bluff just to the north and taking the short dinghy ride upriver to the park docks.

The park itself can be reached only by boat. It is a fascinating, undeveloped region, with two large mounds of snail shells left more than three centuries ago by the Timucuan Indians. Extensive picnic grounds, a nature trail, and an elevated observation platform are available to visitors. The park also features a replica of an Indian totem pole discovered on the island in 1955. All in all, this is a great place to rest from your cruise for a few hours.

Hontoon Dead River (28 57.295 North/081 21.789 West)

The narrow but deep body of water known as Hontoon Dead River makes off from the St. Johns' western banks opposite flashing day-beacon #53. The Hontoon is a truly lovely stream that exhibits some of the very best natural scenery along the St. Johns. Deep cypress shores stretch far back from the water and look as if they have never been disturbed by man. If it were not for the stream's popularity with small craft, you could easily imagine that you had somehow slipped back to a far-removed, simpler time.

Hontoon Dead River maintains minimum depths of 6 feet along its midwidth, with most soundings in the 10- to 20-foot range. Cruising craft under 36 feet should not hesitate to enter. Because of the stream's winding path, however, boats larger than 36 feet may find the going a little tight. If you pilot one of these larger vessels,

perform your explorations by dinghy.

Hontoon Dead River is a bit too narrow over most of its navigable length for anchorage by any except small craft. However, as chart 11495 shows, the river eventually opens out into a lagoonlike body of water. On-site research revealed that 5-foot depths could be maintained for more than 100 yards into the body of the lagoon. Adventurous skippers who pilot craft of 36 feet or less, which draw no more than 4 feet (and preferably a bit less), can drop the hook here in about as far removed a setting as you are ever likely to find.

Hontoon Landing Marina (28 58.569 North/081 21.496 West)

The docks of Hontoon Landing Marina (386-734-2474) lie abeam of the state park piers on the river's northern shore, near unlighted day-beacon #55. Unfortunately, the majority of the available dockage at Hontoon Landing Marina is occupied by rental and resident craft. Transient berths are pretty much relegated to small craft whose owners are lodging at the adjacent motel. Short of supplies and gasoline, this facility no longer offers much in the way of services for cruising-size craft.

On the plus side, the adjoining motel was completely remodeled several years ago, and the on-site ship's, variety, and clothing store is worth a look. There is also a snack bar on site. The rental houseboat fleet offered by Hontoon Landing is large and impressive. There is also a swimming pool on the grounds open to visitors. Gasoline is sold at a fuel pier behind the store, fronting directly on the river.

Lake Beresford Yacht Club and Anchorage (Various Lats/Lons—see below)

East and south of unlighted daybeacon #58, the St. Johns channel borders on the southwesterly reaches of Lake Beresford. Friendly Lake Beresford Yacht Club gazes out upon the lake's westerly banks, well north of unlighted daybeacon #61 (near 28 59.559 North/081 21.120 West). An essentially unmarked and somewhat difficult channel leads first east and then north from #61 into the lake's deeper center section. The club is located on the small, charted, L-shaped body of water between the 4- and 2-foot soundings along the western banks, pictured on chart 11495. Minimum depths on this passage are around 5 feet. Be sure to read the navigational account of Lake Beresford presented in the next section of this chapter before attempting first-time entry!

The Lake Beresford club is glad to accept cruising visitors from other yacht clubs with appropriate reciprocal agreements. Dockmasters are only in attendance on weekends, so be sure to make advance arrangements if you intend to arrive during the week. Berths are at sturdy, fixed wooden piers with 30-amp power hookups and fresh-water connections. There are also a few inner, covered slips just behind the clubhouse, but these are obviously set aside for members. Depths at the docks run 4 to 5 feet. All berths are wide open to strong winds blowing from the east across the lake or north and south up and down the lake. Showers are available in the clubhouse. During our last visit, the entire club's fleet seemed to be composed of power craft.

Lake Beresford Yacht Club is open Tuesday through Friday, 4:00 to 11:00 P.M.; from 11:30 A.M. to 11:00 P.M. Saturday; and on Sunday, 8:00 A.M. to 8:00 P.M. The club dining room serves dinner Tuesday through Saturday from 5:30 to 9:00 P.M. Lunch is available Saturday, and breakfast is served on Sundays.

Lake Beresford Yacht Club (386) 734-3854

Approach depths—5 feet
Dockside depths—4-5 feet
Accepts transients—members of other yacht clubs with appropriate reciprocal arrangements
Fixed wooden piers—yes
Dockside power connections—30 amps
Dockside water connections—yes
Showers—yes
Restaurant—on site (some hourly limitations)

Those lacking yacht-club credentials, or just wanting to anchor off, might consider the deep waters of central Lake Beresford in light airs (anywhere near 28 59.356 North/081 20.821 West). Depths run to a minimum of 5 feet but typically have 6-7-foot soundings. There is ample swinging room, but there is no shelter from blows in any direction. Nevertheless, this writer and his mate have spent several wonderful evenings anchored on mid-Lake Beresford in fair weather, watching the light fade from the surrounding waters. The shores show light-to-moderate residential development that seems to add to rather than detract from the lake's appeal.

Note that members of the Lake Beresford Yacht Club have warned this writer that the holding ground in Lake Beresford is soft mud and not really appropriate for heavy weather. Considering the open character of this anchorage, it would be far better to select another overnight haven, anyway, when the wind has its dander up.

Starks Landing Cutoff Loop (28 56.756 North/081 20.879 West)

West of flashing daybeacon #69, a small loop cuts into the river's western banks. This stream's all-natural shorelines are hauntingly beautiful and provide good protection for overnight anchorage. Minimum depths of 6 feet or more are held throughout the creek's northern and rearward sections. By contrast, soundings on the south side of the loop have now risen to grounding levels. Be sure to enter this anchorage exclusively by its northern mouth. First-timers, check out our navigational account of this loop below.

The best spot to drop the hook is found on the wider, rear (western) portion of the loop. Here craft as large as 36 feet can anchor in an idyllic setting.

Blue Springs State Park

From flashing daybeacon #69 south to unlighted daybeacon #77, the St. Johns passes through the confines of Blue Springs State Park. Numerous signs inform visiting cruisers that these waters are a manatee sanctuary and all boats must proceed at idle speed only! Keep a close watch as you pass and you may be lucky enough to catch sight of one or more manatees. You might wonder how ancient sailors could ever have mistaken these docile, rather ugly creatures for mermaids.

Blue Springs State Park (386-775-3663) is a well-known home of Florida's manatees. The natural springs disgorge 112 million gallons of 72-degree water every day, providing a perfect winter refuge for these gentle creatures. Park recreational activities include camping, picnicking, swimming, scuba diving, and canoeing in Blue Springs Run. Unfortunately, as there is virtually no access for cruising craft, you will most likely have to obtain motorized land transportation to visit the park.

You will spy the park's principal recreation area on the southeastern shore immediately southwest of flashing daybeacon #71. The entrance into Blue Springs Run is largely sealed off by a wooden breakwater. Powered craft should not attempt entry.

If your vessel is less than 38 feet in length, you might be able to anchor in the river, and row ashore to the recreation area. Don't try it if the river is busy with traffic.

If you do make it to shore, be sure to follow the nature trail up Blue Springs Run to the springs themselves. Divers sometimes descend deep into the springs' waters, but they certainly have more nerve than this writer!

The Snake Creek loop that cuts to the northwest at unlighted daybeacon #75 within the park boundaries has shoaled significantly since the soundings recorded on chart 11495. There are currently some 3- to 4-foot depths on the western reaches of the loop. Cruising mariners are advised to avoid this errant stream entirely.

Blue Springs State Park ends at unlighted daybeacon #77, and a sign on the eastern shore informs captains that they may resume normal speeds. The park is quite impressive; don't be in such a hurry that you pass it by without a thought.

Dutchmans Bend Anchorage (28 55.227 North/081 21.114 West)

South of flashing daybeacon #81, a deep channel parallels the river's eastern shore and runs behind a small island. Eventually the stream leads to a lagoonlike area that is choked with weeds on its western border. A deep, narrow creek leads off to the south.

Minimum depths of 6 feet are maintained between the stream's northerly entrance and the lagoon. Boats up to 34 feet can drop the hook here with care. Pick your spot carefully to avoid swinging into the shallow water to the west and south. Protection is excellent from all winds, and there is no development nearby.

With judicious navigation, this can be a great foul-weather hidey-hole. However, under no circumstances should you attempt to enter or leave this haven by way of its southerly entrance.

The small creek leading to the south has a beautifully natural, well-wooded shoreline, but is so narrow that craft over 28 feet could encounter serious maneuvering problems. Consider dropping the hook on the lagoon's waters and exploring the creek by dinghy. Some great natural scenery will be your reward.

Emmanuel Bend Anchorage (28 52.734 North/081 21.765 West)

South of flashing daybeacon #93, undeveloped Emmanuel Bend Creek heads south, while the main channel cuts a bit to the west. Minimum depths of 6 feet are carried in the bend channel until it rejoins the St. Johns at unlighted daybeacon #97. However, there are several unmarked shoals to be avoided. You must take care when anchoring to avoid swinging into the adjoining shallows. For this reason, boats 36 feet or larger would do well to consider another overnight stop.

Craft under 36 feet can find their way to one good anchorage. As the stream begins to bend sharply to the west and heads back into the St. Johns, a large bubble of 6-foot water covers the stream's midwidth. These waters provide fairly good swinging room and excellent protection. Again, you must take care to avoid the shallows to the south and west. Read the Emmanuel Bend navigation information below before entering.

Wekiva River

The upper reaches of Wekiva River intersect the western banks of the St. Johns at flashing daybeacon #96. The entrance is surrounded by several small islands and is littered with unmarked shoals. On the positive side, the stream's banks are composed of deep, almost mysterious cypress swamps. Exploration of the river by small craft is a rewarding ecological experience. Consider anchoring in the river or on nearby Emmanuel Bend and exploring this fascinating stream by dinghy.

Butchers Bend Anchorage (Various Lats/Lons—see below)

Butchers Bend is the best anchorage for craft under 37 feet north of Lake Monroe. The creek loops north from unlighted daybeacon #110 and eventually rejoins the St. Johns at unlighted daybeacon #111. While there are a few shallows (particularly adjoining the creek's southerly section), most of the stream maintains minimum depths of 5 feet. Boats that require generous swinging room can anchor at the creek's mouth, just north of #110, near 28 51.485 North/081 21.142 West. For more shelter, craft that draw less than 4½ feet can cruise to the west of the small island circumvented by the creek and drop the hook with excellent protection from heavy weather near 28 51.476 North/081 21.276 West. The creek's shores are still in their natural state, and it is unlikely that you will need to share the stream with fellow cruisers.

Hidden Harbour Marina (28 50.128 North/081 19.696 West)

Hidden Harbour Marina is tucked snugly into the charted offshoot on the southwestern shoreline just to the northwest of the first (railroad) bridge that spans the St. Johns before you reach Lake Monroe. This facility is one of the finest marinas on the whole of the St. Johns. Apart from diesel fuel, Hidden Harbour offers just about everything, even a swimming

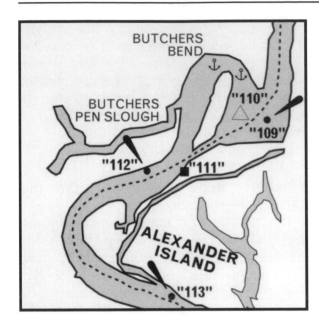

pool open to transients.

Visiting cruisers will find dock space at floating wooden piers in a well-protected harbor. All slips feature fresh-water hookups and 30- and 50-amp power connections. Strangely enough, depths on the outermost slips run around 5½ to 6 feet, while the innermost berths boast 6½ to 7 feet of water, just the opposite of what you might expect. Gasoline is available, and there is also a marine canvas dealer on the grounds.

Showers and a Laundromat are found shoreside. The showers are located on the north side of the complex near the restaurant. Hidden Harbour General Store is a combination ship's and variety store plus deli and snack bar. It is within an easy step of the dockage basin. Otter's Riverside Restaurant (407-323-3991) guards the complex's northern tier. Judging from its number of patrons, the food here must be pretty good.

The marina maintains a 20-ton travelift that facilitates haul-outs and below-waterline repairs. Have you checked your bottom lately?

Hidden Harbour Marina (407) 322-1610

Approach depths—8-10 feet
Dockside depths—5½-7 feet
Accepts transients—yes
Transient dockage rate—below average
Floating wooden piers—yes
Dockside power connections—30
**   and 50 amps**
Dockside water connections—yes
Showers—yes
Laundromat—yes
Gasoline—yes
Below-waterline repairs—yes
Mechanical repairs—yes
Ship's and variety store—yes
Deli and snack bar—yes
Restaurant—on site

Last Anchorage (28 50.332 North/081 19.325 West)

The charted offshoot between the second and third bridges leading into Lake Monroe, cutting into the river's northern shore, can serve as an ideal anchorage for boats up to 40 feet, drawing less than 4 feet. Minimum depths run to 5 feet with typical 6- to 8-foot soundings. The northern tip of the cove serves as a local launching area. Otherwise, protection is excellent and even sufficient for use in heavy weather.

This anchorage also offers an unexpected source of minimal food supplies. Use your binoculars to pick out the Lake Monroe Park Store overlooking the cove's westerly banks. Break out the dinghy and tie it off temporarily to one of the small piers associated with the public launching ramps. It's then only a quick walk to the store, where you will find beer and hot dogs as well as the usual variety store fare.

Lake Monroe

Popular Lake Monroe is the largest body of water on the St. Johns River north of Sanford, except for Lake George. It is consistently deep on its midsection, and weekends usually find many power craft and sailing vessels wafting along on its broad surface. Lake Monroe is a singularly attractive body of water, and few visiting mariners will soon forget this stretch of their cruise to Sanford.

Except for the facilities at Sanford, Lake Monroe lacks any sheltered harbors along its shores. In fact once you have finished admiring its beauty, there is little else to do except visit the marina at Sanford.

Sanford and Monroe Harbour Marina (28 48.879 North/081 15.885 West)

The thriving city of Sanford perches on Lake Monroe's southern banks. Its history stretches far back to the period before Florida's rise to national prominence. Sanford has often looked to the commerce of the St. Johns for its livelihood, and even today, barges still make the 148-nautical-mile trip from the river's inlet to Sanford.

For cruisers, Sanford offers superb marine facilities as well as access to any number of shoreside businesses. Monroe Harbour Marina features two enclosed, well-protected basins on the Sanford waterfront. These two dockage areas are separated by the charted point, just to the south of unlighted daybeacon #4.

What can this writer say about Monroe Harbour Marina except perhaps to note that it is one of the finest marina facilities on either coast of Florida? Extensive, well-sheltered dockage is combined with full repair services and one of the most knowledgeable and

friendly staffs that you will ever find.

In the early 1990s, Monroe Harbour Marina underwent a massive expansion. One hundred new slips were added, and all the existing docks were refurbished. This expansion and face-lift added to the already impressive aura of this facility. It has not diminished to the present day.

Transients are accommodated in Monroe Harbour if space is available. The marina is currently rather full. Call ahead of time to check for slip availability. Fresh water and 30-50 amp power connections are in the offing. Telephone hookups are also available for resident craft. Gasoline can be purchased dockside in the eastern basin. Arrangements can be made for substantial quantities of diesel fuel dispensed from a shoreside tanker truck. Showers and a full-service Laundromat are available, as is a wide-ranging ship's and variety store. Monroe Harbour features both a fixed waste pump-out site at the fuel dock and a portable unit that can be used throughout the marina.

Full mechanical repairs are also offered. Diesel work is usually subcontracted out to local independents, but you can count on Captain Luke and his staff to find the best technicians available. Haul-outs are readily accomplished by a 35-ton travelift.

If you're in the market for dry-stack storage of your smaller power craft, look no farther. One look at Monroe Harbour's massive storage building should be convincing enough.

A large motel with restaurant occupies the point of land separating the two dockage basins. This hostelry is very convenient if you want to take a break from the live-aboard routine. The motel restaurant overlooks the western docks and features huge plate-glass windows gazing out over Lake Monroe.

Newly revitalized downtown Sanford is

only a three-block walk away. Here you will find the local post office and library, as well as a drugstore and any number of restaurants. Among others, you might want to visit the Colonial Room Restaurant (407-323-2999). Be sure to check out the new Riverwalk, which borders much of Lake Monroe and is adjacent to downtown Sanford.

Monroe Harbour Marina (407) 322-2910

Approach depths—6-8 feet
Dockside depths—6 feet
Accepts transients—yes
  (call ahead to check on slip availability)
Transient dockage rate—average
Floating concrete piers—yes
Dockside power connections—30
  and 50 amps
Dockside water connections—yes
Showers—yes
Laundromat—yes
Waste pump-out—yes
Gasoline—yes
Diesel fuel—larger quantities only
Below-waterline repairs—yes
Mechanical repairs—yes
Ship's and variety store—yes
Restaurant—on site and others nearby

Sanford History   In 1837 a large force of Seminole Indians staged a surprise attack on a squadron of U.S. soldiers along the southern banks of Lake Monroe. The soldiers drove off the Indian attack with the sole loss of Capt. Charles Mellon. Later a fort built on the battle site was named Fort Mellon in his honor.

Following the Seminole War, in the 1840s, settlers began to filter slowly into the Lake Monroe region. A trading post was established near the site of the old fort and was dubbed Mellonville. One of these early settlers was Capt. Jacob Brock, who foresaw the great sport and tourism potential of the lands about Lake Monroe. He established the settlement of Enterprise opposite Mellonville, where he built an inn that became known as "a paradise for sportsmen."

In 1870 Gen. Harry S. Sanford, a New Englander by birth, visited the inn at Enterprise and was so impressed with the area that he decided to form his own empire on the shores of Lake Monroe. By 1876 he had acquired twenty-two square miles on the southern shores of the great lake. Dense growth lining the shore was cleared away, several broad avenues were built from the lake to the new settlement, and a large sawmill was soon in operation. A pier more than 600 feet long was built out into the waters to receive and dispatch commerce, and a collection of storehouses was built from the planks cut in the new sawmill. Finally, to attract visitors, the general built the Sanford Motel, one of the finest hostelries in the state at that time. By 1886 the town of Sanford had a bank, two newspapers, a telegraph office, and six hotels.

General Sanford also believed that the warm, humid climate of the Lake Monroe shores would be ideal for growing tropical fruits. At various times he experimented with almonds, tamarinds, mangos, figs, pomegranates, loquats, Barbados cherries, pecans, peaches, olives, and even pineapples. While most of these exotic plants flourished in the spring and summer, every winter a vagrant frost killed most of the general's prizes.

It was only after General Sanford's death in 1890 that farmers discovered the Lake Monroe climate was ideal for growing celery. For many years now, the southern shores of Lake Monroe have produced as many as 1,719,027 crates of celery in a single season.

Upper St. Johns River

This account of the St. Johns River ends at Sanford. Although the river continues south for many miles, the stream splinters into numerous branches and depths become much too uncertain for larger cruising craft. If you happen to be in the area with a small outboard or I/O boat, you might give the St. Johns' upper reaches a try for some truly unforgettable natural scenery.

LAKE GEORGE TO SANFORD NAVIGATION

Successful navigation of the upper St. Johns River is mostly a simple matter of following the well-marked channel. In contrast to the river north of Lake George, the route to Sanford is mostly free from encroaching shoals. The two exceptions to this river's generally forgiving nature are found where the channel traverses Lake Dexter and Lake Beresford. You must exercise caution on these waters or risk a most unpleasant grounding.

Entrance from Lake George   From flashing daybeacon #15 the St. Johns channel passes between twin wooden breakwaters and follows a dredged cut through Volusia Bar into the deeper reaches of the river to the south. This is a very tricky section, with shallow water and numerous submerged piles and snags lining both sides of the channel. Proceed with caution and keep a wary eye on the sounder.

Come abeam of flashing daybeacon #17, at the southern foot of the twin breakwaters, to its fairly immediate westerly side and set a new course to come abeam of flashing daybeacon #18 to its fairly immediate northeasterly side. Take great care during this run. Waters surrounding this portion of the channel can run to 1-foot depths, and snags are numerous.

From #18, turn to the east-southeast and set course to come abeam of flashing daybeacon #19 to its southwestern side. Take care to avoid drifting to the north or northeast during this run. As chart 11495 shows, numerous submerged piles guard this side of the channel.

Don't attempt to enter the small creek that enters the St. Johns to the northeast of #19. In spite of soundings shown on chart 11495, entrance depths have shoaled to 4 feet or less.

South of #19 several shallow creeks intersect the river. Avoid all of these errant cuts and continue on the marked route.

At flashing daybeacon #19, the river swings sharply to the south-southeast and flows past flashing daybeacons #21 and #23. Pass both these aids to their westerly sides. Next you will come abeam of unlighted daybeacon #24 to its easterly quarter. South of #24 the channel becomes mostly deep and easy to follow on its way to Astor.

Morrison Creek   Enter Morrison Creek by way of its northerly mouth (only!) on the stream's midwidth. Boats that draw 3 feet or more should cease their exploration before passing through the loop creek's easterly tip. Soundings on the southern branch of the stream run as shallow as 4 feet.

Take note that the entire length of Morrison Creek is an official manatee no-wake zone. Power craft should be sure to proceed strictly at idle speed.

Astor South of flashing daybeacon #28, official signs warn that all the waters in and around Astor are a no-wake zone. Continue at idle speed until you see the "Resume Normal Operation" sign well south of the Astor bridge.

Soon after passing #28, you will catch sight of a large fish camp on the eastern shore. Several more such camps line the banks north of the Astor bridge.

The Astor span has a closed vertical clearance of 20 feet and opens on demand. Blackwater Inn and Midway Marine line the westerly banks, south of the bridge, while Astor Bridge Marina and Motel flanks the easterly shore.

Immediately south of the Astor bridge, the channel passes under an overhead power cable with a charted clearance of 50 feet. Local cruisers have warned this writer that only 45 feet of clearance can be expected at this time.

On the St. Johns South of Astor the river deepens almost from shore to shore. Watch for a profusion of manatee slow-speed and no-wake zones all the Way to Lake Monroe. These zones have hatched here, there, and yonder over the last several years.

South of the Astor bridge, there are no markers for several miles. Eventually you will sight flashing daybeacon #1 north of Lungren Island. Follow the marked channel west of the island. Before long you will come abeam of flashing daybeacon #4. South-southeast of #4, the main river channel begins its run through the otherwise shallow waters of Lake Dexter.

Lake Dexter The passage across Lake Dexter is the most exacting part of the entire run from Lake George to Sanford. The channel isn't just tricky; it can be downright dangerous. Very shallow water and numerous snags line the improved cut. Markers are not really as close together as they should be, and leeway can ease you out of the channel, even when you think you are following the correct course. Proceed with the greatest caution, check the track over your stern for leeway, and keep a weather eye on the sounder.

Come abeam of flashing daybeacon #8 by some 20 yards to its easterly side. Turn almost due south, and set course to come abeam of unlighted daybeacon #10 to its immediate easterly side. Bend your course just a tiny bit farther to the east, and point to come abeam of flashing daybeacon #12 to its immediate eastern quarter.

From #12, the channel turns to the south-southeast. Set a new course to come abeam of and pass unlighted daybeacon #13 by some 10 yards to its westerly side and come abeam of flashing daybeacon #15, to its northwesterly quarter. Between #13 and #15, be especially vigilant against leeway to the east and southeast. Waters with only 1 foot of depth parallel this side of the channel.

At flashing daybeacon #15, the channel turns yet again, this time sharply to the west-southwest. From #15 point to pass flashing daybeacon #16 to its easterly quarter and follow the river channel as it curves around the charted point and swings to the southeast. Deep water again spreads out almost from bank to bank east and south of #16. Stick to the river's midline and all will be well.

Don't attempt to enter Adams Lake south of unlighted daybeacon #23. Depths of 2 feet at the entrance are waiting to greet your keel. Similarly, Horseshoe Mud Lake, south of unlighted daybeacon #24, is quite shoal. Even small craft may find the bottom trying to cruise into this errant body of water.

Loop Creek Favor the port shore slightly when entering the northern mouth of the small loop creek south of flashing daybeacon #30. Continue to favor this shoreline as the creek follows a hairpin turn to the north on its way to rejoin the St. Johns.

At this point the channel splits. While the offshoot running toward flashing daybeacon #32 holds good 8-foot depths, it is unmarked and borders on a shoal to the south. The western cut is more reliable. Hold to the midwidth and pass between the large island to port and the smaller charted landmass to starboard until you rejoin the river.

River Forest Anchorage To enter the loop creek north of River Forest, leave the St. Johns by passing just to the southwest of unlighted daybeacon #36. Hold to the center as you pass into the creek's mouth.

Once on the stream's interior reaches, begin favoring the western (starboard) banks slightly. Continue to favor this shore as the creek follows a sharp bend to the east-northeast. Be careful to avoid the charted patch of shallow water on the southern side of the stream's western tip. Favor the port side banks to bypass this hazard. Cruise back into the St. Johns by passing just to the south of unlighted daybeacon #38.

On the St. Johns South of flashing daybeacon #39, the St. Johns River passes under a power line with 83 feet of vertical clearance in the body of a knuckle-like turn. Soon you will begin your approach to the De Land/Whitehair bascule bridge. Slow to idle speed as you approach the span, and continue at slow speed for several hundred yards south of the bridge. Boat Show Marina will be obvious on the northeasterly banks, north of the bascule bridge, as will Pier 44 Marina on the western shoreline, south-southeast of the span.

The De Land/Whitehair Bridge has a closed vertical clearance of 15 feet, but fortunately it opens on demand.

Drigger Island Loop Be sure to enter Drigger Island loop by way of its northern entrance abeam of flashing daybeacon #41. The southerly portion of this stream (opposite flashing daybeacon #42) is now choked with lily pads and snags. Larger cruising craft should avoid this southerly leg of the loop.

Stick to the midwidth as you cruise into the northerly branch of Drigger Island loop. Drop the hook or discontinue your exploration short of the stream's sharp turn back to the west-southwest on its way to rejoin the St. Johns.

On the St. Johns South of the Drigger Island loop, the channel takes a hard jog to the east at flashing daybeacon #42. South of #42, several of the daybeacons on the river are hard to spot. Flashing daybeacons #45, #47, and #49 tend to blend with the northern and eastern shorelines, and can easily be missed. Keep a sharp watch to identify each aid as you approach its position.

South of flashing daybeacon #47, the river's track borders some fairly extensive residential development along the northeastern banks near the charted position of Lambs Bluff. The docks of Holly Bluff Marina will also be spotted along this stretch.

At flashing daybeacon #49, the river sweeps to the southwest and begins its approach to Hontoon Dead River, Hontoon Island State Park, and Hontoon Landing Marina. Slow to idle speed south of #49 until you are well past all these attractions.

Hontoon Dead River   The mouth of Hontoon Dead River strikes into the westerly banks of the St. Johns opposite flashing daybeacon #53. Enter the stream on its midwidth while keeping a careful watch for snags. Continue following the centerline as you track your way upriver at slow speed.

Eventually, the Hontoon follows a sharp turn to the east, and then strikes south into a wide lagoon. Boats drawing 4 feet or less can track their way safely to the south on the midline of the lagoon for a maximum of 100 yards (no farther). Be sure to anchor or come about well before reaching the charted 4-foot shallows farther to the south.

Lake Beresford   The St. Johns channel follows another dredged cut across the southwesterly reaches of Lake Beresford. The easterly quarter of the channel borders shoal water for the most part. Be on guard against lateral slippage to the east.

Come abeam of flashing daybeacon #60 to its immediate northeasterly side. Curl around to the south-southeast and set course to come abeam and pass unlighted daybeacon #62 to its immediate eastern quarter. Continue on this course, pointing to come abeam of flashing daybeacon #63 by some 10 yards to its westerly side. The channel leaves Lake Beresford south of #63, and successful navigation becomes far less complex.

To make good your passage into Lake Beresford, and perhaps eventually to the yacht club of the same name, depart the main cut immediately north of unlighted daybeacon #61. Watch to the north and you will spy a series of small pilings, some barely above the water's surface, which outlines the northern edge of the channel leading into the lake. Stay some 20 to 25 yards south of these pilings and follow them along as you curl around to the north and enter the main body of Lake Beresford. Soon depths improve. Hold to the lake's center section until the yacht club docks come abeam to the west. You can then cut directly into the basin, or anchor anywhere on the large tongue of correctly charted deeper water lying along Lake Beresford's central axis.

On the St. Johns   South of flashing daybeacon #63, stick strictly to the river's midwidth until reaching flashing daybeacon #69. Both shorelines are shoal in this area.

At #69 be prepared to slow down and proceed through the Blue Springs Park area at idle speed. Continue at no-wake speed until reaching the "Resume Normal Operation" sign south of unlighted daybeacon #77.

Starks Landing Loop   Starks Landing loop must now be entered strictly by way of its northerly mouth. The southern portion of the creek has become shoal and choked with lily pads.

While cruising into the loop's northerly entrance, be on guard against the charted but unmarked shoal that flanks the northwestern tip of the stream's mouth. Feel your way in at idle speed and use the sounder.

Enter the main body of the loop on its midwidth and continue on the middle until the creek begins to pass through the hairpin curve leading back to the St. Johns. Discontinue your forward progress at this point and retrace your steps back through the northern branch of the loop when it's time to leave.

On the St. Johns   Remember to avoid the Snake Creek loop that cuts to the northwest at flashing daybeacon #73. In spite of depths shown on chart 11495, recent shoaling has raised soundings in a few spots on this creek to grounding levels.

Dutchmans Bend Anchorage   To enter Dutchmans Bend anchorage, pass flashing daybeacon #81 to its immediate westerly side and cruise into the midline of the small lagoon bordering the eastern banks. Set the hook before coming abeam of the southeastern tip of the small island to the west.

Even though chart 11495 shows a channel leading back into the St. Johns south of the small island, this cut is now completely closed by lily pads and hyacinths.

Boats over 28 feet should not attempt to enter the creek leading south from Dutchmans Bend. While minimum depths of 6 feet continue for quite some distance upstream, the creek's width is so constricted that larger craft will not find enough room to maneuver.

Emmanuel Bend   Enter Emmanuel Bend south of flashing daybeacon #93. Favor the eastern banks as you cruise through the stream's northerly mouth. Consider dropping the hook just before the creek follows a sharp bend to the west and heads back to the St. Johns.

It would probably be best for larger craft to retrace their steps back to the north when leaving. As chart 11495 shows, there is a southern channel leading back to the St. Johns, but there are also several unmarked shoals along the way.

If you should attempt this southerly route, favor the starboard shore as you round the sharp bend in the creek and head back to the west. There is very shallow water just south of the channel. Continue favoring the starboard banks until coming abeam of the sharp point of land to the south just before rejoining the St. Johns. Cruise back to the midwidth once abeam of the southerly point and continue on the centerline out into the main body of the St. Johns.

Butchers Bend   Cruisers following a path into Butchers Bend should head straight for unlighted daybeacon #110. Some 20 yards before reaching this marker, turn sharply to the north-northwest and enter the bend by favoring the starboard shore. As the northern tip of the small island to port comes abeam, begin favoring the island's shores. The waters with the most swinging room are found abeam of this point. There is little in the way of surrounding shallows into which you might drift. Continue favoring the eastern (island) shores as the creek loops back to the south and eventually rejoins the St. Johns.

On the St. Johns   From Butchers Bend south to Lake Monroe, the channel is uniformly deep and well marked. Simply hold to the river's midwidth and observe the various aids carefully.

East of flashing daybeacon #116, you will catch sight of three red and white, candy cane striped smokestacks in the distance. These stacks are associated with a large power plant. As you come abeam of the plant, Hidden Harbour Marina will come abeam in the sheltered offshoot on the southwesterly banks.

Moving farther to the east, you will begin your approach to Lake Monroe and the three bridges crossing the path into the lake.

Lake Monroe Bridges   Three bridges guard the approach from the St. Johns River into Lake Monroe. First comes a railroad bridge with a bare 7 feet of closed vertical clearance. This span supposedly opens on demand unless a train is due. The operator has been known to be a little slow on the draw.

East of the railway span, the fixed Highway 17, high-rise bridge crosses the river. The old swing bridge that once spanned the river at this point has been moved to the southern banks and is now

part of a small park. The current bridge has a vertical clearance of 45 feet.

Once through this span, favor the northerly side of the channel slightly. Take our bent prop's word for it, a patch of shallows lies to the south around the park's launching ramps.

Continue on course, pointing for the pass through of the third and last (Interstate 4) bridge. This fixed span also has a vertical clearance of 45 feet.

The entire stretch between the three bridges is an official no-wake zone. Proceed at idle speed until you are south of the final span.

Last Anchorage   The wide cove on the river's northern shore between the two highway bridges offers excellent overnight anchorage. Enter the cove on its midwidth and drop the hook before approaching to within 50 yards of any shoreline.

Lake Monroe   The Lake Monroe channel is well marked and the current edition of chart 11498 pretty much reflects the correct configuration of aids to navigation. The scheme of markers leading to Monroe Harbour Marina must have been thought up by some Washington bureaucrat.

From the last 45-foot span you must follow the marked channel carefully east to unlighted daybeacon #6. Very shallow water borders both sides of the channel from the bridge to #6.

Set a course from #6 to come between flashing daybeacon #8 to its northerly side and unlighted daybeacon #7 to its southerly quarter. Look to the north of #7 and you will see a marked channel leading to the northerly shores of the lake. This cut, known as the Enterprise Landing channel, is used by commercial barges passing to and from a huge power plant that can easily be seen from the lake.

East of #7 and #8, good depths open out on the midwidth of Lake Monroe. However, as chart 11495 shows, there are several shallow spots bordering the intersection of the Lake Monroe and Enterprise Landing channels. Avoid these shoals (denoted on the water by small, uncharted floating markers) like the plague—the bottom is foul.

If you choose to cruise on the lake's broad, deep section, as many local craft regularly do, it would be best to follow the Enterprise channel north to unlighted daybeacon #3. From this aid you have a clear passage into the deep water to the east.

The principal Lake Monroe channel continues southeast toward the Sanford waterfront from #7 and #8. This passage is straightforward as far as unlighted daybeacon #10. Southeast of #10, an alternate channel leads due south, straight toward the Sanford waterfront, While this cut is consistently deep, it leads only to a large condo development. Visiting pleasure cruisers will find the direct route to flashing daybeacon #5 shorter. However, the westerly channel is perfectly safe, so if you want to view a bit more of the city waterfront, don't hesitate to use this cut.

Follow either the waterfront or the direct channel until flashing daybeacon #5 comes abeam to its southerly side. From #5, the route to Monroe Harbour Marina gets a little crazy, but at least all (but one) of the markers are now where they should be on chart 11495.

Once abeam of #5 to its southerly side, look east and you will spy the entrance to Monroe Harbour's western dockage basin. Before venturing on, note the octagonal, glass-enclosed structure on the northern point of the west basin's entrance. This building houses the restaurant associated with the motel adjacent to Monroe Harbour.

To reach the eastern dockage basin, cruise east from #5 for a very short distance (no more than 10 to 15 yards) and then cut sharply to the north. Cruise slowly on this heading until the gap between unlighted daybeacon #1 and the charted position of unlighted daybeacon #2 come abeam to the east. Then, turn sharply to the east and point to pass between #1 and #2.

Just to make matters a bit more interesting, unlighted daybeacon #2 has been missing for some time, and the United States Coast Guard does not seem in a real hurry to replace this important aid to navigation. Consequently, it may or may not be in place by the time of your arrival. If you should find #2 absent, my best recommendation is to point to pass unlighted daybeacon #1 by some 20 yards to its southerly side. Good luck—you may need it!

Once abeam of #1 (or between #1 and #2 if #2 should have been replaced), continue on the same course, eventually passing unlighted daybeacon #4 by some 5 to 10 yards to its northerly side, and come abeam of unlighted daybeacon #6 by about the same distance to its northerly quarter.

Some local captains have told this writer that it is possible to shorten this trek to #6 by cruising directly from flashing daybeacon #5 to unlighted daybeacon #4. However, an unmarked shoal borders the northwestern quarter of this run. Visiting cruisers are strictly advised to make the run to #1 and #2 before making the turn to #4.

After passing unlighted daybeacon #6, turn sharply to starboard and cruise through the entrance in the wooden breakwater protecting Monroe Harbour's eastern dockage basin, leaving a second unlighted daybeacon #2 to your starboard side. As you pass through the breakwater, watch for a second, privately maintained daybeacon, marked as #6. Pass this second #6 close by your starboard side.

If all this seems a bit confusing, Monroe Harbour will be glad to talk visiting navigators in via VHF. Even if you think you can follow the account presented above, it might be a good idea to check with the marina anyway to see if conditions have changed since the time of this writing. Give the marina a call on channel 16.

South of Sanford   South of Sanford an indifferently marked channel continues into a small canal, which eventually leads to Sanford Boat Works and Marina. However, the route to this facility borders on several unmarked shoals, and local knowledge is probably necessary to navigate this passage safely.

Farther to the south, the St. Johns splits into numerous branches, and shallow depths become common. The upper reaches of the St. Johns are strictly not recommended for larger cruising boats. However, exploration by outboard or I/O, whether for sightseeing or for black bass, can be most rewarding.

Jacksonville Beach to St. Augustine

The waters between Jacksonville Beach and St. Augustine have a strikingly varied historical heritage. To the north, modern development predominates in the resort community of Jacksonville Beach. This is a very popular tourist mecca that has developed mostly since World War II.

Conversely, the timeless city of St. Augustine guards the lower reaches of the region covered in this chapter. From the earliest era of Spanish colonization, the story of St. Augustine is the history of eastern Florida well into the nineteenth century. Even though it covers only a few nautical miles, for cruisers interested in the state's heritage, this stretch of the ICW is one of the richest finds in all of Florida.

With but one exception, anchorages are practically nonexistent south of the St. Johns River to Jacksonville Beach. However, as you approach St. Augustine, sheltered havens become more numerous, and at least one spot is sufficient for heavy-weather anchorage.

Full-service marina facilities are found all along this stretch, though veteran cruisers will look in vain for what was once perhaps the best marina in Jacksonville Beach. There are still any number of excellent pleasure-craft facilities in this region, and St. Augustine can boast some truly topflight marine accommodations.

This is one of the most historically important sections of the entire Florida ICW. For this reason, we have devoted an entire chapter to this relatively small region. Visiting cruisers should allow sufficient time in their itinerary to take full advantage of the many rich cultural and historical adventures these waters can afford.

Charts Two charts detail the ICW between the St. Johns River and St. Augustine:
11489—follows the Waterway from the St. Johns to the northern section of Tolomato River

11485—continues coverage of the ICW past St. Augustine and on to points south. This chart also details the passages on Salt Run and San Sebastian River

---

Bridges
San Pablo/Atlantic Boulevard Bridge—crosses ICW at Standard Mile 744.5—Fixed—65 feet
B. B. McCormick/Beach Boulevard Bridge—crosses ICW at Standard Mile 748—Bascule—37 feet (closed)—April-May and October-November opens only on the hour and half-hour 7:00 A.M. to 9:00 A.M. and 4:30 P.M. to 6:30 P.M. weekdays; during weekends, federal holidays, opens on the hour and half-hour noon to 6:00 P.M.; at all other times opens on demand
J. Turner Butler Bridge—crosses ICW at Standard Mile 749—Fixed—65 feet
Palm Valley Bridge—crosses ICW at Standard Mile 759—Fixed—65 feet
Vilano Beach Bridge—crosses ICW at Standard Mile 776, just north of ICW's intersection with St. Augustine Inlet—Fixed—65 feet
Bridge of Lions—crosses ICW at Standard Mile 778, in downtown St. Augustine—

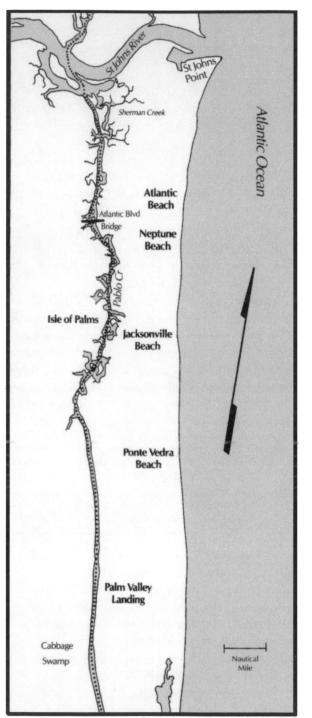

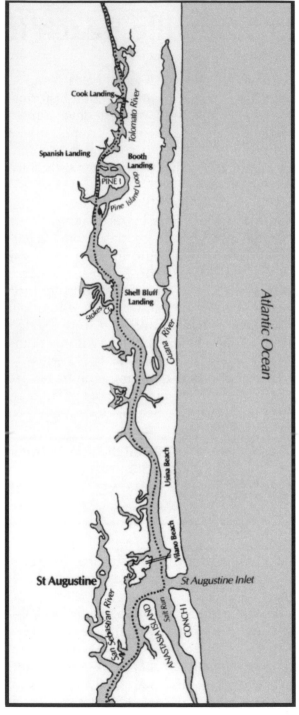

Bascule—25 feet (closed)—opens only on the hour and half-hour 7:00 A.M. to 6:00 P.M. weekdays except there are no openings at 8:00 A.M., noon, and 5:00 P.M.; weekends, opens on the hour and half-hour, 7:00 A.M. to 6:00 P.M.; at night opens on demand

Chapter 3 Anchorage Summary (Anchorages are listed in geographic order, moving north to south.)

One and Only Anchorage—(Standard Mile 744)—located near 30 19.709 North/081 26.212 West, south of flashing daybeacon #17, and just north of the San Pablo Bridge—10-foot depths—reviewed on pages 173, 182

Pine Island Loop Anchorage—(Standard Mile 765)—located near 30 03.059 North/081 21.951 West, south of unlighted daybeacon #25, off the eastern banks of the Waterway—7-foot depths—reviewed on pages 176, 184-85

Shell Bluff Anchorage—(Standard Mile 767.5)—located near 30 01.342 North/081 20.977 West, north-northwest of flashing daybeacon #35—6-foot depths—reviewed on pages 176, 185

Open Anchorages—(Standard Mile 769)—located off the easterly flank of the ICW, between flashing daybeacons #41 and #44—various lats/lons (see detailed account)—8-foot depths—reviewed on pages 176-77, 185

Guana River Anchorage—(Standard Mile 770.5)—located off the eastern side of the ICW, south of flashing daybeacon #45—various lats/lons (see detailed account)—5-foot depths, but be advised that this is a navigationally difficult anchorage—reviewed on pages 177, 185-86

Waterway Anchorage—(Standard Mile 775)—located near 29 55.628 North/081 18.247 West, south-southeast of flashing daybeacon #55—8-foot depths—reviewed on pages 178, 186

Salty Run Anchorages—located on the waters of Salt Run, south-southeast of unlighted daybeacon #11—various lats/lons (see detailed account)—5½-foot depths—reviewed on pages 190-91, 206

St. Augustine City Northern Anchorage—(Standard Mile 778)—located near 29 53.776 North/081 18.587 West, north of the Bridge of Lions—8-foot depths—reviewed on pages 192, 206

St. Augustine City Southern Anchorage—(Standard Mile 778.5)—located near 29 53.402 North/081 18.445 West, south of the St. Augustine City Marina—*Be sure to anchor south of a point abeam of the Santa Maria Restaurant and Dock*—6-foot depths, typical 10-foot soundings—reviewed on pages 194, 207

Chapter 3 Marina and Yacht-Club Summary (Marinas are listed in geographic order, moving north to south.)

Palm Cove Marina—(904) 223-4757—(Standard Mile 747)—located near 30 17.378 North/081 25.821 West, south of unlighted daybeacon #31, off the western shores of the ICW—transient dockage available—gasoline and diesel fuel available—4-foot minimum depths—reviewed on pages 173-74, 183

Beach Marine—(904) 249-8200—(Standard Mile 748)—located near 30 17.310 North/081 25.206 West, south of unlighted daybeacon #34, and just north of the B. B. McCormick/Beach Boulevard bascule bridge—transient dockage available—gasoline and diesel fuel available—6-foot minimum depths—reviewed on pages 174-75, 183

Camachee Cove Yacht Harbor—(904) 829-5676—(Standard Mile 775.5)—located near

29 55.061 North/081 18.518 West, off the Waterway's western shoreline, south of unlighted daybeacon #57 and just north of the Vilano Beach Bridge—transient dockage available—gasoline and diesel fuel available—6-foot minimum depths—reviewed on pages 178-80, 186

Conch House Marina Resort—(904) 824-4347—located near 29 53.722 North/081 17.745 West, along the western shores of Salt Run, just to the west of unlighted daybeacon #11—transient dockage available—gasoline and diesel fuel available—7-foot minimum depths—reviewed on pages 189-90, 205-6

St. Augustine City Marina—(904) 825-1026—(Standard Mile 778)—located near 29 53.530 North/081 18.513 West, overlooking the western shoreline, just south of the Bridge of Lions—transient dockage available—gasoline and diesel fuel available—7-foot minimum depths—reviewed on pages 192-94, 207

Fish Island Marina—(904) 471-1955—(Standard Mile 780)—located near 29 52.265 North/081 18.175 West, overlooking the Waterway's eastern flank, just north of the intersection with San Sebastian River—transient dockage available—diesel fuel available—8-foot minimum depths on outer docks—0 feet of water at low tide in inner harbor—reviewed on pages 194-95, 207

St. Johns River to St. Augustine

After crossing the St. Johns River, the ICW follows a canal-like passage for several miles south to Jacksonville Beach. The Waterway then flows through the Palm Valley Cut until intersecting Tolomato River's northern headwaters. This stream leads mariners in turn to the storied city of St. Augustine and the inlet bearing the same name. While there are undeveloped sections of the shoreline on the northerly portion of this run, most of the banks exhibit fairly heavy development. In the Jacksonville Beach region, commercial businesses of all descriptions and several marinas line the Waterway. To the south, private residences overlook the ICW for several miles. On the Tolomato River section of the Waterway, much of the shoreline is in its natural state. All in all, this is a pleasant run, though numerous no-wake zones along the way may try the patience of power captains.

The Waterway follows its usual well-marked course to St. Augustine, but strong currents flow through this section of the ICW and demand more than the usual caution. Low-powered craft such as trawlers and sailboats should be on guard against excessive lateral leeway. Outside of the marked channel, depths quickly rise to grounding levels.

The Waterway is well sheltered around Jacksonville Beach, offering smooth passage, even in high winds. Heavy weather can raise a steep chop on Tolomato River, but cruising-size boats should still be able to track their way to the St. Augustine inlet without too many fillings being jarred out of captains' teeth.

There are numerous no-wake zones between Jacksonville Beach and St. Augustine. Most are amply marked, with signs saying, "Idle Speed—No Wake" at the beginning of each zone and "Resume Normal, Safe Operation" at the end of the restricted area. While these pests can play havoc with your cruising schedule, skippers are advised to observe the regulations. The Florida Marine Patrol is ever on guard throughout this stretch, and a stiff fine can ruin your day. The major no-wake zones will be outlined later in this chapter, but there have been frequent additions in recent years to these Waterway speed traps. Don't be surprised to find new restricted zones that have been added since the time of this writing.

With a single exception, there are no acceptable anchorages north of Spanish Landing at Standard Mile 764. Consequently, cruisers must either make use of the facilities around Jacksonville Beach or continue their trek south for a good distance before dropping the hook.

Jacksonville Beach

The northerly portion of the run from the St. Johns River to St. Augustine is dominated by the community of Jacksonville Beach. Two good marinas flank the Waterway along its run through Jacksonville Beach, but as mentioned above, one old friend is now lacking.

The One and Only Anchorage (Standard Mile 744) (30 19.709 North/081 26.212 West)

Just south of flashing daybeacon #17, a wide stream on the Waterway's eastern banks offers the only protected anchorage for many miles. The creek boasts minimum depths of 10 feet, with most of its waters considerably deeper. Its mostly undeveloped shores give excellent protection from all winds. This stream eventually runs south to a basin that used to serve Pelican Creek Marina (now long out of business), but there is plenty of room on the creek's northerly reaches for boats up to 38 feet to anchor in some 10 to 15 feet of water.

Don't attempt to cruise into or exit this anchorage by its alternate entrance east of

unlighted daybeacon #19 (charted on the current edition of 11489 as unlighted can buoy #19). This cut is quite shallow, even at high water.

Pablo Creek Marina (Standard Mile 744.5)

For many years Waterway cruisers counted on a stop at Pablo Creek Marina, just south of the 65-foot San Pablo Bridge. This facility used to be located in the charted harbor making into the ICW's westerly banks, opposite unlighted can buoy #19A.

Sadly, Pablo Creek has recently been destructed, preparatory to the beginning of a condominium development on this site. A conversation between this writer and one of the developers has given us some reason to believe that, when complete, the new complex may offer some services for visiting cruisers. However, in keeping with my longstanding policy of not reviewing a facility until I can inspect it personally, we will have nothing more to say about this new condo/marina here. Watch our free, on-line newsletter, the *Salty Southeast,* for updates. Remember, all you need do to subscribe to the *Salty Southeast* is to send an e-mail to opcom@cruisingguide.com containing the word "subscribe."

Palm Cove Marina (Standard Mile 747) (30 17.378 North/081 25.821 West)

The marked channel leading to shiny, new Palm Cove Marina makes off to the west at unlighted daybeacon #31. Waterway veterans will remember this site as the old location of Jacksonville Yacht Basin. Things have changed since those days. Transients are accepted at new, concrete-decked, floating piers featuring full 30- and 50-amp power and fresh-water connections. Unfortunately, low water-depths are now only at 4-foot levels, but Palm Cove is in the process of acquiring the necessary permits to dredge, and it is to be hoped that, as a result of this project, soundings will be much improved by the fall of 2004.

Gasoline, diesel fuel, waste pump-out, an on-site Laundromat, and climate-controlled, shoreside showers are also available. Mechanical servicing for gasoline power plants and haul-outs by way of a 35-ton travelift can be arranged through the on-site, independent contractor known as Isle of Palms Marine Service (904-821-0992). These seem to be genuinely nice folks. Give them a try!

Still not enough for you? Well, check on the marina ship's store and dive shop. A convenience store, deli, and shopping center are a scant block away. Clearly, Palm Cove has much to offer.

Palm Cove Marine (904) 223-4757
  http://www.palmcovemarina.com

Approach depths—4 feet MLW
Dockside depths—4 feet MLW
Accepts transients—yes
Transient dockage rate—average
Concrete floating docks—yes
Dockside power connections—30
  and 50 amps
Dockside water connections—yes
Showers—yes
Laundromat—yes
Gasoline—yes
Waste pump-out—yes
Diesel fuel—yes
Mechanical repairs—gasoline engines only
Below-waterline repairs—yes
Ship's store—yes
Restaurant—several within walking distance

Beach Marine (Standard Mile 748) (30 17.310 North/081 25.206 West)

Waterway cruisers will spy the clearly charted Beach Marine dockage basin on the Waterway's eastern banks, just north of the B. B. McCormick/Beach Boulevard Bridge and south of unlighted daybeacon #34.

Transients are eagerly accepted at Beach Marine's floating, wooden-decked piers fitted out with full power and water connections. Depths in the harbor run around 6 feet or better. Gasoline and diesel fuel are readily available, and waste pump-out service is offered as well. There are four full sets of showers on the marina's extensive grounds. Obviously, these good people are intent on allowing cruisers every opportunity to wash away the day's salty accumulation. A full Laundromat with a small paperback exchange library is located in the main

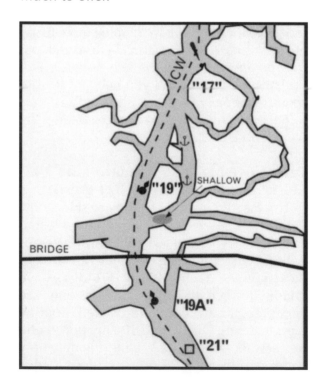

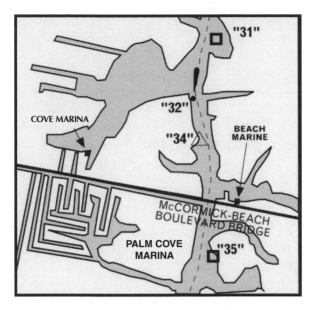

building, hard beside a small cruiser's lounge and a surprisingly well-equipped exercise room.

Service work at Beach Marine is performed by an independent operator that leases space from Beach Marine. The docks and work barns of the Boat Tree (904-249-0099) overlook the harbor's easterly tip. Mechanical repairs for both diesel and gasoline power plants are on hand, and boats can be hauled via a 20-ton travelift.

Beach Marine also features its own on-site restaurant, Billy's Boat House Grill (904-241-9771). We did not get to dine here, but we did check out the menu and were much impressed. Give it a try and let us know what you think!

Beach Marine (904) 249-8200
http://www.jaxbeachmarine.com

Approach depths—6-7 feet
Dockside depths—6-7 feet
Accepts transients—yes

Transient dockage rate—average
Floating wooden piers—yes
Dockside power connections—30 and 50 amps
Dockside water connections—yes
Showers—yes
Laundromat—yes
Waste pump-out—yes
Gasoline—yes
Diesel fuel—yes
Below-waterline repairs—yes
Mechanical repairs—yes
Ship's store—yes
Restaurant—on site

Palm Valley Cut No-Wake Zone (Standard Mile 750)

Immediately south of flashing daybeacon #48, one of the longest and strangest no-wake zones in all of Florida begins. Stretching for better than six statute miles from #48 to a point just south of the Palm Valley Bridge, this canal-like section of the Waterway actually borders on very few docks with boats in attendance. Why then is the no-wake zone necessary? Search me, dear reader. There is heavy residential development along the easterly banks, but few of these home support large craft in wet slips, and most residents seem to wisely keep their smaller vessels securely out of the water on davits.

As you might imagine, this is a very controversial, restricted speed zone. Some of "those in the know" in Jacksonville have told this writer for a fact that while, for some years, this no-wake zone was not really officially sanctioned, it has now been recognized by the Army Corps of Engineers. Others in the same region swear that it is still nothing more than a few signs erected by local boat owners. At this time, we cannot seem to resolve this schism of information. Sorry as I am to say it, we still suggest that you traverse this long stretch at slow speed.

Pine Island Loop Anchorage (Standard Mile 765) (30 03.059 North/081 21.951 West)

Some 14 nautical miles south of Jacksonville Beach (near Standard Mile 765), cruisers finally have the opportunity to anchor in relative security. A large creek makes into the eastern banks of the ICW immediately north of flashing daybeacon #23. This stream eventually loops Pine Island, rejoining the Waterway to the south at unlighted daybeacon #25. The creek's northern entrance at #23 is tricky and should not be attempted by strangers. However, the southerly mouth of the stream holds minimum 7-foot depths and is easily entered. Boats up to 48 feet can drop the hook with ample protection in the wide reaches of the

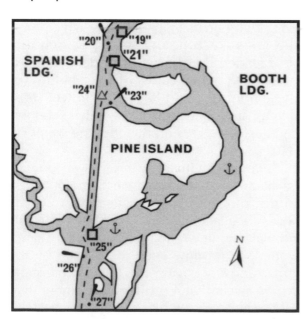

creek near the southern entrance. Adventurous skippers can follow the creek into its easterly reaches, but you must be careful to avoid several charted but unmarked shoals along the way. Also, swinging room on the rearward section of the loop is sufficient for anchorage only by craft up to 34 feet. Depths here run 8 to 9 feet in the unmarked channel. A good portion of the stream's shoreline is undeveloped saltwater marsh, with some higher ground to the east.

Shell Bluff Anchorage (Standard Mile 767.5) (30 01.342 North/081 20.977 West)

North-northwest of flashing daybeacon #35, chart 11489 correctly identifies a large patch of deep water bordering the northeastern shoreline. While it is quite open to strong northwestern and westerly blows, boats up to 36 feet can feel their way carefully north-northwest from #35 and drop the hook within 50 yards or so of the northeastern banks. You will be exposed to the wake of passing vessels, and there is an unmarked shoal that must be avoided when you enter. Frankly, there are better anchorages not far to the north and south, but if darkness is quickly coming on, you might consider spending the night here.

Open Anchorages (Standard Mile 769) (Various Lats/Lons—see below)

Look at 11485 and note the deepwater channel running to the northwest, east and northeast of flashing daybeacon #41. Cruising captains in need of immediate anchorage can drop the hook near 30 00.061 North/081 20.231 West, but protection is sufficient only in light to moderate breezes. There is enough swinging room for boats up to 40 feet. You will be buffeted by the wake of all passing boats, and a westerly wind could raise a most unwelcome chop. Given its tricky entrance, this anchorage should only be used when there is some good reason not to continue.

Alternately, you might try easing in toward the eastern banks from flashing daybeacon #44 (Standard Mile 769.5, 29 59.782 North/081 19.874 West). During an earlier cruise through these waters, we observed two sailcraft anchored snugly on these waters. Good depths of 10 feet or better run to within 75 to 100 yards of the easterly shoreline. Avoid the charted submerged pile area just to the north. Protection is good in easterly and southeasterly breezes, and fair during westerly and southwesterly winds. Strong blows from the northwest or the south are quite another story. As with the anchorage detailed above, you will be exposed to the wake of all passing vessels.

Guana River (Standard Mile 770.5) (Various Lats/Lons—see below)

The westerly reaches of unspoiled Guana River intersect the ICW's easterly banks, south of flashing daybeacon #45. While this stream can serve as a very protected anchorage for boats as large as 40 feet, the river's entrance is navigationally difficult and should only be attempted by devil-may-care skippers piloting boats that draw 4 feet or preferably less. Minimum depths in the channel run about 5 feet with low-water soundings of 6 to 9 feet typical. However, an errant trip outside of the scantily marked channel can quickly land you in 1 to 2 feet of water.

If you do make it past the tricky entrance, consider anchoring on the midwidth of the river, upstream of its first swing to the north, near 29 59.612 North/081 19.304 West.

Here boats up to 45 feet will find plenty of swinging room with fair protection in 6½- to 8-foot depths.

Better shelter can be found farther upstream, where the charted, high ground borders the river on its western banks (near 30 00.019 North/081 19.583 West). Unfortunately, the river narrows and swinging room is sufficient only for boats up to 34 feet. If this restriction is not a problem, you could ride out a heavy blow anchored snugly in this spot, always supposing you get past the difficult entrance.

Farther upriver, good depths continue to within 200 yards of a dam that blocks the Guana's upper reaches. Larger cruising craft would be well advised to discontinue their exploration long before reaching this point.

Cap's Seafood Restaurant (Standard Mile 773.5)

East of unlighted daybeacon #52, passing

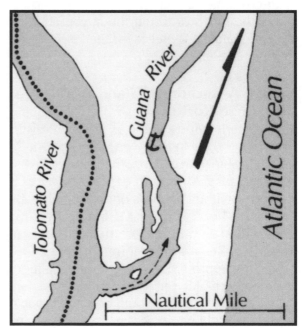

mariners will note the single, low-level floating dock of Cap's Seafood Restaurant (904-824-8794). Visiting craft are welcome to tie up while dining. The pier features minimum 5½- to 6-foot depths, and there should be enough room to squeeze in one 38-footer.

Let's not beat around the bush with this one. Don't let Cap's modest exterior fool you. It serves some of the best seafood that you will ever enjoy. While good old fried and broiled catch of the day is certainly available, many of the seafood and landlubber dishes are sophisticated concoctions that seem to have been prepared in paradise. The Shrimp Etouffée, Shrimp and Scallops Sauté, and Mediterranean Catch are to die for. This last dish consists of whatever fish of the day is freshest, sautéed with olives, capers, feta cheese, and marinara sauce, served on a bed of pasta. Yuuummm! We have never been disappointed with a selection at Cap's, and we hazard to assert that you won't be either. If your cruise takes you anywhere near Cap's at either the lunch or dinner hour, you couldn't do your palate a better favor than tarrying for an hour or two.

Waterway Anchorage (Standard Mile 775) (29 55.628 North/081 18.247 West)

In easterly winds, some Waterway cruisers drop their hooks in the deep water just southeast of flashing daybeacon #55, near the river's eastern banks. Minimum depths of 8 feet are carried to within 50 yards of the shoreline. Be sure your hook is well set before heading below to start dinner. The tidal currents in Tolomato River are nothing to sneeze at. While not appropriate in strong or even moderate breezes blowing from any other than an easterly direction, this would be a good spot to spend the night while waiting for the morning

light to navigate tricky St. Augustine Inlet and the adjacent Waterway channel.

Camachee Cove Yacht Harbor (Standard Mile 775.5) (29 55.061 North/081 18.518 West)

Look to the west-southwest, just south of unlighted daybeacon #57, and you will quickly spot a collection of unlighted daybeacons leading to the well-sheltered dockage basin at Camachee Cove Yacht Harbor. Camachee Cove is another of those large, incredibly well-appointed facilities that seem to abound in eastern Florida. Boasting every imaginable service and convenience for transient cruisers, along with ultramodern dockage, this facility also has the deserved reputation for assisting visitors in every way. Few will count a stay at Camachee Cove as anything but a pleasant experience.

Camachee Cove welcomes cruising visitors to an extensive array of transient slips. Dockage is at modern, concrete-decked, floating piers with full power and water connections, including 100-amp service. Captains can now expect low-water entrance and dockside depths of 6 to 8 feet. The harbor is very well sheltered from all winds and would make a good spot to ride out really heavy weather. Gasoline and diesel fuel are readily available at the marina's fuel dock.

Shoreside, cruisers will discover top-notch, climate-controlled showers spread about the marina grounds in three separate locations. There is also an extensive on-site Laundromat alongside an extra-nice, air-conditioned cruiser's lounge, featuring free coffee, a weather computer, color television, and paperback exchange library. On-line captains can even check their e-mail here by way of a special hookup.

Full mechanical repairs for both gasoline

and diesel engines are offered by Camachee Yacht Yard (904-823-3641), one of the many, independent marine firms located within the yachting complex. This facility is found at the southerly tip of the yacht harbor. The yard has a 37-ton trovelift for haul-outs.

If you need marine supplies or repairs, this writer suggests that you make the acquaintance of First Mate Yacht Services (904-824-9300). Their building overlooks the eastern shores of the harbor, south of the entrance. In addition to offering an unusually complete collection of nautical hardware and publications in their ship's store, First Mate also provides service work on marine generators and engines (gas and diesel). E-mail can be checked for a nominal charge of $1.50 per use. We have found the personnel at First Mate to be extrafriendly and ready to go that extra mile to be sure that the job is done right.

A chain of retail shops fronts the Camachee Cove dockage basin to the south. Here, you will find a surprisingly good selection of foodstuffs, a few nautical items, and some truly

Camachee Cove Yacht Harbor

yummy deli sandwiches, plus homemade soups at the Camachee Cove Market (904-824-3780). If you have the need for any fishing gear, check out the adjacent Hook, Line and Sinker Bait and Tackle Shop (904-829-6073).

Camachee Cove has just one on-site restaurant, but it's a good one. Peerces Café (904-823-1188) serves lunch and dinner Monday through Saturday, and Sunday brunch. The crab cakes, and particularly the crab soup, are awesome.

For those who would like to take a break for a night or two from the live-aboard routine, The Inn at Camachee Cove (904-825-0003) is conveniently located on the yacht harbor's grounds. We have never had the opportunity to visit here, but have been told that the accommodations are absolutely first rate.

Cruisers looking to charter a sailcraft in the St. Augustine region can contact St. Augustine Sailing (800-683-7245), also located at Camachee Cove. This firm offers sailing vessels from 30 to 40 feet for charter and instruction.

Still not convinced? Well, consider that Camachee Cove is home to the St. Augustine Yacht Club (904-824-9725). This salty organization was originally chartered in 1876, and it remains one of the most venerable yacht clubs in eastern Florida (fourth oldest in the U.S.). Visitors who are members of other yacht clubs with appropriate reciprocal agreements are accepted for dockage and clubhouse privileges. Transient berths are very limited, and the club requires that potential visitors contact the club's manager to make slip arrangements at least 24 hours in advance. The St. Augustine Yacht Club does not employ a regular dockmaster. Showers are available in the clubhouse

and there is an adjacent swimming pool. The club dining room is open for lunch Wednesday through Saturday, and in the evening Friday and Saturday. There is also a Sunday brunch.

All but the most dedicated hikers will find the St. Augustine historic district too far away for walking from Camachee Cove. Call Ace Taxi at 904-824-6888.

Well, are you as tired out from reading about the many attractions at Camachee Cove as this writer is from noting them down for you? Suffice it to say that if you can't find it here, better give some thought to leaving the cruising life behind. There are no marinas in eastern Florida, to this writer's knowledge, that offer more services and amenities than Camachee Cove.

Camachee Cove Yacht Harbor
   (904) 829-5676
   (800) 345-9269
   http://www.Camacheeisland.com

Approach depths—6-8 feet (minimum)
Dockside depths—6-8 feet (minimum)
Accepts transients—yes
Transient dockage rate—above average
Floating concrete piers—yes
Dockside power connections—30,
   50, and 100 amps
Dockside water connections—yes
Showers—yes
Laundromat—yes
Gasoline—yes
Diesel fuel—yes
Below-waterline repairs—yes
Mechanical repairs—yes
Ship's and variety store—yes
Restaurant—on site

ST JOHNS RIVER TO ST AUGUSTINE NAVIGATION

While well marked and straightforward, the ICW route from the St. Johns River to St. Augustine Inlet does call for caution. Strong tidal currents can set you outside of the channel into shallow water far more quickly than you might expect. You must make corrections for excessive leeway immediately, before you reach shoal water.

These same currents can be a problem if you have to wait along the way for a bridge to open. Fortunately, all but one of the spans north of St. Augustine have been replaced by fixed, high-rise structures. This happy state of affairs is not true for the B. B. McCormick/Beach Boulevard span, which remains a bascule structure with 37 feet of closed vertical clearance.

Low-powered craft can all too easily be swept into the surrounding shallows while waiting for the sometimes slow bridge operator to open this span. Sound your signal well in advance and try to time your arrival to coincide with the bridge opening. This is a lot easier said than done, but it is a great way to avoid any problems.

This is a not the place to doze at the wheel. Keep alert, watch your stern as well as the track ahead, and you should come through with nothing worse than a sunburn.

Entry from St. Johns River   After leaving the mouth of Sisters Creek, angle your course to the south-southeast across the main body of the St. Johns River, and point to come between unlighted nun buoy #2 and flashing daybeacon #1. Be ready for strong tidal currents between Sisters Creek and the gap between #1 and #2. The moving waters will attempt to sweep you up- or downriver, depending on the set of the tide.

Stay away from flashing daybeacon #1. This aid to navigation is set on the outer tip of a rock breakwater that protects the channel's northeasterly flank. At or near low tide, this jetty is obvious, but it partially covers at high water.

A long, manatee no-wake zone begins at #1 and #2 and stretches south to flashing daybeacon #9 and unlighted daybeacon #8. Proceed strictly at idle speed through this current-plagued section of the Waterway.

Once between #1 and #2, continue on the same track, coming abeam and passing unlighted daybeacon #5 to its southwesterly side. Unlighted daybeacon #5 sits southwest of the rock breakwater, not directly on top of this structure as does #1. You should eventually come abeam of flashing daybeacon #6 to its easterly quarter.

Once abeam of #6, the Waterway cuts to the south-southeast. Set a new course to pass unlighted daybeacon #7 to its westerly side and then come between unlighted daybeacon #8 and flashing daybeacon #9. Near #8 you should spot a "Resume Normal, Safe Operation" sign.

This stretch has chronic shoaling problems and strong tidal currents. Don't be surprised to find additional markers leading you south into the Waterway canal. Take your time, watch the sounder, and check your course over your stern as well as the track ahead to catch quickly any leeway.

South to Jacksonville Beach   South-southeast of unlighted daybeacon #8 and flashing daybeacon #9, the ICW follows a long, canal-like passage leading to Jacksonville Beach. There are only a few markers along the way north of the San Pablo/Atlantic Boulevard Bridge. Stick to midwidth, as both shorelines are shoal.

North of unlighted daybeacon #12, two small, privately maintained daybeacons mark a tiny channel cutting in to the westerly banks. This small cut leads to several private docks. Visiting cruisers are advised to keep clear.

After coming abeam of unlighted daybeacon #12 to its easterly side, follow a careful course to the south, designed to come abeam of the next southerly aid, unlighted daybeacon #13, to its immediate western side. Both sides of the channel are particularly shoal between #12 and #13.

The One and Only Anchorage   South of flashing daybeacon #17 you will soon catch sight of the large stream on the eastern shore that provides the only safe anchorage in the Jacksonville Beach region. Enter on the midwidth. For best shelter, set the hook before cruising too far south into the old marina anchorage basin. Don't attempt to rejoin the Waterway via the charted entrance (from the anchorage), south of unlighted daybeacon #19 (charted as unlighted can buoy #19 on the current edition of 11489).

On the ICW   The Waterway channel just north (and south) of the San Pablo/Atlantic Boulevard Bridge, south of flashing daybeacon #17, is subject to continual shoaling. Over the past decade the Army Corps of

Engineers has changed and rechanged the markers north of the bridge at dizzying speed. Sometimes a floating buoy has marked the eastern side of the channel, at other times it has been an unlighted daybeacon. At the time of this writing the latest edition of chart 11489 shows an unlighted can buoy #19 on the easterly flank of the channel. On-site research revealed an unlighted daybeacon #19 in place at this time, but you may well find some different form of marker when you arrive.

In any case, it is critically important that you pass well to the west of #19, or any other green, odd-numbered aid that you find present. There is very shallow water to the east. On the water, you may also note that unlighted daybeacon #19 seems much farther from the eastern shoreline than a cursory study of chart 11489 might lead you to believe. Apparently the shoal it marks is building outward continually. Slow down as you approach the San Pablo/Atlantic Boulevard Bridge and make sure to pick out any aids to navigation before proceeding. Be on guard against this region's usual swift tidal currents as you approach and pass under the bridge.

Just north of the San Pablo span, a large commercial barge facility will come abeam on the western shore. You are certainly free to look, but pleasure craft are advised not to enter this busy basin.

The San Pablo/Atlantic Boulevard Bridge is a fixed span with 65 feet of vertical clearance. However, we have been informed by fellow cruisers that this bridge has, at least as of late 2003, a height gauge (also known as a "height board") that is wrong. In our online newsletter, the *Salty Southeast,* we recently presented an account of a sailboat with a 65-foot mast that spotted the gauge, showing a clearance of only 59 feet, and tried to reverse their course. The craft was not able to stop and went under the bridge sideways with 6 inches to spare. Perhaps this errant board will be removed by the time of your arrival, perhaps not.

Trouble Spot   The ICW channel just south of the San Pablo/Atlantic Boulevard Bridge is subject to shoaling and can be a ready source of difficulty. Older versions of chart 11489 may show an unlighted daybeacon #20 just south of the span. This aid has been gone for some time now and navigators will now discover an unlighted can buoy #19A marking the channel's easterly flank. Be sure to pass west and southwest of #19A.

Shoaling has also encroached on unlighted daybeacon #21 south of the bridge. Don't approach this aid closely. Pass #21 by at least 20 yards to its southwesterly side.

Even if you follow the above procedure faithfully, don't be surprised to see some 8-foot readings on your sounder. Proceed at idle speed and be ready to take corrective action if depths start to rise. The Corps of Engineers dredges this trouble spot regularly, but the problems reappear between maintenance cycles.

On to Jacksonville Beach   The channel between the San Pablo/Atlantic Boulevard and B. B. McCormick/Beach Boulevard spans is well marked and easily traveled. Southeast of unlighted daybeacon #23, the ICW passes under an overhead power cable with 90 feet of clearance.

West of flashing daybeacon #32, you will spot the channel leading to Palm Cove Marina. Remember, at the time of this writing, this cut only carries 4 feet of water at low tide. Hopefully, dredging will soon deepen these soundings, but we suggest that captains piloting vessels that draw more than 3½ feet call the marina dockmaster ahead of time to check on current depths.

South of flashing daybeacon #32, slow to idle speed. No-wake regulations are in effect as far as unlighted daybeacon #35, south of the B. B. McCormick/Beach Boulevard Bridge. These prohibitions protect the dockage facilities clustered around the bridge. Remember, you are legally responsible for any damage caused by your wake.

South of unlighted daybeacon #34 and just north of the B. B. McCormick/Beach Boulevard span, Beach Marine will come abeam to the east. If you enter, hold to the midwidth of the marina channel. The dockmaster's office will be spotted to starboard, perched on the outer tip of a large floating dock, near the western side of the complex.

The B. B. McCormick/Beach Boulevard span has a closed vertical clearance of 37 feet and, to make life a little more interesting, it has restrictive opening hours for some of the busiest boating months. Currently, the bridge opens on demand except during the months of April, May, October, and November. If you happen to be cruising through during these months, the span opens only on the hour and half-hour from 7:00 A.M. to 9:00 A.M. and between 4:30 P.M. and 6:30 P.M., Monday through Friday. On Saturdays, Sundays, and federal holidays, during the restricted months, the bridge opens on the hour and half-hour from noon to 6:00 P.M. At all other times the span does condescend to open on demand. Most power craft will be able to proceed without having to bother with a bridge opening. However, sailors are faced with a very different situation. Swift currents can quickly sweep unwary sailing skippers onto either shore, or—perish the thought—into the bridge itself. Approach with caution and be ready to take immediate action if your craft is caught by the current.

On the ICW   As you move farther south from the B. B. McCormick/Beach Boulevard span, numerous streams flank both shores of the Waterway for several miles along the way. Without exception, these are shallow and should not be entered. We have been lured into several of these cuts by the sight of large craft moored to private piers. Too late, the extra dings in our prop told us that they must have entered at high water.

Just south of flashing daybeacon #44, the Waterway passes under the fixed J. Turner Butler Bridge with 65 feet of vertical clearance. This span does not present any problems.

The controversial 6-mile no-wake zone discussed above begins at flashing daybeacon #48 and restricts speed to a point just south of the Palm Valley span. Slow to idle speed and muse on Waterway politics!

Be on guard against a very prominent shoal shelving out from the ICW's easterly banks, opposite flashing daybeacon #48. Favor #48 and the western side of the Waterway channel a bit in order to stay well clear of this hazard.

The Palm Valley Bridge comes up south of unlighted daybeacon #2. While still charted as a 9-foot bascule structure, this span is now a fixed 65-footer.

Just north of the Palm Valley span, passing cruisers will sight a long face dock associated with Annie's Palm Valley Crossing restaurant abutting the easterly banks. Don't attempt to tie up. Depths are absolutely nil at low water.

The ICW's southward track past the Palm Valley Bridge is easily navigable into the headwaters of the Tolomato River. The first good anchorage south of Jacksonville Beach comes up on the ICW's easterly banks at unlighted daybeacon #25.

Pine Island Loop   Remember to enter the Pine Island loop creek only by its southern entrance. Cruise south of unlighted daybeacon #25 on the Waterway channel for a short distance, and then turn immediately into the loop stream's entrance, favoring the northern shore a bit. Craft over 32 feet should consider dropping the hook on these waters.

Adventurous captains piloting smaller boats may choose to continue around to the eastern portion of the loop. If you attempt this passage, begin favoring the starboard banks slightly as you approach the finger of marsh sweeping west from the southern shore of the charted marsh island. Be sure to pass south of this marsh. Very shallow water lies south of the grass. As you cruise into the loop's easterly extreme, reenter the midwidth. The best spot to drop the hook on this stretch is where the high ground south of Booth Landing comes closest to the creek's eastern shores.

Don't attempt to reenter the ICW through the loop's northerly entrance. Numerous unmarked shoals make this passage too difficult unless you have specific local knowledge.

On the ICW South of unlighted daybeacon #25, the ICW exchanges greetings with Tolomato River. Southbound ICW cruisers will follow this body of water to St. Augustine.

The Waterway channel between unlighted daybeacon #29 and flashing daybeacon #35 calls for caution. Chart 11489 correctly portrays a finger of shallow water encroaching on unlighted daybeacon #30 to the west and a similar shoal to the north of unlighted daybeacon #33. The shallows near #33 appear to be building ominously. To avoid these shallows, pass #30 by a good margin to its easterly side and #33 by about the same distance to its westerly quarter. Don't approach either aid closely and you should pass through unscathed.

Flashing daybeacon #35 is often difficult to spot, and it is all too easy for careless navigators to drift into the shallow water to the northeast. Use your binoculars to pick out #35 and pass it well to its southwestern side.

Shell Bluff Anchorage To enter the deep-water bubble north-northwest of flashing daybeacon #35, come abeam of this aid to its southwesterly side. Turn straight in toward the northeastern banks and head directly for #35. Just before reaching the beacon, swing 90 degrees to the north-northwest and follow the shoreline into the anchorage. Stay at least 50 yards but no farther than 100 yards away from the shore and you will avoid the charted shallows to the west and southwest. If depths should start to rise as you enter the anchorage, give way to the east and northeast. This should place you back into deeper water unless you are in the shallows close by the northeastern shoreline.

On the ICW The run south from flashing daybeacon #36 to unlighted daybeacon #37 is a long one. Use your binoculars to pick out #37 and be sure to come abeam of this aid well to its westerly side. At #37, the channel turns to the southeast, and borders a long shoal to the north and northeast. At this point, it's time to retire our old friend chart 11489, and break out 11485.

Southeast of #37, favor the southern and southwestern side of the channel slightly, and be sure to pass southwest of unlighted daybeacon #39 and flashing daybeacon #41 to avoid this hazard. From #41, point to come abeam of unlighted daybeacon #42 to its fairly immediate northeasterly side. Shoal water continues to flank the Waterway to the north between #41 and #42.

Open Anchorages Come abeam of flashing daybeacon #44 before turning into the eastern banks. Carefully feel your way toward the banks, making sure not to approach the shoreline any closer than 100 yards. You can anchor here or attempt the tongue of deep water to the northwest. If you choose this latter haven, turn again, this time to the northwest, and cruise into the patch of deep water to the east and northeast of #41. Proceed at idle speed and keep a weather eye on the sounder. This is a tricky procedure for larger vessels and demands extra caution.

Guana River Remember, it is difficult to enter Guana River and only bold captains who pilot craft less than 36 feet long that draw less than 4 feet should attempt it. Feel your way carefully through the entrance and maintain a steady watch on your sounder to avoid an unpleasant grounding.

Chart 11485 denotes several small private markers that supposedly outline the channel into Guana River. Some of these doubtful aids to navigation, consisting of white PVC pipes, have been present during our various visits to this stream, and some have not! Even those that were there could not be relied upon to provide channel markings for visiting cruisers, and none have ever looked very permanent. I suggest that you use these markers with a healthy helping of skepticism.

Enter the river's mouth by favoring the southern shore. You may or may not see a small private marker that defines the northern edge of the channel. As you begin to approach the first cove to the south, start edging back toward the midwidth of the passage between the southern banks and the charted marsh island that bisects the river's entrance. You should be back on the centerline by the time the northeastern tip of this small landmass comes abeam to the northwest.

Continue on the middle ground as you follow the river through its sharp turn to the north. As the river straightens on its passage to the north, good water opens out in a fairly wide swath along the stream's midsection. Larger boats would do well to anchor here.

Cruisers continuing farther upstream should begin favoring the westerly side of the river some 200 yards before coming abeam of the charted high ground on the western banks. As chart 11485 shows, a long slice of shallow water and marsh sits astride the midwidth of the Guana River in this area. The waters abeam of the high ground offer maximum protection if your craft can stand the reduced swinging room.

On the ICW   South of Guana River, the ICW continues mostly deep and readily navigable to the Vilano Beach Bridge. A large patch of shallow water abuts the Waterway's northeastern flank between flashing daybeacons #48 and #49. Be sure to come abeam and pass #49 well to its southwesterly side.

Waterway Anchorage   If the weather is fair, and you choose to anchor in the waters near flashing daybeacon #55, feel your way carefully toward the eastern banks. Good depths of 6 feet or (usually) more are held to within 50 yards of the shoreline, north of #55.

On the ICW   South of unlighted daybeacon #57, the well-marked channel leading west-southwest to Camachee Cove will come abeam. This cut is currently outlined by a whole series of unlighted daybeacons, and it also features a set of lighted (shoreside) range markers. The northern flank is protected by a rock breakwater, nearer to shore. Simply cruise between the various markers and keep on the range, always remembering your good old red, right, returning rule. The harbor entrance will soon be obvious dead ahead.

A bit farther south of #57, the Waterway exchanges greetings with the Vilano Beach Bridge. This fixed, high-rise span has a welcome vertical clearance of 65 feet.

The ICW rushes south from the Vilano

bridge to St. Augustine Inlet and Matanzas River. This stretch suffers from chronic shoaling problems. Be sure to read the navigation information presented in the upcoming section of this chapter before beginning your approach to St. Augustine.

St. Augustine

. . . the first 256 years after the founding of St. Augustine, the major occurrences in and around that place were largely a part and parcel of the history of Florida. . . . For more than seventy-five years after 1565, the settlement founded by Menendez was the chief American outpost held by a European nation north of Mexico, and for more than one hundred years it was the chief center from which the red men were influenced or controlled.

This description of St. Augustine's role in Florida history appears in W. T. Cash's *The Story of Florida*. It is entirely apt. One cannot read the early history of Florida without coming across constant references to St. Augustine and the events that transpired around the coquina walls of the Castillo de San Marcos. This imposing structure has guarded the approaches to St. Augustine since the late seventeenth century.

Visitors who stroll the parapet of the Castillo or the recreated Spanish village on St. George Street cannot but come away with a pervasive sense of this timeless city's remarkable past. Many Americans think of their colonial history as exclusively English in origin. A visit to St. Augustine demonstrates that the Spanish also had a significant influence in those early times.

Today, St. Augustine stands ready to greet visitors with a wide array of motels, lodges, restaurants and, of course, its historical attractions. Marinas are fairly numerous, and one particularly notable facility offers ready access to the historical district. Cruisers could easily dock at St. Augustine for a week and not begin to exhaust the city's offerings.

Numbers to know in St. Augustine:
Ace Taxi—904-824-6888
Avis Rent A Car—904-829-3700
Enterprise Rent-A-Car—904-829-1662
First Mate Yacht Services—904-824-9300
Sea Tow—904-824-9969
Chamber of Commerce—904-829-5681
St. Augustine Visitor's Center—
   904-825-1000

St. Augustine Waters

The waters of St. Augustine had more than a little to do with the city's prominence in early Florida history. Take a few moments when you

Castillo de San Marcos, St. Augustine

visit the Castillo de San Marcos to ascend the tall watchtower facing St. Augustine Inlet. First look northeast and note the inlet's wide passage, which leads directly to the open sea. Now look to your right and notice the broad, protected harbor formed by the northern headwaters of Matanzas River. With this view in mind, you can readily understand why St. Augustine was a natural settlement for the early Spanish colonists, and a central point of government and commerce thereafter.

St. Augustine Inlet (Standard Mile 776.5)

This inlet falls somewhere between those treacherous seaward cuts that are best bypassed and those inlets that are well charted and relatively easy to run. Aids to navigation are not charted in St. Augustine Inlet, as they are frequently shifted to follow the ever-changing channel. Swift currents scour the cut with each tide, and all vessels must be on guard against leeway that could set them outside of the channel and result in a dangerous grounding. When wind and tide oppose each other, the inlet can spawn a very healthy chop. By all accounts this inlet is a real bear in strong easterly blows.

On the other hand, the inlet is used regularly by local captains and appears to be well marked. If you do plan to cruise seaward, stop at one of the local marinas and inquire about the latest conditions on the cut. Even better, watch for a local fisherman putting out to sea and follow in his wake.

St. Augustine waterfront

The intersection of the ICW and St. Augustine Inlet is a very real problem stretch. The shoal west of unlighted nun buoys #58E and #60 seem to be building ever to the east. Be sure to read the navigational account below before attempting the ICW passage across St. Augustine Inlet.

Salt Run (Standard Mile 776.5) (Various Lats/Lons—see below)

Salt Run is a long, narrow body of mostly deep water that separates Conch and Anastasia islands south of the St. Augustine Inlet. The run has minimum depths of 5½ to 7 feet in its prolifically marked channel, but patches of shallows are found on the entrance's southwesterly flank with less than 3 feet of water. There are now many more aids to navigation marking the Salt Run cut than are pictured on the current edition of chart 11485. Craft as large as 45 feet, piloted by cautious skippers, should be able to enter this stream with minimal problems.

Salt Run features two anchorages and one marina facility. Conch House Marina Resort lines the western shores of Salt Run, just to the northwest of unlighted daybeacon #14, near 29 53.722 North/081 17.745 West. This is a friendly, first-rate facility. Transients are gratefully accepted for overnight or temporary dockage at mostly floating, concrete-decked piers with full power and water connections. Depths alongside run 8+ feet on the outer piers and 7+ feet at the innermost slips. Good showers and a Laundromat are found on the docks. Gasoline and diesel fuel are available, and a small but well-stocked ship's and variety store is located on the docks, sharing its headquarters with the dockmaster's office. Cruisers will find a convenient paperback exchange library in the ship's store. Some mechanical

repairs can be arranged through independent contractors.

If you arrive at Conch House Marina hungry, you are indeed a fortunate cruiser. If the mood strikes, you might first want to slake your thirst at the lounge built directly on the docks. This watering hole is found only a short step away from the slips and is most convenient.

For heartier appetites, Conch House Restaurant overlooks the marina docks from the shore. This dining spot has a reputation far and wide for serving good seafood. It is quite popular, with long waits on weekends. We found the food to be very good, but the rates could not be described as inexpensive. Free dockage is available to dining patrons who do not plan on an overnight stay.

Should you want to spend a night ashore, the adjacent Conch House motel is ideal. Here you will find a cooling swimming pool open to both motel guests and visiting cruisers.

So, it does not require too much imagination to discern that Conch House Marina Resort is a well-appointed, friendly facility that many Waterway veterans visit time and time again. You would not do badly to imitate their practice.

Conch House Marina Resort (904) 824-4347
http://www.conch-house.com/marina.htm

Approach depths—8+ feet
Dockside depths—7+ feet
Accepts transients—yes
Transient dockage rate—above average
Floating concrete piers—yes (mostly)
Dockside power connections—30
   and 50 amps
Dockside water connections—yes

Showers—yes

Laundromat—yes

Gasoline—yes

Diesel fuel—yes

Mechanical repairs—limited
    (independent contractors)

Ship's and variety store—yes

Restaurant—on site

Farther south on Salt Run, some craft anchor around unlighted daybeacon #14, just off of the main channel (near 29 53.518

North/081 17.389 West). This is the smaller of the two anchorages, and we have seldom seen more than two or three boats swinging on the hook here at one time. Depths run 5½ to 6 feet, and there is only enough room for vessels as large as 40 feet to swing comfortably. As with both anchorages on Salt Run, there is good protection to the east and west, and fair shelter to the south. Strong winds from the northwest could make this haven less than ideal. The westerly banks are overlooked by moderate residential development, and the

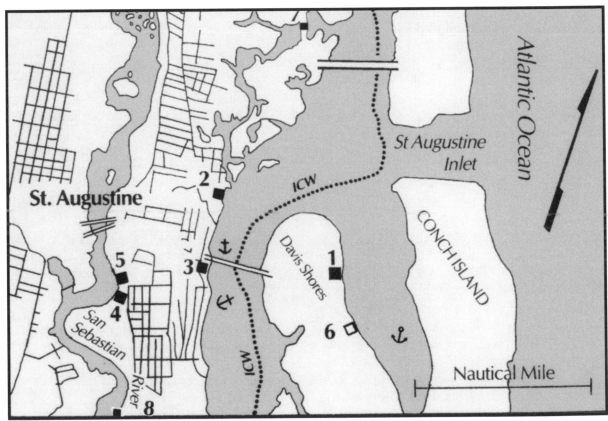

1 Conch House Marina Resort

2 Castillo de San Marcos

3 St. Augustine City Marina

4 Harry Xynides Boat Yard

5 Oasis Boat Yard

6 St. Augustine Lighthouse

7 Camachee Cove Yacht Harbor

8 St. Augustine Marine

St. Augustine Lighthouse

tall eye of the St. Augustine Lighthouse is readily visible to the south. The easterly shoreline is completely in its natural state.

Most skippers anchoring in Salt Run make use of the waters south of unlighted daybeacon #15, near 29 53.363 North/081 17.179 West. Here, a fairly large bubble of 6- to 8-foot water stretches from the channel well in toward the eastern banks. During our last visit, there must have been two dozen vessels of various sizes and types anchored in this haven. Holding ground seems to be good, and, again, there is good shelter from all but strong northwesterly blows. Shoreside scenery is very much as described in the haven above, with the St. Augustine Lighthouse still quite visible.

Cruisers plying the waters of upper Salt Run will quickly catch sight of the 161-foot St. Augustine Lighthouse gazing serenely over the eastern banks of Anastasia Island. This old landmark is sure to remind mariners from North Carolina of the famous Cape Hatteras Lighthouse. They are both painted with a black and white spiral design. Cruisers interested in a closer look can safely cruise on the run's midwidth until the lighthouse comes abeam to starboard.

The St. Augustine Lighthouse is open to the public, and, after paying a modest fee, visitors can ascend its winding stairs for a breathtaking view of St. Augustine and the surrounding waters. Call the St. Augustine Lighthouse and Museum (904-829-0745, lighthouse@staug.org) for more information. Unfortunately, the lighthouse is much too far from the water and any available dockage for walking. Take a taxi. It's really worth the additional effort and expense.

While good depths do continue south of the lighthouse, you will encounter shoal water well short of the shallows shown on chart 11485.

Approach to St. Augustine
The ICW turns sharply to the west-southwest just southeast of unlighted nun buoy #2 and flows quickly to the St. Augustine waterfront. Along the way, you will undoubtedly spot a huge cross overlooking the northwestern shore, near flashing daybeacon #6. This impressive stainless steel structure is a part of Our Lady of la Leche shrine. The cross commemorates the place where the Spanish conquistador Menendez and his followers first celebrated Mass on the shores of Florida. It was later the site of the Nombre de Dios mission, the first Roman Catholic mission established in the land that would one day become the United States.

St. Augustine Facilities and Anchorages (Standard Mile 778) (Various Lats/Lons— see below)

As you round the turn from flashing daybeacon #6, the Castillo de San Marcos will be prominent to the west, while the Bridge of Lions crosses your course dead ahead. You can anchor just north of the bridge in the deep water that abuts the western banks (near 29 53.776 North/081 18.587 West). Minimum depths of 8 feet or more are held to within 100 feet of the concrete seawall. Unfortunately, there are no dinghy docking facilities in the immediate area. To go ashore, you will have to make a fairly long dinghy trip south to the city marina.

This anchorage is far more open to foul weather than its counterpart south of the Bridge of Lions (see below). Also, captains anchoring their craft on these waters might very well want to set two anchors. Dragging anchor into the nearby Bridge of Lions does not bear contemplation.

The St. Augustine City Marina (Standard Mile 778, 29 53.530 North/081 18.513 West)

St. Augustine anchorage, north of Bridge of Lions

overlooks the western shoreline, just south of the Bridge of Lions. Visitors will discover modern, concrete, floating piers with all power and water connections. In particularly strong blows from the north or south, the waters can get bumpy in the slips, but in most weather, you are reasonably well protected. Be on guard against strong tidal currents as you approach the marina's piers.

Transients are readily accepted, and slip space for visitors is extensive. Nevertheless, considering the popularity of this marina, it might be best to make advance reservations, particularly during the spring and fall snowbird seasons. Good, climate-controlled showers and an air-conditioned, full-service Laundromat are found in the dockmaster's building on the mainland side of the piers. It is a bit of a walk from your slip to this building, but most mariners will not find this to be a great problem. An excellent ship's store, under the auspices of First Mate Yacht Services (904-824-9300), whom we first met in our discussion of Camachee Cove Yacht Harbor above, is also located in this building. This firm is highly recommended by this writer if you are in need

of anything in the way of nautical equipment or service work. Gasoline and diesel fuel can be purchased at the marina's outermost dock, and waste pump-out services are also available on this pier. Mechanical repairs can be arranged through First Mate Yacht Services.

St. Augustine City Marina also features a climate-controlled cruiser's lounge. Surprisingly, there is not a paperback exchange library located here, but you will find just such a useful service in First Mate Yacht Services. The marina provides a most useful dinghy dock (see below), which is a wonderful service to the many vessels that regularly choose to anchor off on the immediately adjacent waters.

Of course, one of St. Augustine City Marina's principal advantages is the facility's location within the heart of the city's historical district. This can also be a real advantage come dinnertime. There are many excellent dining choices within easy walking distance. Consult the review of St. Augustine restaurants below. If you should need motorized land transportation, call Ace Taxi at (904) 824-6888, Enterprise Rent-A-Car at (904) 829-1662, or Avis Rent A Car at (904) 829-3700.

St. Augustine City Marina provides the only readily available transient dockage within walking distance of the St. Augustine historic district. This fortunate location, coupled with the marina's excellent services, should be enough to call for making a red circle on any cruiser's chart.

St. Augustine City Marina (904) 825-1026

Approach depths—10+ feet
Dockside depths—7 feet
Accepts transients—yes
Transient dockage rate—above average
Floating concrete piers—yes

St. Augustine City Marina

Dockside power connections—30
and 50 amps
Dockside water connections—yes
Showers—yes
Laundromat—yes
Waste pump-out—yes
Gasoline—yes
Diesel fuel—yes
Mechanical repairs—yes
Ship's store—yes
Restaurants—many nearby

The old Santa Maria Restaurant resides atop a series of pilings, built out over the waters just south of the St. Augustine City Marina. This dining spot offers some floating, wooden decked docks for its patrons. You are welcome to tie up while dining, but no overnight stays, nor dockside power or water connections, are available. Depths at the piers run 8 to 9 feet.

Don't *attempt to anchor abeam of Santa Maria Restaurant and then dinghy in to the docks.* An underwater power cable crosses the river at this point. Be sure to anchor south of the restaurant (see below).

The patch of deep water south-southeast of

Santa Maria Restaurant, St. Augustine

the city marina is a popular anchorage for visiting cruisers. Minimum depths of 10 feet can be expected near 29 53.402 North/081 18.445 West. Protection is not adequate for gale-force winds blowing from the north or south, but otherwise the anchorage is reasonably secure. While the city of St. Augustine has reduced the size of this anchorage within the last two years, many boats still drop anchor here year after year and enjoy St. Augustine by dinghying ashore. The city marina maintains a dinghy dock on its innermost rank of piers, striking out from the north side of the main dock. Visitors are welcome to tie up here after checking with the dockmaster on duty. For a fee of $7 a day, cruisers riding at anchor can make use of all the city marina facilities including showers and Laundromat.

Some fellow mariners have reported that anchors tend to drag in the mud of the St. Augutine anchorage when the weather turns really nasty. We have not had this problem, but, to be on the safe side, consider setting two anchors if the NOAA broadcasts call for heavy weather.

During one of our visits to this anchorage, we noticed a sailboat hard aground on the charted tongue of 3-foot shoals bordering the southern flank of the deeper waters. Avoid this hazard like the plague. Also, be sure to anchor south of the Santa Maria Restaurant to avoid an underwater power cable!

The piers of Fish Island Marina (Standard Mile 780, 29 52.265 North/081 18.175 West) overlook the Waterway's eastern flank, just north of the intersection with San Sebastian River. A series of older piers are found in an inner harbor on the upstream limits of the charted creek, indifferently marked by (charted) unlighted daybeacons #2, #4, and

#5. We specifically do not recommend docking in Fish Island's inner harbor. Depths at low water are practically nil. During an earlier visit, we found several sailcraft moored at the inner docks, during low water, with their keels completely buried in the black ooze.

Conversely, the newer, outer, concrete-decked floating docks have minimum depths of 9 feet and offer plenty of space for transients. Power (30 amp) and water connections are in the offing, and diesel fuel (no gasoline) can be purchased at the deep-water piers. These berths are exposed to the wake of passing vessels, and they are rather open to strong winds blowing from the north or south. Mechanical repairs for both gasoline and diesel engines are offered as well.

Fish Island Marina (904) 471-1955

Approach depths—9+ feet (outer docks)
3-4 feet (minimum—inner harbor)
Dockside depths—8-9 feet (outer docks)
0-1 feet (minimum—inner harbor)
Accepts transients—yes
Transient dockage rate—below average
Floating concrete piers—yes (outer docks)
Fixed wooden piers—yes (inner docks)
Dockside power connections—30 amps
Dockside water connections—yes
Showers—yes
Diesel fuel—yes
Mechanical repairs—yes

San Sebastian River (Standard Mile 780)

The San Sebastian River intersects the ICW's western reaches south-southwest of unlighted daybeacon #12, at unlighted daybeacons #1 and #2. The channel cuts generally to the west and northwest behind St. Augustine and leads upstream for several miles to a low-level fixed bridge that bars farther passage. Low-water depths in the channel run 8 feet or better. Many local shrimpers and trawlers dock along the river, and the well-protected banks are lined with commercial facilities to serve these craft. However, there are at least three establishments that also cater to pleasure craft. Transient dockage, however, is virtually nonexistent.

Anchorage is not a practical consideration on narrow San Sebastian River. By the time you set the hook, a passing trawler would probably oblige you to move. On the other hand, if you have the time for a side trip, cruising up the San Sebastian as far as the low-level fixed bridge can be rewarding. The many trawlers and large repair yards make for interesting sightseeing.

A repair facility will be spied on San Sebastian River's easterly shores, north of unlighted daybeacon #10, near 29 52.646 North/081 18.861 West. St. Augustine Marine (904-824-4394) obviously caters to repair work for larger power craft. Any number of these monsters were hauled out and resting on cradles during our last visit. Full mechanical repairs for both gasoline and diesel engines are in the offing. Haul-outs are accomplished by 75- and 100-ton travelifts.

Old Harry Xynides Boat Yard (904-824-3446) is found on the San Sebastian's eastern banks between unlighted daybeacons #15 and #17, near 29 52.788 North/081 18.887 West). You don't see many yards left like this one. Harry's place usually looks as if it has just been visited by a tornado. Nevertheless, in spite of all the seemingly haphazard junk lying about, my mate and I cannot help but find this yard charming. It recalls a different, simpler era in pleasure boating that is quickly fading into the fabric of the past. We are pleased to report that amidst all the modern changes, Harry is still in business. Haul-outs are accomplished by a marine railway, and some mechanical repairs are offered as well.

Oasis Boat Yard (904-824-2520) guards the eastern banks just upstream from Harry Xynides, near 29 52.803 North/081 18.906 West. This yard is very popular with visiting cruisers as they offer do-it-yourself yard facilities. Haul-outs are accomplished by a 25-ton travelift. Mechanical service work is offered for both gasoline and diesel power plants, and if you don't want to do bottom work for yourself, the yard personnel will gladly take on the job for you. There is also an on-site ship's and parts store that is most convenient for those doing their own service work. On-site showers and a Laundromat are an extra bonus for those engaged in their own repair work. All wet-slip dockage (7½-8 feet) is reserved for service customers.

St. Augustine Lodging

St. Augustine is the perfect place for captains and crew who need to get solid ground under their feet for a night or two. The city boasts a wide assortment of hotels, motels, and, particularly, bed and breakfast inns.

Most of these inns are housed in historic homeplaces, which seems ever so appropriate for those staying ashore in this timeless community. Listed below are just a few of the choices you might consider.

Carriage Way Bed and Breakfast Inn (70 Cuna Street, 904-829-2467) is located in a beautiful 1883 Victorian home. We have happily spent a few days as guests of this intimate inn from time to time. From the upper balcony, you can catch a glimpse of the tall spires of the former Ponce de Leon Hotel. Carriage Way features canopy beds, newspapers at your door each morning, and bicycles.

The Southern Wind Bed and Breakfast Inn (118 Cordova Street, 904-825-3623) is one of the larger St. Augustine inns. It has central air, queen-size beds, cable television, private baths, and a full buffet breakfast.

The Old Powder House Inn (38 Cordova Street, 904-824-4149) is a Victorian-flavored hostelry built on the site of an old gunpowder storage house. This inn has wraparound verandas, elaborate woodwork, and a charming antique decor.

St. Augustine Restaurants

Dining in St. Augustine will never be dull. More than thirty-two restaurants stand ready to satisfy the famished cruiser, only a few of which can be mentioned here.

The Columbia House Restaurant (904-824-3341) on St. George Street serves some of the most authentic Spanish fare in St. Augustine. We found the food good to very good, but not inexpensive. This is one of those dining spots for which you will probably want to dig out your last clean shirt—you know, the one buried under the forward V-berth.

For the best breakfast in town, not to mention a memorable lunch or dinner, give the Athena Restaurant (14 Cathedral Place, 904-823-9076) your most serious gastronomical attention. Besides offering excellent cuisine, this dining spot has the advantage of being only a very quick step away from the city marina docks.

For the evening meal, consider Harry's Seafood Bar & Grille (46 Avenida Menendez, 904-824-7765). This member of the popular Harry's chain, also within an easy step of the city marina, features New Orleans style cooking. We were most impressed with our dinner here, even if the service was a bit slow.

Cruisers looking for a few good sandwiches, or just first-class deli supplies to take back to the galley, should check out the Basket Case

(98 King Street, 904-810-2299). Located almost across the street from the city marina, this is a great spot for visiting mariners to pick up a quick but good meal.

Those up for something a little more lively might try the A1A Ale Works (1 King Street, 904-827-2977). We have not yet checked this spot out for ourselves, but the good people at First Mate Yacht Services have recommended this establishment to us. It is also just across the street from the city marina.

The Santa Maria Restaurant (904-829-6578) is built out over the water, just to the south of the city docks. It is only a short walk from the city marina, and the Santa Maria boasts wooden, floating docks of its own (see above). We recommend the fried seafood at Santa Maria. It's good, if not great. One of the real delights in partaking of a meal at this restaurant has little to do with the food. Beside most tables is a small trapdoor, which can be opened to "feed the fish" that gather in the waters below in surprising numbers. Stale bread is provided by the restaurant for this activity.

Just across the Bridge of Lions from the St. Augustine waterfront, cruisers willing to take a hike (or a taxi ride) for their meal will find what must surely rank as the best purely seafood restaurant in the city (ask any local for directions). O'Steens Seafood Kitchen (205 Anastasia Boulevard, 904-829-6974) has become something of a legend in northeastern Florida. Located directly on Highway A1A, a short hop east of the Bridge of Lions, the place sees crowds gathering by 5:30 P.M. To avoid long waits, get there as early as possible. What else can we add except to say that the seafood is simply wonderful.

St. Augustine Attractions

You could spend weeks exploring St. Augustine's many sights, but fortunately most can be enjoyed in the space of a few days. The information presented below will provide you with a good basic reference for your visit.

Perhaps St. Augustine's star attraction is the Castillo de San Marcos National Monument, which is still very much as it was when it defied Sir James Moore and General Oglethorpe (see below). Visitors are free to visit the deep vaults and walk the parapets as did the Spanish soldiers more than 200 years ago. Just walking through the old fortification can be quite rewarding. Push-button message boxes are located at strategic points throughout the monument and give a good overview of the fort's history. Lectures are provided hourly by a Park Service ranger, beginning in the southwestern corner of the interior courtyard.

The old Ponce de Leon Hotel at 74 King Street is one of the most striking edifices in St. Augustine. It is currently the home of Flagler College. Visitors by the hundred still gaze in awe at this incredible example of opulence from an age of luxury that will never come again. Built by Henry Flagler as the genesis of his eastern Florida development, the old Ponce de Leon was the first building in America of any size to be constructed of poured concrete. The interior is decorated with vast marble slabs, carved oak panels, and massive murals. The many stained-glass windows are the creation of Louis C. Tiffany.

The Ponce de Leon was a success from the very first. Wealthy, aristocratic visitors arrived by the carload. The new hotel was called "the foremost winter resort in America." In 1893 *Vogue* magazine wrote, "It is as if some modern Horoun-Al-Raschid deserted his own palace and turned it into a hotel."

By the early 1960s, the Ponce de Leon had

fallen on hard times as had so many hostelries dating from the early part of the century. The old hotel was converted to a college, which was named after the man who had done so much for eastern Florida. Today, Flagler College is a constant reminder of the vanished opulence and prestige of the early American "wateringhole." Inequitable as those times may have been, who among us cannot stare in wonder at Flagler's creation and envy those who lodged there in its heyday?

The old Alcazar Hotel, another Flagler creation, is located near Flagler College at 75 King Street. While it was originally created as an annex to the more famous Ponce de Leon, it is also well worth your attention. Its architectural style reflects both Spanish and Moorish influences. In modern times, the St. Augustine city hall has relocated on the old Alcazar's first floor, and Lightner antique mall occupies the second story. This latter establishment contains what must surely be one of the largest collections of antique shops in the United States.

Just across the street from the old Alcazar is the building that once housed the Cordova

Carriage tours in St. Augustine

Hotel. It was not originally built by Flagler, but the wealthy developer acquired the building during his development of St. Augustine's tourist facilities and extensively remodeled the interior. Like its sisters, the Alcazar and the Ponce de Leon, the Cordova recalls the faded grandeur of earlier days. This structure underwent a thorough renovation in 2000, and it now houses the Casa Monida Hotel (904-827-1888). This Casa Monida features 138 rooms and a four star-restaurant, "the 95 Cordova," offering all three meals of the day.

St. George Street is a favorite attraction among visitors. Much of the street is lined by retail shops and restaurants that are decorated in an old Spanish style, but there are also several direct links with the city's past. Chief among these is the San Augustin Antiguo. Sponsored by the state of Florida, the Antiguo is a recreation of an eighteenth-century Spanish-American village. The exhibit contains several authentic colonial homes dating to the eighteenth century and a working forge. Each exhibit is occupied by participants dressed in period costume and going about the everyday tasks of eighteenth-century housewives, soldiers, and craftsmen. They are always happy to answer questions and are particularly helpful in fostering an understanding of everyday life in colonial Florida.

The Old Market and Plaza de la Constitution are comprised of an open-air, parklike area that divides the eastern portions of King Street and Cathedral Place. The plaza dates back to St. Augustine's earliest settlement. In the sixteenth century a royal Spanish law required each town to be built around a central plaza that served as a market and meeting place for the citizenry.

Today, an 1887 recreation of the old Spanish market occupies the eastern portion of the plaza. West of the market is an open expanse with a bandstand built around 1900 and a monument commemorating the liberal Spanish constitution of 1812. Two other memorials honor those who gave their lives in the Civil War and later conflicts. There is also a statue of Ponce de Leon at the plaza's eastern tip.

The Cathedral of St. Augustine looks over the street known as Cathedral Place just north of the plaza. The parish dates back to 1594, but the present structure was built in 1888.

The cathedral represents the oldest Roman Catholic congregation in the United States.

Just north of the Plaza de la Constitution is the building that has long been known as Government House. It was on this site that many Spanish and English governors lived during colonial times. The present structure was built in the 1930s from a British plan dating back to 1764.

St. Augustine is one of those rare cities that seems to offer a different attraction around

Plaza de la Constitution, St. Augustine

each bend of the road. Strike out on your own and discover this timeless community for yourself. Who knows, if you go slowly and quietly enough, you may still hear harsh orders being shouted from the Castillo's parapet or the harmonious guitar of a Spanish party. For those who seek to understand our Spanish-American heritage, St. Augustine never fails in her reward.

Walking Tour

Several commercial tours are available in St. Augustine. One of these stops at the old house just behind the city marina. If you are new to St. Augustine, this is an excellent means of getting to know the city.

Once you have a feeling for St. Augustine, a walking tour is a great way to take in the sights. Our favorite route is outlined below.

Turn right from the city docks and walk north for one block along Avenida Menendez. Turn left onto King Street. Watch to your right and you will be able to admire the statue of Ponce de Leon, the old market, and the Plaza de la Constitution.

Continue walking west on King Street past the St. George Street intersection. Watch for the Government House to your right, just past the junction.

Turn left onto Cordova Street. You will soon pass the entrance to the old Cordova Hotel on your left and the Lightner antique mail (the old Alcazar Hotel) will be to the right. If you are interested in antiques, a stop here is a must.

Retrace your steps to the north and continue past King Street on Cordova. Soon you will spy Flagler College (once the Ponce de Leon Hotel) on the western side of the street. It occupies an entire block and is about as striking a sight as you are ever likely to come across.

Turn right at Cathedral Place and walk one block to the Cathedral of St. Augustine. Pause to admire the quiet grandeur of this beautiful church and the lovely stained-glass windows that depict the life of the city's patron saint, San Augustin. Respectful visitors are welcome inside.

Walk back to the west for a short distance on Cathedral Place and turn right onto St. George Street. Farther on, St. George Street is closed to traffic. Begin watching to your right for the entrance to San Augustin Antiguo. Take your time at this fascinating exhibit. The costumed attendants are well versed in St. Augustine history and culture and are eager to share their knowledge with the sensitive visitor.

To continue your tour, walk north on St. George Street until you reach the old city gates. These venerable pillars were originally part of the outworks built during the early eighteenth century to strengthen the city's defenses.

After admiring the old gates, continue walking north on San Marco Avenue. Watch to your left for the St. Augustine Visitor Center. Here you can purchase maps or guidebooks and watch a free movie that serves as an excellent introduction to the city's heritage.

Upon leaving the Visitor Center, turn back to the south on San Marco and follow the street as it swerves to the east. Soon you will see the massive walls of the Castillo de San Marcos National Monument to the left. Walk through the parking lot and follow the marked path to the fort's entrance. There is a small entry fee, but the monument is worth every penny.

After touring the fort, you will probably be more than ready for a refreshing break. Why not stop for a cool drink at one of the many restaurants lining Avenida Menendez as you walk south back to the city docks?

St. Augustine History   The history of St.

Augustine stretches back to the earliest Spanish explorations of North America. St. Augustine is the oldest European settlement in the United States and Canada. When you consider that the English colony at Jamestown was founded almost fifty years after the settling of St. Augustine, the city's heritage seems impressive indeed.

Some historians claim that Juan Ponce de Leon, the Spanish discoverer of Florida, landed in the vicinity of the future St. Augustine. There has been a persistent legend that Ponce was searching for the fabled "fountain of youth," but while the Spanish conquistador was probably aware of this legend, all historical evidence suggests that he was actually on his way to assume the governorship of Bimini. History notwithstanding, the Fountain

of Youth Archaeological Park today stands north of the city and claims to commemorate Ponce de Leon's first landing in Florida.

The first permanent settlement of St. Augustine came about as a direct result of Spanish resolve to prevent settlement in Florida by other European powers. Though this new land lacked the gold and precious metals that gave rise to Spanish exploration and domination in South America, eastern Florida lay along the route that Spanish treasure ships usually followed from South America to Spain.

Consequently, in 1564 King Philip dispatched Pedro Menendez de Aviles to found a permanent colony in this new land. He was also instructed to destroy any usurpers he might encounter. The story of how Menendez carried out his mission mercilessly on the

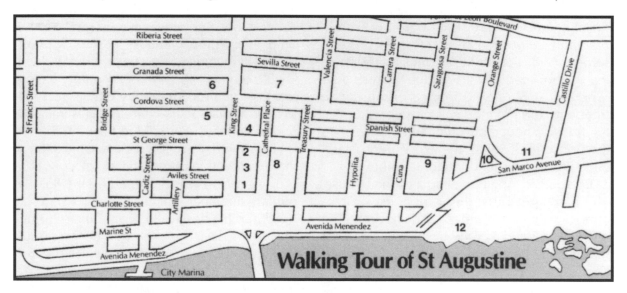

1 Statue of Ponce de Leon	7 Flagler College
2 Plaza de la Constitution	8 Cathedral of St. Augustine
3 Old Market	9 San Augustine Antiguo
4 Government House	10 Old City Gates
5 Cordova Hotel	11 St. Augustine Visitors Center
6 Lightner Antique Mall	12 Castillo de San Marcos National Monument

French inhabitants of Fort Caroline will be told in the last chapter of this guidebook. Before engaging in battle, however, Menendez quickly founded a settlement at the River of Dolphins. The Spanish renamed the harbor San Augustin, having reached their destination on the festival day of that saint.

With French opposition eliminated, Menendez began to establish a stable outpost for his king in a hostile wilderness. It was a long and often-thankless job.

Besides disease, crop failure, and frequent storms, the Spanish also had to contend with an often-hostile Native American population. Until the beginning of British rule in 1764, Spanish authorities attempted to solve the Indian problem by establishing a mission system throughout Florida. During the colony's early years, these missions extended as far north as present-day South Carolina. While first the Jesuits and later the Franciscans had some success converting the Indians and holding them under the sway of the Spanish government at St. Augustine, rebellions were frequent, and the plan was never as successful as it was hoped it would be. The English to the north finally dealt the experiment a fatal blow with their superior trading ability.

By 1585 St. Augustine had a council house, a church, several stores, and houses for its almost 300 men, women, and children. The city also boasted a crude wooden fort, but not for long. In 1586 it was destroyed by Sir Francis Drake, England's most famous buccaneer.

After Drake's raid, aid was rushed to St. Augustine, but the rebuilding process was slow. Furthermore, a disastrous fire in 1599 burned the Franciscan friary and many other thatched-roof buildings.

Following another successful raid by English pirates in 1668, it became obvious that St. Augustine needed some sort of reliable military protection if the colony was to be maintained. In 1672 construction began on the Castillo de San Marcos. This formidable structure was built directly on the St. Augustine waterfront and commanded an imposing view of the inlet and harbor. The basic construction took some fifteen years, though it was several more decades before all the supporting structures were completed.

Stone for the fort was quarried on nearby Anastasia Island. The material selected for the walls was known as coquina, a natural mixture of crushed sea shells and sand. The name was derived from the Spanish term for shellfish or cockle. When first mined, coquina is soft, allowing the Spanish craftsmen to shape the stone to their purposes. Once exposed to air and allowed to dry, coquina becomes practically as hard as modern concrete. Yet this unique building material was to display a spongelike quality that concrete lacks. Many English gunners over the next century were to learn of coquina's durability under fire, much to their dismay. Years later an English attacker under Oglethorpe is said to have exclaimed, "What's the use . . . it's just the same as sticking a knife into a round of cheese!"

The Castillo was designed by the Spanish military engineer Ignacio Daza. He incorporated into his design the best military principles of his day. The extended corners of the fort allow attacking forces to receive fire from three sides. Many heavy cannon were carefully placed along the parapets. These imposing guns commanded both the inlet and harbor as well as the only practical approach by land. So effective were the design and the construction of the Castillo that it was never taken by a hostile force in more than 150 years of off-and-on warfare.

In 1702 the Castillo underwent its first test. South Carolina forces under Gov. Sir James Moore attacked St. Augustine by sea. The city was quickly evacuated and the entire population took shelter within the Castillo's walls. Moore's cannon had no effect on the coquina walls, and the intrepid palmetto general dug in for a long siege. When four heavily armed Spanish warships appeared, the attackers hastily withdrew, but not before burning the entire town yet again.

Following Moore's attack, the Spanish ringed the city with earthen walls. In 1704, to the north they built the Cubo Line, which incorporated the main city gate. By 1706 the Fort Nombre de Dios and its palisade had been erected to the north. To the west, the Rosario Line was thrown up in 1718 to strengthen the defenses further.

English forces returned in 1739, this time under the command of Gen. James Oglethorpe, founder of the Georgia colony. Oglethorpe repeated Moore's mistake of arriving with only light cannon. While the fort was soon ringed with hostile batteries, the Castillo remained impregnable to English attack. In a replay of the earlier drama, seven Spanish men-of-war sailed boldly into St. Augustine harbor, and Oglethorpe retired to the north.

For a brief period Spanish forces went on the offensive. Raids were regularly conducted on the English colonists in Georgia. However, in 1742 Oglethorpe won the Battle of Bloody Marsh in Georgia, and the Spanish threat was at an end.

For the next twenty years, St. Augustine was free from attack, but ironically the fate of Spanish Florida was to be decided elsewhere. During the eighteenth century, Spain became seriously worried about the rise of English power. When it appeared that France would lose the Seven Years War (known as the French and Indian War in America) to England, Spain joined with France shortly before the conclusion of the conflict in an effort to reverse the outcome. England was soon victorious over her combined foes, and in the treaty negotiations, Spain ceded Florida to England.

Lt. John Hedges received St. Augustine from the Spanish governor in 1764. Soon James Grant, a prominent South Carolinian, arrived to assume the governorship. Grant was a fortunate choice as governor. He was able to make peace with the Indians by shrewd trading practices, and, most importantly, his far-reaching connections among South Carolina planters helped to attract a good number of this prosperous breed to Florida. Before long, large plantations were springing up around and to the south of St. Augustine.

St. Augustine prospered under British rule. The city soon became a major shipping port. From 1766 to 1768, pine boards, oak staves, mahogany, shingles, tar, turpentine, indigo, rice, deerskins, tanned leather, raw hides, calfskins, and some 65,000 oranges left St. Augustine bound for European ports.

During the Revolution, Florida and St. Augustine remained loyal to England. Loyalists from the north fled to Florida in large numbers expecting to return shortly to their homes, but of course the refugees' hopes were to be bitterly disappointed.

There was little military activity in Florida during the war, but the old fort played an interesting role during the conflict's latter stages. In 1780 the British transferred sixty-three "important" hostages to the old Castillo for safekeeping. Among this group were such notable American patriots as Arthur Middleton, Edward Rutledge, and Thomas Heyward, all three signers of the Declaration of Independence.

The Treaty of Paris ended the American Revolution and returned Florida to Spanish rule. Spanish power at that time was only a shadow of its former glory in the days of South American domination. Soon the young, land-hungry United States to the north would begin to view Florida with an eye for acquisition.

The seat of Spanish government during the second period of Spanish rule was again St. Augustine. It was not long before Florida became a haven for runaway slaves and renegade Indians. The Spanish governor could do little to control these outlaws. Given American land hunger as well, it is not surprising that scheming military officers and adventurists soon began to hatch plans to bring Florida into the new nation. Several abortive Florida revolutions have already been described. St. Augustine was never seriously threatened by any of these schemes, however, and it was through negotiation that Florida finally came under American control in 1821.

Under American control St. Augustine gradually began to lose its political importance. However, the old city was still to have a place in later historical events. During the Seminole Indian wars of the 1830s and 1840s, the settlements south of St. Augustine were laid waste by Indian attacks. Refugees streamed north to the protection of St. Augustine. Several of the great Seminole chiefs were imprisoned in the old Castillo. Among these notable Native Americans were Osceola and Coacoochee. Both were captured under flags of truce on the grounds that it was more humane to end the struggle through any means rather than honor the traditional rules of war.

Osceola was eventually transferred to Fort Moultrie, where he died, but Coacoochee engineered a miraculous escape. Late one night, under their chief's instructions, the Indians formed a human ladder by standing atop each other's shoulders. Coacoochee and twenty of his comrades clambered up this human chain and squeezed through the small window at the top of their cell. Then they slipped undetected down the fort's wall into the moat. Coacoochee went on to command his people in the disastrous Battle of Okeechobee, but that is a story for a later time.

Even as St. Augustine declined as a seat of government, it began its growth as a tourist resort. The healing power of the St. Augustine winters was a great lure for Americans trapped in the ice and snow of the north.

St. Augustine's popularity was temporarily ended by the Civil War. The old port city itself was only nominally involved in the War Between the States. Early in the conflict, Confederate forces stripped the old Castillo of all its guns and in March 1862 Union forces occupied the city without opposition.

After the war and Reconstruction, beginning in 1885, the remarkable Henry M. Flagler began his single-handed development of eastern Florida as a tourist mecca. Mr. Flagler's story will be told later; for now we need only note that between 1885 and 1890 he oversaw the construction of the fabulous Ponce de Leon and Alcazar hotels in St. Augustine. The Ponce de Leon cost more than a quarter of a million dollars and could accommodate 450 guests.

Since then St. Augustine has become ever more popular. In modern times, one of the most dramatic developments has been the recreation of the atmosphere of a Spanish village on St. George Street. If you visit it, you are sure to come away with an increased understanding of life in those very early colonial days.

ST. AUGUSTINE NAVIGATION

The waters surrounding St. Augustine are well marked and reasonably easy to navigate, though tidal currents do flow swiftly. The only source of real concern is the passage around the St. Augustine Inlet. This can be a difficult portion of the ICW and you should approach these waters with caution.

ICW to St. Augustine Inlet   As the ICW runs past the westerly reaches of St. Augustine Inlet, the channel comes within sight of the open sea. This portion of the Waterway is subject to shoaling, strong tidal currents, and wicked chop in high winds. Take special care to watch for excessive leeway as you run past the inlet's entrance.

After leaving the Vilano Beach Bridge behind, be ready for new and uncharted aids to navigation. Southbound cruisers should take all red, even-numbered aids to their (the cruisers') starboard side and pass green markers to port. At the present time, unlighted nun buoy #58C, flashing daybeacon #58D, and unlighted nun buoy #58E mark the channel's westerly limits. Be sure to pass well *east* of all these aids to navigation. Continue on, pointing to pass the large, unlighted nun buoy #60 well to its easterly side.

For many years now, NOAA chart 11485 has *incorrectly* shown the magenta ICW fairway line passing west of #58E and #60. In spite of repeated protests by this writer, and any number of others within the cruising community, this mistake persists to the present day. If you do pass west of either #58E, #60, or #2, *you will run aground!* Be sure to stay well east of #58E, #60, and #2.

If you need a little visual explanation for all of this, note the correctly charted tongue of building shoals west of #2. These shallows seem to be stretching ever farther to the east. Take great care to stay clear.

After rounding #60, curl your course back around almost 90 degrees to the west-southwest, and point to come abeam of unlighted nun buoy #2 to its southerly side. Flashing daybeacon #1, marking the southern side of the channel, will come abeam south of your course line.

Short of #1 and #2, cruisers putting to sea can cut to the east-northeast and follow the reasonably well marked St. Augustine inlet channel out to sea, or, alternately, a turn to the south will bring you into Salt Run.

St. Augustine Inlet   The seaward passage through the inlet is subject to continual change, and markers are not charted owing to their frequent relocation. Local craft use the cut regularly, and visiting cruisers who exercise reasonable care should be able to run the channel. Check at one of the local marinas before making the attempt or, better yet, watch for a local captain putting out to sea and follow in his or her wake.

Salt Run   There are far more unlighted daybeacons outlining the Salt Run channel than are shown on the current edition of 11485. The prolific quantity of these markers makes navigation of the cut rather simple (once past the current plagued entrance) during daylight, at least as far as Conch House Marina. At night, it could be a different story for strangers.

To slip successfully into the northerly entrance of Salt Run, pass flashing daybeacon #1 to its easterly side and immediately set course to pass between Salt Run's outermost pair of markers, unlighted daybeacons #1 and #2. Be ready for strong currents as you enter the run.

The close proximity of two aids to navigation, both labeled as #1, can be a source of confusion. Flashing daybeacon #1 is part of the combined ICW-St. Augustine Inlet channel, while unlighted daybeacon #1 is the northernmost aid to navigation on the Salt Run cut.

Continue into the main body of Salt Run by passing between the many pairs of (mostly uncharted) unlighted daybeacons. As correctly portrayed on chart 11485, a large shoal lies west and southwest of your course track. Avoid any slippage to the west or southwest. Eventually, the profusely marked channel turns to the southwest, and Conch House Marina will be obvious along the westerly banks.

At this point, the channel turns to the south-southeast and follows the main body of Salt Run. As you would expect, pass all subsequent red, even-numbered aids to your starboard side and take green markers to port.

The first anchorage comes abeam at unlighted daybeacon #14, while the larger, more popular, haven is clustered south-southeast of unlighted daybeacon #15. Larger, deep-draft boats are urged to make use of this latter anchorage. Good water stretches south-southeast from #15 well in toward the easterly banks.

South-southeast of the charted position of the St. Augustine Lighthouse, depths soon begin to decline in spite of the soundings recorded on chart 11485. We discovered soundings of 4 feet past the charted, sharp point of land on the eastern shore, upstream of the lighthouse. Larger cruising craft are strictly advised to avoid the extreme southeasterly reaches of Salt Run.

On to St. Augustine   West-southwest of flashing daybeacon #1 and unlighted nun buoy #2, the run to the St. Augustine waterfront becomes well marked and fairly straightforward. At flashing daybeacon #6, the Waterway takes a sharp turn to the south and flows quickly into the headwaters of Matanzas River and toward the Bridge of Lions.

By the time you reach #6, you will have a good view of the old Castillo to the west. If you want to anchor north of the bridge near the fort, continue on the Waterway channel until you are within 100 yards of the bridge. Then cut in sharply toward the western banks. You can approach to within 40 yards of the St. Augustine seawall and hold excellent depths. To anchor closer to the old fort, feel your way north for several hundred yards, but be sure to stop well short of the charted shallows, north of the Castillo's position.

Slow to idle speed as you approach the Bridge of Lions, and continue cruising slowly until you are past the St. Augustine waterfront, south of unlighted daybeacon #12. The Bridge of Lions (closed vertical clearance, 25 feet) opens only on the hour and half-hour from 7:00 A.M. to 6:00 P.M. on weekdays except there are no openings at 8:00 A.M., noon, and 5:00 P.M. On weekends, the span opens on the hour and half-hour during the day. At night, the bridge opens on demand.

On the ICW South of the Bridge of Lions, you will soon see the city marina to the west followed by the docks of the Santa Maria Restaurant and the popular adjacent anchorage a bit farther to the south. Remember, if you anchor on these waters, be sure to anchor south of the Santa Maria Restaurant. Also, be on guard against the correctly charted tongue of 3-foot waters, lying just south of the anchorage. Stay well north of this obstruction.

The Waterway channel continues south on its usual well-marked, easily followed way to the intersection with San Sebastian River. Don't drift too far to the west between unlighted daybeacons #10 and #12. Shallows strike out from the westerly shores between these two markers.

Slow to idle speed again as you near the San Sebastian River juncture. This wise practice will protect the boats berthed at Fish Island Marina's piers opposite the river's entrance.

San Sebastian River The San Sebastian River channel is unusually well marked. Enter the river by breaking off from the Waterway channel as you come abeam of unlighted daybeacons #1 and #2 to the west. Swing sharply to the west and point to pass between #1 and #2. To continue upstream, you need only pass red markers to your starboard side and take green beacons to port. There is a fair amount of tidal current, so be ready for it as you cruise along.

Don't attempt to enter the small marina west of unlighted daybeacon #9 unless you can stand low-water depths of 3 feet or less.

After passing unlighted daybeacon #9, the river turns to the north-northeast. Soon St. Augustine Marine repair yard will come up along the easterly banks. Don't attempt to tie to the long, wooden pier stretching south from this yard. This structure is in poor repair, and is apparently unused.

Just upstream from St. Augustine Marine, Harry Xynides Boat Yard and Oasis Boatyard will also come abeam to the east. Between unlighted daybeacon #18 and #20, a huge marine manufacturing plant owned by Luhrs Yacht Corporation guards the westerly shores.

Eventually, San Sebastian River is blocked by a low-level, fixed bridge north of unlighted daybeacon #33. Larger cruising craft will want to cease their explorations well before reaching the fixed span. Maneuvering room becomes tight on the river's upstream limits.

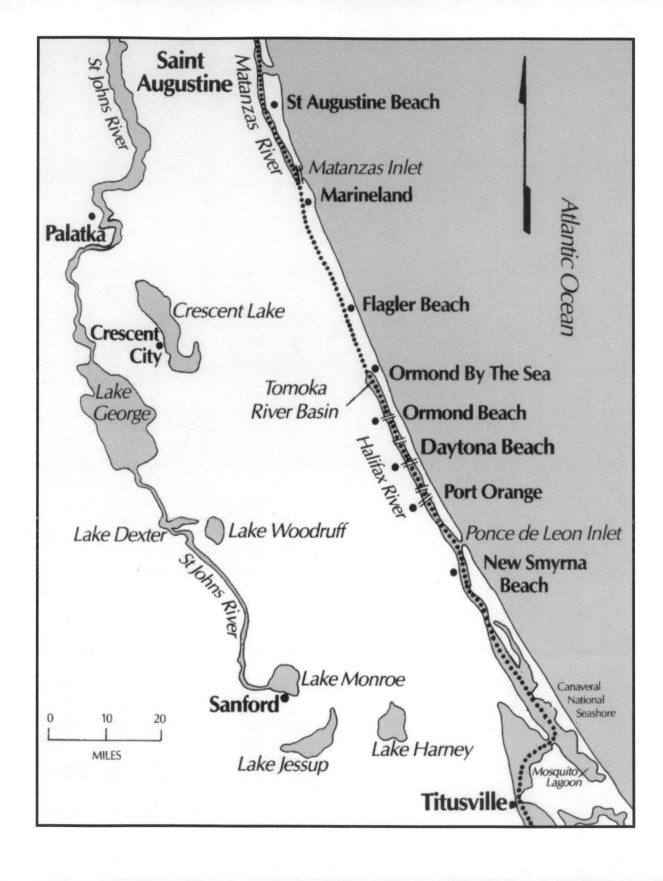

Matanzas River to Indian River

South of St. Augustine, the ICW runs generally south toward the headwaters of mighty Indian River. First the Waterway snakes its way through the Matanzas River until reaching its inlet; then the ICW passes into a mostly man-made cut until it intersects Tomoka Basin and Halifax River. The popular resort city of Daytona Beach sits astride the Halifax and offers every service imaginable for visiting cruisers. Leaving Daytona, the Waterway channel follows Halifax River south to Ponce de Leon Inlet. This capricious cut boasts several side trips for bold captains.

Some 56 nautical miles south of St. Augustine, ICW cruisers will discover New Smyrna Beach. The story of this historic community is one of the most extraordinary in all of Florida. From New Smyrna, the Waterway tracks its way through an improved channel lined by mud flats and oyster beds. Eventually, it leads to mostly shallow Mosquito Lagoon. Although the name tells all as far as the local insect population is concerned, traversing the huge lagoon is nonetheless fascinating.

Finally, southbound cruisers will find their way through Haulover Canal into the headwaters of Indian River. Along the course of the canal, passing mariners can sometimes observe an impressive collection of wildlife.

Taken as a whole, this stretch of the ICW is a mixed bag, with something for everyone. Good facilities, large resort communities, and isolated anchorages are all available to fortunate cruisers who have the time to tarry along the way and rest from their travels.

Charts   Only one NOAA chart is needed for complete navigational coverage of the waters from San Sebastian River to Indian River:

11485—an ICW chart that details the Waterway and all the intersecting inlets from St. Augustine to Indian River

---

Bridges

State Road 312 Bridge—crosses ICW at Standard Mile 780, south of the Waterway's intersection with the San Sebastian River—Fixed—65 feet

Crescent Beach Bridge—crosses ICW at Standard Mile 789, southeast of flashing daybeacon #58—Bascule—25 feet (closed)—opens on demand

Palm Coast Parkway Bridge—crosses ICW at Standard Mile 803—Fixed—65 feet

Flagler Beach Bridge—crosses ICW at Standard Mile 811, well south of flashing daybeacon #13—Fixed—65 feet

J. B. Knox/Bulow/High Bridge—crosses ICW at Standard Mile 816, south of unlighted daybeacon #24—Bascule—15 feet (closed)—opens on demand

Ormond Beach Bridge—crosses ICW and Halifax River at Standard Mile 825, south-southeast of unlighted daybeacon #18—Fixed—65 feet

Seabreeze Bridge—crosses ICW at Standard Mile 829, south-southeast of unlighted daybeacon #30—Fixed—65 feet

Main Street Bridge—crosses ICW at Standard

Mile 830, south-southeast of unlighted daybeacon #32—Bascule—22 feet (closed)—opens on demand

Broadway Bridge—crosses ICW at Standard Mile 830.5, south-southeast of unlighted daybeacons #33 and #34—Fixed—65 feet

Memorial Bridge—crosses ICW at Standard Mile 830.5, south-southeast of unlighted daybeacon #36—Bascule—21 feet (closed)—does not open at all Monday to Saturday between 7:45 A.M. and 8:45 A.M. and 4:45 P.M. and 5:45 P.M. except it does open 8:15 A.M. and 5:15 P.M.; at all other times opens on demand

Port Orange Bridge—crosses ICW at Standard Mile 835.5, south-southeast of unlighted daybeacon #56—Fixed—65 feet

Coronado Beach Bridge—crosses ICW south of flashing daybeacon #29—Bascule—23 feet (closed)—opens on the hour and every 20 minutes thereafter from 7:00 A.M. to 7:00 P.M., seven days a week, year round—current edition of chart 11485 still shows the old 14-foot restricted span here but it has been removed entirely and replaced with this structure

New Smyrna/Harris Saxon Bridge—crosses ICW at Standard Mile 846.5, south of flashing daybeacon #38—Fixed—65 feet

Allenhurst Haulover—crosses ICW's track through Haulover Canal at Standard Mile 869—Bascule—27 feet (closed)—opens on demand

Chapter 4 Anchorage Summary (Please note that anchorages are listed in geographic order, moving north to south.)

Emergency Anchorages—(Standard Mile 781)—located west and south of flashing daybeacon #18, and northeast and south of flashing daybeacon #31—various lats/lons (see detailed account)—6-foot depths—reviewed on pages 212-13, 226

South Channel Anchorage—(Standard Mile 843)—located near 29 03.557 North/080 54.846 West, north-northeast of the ICW's flashing daybeacon #19—7-foot depths—reviewed on pages 235-36, 246

Chapter 4 Marina and Yacht-Club Summary (Please note that marinas are listed in geographic order, moving north to south.)

Palm Coast Marina—(386) 446-6370—(Standard Mile 802)—located near 29 34.620 North/081 11.607 West, on the southern shores of the first westward-striking canal, north of the Palm Coast high-rise bridge—transient dockage available—gasoline and diesel fuel available—6-foot minimum depths—reviewed on pages 215-16, 228

Caribbean Jack's Marina—(386) 253-5647—(Standard Mile 830)—located near 29 13.650 North/081 01.358 West, off the western banks of the ICW/Halifax River, south of unlighted daybeacon #32—transient dockage available—gasoline and diesel fuel available—6-foot minimum depths—reviewed on pages 221-22

Halifax Harbor Marina—(386) 671-3600—(Standard Mile 831)—found near 29 12.216 North/081 00.755 West, guarding the western shores of the ICW/Halifax River, south of unlighted daybeacon #39A—transient dockage available—gasoline and diesel fuel available—6½-foot minimum depths—reviewed on pages 222-24, 229-30

Halifax River Yacht Club—(386) 255-7459—(Standard Mile 831)—found near 29 12.463 North/081 00.978 West, overlooking the western shoreline of the northern Halifax Harbor Marina dockage basin—transient dockage available for members of other yacht clubs with appropriate reciprocal privileges—6-foot minimum depths—reviewed on page 224

Daytona Marina and Boat Works—(386) 252-6421—(Standard Mile 831)—found near 29 12.097 North/081 00.671 West—entrance channel runs west-southwest from the Waterway south of unlighted daybeacon #39A and the southerly entrance cut for Halifax Harbor Marina—transient dockage available—gasoline and diesel fuel available—7-foot minimum depths—reviewed on pages 224-25, 230

Seven Seas Marina & Boatyard—(386) 761-3221—(Standard Mile 835)—located near 29 09.251 North/080 58.567 West, east-northeast of unlighted daybeacon #56 and just north of the Port Orange high-rise bridge—transient dockage available—gasoline and diesel fuel available—4-foot minimum depths but typical 6-foot soundings—reviewed on pages 231, 244

Adventure Yacht Harbor—(386) 756-2180—(Standard Mile 837)—found near 29 07.935 North/080 57.695 West, east and south of the ICW between flashing daybeacon #59 and unlighted daybeacon #60—transient dockage available—gasoline and diesel fuel available—5-foot minimum depths—reviewed on pages 232, 244-45

Inlet Harbor Marina—(386) 767-3266—found near 29 05.481 North/080 56.435 West, northwest of Ponce Inlet's unlighted nun buoy #2—transient dockage available—gasoline and diesel fuel available—5-foot minimum depths—reviewed on pages 233-34, 245

Lighthouse Boat Yard—(386) 767-0683—found near 29 04.743 North/080 55.596 West, hard by the charted location of the Ponce Inlet Lighthouse—limited transient dockage available—gasoline and diesel fuel available—5½-foot minimum depths—reviewed on pages 234-35, 245-46

North Causeway Marine—(386) 427-5267—(Standard Mile 846)—located near 29 01.789 North/080 55.163 West, behind two spoil islands west of unlighted daybeacon #37—limited transient dockage—gasoline available—5-foot minimum depths—reviewed on pages 236-37, 248

Smyrna Marina—(386) 428-1430—(Standard Mile 846)—located near 29 01.647 North/080 55.277 West, on the New Smyrna Beach waterfront, west of flashing daybeacon #38—transient dockage available—7-foot minimum depths—reviewed on pages 237-38, 248

Smyrna Yacht Club—(386) 427-4040—(Standard Mile 847.5)—located near 29 00.684 North/080 54.870 West, southeast of unlighted daybeacon #46—transient dockage available for members of other yacht clubs with appropriate reciprocal privileges—5-foot minimum depths—reviewed on pages 242, 249

San Sebastian River to Daytona Beach

South of San Sebastian River and St. Augustine, the ICW track to Matanzas Inlet is a lonely stretch with precious few anchorages and no facilities. If your tanks are low, be sure to fill up at St. Augustine before leaving the city's marinas behind.

From Matanzas Inlet, the Waterway flows through a sheltered passage for more than 20 nautical miles. The popular facility at Palm Shores is found along this stretch.

Eventually the ICW wends its way south to the Tomoka River basin and the headwaters of Halifax River. Here perhaps more than any-where else, Florida's British period made its greatest mark and then suddenly disappeared forever. The story of the rise and fall of Tomoka's great sugar plantations is one of the most tragic tales in this storied state.

Sitting astride the Halifax River, Daytona Beach combines numerous marina facilities, world-famous beaches, and a mind-boggling array of sporting attractions. No wonder cruis-ers have chosen Daytona as one of the most popular ports of call in northern Florida for many a year.

The Waterway channel to Daytona is easily run, with only a few trouble spots. Tidal cur-rents do run swiftly so you must still watch for excessive leeway. The Waterway's intersection with Matanzas Inlet has almost continual shoaling problems and calls for extreme cau-tion. Otherwise, simply keep to the channel and enjoy the sights.

Anchorages between St. Augustine and Daytona Beach are sparse. A few spots do pro-vide good protection and adequate swinging room for larger craft, but it can be a long cruise between these havens.

South of Matanzas Inlet, marina facilities are numerous and of good repute. Conversely, there is not a single facility available to cruis-ing craft between San Sebastian River and the inlet.

Your cruise from St. Augustine to Daytona should be interesting and relaxing. Keep alert and you should have an enjoyable run.

Matanzas River

The Waterway channel down Matanzas River is wide and well marked, but it does wind a bit. Tidal currents can still ease unwary navigators out of the channel onto an inop-portune shoal. However, north of Matanzas Inlet, most mariners will be able to traverse the Waterway with few concerns.

Anchorages are practically nonexistent along this stretch. A few deepwater bubbles alongside the Waterway do allow for emer-gency stops, but none of these offers any shel-ter from inclement weather.

There are no facilities on the Matanzas catering to pleasure craft between San Sebastian River and the inlet. This can be a lonely stretch, so be sure your fuel (not to mention your beer and food) supply is ade-quate to see you through.

The Matanzas shoreline alternates between undeveloped saltwater marsh and higher shores, which exhibit moderate residential development. To the west of unlighted day-beacon #28, you can see a beautiful old house marked as "Cup" on chart 11485. This struc-ture was built in 1885, and it is apparently now abandoned. The house and its outlying lands are private property, so don't attempt going ashore.

The southerly portion of Matanzas River borders the twin communities of Butler and Crescent beaches to the east. Despite the resi-dential development, there are no facilities for visiting cruisers, and no-wake restrictions are in effect for these waters.

Emergency Anchorages (Standard Mile 781) (Various Lats/Lons—see below)

If for some reason you simply have to set the hook immediately south of St. Augustine, there are two patches of deep water along the Waterway that could serve as anchorages in light air. Both are open to wind and wake, but if you simply can't proceed on or return to St. Augustine, they are your best bet.

West of flashing daybeacon #18, a large tongue of deep water strikes to the south-southeast. Minimum depths of 8 feet are carried along this stretch and to within 75 yards of the extensive, charted mud banks lining the westerly shoreline near 29 50.994 North/081 18.260 West. These flats cover at high tide, and you must take care to stay in the deeper waters, or you could awake perched atop the mud. Swinging room should be sufficient for most cruising-size craft, and the adjacent shoreline does give some protection in moderate western and southwestern winds. There is not enough shelter for anything approaching heavy weather.

A deep channel runs along the river's eastern shores south and northeast of flashing daybeacon #31, near 29 49.010 North/081 17.550 West. While there is an unmarked shoal to avoid, this anchorage does offer some protection from easterly breezes. Swinging room should be sufficient for boats up to 36 feet. Minimum depths run 6 to 8 feet in the channel.

Matanzas Inlet and the ICW (Standard Mile 792.5)

Matanzas Inlet is an impassable seaward cut crossed by a low-level fixed bridge. Matanzas River leads generally northwest from the seaward channel to the Waterway.

South of flashing daybeacon #81 the ICW channel breaks off to the south, skirts across the headwaters of Matanzas River, and ducks into a dredged cut running behind Rattlesnake Island. The run across the river is one of the trickiest sections of the eastern Florida ICW.

Don't attempt to enter the northwesterly

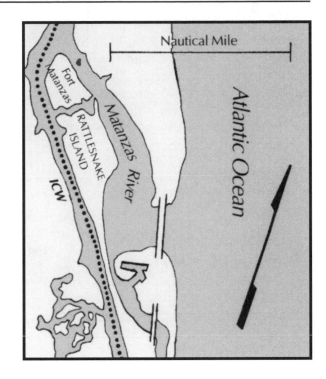

headwaters of Matanzas River, abandoned by the Waterway, near the old fort (see below). These waters are too changeable for all but small, shallow-draft power boats or those with specific, up-to-date local knowledge. Fortunately, you can still catch a good view of the old fort from the Waterway.

Matanzas Inlet History It was late September 1565 and Pedro Menendez de Aviles, the founder of St. Augustine, was rushing back to his new settlement following the surprise victory over French forces at Fort Caroline on St. Johns Bluff. As far as Menendez knew, the French fleet under Jean Ribault was still on the high seas ready to pounce on the few ships and men left at St. Augustine.

However, Menendez found no news of the French force when he arrived. A few days later friendly Indians brought word of a large body of shipwrecked Europeans on the southern side of present-day Matanzas Inlet. Menendez hastily gathered his forces and marched south with 50 men. He discovered some 300 destitute French soldiers and learned that the entire French fleet had been destroyed in a great storm. The 300 were but a portion of the shipwrecked French crews.

Menendez must have felt that divine intervention had aided his cause, but his next actions were certainly not attributable to Christian charity. After bargaining with the French and promising fair treatment, the Spanish took all 300 prisoners and proceeded to give the starving refugees a much-needed meal. It was to be their last. After they had eaten, Menendez put all his captives to the sword except 10 who professed to be Catholics.

By October 10, Menendez learned that Ribault himself with some 320 of his men were miserably encamped south of Matanzas Inlet. Again the Spaniards marched out with vastly inferior numbers to meet their foes. Lacking any means of resistance and obviously ignorant of their fellows' fate, 120 of the French refugees, including Ribault, agreed to surrender. The captives were ferried across the inlet and then killed.

The remaining French forces retreated south to present-day Cape Canaveral and began to build a fort. Menendez marched south yet again, and convinced this group to surrender by promising that they would all be transported safely to Havana. Strangely enough, Menendez honored this bargain.

The bloody Spanish massacres gave the name Matanzas or place of slaughter to the nearby inlet and river. Some historians have defended Menendez as only doing what was required to protect his numerically inferior

Fort Matanzas

forces. Most, however, have condemned the Spanish actions as the callous bloodbaths they really were.

Many years after Menendez's treachery, English forces attempted to use Matanzas Inlet as a "back door" route to attack St. Augustine. The Spanish countered by erecting a small fort on Rattlesnake Island in the late 1660s. Surprisingly, this coquina fortification proved successful in helping defend St. Augustine while the great Castillo de San Marcos was under construction. This same fort can be seen today overlooking the river and inlet it has guarded for more than 300 years.

Marineland (Standard Mile 796.5)

Marineland Marina used to sit along the Waterway's eastern banks some 3 nautical miles south of the ICW's intersection with Matanzas Inlet, between flashing daybeacon #87 and unlighted daybeacon #89. This facility is apparently out of operation as this account is being tapped out on the keyboard. Only the future will tell what, if any, services may some-day be available here for passing cruisers.

Palm Coast Marina (Standard Mile 802) (29 34.620 North/081 11.607 West)

A mile or so south of flashing daybeacon #109, the popular resort community of Palm Coast lines the Waterway's western banks for several miles. This resort boasts many beautiful homes and a labyrinth of small canals.

Of greater importance to visiting mariners is the full-service Palm Coast Marina. This excellent facility offers a whole array of attractive and unusual amenities for waterborne transients. The marina is found on the southern shores of the southernmost Palm Coast canal. This stream makes into the Waterway's westerly banks, just a short hop north of the high-rise Palm Coast bridge.

Palm Coast Marina is one of our favorite stops in northeastern Florida. Seldom will cruisers find a facility that offers such an impressive variety of services. Extensive transient dockage at concrete, fixed piers, along

Palm Coast Marina

with full fueling facilities and waste pump-out service, is, of course, readily available. Approach and dockside depths maintain minimum 6- to 6½-foot levels with typical soundings in the 7-foot region. Full power and water connections are at hand, as are cable-television hookups in the larger slips. There is even the opportunity to connect the laptop to a local Internet service to check e-mail. The adjacent climate-controlled showers and Laundromat are extranice and squeaky clean. Mechanical repairs can be arranged through independent contractors. The on-site ship's and variety store is very impressive. It is one of the finest nonchain stores of this ilk that we have ever reviewed. Bicycles can be rented here as well.

If the marina's variety store cannot meet your galley supply needs, a complimentary ride to the local grocery and other retail stores is cheerfully furnished. Cruisers who are docking in the marina and want to rest ashore for awhile receive special rates at the adjacent hotel (800-654-6538). Fine dining is also available at the hotel's Flagler's Restaurant and adjacent Henry's Lounge, both within easy walking distance of the docks. In fact, Flagler's

now offers dockside delivery of takeout food items. Just call (386) 445-6357.

Palm Coast offers more than a few opportunities to leave your craft behind and enjoy all sorts of outdoor and recreational activities. You can make use of the adjacent swimming pools and Jacuzzi at no additional charge, and guest rates are in effect for the tennis courts and five golf courses. Complimentary trams are available to ferry-visiting cruisers to these various amenities. Bike rentals are conveniently available at the harbor.

> **Palm Coast Marina (386) 446-6370**
> **http://www.palmcoastresort.com**
> **/marina.htm**
>
> **Approach depths—6-10 feet**
> **Dockside depths—6-7 feet (minimum)**
> **Accepts transients—yes**
> **Transient dockage—average**
> **Fixed concrete piers—yes**
> **Dockside power connections—30,**
>   **50, and (a few) 100 amps**
> **Dockside water connections—yes**
> **Showers—yes**
> **Laundromat—yes**
> **Waste pump-out—yes**
> **Gasoline—yes**
> **Diesel fuel—yes**
> **Mechanical repairs—yes**
>   **(independent contractors)**
> **Ship's and variety store—yes**
> **Restaurant—on site**

Flagler Beach Marina (Standard Mile 808.5)

Passing cruisers will note a marked, eastward-running channel between unlighted daybeacons #7 and #9. This cut once led to poorly maintained Flagler Beach Marina. This operation has now been closed for several years, and the old piers are in very poor condition. Don't even think about attempting entry.

Concrete Plant Canal (Standard Mile 809)

Between unlighted daybeacon #11 and

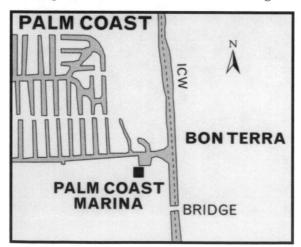

flashing daybeacon #13, a deep creek makes into the Waterway's western shoreline. This stream, which served as a popular anchorage for many years, is no longer a ready haven for the cruising community. A concrete plant sits at the westerly tip of the creek. After being closed for time out of mind, it has reopened, and barge traffic is once again regularly making use of the passage from the Waterway to the plant. There is also a Sea Ray manufacturing facility on the stream's southern banks. With all this activity, we strongly suggest that you look elsewhere for secure overnight anchorage.

Tomoka River Basin and Halifax River (Standard Mile 819)

South of unlighted daybeacon #32, the ICW flows into the headwaters of broad but shallow Halifax River, with Tomoka Basin just to the west. Like most of the waters outside the Waterway channel along Halifax River, the Tomoka Basin is quite shallow, with depths of 2 to 4 feet being the norm. A marked channel between unlighted daybeacon #6 and flashing daybeacon #7 leads west and then north to Tomoka River itself. While the river is quite deep, the channel through the basin exhibits consistent 3- to 4-foot soundings at low water.

This cut's shallow depths prohibit all but shoal-draft boats from cruising the Tomoka. This lovely stream has beautifully natural banks with lush tropical foliage and abundant wildlife. Those lucky enough to visit the Tomoka often report sighting alligators, dolphins, pelicans, and birds of all descriptions.

Adding insult to injury, the river also provides access to Tomoka State Park (386-676-4050). This intriguing 914-acre recreational facility was once the site of a Timucuan Indian village, and later Mount Oswald Plantation. Today, the park offers camping, fishing, picnic grounds, nature trails, a historical museum, and a magnificent statue of Chief Tomokie, who ruled the land hereabouts long before European domination. Canoe rentals are also available for trips down dreamlike Tomoka River.

Captains of most cruising-size vessels will have no choice but to arrange for land transportation from one of the Daytona Beach marinas in order to visit this memorable park. Otherwise, you will most likely have to pass by this wonderful attraction, though perhaps not without a few sighs of longing.

Tomoka and Halifax River History The history of the Tomoka and Halifax River Basin stretches far back into the era when only Native Americans wandered Florida's land and waters.

In 1605 Alvaro Mexia Ybarra visited a cove on Tomoka River called Nocoroco. There he saw four Indian villages huddled on the shores of the cove. According to Alice Strickland in her fascinating book *The Valiant Pioneers,* Nocoroco was probably the location where "the Timucuans made their last stand against the overwhelming encroachment of the white man." Today, you can still visit the historic site of Nocoroco; it is now known as Fairland and is part of Tomoka State Park.

As interesting as the prehistory of the Tomoka and Halifax rivers is, for many the real historical interest of the region centers on the tragic story of the vast plantations that once graced the two rivers' shores. During the second period of Spanish rule, which began in 1783, Florida's governors encouraged development of the land by all who were willing to take an oath of loyalty to the Spanish king. One hundred acres were to be allotted to the head of every foreign household, with an additional fifty acres for all other members of the family.

Many arrived in Florida during this period to take advantage of Spain's generous offer. From the nearby Bahama Islands came the Russell, Williams, McHardy, Kerr, Bunch, Addison, and Ormond families. In a surprisingly short period, these dedicated settlers had begun to carve vast landholdings out of the wilderness surrounding the twin rivers.

In 1821 the heirs of John Russell sold over 4,000 acres of their family land to Charles W. Bulow of Charleston. Bulow wasted no time in settling on his estate, naming it Bulowville. To the south, Samuel Williams founded Orange Grove on the site of modern Daytona Beach, and in April 1816, Capt. James Ormond was granted 2,000 acres of fine land on the Halifax River at a place called Damietta. Many years later, the settlement of Ormond Beach would take its name from the one-time presence of this hardy family.

By 1821 when Florida finally came under American control, it is estimated that as many as sixteen plantations occupied the rich lands between the Tomoka Basin and New Smyrna. Though cotton, rice, and other crops were grown with success, it was the cultivation of sugarcane that brought great wealth to the twin river planters. Before the 1820s, many sugar mills had been built on the various plantations from the native coquina rock. Several of these plants were outfitted with new steam engines to turn the massive rollers that crushed the sweet cane to syrup.

Meanwhile, since the mid-eighteenth century various branches of the Creek Indian nation had been drifting into Florida. The territory's native Indians had completely disappeared by this time, and the new arrivals quickly adapted their life-style to Florida's swampy resources. In time, these various subtribes became the Seminole Indian nation.

By the 1830s, pressure was being brought to bear on the federal government in Washington to remove the entire Seminole population to western lands. Many unscrupulous settlers had already driven the Indians ruthlessly from their lands. These self-serving developers saw the Seminoles' mass migration as a quick way to open the rest of Florida to settlement. Tragically, the federal government responded with an ill-planned offer to move the Indians to Oklahoma in exchange for money and land.

The Seminoles had already learned to distrust their white neighbors. When the various tribes heard of the plan to evict them from their lands, they were enraged. In December 1835, the long and bloody seven-year Seminole War began. The Tomoka and Halifax plantations were some of the first lands to fall victim to this senseless struggle.

By 1835, Bulowville was being managed by Charles Bulow's son, John Joachim Bulow. With the threat of hostilities in the air, Maj. Benjamin Putnam marched south from St. Augustine to protect the twin-river plantations. Bulow had been on excellent terms with the local Seminoles until now and did not welcome Putnam's protection. He correctly foresaw that the militia's presence might well incite the Indians to violence.

Bulow therefore summarily ordered the soldiers off his land. Putnam refused and Bulow became a prisoner in his own home. A makeshift fort was thrown up around Bulowville, and with the onset of Indian attacks, the region's planters rushed to the fortified house for protection.

Eventually, after an abortive engagement with a strong Seminole war party under their great chief Coacoochee (Wildcat), Putnam was ordered to retreat. Bulow was not allowed to carry away any of his personal possessions. The soldiers had barely departed before Seminole warriors descended on Bulowville and burned it to the ground.

All the once-proud plantations of the Tomoka and Halifax rivers were laid waste in the long war. Even after peace was restored seven bloody years later, the plantations never revived. Many a field that had once waved proudly with sugarcane or snowy cotton was reclaimed by the wilderness. The coquina walls of the sugar mills were hidden by green vines, and the remains of the plantation homes vanished in a riot of undergrowth.

For many years the once-developed lands about the Tomoka and Halifax rivers remained a veritable wilderness. Eventually, however, the region recovered. During the 1850s a small settlement known as Tomoka grew up some four miles west of present-day Ormond Beach, but this community was abandoned after the destructive freezes of 1894-95. By 1866, the New Britain community had been founded on the banks of Halifax River by the Bostrorn family (New Britain would eventually grow into the resort community of Ormond Beach) and in 1870 Mathias Day founded Daytona to the south.

In *The Valiant Pioneers,* Strickland tells of the return of John Bulow as an elderly man to the Ormond settlement. With the aid of several prominent townspeople, he was able to locate the ruins of his old homeplace. Who among us cannot but wonder at his bitter thoughts on that sad occasion? Looking from the long-overgrown fields to the shattered remnants of his plantation home, Bulow must have wondered where it had all gone.

Daytona Beach (Standard Mile 830)

South of the Ormond Beach Bridge and unlighted daybeacon #18, only passing cruisers who have lost the power of sight could miss the increased development along both shorelines. You are now beginning your approach to the resort city of Daytona Beach and its various nearby supporting communities.

Daytona Beach is the most popular resort on Florida's east coast north of Palm Beach. When you consider the vast number of tourists who flock to eastern Florida each winter, that is quite a claim to fame.

Daytona's popularity is certainly deserved. The packed sand beaches in the area have been famous for many years. In fact, some of the first automobile races in the United States were held on the sands of Ormond and Daytona beaches.

Daytona Beach boasts many attractions for visitors. For those who can obtain automobile transportation, a visit to The Casements (25 Riverside Drive, 386-676-3216) in nearby Ormond Beach is highly recommended. Once the winter home of multimillionaire John D. Rockefeller, this famous homeplace now serves as a cultural center and museum for the city of Ormond Beach. Regular attractions include art exhibits, the Hungarian Historic Room, and the historic Rockefeller exhibit. Operating hours are 9:00 A.M. to 9:00 P.M. Monday through Thursday, 9:00 A.M. to 5:00 P.M. Friday, and 9:00 A.M. to noon Saturday.

The downtown Halifax Historical Museum (252 South Beach Street, 386-255-6976) is within walking distance of both Halifax Harbor Marina and Daytona Marina and Boat Works. The museum is housed in the old

Merchant's Bank building. Spanish artifacts, plantation memorabilia, and mementos of the early days of beach automobile racing are featured. A film is also offered outlining the history of Daytona Beach and its surrounding communities.

Again, those lucky enough to have car rentals or other motorized transportation should make every effort to visit the Bulow Plantation Ruins State Historic Site (Old Dixie Highway north of Ormond Beach). Here you can view the remains of the proud plantation that we met in our historic review of Halifax River above. The coquina ruins of a sugar mill, springhouse, and the Bulow home's foundation are all fascinating. There is also an open-air museum featuring Seminole Indian relics and artifacts. The site is open from 9:00 to 5:00 daily.

Those who love sports will find plenty to do in Daytona. In February there is the 24 Hours of Daytona auto race, followed by the world-famous Daytona 500. January brings the women's South Atlantic Golf Tournament, and spring finds the Montreal Expos in training camp at Daytona. It's often possible to catch an exhibition baseball game in March or April. Of interest to sailors, the Daytona to Bermuda sailing race begins just offshore in May. If Harley Davidson motorcycles happen to be your thing, don't dare miss Bike Week every March. This event grows ever larger with each passing year.

It is also possible to join one of the bus tours to Disney World. Daytona is the northernmost point from which shoreside transportation is readily available to this magical wonderland.

As you might imagine, Daytona Beach offers a host of shoreside businesses and yachting services. You should be able to satisfy almost any need in the Daytona region, from groceries to a new fuel pump. Many merchants are within walking distance of the city marinas. Others can be reached by a short taxi ride.

Daytona also offers excellent transportation facilities. From the Daytona airport many major airlines fly regularly to points north. You could arrange to dock your boat here for several weeks and fly back home to check on whoever's minding the store.

Daytona Beach, as you might imagine, offers a wide array of dining attractions. By all accounts, consider a visit to the Cellar Restaurant (220 Magnolia Avenue, 386-258-0011). It is within walking distance of Halifax Harbor Marina and Daytona Marina and Boat Works. This bistro-style restaurant features outside dining and yummy French pastries.

Yet another choice is Live Oak Inn and Restaurant (448 South Beach Street, 386-252-4667), directly across the street from Halifax Harbor Marina. This outstanding "country inn" is housed in the oldest home in Daytona, originally built in 1871. It serves some truly elegant cuisine. The restaurant is open to the public beginning at 5:30 P.M., Tuesday through Saturday.

The good people at Halifax Harbor Marina (see below) have told us that many cruisers berth in Daytona year after year just to visit Stavros Original Pizza Restaurant (262 Beach Street, 386-258-5041). Also within walking distance of the two main dockage basins, this establishment serves simply outstanding Greek and Italian style food.

Numbers to know in Daytona:
Yellow Cab—386-255-5555
Enterprise Rent-A-Car—386-252-1224
Budget Car Rental—386-255-0539
AAA Rentals—386-304-2727
Alamo Rent A Car—386-255-1511
West Marine—386-226-9966

Chamber of Commerce—386-255-0981

While the hustle and bustle of the greater Daytona region may be a bit much for mariners who prefer a quiet anchorage, there is no denying the city's popularity with tourists and cruisers alike. It's a great place to rest from your travels for a day or two. Remember, there is no metropolitan complex to compare with Daytona north of Palm Beach. That fact may entice you to stay or pass on by, depending on your particular taste.

Daytona's Bridges

Four bridges span the Halifax River-ICW channel in Daytona Beach. In years past, a cruise through these waters was a real steeplechase. Now, thankfully, two of these former impediments to navigation have been replaced by fixed, high-rise structures. Only the southernmost span, Memorial Bridge, retains any opening restrictions. Things do improve sometimes!

Daytona Marina Facilities (Various Lats/Lons—see below)

With only a few exceptions, the marinas in the Daytona region are of good reputation and can be confidently used by visitors. Two large facilities offer just about everything passing cruisers could desire. There is also one smaller firm that might be considered as well.

South-southeast of unlighted daybeacon #30, a marked channel once led west-southwest to Aloha Marina. This facility is now completely closed.

Next up is Caribbean Jack's Marina (formerly English Jim's Marina, near 29 13.650 North/081 01.358 West). This facility lies along the southwesterly banks, south-southeast of unlighted daybeacon #32. Caribbean Jack's changed ownership in March of 1999, and while many new and welcome services have been added, many of us still fondly remember the warm greeting we used to receive from longtime English Jim's dockmaster Gary Crane.

Caribbean Jack's Marina does accept transients, and visitors will find berths at fixed wooden piers featuring water hookups and 30- and 50-amp power connections. Caribbean Jack's has two sets of docks. The newer piers face directly onto the Halifax River, while the remaining docks are located in a protected basin dredged out of the shoreline. Obviously, better protection is afforded by the inner harbor slips. Both sets of docks are subject to some chop in particularly strong easterly and northeasterly winds. Depths alongside run from 6 to 8 feet at most berths. New, climate-controlled showers, a full Laundromat, a cruiser's lounge complete with Internet connections, plus gasoline and diesel fuel are all ready at hand. There's even a new, on-site, heated swimming pool.

Another new addition at Caribbean Jack's is a large, on-site restaurant of the same name. We have not yet had the good fortune to dine here, but the huge deck overlooking the Halifax River looked ever so inviting as we cruised past. Parks Seafood Restaurant (951 North Beach Street, 386-253-0681) is within a long walk of Caribbean Jack's. This well-known dining spot is a family operation, and the seafood is obviously prepared with a special pride. For those who prefer to cook the catch of the day themselves, Parks also has a seafood deli.

Caribbean Jack's Marina (386) 253-5647
http://www.caribbeanjacks.com

Approach depths—6-10 feet
Dockside depths—6-8 feet

Accepts transients—yes
Transient dockage rate—above average
Fixed wooden piers—yes
Dockside power connections—30
   and 50 amps
Dockside water connections—yes
Showers—yes
Laundromat—yes
Gasoline—yes
Diesel fuel—yes
Restaurant—on-site and another nearby

Cruisers who have suffered through a long absence from the shores of Halifax River will be in for quite a shock when they go searching for the old Daytona Municipal Marina. Study the "Daytona Beach Municipal Yacht Basin" inset on chart 11485 for a moment. Both of the basins pictured in the inset are now part of huge Halifax Harbor Marina (near 29 12.216 North/081 00.755 West).

In the 1980s, the old municipal marina

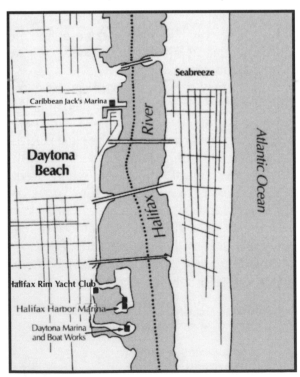

came under private management. In addition to the longtime harbor to the north (whose entrance runs west-southwest from the ICW, just south of the Memorial bascule bridge), the onetime small-craft dockage basin to the south was enlarged, dredged, and completely reconstructed as a second dockage basin. The entrance to this complex runs to the west-southwest, just south-southeast of unlighted daybeacon #39A.

There are now a total of 550 slips available to cruising craft between the two harbors. Berths in the older, north harbor feature fixed, wooden piers, while the south basin is graced by ultramodern, floating, concrete-decked docks. Low-water entrance and dockside depths in the north harbor run some 6½ to 7 feet of water, with 7½- to 9-foot soundings to be expected in the south basin. Protection from inclement weather is excellent in both enclosed harbors.

Transients are usually accommodated in the south harbor. Some slips have 50-amp and others have 30-amp power connections, while fresh water is on hand at all berths. A waste pump-out unit is available at the fuel dock. Some mechanical repairs can often be arranged through local, independent contractors.

The management of Halifax Harbor has warned this writer that more and more of their slips are being occupied by resident or seasonal vessels. It might be a good idea to make advance dockage reservations rather than risk disappointment.

Shoreside, there is much to see and do. Showers and Laundromats are spread in several convenient locations around both basins. Visit the dockmaster's building, just behind the fuel dock in the south harbor, and you will discover a nice captain's lounge graced by a

Halifax Harbor Marina, Daytona Beach

paperback exchange library. A second lounge is located on the second floor of the old north basin dockmaster's office, overlooking this harbor's entrance. There is also a small ship's store in the south harbor dockmaster's building.

When it comes time to tame a hearty appetite gleaned from a day on the water, all of the restaurants reviewed above are either within walking distance or only a quick taxi ride away. There are many other choices as well. Ask the friendly marina staff for directions.

Unfortunately (and surprisingly), all of the restaurants that once made their home in the building known as Columbia Plaza (which sits between Halifax Harbor's two dockage basins) were closed some years ago. However, plans call for a new "dining and dancing" attraction, to be known as the "Stock Exchange," to open in this complex by the time this account finds its way into your hands. Let us know if you have a good (or less-than-good) experience when you slake a healthy appetite here. Please send your impressions to opcom@cruising-guide.com.

For many years West Marine has maintained a store in the same building that will soon house the Stock Exchange. Give them a call at (386) 226-9966 for anything nautical.

Cruisers looking to restock their galley larders will need to take a taxi or find some other means of landside motorized transportation. The nearest supermarket is some two miles from the dockage basin. Ask any of the marina staff for directions.

Still not convinced? Well, consider two more attributes of Halifax Harbor. First of all, the marina is located in the heart of downtown Daytona Beach. Retail businesses of all descriptions are within walking distance. You'll also be close to the action when Daytona is hosting one of its many festivals. During one of our earlier visits, it was "Biker's Weekend." We have never seen so many Harley Davidsons.

Then, there is the attitude that we have always encountered when visiting Halifax Harbor. All too often, large supermarinas of Halifax Harbor's vintage have a cold, distant reception for visiting cruisers, but not so here! We have never failed to find a friendly, helpful, and caring attitude during our many stays. The dockmaster and his staff do a wonderful job of making one and all feel welcome.

Well, if you still aren't convinced, better consider some other avocation besides cruising. We give Halifax Harbor our highest recommendation.

Halifax Harbor Marina (386) 671-3600
http://www.halifaxharbor.net

Approach depths—6^1/$_2$-7 feet (north harbor)
   7^1/$_2$-9 feet (south harbor)
Dockside depths—6^1/$_2$-7 feet (north harbor)
   7^1/$_2$-9 feet (south harbor)
Accepts transients—yes
Transient dockage rate—average
Fixed wooden piers—yes (north basin)
Floating concrete docks—yes (south basin)
Dockside power connections—30

and 50 amps (not every
slip has both connections)
Dockside water connections—yes
Showers—yes
Laundromat—yes
Waste pump-out—yes
Gasoline—yes (south harbor only)
Diesel fuel—yes (south harbor only)
Mechanical repairs—yes
(independent contractors)
Ship's store—yes (south harbor)
Restaurant—several nearby

Approach depths—6-7 feet
Dockside depths—7 feet
Accepts transients—members of other
yacht clubs with appropriate
reciprocal arrangements
Fixed wooden piers—yes
Floating wooden piers—yes (for smaller craft)
Dockside power connections—30 amps
Dockside water connections—yes
Showers—yes
Laundromat—yes
Restaurant—on site and others nearby

The north dockage basin of Halifax Harbor is home to the good folks at Halifax River Yacht Club. The clubhouse and docks overlook the western shoreline in this harbor near 29 12.463 North/081 00.978 West. Guest dockage is afforded to members of other yacht clubs with appropriate reciprocal arrangements. Two hundred feet of fixed, wooden piers are set aside for transients, as well as a number of slips built around wooden-decked floating piers for smaller craft. Depths alongside run an impressive 7 feet or better. The club has a dockmaster in attendance from 8:00 A.M. to 6:00 P.M. "most days." Showers, ice, and a Laundromat are available in the clubhouse. The club's dining room is open for lunch and dinner seven days a week. Reservations are requested for the evening meal.

In 1997 this writer was privileged to hold a seminar at Halifax River Yacht Club on cruising the waters of eastern Florida. The meeting was thrown open to the public, and before it was all over, you could not have stuffed another cruiser into the clubhouse with a shoehorn. This writer will always be grateful to the members of HRYC for this memorable evening.

Halifax River Yacht Club (386) 255-7459
http://www.hryc.com

If by now you are getting a bit tired of hearing me discuss first-class Daytona-based marinas, prepare to be bored anew. If Halifax Harbor is the best semipublic facility in Daytona, then certainly Daytona Marina and Boat Works (near 29 12.097 North/081 00.671 West) is the best privately owned marina and boatyard, particularly for power craft. The entrance channel leading to the marina's well-sheltered dockage basin cuts west-southwest from the ICW track, a short hop south-southeast of unlighted daybeacon #39A and the southerly Halifax Harbor entrance cut. The channel is clearly charted as the southernmost cut on the "Daytona Beach Municipal Yacht Basin" chart 11485 inset.

Daytona Marina and Boat Works combines extensive transient dockage with an impressive array of repair services. Visiting craft are accommodated at both fixed wooden and one floating wooden pier. Currently, minimum entrance depths run 8 to 8½ feet. Depths in most of the dockage basin are about 10 feet, but against some of the docks, water levels are at 7-foot levels. Power connections run the full gamut with 30-, 50-, and even 100-amp hookups (including three-phase), alongside the usual freshwater connections. The fully air-conditioned showers and Laundromat are as first class as it gets, as is the impressive captain's lounge with color television. To give you some idea of how this firm treats its customers, fresh coffee and a wide variety of donuts are complimentary every morning in the lounge. Gasoline, diesel fuel, and waste pump-out are on hand at the fuel dock, sitting astride the dockmaster's office and the marina entrance. A small but well-stocked ship's and variety store is also found in this building.

Daytona Marina and Boat Works offers full-service mechanical repairs for both gasoline and diesel engines, plus haul-outs and below-waterline repairs by way of a 55-ton travelift. It's really good news that this sort of full-service work is available in Daytona after an absence of several years.

As if all these amenities were not enough, the marina also features its own top-line dining spot, the Chart House Restaurant and Lounge (386-255-9022). Housed in a glass-encased, many-sided building, the restaurant overlooks the harbor and its collected craft. Patrons sit amid many lush plants and can

Chart House Restaurant at Daytona Marina and Boat Works

enjoy the freshest seafood or fine steaks and prime rib. The food is wonderful, but this is the sort of dining spot that may blow the weekly budget. We suggest trying it at least once during each visit to the marina, though. It's really that good.

Daytona Marina and Boat Works
(386) 252-6421
http://www.daytonamarina.com

Approach depths—8-8$^{1}/_{2}$ feet
Dockside depths—7-10 feet
Accepts transients—yes
Transient dockage rate—slightly above average
Fixed wooden piers—yes
Floating wooden pier—yes
Dockside power connections—30, 50, and 100 amps
Dockside water connections—yes
Showers—yes
Laundromat—yes
Waste pump-out—yes
Gasoline—yes
Diesel fuel—yes
Below-waterline repairs—yes
Mechanical repairs—yes
Ship's and variety store—yes (small)
Restaurant—on site and others nearby

Daytona Marina and Boat Works

MATANZAS RIVER TO DAYTONA BEACH NAVIGATION

South of its intersection with San Sebastian River, the ICW follows the winding course of Matanzas River for just over ten nautical miles before ducking behind Matanzas Inlet and Rattlesnake Island. While, as usual, the Waterway is well marked, strong tidal currents scour this stretch. The swiftly moving waters can ease you onto the shoals flanking both shorelines. Check the track over your stern frequently for excessive leeway.

The intersection of the ICW and the upper reaches of Matanzas River (leading to an inlet of the same name) is a problem stretch with chronic shoaling. Proceed at maximum alert and be ready for new and different aids to navigation than those shown on chart 11485 or those described in this text.

From Matanzas River to the Tomoka Basin, the ICW is well protected and easily run. The Waterway follows a dredged channel through the headwaters of Halifax River to Daytona Beach. The consistently shallow depths outside of the ICW cut call for careful attention to markers north of Daytona.

On the ICW A short distance south of the ICW's intersection with San Sebastian River, the Waterway passes under the State Road 312 fixed bridge with 65 feet of vertical clearance. After clearing the span, be sure to pass west of unlighted daybeacon #15. Shallow water lies east of this aid to navigation.

At unlighted daybeacon #17, the ICW rounds a turn and strikes to the southeast. Soon the first possible anchorage comes abeam at flashing daybeacon #18.

Waterway Anchorage To enter the patch of deep water west and southwest of flashing daybeacon #18, break off from the ICW about 200 yards northwest of #18. Point to pass #18 by some 100 yards to its westerly side. You can continue on this course to the south-southeast and hold minimum 8-foot depths for at least .3 nautical miles.

On the ICW Pass well to the east of unlighted daybeacons #20 and #22, and flashing daybeacon #24. As correctly portrayed on chart 11485, shallows lie west of these markers.

Open Anchorage You can enter the open anchorage southeast of flashing daybeacon #31 by tracking your way carefully toward the eastern banks of the river as you come abeam of unlighted daybeacon #30. After approaching to within 75 yards or so of the eastern shoreline, curve around to the south-southeast and point to pass #31 by some 100 yards to its easterly side. You continue to feel your way south-southeast for a good distance in 6-foot minimum depths, but be on guard against the tongue of 2-foot shallows to the west. We have seen people standing at high tide on this shoal in water only up to their knees.

On the ICW Watch out for the prominent shoal abutting the Waterway's southerly flank in the charted bend between unlighted daybeacons #38 and #40. Be sure to come abeam and pass #38 to its northerly side and take #40 to its easterly quarter. Flashing daybeacon #39 lies between #38 and #40, in the body of the turn. Pass #39 by some 20 yards to its southwesterly side.

Chart 11485 shows a small channel adjacent to the Butler Beach waterfront southeast of unlighted daybeacon #44. Shoaling not noted on chart 11485 has rendered this cut unusable by cruising-size vessels. Currently, you will encounter 3- and 4-foot depths as you move southeast on the one-time channel.

While passing between unlighted daybeacon #54 and flashing daybeacon #57, you will likely spy a series of unlighted daybeacons leading toward the eastern shore. These mark a small channel used by local vessels in the Crescent Beach community. The cut does not lead to any facilities and is best avoided by Waterway cruisers.

Southeast of unlighted daybeacon #58, you will soon encounter the Crescent Beach Bridge. This span has a closed vertical clearance of 25 feet and opens on demand.

Just northwest of this bridge, a sign on the northeastern side of the channel warns that the next 3 miles are a minimum-wake zone. The restricted stretch ends near flashing daybeacon #74, where you will see a "Resume Normal, Safe Operation" sign.

Pay particular attention to markers south of the Crescent Beach span. Both sides of the channel are quite shoal.

Between unlighted daybeacons #66 and #68, flashing daybeacon #67 marks the eastern boundary of the ICW channel. This flasher is almost on shore and can be difficult to see for both north- or southbound navigators. As the channel is rather broad here, there is no great cause for concern.

Past Matanzas River   South of flashing daybeacon #78, the Waterway begins its approach to the passage across the headwaters of Matanzas River. As has been stated repeatedly throughout this chapter, the stretch of the ICW is subject to continual shoaling and can be quite tricky. Markers are frequently shifted and changed to follow the ever-moving sands.

With this in mind, we will not pretend to outline the current configuration of aids to navigation in this account. They would undoubtedly be different by the time you arrive. As usual, southbound craft should pass all red, even-numbered markers to their (the cruisers') starboard side and take green beacons to port. In general, favor the western (mainland) side of the channel as you move past the Matanzas River intersection, and watch out for strong tidal currents. Eventually, the cut skirts behind Rattlesnake Island, and most of the problems are left behind. Flashing daybeacon #82 is the first marker south of the turn behind Rattlesnake Island. It is a welcome sight.

Remember, we no longer recommend that cruising craft attempt to anchor in Matanzas River, abeam of the old fort. Leave these highly changeable waters to local power captains.

On the ICW   The lower reaches of Matanzas River leading south from the inlet make into the Waterway's eastern shore at flashing daybeacon #86. Avoid this cut! It is crossed by a low-level fixed bridge, and unmarked shoals are rampant.

The various Marineland buildings will appear to the southeast as you come abeam of flashing daybeacon #87. Remember, at least for the moment, this facility is not in operation.

Past Marineland, the ICW follows a dredged cut through the shallow waters of Pellicer Flats. South of flashing daybeacon #109, the Waterway enters a sheltered canal that eventually leads to Tomoka Basin and the headwaters of Halifax River.

Begin watching to the west as you track your course south from #109 and you will soon catch sight of the homes and canals associated with the Palm Coast development. The eastern banks also exhibit fairly heavy residential development, though the houses are certainly a step or two down the ladder of luxury from the Palm Coast homes.

Eventually, you will spot a sign advertising Palm Coast Marina just off the mouth of the southernmost of the resort's canals. To enter, remain on the Waterway's midwidth until coming directly abeam of the canal's midwidth. Then turn in on the centerline and follow the canal west to the marina complex. The fuel docks front the stream itself while the dockage basin is carved out of the southern banks.

Just south of the entrance to Palm Coast Marina, cruisers will come upon the Palm Coast Parkway Bridge. Fortunately, this fixed span has a full vertical clearance of 65 feet and does not present any problems.

Unlighted daybeacon #1 south of Palm Coast marks the northerly entrance to an abandoned loop of the ICW that reenters the present-day Waterway at flashing daybeacon #3. This old cut has now shoaled badly, with depths of 3 to 4 feet being the norm. Cruising skippers are strictly advised not to attempt entry at either end of the loop.

The old channel that once led to Flagler Beach Marina will come up to the east-northeast, south of unlighted daybeacon #7. This cut is now quite shoal and the marina is closed. Don't attempt to enter.

Please remember that we no longer recommend anchorage on the westward running stream, south of unlighted daybeacon #11. With the reopening of the concrete plant overlooking this stream's westerly tip, barge traffic is too great a possibility for a comfortable overnight stay.

On to Daytona   Some 1.1 nautical miles south of flashing daybeacon #13, the Flagler Beach high-rise bridge crosses the Waterway, with 65 feet of vertical clearance.

South of unlighted daybeacon #24, passing cruisers will come upon the J. B. Knox/Bulow bascule bridge (also known as High Bridge). This span has a closed vertical clearance of 15 feet, but it opens on demand.

South-southeast of unlighted daybeacon #32, you will begin to catch sight of the wide Tomoka River basin across the small spoil islands to the west and southwest. South of #34, for some unknown reason, the numbering sequence on the ICW's aids to navigation begins anew. The next marker (moving south from #34) is flashing daybeacon #2, marking the channel's westerly limits.

Unlighted daybeacon #6 ushers cruising mariners into the wide but shallow reaches of Halifax River. Remember to keep strictly to the marked channel while on the waters of the Halifax. With but a few exceptions, grounding depths are quickly encountered outside of the Waterway.

Between unlighted daybeacon #6 and

flashing daybeacon #7, the marked, but shallow, channel leading to Tomoka River breaks off to the west. Don't attempt to enter unless you can stand consistent 3- to 4-foot depths.

Ormond Beach Bridge spans Halifax River south-southeast of unlighted daybeacon #18. The bridge is a fixed span with a vertical clearance of 65 feet.

South of unlighted daybeacon #19, the heavy development associated with Daytona Beach and its surrounding communities begins to encompass both shorelines.

Daytona Beach Bridges   Passage through the waters adjoining Daytona Beach has now been vastly simplified by the replacement of both the old Seabreeze bascule bridge and Broadway bridges with modern, fixed, high-rise structures. Only the southernmost Memorial Bridge still features a restrictive opening schedule.

The Seabreeze Bridge comes up south-southeast of unlighted daybeacon #30. As alluded above, this span's 65 feet of vertical clearance is a welcome addition to the eastern Florida ICW.

The next span, known as the Main Street Bridge, comes up south-southeast of unlighted daybeacon #32. It has a closed vertical clearance of 22 feet, but opens on demand.

The Broadway Bridge crosses the ICW south-southeast of unlighted daybeacons #33 and #34. Thankfully this span is now a 65-foot fixed bridge as well.

On the other hand, the Memorial Bridge, which spans the Waterway south-southeast of unlighted daybeacon #36, features a closed vertical clearance of 21 feet and a restrictive opening schedule. This span is closed Monday to Saturday from 7:45 A.M. to 8:45 A.M. and 4:45 P.M. to 5:45 P.M. However, it does open at 8:15 A.M. and 5:15 P.M. At all other times, it opens on demand.

Memorial Bridge can present a difficult problem while you await an opening. Shallows guard both flanks of the channel. It's no easy task keeping your craft in the deep water during high winds. In foul weather, time your arrival to coincide with the hours when the bridge opens on demand.

No-wake regulations are strictly enforced between the Seabreeze and Main Street bridges. In fact, it is a good idea to proceed with minimal wake along the entire Daytona Beach waterfront. Even if you are operating on unrestricted waters, every captain is legally responsible for any damage resulting from his or her wake.

Daytona Marinas   North of Seabreeze Bridge, the old channel that once led to Aloha Marina makes off to the southwest. It is marked on chart 11485 as "7 feet rep." This marina is now closed. Bypass this cut entirely.

South of unlighted daybeacon #36, switch to the "Daytona Beach Municipal Yacht Basin" inset on chart 11485 for better resolution. The marked entrance channel to Halifax Harbor's northern dockage basin comes up to the west-southwest, just south of the 21-foot Memorial Bascule Bridge. Successful navigation of the entrance channel is a simple matter of tracking your way between the various markers (remember your red, right, returning rule), taking red aids to navigation to your starboard side and passing green marks to port. Don't wander outside of the marked cut. This channel is flanked by partially submerged stone breakwaters, particularly to the north.

Another well-marked passage, this one leading west-southwest to Halifax Harbor's southerly dockage basin, will be spied just south-southeast of unlighted daybeacon #39A. Remember, the vast majority of transient craft visiting Halifax Harbor are accommodated in this basin. Follow the markers (did you remember red, right,

returning?) until the channel takes a 90-degree swing to the north-northwest. Soon after you cut around this bend, the fuel dock and dockmaster's office will come abeam to starboard.

The well-outlined entrance to Daytona Marina and Boat Works comes up on the Waterway's west-southwesterly flank, also south-southeast of #39A and the southerly Halifax Harbor entrance channel. Simply pass between the marks. It doesn't get much simpler than this.

Port Orange to Indian River

From Port Orange, just south of Daytona Beach, the ICW follows the narrowing reaches of Halifax River to Ponce de Leon Inlet. Several miles north of the inlet, the Waterway abandons the Halifax and follows a man-made cut behind the various channels and small islands associated with this seaward passage.

The main body of Halifax River continues southeast to the inlet. As the stream swings southeast into the seaward cut, Rockhouse Creek splits back to the southwest and rejoins the ICW east of flashing daybeacon #10. Another cut, known locally as the "South Channel," leads southeast from Ponce de Leon Inlet and intersects the Waterway at flashing daybeacon #19. This entire region is subject to astonishingly swift tidal currents and chronic shoaling problems.

The friendly, almost sleepy port city of New Smyrna Beach makes its appearance on the ICW south of the inlet's waters. Boasting good marina facilities for visiting cruisers and a friendly yacht club, New Smyrna is a popular

stopover between Daytona and Titusville.

From New Smyrna the Waterway flows south via an improved channel that passes through a long series of mud flats and oyster banks. Eventually, the eastern shore falls away and mariners cruise into broad but mostly shallow Mosquito Lagoon. After a run of some 10 nautical miles through this vast water body, the ICW passes quickly through Haulover Canal and out into the headwaters of mammoth Indian River.

Anchorages are again fairly few, though a couple of sidewaters do offer a safe haven for the night. Marina facilities are available at Port Orange, Ponce de Leon Inlet, and New Smyrna. In between are long, barren stretches of often-undeveloped shores. You should be sure your tanks are topped up and your craft in first-rate operating condition before tackling the lonely stretch from New Smyrna to Indian River.

The run from Port Orange to Indian River is quite interesting, with a wide variety of scenery and wildlife. There are some trouble spots along the way, however, and the wise captain will stay alert for problems. You should have a pleasing but challenging run south to Indian River.

Port Orange and Seven Seas Marina & Boatyard (Standard Mile 835) 29 09.251 North/080 58.567 West

The ICW tracks its way south from Daytona Beach through the shallow waters of Halifax River and eventually passes under the high-rise Port Orange Bridge. Several small islands border the Waterway channel to the east and west on both sides of the Port Orange span. These small plots are sometimes covered with an incredible variety of pelicans, egrets, and other sea birds. You are, of course, welcome to look, but regulations prohibit landing.

Seven Seas Marina & Boatyard welcomes visiting cruisers on the eastern banks just north of the Port Orange Bridge. The marked and charted entrance channel cuts east-northeast almost directly abeam of unlighted daybeacon #56. This facility has a long-standing and richly deserved reputation for hospitality with Waterway cruisers.

Transients are accommodated at fixed, wooden piers set in a narrow, east-to-west-running basin. Protection is quite good from all but strong westerly and southwesterly winds, which blow directly across the river and into the harbor's entrance. All slips have full water and power connections. Approach depths run 6 to 8 feet, with at least 8 feet of water in the outer slips. Closer to shore some berths display soundings of 6 feet to as little as 4 feet for the innermost slips.

Step ashore for good showers, a Laundromat, and a full-line ship's store. Hungry? The on-site Pat's Riverfront Café

(386-756-8070) is open for breakfast and lunch. The seafood offerings during the mid-day meal are absolutely yummy. The locals have long ago discovered this rustic dining spot, so come early. Several additional restaurants and other shoreside businesses are within walking distance. Complimentary transportation is also provided to a nearby grocery store. Ask the friendly marina staff for help.

Seven Seas features haul-outs by way of a 30-ton travelift. Once your craft is out of the water and set upon its chocks or cradle, you may choose to do your own bottom work or leave the job to the yard professionals. Mechanical servicing is also available through arrangements with independent contractors. Judging from the numbers of hauled craft that we always observe during our visits to Seven Seas, this is a very popular yard with those who go cruising under sail.

Seven Seas Marina & Boatyard (386) 761-3221

Approach depths—6-8 feet
Dockside depths—6-9 feet
  4 feet (innermost slips)
Accepts transients—yes
Transient dockage rate—well below average
Fixed wooden piers—yes
Dockside power connections—30
  and 50 amps
Dockside water connections—yes
Showers—yes
Laundromat—yes
Gasoline—yes
Diesel fuel—yes
Below-waterline repairs—yes
Mechanical repairs—yes
  (independent contractors)
Ship's store—yes
Restaurant—on site and others nearby

While visiting in the Port Orange community, cruising visitors with automobile transportation may want to check out the Gamble

Place at Spruce Creek Preserve (386-255-0285). The preserve is home to hundreds of wildlife species, ancient cypress trees, and a profusion of plant life. A self-guided nature walk is available and pontoon boat trips on Spruce Creek are scheduled on a regular basis. Tours of the Gamble Place home are offered every Wednesday and Saturday. Reservations are required.

Adventure Yacht Harbor (Standard Mile 837) 29 07.935 North/080 57.695 West

Between flashing daybeacon #59 and unlighted daybeacon #60, a marked channel leads east and southeast to Adventure Yacht Harbor. New ownership took over this marina in June 1999, and things have been looking up ever since.

Adventure Yacht Harbor itself is glad to welcome visiting cruisers to fixed wooden piers featuring full power and water connections. Some 5-foot depths in the entrance channel might be a problem for long-legged vessels, but otherwise cruisers can make use of this small, well-sheltered marina with confidence. Showers and a Laundromat are found in the dockmaster's building just behind the piers. Here also you will find a petite ship's store. Gasoline and diesel fuel can be purchased at the newly rebuilt fuel pier, and the staff can sometimes arrange for mechanical repairs through local, independent contractors. Waste pump-out service is planned for the future.

Still not enough for you? Well, consider Adventure Yacht Harbor's location a scant two and a half blocks from the public beach. It's only a very short walk to the sun and sand scene.

Of course, all visitors will also want to take a very long look at the on-site Boondock's Restaurant and Bar (386-760-9001). This utterly funky dining spot features "under tent" dining. Besides the extensive menu, which boasts more than a few "sea creatures," this entire establishment has a real "Key West" feeling. Our impression is that a good time is usually had by all those fortunate enough to find their way through Boondock's tent flap!

Over and above these vital statistics, we could not help but be impressed by the owner's commitment to providing a warm and knowledgeable welcome to all cruisers. We think you will agree that Adventure Yacht Harbor is well worth a visit.

Adventure Yacht Harbor (386) 756-2180
http://www.adventureyachtharbor.com

Approach depths—5-6 feet
Dockside depths—6-8 feet
Accepts transients—yes
Transient dockage rate—below average
Fixed wooden piers—yes
Dockside power connections—30
and 50 amps
Dockside water connections—yes
Showers—yes
Laundromat—yes
Gasoline—yes
Diesel fuel—yes
Mechanical repairs—limited
(independent contractors)
Ship's store—yes (small)
Restaurant—on site

Ponce de Leon Inlet Channels, Facilities, and Lighthouse (Standard Mile 839.5) (Various Lats/Lons—see below)

The ICW flows south from unlighted daybeacon #72 to meet the northernmost channel leading to Ponce de Leon Inlet. This body of water is actually the southernmost waters of Halifax River, abandoned by the Waterway. Ponce de Leon Inlet is a treacherous seaward cut that is nevertheless used regularly by local captains. Twin stone breakwaters flanking the seaward entrance and regular dredging do serve to keep the cut open, but the passage is regularly exposed to deep swells and strong tides.

To say the very least, tidal currents boil through the various streams approaching Ponce de Leon Inlet. Seldom before have we seen such swiftly moving waters south of St. Marys River. Sailboats and trawlers must take extra care to see that they are not picked up and shoved onto one of the surrounding shoals.

The northerly, lower Halifax River, approach to the inlet boasts a wide channel with (currently) minimum 7-foot depths, but there is a definite scarcity of aids to navigation. In fact, at the current time, there are only three markers on this changeable cut. This coupled with the unusually strong tidal currents running through this lowest section of Halifax River will put navigators to the test. It is still possible to traverse the north channel in daylight, during fair weather, but it is an exacting process calling for more than the usual share of caution.

The first of Ponce Inlet's marina facilities gazes out over the northerly approach channel's northeasterly shores at the charted location of "Inlet Harbor" (northwest of correctly charted unlighted nun buoy #2 and near 29 05.481 North/080 56.435 West). Inlet Harbor Marina has been going through a slow upgrade process for the past several years. While we still could not accurately describe Inlet Harbor as first class in all respects, it does merit cruisers' attention, particularly those who pilot power craft less than 50 feet in length.

Overnighters are accepted at fixed wooden piers with water hookups and 30- and 50-amp power connections. Most of the basin is well sheltered, though a few slips and the fuel dock do front directly onto the inlet channel. As is true throughout this entire region, tidal currents on this main body of water can be swift indeed. Depths at Inlet Harbor's various slips vary widely from low-water soundings of 7 to as little as 5 feet. Some medium-quality showers are available, and both gasoline and diesel fuel can be purchased at the fuel dock fronting directly onto the inlet approach channel. A dry-stack storage building to accommodate smaller power craft is located on the marina grounds. There is also a tackle store just behind the fuel dock that offers a few marine items.

There is an on-site restaurant that goes by the name of Inlet Harbor Restaurant (386-767-5590), and judging from the number of cars we saw in the parking lot, it seems quite popular.

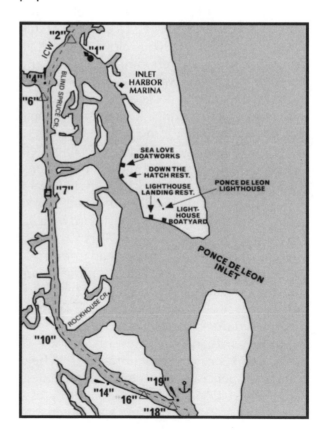

Inlet Harbor Marina (386) 767-3266
http://www.inletharbor.com

Approach depths—7-10 feet
Dockside depths—5-7 feet (minimum)
Accepts transients—yes
Transient dockage rate—above average
Fixed wooden piers—yes
Dockside power connections—30
    and 50 amps
Dockside water connections—yes
Showers—yes
Gasoline—yes
Diesel fuel—yes
Mechanical repairs—yes
    (smaller gasoline only)
Tackle store—yes
Restaurant—on site

South of unlighted nun buoy #2, several charter-boat docks line the eastern shore at the charted point of land, southeast of Piddler Island. You will also spy Down the Hatch Restaurant (386-761-4831) along this stretch. This popular spot offers outdoor dining and dockage for patrons who arrive by water. Most of the fixed, wooden docks seemed to be filled with resident craft during our last visit, but there should be enough room for at least one 30 footer. Depths alongside are a respectable 6 feet or better. Again, captains are cautioned against swift currents when approaching these docks.

A repair facility, Sea Love Boat Works (386-761-5434), is located just northwest of Down the Hatch Restaurant. This yard specializes in haul-outs by way of an impressive 70-ton travelift. Mechanical repairs are arranged through independent technicians, and diesel fuel can be purchased. There is no wet-slip dockage for visitors.

Southeast of the just described point of land, a series of charted, unlighted daybeacons leads generally north to Lighthouse Boat Yard (near 29 04.743 North/080 55.596 West). This is a very friendly marina and repair yard that goes the extra mile to help visitors. Transients are always welcome unless the docks are full. Berths are found at fixed wooden piers in an artificially enclosed basin, with good depths alongside of 6 to 8 feet. Some 5½- to 6-foot soundings are discovered in the marked entrance channel at low tide. Considering the somewhat limited number of slips at this marina, it would be best to call ahead of time and check on berth availability before planning an overnight stay. Full power and water connections are found at every slip, and there is a single, fair, non-air-conditioned shoreside shower. Gasoline and diesel fuel can be purchased dockside. The on-site ship's store has been recently expanded, and it is now worth everyone's attention who might be in the market for anything nautical.

Lighthouse Boat Yard's repair facilities are very active and obviously quite popular. We have never visited here without finding a whole collection of hauled boats undergoing service work of all varieties. The yard offers every imaginable mechanical, electrical, and below-the-waterline repair service. The on-site travelift is rated at 70 tons.

Hungry patrons of Lighthouse Boat Yard have the opportunity to satisfy their appetites at one of the most "funky and fun" dining spots in eastern Florida. Lighthouse Landing and Raw Bar (386-761-9271) is within a quick step of the marina basin. Here you will find the atmosphere of a Bahamian bar with outside (and inside) dining, superb seafood, and a warm crowd. During one of our earlier visits, a contingent of bikers had journeyed all the way from Biker's Weekend in Daytona just to partake of the crab and grouper sandwiches, not to mention a few cold ones. We have thoroughly enjoyed all our times at Lighthouse Landing, and feel that you will have a similar happy experience.

Lighthouse Boat Yard (386) 767-0683

Approach depths—5½-6 feet (minimum)
Dockside depths—6-8 feet
Accepts transients—limited (when
    space is available)
Transient dockage rate—average
Fixed wooden piers—yes
Dockside power connections—30
    and 50 amps
Dockside water connections—yes
Showers—yes
Gasoline—yes
Diesel fuel—yes
Below-waterline repairs—yes (extensive)
Mechanical repairs—yes (extensive)
Ship's store—yes
Restaurant—next door

Historic Ponce de Leon Lighthouse (386-761-1821) is literally just across the street from Lighthouse Boat Yard. This old sentinel of the sea has guarded Ponce Inlet for more than one hundred years. Visitors brave enough to ascend its 203 spiral steps are rewarded with a spectacular view of the surrounding land and waters.

The on-site museum features a variety of lighthouse artifacts and a gift shop. There is also a most interesting film shown regularly that depicts the history of Ponce Inlet as well as highlights from the days of beach racing in the area.

Southwest of the main inlet channel, Rockhouse Creek leads back to a juncture with the ICW southeast of flashing daybeacon #10. This creek has now shoaled badly and all but the smallest and shallowest-draft vessels are strictly warned against entering this errant body of water.

Southeast of the inlet, another marked channel (known locally as the "South Channel") forms a third link with the Waterway. This cut intersects the ICW at flashing daybeacon #19. While this stream is subject to chronic shoaling

along the edges of its channel, it currently holds minimum 7-foot depths along a broad passage between a barrier island to the east and a prominent shoal to the west. Two charted aids to navigation define a portion of the channel's flanks, but there is a lot of navigation by eye to be done between flashing daybeacon #11 and Ponce Inlet's flashing buoy #9.

It is far easier to enter the South Channel from the ICW at #19, rather than its northern intersection with Ponce Inlet at flashing buoy #9. Cautious navigators can probably run the South Channel successfully as far north as flashing buoy #9 during daylight, and in fair weather. Be warned, though; the partially unmarked shoals to the west and the usual swift currents are real hazards.

The lower (southeasterly) reaches of the South Channel can serve as a fair-weather overnight anchorage for boats of almost any size and draft. Protection from all but northerly blows is good, but you will have to contend with the water's strong currents. There is some condo development on the eastern shore, but to the west and southwest there is only marsh and undeveloped higher ground. If you drop the hook here, consider anchoring within 200

Lighthouse Boat Yard, Ponce de Leon Inlet

yards or so of the Waterway intersection (near 29 03.557 North/080 54.846 West). An anchor light is a necessity in this haven. Be sure your anchor isn't dragging before beginning your work below in the galley. A second anchor might also be a good plan indeed considering the swiftly moving waters.

Sheephead Cut (Standard Mile 845.5)

It is always a sad experience for us to report on an anchorage that in years past was a fine haven, but has now been pretty much negated by encroaching development. We are sorry to say that this now describes the once-popular overnight stopover on Sheephead Cut. This loop stream breaks off from the Waterway's southern shores at flashing daybeacon #33 and rejoins the ICW just north of the New Smyrna fixed bridge.

While minimum 8-foot depths are still held in the cut's channel, the southern shores are now guarded by a closely packed maze of low-rise condos. Just to make matters worse, most of the stream's channel, including its westerly intersection with the ICW, has now been marked, thereby promoting far more through traffic on these waters than was true in times past. It is difficult if not downright impossible to find enough room off the marked passage to anchor comfortably, and we all know that dropping the hook inside a marked cut is a definite no-no. So, all in all, we now suggest that you continue past Sheephead Cut to the marina facilities at New Smyrna Beach, but perhaps not without a backward sigh.

New Smyrna Beach (Standard Mile 846)

Southbound cruisers rounding the bend from Sheephead Cut will get their first view of the storied city of New Smyrna Beach. New Smyrna is one of the friendliest and most easygoing of the many Florida river towns we have visited. Noticeably absent is the hustle and bustle of a Fort Lauderdale or Palm Beach. Most of the residents of New Smyrna seem intent on enjoying the Florida life-style and are not terribly interested in transforming their community into another world-famous resort. The visiting cruiser is one beneficiary of this laid-back style. Stopping for an evening, a week, or even longer at one of the city's several marinas is a study in relaxation. Fortunately, transient dockage in New Smyrna is now a bit more available than it has been during the past several years.

All of the community's pleasure-craft facilities are within walking distance of a supermarket, drugstore, and other shoreside businesses. There is even one historical attraction of note within a short step of Smyrna Marina. The old ruins sometimes described as Turnbull's Castle can readily be seen just down the street from the marina.

Those interested in historical sites should inquire at any of the marina offices about transportation to the old sugar mills nearby. Prior to the Seminole wars of the 1830s, as many as ten sugar mills in New Smyrna processed the raw cane grown on the large plantations to the north.

Numbers to know in New Smyrna Beach:
Yellow Cab—386-252-5536
Silver Bullet Cab—386-424-1444
Enterprise Rent-A-Car—386-252-1224
Budget Car Rental—386-427-4700
Chamber of Commerce—386-428-2449

New Smyrna Beach Facilities (Various Lats/Lons—see below)

The northernmost of New Smyrna's facilities catering to cruising craft is North Causeway Marine. This facility is located in a small harbor

Sheephead Cut, New Smyrna Beach

Dockside power connections—30 amps
Dockside water connections—yes
Gasoline—yes
Mechanical repairs—limited
Ship's store—yes
Restaurant—nearby

behind two spoil islands west of unlighted day-beacon #37, near 29 01.789 North/080 55.163 West. The marina can be readily recognized by the large metal, small-craft (dry-stack) storage building just behind the docks. Be sure to enter from the northeast at #37, as the southwesterly passage between the islands is quite shoal.

North Causeway Marine has one or two slips for transients up to 50 feet in length. The marina's single, fixed, wooden dock features water hookups and 30-amp power connections. Advance arrangements are recommended. Gasoline and a ship's store are also available on the premises. A supermarket is found just across the street, and the Sea Harvest Restaurant and the attractions on Canal Street (see below) are within walking distance.

North Causeway Marine (386) 427-5267
http://www.northcausewaymarine.com

Approach depths—6-9 feet
Dockside depths—5-6 feet
Accepts transients—limited
Transient dockage rate—above average
Fixed wooden pier—yes

Most cruising visitors dock at Smyrna Marina (formerly Sea Harvest Marina), which graces the shores of New Smyrna Beach west of flashing daybeacon #38 (near 29 01.647 North/080 55.277 West). This is without a doubt one of the most unique marinas in all of Florida. Where else can you find two-day transient dockage and ice paid for on the honor system? There is a laid-back, Bohemian feel to Smyrna Marina that is far more reminiscent of the Florida Keys than the upper east coast of the Sunshine State. With its easy, foot access to the wonderful Sea Harvest Restaurant and the New Smyrna Beach downtown business and historical district on nearby Canal Street, this facility deserves a red circle on any cruiser's chart (at least those not looking for the latest in glitzy nightlife).

As alluded to above, transients are accepted at Smyrna Marina for two-night stays. Longer

First-rate first mate at New Smyrna Beach waterfront

stopovers can be arranged with the live-aboard dockmaster. Ask anyone in the marina where to find his boat. Payments for the first two days should be made in a box that you will find in the shoreside support building just behind the piers. While this fee arrangement does work on the honor system, a sign warns of retribution against those who abuse this system.

Berths at Smyrna Marina are provided at the protected basin's fixed, wooden piers, with at least 7 feet of water in each slip. Typical low-water soundings run 8 to 13 feet. Full power and water connections are available as well. Some mechanical repairs can be had through local, independent contractors.

In the 1990s the block building that overlooks the main pier was converted from a dockmaster's office to an attractive, air-conditioned captain's lounge with a small paperback exchange library. Here, as mentioned above, you can purchase ice on the honor system. The adjacent showers are also fully climate controlled and really quite nice. The on-site Laundromat is a bit on the small side but perfectly acceptable. Visiting cruisers will find keys allowing access to the showers and Laundromat in the captain's lounge. Just be sure to return them to their proper spot after you are finished.

Galleys can be restocked via a three-block walk to the supermarket just across from North Causeway Marine mentioned above. You will find this store on the north side of Highway 44. It is also a mere one-block walk to the downtown Canal Street business district (see below). What more could one want?

Cruisers who arrive at Smyrna Marina with a good appetite and a taste for seafood are in luck. Sea Harvest Restaurant (386-426-5301) sits perched on the harbor's southeasterly tip. You can't miss its blue, metal-sided building and fishing-fleet docks to port as you enter the dockage basin. Suffice it to say that the seafood here is about as good and fresh as it gets. Also, be assured New Smyrna's easygoing, laissez-faire attitude is perfectly mirrored at Sea Harvest. Several years ago the menu was expanded a bit, and while fried catch of the day is still very much in evidence, there are many other delectable choices. While inside, climate-controlled dining is available at Sea Harvest, in clement weather opt for the picnic tables set outside (some under a canvas canopy) overlooking the Waterway. It's one of the nicest experiences in all of Florida to be munching away on Sea Harvest's bountiful fare while watching pleasure craft wend their way up or down the ICW. Those who prefer to prepare their seafood aboard will discover that pretty much everything on the menu can be purchased uncooked. Trust me on this one, reader. Don't miss Sea Harvest!

Smyrna Marina (386) 428-1430

Approach depths—8-10 feet
Dockside depths—7-13 feet
Accepts transients—yes
Transient dockage rate—below average
Fixed wooden piers—yes
Dockside power connections—30
    and 50 amps
Dockside water connections—yes
Showers—yes
Laundromat—yes
Mechanical repairs—limited
    (independent contractors)
Restaurant—on site and others nearby

Fishing Cove Marina (386-428-7827) lines the southerly shore of the Smyrna Marina basin. This facility is primarily concerned with dry dock storage of small craft. Gasoline can be purchased and there is a variety and tackle store adjacent to the docks.

Private Angler's Yacht Club (386-428-8424)

lines the northern shores of the Smyrna Marina harbor. The clubhouse is readily visible from the docks.

New Smyrna Downtown

Fortunate cruisers who find their way to a slip in Smyrna Marina are only a single-block walk away from the rejuvenated New Smyrna Beach downtown business district lining both sides of Canal Street (Highway 44). Here you will find a wonderful collection of drugstores (two), restaurants, and, would you believe, an antique mall. Begin your visit with a stop at the local Chamber of Commerce (115 Canal Street). They can usually help with information and any questions you might have. Next up, try a breakfast or lunch stop at the Deli Touch Restaurant (135 Canal Street, 386-424-9878) or Mahoney's Oyster Bar (also open evenings—147 Canal Street, 386-424-1312). If you are into antiques, don't miss the Smyrna Antique Mall (419 Canal Street, 386-426-7825). We found the selection here to be quite fascinating. Do you need bicycle repair? Well, there is a bike shop along Canal Street as well.

By all accounts, don't miss a stroll along Canal Street. Even if you are not in the market for anything, it is all too rare these days to encounter a downtown Floridian business district that can still be accurately described as quaint. Please let us know what you think!

New Smyrna History The early history of New Smyrna is more than fascinating. It begins with the period of British rule in Florida. The new English governor and his council found the land in great need of settlers. The mass exodus of the Spanish left the future state almost completely depopulated. It soon became the policy of the British Crown to encourage any reasonable offer of settlement in the region. Free land could be had almost for the asking if only one were willing and able to clear and plant the ground.

One Englishman who became fascinated with this opportunity was Dr. Andrew Turnbull, a successful and wealthy London physician and businessman with many highly placed contacts in the British cabinet. He formed a plan for a vast Florida plantation that would produce cotton, silk, indigo, and other cash crops. The problem remained,

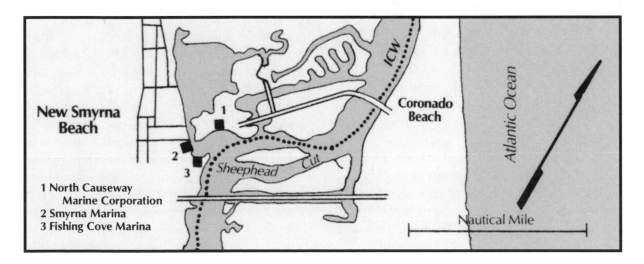

New Smyrna Beach

1 North Causeway Marine Corporation
2 Smyrna Marina
3 Fishing Cove Marina

Coronado Beach

Atlantic Ocean

ICW

Sheephead Cut

Nautical Mile

however, of peopling the large holding.

Turnbull found his answer in the writings of the British undersecretary of state for American affairs, William Knox, who had conceived the idea of recruiting people of Greek extraction for a Florida colony. Turnbull was very much taken with Knox's novel concept. His wife was Greek, and his first son had been born in the town of Smyrna. Through his wife's family, he knew that because of religious persecution and famine many Greek families in the Levant region could undoubtedly be persuaded to journey to a new world of hope and promise.

Along with a partner, Turnbull received a grant for 40,000 acres of land in east Florida in June 1776. In November Turnbull arrived in St. Augustine to choose a site for his colony. He immediately reported to Governor Grant, and the two struck up a friendship.

At Grant's suggestion a large tract of land was surveyed some 75 miles south of St. Augustine near Mosquito Inlet. It is only in modern times that this seaward passage has become known as Ponce de Leon Inlet. Turnbull was ecstatic about the site. He hired a skilled planter and began a cotton plantation. Workers were engaged to clear the land and begin building houses for the 500 Greeks he intended to import. After only three months, with his project well under way, he returned to England.

Back home Turnbull found that several prominent politicians, including Lord Grenville, the prime minister, wanted to join the venture. With the backing of so many formidable people, he obtained the use of a sloop of war and in June he departed for the Levant.

Turnbull secured willing Greek and Italian settlers in such diverse places as Minorca, Leghorn, Smyrna, Messenia, Crete, and Corsica. On March 28, 1768, about 1,200

men, women, and children departed the port of Mahon for St. Augustine.

In return for their passage, the settlers promised to indenture themselves to Turnbull and his company for ten years. As a group, they were also promised one half of the profit from the crops produced in the new colony after expenses for the crossing were deducted. In practice, this pact was never kept.

Upon their arrival Turnbull immediately ferried his diverse group south to the high west banks of the Halifax River, where a few hastily built shacks represented the beginnings of the New Smyrna colony. There was trouble from the very beginning. Food was short and disease ran rampant. A ship ferrying black slaves to the new colony was lost at sea. Now the settlers themselves had to begin the backbreaking job of clearing fields for planting.

Perhaps Turnbull's greatest mistake was in hiring former noncommissioned officers from the British army as overseers. These heartless men drove the colonists relentlessly and even beat those who claimed they were too sick to work. The inevitable revolt came on August 18 while Turnbull was visiting a nearby plantation. The storehouses were broken into and some 300 of the settlers commandeered a ship that had just arrived from St. Augustine with supplies. They decided to sail for Havana and ask the Spanish authorities for sanctuary. Meanwhile, Turnbull, who had been warned of the revolt, appealed to Governor Grant for help. Grant dispatched two armed sloops to Mosquito Inlet and ordered a body of troops to march overland to New Smyrna. One of the ships caught the rebel vessel at anchor in Mosquito Inlet. A single cannon shot produced a flag of surrender, and the New Smyrna revolt was over. Three of the ringleaders were sentenced to death and the others returned to their back-breaking tasks.

In spite of its difficulties, the New Smyrna colony did succeed economically as the years went past. By 1769 the various families had established farms along the river's bank. Most huts had their own vegetable gardens, which proved to be an invaluable aid in fighting scurvy. Sugar production began and the cultivation of corn went forward at an impressive pace. In 1777 Turnbull marketed 5,000 bushels of corn in St. Augustine and the surrounding region. Tar, pitch, and turpentine were also produced from the surrounding pine forests. These so-called naval products were very much in demand by the British navy and merchant fleet.

However, it was the successful production and processing of indigo that was to bring Turnbull's enterprise its greatest return. Indigo was much valued as a dye in the British textile community. The government was anxious to reverse the drain on the country's capital derived from the purchase of indigo abroad. Consequently, the Crown paid a generous bounty for the successful manufacture of indigo dye on British soil.

The end of the New Smyrna colony came about largely as the result of political infighting in east Florida. With the departure of Turnbull's friend, Governor Grant, leadership was assumed by Lt. Gov. William Moultrie. Moultrie was ever at odds with Florida's chief justice, William Drayton, and Turnbull and Drayton were fast friends. Soon political factions formed around Moultrie on the one hand and Turnbull and Drayton on the other.

In 1773, Col. Patrick Tonyn arrived from England to assume the governorship. He immediately sided with the Moultrie faction, and Turnbull suddenly found himself outside the innermost ring of power. As tidings of revolution spread south from the northern colonies, Tonyn tried to implicate Drayton and Turnbull as patriot sympathizers. Tonyn dismissed the chief justice from his post and removed Turnbull from the governor's council.

In 1776 both Drayton and Turnbull left Florida for London, Drayton to seek reinstatement, and Turnbull to attempt to have the governor removed from office. With the American Revolution in full swing, however, the British government could not simply dismiss the governor of the only American colony not in revolt. Turnbull remained in London for more than a year pleading his case. When he returned, the fate of the New Smyrna colony had already been sealed.

For a time, all was well in New Smyrna after Turnbull's departure. The colony was under the supervision of the doctor's nephew, and the spring planting went forward. Tradition tells us that the end came when an unknown group of Englishmen was visiting the colony from St. Augustine. Observing the harsh treatment by the overseers and the deplorable living conditions, the visitors are supposed to have said to the colonists, "if these people knew their rights, they would not suffer this kind of slavery." A young boy who understood English happened to be within earshot, and the news spread through the community like wildfire.

Under the pretext of a fishing expedition, three of the settlers' leaders journeyed to St. Augustine and met with Governor Tonyn, who assured them that the government would guarantee them their rights. With this assurance, by late April the entire colony began a mass march to St. Augustine. Turnbull's nephew begged the people to return, but his pleas fell on deaf ears.

In St. Augustine, the new arrivals made depositions as to their living conditions and treatment in New Smyrna. Tonyn immediately ordered all their indenture canceled. The settlement may have failed, but afterward, this group of hardy people became a valuable part of the St. Augustine community, contributing much to the town's progress.

Smyrna Yacht Club (Standard Mile 847.5) (29 00.684 North/080 54.870 West

South of flashing daybeacon #38, the ICW flows under the high-rise New Smyrna/Harris Saxon Bridge and leaves the principal New Smyrna waterfront on its way to Mosquito Lagoon. There is one other possible stop to consider in the New Smyrna region before our review of this passage.

A marked channel leads southwest from a position just southeast of unlighted daybeacon #46, to the Smyrna Yacht Club. This friendly organization is glad to accommodate members of other yacht clubs with appropriate reciprocal privileges. There are two sets of slips. The larger, deeper docks front directly on the ICW. Boats larger than 35 feet must moor to these piers. A second set of better-sheltered docks is located behind the club. Depths at the outer berths run 8 feet or better. The inner slips have some 5-foot soundings, though typical depths run from 6 to 8 feet. Fresh-water connections and 30- and 50-amp power hookups are available. The club's dining room is open for lunch and dinner Tuesday through Saturday. There is also a Sunday brunch.

The only real disadvantage to docking at Smyrna Yacht Club is the longer walk that you must undertake to reach the downtown business district with its restaurants, grocery stores, and drugstore. If you're not up to an eight- to ten-block stroll, call one of the New Smyrna taxi services listed above.

Smyrna Yacht Club, New Smyrna Beach

Smyrna Yacht Club (386) 427-4040

Approach depths—5 feet
Dockside depths—5-8 feet
Accepts transients—members of other yacht clubs with appropriate reciprocal arrangements
Fixed wooden piers—yes
Dockside power connections—30 and 50 amps
Dockside water connections—yes
Restaurant—on site

Mosquito Lagoon (Standard Mile 857)

After a long cruise south from New Smyrna Beach through a dredged cut running between shallow sloughs and small bays (and several long, no-wake zones), the ICW begins its trek across Mosquito Lagoon southeast of flashing daybeacon #5. The immensity of Mosquito Lagoon can be a bit of a shock after tracking through the relatively narrow Waterway channel leading south from New Smyrna. In spite of its impressive size, much of Mosquito Lagoon is shallow, with depths of 3 to 5 feet the norm. Chart 11485 does show some 6- to 7-foot soundings, but on-site research has proved that these readings cannot be trusted. We have tried to find these deepwater patches several times, only to hit 3- and 4-foot depths on each occasion.

Mosquito Lagoon is extremely popular with local fishermen, who regularly ply these waters in their small skiffs. If you pass close by any of these sportsmen, please be courteous and reduce your wake.

Some other cruising publications suggest anchoring off the channel in Mosquito Lagoon. However, we must strictly warn you against this practice. With the uncertain depths, you could easily swing onto a shoal at night. Any sort of wind is bound to raise a most unwelcome chop on the wide, unprotected waters and could make for a very uncomfortable evening. Also, the lagoon is aptly named, and our whining, winged friends make their appearance during the nighttime hours. Waterway visitors are advised either to stop at New Smyrna or to continue cruising south to the facilities at Titusville.

Haulover Canal (Standard Mile 868.5)

At flashing daybeacon #45 and unlighted daybeacon #46, the ICW takes a sharp swing to the southwest and leaves Mosquito Lagoon behind as it enters Haulover Canal. This narrow body of water leads to the wide but shallow

Haulover Canal

headwaters of Indian River. The canal is a short, straightforward passage spanned by a single bascule bridge (closed vertical clearance, 27 feet).

Shortly after passing under the Haulover bridge, you will see a small basin with a launching ramp on the southeastern shore. This cove has been dredged and surrounded with a concrete seawall. Considering the high degree of launching-ramp activity, particularly during weekends, we no longer recommend that cruisers attempt to anchor in this basin.

Haulover Canal and the spoil islands along the Indian River channel to the southwest are a bird watcher's paradise. We have observed numerous ospreys, hawks, pelicans, and terns. Several always seem to perch in the trees along the canal and whistle at us as we go along. One time, on our way back to Mosquito Lagoon, a large raccoon lumbered down to the shore, washed his hands, and watched us quizzically as we motored by. Those who go quietly through the canal and have their cameras ready may come away with some prize wildlife photos.

PORT ORANGE TO INDIAN RIVER NAVIGATION

The run from Daytona to Indian River presents some varied navigational conditions. To the north, the ICW continues to track its way south via a narrow but well-marked, improved channel through the shallow reaches of Halifax River. Below Port Orange, cruisers must contend with swift currents and shoaling problems associated with Ponce de Leon Inlet. Then there is the narrow channel leading through extensive mud flats and oyster banks south of New Smyrna. Though tidal currents are mostly absent here, you must take great care to stay in the channel. Finally, the ICW follows the westerly reaches of wide but shallow Mosquito Lagoon to Haulover Canal. Strong winds from the south and east can raise a considerable chop on the lagoon. A straight shot through Haulover Canal leads to the vast but shallow headwaters of Indian River. To say the least, this is not a dull or repetitive passage.

Port Orange At unlighted daybeacon #56, two sets of privately maintained daybeacons lead east to Seven Seas Marina & Boatyard. Between #56 and the Port Orange Bridge, shoal islands flank both sides of the ICW. These are often the nesting places for all sorts of coastal birds. Feel free to look, or even take pictures with a telephoto lens, but landing on the islands is forbidden.

The Port Orange Bridge is a fixed, high-rise structure with a fortunate 65 feet of vertical clearance. Those of us who can remember the old, low-level span are most thankful for this new bridge.

On the ICW South of the Port Orange Bridge, tidal currents become swifter as you approach the passages to Ponce de Leon Inlet. Keep a sharp watch for excessive leeway and stay strictly to the channel. Outside of the marked cut, you will quickly encounter grounding depths.

South-southeast of flashing daybeacon #59 and unlighted daybeacon #58, the marked channel to Adventure Yacht Harbor, breaks off to the east. Simply follow the markers through the winding entrance cut. Eventually the harbor will open out to your port side.

Passages to Ponce de Leon Inlet   South of unlighted daybeacon #72, the ICW markers begin a new numbering sequence. The Waterway abandons Halifax River at unlighted daybeacon #2. While the ICW passes to the west via a man-made landcut, the Halifax snakes its way southeast to Ponce de Leon Inlet. This passage, known locally as the North Channel, holds minimum 7-foot depths but markers are scarce. Currently, there are only three aids to navigation on the North Channel.

Generally, good water parallels the eastern and northeastern banks, with a whole bevy of shoals lying to the west and southwest. During daylight and fair weather, you may well be able to avoid these hazards and track your way safely to the Lighthouse Boat Yard channel. None of the various aids along the channel is lighted and nighttime entry would be especially hazardous.

It's been said before, but it's worth repeating: tidal currents in and around Ponce Inlet are absolutely fierce. Watch for them whether you are simply cruising the channel or approaching a dock. First-time visitors will soon discover why this writer has repeatedly issued this warning.

To enter the North Channel from the ICW, depart the Waterway abeam of unlighted daybeacon #2. Set a course to the southeast, designed to bring correctly charted unlighted can buoy #1 abeam by some 50 yards to its southerly side. Be mindful of the shallows to the southwest during this run.

Southeast of unlighted can buoy #1, the docks of Inlet Harbor Marina will come abeam on the northeastern banks at the charted position of "Inlet Harbor." Continue cruising southeast on the main channel until the midwidth of the docks are directly abeam to the northeast. Then, turn straight into the facility.

To continue southeast toward Lighthouse Boat Yard and Ponce Inlet, begin favoring the northeastern banks as you begin to round the point, well east of Piddler Island (occupied by Down the Hatch Restaurant and Sea Love Boat Works). The charted shoal to the west and southwest is building into the channel. These shallows are marked by unlighted nun buoy #2 and uncharted unlighted nun buoy #4. Obviously you should stay east and northeast of #2 and #4.

Southeast of the point, a series of privately maintained daybeacons leads generally north to Lighthouse Boat Yard. Surprise, surprise, pass all red markers to your starboard side and take green markers to port. At unlighted daybeacon #5 the channel takes a sharp jog to the north. Turn smartly to port and pass between #5 and #6, then between #7 and #8. Finally, you will pass #9 to port and see the marina facilities dead ahead.

Southeast of Lighthouse Boat Yard, the channel leading to Ponce Inlet is now wholly unmarked. You must navigate by eye in order to reach the buoyed seaward passage, beginning with flashing buoys #7 and

#8. Don't head toward flashing buoy #9 to the southeast. Shoal water lies between your position and this marker.

The passage southeast of Lighthouse Boat Yard is, quite simply, treacherous and should only be attempted by the adventurers among us, or those with specific local knowledge. Perhaps in the future this cut will again be marked, but for now, it is a white-knuckle experience.

The marked inlet channel east of flashing buoys #7 and #8 is not for the faint of heart. Heavy swells and strong currents are regular companions. If you should stray out of the channel, a grounding on an adjacent shoal could be extremely dangerous. At the least, check at Lighthouse Boat Yard for the latest navigational information before attempting the inlet. If you are approaching from sea, call the marina on VHF channel 16.

None except locals piloting small, outboard skiffs should attempt entry into Rockhouse Creek from either the inlet or the ICW. This stream has shoaled markedly over the last several years, and much of its track is now quite shallow.

The so-called South Channel leading to Ponce de Leon Inlet strikes north-northwest from the ICW at flashing daybeacon #19. While this cut is also subject to chronic shoaling along its edges, there is currently a wide, deep channel leading north-northwest to flashing buoy #9. There are only two markers to help you along the way. Generally, you should favor the eastern and northeasterly shoreline. A large, charted shoal flanks the western side of the channel all the way north to flashing buoy #9. Avoid these shallows like the proverbial black plague.

To enter the South Channel, leave the ICW some 100 yards southeast of flashing daybeacon #19. Turn sharply to the north-northwest, and cruise into the cut by favoring the easterly and northeasterly shoreline. Pass correctly charted flashing daybeacon #12 well to its easterly and northeasterly side. Daybeacon #12 sits hard by the west-side shallows. Continue tracking your way north past #12, keeping some 75 to 100 yards (no more) off the eastern banks.

A series of private condo docks flanks the eastern shore between #12 and the next northerly aid to navigation, flashing daybeacon #11. Larger power craft should probably slow to no-wake speed while passing these piers.

Next up is flashing daybeacon #11. This aid to navigation is actually located on the outer portion of a concrete pier associated with the adjacent (charted) U.S. Coast Guard station. Pass #11 by some 50 yards to its westerly side. Larger power vessels should slow as they cruise past the Coast Guard piers.

Wise skippers looking to anchor on the South Channel would do well to drop the hook between the intersection with the ICW at unlighted daybeacon #19 and flashing daybeacon #12. Farther to the north-northwest, there is even less shelter. Be sure to set your hook so as to swing well away from the shallows to the west and southwest.

Wild-eyed captains who simply must cruise the entire length of the South Channel, north of flashing daybeacon #11, should proceed at idle speed with a weather eye on the sounder. Continue to follow the deep water as it parallels the easterly banks. Be sure to avoid any slippage to the west and southwest into the charted shoals.

Eventually you will spy flashing buoy #9 ahead. You're on your own after that! This is a tricky passage indeed. Good luck!

On the ICW   South of unlighted daybeacon #2, the ICW follows a sheltered landcut to the west and southwest of the Ponce de Leon Inlet channels. North-northwest of unlighted daybeacon #7, a shallow stream leading to the inlet makes into the Waterway from the northeast. Don't attempt to enter. This passage is shoal and treacherous.

Southeast of flashing daybeacon #10, the Waterway intersects Rockhouse Creek. A large shoal is building southwest into the Waterway from the creek's mouth. Favor the southern (mainland) side of the channel as you cruise past the stream's entrance. Eventually, you will leave this hazard behind as you come abeam of unlighted daybeacon #12 to its northerly side.

On to New Smyrna Beach   South-southeast of flashing daybeacon #19, shoal water is encroaching on the western and southwestern side of the Waterway channel. The shallows stretch on to the south, even past the Coronado Beach bascule bridge. Chart 11485 correctly forecasts shallow water near unlighted daybeacon #20. Between #19 and unlighted daybeacon #32, favor the easterly and northeasterly side of the channel. Stay well east and northeast of #20. This marker is found in shoal water.

A long, marshy island flanks the Waterway's westerly extreme between unlighted daybeacon #24 and unlighted daybeacon #28. This small parcel of land is often covered by an incredible collection of birds. Shallows seem to be encroaching on #24. Again, favor the eastern side of the channel slightly to avoid this potential obstruction.

At flashing daybeacon #26, the channel takes a jog to the south and runs hard by the easterly banks. Flashing daybeacon #29 sits perched quite close to the eastern shore, and it can be hard to spot. Use your binoculars to help pick it out of the clutter.

South of #29, there is a long, markerless stretch leading to the Coronado Beach bascule bridge. For best depths, continue favoring the easterly side of the channel. Shoal water abuts the westerly extremes of the Waterway from this point to well south of bridge.

The Coronado Beach bascule bridge has a closed vertical clearance of 23 feet and, you guessed it, a restricted opening schedule. Year round, seven days a week, this span opens only on the hour and every 20 minutes thereafter from 7:00 A.M. to 7:00 P.M. The Coronado Beach Bridge can be a real navigational impediment for sailboats and larger powercraft. Try to time your arrival for a scheduled opening, rather than having to pass time in the current strewn water.

Sheephead Cut Anchorage   Sheephead Cut breaks off from the ICW's track southwest of flashing daybeacon #33. As mentioned above, this once popular anchorage is now flanked by heavy condo development to the south, and its southwesterly intersection with the Waterway just north of the New Smyrna fixed bridge has been marked. Both these aspects have promoted far more waterborne traffic on Sheephead Cut than was true in times past. For these reasons, we no longer recommend anchorage on these waters.

Should you choose to enter Sheephead Cut anyway, depart from the Waterway channel once abeam of flashing daybeacon #33. Cruise directly into the midwidth of the wide stream, which will be obvious to the southwest. Soon you will sight the first set of new markers, unlighted daybeacons #1 and #2, ahead. Good depths can be held all the way to the stream's southwesterly juncture with the Waterway, a short hop north of the New Smyrna high-rise bridge, by passing all subsequent red, even-numbered aids to navigation to their (the markers') southerly sides and taking green beacons to their northerly quarters.

New Smyrna Waterfront   No-wake speed restrictions are in effect from the Coronado Beach span to the high-rise New Smyrna/Harris Saxon Bridge. This limitation protects docks along the New Smyrna Beach waterfront. Passage through New Smyrna's waters is a simple matter of following the well-defined channel to the high-rise bridge.

Be sure to pass unlighted daybeacons #32 and #34 to their southerly sides. The charted shoal to the north seems to be building south. Additionally, #34 sits well out into the water, and, for some reason, it often seems to be missed by southbound captains.

North Causeway Marine will be spotted to starboard at unlighted daybeacon #37. Enter by passing northeast of the small marsh island. Hug the docks as you cruise southwest to the fuel pier.

The wide entrance to Smyrna Marina's dockage basin will be obvious west of flashing daybeacon #38. Cruise into the harbor's middle line, avoiding the northside entrance point and its adjacent marsh island.

South of flashing daybeacon #38, you will exchange greetings with the high-rise New Smyrna/Harris Saxon with its happy vertical clearance of 65 feet.

North on the ICW   Northbound ICW cruisers passing under the high-rise New Smyrna bridge must now be on guard against mistaking the westernmost markers on the Sheephead Cut channel, unlighted daybeacons #7 and #8, for aids to navigation outlining the Waterway. Ignore #7 and #8, and continue cruising generally north, pointing to pass between flashing daybeacon #38 and unlighted daybeacon #39.

South of the High Rise   Captains cruising south of the New Smyrna high rise should proceed with caution. This is a narrow, changeable stretch of the Waterway. Point to pass east of flashing daybeacon #42 and west of unlighted daybeacon #43. Adjust course slightly to the south-southeast and point to pass between flashing daybeacon #45 and unlighted daybeacon #46. The channel now widens a bit, and you can breathe easier.

Northbound captains must take care to

pass unlighted daybeacon #43 to its westerly side. You cannot make a straight run from the gap between unlighted daybeacon #46 and flashing daybeacon #45 to the high rise's central pass through unless finding the bottom is in your game plan. Cut to the north-northwest from #45 and #46 and be sure to clear #43 before making your approach to the bridge.

Smyrna Yacht Club   The marked entrance channel leading to Smyrna Yacht Club strikes into the Waterway's western flank, southeast of unlighted daybeacon #46. Simply follow the markers into the docks, remembering the red, right, returning rule. Larger vessels must moor to the outer docks, facing the ICW.

On to Mosquito Lagoon   From New Smyrna, the ICW tracks its way through a large expanse of mud flats and oyster banks, Depths outside of the improved channel run in inches. It is very important to keep to the marked Waterway cut and maintain a steady watch on the sounder during the entire run from New Smyrna to Indian River. If depths start to rise, slow down and make immediate corrections before grounding depths are reached. Also, be prudent and watch over your stern for leeway. Though tidal currents are not as strong here as to the north, the water flow can still set unwary skippers outside of the channel just when it appears that they are pointed on the proper course.

From flashing daybeacon #49 to unlighted daybeacon #52, a no-wake zone restricts speed on the Waterway. Be advised that the local water cops have become infamous in the cruising community for passing out speeding tickets along this stretch. Be sure you aren't throwing a wake!

These waters call for caution anyway. An extensive community park lines the banks between the two aids, and the adjacent waters are often used for swimming. The large point of land adjacent to the "Edgewater" designation on chart 11485 seems to be building northeast into the Waterway channel. It can be a bit unnerving to see swimmer standing in water only up to their knees barely 50 feet from your track! Favor the eastern side of the channel slightly as you pass #50.

Shockingly enough, a slow-speed manatee zone is in effect all the way from unlighted daybeacon #64 into the northerly headwaters of Mosquito Lagoon. This 5+-mile no-wake zone seems to go on and on forever.

Keep your eyes open between flashing daybeacon #69 and Mosquito Lagoon. We have spied manatees along this stretch, and on several occasions, friendly, bottle-nosed dolphins have followed us for some distance.

Mosquito Lagoon   The entrance into Mosquito Lagoon south-southeast of flashing daybeacon #75 also calls for caution. Very shallow water abuts both sides of the channel between #75 and flashing daybeacon #13. Stay strictly to the channel, observe all markers carefully, and keep a sharp watch for lateral leeway.

A small channel leads west from unlighted daybeacon #8 to a launching ramp. Cruising craft should not attempt entry.

South of flashing daybeacon #13, the wide swath of Mosquito Lagoon begins to open out to the southeast. First-time visitors could be readily excused for thinking they are headed out into the open sea.

From #13 to the Haulover Canal entrance, the Waterway route is generally simple to navigate. As you are now heading south with standard Waterway markings in effect, pass all red, even-numbered aids to navigation to your starboard side and take green beacons to port.

Some markers along this stretch can be hard to spot. Have your binoculars handy to pick out any hard-to-see aids.

Haulover Canal   The northeasterly entrance into Haulover Canal is a changeable area that is subject to shoaling. It is prolifically marked, but we have never cruised through this stretch without finding a slightly different configuration of aids to navigation than that pictured on chart 11485. Be ready for different markings than those shown on the chart or discussed in the account below.

To begin a northerly approach to Haulover Canal, come between flashing daybeacon #38 and unlighted daybeacon #37. The Waterway now takes a very slight jog farther to the south-southeast. Set course to eventually come between unlighted daybeacon #41 and flashing daybeacon #42. Between #37 and #42, you will pass unlighted daybeacon #40 to its easterly side.

From #41 and #42, point to come abeam of unlighted daybeacon #43 to its southwesterly quarter. Once abeam of #43, begin a slow, lazy turn to the southwest into the mouth of Haulover Canal. Unlighted day-beacons #44 and #46 define the channel's western and northwestern edge through this turn and into the canal, as does flashing daybeacon #45 and unlighted daybeacon #47 for the cut's eastern and southeastern extreme. Obviously, you should pass between all these beacons as you work your way into the canal's mouth. Stay east and southeast of #44 and #46 and west of #45.

Good depths are held on the canal's mid-width into the headwaters of Indian River. Take a break from the sounder and enjoy the scenery and the abundant wildlife. The entire canal is an official no-wake zone anyway, so you have little choice but to take your time.

The Allenhurst (Haulover Canal) bascule bridge spans the cut about halfway between Mosquito Lagoon and the juncture with Indian River. The bridge has a closed vertical clearance of 27 feet and opens on demand.

Southwest of the bridge, watch the southeastern banks and you will soon catch sight of the small launching-ramp basin described earlier. Remember, anchorage is no longer recommended in this cove.

The southwesterly mouth of Haulover Canal empties into the wide but shallow upper reaches of mighty Indian River. After leaving the canal, point for the gap between flashing daybeacon #1 and unlighted daybeacon #2. Keep your stern lined up with the canal's midwidth as you head toward a position between #1 and #2. Shallows line both sides of the channel along this stretch. There are even some rocks visible at low water just northwest of Haulover Canal's southwesterly mouth. A continuing account of the ICW resumes in the next chapter.

Titusville to Vero Beach

Cruisers leaving the southwestern entrance of Haulover Canal are suddenly reminded of the wide diversity presented by the waters of eastern Florida. Gone are the sheltered, almost timid passages to the north. Now visiting cruisers are faced with the broad and impressive body of water known as Indian River.

Some years ago, this writer and his first-rate, first mate cruised into the northern reaches of this great river late on a fall afternoon. The golden sunlight reflected on the wide waters and sparkled in the light chop. Hundreds of birds wheeled around the small spoil islands lining the channel, calling to each other with raucous voices. As far as the eye could see there was not another boat or any other sign of civilization. It was one of those moments unique to those who go cruising on the water. We hope you too will have the chance to experience this Indian River magic for yourselves.

Beginning north of Titusville and running to Stuart, the ICW follows Indian River's track south for some 100 nautical miles. While the entire passage is well marked, captains must now take the latest weather forecast into account. Winds over 15 knots can foster a very uncomfortable chop on the ICW channel, and blows over 25 knots can be dangerous for smaller cruising craft.

Fortunately, there is little tide or tidal current to worry about on Indian River north of Vero Beach. You should be able to take a welcome break from your guard against excessive lateral leeway.

The northern portion of the Indian River passage presents a wide variety of cruising possibilities and overnight facilities. The old river village of Titusville guards the northern reaches of this run and offers excellent marina service. To the east, Merritt Island, Cape Canaveral, and Spaceport, USA can be reached by the Trans-Florida Barge Canal. This useful cut provides reliable access to the open sea and Banana River.

The Banana is a weak sister when compared to Indian River, but those who must cruise where none have gone before can still enjoy its waters. Mariners fortunate enough to be plying these waters when a space launch is scheduled can anchor in the northern reaches of Banana River for a spectacular view of the liftoff.

Cruisers moving south on Indian River will find diverse overnight facilities at Cocoa, Melbourne, and Vero Beach. Additionally, many other marinas beckon from the river banks in more isolated settings.

Anchorages are scarce between Titusville and Vero Beach. A few coves on Indian River have sufficient depth and enough protection for a snug overnight stay, and the lower reaches of Banana River also offer several protected spots where you can drop the hook.

In short, captains and crew traveling the ICW between Titusville and Vero Beach will find much to see and do while mooring at an impressive variety of marinas. Visiting cruisers who fail to take advantage of Indian River's charms north of Vero Beach have only themselves to blame.

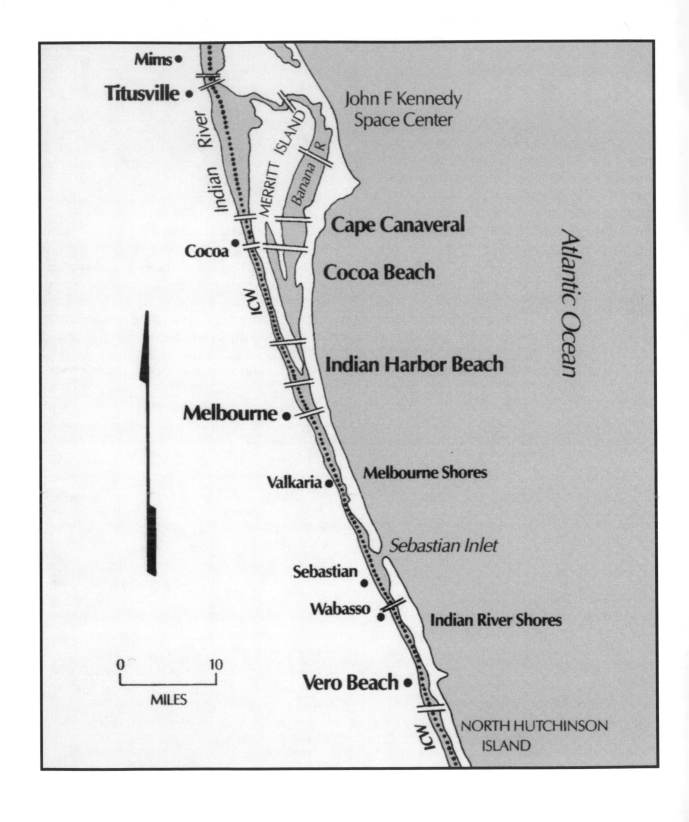

Charts   Several charts are required for complete navigational detail of all the waters between Haulover Canal and Vero Beach:
11485—covers the ICW from Haulover Canal to Palm Shores
11472—details the ICW south to Vero Beach
11476—provides coverage of most sections of Banana River

11478—a detailed chart that covers the Canaveral Barge Canal and its inlet. This is an excellent chart to have on board if you are planning to cruise this passage
11484—presents navigational detail of the northern section of Banana River (most cruisers will not need this chart)

Bridges

Jay-Jay/NASA Railway Bridge—crosses ICW at Standard Mile 876.5, south of flashing daybeacon #19—Bascule—7 feet (closed)—usually open unless a train is due (flashing green light means it's OK to proceed; flashing red light warns of an imminent closing)

Titusvulle/Max E. Brewer Bridge—crosses ICW at Standard Mile 879, southeast of unlighted daybeacon #27—Swing bridge—9 feet (closed)—does not open at all weekdays between 6:00 A.M. and 7:15 A.M. and 3:15 P.M. and 4:30 P.M.; at all other times opens on demand

Addison Point Bridge—crosses ICW at Standard Mile 885, south of flashing daybeacon #43—Bascule—27 feet (closed)—does not open at all weekdays between 6:30 A.M. and 8:00 A.M. and 3:30 P.M. and 5:00 P.M.; at all other times opens on demand

State Road 3 Bridge—crosses Canaveral Barge Canal well east of flashing daybeacon #10—Bascule—25 feet (closed)—does not open at all weekdays (except holidays) between 5:15 A.M. to 7:45 A.M. and 3:30 P.M. to 5:15 P.M.; at all other times opens on demand, except during nighttime hours after 10:00 P.M. it opens only with three hours' notice

State Road 401 Triple Bridges—cross Canaveral Barge Canal east of the lock—Bascule—25 feet (closed)—do not open at all weekdays (except holidays) between 5:30 A.M. and 8:00 A.M. and 3:45 P.M. and 5:00 P.M.; at all other times open on demand

Highway A1A Bridge—crosses Banana River immediately south of the river's intersection with the Canaveral Barge Canal channel—Fixed—36 feet

Highway 520 Bridge—crosses Banana River south of unlighted daybeacon #28—Fixed—36 feet

Highway 404 Bridge—crosses Banana River south of unlighted daybeacon #6A—Fixed—43 feet

Mathers Bridge—crosses Banana River north of Dragon Point—Swing bridge—7 feet (closed)—opens on demand 6:00 A.M. to 10:00 P.M.; during the nighttime and early morning hours, it normally doesn't open at all

City Point Twin Bridges—crosses ICW at Standard Mile 894, south of flashing daybeacon #67—Fixed—65 feet

Cocoa Twin Bridges—cross ICW at Standard Mile 897, south of unlighted daybeacon #76—Fixed—65 feet

Palm Shores Pineda Causeway Bridge—crosses ICW at Standard Mile 909, south of flashing daybeacon #95—Fixed—65 feet

Eau Gallie Bridge—crosses ICW at Standard Mile 914, south of unlighted daybeacon #102—Fixed—65 feet

Melbourne Bridge—crosses ICW at Standard Mile 918, south-southeast of flashing daybeacon #5—Fixed—65 feet

Wabasso Bridge—crosses ICW at Standard Mile 943, southeast of unlighted daybeacon #80—Fixed—65 feet

Vero Beach/Merrill Barber Bridge—crosses ICW at Standard Mile 952, south of flashing daybeacon #137—Fixed—65 feet

Chapter 5 Anchorage Summary (Note that anchorages are listed in geographic order, moving north to south.)

Titusville Anchorage—(Standard Mile 879)—located near 28 37.310 North/080 48.211 West, south of the Titusville harbor entrance channel—4½-foot depths—reviewed on pages 259-60, 263-64

Indian River Spaceport Anchorage—(Standard Mile 882)—located near 28 34.527 North/080 45.824 West, east-northeast of flashing daybeacon #38—6-foot depths—reviewed on pages 261, 264

Addison Point Bridge Anchorages—(Standard Mile 885)—located north and south of the Addison Point Bridge, east and west of the ICW channel—various lats/lons (see detailed account)—7-foot depths—reviewed on pages 261-62, 264-65

Cocoa Anchorages—(Standard Mile 897)—located east and west of the Waterway channel, a short hop south of the Cocoa twin bridges—various lats/lons (see detailed account)—6-foot depths—reviewed on pages 281-82, 302

Open Anchorage—(Standard Mile 901.5)—located near 28 18.799 North/080 41.745 West, on the charted deep-water patch southeast of flashing daybeacon #83—6-foot depths—reviewed on pages 282, 303

"The Point" Anchorages—(Standard Mile 904.5)—found on the charted deep-water coves to the north and south of "The Point," southeast of unlighted daybeacon #89—various lats/lons (see detailed account)—5-foot depths—reviewed on pages 282-83, 303

Banana River Anchorages—(Standard Mile 914)—located on the waters of extreme southern Banana River, north and south of the charted, Mathers, 7-foot swing bridge—various lats/lons (see detailed account)—8-foot depths—reviewed on pages 287-88, 304

Island Anchorages—(Standard Mile 925.5)—located to the south and west of the series of small islands lying off the Waterway's western flank between unlighted daybeacons #18 and #24—various lats/lons (see detailed account)—6-foot depths, but far shallower waters are nearby—reviewed on pages 293-94, 306

Secluded Anchorage—(Standard Mile 945)—located near 27 44.273 North/080 23.634 West, behind the small charted island, northeast of unlighted daybeacon #102—5-foot depths—reviewed on pages 297, 307-8

Vero Beach Mooring Field—(Standard Mile 952)—located near 27 39.547 North/080 22.251 West, on the waters of Bethel Creek, moving northeast and north from the Vero Beach/Merrill Barber high-rise bridge, south of flashing daybeacon #139—7-foot depths—reviewed on pages 299-300, 308-9

Chapter 5 Marina and Yacht-Club Summary (Note that marinas and yacht clubs are listed in geographic order, moving north to south.)

Titusville Municipal Marina—(321) 383-5600—(Standard Mile 879)—located near 28 37.224 North/080 48.551 West, on the southwest banks of the charted harbor south of unlighted daybeacon #27—transient dockage available—gasoline and diesel fuel available—minimum 5-foot depths, but typical 7½ feet or better—reviewed on pages 257-59, 263

Kennedy Point Yacht Club & Marina—(321) 383-0280—(Standard Mile 882.5)—located near 28 33.276 North/080 47.773 West, west of unlighted daybeacon #39—transient dockage available—gasoline and diesel fuel available—minimum 4-foot depths—reviewed on pages 260-61, 264

Harbor Square Marina—(321) 453-2464—located near 28 24.368 North/080 42.591 West, off the southern shores of the Canaveral Barge Canal between its western mouth and the charted, 21-foot, bascule bridge—transient dockage available—diesel fuel available—5½-foot minimum depths—reviewed on pages 266-68, 275

Tingleys Marina—(321) 452-0504—located near 28 24.439 North/080 42.427 West, off the southern shores of the Canaveral Barge Canal between Harbor Square Marina (see above) and the charted, 21-foot, bascule bridge—very limited transient dockage available—gasoline available—6-foot minimum depths—reviewed on pages 268, 275

Harbortown Marina—(321) 453-0160—located near 28 24.537 North/080 40.496 West, off the southern shores of the Canaveral Barge Canal between Sykes Creek and the Banana River—transient dockage available—gasoline and diesel fuel available—6-foot minimum depths—reviewed on pages 268-69, 275

Banana River Marine—(321) 452-8622—located near 28 20.054 North/080 39.650 West, flanking the Banana River's western banks near unlighted nun buoy #24—transient dockage available—minimum 4½-foot depths—reviewed on pages 271-72, 276-77

Scorpion's Marina—(321) 784-5788—located near 28 24.477 North/080 37.807 West, on the southwestern shores of the westernmost cove of the Canaveral Barge Canal, between the lock and the channel's inlet to the briny blue—transient dockage available—gasoline and diesel fuel available—10-foot minimum depths—reviewed on pages 272-73, 275-76

Cape Marina—(321) 783-8410—located near 28 24.466 North/080 37.679 West, on the southeastern banks of the westernmost cove of the Canaveral Barge Canal, between the lock and the channel's inlet to the briny blue (opposite Scorpion's Marina)—transient dockage available—gasoline and diesel fuel available—10-foot minimum depths—reviewed on pages 273, 275-76

Indian Cove Marina—(321) 452-8540—Standard Mile 897—located near 28 21.481 North/080 42.459 West; at the easterly tip of the east-bank cove; immediately north of the Cocoa, twin, high-rise bridges; south-southeast of unlighted daybeacon #76—marina in transition; visitor services still in question—reviewed on pages 279, 302

Whitley Bay Marina—(321) 632-5445—Standard Mile 897—located near 28 21.431 North/080 43.507 West, at the western foot of the charted westward-running channel, immediately north of the Cocoa, twin, high-rise bridges—transient dockage available—5½-foot minimum depths—reviewed on pages 279-80, 302

Diamond 99 Marina—(321) 254-1490—(Standard Mile 910.5)—located near 28 10.691 North/080 38.966 West, west of unlighted daybeacon #99—transient dockage available—gasoline and diesel fuel available—4½-foot minimum depths—reviewed on pages 283-84, 303

Anchorage Yacht Basin—(321) 773-3620—(Standard Mile 914)—located near 28 08.348 North/080 36.071 West, at the southern foot of the Banana River, south of Dragon Point and unlighted daybeacon #1—transient dockage available—gasoline and diesel fuel available—5-foot minimum depths—reviewed on pages 285, 304

Eau Gallie Yacht Club—(321) 773-2600—(Standard Mile 914)—located near 28 08.671 North/080 36.127 West, on the Banana's eastern banks north of Anchorage Yacht Basin (see above)—guest dockage available for members of other yacht clubs with appropriate reciprocal privileges—5-foot minimum depths—reviewed on pages 285-86, 304

Telemar Bay Marina—(321) 773-2468—(Standard Mile 914)—located near 28 08.977 North/080 36.208 West, guards the Banana River's easterly banks, just south of the charted, 7-foot, swing bridge and a short hop north of Dragon Point—transient dockage available—gasoline and diesel fuel available—6-foot minimum depths—reviewed on pages 286-87, 304

Eau Gallie Yacht Basin and Boat Works—(321) 242-6577—(Standard Mile 915)—located near near 28 07.556 North/080 37.496 West, north and west of the ICW's flashing daybeacon #2 and just south of the Eau Gallie high-rise bridge—very limited transient dockage available (advance reservations required)—6-foot minimum depths—reviewed on pages 288-89, 304-5

Waterline Marina—(321) 254-0452—(Standard Mile 915)—located near 28 07.342 North/080 37.789 West, on the westerly extreme of the charted channel north and west of the ICW's flashing daybeacon #2 and just south of the Eau Gallie high-rise bridge—transient dockage available—4½-foot minimum depths, but typically 5+ feet of water—reviewed on pages 289-90, 304-5

Intracoastal Marina of Melbourne—(321) 725-0090—(Standard Mile 916.5)—located

near 28 05.956 North/080 36.665 West, entry channel cuts west between unlighted daybeacon #3 and flashing daybeacon #5—transient dockage available—gasoline and diesel fuel available—minimum 6-foot depths—reviewed on pages 290-91, 305

Melbourne Harbor Marine—(321) 725-9054—(Standard Mile 919)—located near 28 04.632 North/080 36.005 West, entrance channel cuts west, abeam of unlighted daybeacon #6, south of the Melbourne twin, high-rise bridges—transient dockage available—gasoline and diesel fuel available—5½-foot minimum depths, but typical 6+-foot depths—reviewed on pages 291-93, 305

Sebastian River Marina & Boat Yard—(772) 664-3029—(Standard Mile 934)—located near 27 52.395 North/080 29.809 West, entrance channel cuts to the west, south of unlighted daybeacon #55—limited transient dockage available—gasoline and diesel fuel available—3-foot minimum depths—reviewed on pages 294, 307

Sebastian Inlet Marina—(772) 589-4345—(Standard Mile 938)—located near 27 49.493 North/080 28.308 West, west of unlighted daybeacon #66—limited transient dockage available—gasoline and diesel fuel available—4½-foot minimum depths—reviewed on pages 294-96, 307

Grand Harbor Marina—(772) 770-4470—(Standard Mile 948.5)—located near 27 41.519 North/080 23.692 West, west and a bit south of the ICW's unlighted daybeacon #122—transient dockage available—gasoline and diesel fuel available—6-foot minimum depths—reviewed on pages 297-98, 308

Vero Beach Yacht Club—(772) 231-2211—(Standard Mile 952)—located near 27 39.451 North/080 22.200 West, on the eastern shores of Bethel Creek, moving northeast and north from the Vero Beach/Merrill Barber high-rise bridge, south of flashing daybeacon #139—guest dockage available for members of other yacht clubs with appropriate reciprocal arrangements—6-foot minimum depths—reviewed on pages 298-99, 308

Vero Beach Municipal Marina—(772) 231-2819—(Standard Mile 952)—located near 27 39.497 North/080 22.210 West, on the eastern shores of Bethel Creek, moving northeast and north from the Vero Beach/Merrill Barber high-rise bridge, south of flashing daybeacon #139—transient dockage available—gasoline and diesel fuel available—6½-foot minimum depths—reviewed on pages 299-301, 308-9

Indian River Entrance to Canaveral Barge Canal

The ICW enters Indian River from the southwestern terminus of Haulover Canal via a narrow but well-outlined channel. This passage runs first to the southwest and then curves to the south and heads for the charming river city of Titusville. Depths outside of the Waterway in this section are suspect at best. Soundings of 3 to 4 feet are all too common. North of flashing daybeacon #16, you should probably keep to the marked cut unless you have specific local knowledge.

Titusville (Standard Mile 879)

Titusville is a thriving community, but while modern development is in evidence everywhere, we have never witnessed the "high-speed" lifestyle of southeastern Florida. People seem friendly and more than willing to lend visiting cruisers a helpful hand. We have always liked Titusville and think you will have a similar experience.

Bus tours depart regularly from Titusville for Disney World and the Spaceport exhibit at Kennedy Space Center. You can check at one of the marina offices for schedules and pickup locations. We have found both Titusville marinas more than willing to help with a ride to the bus terminal.

Numbers to know in Titusville:

Yellow Cab—321-267-7061
Yellowtop Taxi—321-264-1700
Brevard Express (Shuttle)—321-267-7179
Enterprise Rent-A-Car—321-383-9934
Budget Car Rental—321-269-4155

Titusville Facilities (Various Lats/Lons—see below)

Titusville boasts two full-service marina facilities, one of which is eager to greet transient visitors. The marinas are located in a well-protected harbor just north of the city. A marked channel leads southwest from the ICW channel to the dockage basin between unlighted daybeacon #27 and the Titusville bridge. Cruisers can count on approach depths ranging from 7½ to 10 feet.

Titusville Municipal Marina overlooks the southwestern banks of the basin near 28 37.224 North/080 48.551 West. Cruise straight ahead from the harbor entrance and you will wind up dead center at the marina docks. This is another in northeastern Florida's collection of impressive municipal marinas. We have always found the staff friendly, knowledgeable, and schooled in providing whatever services visitors might require. You simply can't find a better municipal facility anywhere.

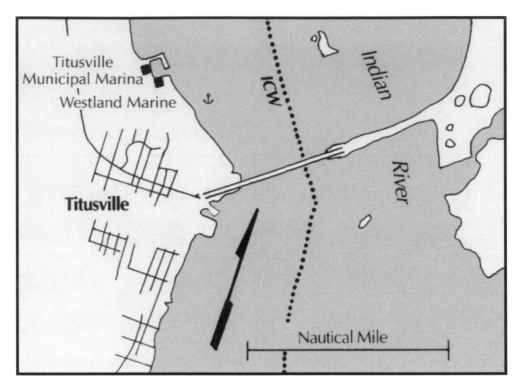

Transients are welcomed at modern, floating, concrete docks with 30-50 amp power and water connections. Dockside fiberglass storage boxes are provided with every slip. Minimum depths at most berths are 8 feet or better, but a very few inner slips have only 5 to 6 feet of water. Long-term marina residents have access to cable-television and telephone hookups. First-class, climate-controlled showers, a Laundromat boasting three washers and dryers, plus a paperback exchange library are found shoreside. Waste pump-out is available both at the fuel dock and by way of a mobile pump unit. Gasoline and diesel fuel are sold at a centralized pier. Mechanical repairs are sometimes possible through independent contractors. Titusville Marina maintains a small but well-stocked ship's and variety store on the grounds.

Mariners anchored along the Titusville waterfront (see below) can now make use of a convenient dinghy dock at Titusville Municipal Marina. There is no charge just to use the dock, but for a measly $5, you can have use of the bathrooms, showers, and Laundromat. How's that for a great deal?

Titusville Marina also provides a thoroughly convenient dockside (undercover) telephone hookup for your laptop computer. This is a great place to check your e-mail, and the local AOL access number is posted just beside the connection. Look for this novel service on the wall of the ship's store facing the dockage basin.

Both a convenience store and a supermarket are within a two-block walk. This is an excellent spot to obtain provisions without the necessity of a taxi ride.

Come dinnertime, there is one dining spot in Titusville that demands your immediate attention. Dixie Crossroads Restaurant (1475 Garden Street, 321-268-5000) is one of those places where cruisers will plan to stop at Titusville just to dine. They are famous for their "rock shrimp," and you can't go wrong with anything on the menu. The serving sizes are legendary. It doesn't get any better than this, gang. The word has long been out about Dixie Crossroads, so go early, or be prepared for a long wait, particularly on weekends. Complimentary transportation is available to Dixie Crossroads. Simply obtain a coupon from any of the marina staff and then call Yellowtop Taxi.

Considering the many services and deserved popularity of Titusville Municipal Marina, advance reservations would be a very wise precaution. Tell them we sent you.

Titusville Municipal Marina (321) 383-5600
http://www.titusville.com/marina

Approach depths-7½-10 feet (minimum)
Dockside depths—8-12 feet
  5-6 feet (some inner docks)
Accepts transients—yes
Transient dockage rate—average
Floating concrete piers—yes
Dockside power connections—30
  and 50 amps
Dockside water connections—yes
Showers—yes
Laundromat—yes
Waste pump-out—yes
Gasoline—yes
Diesel fuel—yes
Mechanical repairs—limited
  (independent contractors)
Ship's and variety store—yes (small)
Restaurant—several nearby

Westland Marine, Titusville Harbor

The docks of Westland Marine (also known as Nelson's Harbor, 321-267-1667) occupy the harbor's southeastern shore near 28 37.166 North/080 48.424 West. This friendly, family owned operation offers extensive repair services, but transient dockage is no longer available. Depths alongside are mostly 8 feet or better, but we did sound a few 5-foot readings on some of the innermost slips. Gasoline and diesel fuel are on hand, and Westland has the reputation of offering very competitive fuel prices.

It takes only one look to realize that below-waterline repairs are the specialty of Westland Marine. During our many visits, we have never failed to observe a host of hauled craft sitting on blocks and cradles. Haul-outs are accomplished via a 40-ton travelift. Once your craft is out of the water, you have the option of doing your own bottom work or leaving it to the yard professionals. Full mechanical servicing for both diesel and gasoline engines is also available. Westland Marine also maintains a large, full-line ship's store.

Titusville Anchorage (Standard Mile 879) (28 37.310 North/080 48.211 West)

A few boats occasionally anchor in the

4½- to 6-foot waters southeast of the Titusville Harbor entrance channel, between this cut and the 9-foot swing bridge. Clearly, this anchor-down spot is only a consideration for boats drawing less than 4 feet. There is some protection from westerly and southwesterly winds, but virtually no shelter from any other quarter. We certainly wouldn't want to be caught in these waters during a thunderstorm. About the only positive attributes of this potential haven is virtually unrestricted swinging room and access to the dinghy dock at Titusville Municipal Marina (see above). The westerly shoreline plays host to a large municipal park, and it shows surprisingly light development.

Spaceport, USA

Highway 405 (also known as NASA Parkway), just south of Titusville, provides public automobile access to Spaceport, USA, one of the most popular exhibits in Florida. The port and its exhibits are located in the heart of the Cape Canaveral complex. Visitors are treated to a two-hour tour. The tours begin at 9:45 A.M. and run continuously until two hours after dark. First up is an inspection of Space Shuttle Launch Complex 39, including the massive Vehicle Assembly Building, launch pads A and B, and an authentic Saturn V Moon Rocket. Back at the visitor center, displays of various space hardware, including full-scale models of many rockets, still draw vast crowds every day. Perhaps most impressive are two beautifully composed "IMAX" films. Both *The Dream Is Alive,* an inspiring film of the Space Shuttle program, and *Blue Planet,* an in-depth look at the earth's environment from the perspective of space, are shown on a screen 5½ stories high and 70 feet wide. Narrated by Walter Cronkite and filmed

by the Shuttle astronauts in flight, the films offer breathtaking visual and auditory effects. Allow five hours to fully experience the sights and sounds of Spaceport, USA. For more information, call (321) 452-2121.

Kennedy Point Yacht Club & Marina (Standard Mile 882.5) (28 33.276 North/080 47.773 West)

South of Titusville a charted, well-marked channel leads west from unlighted daybeacon #39 to Kennedy Point Yacht Club & Marina. This privately owned club and marina is happy to accept visitors (without the need for reciprocal agreements), and there is much to recommend this facility to visiting cruisers.

Slips are composed of fixed, wooden piers with full power and water connections. The harbor is sheltered by a wooden breakwater. Entrance depths are now in the 6- to 6½-foot range at MLW, while soundings alongside run from 5 to 7 feet in most slips, with as little as 4 feet on the innermost berths. Gasoline and diesel fuel are available at the club's fuel dock, and, again, you do not have to be a member of another yacht club to purchase fuel.

Excellent, climate-controlled showers, a Laundromat, and an e-mail hookup are available in the clubhouse overlooking the harbor. Here visitors are also afforded privileges to use

Kennedy Point Yacht Club & Marina, Titusville

the Jacuzzi, swimming pool, sauna, exercise room, racquetball court, and wide-screen television. Tennis courts are also available on the grounds.

Surprisingly for a facility of this ilk, Kennedy Point operates a tiny ship's store in the clubhouse with a paperback exchange library. On Sunday mornings, complimentary donuts are served. This practice only hints at the can-do and accommodating attitude that this club and its personnel take toward visiting and resident mariners alike.

While the club does not usually have on-site dining, Dixie Crossroads Restaurant (described above in our account of Titusville Municipal Marina) will dispatch a car to Kennedy Point to pick up and return visiting cruisers interested in partaking of this dining firm's superb fare. Cruising chefs in the mood to prepare a fresh catch of the day in their own galleys can easily walk just a bit north on adjacent Highway U.S. 1 to Titusville Seafood Market (4700 South Washington Avenue, 321-383-9912).

So, all in all, this writer is willing to go out on the proverbial limb and heartily recommend Kennedy Point Yacht Club & Marina to all skippers, save those piloting especially deep-draft vessels. We hope you have as good a time as we always do!

Kennedy Point Yacht Club & Marina
(321) 383-0280
http://www.kennedypointmarina.com

Approach depths—6-6½ feet
Dockside depths—4-7 feet
Accepts transients—yes
Transient dockage rate—average
Fixed wooden piers—yes
Dockside power connections—30 and 50 amps
Dockside water connections—yes
Showers—yes

Laundromat—yes
Waste pump-out—yes
Gasoline—yes
Diesel fuel—yes
Ship's store—yes (tiny)
Restaurant—nearby

Indian River Spaceport Anchorage (Standard Mile 882) (28 34.527 North/080 45.824 West)

Chart 11485 correctly identifies a large patch of deep water east-northeast of flashing daybeacon #38. While this spot is wide open to wind and wave and would therefore not be considered a good anchorage under other circumstances, it is a great spot from which to watch a launch of the Space Shuttle or other NASA rocket. The huge NASA Vehicle Assembly Building is also readily visible to the east.

Cruising craft of almost any size drawing less than 5½ feet can feel their way east from #38 for 1.8 nautical miles and hold 6- to 7-foot depths. During a scheduled launch this anchorage is often crowded, but it is large, and there's usually room for one more.

Captains entering the launch anchorage should take care to avoid the charted shoal islands and 2-foot shallows east of the ICW channel. Be sure to read the navigation information before attempting entry.

Addison Point Bridge Anchorages (Standard Mile 885) (Various Lats/Lons—see below)

South of flashing daybeacon #43, the Addison Point/NASA Parkway bridge crosses Indian River and the ICW's path. Both sides of this span are connected to long causeways that can provide fair shelter for overnight anchorage, depending on the prevailing wind. All these potential havens have plenty of swinging room and the surrounding shorelines are essentially undeveloped (except, of course, for the bridge). After 6:30 P.M., we have seldom found the headlights or automobile noise to be a problem.

In southerly blows, cruisers can work their way carefully into the charted deep water to the west, just north of the bridge, near 28 31.755 North/080 46.181 West. These waters are easily entered and hold minimum 8-foot depths. However, you must be careful not to cruise into the charted shallows to the west.

Probably the best, though certainly not the most easily navigated, of the Addison Point Bridge overnight stops lies north of the span, east of the main channel. To reach this haven safely you must depart the ICW immediately south of flashing daybeacon #43. This procedure will help you avoid the correctly charted 2- and 3-foot patches farther to the southeast. From #43, you can track your way through good depths to a point just west of the charted spoil island to the east-southeast (near 28 31.889 North/080 45.140 West). Drop the hook some 100 yards off this small landmass's westerly banks. Now you have good shelter to the east and south, but winds from the north

or west are still a problem. During one of our earlier visits to these waters, we found two large sailcraft ensconced in this anchorage during a wicked southerly blow.

South of the bridge, the best anchorage is in the deep water to the west, near 28 31.564 North/080 46.204 West. Good depths of 7 feet or more are held for several hundred yards west of the ICW channel. If you make use of this southerly anchorage, keep a sharp watch to the west as you are entering. You should spot the charted missile exhibit on the western shore. Don't attempt to approach this attraction unless you can stand depths of less than 3 feet. Now, there is shelter to the north and west, but none to the south and precious little to the east.

It is also possible to anchor south of the bridge in the lee of the causeway to the east, amidst 7-foot depths, near 28 31.514 North/080 45.350 West. Unfortunately, several unmarked and incorrectly charted shoals make navigation of these waters a bit tricky. Unless there is some particular reason why you prefer the eastern anchorage, you should probably choose the haven on the opposite side of the Waterway.

INDIAN RIVER ENTRANCE TO CANAVERAL BARGE CANAL NAVIGATION

Navigation of the ICW from Haulover Canal to the Canaveral Barge channel is a matter of holding to the Waterway channel. On the northerly portion of this run, depths outside of the ICW are highly suspect. Farther south, some deep water abuts the Waterway, but even here there is little purpose in cruising outside of the marked ICW channel except to enter the anchorages and facilities discussed

above. There are no sidewaters with sufficient depth for cruising craft, and the river itself is far too broad for anything but emergency anchorage.

ICW to Titusville   The ICW leaves the southwestern entrance of Haulover Canal behind and follows a narrow but well-defined channel out into the headwaters of Indian River. While some waters outside of the marked cut hold 5- to 6-foot depths, others fall off to the 3- and 4-foot level. Skippers piloting boats more than 28 feet long and drawing more than 3½ feet are advised to stay to the ICW channel north of flashing daybeacon #16.

Several years ago we heard rumors that in spite of depth readings shown on chart 11485, some deep water was to be found near the small islands flanking the northwestern tier of the channel between flashing daybeacons #1 and #12. However, extensive on-site research on several occasions has revealed 3- and 4-foot soundings every time we attempt to leave the ICW channel behind. With these findings in hand, only small outboard craft should consider approaching these islands.

The shallow depths outside of the channel need not keep you from observing the many hundreds of birds that are regularly sighted in and around these small islands. We spotted numerous species, varying from ospreys to common seagulls and pelicans.

At flashing daybeacon #12, the ICW turns sharply to the south and begins to track its way down the course of Indian River. South of flashing daybeacon #16, a narrow buffer of deep water flanks the Waterway channel to the east. Owing to their total lack of shelter, these waters are only useful as an emergency stop.

Between flashing daybeacon #19 and unlighted daybeacon #23, the channel passes through the Jay-Jay/NASA Railway Bridge. This span has a closed vertical clearance of only 7 feet, but it is kept open unless a train is due. The bridge closes automatically some eight minutes before a train is scheduled to pass through. Flashing red lights and a repeating siren warn skippers that the bridge is about to close. If you happen to arrive while these signals are on, please wait for the train to pass rather than be caught under the lowering span. Once the tracks are clear, the bridge will reopen automatically. A flashing green light means that it is safe to proceed.

It's only a short run from the railway span to the Titusville/Max E. Brewer highway bridge. The entrance channel to the city facilities will come abeam to the southwest between unlighted daybeacon #27 and the highway span.

Titusville Harbor Channel To enter well-sheltered Titusville Harbor, you need only pass between the various pairs of unlighted daybeacons and enter the harbor inlet on its midwidth. Prudent navigators will continue south on the Waterway channel until the northeastern most set of markers (unlighted daybeacons #1 and #2) are directly abeam to the southwest. You can then turn into the channel's centerline without any danger of encroaching on the shallower water to the north.

Titusville Anchorage Remember that depths on the anchorage southeast of the Titusville Harbor channel can run less than 4½ feet. If you can stand these sorts of soundings, depart the ICW some 300 yards south of its intersection with the Titusville cut. Track your way at idle speed to the southwest, keeping your sounder under close observation. The farther you cruise from the Waterway, the more the bottom will shelve up. By all accounts, stay at least 300 to 400 yards off the southwesterly shoreline.

Titusville/Max E. Brewer Highway Bridge
The Max E. Brewer swing bridge spans the Waterway well southeast of unlighted daybeacon #27. This bridge often obstructs Waterway traffic during the early morning and late afternoon. The span has an official closed vertical clearance of 9 feet, but another foot or so can be carried if you pass through the side spans adjoining the central pass through. Currently, the bridge is closed from Monday to Friday between the hours of 6:00 A.M. to 7:15 A.M. and from 3:15 P.M. to 4:30 P.M. Southbound cruisers planning an early morning start or northbound captains approaching Titusville during the afternoon hours should take this restricted period into account.

On the Waterway   The run from the Titusville swing bridge to flashing daybeacon #38 is a nearly straight shot down the easily defined ICW channel. Again, it is a good idea to stay in the marked passage until reaching the deep waters abeam of #38. At this aid, the waters to the east-northeast can serve as an ideal site from which to watch Space Shuttle launches.

Indian River Spaceport Anchorage   To enter the anchorage east-northeast of #38, set a compass course from the daybeacon to avoid the charted spoil shoals to the north and south. Once between these two obstructions, you can continue cruising east-northeast for 1.5 nautical miles before encountering any shallows. The Space Shuttle launch pad is only some 5 miles away, and you should have an excellent view of the liftoff.

Kennedy Point Yacht Club & Marina   To enter the Kennedy Point Yacht Club & Marina channel, continue cruising south on the Waterway past unlighted daybeacon #39. Watch to the west for the easternmost pair of unlighted daybeacons on the Kennedy Point channel. Simply pass between the first pair, #1 and #2, and continue tracking your way to the west-southwest to the harbor's entrance by passing all red, even-numbered aids to your starboard side and taking green markers to port. There are now more markers in this cut than appear on the current edition of chart 11485.

On the ICW   The Waterway continues south down a mostly straight path to Addison Point bascule bridge, south of flashing daybeacon #43 and unlighted daybeacon #44. Between unlighted daybeacon #40 and flashing daybeacon #43, shallow water flanks the western quarter of the channel. Be on guard against excessive lateral leeway easing you onto this shoal.

The Addison Point span has a restricted opening schedule, but with its 27-foot closed vertical clearance, many powerboats do not have to worry about this limitation. Sailcraft that cannot clear this height will have to contend with early morning and late afternoon delays. The bridge will not open on weekdays (year round) from 6:30 A.M. to 8:00 A.M. and 3:30 P.M. to 5:00 P.M.

Addison Point Anchorages   Cruisers anchoring north of the westside Addison Point causeway need only work their way carefully under the lee of land to the south. Be sure to set the hook well before coming abeam of the charted tongue of shoal water to the north. Chart 11485 notes an "Obstn" (Obstruction) on these waters.

The eastside anchorage north of the bridge should be approached by leaving the ICW immediately south of flashing daybeacon #43. Set course for a point 100 yards north of the spoil island to the east-southeast. After approaching to within .2 nautical miles of this small island, you can begin to point for its north-to-south midpoint. This maneuver will serve to avoid the correctly charted twin patches of 2- and 3-foot waters to the south. Be mindful of these shallows on your run from #43 to the island. If depths start to rise, try giving way to the north. Drop anchor at least 100 yards west of the small island. Closer to shore, depths rise to 3 feet or less.

To visit the western haven south of the bridge, turn 90 degrees to the west some 75 to 100 yards south of the span. By staying 75 yards off the northerly banks, and north of the charted 4-foot finger of shoal water to the south, you can track your way easily under the lee of the causeway to the north. Depths of 6 to 7 feet hold for some 200 yards to the west. Farther in toward the westerly banks, the bottom shelves upward sharply.

Approach the tricky easterly anchorage south of the bridge by setting a careful compass course to the northeast from unlighted daybeacon #47. Point to avoid the charted shoals to the north and south. On-site research has revealed that both these danger areas are now considerably larger than they appear on chart 11485. Plot your course directly between the two shallow patches, proceed at idle speed, and keep a wary eye on the sounder.

On the ICW From Addison Point Bridge the ICW darts quickly south down a nearly arrow-straight passage to its intersection with the Canaveral Barge Canal. While some deep water abuts the channel during this run, there are also some shallow spoil areas west of the Waterway between the bridge and flashing daybeacon #55. Again, the prudent captain would do well to hold to the established channel.

South of unlighted daybeacon #47, you will catch sight of two pairs of red and white horizontally banded smokestacks on the western shoreline. These colorful signposts mark two large power plants, which are served by their own indifferently marked channels. The northernmost cut breaks off to the west just south of unlighted daybeacon #52, while the southern channel is found south of unlighted daybeacon #56. Many of the markers shown on chart 11485 were absent during our research. Even if they are all present, pleasure craft should keep clear of both cuts and the dockage basins beyond.

Between unlighted daybeacons #53 and #62, chart 11485 shows two channels striking east to Merritt Island. Neither of these cuts has been used for some time, and both are best avoided by visiting cruisers.

South-southeast of unlighted daybeacon #66, the ICW passes under an overhead power line with a charted overhead clearance of 85 feet "over the main channel." While this is sufficient clearance for virtually any pleasure craft, cruising under these shocking structures always makes us a bit uneasy.

South of flashing daybeacon #67, mariners are faced with a choice of two routes. The ICW continues south through twin fixed bridges, while the Canaveral

Barge Canal runs off to the east. We shall first consider the barge canal route and its adjoining inlet. Continued coverage of the ICW will resume in the next subsection.

Canaveral Barge Canal, Merritt Island, and Banana River

The Canaveral Barge Canal provides reliable access to the open sea and the northerly reaches of Banana River. The canal first cuts through the heart of Merritt Island as it tracks its way east to Banana River. Three marinas guard this portion of the route. One offers superb services for visiting cruisers.

The barge channel crosses Banana River, flows through a single lock, and enters another sheltered cut leading to the ocean. Two marinas on the southerly banks between the lock and oceanside inlet offer additional first-class facilities for visiting cruisers.

The barge canal inlet is well maintained and carefully marked. Unless there happens to be some problem with the lock doors, skippers can use this passage to and from the Atlantic with confidence.

Banana River offers a very mixed bag of cruising opportunities. The river's northerly reaches border on the heart of Cape Canaveral and Spaceport, USA. There are several anchorages on these waters from which cruisers can watch Space Shuttle launches. The southerly passage down the length of Banana River to Dragon Point is very tricky indeed and not for the fainthearted.

Western Barge Canal

The approach channel to the western entrance of the Canaveral Barge Canal makes into the ICW just south of flashing daybeacon #67 (Standard Mile 894). This portion of the Barge Canal route consists of a narrow but deep cut that tracks its way to Banana River through two arrow-straight runs. Typical depths in the canal and its passage across Banana River at the time of this writing are 11 to 15 feet.

Most of the shoreline is in its natural state. A few buildings break the landscape here and there, but for the most part, visitors have the opportunity to see what Merritt Island was like before it was radically altered by high-tech development.

Western Barge Canal Facilities (Various Lats/Lons—see below)

As you move from west to east, the first facility on the Canaveral Barge Canal comes up in the charted cove on the southern shore, west of the charted bascule bridge, near 28 24.368 North/080 42.591 West. Harbor Square Marina features one of the most protected harbors you will ever encounter. A small stream provides entry into the man-made dockage area, which is almost completely surrounded by grassy, high, earthen banks. Protection should be adequate for almost any sort of weather short of an intense hurricane. Theoretically, transients are accepted at modern, fixed, wooden piers with full power and water connections. Depths alongside range from 5½ to as much as 8 feet. However, after at least a half-dozen visits to this facility, we have yet to meet an actual dockside attendant. We have been assured by fellow cruisers that a dockmaster can be found most of the time, but you wouldn't know it by us.

A single, fair (non-air-conditioned) shoreside shower overlooks the harbor's southwesterly corner. Mechanical repairs are offered, and the marina staff can arrange for haul-out services at nearby facilities. They will even deliver your boat to the travelift and return it to its slip after the work is completed. While there is not a formal ship's store on the grounds, the marina does maintain a good inventory of parts and supplies. Diesel fuel, but no gasoline, can be purchased in the harbor. One very low-key restaurant is available within walking distance at Tingleys Marina (see below), and there is a good Chinese restaurant a short step farther.

Harbor Square Marina (321) 453-2464

Approach depths—8-10 feet
Dockside depths—5$\frac{1}{2}$-8 feet
Accepts transients—yes
Transient dockage rate—below average
Fixed wooden piers—yes
Dockside power connections—30

Harbor Square Marina, Merritt Island

and 50 amps
Dockside water connections—yes
Showers—yes
Diesel fuel—yes
Below-waterline repairs—yes
    (independent contractors)
Mechanical repairs—yes
Restaurant—nearby

Tingleys Marina (28 24.439 North/080 42.427 West) comes abeam next on the southern shore, just west of the bascule bridge. This folksy (rather seedy) facility occasionally accepts transients, but the fixed, wooden docks are decidedly low key and only appropriate for smaller cruising craft. Depths alongside run 6 to 9 feet. There is a small, dockside restaurant with an adjacent tackle and variety store that operates from 6 A.M. to 7 P.M. Gasoline, but no diesel fuel, can be purchased. The marina is adjacent to a large trailer and camper park under the same ownership. There is a decided flavor of inland sportfishing at this small facility.

Tingleys Marina (321) 452-0504

Approach depths—10+ feet
Dockside depths—6-9 feet
Accepts transients—limited
Transient dockage rate—below average
Fixed wooden piers—yes
Dockside power connections—mostly
    20 amps
Dockside water connections—yes
Gasoline—yes
Variety and tackle store—yes
Restaurant—on site

Those who have not visited the Canaveral Barge Canal since 1997 are in for quite a surprise. Where once there was a small nondescript facility known as Abbey's Marina flanking the canal's southern banks about halfway between the bascule bridge and the stream's juncture with Banana River, cruisers will now find a large, full-service, pleasure-craft haven known as Harbortown Marina (28 24.537 North/080 40.496 West).

Harbortown is really quite a place. It served as the site for the 1999 Marine Trader Owner's Association Rendezvous, at which this writer was privileged to speak.

The well-sheltered harbor has been thoroughly dredged and ringed by a concrete seawall. Depths alongside are typically 8 feet with a few 6-foot soundings on the extreme interior slips. Transients are eagerly accepted, and there seems to be an impressive number of slips set aside for visiting cruisers. Berths are afforded at modern, fixed, wooden piers featuring full power and fresh-water hookups. Gasoline, diesel fuel, and waste pump-out services are all readily available.

Shoreside, visiting cruisers will discover good (but not climate-controlled) showers and a full Laundromat. Overlooking the dockage basin, there is also a welcome swimming pool at which visiting mariners are welcome.

Full mechanical servicing (gasoline and diesel power plants) is complemented by below-waterline repairs. Haul-outs are accomplished by way of a 70-ton travelift. We have been impressed by the facility's commitment to full service. Captains can place their vessels in the hands of these yard professionals with confidence.

There is also on-site dry-stack storage for power craft as large as 35 feet. You can't miss the storage building overlooking the harbor's westerly banks.

The on-site restaurant is now known as Nautical Spirits (321-452-5090) It is open for the evening meal seven days a week, with lunch served Monday through Saturday and brunch served on Sundays.

You will need to take a taxi or arrange for a rental car in order to undertake any serious provisioning, to visit other restaurants, or to make the acquaintance of nearby Spaceport, USA. The marina staff will be glad to arrange for this sort of landside transportation, but Harbortown does not maintain a courtesy car.

All these dry statistics, impressive as they are, do not really convey the helpful, can-do attitude that we have encountered at Harbortown Marina during our two visits. We are happy to go out on a proverbial limb and give this facility our most hearty endorsement.

Harbortown Marina (321) 453-0160
   http://www.harbortownmarina.com
   /Canaveral/frames1.htm

Approach depths—8-10 feet
Dockside depths—6-8 feet
Accepts transients—yes
Transient dockage rate—average
Fixed wooden piers—yes
Dockside power connections—30
   and 50 amps

Harbortown Marina, Merritt Island

Dockside water connections—yes
Showers—yes
Laundromat—yes
Waste pump-out—yes
Gasoline—yes
Diesel fuel—yes
Below-waterline repairs—yes
Mechanical repairs—yes
Restaurant—on site

Merritt Island

South of Mosquito Lagoon the thin barrier island that separates the ICW from the Atlantic Ocean suddenly bulges out to form a significant body of land. This vast isle is bisected by Banana River, thereby forming Cape Canaveral to the east and Merritt Island to the west. Today we think of this entire region as Spaceport, USA.

However, rockets were not on Vernon Lamme's mind when, on February 22, 1912, he and his father journeyed by boat to Merritt Island to pick out a home site. The hitherto uninhabited island had been set aside by former president Theodore Roosevelt as a national forest, but now President Taft had elected to throw open the island to homesteading. The pioneering Lamme family had decided to try its luck on this fresh body of land. In his now-famous chronicle *Florida Lore Not Found in the History Books,* Vernon Lamme comments:

> When the homesteaders came to Merritt Island . . . we didn't even ask the government to reduce the requirements of the homestead code. . . . We bought grub hoes and yanked out acres of palmetto roots at the rate of one acre every 30 days. . . . I just happened to think that if we placed all those homesteaders' homes along one side of any city today—boy, that would be a slum to shame all slums. However we didn't realize it—we were poverty stricken and didn't know it. . . .

Way back in 1912 when I first inhaled the heavenly aroma of orange blossoms on Merritt Island, folks, even those with "schoolin" had few of the worries that attack us today. Not only did they never dream of a guided missile, carrying utter destruction . . . but actually knew little of the Nation's economy—and cared less.

The story of Merritt Island and Cape Canaveral took a radical turn during World War II when the federal government established the 1,822-acre Banana River Naval Air Station to watch for enemy submarines. The base was reactivated in 1949 as a long-range proving ground to be shared by all the armed forces. Eventually the government acquired the remainder of Merritt Island and Cape Canaveral and began a rocket testing program. This first launch of a modified German V2 rocket was on July 22, 1950.

Today, more change has come to Cape Canaveral and Merritt Island. After discovering that it had acquired more land than it needed, the federal government established the Merritt Island National Wildlife Refuge north of Kennedy Space Center. Here in a totally natural environment more than 70,000 ducks, 4,000 alligators, 500 manatees, and numerous sea cows, porpoises, loggerhead and green sea turtles, armadillos, eagles, bobcats, otter, skunk, deer, and wild hogs make their home.

South of the space center Patrick Air Force Base overlooks the banks of Banana River and remains a very active center of military activity. Residential communities jostle each other for space near the southern tip of Merritt Island and the cape. It is all far removed from Vernon Lamme's day.

Banana River

Captains should consider Banana River as two very different cruising grounds. North of the barge canal channel, cruising craft are permitted to explore the river as far as the first bridge by a deep, well-marked passage. Beyond this point, NASA does not allow any public water traffic. Numerous deepwater patches flank the northern channel's westerly reaches short of the bridge. While none of these potential anchorages are sheltered, they all make a great place to drop the hook when a space launch is due. Fellow cruisers report that liftoffs seen from northerly Banana River are nothing short of spectacular.

South of the Canaveral Barge Canal intersection, the passage down Banana River to the Dragon Point is poorly marked and fraught with peril. There are also a couple of fixed bridges along the way with as little as 36 feet of vertical clearance. While it is possible for local captains to follow the so-called channel all the way to Dragon Point and hold 5-foot depths, there are many opportunities for even careful cruisers to stray into shoal waters, with a hard grounding as the result. While navigation of this tricky channel will be described later in this chapter for the devil-may-care skippers among us, visiting mariners who enter this cut do so with considerable risk of bottom and prop damage.

Between the Banana's southernmost bridge and the stream's intersection with its big brother, Indian River, the river's character changes yet again. The southernmost reaches of Banana River (known as the Dragon Point region) are deep and chock-full of facilities catering to cruising craft. As the Dragon Point section of the river is normally approached almost exclusively by way of the Indian River-ICW route, these regional facilities will be discussed later as part of the Waterway passage to Vero Beach.

Northern Banana River Anchorages (28 29.407 North/080 37.619 West)

Since the September 11 atrocities, security has, understandably, become a much greater concern at Cape Canaveral. You may discover that the anchorages described below are no longer accessible to cruising craft, particularly when a launch is imminent. All we can advise is to watch for warning signs or patrol boats. Good luck!

Assuming it's still allowed at all, your decision where to anchor in northern Banana River before a scheduled rocket or shuttle launching will be heavily influenced by the time of your arrival. Probably the best spot is in the charted 6-foot water west of the marked channel between flashing daybeacon #29 and unlighted daybeacon #31 (near 28 29.407 North/080 37.619 West). Here navigators can carefully sound their way for some 100 yards to the west before depths begin to deteriorate.

Unfortunately for late arrivals, these waters are usually filled as much as twenty-four to forty-eight hours before scheduled liftoff. As more and more boats arrive, the available anchorages are usually filled beginning in the north and moving south. Your best bet is to cruise as far north as you can while there is still a spot to the west where you can anchor with sufficient swinging room.

Banana River Marine (28 20.054 North/080 39.650 West)

Surprisingly, there is one facility on southern Banana River, between the barge canal intersection and the Dragon Point facilities, that caters to cruising craft, at least those of the powered persuasion. Vessels cruising south from the Canaveral Barge Canal-Banana River intersection must pass under a fixed span with 36 feet of clearance, and those journeying north on Banana River from Dragon Point must contend with a 43-foot fixed bridge. Obviously the waters along the central section of Banana River are pretty much relegated to powerboats or smaller sailcraft.

Friendly Banana River Marine lines the river's western banks near unlighted daybeacon #24. A pile-marked channel leads cruising visitors through a small drawbridge into an ultrasheltered dockage basin behind the large ship's store. The management has informed this writer that transients are gladly accepted, though thus far few have made the lengthy trek off the ICW. Most berths are provided at a long, fixed, concrete pier with minimum depths of 5 to 6 feet alongside. There is one 4½-foot lump at the easterly end of the entrance channel, and it sets the depth limit for this facility. Water hookups and 30- and 50-amp power connections are readily available, and those who plan to stay for a while can arrange for telephone and cable-television hookups via the already-in-place wiring. Fair showers and a Laundromat are found on the premises. The on-site ship's store is extensive and well supplied. If you need anything nautical, you need look no further. It would take a very long hike indeed to reach a restaurant, so be sure to bring along all your galley needs.

Another company, Coastal Marine Repair (321-453-1885), is located on the grounds (and under the same family ownership). Full mechanical (gas and diesel) repairs are offered, and the yard hauls boats via a 30-ton travelift. The old marine railways have now been removed. Do-it-yourself work is allowed, or you may choose to let the yard professionals handle all your bottom-work needs.

If you, like this writer, enjoy marinas that are a bit off the beaten path, then give Banana River Marine a try. We have consistently found the management to be accommodating and willing to go that extra mile to meet all their patrons' needs.

Banana River Marine (321) 452-8622

Approach depths—4½-6 feet
Dockside depths—5-6 feet (minimum)
Accepts transients—yes
Transient dockage rate—below average
Fixed concrete pier—yes (mostly)
Dockside power connections—30
  and 50 amps
Dockside water connections—yes
Showers—yes
Laundromat—yes
Waste pump-out—yes
Below-waterline repairs—yes
Mechanical repairs—yes
Ship's store—yes

Eastern Canaveral Barge Canal Facilities (Various Lats/Lons—see below)

From Banana River, the barge canal channel

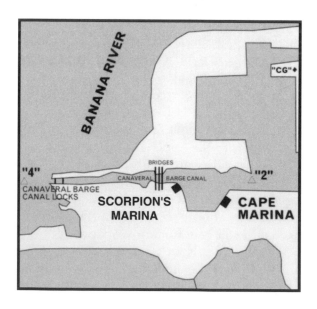

Entering Canaveral Barge Canal lock

flows through a single lock and then enters an artificial cut leading to the ocean. This portion of the passage is lined by deep bays making into both shorelines. All but one of these coves are dominated by commercial shipping traffic and should be avoided by cruising craft except for sightseeing.

Over the past several years the lock giving access to the easterly section of the Canaveral Barge Canal and its reliable inlet has operated without mechanical problems. However, in times past, this lock has been closed for long periods of repair. To be on the safe side, contact one of the local marinas about present conditions before committing absolutely to this passage.

The first large bay on the southern banks, east of the lock, is home to two marinas catering to transient craft. In addition to dockage, both facilities offer extensive repair service.

Scorpion's Marina (formerly New Port Marina) is located on the southwestern shore of the bay, near 28 24.477 North/080 37.807 West. This large, marine complex accepts transients at fixed, steel-decked piers featuring full power and water connections. Depths alongside are an impressive 10 feet or better. Fair showers and a Laundromat are readily available. There is also a medium-sized, on-site ship's store. Gasoline and diesel fuel can be purchased, and the marina offers full mechanical repairs for both gas and diesel power plants. Haul-outs are accomplished by a 75-ton travelift. Bottom and fiberglass repair services are extensive.

Scorpion's also maintains a huge dry-stack storage building, where many smaller power craft are stored. This mammoth structure is more than apparent from the water.

While it's a bit of a walk, most visiting cruisers won't mind the trek to several nearby restaurants. Ask the marina personnel for advice.

Scorpion's Marina (321) 784-5788

Approach depths—12+ feet
Dockside depths—10 feet (minimum)
Accepts transients—yes
Transient dockage rate—above average
Fixed metal piers—yes
Dockside power connections—30,
    50, and 100 amps
Dockside water connections—yes
Showers—yes
Laundromat—yes
Gasoline—yes
Diesel fuel—yes
Below-waterline repairs—yes
Mechanical repairs—yes
Ship's store—yes
Restaurant—several within walking distance

Cape Marina is found on the first cove's eastern banks just across from Scorpion's, near 28 24.466 North/080 37.679 West. This large, full-service facility has been very popular with cruising captains for many a year. Transients are welcomed at fixed, metal-decked piers with all power and water connections. Again,

dockside soundings are quite deep, 10 feet or better. First-class, fully climate-controlled showers and a Laundromat are found shore-side, as is an extensive ship's and variety store. Waste pump-out is also available.

Gasoline and diesel fuel are ready for pumping. Full mechanical repairs (gas and diesel) are offered and Cape Marina boasts two 50-ton travelifts. We have always observed a fleet that resembles the Spanish Armada here perched atop their cradles and stand-offs waiting for service. There are few surer signs of a popular repair yard.

Several good restaurants are found within a quick step of Cape Marina. Ask any of the dock personnel for recommendations.

Given its obvious popularity and our own consistently friendly reception, this writer is ready to go out on the proverbial limb and recommend Cape Marina without reservation.

Cape Marina (321) 783-8410
    http://www.capemarina.com

Approach depths—12+ feet
Dockside depths—10 feet (minimum)
Accepts transients—yes
Transient dockage rate—above average
Fixed metal piers—yes
Dockside power connections—30
    and 50 amps
Dockside water connections—yes
Showers—yes
Laundromat—yes
Waste pump-out—yes
Gasoline—yes
Diesel fuel—yes
Below-waterline repairs—yes
Mechanical repairs—yes
Ship's and variety store—yes
Restaurant—several nearby

Cape Marina, Port Canaveral

A few additional services are provided by Sunrise Marina (321-783-9535) on the canal's southern banks, opposite the charted "Tower" between the second and third (moving from west to east) coves on the cut's northern shore. This facility has very limited dockage. There is a well-stocked bait and tackle-variety store on the premises and full fueling services (gas and diesel) are readily available. Above the store, a deli offers taste-tempting sandwiches. Some 4-foot dockside depths will limit this marina's accessibility for cruising-size vessels.

Canaveral Barge Canal Inlet

As long as the canal's locks are operating without delays, the barge channel's inlet is one of the most reliable seaward passages in all of eastern Florida. This seaward cut combines exceptionally well prepared markings with a stable channel and a general absence of strong tides. While this passage, like all seaward channels, can be a bit rough in bad weather, the facilities nearby allow mariners to wait for favorable conditions before proceeding to sea. If you plan to cruise offshore from Indian River, this inlet would be your best bet north of Fort Pierce.

CANAVERAL BARGE INLET AND BANANA RIVER NAVIGATION

Navigation of these waters will be reviewed in three separate discussions. First, the canal itself will be covered from its intersection with Indian River to its inlet; second, successful passage of northern Banana River will be discussed; and finally this river's southerly reaches will be reviewed.

Canaveral Barge Canal   Cruisers can follow the Canaveral Barge Canal channel with great confidence and relative ease. The entrance channel makes off to the east from the ICW south-south-east of flashing daybeacon #67. To enter the canal turn east off the Waterway about halfway between #67 and unlighted daybeacon #13. Set course to come between the first pair of aids on the entrance channel—flashing daybeacon #12 and unlighted daybeacon #11. Once between these markers, continue on course, pointing to pass between flashing daybeacon #10 and unlighted daybeacon #9. We found that, surprisingly enough, #9 and #10 can be a bit hard to spot from a position between #11 and #12. Have your binoculars handy to help pick out these markers. Identification is important, as shoal water lies immediately north and south of the marked cut.

After passing #9 and #10, continue straight on to the canal's mouth. Once on the canal's interior reaches, simply hold to the centerline for problem-free cruising all the way to Banana River.

Soon you will sight the one and only bridge (State Road 3) crossing the canal's westerly passage, dead ahead. Slow down—no-wake regulations are in effect from several hundred yards west of the bridge to well east of the span. Before reaching the bascule, the entrance to Harbor Square Marina will come abeam along the southerly banks, followed by the face dock of Tingleys Marina (just short of the bridge).

The State Road 3 span has a closed vertical clearance of 25 feet and it sports a restricted opening schedule. This span usually opens on demand, except that the draw is closed between 5:15 A.M. and 7:45 A.M., and from 3:30 P.M. to 5:15P.M., weekdays only (except holidays). Nighttime openings after 10:00 require three hours' notice.

East of the bridge, the channel bisects the shallow reaches of Sykes Creek to the north and south. Avoid these waters' 4-foot depths and hold to the midwidth of the canal channel. Shortly after passing the creek, you will need to switch to chart 11476 for continued navigation. Soon the superbly sheltered harbor belonging to Harbortown Marina will come abeam to the south.

Entry into Banana River calls for caution. Slow down and take a few moments to sort out the various markers. They may not correspond to those pictured on the latest edition of chart 11478. As you are traversing the channel across Banana River to the easterly section of the barge canal, pass all intervening red, even-numbered markers to their southerly sides and all green, odd-numbered aids to their northerly quarters.

It's an arrow-straight shot from the juncture of the canal and Banana River to the barge channel's lock. Set course from the canal's mouth to pass flashing daybeacon #8 to its immediate southerly side and unlighted daybeacon #7 to its immediate northerly quarter. Guard against any slippage to the south between the canal's easterly mouth and #7. A long, uncharted shoal lines the channel in this quarter.

Once abeam of unlighted daybeacon #7, continue on course, pointing to pass unlighted daybeacon #6 to its southerly side, and come abeam of flashing daybeacon #5 to its fairly immediate northerly quarter. At #5, the main Banana River channel makes off to the north while gutsy cruisers can also follow a faint track to the south. Captains headed for the barge canal's inlet should continue on the same course to the east.

After passing unlighted daybeacon #4 to its southerly side, you will see the western doors of the lock dead ahead. Slow to idle speed—the lock's waters are an official slow-speed manatee zone. Give the usual signal, two long, followed by two short blasts on the horn. Moor to the lock bulkhead as directed by the lockmaster and put out plenty of fenders.

Once through the lock, you will follow a straight stretch of canal to the State Road 401 Triple Bridges with 25 feet of closed vertical clearance. These bridges open on demand except during the hours of 5:30 A.M. to 8:00 A.M. and from 3:45 P.M. to 5:00 P.M., weekdays (except holidays), when they don't open at all.

Shortly after you leave the triple bridges behind, the first cove on the southern shore will come abeam. Visiting cruisers can make use of either of the fine marinas here.

Charts 11478 and 11476 correctly identify several more bays flanking the northern side of the canal between the lock and its intersection with the ocean. While all are deep, they are commercially oriented and should only be entered for sightseeing.

As already mentioned, the barge canal inlet is unusually well marked and relatively easy to run. Simply hold to the midline of the buoyed channel and pick a day with fair winds. Under these conditions, you should come through with nothing worse than a little salty spray.

Northern Banana River   Navigation of the north Banana River channel is about as simple a proposition as you are ever likely to encounter. The cut is quite well marked. North of unlighted daybeacon #23, you will need to switch to chart 11484 for coverage of the river's northernmost reaches.

Depths of 5 to 6 feet abut the western side of the channel between unlighted daybeacons #15A and #32. If you do choose to make use of this anchorage, be sure to drop the hook before cruising more than 200 yards from the main channel. Farther to the west, depths deteriorate markedly.

Chart 11484 correctly identifies a second channel running east from flashing daybeacon #29. This cut serves a commercial fuel facility and pleasure boats are advised to keep clear.

North of unlighted daybeacon #36, the NASA Parkway bridge crosses Banana River. Numerous signs warn pleasure craft to discontinue their explorations at this point. The river's waters to the north are strictly off-limits.

Southern Banana River Channel   Remember, navigation of Banana River south of the Canaveral Barge Canal is not really recommended for skippers of deep-draft pleasure craft. The indifferently marked channel is quite tricky. Even when you are in the marked cut, depths can run as little as 4½ to 5 feet. The river's waters are extraordinarily clear in this section. Even when the sounder reads 6 feet, it can be a bit disconcerting to look over the side and see the bottom so clearly.

Sailors should take note of the relatively low, fixed bridges spanning Banana River south of the barge canal intersection. Two have only 36 feet of clearance. Many sailors will find it not only advisable, but also absolutely necessary to approach the southerly marina facilities around Dragon Point by way of the channel cutting directly off the ICW. This passage will be covered later in this chapter.

You should also know that Banana River features a more recent obstruction to navigation. Several years ago, the Florida Department of Transportation affixed new lights to the river's bridges. These lights have been attached in such a way that they hang below the charted bridge clearances. Several fellow cruisers have contacted this writer to warn against this undocumented hazard. Sailors with masted craft should take extra care when passing under the various fixed bridges. By all accounts nighttime passage of Banana River is not recommended.

Between the Bridges   To enter the southern Banana River channel, turn due south just before reaching flashing daybeacon #5 on the barge route. Head straight for the central pass through of the fixed bridge just to the south. This span has a vertical clearance of 36 feet.

After passing through the first span, set a careful compass course to come abeam of and pass unlighted daybeacon #28 to its fairly immediate westerly side. This aid is found north of the second bridge (moving from north to south) across Banana River. It is important to stay west of this daybeacon. To the east, 3- and 4-foot water is immediately encountered. From #28, set course for the second (Highway 520) bridge's pass through. Be on guard against leeway to the east. If depths start to rise, give way to the west.

Once through the Highway 520 span, swing a bit to the west and set course to come abeam of unlighted daybeacon #27 to its easterly side. Some 5-foot depths can be expected on these waters.

From #27 set course to come abeam of and pass unlighted daybeacon #26 to its westerly quarter and unlighted daybeacon #25 to its immediate easterly side. Then point to come abeam of unlighted daybeacon #24 to its immediate westerly quarter. Between #25 and #24, a marked but uncharted track cuts west to Banana River Marine.

South of #24, a series of markers leads south for several more miles. Southbound cruisers should pass red, even-numbered markers to their (the markers') westerly sides and green, odd-numbered aids to their easterly quarter. Expect some 4- to 4½-foot depths in this portion of the channel.

Eventually, those intrepid mariners following the channel south will come between unlighted daybeacons #11 and #12. Past this point all markers cease for a good distance south. This is the most difficult portion of the passage south.

To traverse the markerless section, set a careful compass course from the gap between #11 and #12 to pass through the large patch of deep water to the south, pointing to eventually come abeam of unlighted daybeacon #8 to its immediate westerly side. Just before reaching #8, you should pass unlighted daybeacons #8A and #9 east of your course. Look to the east as you approach #8 and you will spy several runways connected with Patrick Air Force Base.

This channel serves the Patrick Air Force Base area, and pleasure craft should not attempt to cruise east from #8A and #9. Depths deteriorate as you approach #8, and you can expect soundings of as little as 4 to 4½ feet.

A narrow channel extends south from #8 to the third Banana River (Highway 404) bridge. Pass unlighted daybeacons #6B and #6A to their immediate westerly sides. From #6A, point directly for the third bridge's pass through. This fixed span has a vertical clearance of 43 feet.

Between the State Road 3 bridge and the river's southernmost span, markings improve. Several pairs of charted unlighted daybeacons keep you to consistent 6-foot depths. Take your time, watch the markers carefully, and you should finally reach the fourth, southernmost bridge without too much difficulty.

Between unlighted daybeacon #5A and the last span, several small channels lead off to the east. These are used regularly by small craft and serve a series of canals on the eastern banks. Many private homes line these sheltered waterways. As there are no facilities for visiting cruisers in this region, most captains should continue to track their way south.

South of the last (Mathers) swing bridge (7-foot closed vertical clearance), several facilities are available to mariners. These will be covered in the next section of this chapter.

Canaveral Barge Canal to Vero Beach

South of the Highway A1A (City Point) twin bridges and the intersection with the Canaveral Barge Canal, the ICW continues to follow the wide swath of Indian River to Wabasso. A more restricted passage leads south from the Wabasso Bridge to Vero Beach. The channel remains well marked and easy to follow. North of Valkaria, deep water flanks a good portion of the Waterway channel. With judicious use of charts 11485 and 11472, sailors can depart from the marked cut in many places for good cruising without frequent tacks.

Facilities are fairly numerous and of good reputation as far south as the city of Melbourne. Farther south, there are only a few marinas short of Vero Beach. At Vero Beach a large municipal marina and several other facilities welcome cruising craft.

Anchorages are few and far between north of Vero Beach. A few deepwater coves along Indian River's banks can provide some overnight shelter, but even these are not recommended in heavy weather. On the other hand, cruising craft can ride tranquilly on mooring buoys for a modest fee in the Vero Beach anchorage.

The run from Indian River to Vero Beach is decidedly pleasant in fair weather. Along both shorelines natural and developed stretches alternate. Often the undeveloped sections feature tall palm trees and hardwoods. Along some stretches, the river is dotted with small, undeveloped islands verdant with lush tropical foliage. These small dots of land are popular stopovers for weekend outboarders. Very attractive homes overlook the river in many locations and make for a very interesting view from the water. With winds less than 15 knots in the offing, cruisers should find their voyage along Indian River one of the most appealing on the entire Florida ICW.

Cocoa (Standard Mile 897)

The old river town of Cocoa perches on the western shores of Indian River, south of unlighted daybeacon #76, and eagerly waits to greet visiting skippers. The modern community of Cocoa Beach beckons from the eastern shore with teeming streets and bustling thoroughfares.

Captains and crew docking at Whitley Bay Marina on the mainland shores have easy foot access to Cocoa Historic Village. This quaint, downtown district teems with superb restaurants, interesting shops, and more than a little history.

Regular bus service is available from Cocoa to Disney World, and it is only a short taxi ride to Spaceport, USA at the Kennedy Space Center. Inquire at any of the marina offices for details about ground transportation to either attraction.

Though long associated with the high-tech space effort, Cocoa preserves the neighborly traditions of small-town America. The residents have an attitude that is all too absent in the "Gold Coast" to the south, and visiting cruisers can be sure of a warm and courteous welcome. Many mariners visit Cocoa year after year, and it's easy to understand why.

Numbers to know in Cocoa:

Always Available Transportation
  (taxi)—321-453-8294
Yellow Cab—321-636-1234
Budget Car Rental—321-784-0634
Hertz Rent A Car—321-783-7771
Chamber of Commerce—321-459-2200

Cocoa Facilities (Various Lats/Lons—see below)

In regards to marina facilities, things have already changed and will continue to change in Cocoa during the coming months. Where there was once a large repair yard sitting opposite a transient-friendly marina, both of these locations are now "going condo." This changeover has already occurred at Whitley Bay Marina, while Indian Cove Marina will be overlooked by a condo complex by the time this account finds its way into your hands.

Fortunately, all these developments are being undertaken by the same firm, and they have made a solid commitment to the city of Cocoa to offer transient slips at both marinas for the foreseeable future. That is fortunate indeed, as otherwise a visit to this interesting community would be ever so difficult.

Indian Cove Marina currently sits on the easterly tip of the east-bank cove, adjacent to the charted WWBC radio tower, south-southeast of unlighted daybeacon #76 and near 28 21.481 North/080 42.459 West. We

last visited here in April of 2004, and a conversation with the dockmaster revealed that his entire facility was slated for rebuilding and refurbishment as part of the imminent condo development. There is even some question as to whether the current telephone number, (321) 452-8540, will remain in effect following the various upgrades. In keeping with my long-standing policy of not commenting on a marina or repair-yard facility until I can lay my own little peepers on it, I will have nothing else to say about the future version of Indian Cove Marina here.

Let's now turn our attention to the marina on the mainland (western banks). As alluded to above, big changes have already taken place here. For starters this facility is now known as Whitley Bay Marina instead of Whitley Marine (near 28 21.431 North/080 43.507 West). Where once there was a large repair yard, visitors will now quickly spy a condo complex. Not all the news is bad by any means, however.

Under the old regime, the wet slips were wide open to northerly blows and wake from passing vessels. The entire harbor is now breakwater protected by "concrete attenuators."

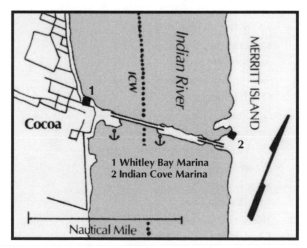

Transients are readily accepted at Whitley Bay, with some 15 slips set aside for visitors. Freshwater connections as well as 30- and 50-amp power hookups (along with one 100-amp service) are to be found at every berth. Shoreside, cruising visitors will find an impressive array of fully climate-controlled, first-class showers and an extensive Laundromat. There's even a sauna open to transients. Waste pump-out is also in the offing, and a ship's store was just getting up and running during our last visit. Contained within this retail facility, the marina has already provided a desk at which captain and crew can connect their laptop to a dial-up connection and check e-mail or surf the web. How's that for *full* service?

Amidst all this good news, we must sadly note the passing of all repair services at this facility. If you need mechanical or below-waterline repairs, better give the nod to Westland Marine in Titusville!

The many shopping and dining choices of the Cocoa Historic Village (see below) are within an easy two-block walk. Here you will discover several topnotch dining attractions.

Whitley Bay Marina (321) 632-5445

Approach depths—6-7 feet
Dockside depths—5½-7 feet
Accepts transients—yes
Transient dockage rate—below average
Fixed wooden piers—yes
Dockside power connections—30 and 50 amps (and one 100-amp service)
Dockside water connections—yes
Waste pump-out—yes
Showers—yes
Laundromat—yes
Ship's store—soon
Restaurant—several nearby

Cocoa Historic Village

Nestled within the confines of downtown Cocoa is one of the real shoreside gems in eastern Florida. The downtown business district traces its history back to the late 1800s. Today, the buildings along the two blocks of Brevard Avenue (and several surrounding streets), adjacent to Highway 520, have been restored and teem with wonderful restaurants and interesting shops. We only have space here to list a few of this writer's favorites, but readers are encouraged to strike out on their own walking tour of discovery.

Those interested in learning more about the history of Cocoa, and Cocoa Village in particular, should contact the volunteers from the Brevard Museum of History and Natural Science, headquartered in beautiful Porcher House (321-639-3500). This elegant homeplace dates to 1916 and makes for a magnificent start to your tour. After you view the old home, the knowledgeable volunteers will lead you on a walking tour through the historic village, explaining fourteen points of interest. This is a great introduction to historic Cocoa, and it is highly recommended by this writer.

Fortunate are those who arrive at Cocoa Historic Village hungry. Not one but two wonderful restaurants guard opposite sides of the street at the northern end of the district (within a very quick step from Whitley Bay Marina). Cafe Margaux (220 Brevard Avenue, 321-639-8343) is tucked in a small piazza on the eastern side of Brevard Avenue. To say that the food here is good is akin to asserting that the sun is slightly bright. Both lunch and dinner, not to mention the Sunday brunch, are fabulous. For your evening meal, consider the Chicken Margaux. This luscious dish consists of chicken breast wrapped in bacon and pan seared in a mushroom-sherry sauce. Want something more in the seafood line? Well, how about the seafood crepes with lobster sauce or the Shrimp and Scallops Margaux (lightly sautéed shrimp and scallops wrapped in bacon and finished with a piccata lemon-butter sauce). We could go on and on, but perhaps you are beginning to get the idea. Cafe Margaux is a good place to have one of those once-a-month dining-out experiences. The prices are commensurate with the quality of food you will receive.

But wait, there's more. Just across the street you will discover the Black Tulip (207 Brevard Avenue, 321-631-1133). Rated as one of the top 100 restaurants in Florida, this dining spot features an award-winning wine list and superb cuisine. The Black Tulip is closed on Sundays.

In the mood for something a little less formal? Well, consider Village Perks at 10 Oleander Street (within a half-block of central Brevard Avenue, 321-638-0038). We found the pastries here to be absolutely yummy.

Another informal dining spot of note is the Paradise Alley Café (234 Brevard Avenue, 321-639-2515). Judging from the crowd of locals

we always see here during the lunch hour, Paradise must be doing something right.

A bit farther to the south on Brevard Avenue, the Village Cappuccino Shop (407 Brevard Avenue, 321-632-5695) will be spied on the western side of the street. Here you can sip on delicious espresso and cappuccino while dining on light sandwiches and other novel fare. We found this establishment absolutely delightful.

Are you in the mood to cook your own? Well, then, spare no pains to look up the Village Gourmet (316 Brevard Avenue, 321-636-5480) on the eastern face of Brevard Avenue. We found an unusually good selection of gourmet foods, wines, and coffees, including a fine assortment of native Floridian concoctions.

Visitors strolling up Brevard Avenue will notice the Cocoa Village Playhouse (300 Brevard Avenue, 321-636-5050). Be sure to check the marquee to see if a production is scheduled during your time in Cocoa. If you are lucky, this local theater company could make for a most memorable evening.

S. F. Travis Company hardware store (300 Delannoy Avenue, 321-636-1441) is found one block east of Brevard Avenue. In addition to a full line of landlubber hardware, they offer an impressive selection of nautically oriented items. Ask the staff at your marina for specific directions.

Not to be repetitive, but the restaurants and shops outlined above are only the tip of the proverbial iceberg. Those who go a-searching in Cocoa Historic Village seldom come away with anything but good memories.

Cocoa Anchorages (Various Lats/Lons— see below)

South of the Cocoa twin high-rise bridges,

Cocoa Historic Village

good anchorage can be found west of the ICW between the causeway and the overhead power lines to the south, near 28 21.267 North/080 43.286 West. Depths of 6 to 8 feet are held well in under the lee of the causeway to the north, and there is good shelter to the north and west. Swinging room is ample for a 45 footer. Fresh southerly blows would obviously make this overnight stop untenable. Don't drop the hook too far to the west, as this shoreline borders on a public launching ramp and a small park. On the other hand, in fair weather you might be able to dinghy ashore to the small ramp docks. Don't try this with a deeper-draft vessel.

Alternately, you can anchor on the correctly charted bubble of deep water, just south of the high-rise bridges, east of the Waterway, near 28 21.313 North/080 42.914 West. While this anchorage is not as snug (at least to us) as the westside haven, reviewed above, it is certainly acceptable with appropriate winds in the offing. Good depths of 6½ feet or better are held on the waters of the eastside anchorage until coming under the lee of the causeway to the north. There is enough room for craft as large as 40 feet. Protection is good from northern and eastern winds, with fair shelter to the west. Winds over 10 knots from the south, southwest, or (to a lesser extent) southeast call for a continued cruise down the Waterway to another haven.

Both these anchorages can suffer from automobile noise and headlights during the night. On weekends, and during morning weekday rush hours, the noise can be a real bother.

Open Anchorage (Standard Mile 901.5) (28 18.799 North/080 41.745 West)

A few skippers occasionally anchor in the charted deep-water patch southeast of flashing daybeacon #83. While 6- to 7-foot depths can be held to within 150 yards of the eastern shoreline, this anchorage is wide open and subject to considerable chop if winds exceed 10 to 15 knots. Cruisers should probably consider dropping the hook here only in light airs.

"The Point" Anchorages (Standard Mile 904.5) Various Lat/Lons—see below

One of the best, though certainly not the most navigationally simple, anchorages between Cocoa and Vero Beach (for boats drawing less than 5 feet) is found on the charted deepwater coves to the north and south of "The Point," southeast of unlighted daybeacon #89. Unfortunately, several charted but unmarked 4-foot shoals make entry into this potential haven a bit tricky. Be sure to read the navigational information on this anchorage in the next section of this chapter before attempting first-time entry.

Assuming you can successfully bypass the 4-foot shallows, minimum depths of 5 to 6 feet extend to within 200 yards of the easterly banks. With winds blowing from the north, you should obviously anchor south of "The Point" (near 28 15.924 North/080 40.283 West), while southerly breezes call for just the opposite strategy, anchoring near 28 16.061 North/080 40.325 West. The easterly shores give good protection when winds are blowing from this quarter, but the anchorage is wide open to westerly blows.

Even with the protection provided by "The Point," this is not a foul-weather hidey-hole. However, given the lack of protected anchorages along Indian River north of Vero Beach, this haven is certainly a consideration in appropriate weather conditions.

The surrounding shores have been developed with a few palatial homes. These "cottages" make a delightful backdrop. With fair breezes, this is one of our favorite overnight stops along the ICW's path through Indian River, though those 4-foot shoals always give us a bit of a scare.

Diamond 99 Marina (Standard Mile 910.5) (28 10.691 North/080 38.966 West)

Cruisers wending their way south on the Indian River-ICW route will discover another facility along the western shore between unlighted daybeacons #98 and #99. A marked entry channel leads to Diamond 99 Marina and a warm welcome for visiting mariners. The harbor is well sheltered and transient dockage is provided at fixed, wooden piers with (mostly) 30-amp power and water connections. Approach depths run some 6½ to 7 feet, while soundings at dockside are 4½ to 5½ feet at low water. Fair showers and a semi-open-air Laundromat are located on the premises, and waste pump-out is now available as well. Gasoline and diesel fuel can be purchased dockside, and full mechanical repairs are offered through an on-site firm known as Carter's Marine Service (321-254-1490). Diamond 99 also features dry storage for smaller power craft. The marina's small ship's store shares its space, providing a classroom for the on-site sailing school (see below). In addition to all these amenities, Diamond 99 features a dockside swimming pool. It's a great place to end a long, hot day of cruising.

Diamond 99 Marina

Captain Katanna's Dockhouse and Bar (4263 Harbor City Boulevard, 321-253-1369) is within walking distance of the dockage basin. We have not had the opportunity to sample the cuisine here, but it is recommended by the Diamond 99 management. A convenience-type variety store is accessible via a half-mile walk. Diamond 99 also features sailcraft rentals and sailing lessons at the only ASA-certified sailing school in the region.

Diamond 99 Marina (321) 254-1490
http://www.diamond99marina.com

Approach depths—6¹/₂-7 feet
Dockside depths—4¹/₂-5¹/₂ feet (minimum)
Accepts transients—yes
Transient dockage rate—average
Fixed wooden piers—yes

**Dockside power connections—mostly
    30 amps**
Dockside water connections—yes
Waste pump-out—yes
Showers—yes
Laundromat—yes
Gasoline—yes
Diesel fuel—yes
Mechanical repairs—yes
Ship's store—yes
Restaurant—nearby

Dragon Point Facilities (Standard Mile 914) (Various Lats/Lons—see below)

As mentioned in the preceding account concerning southern Banana River, this body of water meets its larger sister at the foot of Merritt Island, southeast of unlighted daybeacon #102. Here, within sight of famous Dragon Point, a host of facilities is available

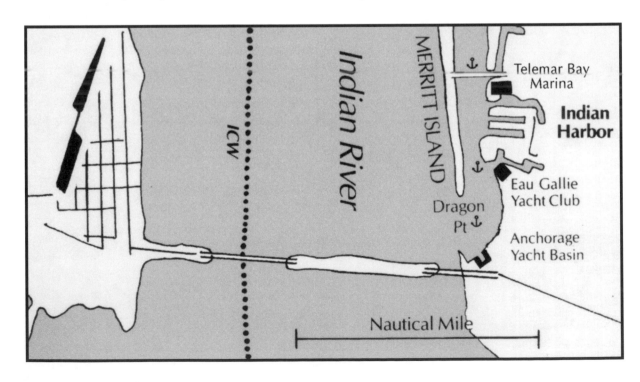

to cruising craft. Entry into these southern-most Banana River waters can be a trifle tricky as you round Dragon Point at unlighted daybeacon #1. Be sure to read the navigational information in the next section before attempting an initial approach to these waters.

As you move from south to north, the first of the Dragon Point facilities will come up on the southeastern banks, soon after you come abeam of unlighted daybeacon #1 (near 28 08.348 North/080 36.071 West). Anchorage Yacht Basin is a well-appointed facility that features plenty of transient dock-age in a well-sheltered, earthen-breakwater-enclosed harbor. Berths are provided at fixed wooden piers with water hookups and 30- and 50-amp power connections. Typical depths in the harbor run 6 to 7 feet, with a few inner slips having some 5 to 5½ feet of water. Fair, non-climate-controlled showers and a Laundromat (with paperback exchange library) are on hand, as are both gasoline and diesel fuel. Mechanical repairs are offered, and the marina has a travelift for haul-outs. Dry-stack storage is available for power craft, and there is even a large dealer in boat sales on the grounds.

Anchorage Yacht Basin maintains a large, well-supplied ship's and variety store. If you need more in the way of foodstuffs, a super-market and drugstores are within a three-block walk. There are any number of fast-food-type restaurants within walking distance as well.

Anchorage Yacht Basin (321) 773-3620

Approach depths—7-8 (minimum)
Dockside depths—5-7 feet
Accepts transients—yes
Transient dockage rate—below average
Fixed wooden piers—yes

Dockside power connections—30
   and 50 amps
Dockside water connections—yes
Showers—yes
Laundromat—yes
Gasoline—yes
Diesel fuel—yes
Below-waterline repairs—yes
Mechanical repairs—yes
Ship's and variety store—yes
Restaurant—several nearby

The fixed, wooden docks of the Eau Gallie Yacht Club lie on the Banana's eastern banks north of Anchorage Yacht Basin, near 28 08.671 North/080 36.127 West. This club accepts members of accredited yacht clubs with appropriate reciprocal privileges for guest dockage at piers featuring full power and water connections. The club's dockmaster is usually on duty from 8:30 A.M. to 4:30 P.M., Tuesday through Sunday.

Transients are free to use the club's bar, dining room, tennis courts, swimming pool, and other facilities. The dining room is open for lunch Tuesday through Friday, and dinner is served Tuesday through Saturday. There is also a Sunday brunch. The entire club is closed on Mondays. Showers are available in a separate "cruiser's building," which is open 24 hours a day. Waste pump-out is in the off-ing for members and accredited guests only.

Eau Gallie Yacht Club (321) 773-2600
http://www.egyachtclub.com

Approach depths—7-8 feet (minimum)
Dockside depths—5-6 feet
Accepts transients—members of other
   yacht clubs with appropriate
   reciprocal arrangements
Fixed wooden piers—yes
Dockside power connections—30
   and 50 amps
Dockside water connections—yes
Waste pump-out—members and accredited

guests only
Showers—yes
Restaurant—on site

The northernmost of the Dragon Point facilities guards the easterly banks, just south of the charted, 7-foot, swing bridge, near 28 08.977 North/080 36.208 West. Telemar Bay Marina is a good stop for any cruising craft, but we did note an absence of the warm welcome that visiting mariners used to receive here when this facility was under its previous ownership.

Most dockage at Telemar Bay is secured in a well-protected, tideless basin with depths of 6 to 8 feet. A few piers front directly onto Banana River, north of the protected harbor's entrance. Berths at fixed wooden piers provide full power and water hookups. Modern, air-conditioned showers and a full Laundromat are complemented by waste pump-out service. Gasoline and diesel are available at the fuel pier, which conveniently fronts directly onto Banana River.

Anchorage Yacht Basin, Dragon Point

Eau Gallie Yacht Club

Full mechanical repairs (gasoline and diesel power plants) are complemented by haul-outs with a 40-ton travelift and dry-stack storage. There is even a nice cruiser's lounge with a paperback exchange library.

A convenience store is located within a three-block walk of the dockage basin and a hike of a half-mile or so will lead you to several supermarkets, smaller grocery stores, and drugstores.

When mealtime comes around, you have several choices. If you're up for some yummy sandwiches, consider Double's Hoagies (1897 S Patrick Drive, 321-773-5341). Those up for a longer (½ mile) hike can find their way to a Chinese restaurant that the marina staff has recommended to this writer. Ask any of the dockmasters for directions.

Telemar Bay Marina (321) 773-2468

Approach depths—6 feet (minimum)
Dockside depths—6-8 feet
Accepts transients—yes
Transient dockage rate—average

Fixed wooden piers—yes
Dockside power connections—30
    and 50 amps
Dockside water connections—yes
Showers—yes
Laundromat—yes
Waste pump-out—yes
Gasoline—yes
Diesel fuel—yes
Below-waterline repairs—yes
Mechanical repairs—yes
Restaurant—several nearby

Banana River Anchorages (Various Lats/Lons—see below)

Many Waterway veterans regularly anchor on Banana River between Anchorage Yacht Basin and the Mathers Bridge at Dragon Point, near 28 08.602 North/080 36.164 West. While good depths ranging from 8 to as much as 18 feet can be expected here, these waters do support considerable small-craft traffic. The wake of passing vessels, particularly on the weekends, can be a little annoying. Otherwise, protection is good in all winds save a strong northerly blow.

Banana River anchorage

Equally sheltered is the patch of deep water just north of the bridge, near 28 09.067 North/080 36.417 West. Here you can anchor in some 10 feet of water and be a little more out of the way. Be sure to set the hook well away from the direct approach to the bridge's central pass through.

Local regulations now limit a stay in the Dragon Point-southern Banana River anchorage to 48 hours. This stricture is being challenged, and the results are uncertain.

The Demise of the Dragon at Dragon Point

Ever since this writer undertook the original edition of this guidebook, he has always been more than fascinated by an almost life-size stone replica of a dragon perched prominently atop appropriately named Dragon Point. It seems that in 1971, an extraordinary woman, Aynn Christal, lived in the house just above the point. One day she decided her children needed something to play on in the backyard. Never one to mess about doing anything in a small way, Aynn hired a sculptor from Tampa to begin a 200-foot statue of a dragon.

Sadly, the great dragon fell to the elements in late 2003, and the broken-up remnants of this extraordinary structure were carted off. Many Waterway veterans, including this writer will look in vain for many years to come for the fire-eating dragon at Dragon Point, with a sigh for what once was and what will be no more.

Eau Gallie Mainland Facilities (Standard Mile 915) (Various Lats/Lons—see below)

Back on Indian River, and the ICW, the next set of facilities appears along the western banks, south of the fixed, 65-foot Eau Gallie Bridge (north and west of flashing daybeacon #2). A marked and charted channel leads into a sheltered basin near the city of Melbourne (formerly Eau Gallie).

After traversing the marked entrance cut (minimum depths, 7 feet), you will first come upon the Eau Gallie Yacht Basin and Boat Works near 28 07.556 North/080 37.496 West. This is one of the oldest marinas in Florida, dating back to 1860. The present owner has a deed signed by no less than Abraham Lincoln.

After going through some very hard years, this facility has been completely rebuilt and modernized. New docks and a new seawall are in the offing, and this writer has been told that "300 loads of junk" were hauled off. That must have been some modernization effort.

The marina portion of this operation is known as the Eau Gallie Yacht Basin. Chuck, the ultrafriendly and superhelpful owner, has informed me that most of his wet slips are now rented out on a long-term basis, but space can occasionally be found for overnight transients. Advance reservations are mandatory, as there is not always a dockmaster present. Berths are discovered at fixed wooden piers with some 6 feet of water alongside. Fresh-water connections and 30- and 50-amp power hookups are featured, and each slip has a waste pump-out connection. Shoreside, visiting cruisers will discovered non-climate-controlled showers, a Laundromat, and a dial-up Internet connection jack.

When it comes time to slake a healthy appetite, it's a very pleasant three-block stroll through the local historic district to Conchy Joe's restaurant (see our review below). Trust me, you won't be sorry!

Full-service repairs are available at this facility, courtesy of Eau Gallie Boat Works

(321-254-1766). Mechanical servicing for (mostly) diesel engines and haul-outs by both a 35-ton travelift and a 75-ton marine railway are featured. Repairs to marine electrical, refrigeration, and air-conditioning systems are also available. In short, if it needs fixing, chances are these folks can help you. Eau Gallie Boat Works also maintains a ship's and parts store on the premises.

Eau Gallie Yacht Basin and Boat Works
    (321) 242-6577

Approach depth—7 feet (minimum)
Dockside depth—6 feet
Accepts transients—limited
    (advance reservations mandatory)
Transient dockage rate—below average
Fixed wooden piers—yes
Dockside power connections—30
    and 50 amps
Dockside water connections—yes
Waste pump-out—yes
Showers—yes
Laundromat—yes
Mechanical repairs—yes
Below-waterline repairs—yes
Ship's store—yes
Restaurant—one nearby

Waterline Marina overlooks the western shores of the same Eau Gallie basin, just south-southeast of the charted 12-foot fixed bridge, near 28 07.342 North/080 37.789 West. This friendly establishment is associated with a large condo project that is quite obvious from the water. Visiting cruisers are accommodated for overnight or temporary dockage. The fixed, wooden piers are in good shape and feature full power and water connections. Dockside depths at most slips run 5 to 7½ feet at low water, but a few inner berths have soundings as slim as 4½ feet.

The entire basin is protected from virtually all winds short of a full gale. This would be a good spot to ride out really heavy weather before tackling the somewhat open Waterway passage on Indian River.

The adjacent single shower is rather cramped, and the Laundromat could only be described as petite. The marina also maintains a portable waste pump-out service. The on-site swimming pool and Jacuzzi are open to visiting cruisers, and a supermarket is accessible by way of a three-block walk.

In addition to a Burger King, Conchy Joe's seafood restaurant (1477 Pineapple Avenue, 321-253-3131) is well worth the while of those who are up to a bit of a walk. The restaurant faces Indian River, immediately north of the Palm Shores Pineda Causeway Bridge, on the mainland shores. Conchy Joe's is a wonderful dining establishment, serving superb conch fritters and lush seafood dishes. The restaurant is built on the site of an old hotel, and a portion of the front hall still bears the original floor from this hostelry. During fair weather, outdoor diners can watch the waters of Indian River and the ICW as they flow tranquilly by. Trust us on this one—don't miss Conchy Joe's if your travels take you anywhere near Melbourne.

Waterline Marina (321) 254-0452

Approach depths—7 feet (minimum)
Dockside depths—5-7½ feet (minimum)
    4½ feet (innermost slips)
Accepts transients—yes
Transient dockage rate—below average
Fixed wooden piers—yes
Dockside power connections—30
    and 50 amps
Dockside water connections—yes
Shower—yes

Waterline Marina, Melbourne

Laundromat—yes
Waste pump-out—yes
Restaurant—several nearby

Numbers to know in Melbourne:
Budget Car Rental—321-725-7737
Avis Rent A Car—321-723-7755
Hertz Rent A Car—321-783-7771
West Marine—321-242-9600
Chamber of Commerce—321-724-5400

Intracoastal Marina of Melbourne (Standard Mile 916.5) (28 05.956 North/080 36.665 West)

Between unlighted daybeacon #3 and flashing daybeacon #5, a marked and charted 7- to 8-foot entrance channel leads west to the enclosed harbor of Intracoastal Marina of Melbourne. The dockage basin is enclosed by a wooden breakwater that affords good shelter in all but the roughest weather. Transient and resident vessels are offered dockage space at fixed, wooden piers with water connections and 30- and 50-amp power hookups. Depths at mean low-water soundings run 6 to 6½ feet.

The on-site showers are air conditioned and in reasonably good condition. Meanwhile, the marina's Laundromat is of the semi-open-air variety. Gasoline, diesel fuel, and waste pump-out services are available at the fuel dock.

Intracoastal Marina offers full repair services, including mechanical work on both gasoline and diesel engines. The 35-ton travelift will be spotted as you enter the harbor. The marina even has a small but well-supplied ship's store adjacent to the dockmaster's office.

The large, on-site dining spot has been reopened as Coral Bay Restaurant (321-733-0431) since the last edition of this guide appeared. We have not dined here yet, but hope to rectify that oversight in the near future.

Additionally, there is a Denny's restaurant within a two-block walk. Those in need of a supermarket will probably require a taxi ride (see above).

Intracoastal Marina of Melbourne
(321) 725-0090

Approach depths—7-8 feet

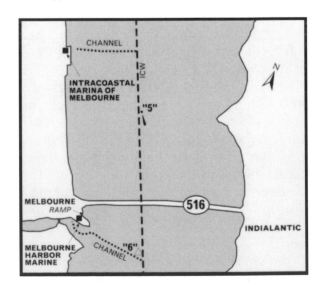

Intracoastal Marina of Melbourne, Indian River

Dockside depths—6-6½ feet
Accepts transients—yes
Transient dockage rate—above average
Fixed wooden piers—yes
Dockside power connections—30
   and 50 amps
Dockside water connections—yes
Showers—yes
Laundromat—yes
Waste pump-out—yes
Gasoline—yes
Diesel fuel—yes
Below-waterline repairs—yes
Mechanical repairs—yes
Ship's store—yes
Restaurant—on site and one nearby

Melbourne Harbor Marine (Standard Mile 919) (28 04.632 North/080 36.005 West)

Cruisers journeying south on the Indian River-ICW route will cross under the Melbourne 65-foot, fixed bridge, south-southeast of flashing daybeacon #5. After leaving this span in your wake, you will catch sight of a westward-running channel as you come abeam of unlighted daybeacon #6.

This cut leads to Melbourne Harbor, a sheltered, enclosed dockage basin with a first-class marina and excellent dining. Most soundings in the entrance channel run 6½ to 7 feet, but there is currently one 5½-foot lump between unlighted daybeacons #6 and #8. As

Melbourne Harbor Marine

you make good your entry into the harbor, the docks will come up to starboard, north-north-west of flashing daybeacon #7, just before the stream turns back to the west-southwest.

Transients are willingly accommodated at modern, fixed, concrete piers featuring almost every conceivable power, water, telephone, and television connection. Dockside depths range from 6 to 8 feet, with most slips being in the deeper range. The showers and Laundromat are in reasonably good shape, and the marina offers waste pump-out service. Mechanical repairs can be arranged through independent contractors. Gasoline and diesel fuel are readily available, and a nice ship's store and nautical gift shop is maintained by the marina dockmasters.

Melbourne Harbor features what may just be the most redoubtable member of the prestigious Chart House restaurant chain (2250 S Front Street, 321-729-6558). It will be prominent on the starboard shore as you round the point at flashing daybeacon #7 and enter the harbor. We have always found the food here to be absolutely succulent. At all risks, don't miss the Caesar salad bar and the dessert selection. Yuuummm! Chart House is open evenings only, and reservations are recommended, particularly during weekends.

For more modest appetites and budgets, Ichabod's (321-952-9532) is located adjacent to the dockmaster's office. This friendly, very popular dining spot is open for lunch and dinner and serves simply wonderful sandwiches that are not to be missed. Outside dining is available in fair weather.

A supermarket is found within a four-block walk of Melbourne Harbor. If you want to take a break from the live-aboard routine, a convenient hotel overlooks the northwestern corner of the harbor. Bus service is available to Disney World and the Kennedy Space Center. The friendly dockmasters can help with the schedules, or can arrange for a rental car.

All in all, Melbourne Harbor has much to offer visiting cruisers. We always make it a point to stop here whenever possible.

Melbourne Harbor Marine (321) 725-9054
http://www.melbourneharbor.com

Approach depths—5½-7 feet
Dockside depths—6-8 feet
Accepts transients—yes
Transient dockage rate—average
Fixed concrete piers—yes
Dockside power connections—30
   and 50 amps
Dockside water connections—yes
Showers—yes
Laundromat—yes
Waste pump-out—yes
Gasoline—yes
Diesel fuel—yes
Mechanical repairs—yes
   (independent contractors)
Ship's store—yes
Restaurant—two on site

Palm Bay Marinas

Two small marinas catering to shallow-draft power craft are located on Turkey Creek, southwest of unlighted daybeacon #13. Entrance depths run as thin as 3 feet and you must be able to clear a 10-foot fixed bridge. Most cruising-size craft will wisely choose to bypass these waters and their facilities.

Island Anchorages (Standard Mile 925.5) (Various Lats/Lons—see below)

South of unlighted daybeacon #18, a series of six, fairly large spoil islands flanks the Waterway to the west. To this writer, these small bodies of dry ground offer one of the most primitive and desirable anchorage opportunities between Melbourne and Vero Beach. Be warned, though; this is not the place to ride out really heavy weather.

These anchorages are not suggested for craft larger than 45 feet, or those drawing more than 5½ feet. Otherwise, if the weather cooperates and you cherish the feeling of spending an evening on the water far from any vestige of civilization, give these waters the nod.

Please read the navigational detail on this entire section below, before attempting first-time entry into this series of anchorages. Some uncharted shoals are present, particularly between the second and third island.

All the islets have spawned fairly dense vegetation and all are completely in their natural state. Island #4 (moving north to south) supports the tallest trees and a vast collection of bird life.

While small, local power craft zip in and out between all the islands, cruising-size craft should leave the ICW north of unlighted daybeacon #20 and cruise between the first and second islands (moving north to south). Probably the best spot to drop the hook is found some 50 to 75 yards off the western shores of the second island (due west of unlighted daybeacon #22, near 27 59.326 North/080 32.663 West). From this side, a wide sand beach runs off the island's shores. Depths of at least 7 feet are held from the Waterway to this haven. Protection is good from the east, but wide open in all other directions. With northerly winds, you can also anchor south of the second island in 6 to 7 feet of water near 27 59.286 North/080 32.592 West. A long sandspit running off island #2's southwesterly corner demands the greatest respect.

You can also drop the hook west (near 27 58.952 North/080 32.600 West) or south (near 27 58.885 North/080 32.512 West) of the third island with similar depths, again keeping 50 to 75 yards off the shoreline. At one time, this island served as a base to reintroduce bottle-nosed dolphins into the wild. You may still spot a breakwater running off the western shore enclosing a pool of water just off the banks. This structure is obviously used in the dolphin training process. There are no buildings on the land, but we once observed several tents pitched ashore. Because of the important, delicate work in progress here, we do not suggest going ashore.

Not to be repetitive, but you may also choose to spend the evening swinging on the hook behind the fourth island (near 27 58.586 North/080 32.527 West), though the navigation here is far more exacting. Frankly, this is our least favorite stop. The island's abundant bird life can get quite noisy early in the morning and the nearby shoals are a bit disconcerting.

Sebastian River Marina & Boat Yard (Standard Mile 934) (27 52.395 North/080 29.809 West)

After passing through a long stretch of Indian River lacking shoreside facilities, passing cruisers will sight the marked channel leading to Sebastian River Marina & Boat Yard west of the Waterway, just south of unlighted daybeacon #55. This facility may well be no longer appropriate for many cruising-size vessels. Entrance depths and soundings in the enclosed harbor have shoaled to 4 feet, or even slightly less at low water. Most of the available dockage is occupied by charter power craft. The long east-west-running (fixed wooden) dock, paralleling the entrance channel, is set aside for transients, but it is wide open to wind, wave, and current. It also suffers from shallow-water problems.

The marina does accept transients on a space-available basis. Most slips have 30-amp power connections and water hookups. Fair showers are available in a building beside the parking lot. Gasoline and diesel fuel can be purchased. Sebastian River maintains a travelift with a 40-ton capacity.

A large restaurant and patio bar guards the northwestern corner of the basin. We found the seafood here to be only fair.

Sebastian River Marina & Boat Yard
   (772) 664-3029

Approach depths—4 feet (minimum)
Dockside depths—3-4 feet (minimum)
Accepts transients—yes (when space
   is available)
Transient dockage rates—below average
Fixed wooden piers—yes
Dockside power connections—mostly 30 amp
Dockside water connections—yes
Showers—yes
Gasoline—yes
Diesel fuel—yes
Below-waterline repairs—yes
Restaurant—on site

Sebastian Inlet Marina (Standard Mile 938) (27 49.493 North/080 28.308 West)

A charted channel strikes west from

Sebastian Inlet Marina (Capt. Hiram's Sebastian Inlet Marina)

unlighted daybeacon #66 to Sebastian Inlet Marina (also known as Capt. Hiram's Sebastian Inlet Marina). This smaller facility offers limited transient dockage at fixed, wooden piers with the usual power and water connections (plus cable-television hookups). The marina has fueling services and offers some repairs for gasoline engines only. The harbor is enclosed to the north and south by a wooden breakwater, but it is wide open to easterly blows. Most of Sebastian Inlet's slips are appropriate for boats 40 feet and under. Depths in the entrance channel run around 5 feet with 4½- to 5-foot soundings dockside. These readings could be a problem for long-legged vessels. The marina's showers and a Laundromat are spotlessly clean, but not climate controlled. Some dry-stack storage is also available for smaller power craft.

A small variety store plus a tiny motel flank the dockage basin to the west. The guest rooms overlook Indian River and the ICW. They are really quite nice. Space is at a bit of a premium, so it might be best to call ahead of time for reservations should you

want to spend a night or two off the water.

The on-site Captain Hiram's Restaurant & Bar is justifiably popular. Featuring three bars and excellent seafood (as well as good sandwiches for lunch), this establishment offers lucky diners tables overlooking the water. Live evening entertainment is often featured on weekends.

If you can stand the somewhat thin depths, Sebastian Inlet Marina is an interesting stop, with good dining and more than a little "partying" flavor.

Sebastian Inlet Marina (772) 589-4345
http://www.hirams.com

Approach depths—5 feet
Dockside depths—4½-5 feet
Accepts transients—limited
Transient dockage rate—below average
Fixed wooden piers—yes
Dockside power connections—30
and 50 amps
Dockside water connections—yes
Showers—yes
Laundromat—yes
Gasoline—yes

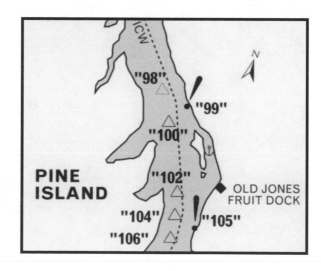

Diesel fuel—yes
Mechanical repairs—limited (gasoline only)
Variety store—small
Restaurant—on site

Pelican Island (Standard Mile 941)

South of Sebastian Inlet, Indian River is delightfully undeveloped. Many species of birds are often observed nesting on the nearby islands. Pelican Island, east-northeast of flashing daybeacon #71, is the nation's first federally sponsored wildlife refuge. Dating from the years of Theodore Roosevelt, this haven continues to support birds of many species.

Jones Dock (Standard Mile 945)

South of flashing daybeacon #79, the ICW enters a more sheltered run through Indian River. Islands to the west shelter the Waterway from this quarter while the beach barrier islands to the east are broad and lush with vegetation.

Jones Fruit Dock

South of Wabasso Bridge, passing cruisers will sight a single, decrepit pier lining the eastern side of the channel near unlighted daybeacon #102. This is the home of Jones Fruit Dock, where once passing cruisers could tie up for the night and buy fresh citrus products grown in the nearby grove.

We had heard that Jones Dock had reopened, and made it a special point to revisit this facility. We did find fresh fruit for sale once again at a tiny roadside stand just across from the dock. However, it was with much consternation that this writer walked the piers. I felt sure that the semi-rotten boards were going to give way at any moment and send me plunging into the waters below. In spite of Jones Fruit Dock's funky, almost Bohemian, and surely backwater atmosphere, we, in all good conscience, cannot recommend a stop here until the piers are extensively repaired.

Secluded Anchorage (Standard Mile 945) (27 44.273 North/080 23.634 West)

Smaller cruising vessels drawing less than 5 feet can anchor in the confines of the protected creek north of the old Jones Dock. By sticking to the midwidth, you will find depths of 5 to 7 feet for some distance to the north-northwest, behind the small island to port. Swinging room should be adequate for craft up to 32 feet, and the creek offers enough shelter to ride out pretty much any storm short of a hurricane. After you pass a single boathouse to starboard, the rest of the creek's shoreline is mostly undeveloped. Several local craft are tied off to mooring buoys along the northerly portion of this stream. A series of private docks lines the eastern banks, just a bit farther to the north-northwest. We suggest anchoring south of the moored craft and entering this haven strictly by way of its southerly entrance, hard by the old fruit dock.

Grand Harbor Marina (Standard Mile 948.5) (27 41.519 North/080 23.692 West)

The entrance channel providing access to Grand Harbor Marina lies along the ICW's westerly banks, just south of unlighted daybeacon #122. This facility's large dockage basin encompasses 144 slips, and it is overlooked by a massive collection of low-rise condominiums.

The harbor is virtually enclosed with a concrete seawall. It would take a severe storm indeed to radically trouble boats docked here. Minimum entrance depths in the well-outlined channel running west from the ICW are around 6 feet, with 8 feet of water in the harbor.

Transients are accepted at the marina's modern, fixed, wooden piers. Full power and water connections are available, as is waste pump-out service. Gasoline and diesel fuel can be purchased at a dock sitting astride the harbor's north-to-south midline. Some mechanical repairs can be arranged through local, independent contractors. A small ship's and variety store sits just behind the fuel pier.

Visiting cruisers (who are not residents of Indian River County) are welcome to make use of the on-site club dining room, swimming pool, and tennis courts. The club golf course is now available to cruising visitors year round.

Grand Harbor Marina (772) 770-4470
http://www.grandharbor.com

Approach depths—6 feet (minimum)
Dockside depths—8 feet

Accepts transients—yes

Transient dockage rate—below average

Fixed wooden piers—yes

Dockside power connections—30
   and 50 amps

Dockside water connections—yes

Waste pump-out—yes

Gasoline—yes

Diesel fuel—yes

Mechanical repairs—limited (independent contractors)

Ship's and variety store—yes

Restaurant—on site

Vero Beach (Associated Facilities and Mooring Field) (Standard Mile 952) (Various Lats/Lons—see below)

South of flashing daybeacon #139, mariners have access to the marine facilities and city mooring field associated with the resort community of Vero Beach.

Numbers to know in Vero Beach:
Yellow Cab—772-589-1234
Klub Car Shuttle—772-567-8539
Community Coach—772-569-0903
Budget Car Rental—772-567-8788
Avis Rent A Car—772-567-3327
Hertz Rent A Car—772-562-4304
Chamber of Commerce—772-567-3491

Vero Beach's facilities line the eastern banks of the charted and well-marked channel that breaks off from the ICW to the east, immediately north of the 66-foot high-rise bridge. Minimum 7½-foot depths are held on this cut, all the way north to the mooring field above the municipal marina. There are now far more unlighted daybeacons outlining this passage than what appears on the current edition of chart 11472. All the many markers make successful navigation (at least during daylight) a fairly simple task. However, be *sure* to read the navigational account of this channel below if you have not run this cut since the bridge was replaced some years ago.

After rounding the bend and passing between unlighted daybeacons #5 and #6, the first facility, Indian River Marina, operated by Hal Jones and Company (772-234-6680), comes up to the east near 27 39.378 North/080 22.184 West. Since the last edition of this guide, new management has taken over here, and virtually all the wet-slip space is now taken up by brokerage boats. I have been told that very occasionally, an overnighter can be accommodated, but clearly this is a rare occurrence.

Mechanical repair work for both gasoline and diesel engines are available through the on-site repair firm of Witicar Boat Works North (772-231-6200). Haul-outs, however, are not offered.

Next up are the docks and impressive clubhouse of Vero Beach Yacht Club (near 27 39.451 North/080 22.200 West). This friendly organization accepts members of other yacht clubs with appropriate reciprocal privileges for guest dockage with advance reservations. Berths are provided at fixed wooden piers with water connections and 30-amp power hookups. Good depths of 6 feet or better are discovered alongside. The dining room is open in the evenings from Tuesday through Saturday (reservations are requested), and lunch is served Wednesday and Friday. Of course, you could also walk to Riverside Cafe or take a taxi over to the beach (see below).

Vero Beach Yacht Club (772) 231-2211
http://www.verobeachyachtclub.com

Approach depths—7 feet

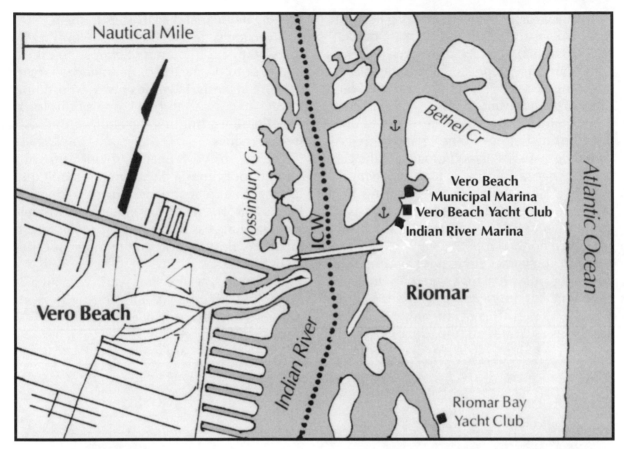

Dockside depths—6+ feet

**Accepts transients—members of other
    yacht clubs with appropriate
    reciprocal arrangements**

Fixed wooden piers—yes

Dockside power connections—30 amps

Dockside water connections—yes

Restaurant—on site and others nearby

Just north of Vero Beach Yacht Club, the wharves of Vero Beach Municipal Marina will come abeam to the east, near 27 39.497 North/080 22.210 West. Seldom have we found a more friendly and helpful municipal facility. For those who prefer dockage to mooring (see below), transient slips are provided at both fixed wooden and concrete-decked piers. The city dockmaster has informed this writer that more than 2,500 visitors a year are accommodated at the docks and moorings. That's a pretty good track record.

Depths at most slips are 6½ feet or better. Full power and water hookups, extranice, climate-controlled showers, a full Laundromat, and multiple waste pump-out units are all readily available. Gasoline and (premium) diesel fuel can be purchased at a convenient fuel dock. There is even a topnotch, air-conditioned cruisers' lounge with color television, a huge collection of magazines, and paperback exchange library.

Vero Beach Municipal Marina manages and

maintains a large, adjacent mooring field, just west and north of the city docks, near 27 39.547 North/080 22.251 West. While there is a nightly charge to pick up a mooring buoy, a free dinghy dock is available on the south shore of the eastward-running canal, just north of the marina docks, for all cruisers tied up in the mooring field. All other marina services, including showers, Laundromat, and the captains' lounge, are available to those paying the mooring fee. Depths in the mooring field range from a low of 7 feet to as much as 12 feet. Protection is good from all winds save gale-force northerlies.

Surprisingly, mechanical repairs are available at the municipal marina through the independent, on-site firm of Helseth Marine (772-567-9552). This dealer also maintains a small ship's store on the docks. Ask the friendly municipal dockmasters for help.

Riverside Cafe (see below) is within walking distance, or you might choose to take a taxi over to the beach or mainland. A small grocery store is 1½ miles away. You could always call a cab to reach one of the local supermarkets, but there is another interesting alternative.

The city of Vero Beach provides free bus service four times a day from the municipal marina to the mainland business district. How's that for a deal? Patrons of this novel service have access to several supermarkets, a Kmart, Wal-Mart, and any number of other retail businesses.

Have you got the idea yet? Vero Beach Municipal Marina is an unusually well appointed facility, particularly for a city-owned property. We suggest that you give it a try.

Vero Beach Municipal Marina

Vero Beach Municipal Marina (772) 231-2819
   http://www.coveb.org/marina/marina.htm

Approach depths—7-8 feet
Dockside depths—6½-8 feet
Accepts transients—yes
Transient dockage fee—below average
Fixed wooden piers—yes
Fixed concrete piers—yes
Dockside power connections—30
   and 50 amps
Dockside water connections—yes
Showers—yes
Laundromat—yes
Waste pump-out—yes
Gasoline—yes
Diesel fuel—yes
Mechanical repairs—yes
Ship's store—yes (small)
Restaurant—several nearby

The barrier-island (east) side of Vero Beach is world famous for its distinctive shops and restaurants. This business strip is located due east of the marina facilities via Highway 60. It is a bit far for walking, but only a quick taxi ride away. If you should arrive during the dinner hour, and your budget is still in good shape, consider an evening repast at the Ocean Grill (1050 Sexton Plaza, 772-231-5409). Highway 60 almost dead-ends at its doorstep. Ask any local for more specific directions. This dining spot overlooks the beach, and the food (particularly the salmon) is out of this world.

The other clothing, gift, and specialty shops on the strip are really something to see. Rivaling the Worth Avenue businesses in Palm Beach, the Vero Beach stores feature some of the newest and most exciting merchandise to be found anywhere.

Should you be seeking a night or two off the boat, a host of motels and hotels is located on the strip. As you might imagine, none are what you would call inexpensive during the winter tourist season.

Immediately south of the high-rise bridge, cruisers whose craft draw less than 4 feet can track their way east through 5- to 6-foot depths to the fixed, wooden docks of Riverside Cafe and Wharf (772-234-5550). This facility used to be located north of the old bascule span, and veteran captains may well be surprised to find it south of the new structure. What was once a small marina is now a large restaurant and bar, with extensive dockside dining. The food at Riverside is quite good. The sandwiches, particularly for lunch, are excellent, and for dinner give the pan-seared salmon with red-onion marmalade a try.

Riverside Cafe actually has two piers. The southern dock is strictly for use by resident craft, while dining patrons may tie to the northern pier. Depths alongside run only 3½ to 4 feet at low water. We do not suggest this dock for boats larger than 38 feet, no matter what their draft.

Riverside Cafe, Vero Beach

CANAVERAL BARGE CANAL TO VERO BEACH NAVIGATION

The ICW channel south of the Canaveral Barge Canal to Vero Beach remains well marked and easily navigated for the most part. Several shoals flanking the channel do call for a bit more caution. Successful entry into some of the anchorages along the way, particularly those around Indian River's small islands, can also be more demanding.

On the Waterway   Immediately south of the barge canal intersection, the Waterway passes under the City Point twin fixed bridges with a vertical clearance of 65 feet, Be sure to pass west of unlighted daybeacon #13, just north of the span. Shallow water lies east of this marker.

Between unlighted daybeacons #71 and #72, a long shoal is building into the Waterway's western flank. Guard against leeway to the west between the two markers. Come abeam of and pass #72 well to its easterly side.

Similarly, be sure to avoid the shallows east and southeast of flashing daybeacon #73. Don't allow leeway to ease you to the east between #73 and unlighted daybeacon #76, the next southerly aid to navigation.

South of #76, the Waterway begins its approach to the Cocoa twin high-rise bridges. Study chart 11485 for a moment and notice the tongue of shallows impinging on the Waterway's western flank between #76 and the bridges. Favor the easterly side of the channel a bit when approaching the twin spans to avoid this potential hazard.

Twin high-rise fixed bridges (with vertical clearance of 65 feet) span Indian River at Cocoa. South of these structures, a portion of the old, low-level bridge has been left to the east and west of the channel for the use of local fishermen.

Cocoa   North of the Cocoa bridges, marked channels lead east and west to the various marinas. The east-side cut is currently outlined by mostly unadorned pilings, but this may change for the better as the above-described condo project at Indian Cove Marina goes forward. A few of these piles do sport daymarks. During daylight, it's relatively simple to cruise between the various piles into the cove to the east.

The western channel is well outlined and reasonably easy to run. It eventually leads to Whitley Bay Marina's new, breakwater-protected dockage basin.

Cocoa Anchorages   South of the bridges, cut to the west, keeping some 50 yards off the northside causeway. You will catch sight of a portion of the old bridge, now used as a fishing pier, north of your course. We suggest that you anchor shortly after coming under the lee of the land to the north. A public launch ramp and park lie farther to the west, and this area will naturally support considerable small-craft traffic, particularly on weekends.

To access the eastside haven, south of the high-rise bridges, leave the ICW some 75 yards south of the bridges. Turn to the east-northeast and carefully track your way under the lee of the causeway to the north. Drop anchor as soon as this point of land comes abeam. Farther to the east, depths decline.

On the ICW   South of the twin Cocoa high-rise fixed bridges, the ICW passes under a power line with 88 feet of vertical clearance.

It is a long run south from the high-rise span to the next southerly aid to navigation, flashing daybeacon #77. Use your binoculars to help pick out #77. Guard against any slippage to the east along this run. A broad band of shallows is building out from the eastern banks.

Shoal water encroaches on the ICW east of the channel between flashing daybeacons #77 and #83. Watch the track over your stern, as well as your course ahead, to be sure contrary winds or currents aren't easing you to the east. Be sure to pass all intervening green markers to their westerly quarters. At #83, the first opportunity for anchorage south of Cocoa comes abeam.

Open Anchorage   Enter the open anchorage south of Cocoa by cruising east from a position some 50 yards south of flashing daybeacon #83. Feel your way in toward the easterly banks, using the sounder. Be sure to set the hook before approaching to within 100 yards of the shore.

"The Point" Anchorage   Successful entrance into the two deep coves north and south of "The Point" (southeast of unlighted daybeacon #89) is complicated by the presence of the correctly charted 4-foot shoals. Of course, if you can stand 4-foot depths then it's easy. Otherwise, you should carefully consider the risks before making use of this potential haven.

Should you decide to make the attempt, we suggest departing the Waterway north of unlighted daybeacon #89. Set a course to the east-northeast toward the eastern banks. Once you are within 200 yards of the shoreline, cut south-southeast into the deeper waters north of "The Point."

To reach the anchorage south of "The Point," stay at least 200 yards off this point of land as you cruise around it to the south-southeast. Continue cruising south-southeast for another 100 yards or so, and then turn carefully east for a short distance. Good depths seem to hold to within 150 yards of the easterly banks south of "The Point." Be sure to set your hook so as to swing well away from the shallows closer to shore. This southerly haven is bounded to the south by a large dock supporting a house built out over the water.

On the Waterway   Favor the eastern side of the Waterway between flashing daybeacon #90 and unlighted daybeacon #91. Shallows and "rocks" have been reported to the west of the ICW track between these two beacons.

Look to the northeast as you pass flashing daybeacon #95 and you should catch sight of a very impressive house overlooking Indian River, north of Mangrove Point. Cruisers will find many such homes well worthy of a few moments' notice on this stretch.

South of #95, the Waterway passes under the Palm Shores Pineda Causeway Bridge, a 65-foot high-rise twin span.

Between unlighted daybeacons #98 and #99, the marked channel to Diamond 99 Marina strikes out from the westerly banks. Use your binoculars to help identify the channel from the Waterway. A sign advertising the marina sits at the northeastern head of the channel.

After leaving unlighted daybeacon #102 behind, there is a long markerless stretch to the high-rise Eau Gallie Bridge. Fortunately, deep water stretches out along a broad band between #102 and the bridge. Some .2 nautical miles north of this span, wise captains will break off to the east-northeast and visit the many attractions of lower Banana River and Dragon Point.

Dragon Point and Southern Banana River

Entry into the southern reaches of Banana River around Dragon Point calls for caution. The channel is squeezed between rocks flanking Dragon Point and the charted finger of shoal water to the south. Approach unlighted daybeacon #1 (marking the shallow water adjacent to Dragon Point) from the west-northwest. Come abeam of and pass #1 by some 25 to 35 yards to its southerly side. Don't pass any closer to #1 to avoid the rocks, and don't stand farther off the marker in order to bypass the charted 4-foot shoal to the south. On-site research has revealed that these southerly shallows are for real. For safety's sake, cruise past #1 at idle speed and keep a weather eye on the sounder until you are well within the deeper water to the east and north.

Once on the interior reaches of southerly Banana River, you can cruise north to the Mathers swing bridge with ease. Anchorage Yacht Basin will come abeam to the southeast, soon after you round #1. Eau Gallie Yacht Club guards the eastern banks to the north, and Telemar Bay Marina also flanks the easterly shores, just south of the charted, low-level Mathers swing bridge. The entrance

to Telemar Bay's protected dockage basin is found just south of the marina's few piers fronting directly onto the river.

The Mathers bridge (closed vertical clearance, 7 feet) opens on demand from 6 A.M. to 10 P.M. During the nighttime and early morning hours, it normally doesn't open at all. Once you're through the swinging span, the northerly Dragon Point anchorage opens out on both sides of the channel. For continuing coverage of the channel striking north from the Mathers bridge, please refer to the Banana River account earlier in this chapter.

On the ICW

South-southeast of unlighted daybeacon #102, the Waterway passes under the Eau Gallie high-rise, fixed bridge. This span has a clearance of 65 feet.

After cruising south of the bridge, set course to come abeam of flashing daybeacon #2 to its easterly side. West of #2 Eau Gallie harbor beckons.

Eau Gallie Harbor

Enter Eau Gallie harbor via its buoyed channel northwest of flashing daybeacon #2. A series of green markers lines the port side of the channel into the dockage basin. Pass all these a short distance to your port side. Charted (red) flashing daybeacon #6 is actually anchored on the northerly point at the entrance to the harbor. This is not the place to try exploring out of the channel. Stick strictly to the marked cut.

Eventually the channel swings to the west-southwest and enters the main body of the harbor. Slow to idle speed after coming abeam of #6. No-wake restrictions are in effect throughout the harbor. Between unlighted daybeacons #9 and #11, the channel borders a public launching ramp park to the south.

Eau Gallie Yacht Basin will soon come up to starboard, To continue upstream to Waterline Marina, pass the remaining green daybeacons to your port side. The docks will appear south-southeast of the charted 12-foot fixed bridge. The condo complex overlooking the piers will be obvious.

On the ICW   Moving south on the Indian River ICW route, you will pass the marked, westward-running Intracoastal Marina of Melbourne entrance channel between unlighted daybeacon #3 and flashing daybeacon #5. Enter by the usual expedient of passing all red markers to your starboard side while leaving green beacons to port.

South of #5 the Waterway soon approaches the fixed high-rise Melbourne Bridge (with 65 feet of vertical clearance). A charted channel leads west, immediately south of this impressive span, to a public launching ramp and small park. Depths are not sufficient for larger vessels. A short distance farther to the south, the cut serving Melbourne Harbor Marine will come abeam to the west.

Melbourne Harbor   Enter Melbourne Harbor via the well-marked channel west of the ICW's unlighted daybeacon #6. After passing between the entrance channel's unlighted daybeacons #5 and #6 (not to be confused with unlighted daybeacon #6 on the Waterway), the channel takes a sharp jog to starboard. Pass between flashing daybeacon #7 and unlighted daybeacon #8 as you cruise into the harbor. Expect some low-water depths of 5½ feet between #6

and #8. This portion of the channel is apparently beginning to shoal, and it may need dredging in the future.

Watch to starboard when passing #8 and you will spy the Chart House Restaurant on the point. Continue cruising north into the heart of Melbourne Harbor. Look to port and you will soon see the Ralph S. Evinrude Marine Operations Center. Several research craft are often moored here.

Eventually the harbormaster's office and fuel dock will come up to starboard, just as the harbor follows a turn to the west-southwest. Check here for dockage or other needs.

On the Waterway   The ICW continues to track its way south from Melbourne down an almost arrow-straight path on Indian River. Take care to avoid the charted shallows west of unlighted daybeacon #8. Be sure to pass well to the east side of #8, and favor the eastern side of the channel until you are about halfway between #8 and the next southerly aid to navigation, unlighted daybeacon #9.

Note the charted Crab Point shoal east-northeast of unlighted daybeacon #9. These shallows appear to be building toward the Waterway. Pass #9 by at least 25 yards to its west-southwesterly side.

Between unlighted daybeacons #15 and #16, favor the eastern side of the Waterway. The charted shoal at Cape Malabar seems to be striking ever farther to the east.

West of unlighted daybeacon #16, passing cruisers may note a marked cut leading into shore. This channel serves a private condo dock that offers no facilities for visitors.

Chart 11472 depicts the ICW channel near unlighted daybeacon #18 as running through slightly shallower water. This problem stretch has never shown up during our on-the-water research. South of #18, bold cruisers have the opportunity to anchor behind the several spoil islands west and southwest of the main track.

Island Anchorages For purposes of our discussion here, the spoil island lying west of the ICW between unlighted daybeacons #18 and #20 will be referred to as the first (or #1) island. Moving north to south, the next bodies of land will be islands #2, #3, etc.

For best depths, break off from the Waterway some 25 yards north of unlighted daybeacon #20 and cruise between islands #1 and #2. We don't suggest anchoring behind island #1. There is less shelter here and, during an earlier visit we noted that someone had beached an old navy landing craft on this isle's western shores, and was apparently living aboard.

To drop anchor behind island #2, cruise in behind the land, keeping some 50 to 75 yards off the western shores. A long sandspit curves off the island's southwesterly point. During daylight, this hazard is obvious at low water, but it covers all too well at high tide. If you continue cruising south to island #3, be sure to give this shoal a wide berth.

Once clear of these shallows, you may also anchor south of island #2, still keeping some 50 yards offshore.

Don't attempt to leave the ICW south of unlighted daybeacon #22 and enter the waters behind the small isles, by cruising between islands #2 and #3. An uncharted bar lies between islands #2 and #3, with $4\frac{1}{2}$- to 5-foot low-water depths. Cruisers anchoring south of island #2 should retrace their steps to the north to rejoin the Waterway.

Stay 50-75 yards off the western shores of island #3 to avoid the dolphin pen. Craft continuing south behind (west of) this isle must avoid yet another long sand shoal striking out from this landmass's southwestern corner.

Swinging room is the slimmest behind island #4. You must carefully pick your way between the island's western shores and the correctly charted 3-foot shallows to the west and southwest. This can be a tricky process, particularly in low light or stormy conditions. Cautious navigators may want to avoid island #4 completely.

Northbound ICW cruisers can depart the main channel just north of unlighted daybeacon #24 and enter the havens behind the various islands by keeping some 50 yards off the northerly shores of island #4. This route also works for southbound boats that have been exploring west of the isles.

On the ICW South of unlighted daybeacon #24, the ICW begins to pass through shallower water on both sides of its track. It's time to pay closer attention to marks and avoid any lateral slippage.

The character of Indian River changes a mite south of flashing daybeacon #28. From #28 to Wabasso, small islands dot both sides of the Waterway channel. Most of these small landmasses are undeveloped, and many are covered with dense tropical vegetation. They are very popular stopovers for small power craft on weekends. It's a great adventure to beach your runabout on the sandy shore and have a picnic or explore the surrounding waters with mask, snorkel, and fins. Unfortunately, the questionable depths around these isles make them too risky a proposition for cruising craft. In most cases, depths rise quickly outside of the ICW cut.

Grant Farm Island, northeast of unlighted daybeacons #39 and #40, is one of the largest of the small isles along this stretch. Several attractive homes have been built here, and they make very interesting viewing from the water. Unfortunately, there are no dockage facilities for visitors.

Between unlighted daybeacon #42 and flashing daybeacon #44, a series of private docks lines the western shore. While this is not an official no-wake zone, skippers of large power cruisers are urged to slow down when passing. Please help to promote good relations between cruisers and landowners.

Sebastian River Marina The buoyed channel (such as it is) to Sebastian River Marina & Boat Yard cuts west just south of unlighted daybeacon #55. While the markers are easy to follow, cruisers are reminded that this cut has shoaled to 4 feet at low tide.

Sebastian Inlet The indifferent markings leading from the ICW to Sebastian Inlet make off to the east-northeast abeam of flashing daybeacon #63. Unless you can find a local craft and follow in its wake, or obtain definite local knowledge from one of the nearby marinas, this seaward cut is best bypassed.

On the Waterway West and a bit north of unlighted daybeacon #66 a prolifically marked channel provides access to Sebastian Inlet Marina. As you would expect, pass all red markers to your starboard side, and all green beacons to port.

A short hop south of unlighted daybeacon #70, a charted channel leads west to a private condo complex. Visiting craft should not attempt to enter.

Southeast of unlighted daybeacon #78, the character of the ICW and Indian River changes again. The Waterway ducks behind a series of large islands in the Wabasso region. These landmasses shelter the Waterway for much of the passage from Wabasso to Vero Beach. Wind and waves are clearly not as much of a concern here as on the wide waters to the north and farther to the south.

Southeast of unlighted daybeacon #80, the ICW encounters the Wabasso 65-foot fixed bridge. Just northwest of the span, a private channel leads southwest to a condo dockage basin. Visiting cruisers should not attempt to enter this cut.

As you pass unlighted daybeacon #90, look east and you should spy a dock associated with an adjacent housing/condo complex. No services are available for transients.

Jones Dock and Anchorage You should spy the old Jones Fruit Dock along the easterly shoreline abeam of unlighted daybeacon #102. The dock itself is in very poor repair.

To enter the sheltered anchorage to the north, cut in toward the centerline of the old fruit dock from the Waterway at idle speed. Some 25 yards short of the pier, swing sharply to the north and enter the midwidth of the wide stream just above the pier. Continue cruising north until you are well under the lee of the undeveloped island to port. Drop your hook near the middle for best depths and swinging room.

Farther to the north, a group of local vessels has established a mooring field on the creek. Visitors are advised to anchor south of the moored boats. Don't attempt to rejoin the Waterway via this stream's northerly entrance. Depths are shallower in this region.

On the Waterway   Watch the easterly shores as you pass between flashing day-beacon #118 and unlighted daybeacon #117. Some gorgeous homes overlook the eastern banks along this stretch.

Grand Harbor Marina   The well-outlined channel to Grand Harbor Marina cuts west from the ICW, immediately south of unlighted daybeacon #122. Simply pass between the many pairs of unlighted day-beacons, composed of concrete piles and daymarks. Soon you will spy the harbor entrance between the arms of a concrete seawall dead ahead. Once inside the basin, turn to port and track your way to the fuel dock. The harbormaster's office and ship's store is just behind this prominent pier.

On the Waterway   South of unlighted day-beacon #135, you will spy the Vero Beach/Merrill Barber fixed, high-rise bridge

dead ahead. Slow down as you approach this span. No-wake speed restrictions are in effect from the high rise, moving south to the next bridge.

Vero Beach-Bethel Creek Facilities and Anchorages   The entrance channel to the Vero Beach facilities on Bethel Creek comes up south of flashing daybeacon #139 and immediately north of the high-rise bridge. This passage is prolifically marked, and any-one who remembers the old red-right-returning rule should not have any problem on the cut's interior reaches. Simply cruise between the various markers, passing all red beacons to your starboard side with green to port. There are now far more aids to naviga-tion on this channel than those pictured on the current edition of chart 11472. All these additional markers help to greatly simplify successful navigation of the cut.

The only tricky section is found along this channel's intersection with the Waterway. Shoals making in from the north are encroaching on flashing daybeacon #139. Stay away from #139 and favor the bridge (south) side of the channel between the ICW and unlighted daybeacon #3. At #3, the cut swerves to the northeast and leaves the correctly charted 2-foot shoal east of #139 behind.

The marked channel continues northeast and then north on Bethel Creek. Soon the docks of Indian River Marina will be spot-ted, overlooking the easterly banks, followed by the Vero Beach Yacht Club and, soon thereafter, Vero Beach Municipal Marina. North of this last facility, the city mooring field will quickly come into view. Check with the city dockmaster before attempting to pick up a mooring buoy, if you should choose to secure your vessel in the mooring field.

On the ICW   The Vero Beach/Merrill Barber high-rise span has a clearance of (you guessed it) 65 feet. Cruising south from this bridge, point to pass flashing day-beacon #140 to its easterly side. Now it's time to contemplate the passage south from Vero to Fort Pierce and eventually to Stuart and an intersection with the Okeechobee Waterway.

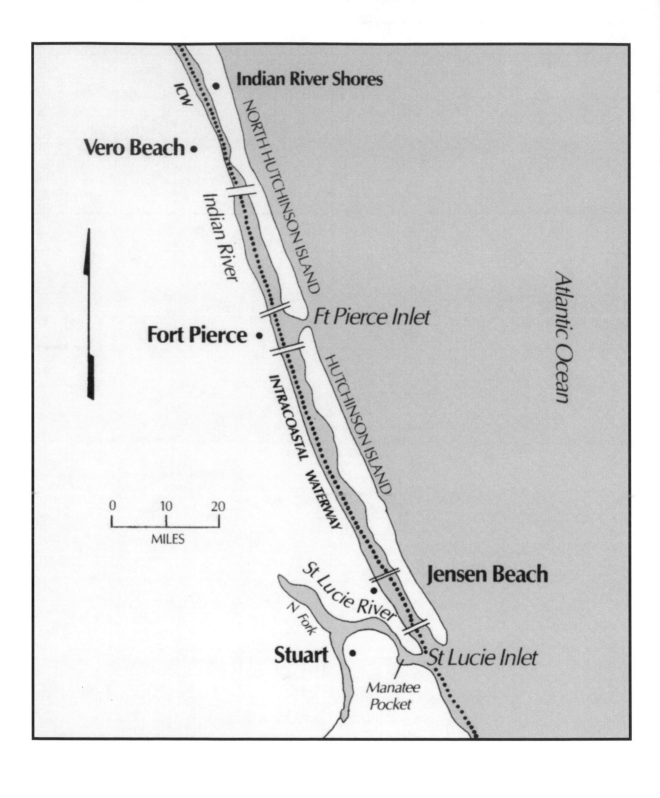

Indian River Shores

Vero Beach •

ICW

Indian River

NORTH HUTCHINSON ISLAND

Fort Pierce •

Ft Pierce Inlet

INTRACOASTAL WATERWAY

HUTCHINSON ISLAND

Atlantic Ocean

0   10   20
MILES

Jensen Beach

St Lucie River

N Fork

Stuart •

St Lucie Inlet

Manatee
Pocket

Vero Beach to Stuart

From Vero Beach it is a run of some 30 nautical miles to the charming city of Stuart, sitting astride the most strategic watery intersection in eastern Florida. From the juncture of the Atlantic ICW, St. Lucie Inlet, and the St. Lucie River, cruisers may choose to continue south to the "Gold Coast," turn west into the intriguing Okeechobee Waterway, or possibly put to sea.

The city of Fort Pierce sits just a little better than 10 nautical miles south of Vero Beach. Boasting an impressive collection of marina and yard facilities, not to mention one of the finest inlets in eastern Florida, this community has been welcoming more and more cruisers.

South of Vero, the Indian River again widens into a most impressive body of water. The ICW tracks its way through the heart of this great river until the waters finally narrow just east of Stuart. This is a very broad, unprotected portion of the eastern Florida ICW. Captains should keep an ear tuned to the weather forecast rather than risk having the fillings jarred out of their teeth. If winds exceed 25 knots, it would be best to wait for fair weather at one of the many Vero Beach or Fort Pierce marinas. Craft under 30 feet should be particularly careful to plan their cruises to coincide with gentle breezes.

Marina facilities are more than adequate on this run, though the various overnight havens do tend to be closely grouped together. A multitude of marinas are found at Fort Pierce and at Stuart; in between, however, there are very few facilities.

Anchorages are practically nonexistent. A few spots do provide enough shelter for a snug stay, but they are few and far between.

The run from Vero to Stuart makes attractive cruising. South of Fort Pierce, the western shores rise to high banks where many sumptuous homes gaze serenely over the river's waters. This is a great time to ease off the throttle and enjoy the sights.

Charts   Only one chart is needed for full coverage of the waters between Vero Beach and Stuart:

11472—details the ICW and all sidewaters south to St. Lucie River and inlet

---

Bridges
17th Street Bridge—crosses ICW at Standard Mile 953, south of flashing daybeacon #145A—Fixed—65 feet
North Fort Pierce Bridge—crosses ICW at Standard Mile 965, south-southeast of flashing daybeacon #182—Bascule—25 feet (closed) (officially listed as 26 feet)—opens on demand
South Fort Pierce Bridge—crosses ICW at Standard Mile 966, south of flashing buoy #185—Fixed—65 feet
Jensen Beach Bridge—crosses ICW at Standard Mile 981.5, south of unlighted daybeacon #219—Bascule—24 feet (closed)—December 1 to May 1, opens only on the hour and half-hour 7:00 A.M. to 6:00 P.M. weekdays; during weekends and at all other times of the day and year, opens on demand

Ernest Lyons/Highway A1A Bridge—crosses ICW at Standard Mile 984, south-southeast of unlighted daybeacon #226—Bascule—28 feet (closed)—December 1 to May 1, opens only on the hour and half-hour 7:00 A.M. and 6:00 P.M. weekdays; during weekends and at all other times of the day and year, opens on demand

Chapter 6 Anchorage Summary (Note that anchorages are listed in geographic order, moving north to south.)

Cook Point Anchorage—(Standard Mile 964.5)—located near 27 28.811 North/080 18.781 West, on the charted Cook Point channel, which leaves the Waterway just north of the North Fort Pierce bascule bridge—6-foot depths—reviewed on pages 315-16, 332

Faber Cove Anchorages—(Standard Mile 966.5)—located on the marked and charted channel running east-northeast from unlighted daybeacon #188—various lats/lons (see detailed account)—5½-foot depths—reviewed on pages 321, 333-34

Open Anchorage—(Standard Mile 970)—located near 27 24.183 North/080 17.492 West, east of unlighted daybeacon #195—6½-foot depths—reviewed on pages 321, 334

Jensen Beach Bridge Anchorages—(Standard Mile 981)—located west of the Waterway, north and south of the Jensen Beach bascule bridge, south of unlighted daybeacon #219—various lats/lons (see detailed account)—5-foot depths—reviewed on pages 322, 334-35

Manatee Pocket Anchorage—(Standard Mile 988)—located near 27 09.239 North/080 11.855 West, on the waters of the large bay indenting the western banks of Manatee Pocket—5-foot depths—reviewed on pages 327, 337

Chapter 6 Marina and Yacht-Club Summary (Note that marinas and yacht clubs are listed in geographic order, moving north to south.)

Riverside Marina—(772) 464-5720—(Standard Mile 964)—located near 27 28.731 North/080 20.053 West, along the western shores of the ICW, south of unlighted daybeacon #180—limited transient dockage available—4-foot minimum depths, but typically 5 feet or better—reviewed on pages 313-15, 331-32

Harbortown Marina—(772) 466-7300—(Standard Mile 965)—located near 27 28.073 North/080 19.702 West, on the northern banks of Taylor Creek, which cuts into the ICW's western flank south of unlighted daybeacon #184—transient dockage available—gasoline and diesel fuel available—6½-foot minimum depths—reviewed on pages 316-17, 332

Pelican Yacht Club—(772) 464-1734—(Standard Mile 965.5)—located near 27 27.875 North/080 18.228 West, on the southern shores of the Fort Myers Inlet, east-southeast of flashing buoy #13—transient dockage available—gasoline and diesel fuel available—6½-foot minimum depths—reviewed on pages 317-19, 332-33

Fort Pierce City Marina—(772) 464-1245—(Standard Mile 966.5)—located near 27 26.995 North/080 19.266 West, entrance channel runs to the northwest, south-southeast of unlighted daybeacon #188—transient dockage available—gasoline and diesel fuel available—7½-foot minimum depths—reviewed on pages 319-21, 333

Outrigger Harbour—(772) 219-8122—(Standard Mile 983.5)—located near 27 13.350 North/080 12.701 West, entrance channel runs to the west-southwest between flashing daybeacon #223 and unlighted daybeacon #224—transient dockage available—gasoline and diesel fuel available—6-foot minimum depths—reviewed in pages 322-24, 335

Hutchinson Island Marriott Marina—(772) 225-6989—(Standard Mile 985)—located near 27 12.511 North/080 10.978 West, south-southeast of the Ernest Lyons/Highway A1A and north of unlighted daybeacon #228—transient dockage available—gasoline and diesel fuel available—5½-foot minimum depths—reviewed on pages 324-25, 335

Sailfish Marina of Stuart—(772) 283-1122—(Standard Mile 988)—located near 27 09.685 North/080 11.745 West, on the western shores of Manatee Pocket, near its northerly entrance—limited transient dockage available—gasoline and diesel fuel available—5½-foot minimum depths—reviewed on pages 325-26, 337

Mariner's Cay Marina—(772) 287-2900—(Standard Mile 988)—located near 27 09.503 North/080 11.725 West), on the western shores of Manatee Pocket, near its northerly entrance—transient dockage available—gasoline and diesel fuel available—4-foot minimum depths, but many slips have 5 to 6 feet of water—reviewed on pages 326-27, 337

Pirate's Cove Resort and Marina—(772) 287-2354—(Standard Mile 988)—located near 27 08.885 North/080 11.751 West, along the western banks of upper Manatee Pocket—transient dockage available—gasoline and diesel fuel available—4½-foot minimum depths—reviewed on pages 327-28, 337

Manatee Marina and Boat Sales—(772) 283-6714—(Standard Mile 988)—located near 27 08.746 North/080 11.755 West, lining the banks between Manatee Pocket's westernmost and central-southern arm—very limited transient dockage available—gasoline and diesel fuel available—3½-foot minimum depths—reviewed on pages 329, 337

Stuart Corinthian Yacht Club—(772) 221-1900—(Standard Mile 988)—located near 27 08.807 North/080 11.538 West, flanking Manatee Pocket's easternmost arm's western banks—limited guest dockage available to members of other yacht clubs with appropriate reciprocal agreements—5-foot minimum depths—reviewed on pages 329-30, 337

Spyglass Harbour (Standard Mile 957)

South of unlighted daybeacon #160, a well-defined channel leads east to what is surely one of the most impressive condo projects north of the "Gold Coast." Spyglass Harbour is a vast collection of attractive townhouses and multifamily units perched directly on the shores of Indian River. There are no facilities available for transients at the present time, but if you are not in too great a hurry, a sightseeing cruise into this fascinating complex is well worth your time.

Riverside Marina (Standard Mile 964) (27 28.731 North/080 20.053 West)

One of the only pleasure-craft-oriented facilities between Vero Beach and Fort Pierce comes up along the westerly banks, south of unlighted daybeacon #180. An indifferently marked but charted channel with 6½-foot minimum depths leads to Riverside Marina. While this facility occasionally accepts transients, clearly its specialty is repair work.

Wet-slip dockage is limited. If you should be successful in securing an overnight berth anyway, the marina features fixed wooden piers with water hookups and 30- and 50-amp power connections. Low-water depths alongside run 4 to 7 feet. Low-key showers are found shoreside near the small ship's store.

Full mechanical repairs for both gas and

diesel motors are available. Haul-outs are accomplished by a 70-ton travelift. Once craft are out of the water, do-it-yourself bottom work is allowed. One look at the host of hauled craft at Riverside, and you will gain the swift and sure impression that more than a few take advantage of the yard services.

One restaurant is located about a mile down U.S. 1. Norris's Ribs (772-464-4000) is acceptable, but not what we would call a premier dining choice. You could always call a taxi (see below) from nearby Fort Pierce and visit the Captain's Galley in the downtown section of this community. Additionally, a mobile lunch wagon visits Riverside most every day. This service is very popular with cruisers working on their own craft.

Riverside Marina (772) 464-5720
  http://www.riversidemarinafortpierce.com

Approach depths—6½-10 feet
Dockside depths—4-7 feet
Accepts transients—limited
Transient dockage rate—below average
Fixed wooden piers—yes
Dockside power connections—30
  and 50 amps

Riverside Marina

Dockside water connections—yes
Showers—yes
Below-waterline repairs—yes
Mechanical repairs—yes
Ship's store—yes (small)
Restaurant—one (a long walk away)

Fort Pierce (Standard Mile 966)

South of flashing daybeacon #182, the ICW soon exchanges greeting with the Fort Pierce waterfront and its like-named inlet. Fort Pierce deserves a red circle on any cruiser's chart for two reasons. First, this handsome city is the home of a half-dozen facilities catering to visiting vessels. Second, it is the site of eastern Florida's most reliable seaward passage north of Palm Beach. Fort Pierce continues to be one of the most popular stopovers on the eastern Florida ICW. During the transient season (September to November and March to May), it's a good idea to call ahead for overnight dockage reservations.

Fort Pierce is a charming collection of parks, restaurants, shopping centers, and shoreside businesses of all descriptions. Sunbathers frequent the nearby beaches, while others may visit the state park north of the inlet. Grocery stores and several restaurants are within a healthy walk of the mainland marinas. To reach the beaches or outlying shopping centers, you will need a taxi or rental car.

Numbers to know in Fort Pierce:
St. Lucie Checker Cab—772-878-1234
Coe Taxi Cab—772-465-2222
Yellow Cab—772-466-6606
Enterprise Rent-A-Car—772-466-7440
Budget Car Rental—772-464-8789
West Marine—772-460-9044
Chamber of Commerce—772-595-9999

Fort Pierce History Fort Pierce was originally established as a military base during the Seminole Indian wars. It was abandoned after the conflict and was not settled as a town until the very late nineteenth century.

Large-scale development came to Fort Pierce with the opening of the Florida East Coast Railroad. The great freeze of 1895 drove large numbers of tourists south to Fort Pierce from their normal haunts in the northern section of the state. Many liked the region so much that they stayed. Since that time, the progress of this likable city has been steady and well planned.

Cook Point Anchorage (Standard Mile 964.5) (27 28.811 North/080 18.781 West)

Note the charted channel on 11472 striking east-northeast immediately north of the 26-foot bascule bridge (south-southeast of flashing daybeacon #182). This cut primarily serves local, small power craft traffic, but it holds minimum depths of 6 feet and there is an interesting opportunity for overnight anchorage. Captains whose vessels draw 5 feet or less and measure no more than 36 feet in length can track their way up the marked cut until the low-level bridge at Cook Point comes abeam to the south-southeast.

Ease your way a bit farther to the east-northeast, past the bridge. Drop your hook in the charted bubble of 8- and 9-foot water here. Favor the southeastern banks and be sure your anchor is set so you don't swing into the correctly charted shoals to the north and northwest. This haven offers superb protection from all but particularly ugly southwest and northeastern blows. The islands to the north and northwest are untouched while the banks to the south and southeast display moderate to light development. During weekends (particularly), early-morning small craft and jet ski traffic could be an annoyance in this anchorage. Be sure to show an anchor light!

Fort Pierce—Taylor Creek Facilities (Standard Mile 965) (Various Lats/Lons—see below)

Immediately south of unlighted daybeacon #184, a marked and charted channel runs west into Taylor Creek. This fortunate body of water is home to a huge marina, two boatyards, and a dry-stack storage facility. The entrance channel boasts minimum depths of 8 feet, with typical soundings in the 9- to 11-foot range.

Mammoth Harbortown Marina occupies the northerly banks of Taylor Creek, just past the stream's mouth (near 27 28.073 North/080 19.702 West). This large, modern facility is a unique operation in eastern Florida. In spite of its impressive size and range of services, Harbortown is not owned by some faceless corporation; rather it is a family enterprise, with father, mother, and daughter all manning the bastions every day. Harbortown is clearly looking to attract large yachts, particularly those of the powered persuasion. However, most any size and type of cruising craft can expect a warm welcome, secure dockage, and any repair services that might ever be needed. Harbortown is also the site of a U.S. Customs clearing station.

To say the least, Harbortown's wet-slip dockage is extensive. How does 340 well-sheltered slips grab you (not to mention 164 dry-stack storage units for smaller power craft)? Transients are eagerly accepted at these fixed and floating wooden piers. Depths alongside run 6½ to 9 feet. The accommodating dockmasters can steer unusually long-legged vessels to deeper berths. Just let them know your requirements ahead of time. Power (30-, 50-, and 100-amp) and fresh-water connections are

Harbortown Marina, Fort Pierce

complemented by telephone and cable-television hookups. First-class, climate-controlled showers and a fair (non-air-conditioned) Laundromat are close by the slips, and waste pump-out service is also available. There is even a heated, year-round swimming pool, which is open to all cruising visitors. Gasoline and diesel fuel can be purchased in the heart of the complex at a fuel pier fronting directly onto Taylor Creek.

Harbortown's repair yard and servicing capabilities are awesome. Just take one look at the mammoth work barn northwest of the docks. No, they don't construct space shuttles in this building; they just perform almost every type of repair service imaginable on the largest pleasure yachts going. Full mechanical (gas and diesel), electrical, marine A/C, and fiberglass repairs are readily available. The yard's two travelifts are rated at 50 and 150 tons.

There are two restaurants in the Harbortown complex. Harbor Cove Restaurant (772-429-5303) occupies the same building as the dockmaster's office, just behind the fuel pier (where you will also find a free e-mail data port). We have found the food at Harbor Cove to be quite tasty. The Harbortown Deli (772-467-8987) is part of a small, retail, office complex fronting the eastern side of the main parking lot.

Besides some yummy deli sandwiches, there are also a few, basic food items (and a paperback exchange library) that can be purchased here and taken back to your galley. This firm is open daily from 6:00 A.M. to 2:00 P.M. It is a quick taxi ride (see numbers above) to grocery stores, drugstores, additional restaurants (including the Captain's Galley), and a host of other shoreside businesses.

Truly Harbortown Marina is one of the most impressive marine establishments in eastern Florida. If things keep growing along at the pace of the last several years, Bahia Mar and Pier 66 had better watch out!

Harbortown Marina (772) 466-7300
http://www.harbortownmarina.com
/FtPierce/frames.htm

Approach depths—8-11 feet
Dockside depths—6½-9 feet
Accepts transients—yes
Transient dockage rate—average
Fixed and floating wooden piers—yes
Dockside power connections—30,
   50, and 100 amps
Dockside water connections—yes
Showers—yes
Laundromat—yes
Waste pump-out—yes
Gasoline—yes
Diesel fuel—yes
Below-waterline repairs—yes
Mechanical repairs—yes
Restaurant—two on site and others nearby

Cracker Boy Boat Works (772-465-7031) guards the southern shores of Taylor Creek, opposite Harbortown Marina, near 27 27.978 North/080 19.676 West. This is a full-service yard offering marine carpentry and haul-outs via a 70-ton travelift. Mechanical repairs are possible courtesy of the on-site, independent firm of Eckel's Marine (772-465-5388). Dockage is available for yard customers only.

Cracker Boy has a second site at Riviera Beach, which we shall meet later in our journey south. This firm has a sure and certain reputation for getting the job done right!

Taylor Creek Marina (772-465-2663) flanks Taylor Creek's southerly shores, just west of Cracker Boy Boat Works, near 27 27.976 North/080 19.745 West. This facility is primarily in the dry stack storage game, though gasoline and diesel fuel can be purchased dockside. Depths alongside run about 7 feet. An extensive ship's and variety store stands just behind the fuel dock.

Fort Pierce Inlet and Pelican Yacht Club (Standard Mile 965.5) (27 27.875 North/080 18.228 West)

The ICW intersects the Fort Pierce Inlet channel between (south-southeast of) flashing bouy #187 and the high-rise South Fort Pierce Bridge. The inlet at Fort Pierce is one of the most reliable seaward passages between St. Johns River and Port Everglades. This cut is used regularly by large commercial freighters and is kept well dredged. Strangers should be able to navigate the channel successfully during daylight, but tidal currents do run swiftly at times, and waves can be formidable when current and wind oppose one another.

Fort Pierce Inlet boasts its own marina. Pelican Yacht Club occupies the eastern banks of the sheltered cove indenting the southern shoreline, between flashing buoys #13 and #11. This facility is another of those rare yacht clubs that accepts transients without the need for any reciprocal arrangements. Visiting cruisers are readily accepted for overnight or temporary dockage, and the list of on-site amenities is truly impressive. Berths

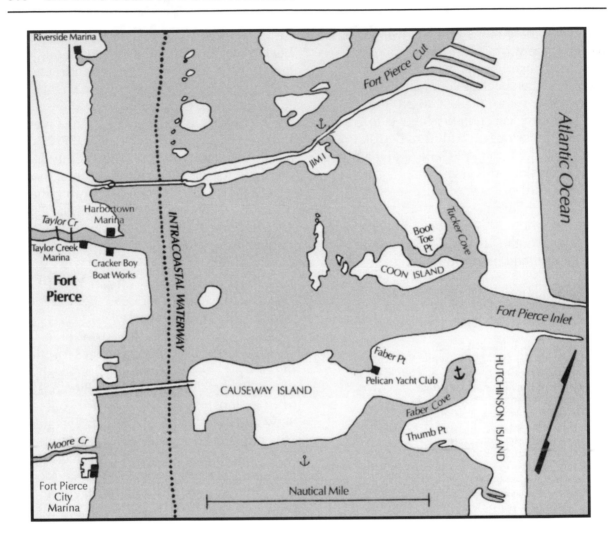

are found at fixed, wooden piers with full power and water connections. Depths alongside run at least 6½ to 8 feet. Watch for the inlet's tidal currents as you make your approach to the docks. The basin is a bit open to strong northerly and northwesterly blows, but otherwise well sheltered.

Good, air-conditioned showers and a small Laundromat are readily available, as are gasoline and diesel fuel. A tiny ship's store is found on the fuel dock, doubling as a dockmaster's office. Pelican Yacht Club's clubhouse features a dining room, swimming pool, and tennis courts, all open to visiting cruisers. While the docks remain open, the club and its dining services are closed on Mondays. Dinner is served Tuesday through Saturday. Within a half-mile stroll you will also discover Mangrove Mattie's Restaurant (1640 Seaway Drive, 772-466-1044), with truly good food, and Chuck's Seafood market (822 Seaway Drive, 772-461-9484). Ask the marina staff for directions.

A far shorter three-block walk will take you to Treasure Coast Foods—a small but full-line grocery and butcher shop. There is also a hardware and convenience store in the same area.

If you are planning to put to (or entering from) sea via Fort Pierce Inlet, and are in need of dockage, give Pelican Yacht Club your most serious consideration.

Pelican Yacht Club (772) 464-1734

Approach depths—8+ feet
Dockside depths—6¹/₂-8 feet (minimum)
Accepts transients—yes
Transient dockage rate—average
Fixed wooden piers—yes
Dockside power connections—30
   and 50 amps
Dockside water connections—yes
Showers—yes
Laundromat—yes
Gasoline—yes
Diesel fuel—yes
Ship's store—yes (small)
Restaurant—on site and others nearby

Alternate Inlet Channel

The Fort Pierce inset of chart 11472 correctly identifies a small channel running north-northwest from the inlet to Jim Island. This cut holds 5-foot minimum depths, and it eventually leads to a small-craft marina and a low-level, fixed bridge. Cruising craft over 30 feet will find the maneuvering room to be a bit tight. Cautious captains of larger vessels should probably bypass this cut.

Fort Pierce Commercial Port

West of the ICW's intersection with the Fort Pierce Inlet channel, the commercial wharves of the Fort Pierce Port facilities lie along the westerly banks. Here you can often see small freighters tied to the wharves. Often loading

is in progress. For those who proceed along at idle speed, it's often quite easy to cruise close enough for a good view.

Fort Pierce City Marina (Standard Mile 966.5) (27 26.995 North/080 19.266 West)

Fort Pierce City Marina's well-marked entrance channel cuts to the northwest, south-southeast of unlighted daybeacon #188. This cut features 7¹/₂- to 9-foot depths and is easily traversed to the marina's two dockage basins.

Veteran Waterway cruisers in the know make it a point to plan a stopover at this superb facility on every sojourn. With its fine array of adjacent restaurants, easy access to downtown Fort Pierce, and very welcoming attitude from the team of city dockmasters, Fort Pierce City Marina is a municipal facility second to none in eastern Florida (or most anywhere else, for that matter).

There are two dockage basins at Fort Pierce City Marina. The outer harbor fronts directly onto the western shores of the ICW and Indian River and consists of modern, floating concrete docks fronted by a protective breakwater. Depths here range from 8 to 9 feet. The inner harbor features fixed wooden piers, with a full 8 feet of water at mean low tide. State-of-the-art, full power and water connections (plus cable-television and telephone hookups) are on hand at every slip. There are two sets of air-conditioned, shoreside showers (one on either side of the harbor), which are absolutely first rate. There is also a (non-climate-controlled) Laundromat in the dockmaster's main building. Extensive waste pump-out service is available both by way of several fixed units and a mobile pump. Gasoline and diesel fuel can be purchased conveniently at a fuel pier located on the inner harbor, where

Fort Pierce City Marina

there is little in the way of tidal current to worry with. While the marina does not offer any repair services of its own, the accommodating staff can usually put you in contact with local, independent technicians for mechanical, canvas, electrical, refrigeration, and air-conditioning servicing as well as fuel filtration.

Visiting cruisers will find a small gift shop in the dockmaster's building, as well as an ATM machine. It is a one-mile walk to a full-line grocery store. You might want to take a taxi (see above). Car rentals can also be arranged through the marina dockmaster's office.

From October through April a local farmers' market is held on the property immediately adjacent to the marina. If you can time your arrival to coincide with this, your galley will be ever so much richer for the effort.

There are two restaurants on site. The recently expanded Tiki Restaurant and Raw Bar (772-461-0880) sits under a grass roof and overlooks the inner dockage basin. The food here is surprisingly good and the prices reasonable. Most any of the seafood entrees are worthy of your attention. Cruisers who are only interested in patronizing the Tiki Bar (as opposed to an overnight or longer stay at the marina) should call the marina in advance for courtesy dockage.

The Mana Tiki Restaurant (772-460-9014) guards the harbor's southwestern corner. This is a very popular, informal dining spot featuring some exotic island cocktails, which once took the tops of our proverbial heads off. The first-rate first mate and I have always been most impressed with our seafood entrees, and the open-air dining is delightful. We recommend this dining spot from the bottom of our collective appetites.

The immensely popular Captain's Galley restaurant (825 N Indian River Drive, 772-466-8495) is located about half a mile to the north of the marina. The food here is quite simply outstanding. Everything is good, and the prices have got to be the best bargain from Jacksonville to Miami. Sadly, the Captain's Galley is now open for breakfast and lunch only. Sniff—we'll miss them for dinner! If you are up for walking, just stroll north on Indian River Drive. The restaurant will appear dead ahead after a half-mile hike. Those not up for the walk can call a taxi.

As if all that weren't enough to warrant a stay at Fort Pierce City Marina, there is the adjacent downtown business district. The local library is located less than a block away. There are also any number of other restaurants, a bakery (on Orange Avenue), and many art galleries within easy walking distance that you might consider. In particular, those with a taste for French cuisine may want to pay a call on Café La Ronde (213 Avenue A, 772-595-1928). Ask the helpful marina staff for other recommendations.

Be sure to check out Fort Pierce City Marina's Web site (see below). It is packed with information about both the marina and its parent community. It receives our vote as one of the best marina Web sites in all of eastern Florida.

Clearly, with its many and ongoing improvements, Fort Pierce City Marina warrants a strong recommendation. Cruisers who pass without a stop here will be less for the omission.

Fort Pierce City Marina (772) 464-1245
   (800) 619-1780
   http://www.FortPierceCityMarina.com

Approach depths—7½-9 feet
Dockside depths—8-9 feet
Accepts transients—yes (extensive)
Transient dockage rate—average
Floating concrete piers—yes (outer harbor)
Fixed wooden piers—yes (inner harbor)
Dockside power connections—30,
   50, 100 amps
Dockside water connections—yes
Showers—yes
Laundromat—yes
Waste pump-out—yes
Gasoline—yes
Diesel fuel—yes
Gift shop—yes
Restaurant—two on site and others nearby

Faber Cove Anchorages (Standard Mile 966.5) (Various Lats/Lons—see below)

A wide, well-marked channel tracks its way east-northeast from unlighted daybeacon #188 to highly developed Faber Cove. Boats up to 45 feet should be able to run this cut without worrying about more than one tricky spot. Minimum depths are currently 5½ feet, with most of the route being considerably deeper.

The first place you might consider dropping the hook is found just south-southeast of the channel between unlighted daybeacons #7 and #9, near 27 27.387 North/080 18.280 West. Here good depths of 10+ feet hold for 100 yards or so south-southeast of the main

cut. Swinging room is virtually unlimited. We found two large sailcraft anchored here during one of our sojourns on these waters. This is a fair-weather anchorage, unless moderate winds are blowing from the north, northeast, or northwest. In this instance, Causeway Island gives good shelter. This anchorage also has the distinct advantage of being far closer to the ICW than Faber Cove itself.

For maximum shelter, continue following the channel east-northeast into the main body of Faber Cove. One small section of 5½-foot depths near unlighted daybeacon #13 could be a bit of a problem for really deep draft vessels. Eventually, the cove will open out into a wide body of water with typical 7- to 10-foot depths. There is ample room for several 50-footers to drop the hook near 27 27.933 North/080 17.739 West. Protection from all winds is superb. Faber Cove is surrounded by a dense collection of houses and condominiums. While it certainly is not a quiet or isolated haven, it does offer good protection in a region that is not exactly blooming with anchorages. Local regulations limit anchoring in Faber Cove to a 96-hour stay.

Open Anchorage (Standard Mile 970) (27 24.183 North/080 17.492 West)

Should you be truly desperate to drop anchor, in fair weather only, the 6½- to 7-foot waters east of unlighted daybeacon #195 are a possibility. There is plenty of room, but virtually no shelter. During light airs, this might be fine, but let any sort of a breeze get its dander up, and you could imitate a lively tennis ball.

Indian River Nuclear Plant (Standard Mile 974)

Moving south on the ICW from Fort Pierce

to Stuart, cruisers have the opportunity to glow in the dark. South-southeast of flashing daybeacon #202, a marked channel cuts east toward a large nuclear power plant on the shores of Big Mud Creek. While you are certainly free to observe the complex from the Waterway, pleasure craft should keep clear of the plant channel. It is used regularly by barges loading and unloading equipment at the power facility.

Jensen Beach Bridge Anchorages (Standard Mile 981) (Various Lats/Lons—see below)

Chart 11472 shows two large patches of deep water bordering the western side of the ICW, to the north and south of the 24-foot Jensen Beach Bridge (south-southeast of unlighted daybeacon #219). Both are potential overnight stops, but the northside haven has some problems.

Depths on the northern site have shoaled to 5-foot levels. We have helped to pull a sailboat off the bottom here where the chart clearly showed 7 feet of water. If that's not evidence enough, consider the wide-open nature of this anchorage. Strong winds from the north, east, or west could set up a very healthy chop. If your boat draws less than 4 feet, and if the forecast is for light winds or moderate southerly blows, you might consider anchoring near 27 15.291 North/080 13.400 West. Otherwise, check out the waters south of the bridge.

The southside patch (near 27 14.998 North/080 13.284 West) has consistent depths of 5½ to 7 feet, but there are a few unmarked shallows to avoid. Read the navigational information below before attempting to access this anchorage. Otherwise good water runs for a considerable distance west-southwest of the Waterway. Anchor at least 300 yards south-southeast of the causeway. Swinging room is adequate for the largest pleasure craft and there is good protection to the north, northwest, and (to a lesser extent) northeast. Obviously, this is not the spot to spend the evening in southerly breezes. The adjacent shoreline exhibits moderate commercial and residential development.

Sun Dance Marine (Standard Mile 981.5)

Sun Dance Marine (772-334-1416) lies adjacent to the southerly anchorage reviewed above. This marina has expanded into a large dry dock storage facility for smaller power craft. Gasoline can be purchased, but no other services are available for transients. Skippers should also know that entrance depths to this marina run as little as 3 to 4 feet.

AA Marine (Standard Mile 983) (27 13.887 North/080 13.060 West)

The well-buoyed channel leading to AA Marine (772-334-0936—formerly Anchors Aweigh Marine) runs west from unlighted daybeacon #222. This facility is now a strictly service-oriented firm, with no transient dockage available. On the other hand, full mechanical (gas and diesel engines) and below-waterline repairs are readily available. Boats up to 50 feet can be hauled on the yard's marine railway and vessels as large as 30 feet are picked from the water with a crane. As the owner, Charles Shoup, put it to this writer, "There's not too much in the way of boat repair that we don't do." Judging from our on-site observations, we would not quibble with that assessment.

Entrance depths at AA range from 6 to 8 feet with 5 to 6½ feet of water dockside. A ship's store fronts the street to the west.

Outrigger Harbour (Standard Mile 983.5) (27 13.350 North/080 12.701 West)

Between flashing daybeacon #223 and

unlighted daybeacon #224, mariners will discover an easily run channel flowing west-southwest to Outrigger Harbour. This facility was once known as Frances Langford's Outrigger Resort and held a personal fascination for this writer. I have a faint memory of myself as a youngster playing on the Morehead City (North Carolina) waterfront docks when about 100 feet of gleaming grey yacht pulled up to the adjacent pier. Being an impetuous youth, I soon made the acquaintance of the illustrious owner, Frances Langford, former actress and wife of Mr. Evinrude himself of outboard fame. According to my mother, Ms. Langford even allowed me to play with her two French poodles on board.

A decade ago, Ms. Langford sold the marina and restaurant. Fortunately, for anyone interested in seeing her magnificent yacht (a newer vessel than the one I played on as a child), she sometimes docks it in the marina's harbor.

Outrigger Harbour

Though a bit small, the marina harbor is extremely well sheltered with modern docks and beautifully landscaped grounds. Transients are accepted for guest dockage. Most of the berths consist of wooden finger piers stretching out from a concrete seawall. There are also some face docks. Depths in the entrance channel run 6½ to 9 feet, with 6- to 7-foot low-water soundings in the harbor. All slips feature full power and water connections. Good (air-conditioned) showers, a Laundromat, gasoline, and diesel fuel are all readily available. There is also a small ship's store at the harbor's southwestern corner complete with paperback exchange library.

As you enter Outrigger Harbour, the Dolphin Bar and Shrimp House restaurant (772-781-5136) will be spotted to port. This restaurant is under the same exemplary ownership as Conchy Joe's in Melbourne, and we feel sure that you will be gastronomically satisfied.

Outrigger Harbour (772) 219-8122

Approach depths—6½-9 feet
Dockside depths—6-7 feet
Accepts transients—yes
Transient dockage rate—above average
Fixed wooden piers—yes
Dockside power connections—30
   and 50 amps
Dockside water connections—yes
Showers—yes
Laundromat—yes
Gasoline—yes
Diesel fuel—yes
Ship's store—yes (small)
Restaurant—on site

Hutchinson Island Marriott Marina (Standard Mile 985) (27 12.511 North/080 10.978 West)

One of the largest resort-style marina complexes in south-central Florida is available to cruising craft just south-southeast of the Ernest Lyons/Highway A1A (north of unlighted daybeacon #228) on the eastern shore. Newly renamed Hutchinson Island Marriott Marina is part of a huge, forty-acre development that includes a mind-boggling array of hotels (including a convention center), restaurants, retail stores, and 1,700 feet of private beach. To the good fortune of all Waterway cruisers, the management has decided to accept transients for overnight and temporary dockage. Just hold onto your wallet when it comes time to fork out for the overnight dockage fee!

After entering through the privately marked channel (minimum 6½-7-foot depths), transients will find fixed concrete piers featuring every power, water, telephone, and cable-television connection imaginable. Depths on the outer slips run 6 to 7 feet, with a few inner berths having 5½-foot soundings. The dockage basin is wide open to strong winds from the south and southwest, but well sheltered to the east and northeast.

World-class, climate-controlled showers and a full (also air-conditioned) Laundromat are available in the large office and retail complex overlooking the dockage basin. As you would expect, all fuels are offered, and some repairs can be arranged through independent contractors.

Considering the popularity of this facility, advance dockage reservations are definitely recommended. During several visits, we have noted that far more large, power vessels than sailcraft are usually berthed at this facility.

Visiting cruisers are welcome to make use of any of the nearby four swimming pools (one with adjacent tiki bar), golf course, thirteen tennis courts, and private beach. The adjacent retail complex includes several restaurants and bars. One particularly noteworthy dining spot is Bahia Grille (772-225-6818). An "emporium" in the retail center features gifts, clothing, sandwiches, cold drinks, and ice cream. A five-minute walk from the docks will lead you to a medium-sized grocery store. Ask the dockmaster for directions.

Hutchinson Island Marriott Marina
(772) 225-6989

Approach depths—6½-7 feet
Dockside depths—5½-7 feet
Accepts transients—yes
Transient dockage fee—well above average
Fixed concrete piers—yes
Dockside power connections—30
   and 50 amps
Dockside water connections—yes
Showers—yes
Laundromat—yes
Gasoline—yes
Diesel fuel—yes
Mechanical repairs—limited
   (independent contractors)
Restaurant—several on site

Manatee Pocket Facilities and Anchorage (Standard Mile 988) (Various Lats/Lons— see below)

South of unlighted daybeacon #239, the ICW

Entrance to Manatee Pocket

runs pell-mell into the easterly genesis of the Okeechobee Waterway at the foot of the St. Lucie River. To the east, the questionable depths of St. Lucie Inlet track their way to the open sea. This intersection is one of the most navigationally difficult portions of the entire passage from Fernandina Beach to Miami. It will be considered in detail in the next section of this chapter.

While the majority of the Okeechobee Waterway will be considered in the next chapter, a whole array of facilities is found just off the ICW on Manatee Pocket. Due to their proximity to the north-south Atlantic ICW, these marinas and boatyards will be reviewed here.

The easternmost section of the Okeechobee Waterway channel, running through the lower reaches of the St. Lucie River between the ICW and Manatee Pocket is a very changeable region. Markers are frequently moved, renumbered, added to, and deleted. Be ready to discover new and different aids to navigation than those that appear on chart 11472, or even in our account below.

The marked entry channel into Manatee Pocket lies southwest of unlighted daybeacon #6. Typical soundings on Manatee Pocket and its marked entry cut are 6 feet or better though a 5½-foot reading will sometimes make an appearance. Some 5-foot depths on the most upstream portion of the pocket could spell problems for deep-draft vessels.

The first two marinas on the pocket are located along western banks. You should spot the docks of the northernmost facility immediately after passing a public park and several launching ramps to starboard.

First up is Sailfish Marina of Stuart, near 27 09.685 North/080 11.745 West. This facility is a power-boat-oriented marina that occasionally accepts transients and features fixed metal decked piers with full water and power connections. Depths alongside range from 5½ to 6½ feet. Shoreside, visiting cruisers will find a climate-controlled shower, a Laundromat, and a huge dry-stack storage building. Gasoline and diesel fuel can be purchased dockside. Full mechanical repairs are available, and boats can be hauled via a 35-ton travelift. A fishing and variety store known as Sailfish Bait and Tackle is located on the premises. A long, long walk is necessary to reach a restaurant, or you could dinghy down Manatee Pocket to one of the restaurants at the rear of the cove.

Sailfish Marina of Stuart (772) 283-1122

Approach depths—6 feet
Dockside depths—5½-6½ feet
Accepts transients—occasionally
Transient dockage fee—below average
Fixed metal piers—yes
Dockside power connections—30
    and 50 amps
Dockside water connections—yes
Showers—yes
Laundromat—yes
Gasoline—yes
Diesel fuel—yes
Below-waterline repairs—yes
Mechanical repairs—yes
Fishing and variety store—yes
Restaurant—long walk

The second of the two facilities near the entrance to Manatee Pocket is Mariner's Cay Marina (27 09.503 North/080 11.725 West). This amiable, unusually well-appointed marine firm is associated with an extensive adjacent condo project. The marina features plentiful, well-sheltered dockage at modern, fixed, wooden piers and a shoreside clubhouse. Low-water depths alongside run as thin as 4 feet. Transients are readily accepted for overnight dockage, and both gasoline and diesel fuel are at hand. Several non-climate-controlled showers are available in the adjacent pool-house, and a full Laundromat is located in the adjacent clubhouse. The marina also features waste pump-out capability. A micro ship's store (with little else other than motor oil) doubles as the dockmaster's office on the docks. Visiting transients are welcome to take a cooling break at the complex's swimming pool. While it's still a bit of a walk, Mariner's Cay is a trifle closer (by foot and dinghy) to the restaurants at the rear of the pocket.

Mariner's Cay Marina (772) 287-2900
Approach depths—6 feet
Dockside depths—4-5 feet (minimum)
Accepts transients—yes
Transient dockage rate—average
Fixed wooden piers—yes
Dockside power connections—30
    and 50 amps
Dockside water connections—yes

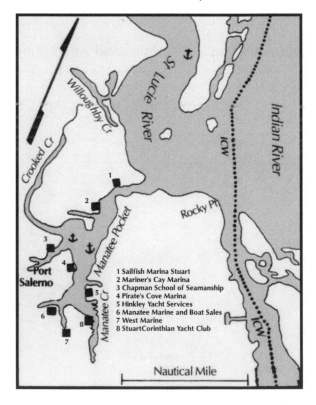

1 Sailfish Marina Stuart
2 Mariner's Cay Marina
3 Chapman School of Seamanship
4 Pirate's Cove Marina
5 Hinkley Yacht Services
6 Manatee Marine and Boat Sales
7 West Marine
8 StuartCorinthian Yacht Club

Nautical Mile

Mariner's Cay Marina, Manatee Pocket

Showers—yes
Laundromat—yes
Waste pump-out—yes
Gasoline—yes
Diesel fuel—yes
Ship's store—yes (small)
Restaurant—long walk

Farther upstream, a large bay indents the western banks of Manatee Pocket. Visiting craft are free to anchor on these waters for 72 hours (near 27 09.239 North/080 11.855 West). Depths run between 5 and 6 feet. There is plenty of swinging room for a 48 footer, with superior shelter from all winds. The surrounding shores are overlooked by heavy but not unsightly residential development. Be sure to show an anchor light to warn away any passing traffic during the night.

Pirate's Cove Resort and Marina guards the westerly banks just south of the cove and anchorage reviewed above, near 27 08.885 North/080 11.751 West. This power-craft-oriented facility continues the pocket's tradition of first-rate services. Transients are readily accepted at the ultramodern, fixed, metal-decked piers. Depths alongside run 5 to 6 feet at most of the docks, with some 4½-foot soundings on the innermost slips. As you would expect, fresh-water connections and 30- and 50-amp power hookups are found at every berth. Good, climate-controlled showers and a Laundromat are just behind the docks, as is an excellent ship's, variety, and tackle store. Waste pump-out service is available at Pirate's Cove as well. Gasoline and diesel can be bought dockside, and full mechanical repairs (both gas and diesel) are also among the marina's offerings. There is even a huge dry-stack storage building for owners of smaller power craft in search of this sort of service.

Now, as if all that were not enough, Pirate's Cove features the Pirate's Loft Restaurant (772-223-5048), a large dining establishment perched over the ship's store with a good view of the docks and Manatee Pocket. We enjoyed our one meal here, and the restaurant seems popular.

Ready for a break from the live-aboard routine? Well, consider the adjacent 50-room motel. We have found the rooms modern, clean, and really quite nice. The on-site swimming pool is also open to transient dockers.

Phew! I'm tired from just listing all of Pirate's Cove's services and amenities. Do yourself a favor and check it out during your next cruise to Manatee Pocket.

Pirate's Cove Resort and Marina
   (772) 287-2354
http://www.piratescoveresortandmarina.com

Approach depths—6 feet
Dockside depths—5-6 feet
   4½ feet (minimum—innermost slips)
Accepts transients—yes
Transient dockage fee—above average
Fixed metal piers—yes
Dockside power connections—30
   and 50 amps
Dockside water connections—yes
Showers—yes
Laundromat—yes

Waste pump-out—yes
Gasoline—yes
Diesel fuel—yes
Mechanical repairs—yes
Ship's, variety, and tackle store—yes
Restaurant—on site

Just opposite Pirate's Cove, Hinkley Yacht Services (formerly David Lowe's Boatyard, 772-287-0923) guards the pocket's eastern shores near 27 08.928 North/080 11.614 West. Besides servicing some of the finest sailing yachts on earth, this huge yard has remained a full-service

Pirate's Cove Resort and Marina, Manatee Pocket

facility for repairs to both sail and powercraft. Full mechanical repairs for both gasoline and diesel power plants are in the offing. Below-waterline repairs and haul-outs are accomplished by one of three travelifts, rated at 50, 88, and 150 tons respectively. Complete marine carpentry, electrical, and electronic repairs are also in the offing. There is even dry-stack storage for 150 smaller vessels. To be succinct, this is one of the finest and most impressive yards in all of eastern Florida. All the available services and associated equipment can only be described as "state of the art" in all respects. Hinkley's mammoth work barn dominates the shoreline, giving you some idea of just how serious they are about handling the largest pleasure craft that come along. This is obviously a highly successful yard that remembers how it got that way!

Though you would be hard pressed to tell it from the chart, Manatee Pocket divides into three arms on its southernmost reaches. This can be a real source of confusion for first timers. Manatee Marina and Boat Sales lines the banks between Manatee Pocket's westernmost and central-southern arm, near 27 08.746 North/080 11.755 West. This facility is largely oriented to sales and dry-stack storage of smaller power craft, but there are several services offered that are of interest to cruising craft as well. Low-water dockside depths of only 3½ to 4 feet will limit this facility's accessibility to many larger vessels.

Manatee Marina does maintain a few wet slips fronting the pocket. These berths consist of small, wooden finger piers stretching out from a concrete seawall. Transients are accepted here if space is available, but this practice is clearly more an exception than the rule. Full power, water, telephone, and cable-television connections are provided. Mechanical repairs for gasoline engines are available, and the staff will

contact independent diesel mechanics for you. Gasoline and diesel fuel are for sale at a fuel dock directly behind Shrimper's Grill and Raw Bar (772-220-3287). This dining spot is located on the grounds, and can be accessed not only from Manatee Marina, but by dinghy as well (though it is a long dinghy ride from the anchorage described above). Shrimper's seems to have gotten it right. The seafood, particularly of the fried variety, is quite good.

Manatee Marina and Boat Sales
   (772) 283-6714

Approach depths—5 feet
Dockside depths—3½-4 feet (minimum)
Accepts transients—very limited
   (when space is available)
Transient dockage rate—above average
Fixed wooden piers—yes
Dockside power connections—30
   and 50 amps
Dockside water connections—yes
Gasoline—yes
Diesel fuel—yes
Mechanical repairs—yes (gasoline only;
   independent contractors for diesel)
Restaurant—on site

Cruisers in need of anything nautical will be most happy to learn that a West Marine store (4545 SE Dixie Highway, 772-223-1515) guards the rear of Manatee Pocket. The center fronts Old Dixie Highway and is within an easy walk of Manatee Marina (or a longer walk or short taxi ride from any of the other Manatee Pocket facilities). Be sure to tell them we sent you.

Finally, the docks of the Stuart Corinthian Yacht Club flank the easternmost arm's western banks near 27 08.807 North/080 11.538 West. This writer has had the rare pleasure of addressing this group on three occasions during the past several years. It was standing room only, with several hundred cruisers in attendance at all these events.

The yacht club has three slips open for visitors. Preferences are first given to local members, then to members of other yacht clubs with appropriate reciprocal privileges. Berths are at modern, fixed, wooden piers with freshwater, 30- and 50-amp power, telephone, and cable-television connections. Approach depths run around 5 feet at low water, with soundings of 5 to 5½ feet dockside. Showers are located in the clubhouse. The club bar manager doubles as a dockmaster. He is on duty Tuesday through Saturday from 10:00 A.M. to 6:00 P.M. Advance arrangements are recommended by this writer.

The club does not maintain a regular dining room, but the bar is open until 6:00 P.M. It's a fairly short walk to Shrimper's Grill and Raw Bar (described above) and West Marine

**Stuart Corinthian Yacht Club
(772) 221-1900
http://www.stucoryc.com**

**Approach depths—5 feet (minimum)
Dockside depths—5-5½ feet
Accepts transients—members of other
 yacht clubs with appropriate
 reciprocal arrangements
Fixed wooden piers—yes
Dockside power connections—30
 and 50 amps
Dockside water connections—yes
Showers—yes
Restaurant—nearby**

Other Stuart Facilities

Many additional marina facilities are available on the St. Lucie River west of Manatee

Stuart Corinthian Yacht Club

Pocket. These will be covered in the next chapter, which details the Okeechobee Waterway.

St. Lucie Inlet

St. Lucie Inlet, lying east of unlighted daybeacon #239, is a capricious cut that is subject to shoaling. This cut is dredged often, but it seems that the mud and sand wash in as fast as the Army Corps can pump it out. If you should attempt this passage, be sure to check at one of the Manatee Pocket marinas about the latest channel conditions and markings. Better yet, watch for a local craft putting out to sea and follow in her wake.

VERO BEACH TO STUART NAVIGATION

Successful navigation of the ICW from Vero Beach to Stuart is straightforward. Stick to the channel's midwidth and don't be lured outside of the Waterway except for well-documented side trips. Tidal currents do pick up markedly near Fort Pierce and St. Lucie inlets. Be on guard against excessive leeway in these areas. Otherwise, the information presented in this account and on chart 11472 should be more than adequate for any captain with a working knowledge of coastal navigation.

On the Waterway South of flashing daybeacon #146 and unlighted daybeacon #147, the ICW channel passes under the 17th Street, fixed, high-rise bridge with 65 feet of vertical clearance.

It is a run of just better than 10 nautical miles from Vero Beach to Fort Pierce. The ICW channel is fairly narrow along this stretch, and depths outside of the dredged passage are more than suspect. Stick to the marked channel and leave your gunkholing for later.

Several charted channels lead off the ICW track between Vero and Fort Pierce. All of these cuts serve private docks, and only one should be entered by visitors.

The charted channel east and a bit south of unlighted daybeacon #160 allows access to Spyglass Harbour and makes a great side trip for those with some extra time on their hands. Simply keep all red markers to your starboard side and take all green beacons to port when entering. At unlighted daybeacon #14, the channel curves sharply to the south. Come abeam of #14 to starboard and then swing slowly around to the south, pointing to come abeam of unlighted daybeacon #18, also to starboard. Don't try to cut the gap between unlighted daybeacons #12 and #18. Cruisers using this false path will find themselves in 3- to 4-foot water.

ICW to Fort Pierce South of unlighted daybeacon #180, be sure to use the Fort Pierce inset (Inset #1) on chart 11472 for navigation of the surrounding waters. Its greater detail makes life a lot easier,

The marked channel cutting west to Riverside Marina comes up a short hop south of unlighted daybeacon #180. Enter between the marina sign and a slow-speed manatee sign. The subsequent aids to navigation are indifferently maintained, but you can still recognize the green and red markers. The north side of this channel is protected by the charted spoil island. Obviously, you should stay in the marked cut and guard against any lateral movement to the north (particularly). Eventually the marina's docks will be sighted dead ahead.

South-southeast of flashing daybeacon #182, the Waterway passes through the North Fort Pierce bascule bridge with 25 feet of closed vertical clearance. Sailcraft skippers will be glad to know that this span opens on demand. Just north of this bridge, visiting cruisers have the opportunity to visit one of the few anchorages afforded by Fort Pierce waters.

Cook Point Anchorage   Break off from the ICW some 50 yards north of the 25-foot bascule bridge, and set course to pass between the westernmost aids to navigation on the Cook Point channel, unlighted daybeacons #20 and #21. Slow to idle speed. This entire channel is an official no-wake zone.

Soon you will pass several launching ramps and a small park to starboard. Continue tracking your way up the channel, passing all red markers to your port side and taking green beacons to starboard. After leaving unlighted daybeacon #14 in your wake, watch the starboard banks for a low-level fixed bridge. Continue cruising northeast on the same channel, past the bridge, by favoring the southeasterly banks. Drop the hook soon after leaving the low-level bridge behind. Farther to the northeast, depths are more suspect and some unmarked shoals are encountered. Set your hook so as to swing well away from the correctly charted shallows to the north and northwest. Be sure to show a bright anchor light.

On the Waterway   South of the 25-foot bascule bridge, set course to come abeam of unlighted daybeacon #184 to its fairly immediate easterly side. Guard against lateral slippage to the east and northeast between the bascule bridge and #184. Chart 11472 correctly identifies 3-foot waters abutting this side of the channel.

No-wake regulations are in effect from the 25-foot bascule to a point well south of the Fort Pierce City Marina channel. Don't look at me, folks—we didn't formulate the rules.

Currents pick up as you approach Fort Pierce Inlet. Be sure to watch your stern as well as your forward course to quickly note any slippage.

Taylor Creek   Fortunate cruisers making for the many facilities on Taylor Creek should follow the channel cutting west, immediately south of unlighted daybeacon #184. Two pairs of unlighted daybeacons lead you into the creek's broad mouth. Pass between both pairs of markers. Soon the extensive docks of Harbortown Marina will come abeam to starboard, followed closely by Cracker Boy Boat Works and Taylor Creek Marina to port.

Fort Pierce Inlet   The substantial Fort Pierce Inlet channel flows into the ICW's east-northeasterly flank south-southeast of flashing buoy #187. Stay on the Waterway channel until the inlet's midwidth comes abeam directly to the east-northeast. Then turn hard to the east-northeast and point to pass between flashing daybeacons #16 and #17. Continue following the well-marked channel out to sea. As you would expect, pass all red markers to your port side and take all green beacons to starboard.

Since the last edition of this guide appeared, many of the aids to navigation in Fort Pierce Inlet have been lighted, and all have had their numbers changed a bit. Be sure to use the latest edition of chart 11472 when navigating these waters.

Most of the inlet channel between its intersection with the ICW and its jettied passage out into the open sea is an idle-speed, manatee zone. Slow down and enjoy the sights along the way.

East-northeast of flashing buoy #13, the deep cove that is home to Pelican Yacht Club will come abeam to the south. The club's docks line the eastern shores of the cove. Cruise into the piers at idle speed.

Twin jetties flank Fort Pierce Inlet's passage out into the briny blue. These fortunate structures make running the inlet as painless as possible. Nevertheless, when wind and tide oppose each other, a formidable chop can develop at the jettied entrance. Batten down the hatches and proceed with caution if you arrive during one of these unfortunate periods.

Alternate Channel   The marked and charted channel leading north-northwest from the Fort Pierce Inlet approach channel, between flashing buoys #12 and #11, should probably be avoided by all but small power craft. The cut is eventually blocked by a low-level fixed bridge, and there is not really enough room to anchor anywhere along the way.

On the Waterway   South of the inlet intersection, the ICW meets up with the South Fort Pierce high-rise bridge. The span has a vertical clearance of 65 feet and poses no

clearance problems. However, tidal currents boil around this bridge. Skippers of slow-moving boats must take great care lest they be pushed into the fenders or pilings. Stay alert and be ready for quick course corrections.

Fort Pierce City Marina Channel   The Fort Pierce City Marina channel strikes northwest from a position some .35 of a nautical mile south-southeast of unlighted daybeacon #188. Southbound mariners should continue cruising on the Waterway channel until the midwidth of the cut is off the stern quarter. Then, curl around quickly to starboard and enter the centerline of the channel.

The channel is well marked with pairs of unlighted daybeacons. While everyone should watch for leeway courtesy of the swift tidal currents that regularly plague these waters, running this channel is a delight compared to the old entrance, which used to run just south of the South Fort Pierce Bridge many years ago.

As you would expect, pass all red markers to your starboard side and take green beacons to port. Once abeam of unlighted daybeacon #8, continue on course to come abeam of unlighted daybeacon #9. At #9, the entrance to the outer harbor is obvious.

Faber Cove Anchorages   To access either of the anchorages on the Faber Cove channel, depart the Waterway channel some 35 yards north-northwest of unlighted daybeacon #188. Set course to pass between unlighted daybeacons #2 and #3. Do not approach #2; it is grounded in shoal water.

The next charted aid to navigation, unlighted daybeacon #4, was absent during our last on-site research. Perhaps it will be replaced by the time of your arrival, perhaps not. Use your binoculars to help pick out unlighted daybeacon #5, marking the channel's northerly edge, considerably farther to the east-northeast.

Between #7 and unlighted daybeacon #9, you may ease south-southeast of the main channel for some 100 yards in good depths. In fair weather, this is an acceptable anchorage.

The remainder of the run into Faber Cove is fairly straightforward as far as unlighted daybeacon #12A. The upstream section of the channel between the next two aids, unlighted daybeacons #13 and #14, has shoaled. Slow to idle speed and start a steady watch on the sounder.

Come abeam of #13 to your immediate port and carefully set course to bring #14 abeam by some 15 yards to your starboard. Favor the port side of the channel between #13 and #14. The shallower water is to the south. Once abeam of #14 you can breathe a sigh of relief and continue into the mid-width of the cove's entrance dead ahead.

On the Waterway South of Fort Pierce, the ICW tracks its way through a rather lonely stretch of Indian River on its way to the St. Lucie River and Inlet. Depths rise quickly for the most part outside of the Waterway channel. This is not the place to explore off the beaten path—stick to the marked cut.

Open Anchorage In light airs only, you might anchor east of unlighted daybeacon #195. Leave the Waterway abeam of #195. Track your way to the east for some 100 yards, well away from any passing ICW traffic, and set the hook. Be sure to avoid the correctly charted shoal water to the east, northeast, and southeast. This writer would suggest breaking out your brightest anchor light.

On the ICW Between flashing daybeacon #202 and unlighted daybeacon #205, the large Herman Bay Nuclear Plant channel cuts off to the east into Big Mud Creek. Entry into the charted channel is not recommended for pleasure craft.

Don't mistake this errant cut's outermost aid to navigation, unlighted daybeacon #1, for a Waterway Marker. Ignore #1 and continue on course to come abeam and pass unlighted daybeacon #205 by some 25 yards to its west-southwesterly side.

Jensen Beach Bridge and Associated Anchorages The Jensen Beach bridge crosses the Waterway south of unlighted daybeacon #219. This span has a closed vertical clearance of 24 feet, and follows restricted opening hours. From December 1 to May 1, the span opens only on the hour and half-hour between 7:00 A.M. and 6:00 P.M. weekdays. On weekends and at all other times of the day and year, the bridge opens on demand.

Captains arriving during the restricted period should be aware of strong tidal currents that regularly sweep the ICW north and south of the bridge. Leave yourself plenty of maneuvering room and stay well back from the span until it is completely open.

Remember that depths on the anchorage north of the Jensen Beach Bridge, west of the ICW, have shoaled to 5-foot levels. If you can stand these soundings, depart the

Waterway at least 300 yards north of the bridge. Use your binoculars to pick out a long pier making out from the causeway to the south. For best depths, stay at least 300 yards north of this pier. Closer to the old dock, soundings rise to 4- and 4½-foot levels. Drop anchor shortly after coming under the protection of the causeway to the south.

To make good your entry into the anchorage south of the bridge (west of the ICW), the trick is again to stay at least 300 yards south the causeway's shores. By following this procedure, good water continues on for at least several hundred yards to the west-southwest. You will most likely spy a host of anchored craft in this haven. Pick out a spot with enough room for your vessel and settle down for the evening.

Immediately south of the Jensen Beach bascule bridge, passing cruisers may spy the charted channel striking east. This petite cut leads to a small park and launching ramp. Larger vessels should keep clear.

On the ICW Immediately south of unlighted daybeacon #222, the channel to AA Marine runs off to the west-southwest. The cut is outlined by small, unlighted daybeacons.

Similarly, the channel to Outrigger Harbour marina will come up to the west-southwest between flashing daybeacon #223 and unlighted daybeacon #224. This passage is outlined by plenty of daybeacons. Eventually, the entrance canal will come up dead ahead. As you enter, the Dolphin Bar and Shrimp House will be passed to port. Continue on—soon the fuel dock will come abeam, also to port.

South-southeast of unlighted daybeacon #226, southbound cruisers will come upon the Ernest Lyons/Highway A1A Bridge, with a closed vertical clearance of 28 feet. Mariners must contend with a restricted opening schedule for this span. From December 1 to May 1, the bridge opens only on the hour and half-hour between 7:00 A.M. and 6:00 P.M. weekdays. On weekends and at all other times of the day and year, it opens on demand.

The well-marked channel to Hutchinson Island Marriott Marina strikes east-northeast a short hop south of the Ernest Lyons bridge. It doesn't get much easier than this. Simply pass between the various markers. The fuel pier and dockmaster's office are located on the outermost dock.

Approaching the St. Lucie River and Inlet
The Waterway channel between the Ernest Lyons bridge and St. Lucie Inlet has chronic shoaling problems and potentially strong tidal currents. Slow down, stay scrupulously to the channel's midwidth, and keep an eagle eye on the sounder. Be prepared to discover new and different markers from those shown on your chart or outlined in the account below. The nearby sands are in flux, and this changeable nature frequently calls for a rearrangement of navigational aids.

South of unlighted daybeacon #230, switch to the St. Lucie River-ICW inset on chart 11472.

From a position abeam of #230, set course to pass between unlighted daybeacon #232 and flashing daybeacon #231. Look west as you come abeam of #232 for a view of a magnificent house overlooking the adjacent shoreline. Continue on the same heading, pointing for the gap between unlighted daybeacon #234 and flashing daybeacon #233.

We have often seen local boats anchored off the western shores of the small island east of flashing daybeacon #233. Obviously they know something we don't. We have tried repeatedly to enter this anchorage from several different angles, only to hit 4-foot depths on each occasion. Visiting cruisers lacking definite local knowledge would do best to bypass this anchorage.

After you pass between #233 and #234, the same track will lead you past unlighted daybeacons #235 and #237 to their westerly sides. Don't ease to the east between #235 and #237. Shoal water lines the ICWs easterly flank along this stretch.

At #237, the channel turns a bit to the south-southeast. Adjust your course and point to pass unlighted daybeacon #238 to its fairly immediate easterly side. The channel now makes a straight run to the intersection with both the St. Lucie River and its like-named inlet.

The small marked and charted channel leading west, west of #237, serves several private homes on nearby Seawall Point. Visiting cruisers are advised to keep clear.

Troubled Waters   The juncture of the ICW, St. Lucie River, and St. Lucie Inlet can be more than mildly confusing. In fact, it is one of the most navigationally difficult sections of the entire eastern Florida ICW. Skippers southbound on the Waterway often mistake the westernmost aid to navigation on the St. Lucie Inlet channel, unlighted daybeacon #17, and/or the easternmost marker on the St. Lucie River-Okeechobee Waterway, flashing buoy #2, for aids to navigation

denoting the Waterway channel. This is one place where it is almost mandatory to have your binoculars close at hand to sort out all the markers.

Let's stop right here for a moment to yet again note the changeability of these waters. The account below is based on our last visit to this important crossroads, but there is no guarantee that the channel and its markers won't have changed by the time you put in an appearance. Be ready for anything!

From a position west-southwest of unlighted daybeacon #239, point to come abeam of flashing daybeacon #240 to its easterly side. Just south of #240, the combined track of the St. Lucie River and the Okeechobee Waterway cuts to the west, while the St. Lucie Inlet strikes off to the east, and just to be contrary, the ICW continues on to the south-southeast.

One (of many) possible source of navigational confusion on these waters is the presence of two markers that are both labeled as #2. One of the two easternmost aids to navigation on the St. Lucie River-Okeechobee Waterway passage is a flashing buoy #2, while the first ICW marker south of flashing daybeacon #240 is an unlighted daybeacon #2. Obviously, the Waterway marker's numbering system begins anew between #240 and unlighted daybeacon #2. Don't let the presence of these two #2s throw you. Study the St. Lucie inset on chart 11472 carefully, and all this will become clear—well, how about, clearer?

From #240, cruisers continuing south on the Atlantic ICW should point to pass the Waterway's unlighted daybeacon #2 by some 25 yards to its easterly quarter. Soon the south-southeasterly running ICW track enters a far more sheltered passage, and eventually, you will pass between flashing daybeacon #4 and unlighted daybeacon #3A. South #4 and #3A, the Waterway once again resumes its straightforward path to the south. Continued coverage of the ICW is presented in chapter 8.

St. Lucie Inlet The St. Lucie Inlet is one of the most frequently dredged seaward channels on Florida's eastern coastline. Nevertheless, if past experience is any guide, this cut may well be shoaling anew as you attempt to pass through. Our best advice is to check at one of the local marinas about the latest inlet channel conditions, or, better yet, find a local craft putting out to sea and follow in his path. Good luck!

St. Lucie River to Manatee Pocket As noted repeatedly above, cruisers tracking their way up the St. Lucie River and the easterly genesis of the Okeechobee Waterway must contend with a very unstable bottom strata. Watch out for new and uncharted aids to navigation, and follow them faithfully.

Navigators bound west on the St. Lucie River and the Okeechobee Waterway should keep red, even-numbered aids to navigation to their (the cruisers') starboard side, and take green markers to port. Depart the Waterway's north-to-south track some .06 nautical miles south-southeast of flashing daybeacon #240. Turn west and point for the gap between flashing buoy #2 and unlighted can buoy #3. Ignore the Waterway's unlighted daybeacon #2, which will be passed south of your course.

Once the gap between flashing buoy #2 and unlighted can buoy #3 is in your wake, point to pass between the next pair of markers, unlighted nun buoy #4 and unlighted can buoy #3A. Continue on more or less the same course, pointing to come abeam of unlighted daybeacon #5 to its northern side.

West of unlighted daybeacon #5, shift your course just a hair farther to the south, and point to come abeam of unlighted daybeacon #6 and unlighted nun buoy #6A by at least 25 yards to their southerly sides. Nun buoy #6A has apparently been placed to warn against a new encroachment of shoal water on the northern side of the St. Lucie River-Okeechobee channel. Be *sure* to stay well south of #6 and #6A.

Once abeam of #6 and #6A, watch to the southwest for Manatee Pocket's outermost aids to navigation, unlighted daybeacons #1 and #2. As soon as the gap between these aids comes abeam, cut sharply to the southwest and pass between #1 and #2 as you make good your entry into the pocket.

From #1 and #2, point for the gap between unlighted daybeacons #3 and #4. After leaving these aids behind, simply stick to the pocket's centerline for best depths.

All the Manatee Pocket waters are an official idle-speed, no-wake zone. Be sure to proceed strictly at idle speed. The Florida Marine Patrol is ever vigilant on these waters.

Soon the first marina will come abeam to the west. Refer to this chapter's description of Manatee Pocket's facilities for locations of the pocket's other marinas and yards.

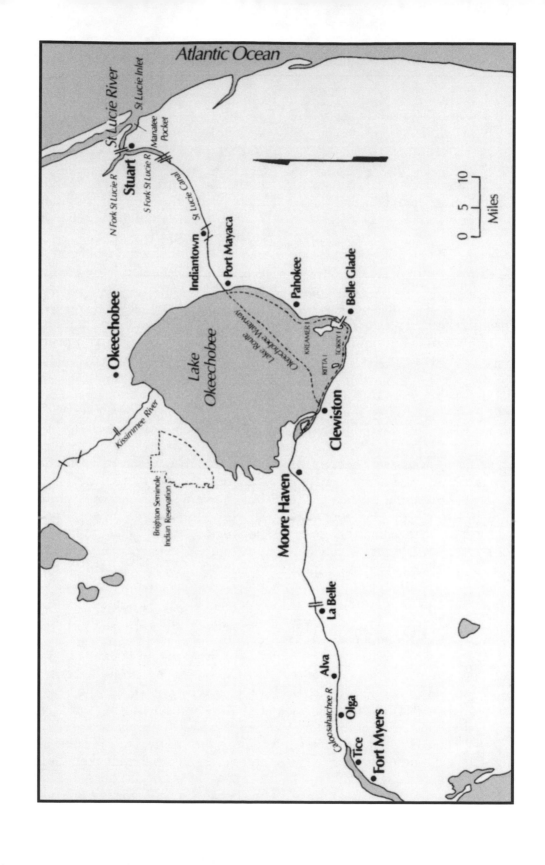

The Okeechobee Waterway

The trans-Florida Okeechobee Waterway brings an entirely new face to eastern Florida's diverse waters. The passage provides quick and reliable access to the state's Gulf Coast, but beyond this practical consideration, it affords visitors the opportunity to experience the "other Florida." It is difficult to comprehend the radical change in character between the east coast and the central section of the Sunshine State that is traversed by the Okeechobee Waterway. Gone are the pleasant, well-populated resorts to the north and noticeably absent is the dense development of the "Gold Coast" to the south. Cruisers wending their way along this trans-Florida waterway will experience a land that is only sparsely developed. The surrounding countryside is incredibly flat, and there is usually little to break the line of sight save the hundreds and hundreds of cows that graze these open ranges. Another familiar sight in this region is fields of waving sugarcane, which stretch to the horizon and then seemingly fall off the earth. Small towns along the way exhibit a definite "cowboy" atmosphere, and they seem as far removed from the likes of Miami and Fort Lauderdale as Florida is from Antarctica. In short, those who enjoy a voyage off the beaten path will find the Okeechobee Waterway one of the most fascinating cruising experiences in all of Florida, perhaps the entire eastern seaboard.

The Okeechobee Waterway breaks off from its sister, the Atlantic ICW, near the city of Stuart and tracks west for some 115 nautical miles to Fort Myers. Initially, the route follows the St. Lucie River to a man-made waterway entered by a tall lock. This canal leads in turn to the budding village of Indiantown and eventually to Port Mayaca, where, after passing through one more lock, cruisers will encounter Lake Okeechobee itself.

Look at any map of Florida and you will quickly spy the immense eye of Lake Okeechobee seemingly looking skyward in the south-central section of the state. It's hard to describe Lake Okeechobee to those who have never visited it. To say the lake is big is truly an understatement: it is the second largest natural fresh-water lake in America. Mariners cruising Okeechobee's midwidth could be readily excused for thinking they are at sea. Perhaps those who have cruised North Carolina's Pamlico Sound or the northern Great Lakes will have some idea of this vast lake's size. First-time visitors should be prepared for a shock when they cruise through the Port Mayaca Lock and catch their initial sight of this incredible body of water.

Two alternate routes cross the great lake and lead mariners to the charming community of Clewiston. Just to the north, cruising craft will enter another canal and lock at Moore Haven. Eventually this track flows through a fourth lock and past the small town of La Belle. A final lock provides access to the waters of Caloosahatchee River. Eventually, this river brings passing cruisers to the attractive, well-developed city of Fort Myers. From this point, Florida's Gulf Coast is only a short cruise away.

The Okeechobee Waterway is well marked and, with the possible exception of the lake crossing, easily run by craft of almost any size. When heading west, pass red markers to your starboard side and take green beacons to port.

High artificial dikes shelter much of the track from high winds. Unfortunately, they also block many fascinating views of the surrounding countryside. Project depth for the Okeechobee Waterway is 8 feet and the *minimum overhead clearance of 49 feet is set by the railroad bridge at Port Mayaca*. Sailcraft that cannot clear this troublesome span must journey south to Marathon in the Florida Keys to make good their crossing into western Florida waters. Of course, if your mast is just a bit taller than 49 feet, you may well be able to use the "Okeechobee Limbo" to pass under the Port Mayaca bridge. Check out our account of this novel procedure below.

Some depth readings down to 6 feet are found on the Lake Okeechobee rim route. Occasionally, long-term drought conditions can lower soundings below these levels. All five locks on the waterway open on demand for pleasure craft from 6:00 A.M. to 9:30 P.M. Bridges on the Waterway west of Stuart tend to open on demand during the same time period. Nighttime bridge openings on the Okeechobee require advance warnings and are a rare event. Since passage of the Okeechobee passage is not recommended after dark, these hours are more than adequate.

Occasionally, the Okeechobee Waterway locks are temporarily closed because of repairs (particularly during the summer months) or drought conditions. Be sure to check with the lockmaster as you pass through the first lock to learn whether the entire passage is open. Better still, give the Corps of Engineers in Clewiston a call at (863) 983-8101 before beginning your cruise. This simple precaution could save you interminable delays on some lonely waters. Other lock telephone numbers to know:

St. Lucie Lock—772-287-2665
Port Mayaca Lock—561-924-2858
Moore Haven Lock—863-946-0414
Ortona Lock—863-675-0616
W. P. Franklin Lock—239-694-5451

A special concern to cruisers running the Okeechobee Waterway locks is Florida's gentle giants, more commonly known as manatees. These ugly but somehow lovable creatures often use the Waterway as a means of travel. Sometimes manatees will "lock through" with several boats. If you happen to spot a manatee in a lock, or while waiting for a lock opening, please proceed with the greatest care.

Facilities along the Okeechobee Waterway are fairly numerous though widely spaced. Some of the marinas are small, low-key establishments, but most are more than happy to accommodate transients. During the winter cruising season, available slips often fill up early. Wise cruisers will call ahead and make overnight reservations rather than risk finding no room at the inn upon their arrival.

Anchorages are relatively few, particularly east of Lake Okeechobee. Even those captains who regularly anchor off may find it advisable to berth at one of the regional facilities rather than risk dropping the hook near the primary channel.

Perhaps because of their relative isolation, the lands about Lake Okeechobee have spawned what is probably the greatest body of folklore in the state. The rugged individualism and lean but generous character of those who have lived about the lake are sure to strike a chord with all those who admire the American spirit of times gone by.

Charts   Surprisingly enough, only one NOAA chart is needed for complete navigation of the Okeechobee Waterway from its intersection with the ICW to Fort Myers:

11428—covers the entire passage from the St. Lucie River to Fort Myers, including Lake Okeechobee and the lower section of Kissimmee River

Bridges

St. Lucie/Steele Point Bridge—crosses Okeechobee Waterway and St. Lucie River northwest of flashing daybeacon #19—Bascule—21 feet (closed)—December 1 to May 1, opens only on the hour and half-hour 7:00 A.M. to 6:00 P.M. weekdays; during weekends and federal holidays, opens on the hour, 20 minutes past, and 40 minutes past from 8:00 A.M. to 6:00 P.M.; at all other times of the day and year, opens on demand

New Roosevelt Bridge—crosses Okeechobee Waterway and St. Lucie River southwest of flashing daybeacon #23—Fixed—65 feet

Britt Point Railway Bridge—crosses Okeechobee Waterway and St. Lucie River southwest of flashing daybeacon #23—Bascule—7 feet (closed)—usually open but closes automatically as much as 30 minutes ahead of time when a train is due (a loud horn and flashing red lights warn of an imminent closing, and eastbound cruisers should also know that the highway bridges will not open when the railway span is closed)

Old Roosevelt Twin Bridges—cross Okeechobee Waterway and St. Lucie River southwest of flashing daybeacon #23—Bascule—14 feet (closed)—open on demand

Palm City Bridge—crosses Okeechobee Waterway and South Fork of St. Lucie River south of unlighted daybeacon #30—Fixed—54 feet

I-95 Twin Bridges—cross Okeechobee Waterway southwest of unlighted daybeacon #43—Fixed—56 feet

Thomas B. Manual/Florida Turnpike Bridge—crosses Okeechobee Waterway southwest of unlighted daybeacon #46—Fixed—55 feet

SSR 76A Bridge—crosses Okeechobee Waterway some 1.9 nautical miles southwest of St. Lucie Lock's western entrance—Fixed—56 feet

Indiantown/Highway 710 Bridge—crosses Okeechobee Waterway some .4 nautical miles west of charted "Micro-Tower" on Waterway's southern banks—Fixed—55 feet

Indiantown Railway Bridge—crosses Okeechobee Waterway .4 nautical miles west of charted "Micro-Tower" on Waterway's southern banks—7 feet (closed)—usually open 6:00 A.M. to 9:00 P.M., unless a train is due—sometimes long waits when a train is scheduled but these are rare—often closed during the evening and nighttime hours

Port Mayaca Railway Lift Bridge—crosses Okeechobee Waterway near the tiny (charted) village of Port Mayaca—Lift bridge—7 feet (closed)—49 feet when fully open—usually open unless a train is due (flashing green light means it's OK to proceed; flashing red light warns of an imminent closing)

Port Mayaca/Highway 98 Bridge—crosses Okeechobee Waterway a short distance east of the Port Mayaca Lock—Fixed—55 feet

Torry/Kreamer Island Bridge—crosses Okeechobee Waterway's Rim Route at Torry Island—Swing bridge—11 feet (closed)—opens on demand 7:00 A.M. to 6:00 P.M. Monday through Thursday and 7:00 A.M. to 7:00 P.M. Friday, Saturday, and Sunday;

closed during the nighttime hours—be warned that it is hand operated and opening can take 15 minutes

Moore Haven Railway Bridge—crosses Okeechobee Waterway south of the Moore Haven lock—Swing bridge—5 feet (closed)—usually open, but should you find it closed, be warned that it is hand operated and opening can be a slow process—be sure to use the easterly pass through

Moore Haven/Highway 27 Bridge—crosses Okeechobee Waterway south of the Moore Haven lock—Bascule—23 feet (closed)—opens on demand except 10:00 P.M. to 6:00 A.M.; during these late-night and early-morning hours, opens only with three hours' notice

La Belle/Highway 29 Bridge—crosses Okeechobee Waterway in the heart of La Belle—Bascule—28 feet (closed)—opens on demand except 10:00 P.M. to 6:00 A.M.; during these late-night and early-morning hours, opens only with three hours' notice

Denaud/SSR 78AW Bridge—crosses Okeechobee Waterway at charted position of Denaud—Swing bridge—9 feet (closed)—opens on demand except 10:00 P.M. to 6:00 A.M.; during these late-night and early-morning hours, opens only with three hours' notice—passing craft are directed by a sign to one of the bridge's pass throughs or another, depending on their direction; westbound vessels should take the northern leg while east-bound boats are directed to the southern pass through

Alva/Broadway Bridge—crosses Okeechobee Waterway at charted position of Alva—Bascule—23 feet (closed)—opens on demand except 10:00 P.M. to 6:00 A.M.; during these late-night and early-morning hours, opens only with three hours' notice

Fort Myers Shores/Highway 31 Bridges—cross Okeechobee Waterway west of unlighted day-beacon #6—Bascule—27 feet (closed)—open on demand except 10:00 P.M. to 6:00 A.M.; during these late-night and early-morning hours, open only with three hours' notice

Interstate 75 Twin Bridges—cross Okeechobee Waterway and Caloosahatchee River west of unlighted daybeacon #15—Fixed—55 feet

SCL Railway Bridge—crosses Okeechobee Waterway and Caloosahatchee River west of unlighted daybeacon #18—Lift bridge with overhang—5 feet (closed)—55 feet when fully open—usually open unless a train is due

Highway 41 Bypass/Thomas Edison Twin Bridges—cross Okeechobee Waterway and Caloosahatchee River southwest of unlighted daybeacon #40—Fixed—55 feet—the two bridges form a Y pattern with the wider gap falling on the southeastern shore and the closed end of the Y on the northwestern banks

Highway 41 Business Bridge—crosses Okeechobee Waterway and Caloosahatchee River southwest of the Fort Myers Yacht Basin—Fixed—55 feet

Chapter 7 Anchorage Summary (Note that anchorages are listed in geographic order, moving east to west.)

Hell Gate Anchorage—(OWW Standard Mile 2)—located near 27 10.676 North/080 11.504 West, east-southeast of flashing daybeacon #15 at Hell Gate Point—6-foot depths—reviewed on pages 346, 359

Hoggs Cove Anchorage—(OWW Standard Mile 4.5)—27 12.998 North/080 12.835 West, northeast of flashing daybeacon #21—6-foot depths—reviewed on pages 346, 360

City of Stuart Mooring Field—(OWW Standard Mile 8)—located near 27 11.997 North/080 15.602 West, off the eastern banks of the South Fork of St. Lucie River, south of the old Roosevelt twin bascule bridges—8-foot depths—reviewed on pages 352-53, 363

St. Lucie Canal Anchorage—(OWW Standard Mile 11.5)—located near 27 08.905 North/080 15.555 West, southeast of unlighted daybeacon #37—7-foot depths—reviewed on pages 353-54, 363

Upper South Fork Anchorage—(OWW Standard Mile 13)—located near 27 07.786 North/080 15.891 West, south of unlighted daybeacon #40—6-foot depths—reviewed on pages 354, 363

Moore Haven Anchorage—(OWW Standard Mile 77.5)—located near 26 50.672 North/081 05.310 West, northwest of the northeasterly approach to the Moore Haven Lock—8-foot depths—reviewed on pages 376-77, 380

South Shore Anchorage—(OWW Standard Mile 120)—located near 26 43.049 North/081 39.780 West, on the charted loop making into the Waterway's southern shore immediately east of charted Hickey Creek—6-foot depths—reviewed on pages 387-88, 400

North Shore Anchorage—(OWW Standard Mile 120.5)—located near 26 43.156 North/081 40.338 West, on the small, charted loop making into the northern banks, a stone's throw to the west of Hickey Creek—6-foot depths—reviewed on pages 388

Triple Loop Anchorages—(OWW Standard Mile 121)—located on several of the charted loops flanking the northern side of the Caloosahatchee River/Okeechobee Waterway, east and west of the W. P. Franklin lock—various lats/lons (see detailed account)—minimum 5-foot depths—reviewed on pages 388-89, 400

Daybeacon Anchorage—(OWW Standard Mile 122)—located near 26 43.555 North/081 42.564 West, west of unlighted daybeacon #2, on the northern side of the Caloosahatchee River/Okeechobee Waterway—5-foot depths—reviewed on pages 389, 401

Olga Loop Anchorage—(OWW Standard Mile 123.5)—located near 26 43.317 North/081 43.012 West, on the charted loop just northwest of the designation "Olga" on chart 11428—6-foot depths—reviewed on pages 389, 401

Southern Shore Anchorage II—(OWW Standard Mile 124)—located near 26 43.117 North/081 43.800 West, along the southern banks of the Caloosahatchee River/Okeechobee Waterway, just west of Jack's Marine—6-foot depths—reviewed on pages 390, 401

Lofton Island Mooring Field and Anchorage—(OWW Standard Mile 135)—located near 26 39.118 North/081 52.412 West, northwest of Lofton Island, opposite Fort Myers Yacht Basin—7-foot depths—reviewed on pages 393-94, 403

Chapter 7 Marina and Yacht-Club Summary (Note that marinas and yacht clubs are listed in geographic order, moving east to west.)

Pelican's Nest Marina—(772) 334-0890—(OWW Standard Mile 6)—located near 27 13.014 North/080 14.181 West, along the St. Lucie River's northern shore, east of flashing daybeacon #22—transient dockage available—5-foot minimum depths—reviewed on pages 346-47, 360

Northside Marina—(772) 692-4000—(OWW Standard Mile 6.5)—located near 27 12.799 North/080 15.377 West, along the St. Lucie's northerly banks, northwest of unlighted daybeacon #22A—transient dockage available—gasoline and diesel fuel available——6-foot minimum depths—reviewed on pages 347-49, 362

American Custom Yachts—(772) 286-2835—(OWW Standard Mile 14)—27 07.093 North/080 16.310 West, near unlighted daybeacon #46—limited transient dockage available—gasoline and diesel fuel available—7-foot minimum depths—reviewed on pages 354-55, 364

Indiantown Marina—(772) 597-2455—(OWW Standard Mile 29.5)—located near 27 00.512 North/080 28.082 West, along the Okeechobee Waterway's northern shore, southwest of the Indiantown/Highway 710 Bridge—transient dockage available—gasoline and diesel fuel available—7-foot minimum depths—reviewed on pages 355-58, 64

Everglades Adventures RV & Sailing Resort—(561) 924-7832—(OWW Standard Mile 50)—located near 26 49.529 North/080 40.064 West, along the southeastern flank of the Okeechobee Waterway Rim Route, near unlighted daybeacon #62—transient dockage available—gasoline and diesel fuel available—6-foot minimum depths, but typical soundings of 10 feet in the enclosed harbor—reviewed on pages 371-72, 378

Slim's Fish Camp—(561) 996-3844—(OWW Standard Mile 61)—located near 26 42.290 North/080 42.827 West, flanking the westerly shores of the Okeechobee Waterway Rim Route, immediately southwest of the Torry/Kreamer Island Bridge—transient dockage available—gasoline available—5½-foot minimum depths—reviewed on pages 372-73, 379

Roland Martin's Marina—(863) 983-3151—(OWW Standard Mile 65)—located near 26 45.508 North/080 55.123 West, on the western shores of the Clewiston canal, south of the charted lock—transient dockage available—gasoline and diesel fuel available—6-foot minimum depths—reviewed on pages 374-75, 379-80

Moore Haven City Docks—(863) 946-0711—(OWW Standard Mile 78)—located near 26 50.079 North/081 05.323 West, along the Moore Haven waterfront, south of the Moore Haven Lock—transient dockage available—6½-foot minimum depths—reviewed on pages 382, 398

Thomas Dockage—(863) 946-1461—(OWW Standard Mile 78)—located near 26 50.046 North/081 05.331 West, along the Moore Haven waterfront, south of the Moore Haven Lock—transient dockage available—5-foot minimum depths—reviewed on pages 382, 398

Port La Belle Marina—(863) 675-2261—(OWW Standard Mile 101)—located near 26 45.975 North/081 24.287 West, along the Okeechobee Waterway's southern banks, 1.8 nautical miles east of the La Belle Bridge—limited transient dockage available—gasoline and diesel fuel available—5-foot minimum depths—reviewed on pages 384, 399

La Belle City Docks—(863) 675-2872—(OWW Standard Mile 103)—located near 26 46.122 North/081 26.291 West, on the southern banks of the Okeechobee Waterway, just west of the La Belle 28-foot, bascule bridge—transient dockage available—5-foot minimum depths—reviewed on pages 385-86, 389

River's Edge Motel Docks—(863) 675-6062—(OWW Standard Mile 103)—located near 26 46.161 North/081 26.347 West, on the northern banks of the Okeechobee Waterway, just west of the La Belle 28-foot, bascule bridge—transient dockage available—5-foot minimum depths—reviewed on pages 386, 399

Rialto Harbor Docks—(239) 728-3036—(OWW Standard Mile 119)—located near 26 43.095 North/081 39.317 West, occupying the loop cutting into the main route's southerly banks near Standard Mile 119, hard by chart 11428's notation "Subm Piles"—transient dockage available—6-foot minimum depths—reviewed on pages 386-87, 400

Jack's Marine South—(239) 694-2708—(OWW Standard Mile 124)—located near 26 43.293 North/081 43.541 West, flanking the southern banks of the Okeechobee Waterway at facility designation #59 on chart 11428—transient dockage available—gasoline available—6-foot minimum depths on outer docks, 4-foot minimum depths on inner docks along the canal—reviewed on pages 389-90

Sweetwater Landing—(239) 694-3850—(OWW Standard Mile 126)—located near 26 42.897 North/081 45.682 West, found along the southern banks of the Caloosahatchee River, just west of the 27-foot, Wilson-Piggott bascule bridge—transient dockage available—gasoline available—5-foot minimum depths on the inner harbor, 10-foot minimum depths on the outer docks—reviewed on pages 391, 401

Fort Myers Yacht Basin—(239) 334-8271—(OWW Standard Mile 135)—located near 26 38.870 North/081 52.180 West, guarding the south-southeasterly banks between (moving east to west) the second and third Fort Myers bridges—transient dockage available—gasoline and diesel fuel available—6-foot minimum depths—reviewed on pages 392-93, 402-3

Centennial Harbour Marina—(239) 461-0775—(OWW Standard Mile 135.5)—located near 26 38.505 North/081 52.574 West, guarding the Caloosahatchee's southeasterly banks, west-southwest of the westernmost Fort Myers high-rise bridge and southeast of flashing daybeacon #49—transient dockage available—6½-foot minimum depths—reviewed on pages 394

Royal Palm Yacht Club—(239) 334-2176—(OWW Standard Mile 135.5)—located near 26 38.197 North/081 52.906 West, entrance channel cuts southeast between flashing daybeacon #54 and unlighted daybeacon #52—transient dockage available for members of other yacht clubs with appropriate reciprocal privileges—6-foot minimum depths—reviewed on pages 394-95

St. Lucie River to Lake Okeechobee

The easterly section of the Okeechobee Waterway is a study in contrasts. North of Manatee Pocket the Waterway tracks its way first north then west on the St. Lucie River to the city of Stuart. Some facilities catering to transients pepper the river's banks north (and west) of Manatee Pocket. There are also several anchorages along the way.

Many attractive homes overlook this portion of the river. The houses bordering the eastern banks north of Manatee Pocket are particularly appealing. The Stuart waterfront also exhibits heavy though not unpleasant development.

West of the St. Lucie Lock, the Waterway enters artificial St. Lucie Canal, and development falls away on both shores. A full-service repair facility graces the Waterway's southern shores between the I-95 twin and Florida Turnpike high-rise bridges. Otherwise, only an occasional house tops the dikes for several miles to the small village of Indiantown. Here stands one of the finest and most interesting marinas on the entire Waterway.

Farther to the west, the Okeechobee continues to track its way along the canal passage until it reaches the tiny community of Port Mayaca. Here a second lock opens onto Lake Okeechobee.

The entire run from the St. Lucie River to Lake Okeechobee encompasses some 32 nautical miles. West of Indiantown, there are no further facilities or anchorages short of Pahokee (Rim Route) or Clewiston (Lake Route). Check your time and make an informed decision about when to start and when and where to stop along this passage.

St. Lucie River to Stuart

The St. Lucie River tracks its way generally north from Manatee Pocket and then turns almost due west at OK Woods Point. Soon the stream begins its passage past the Stuart waterfront. Numerous marina and repair-yard facilities line both the northern and southern banks east of the Old Roosevelt Twin Bridges at Britt Point. Past Britt Point the St. Lucie forks north and south. The northern arm has rarely been visited in the past by transient cruisers. However, at least one good anchorage calls for a closer look at this body of water.

The Okeechobee Waterway follows the south fork of the St. Lucie River past Stuart's popular anchorage to St. Lucie Canal and the Okeechobee's first lock.

Hell Gate Anchorage (Standard Mile 2) (27 10.676 North/080 11.504 West)

East-southeast of flashing daybeacon #15 at Hell Gate Point, deep water runs to within 50 yards of the eastern banks all the way south to Seawall Point. Shoals crowd the anchorage's western flank as you approach Seawall Point. Wise skippers will anchor on the far broader patch of deep water east-southeast of #15. During times of light airs or

easterly breezes, craft of almost any size can drop the hook here in 6 to 20 feet of water. For maximum shelter, set your hook within 50 yards of the easterly banks.

One of the best spots is found just north of a wooden building sitting out over the water, known as Bay Tree Lodge. A sign fronting the river identifies the lodge.

The surrounding shoreline is spotted with sumptuous homes. While the development could only be described as intense, it certainly makes for an interesting view from the water.

Hoggs Cove Anchorage (Standard Mile 4.5) (27 12.998 North/080 12.835 West)

At flashing daybeacon #21, the Okeechobee Waterway and the St. Lucie River make a combined turn to the west. Northeast of #21, 6-foot minimum soundings hold to within 100 yards of the Hoggs Cove shoreline. For best depths, anchor just south of the charted thin line of 2-foot shallows at the very rear of the cove. This spot is well sheltered from eastern, northeastern, and northern winds. Breezes over 10 knots blowing from the west would make an evening spent in this haven downright uncomfortable. Otherwise, you can settle down for a night of peace and security. The surrounding shores are overlooked by moderate residential development.

Pelican's Nest Marina (Standard Mile 6) (27 13.014 North/080 14.181 West)

Pelican's Nest Marina is located on the St. Lucie's northern shore, east of flashing daybeacon #22. The marina's entrance channel is outlined by a series of charted but unadorned pilings. This cut holds minimum depths of 5 to 6 feet with similar soundings dockside.

Pelican's Nest accepts transients for

overnight dockage in its reasonably well-sheltered harbor. Berths are found at wooden finger piers stretching out from a concrete seawall. Fresh-water connections and 30-, 50-, and 100-amp power hookups are featured at each slip. Shoreside, cruisers will discover showers in the building that used to house the marina's ship's store. Some mechanical repairs are available through local, independent contractors. The well-thought-of Lobster Shanty Restaurant (772-334-6400) overlooks the dockage basin. It is quite convenient and reportedly the food is good. You will need to take a taxi (see below) into Stuart to access a grocery store and other restaurants.

Pelican's Nest Marina (772) 334-0890
http://www.pelicansnestmarina.com

Approach depths—5-6 feet
Dockside depths—5-6 feet
Accepts transients—yes
Transient dockage rate—below average
Fixed wooden piers—yes
Dockside power connections—30,
    50, and 100 amps
Dockside water connections—yes
Showers—yes
Mechanical repairs—limited

Pelican's Nest Marina, St. Lucie River

(independent contractors)
Restaurant—on site

St. Lucie Marine (Standard Mile 6.5)

St. Lucie Marine (772-692-2000) is a small repair yard flanking the St. Lucie's northerly shoreline, northwest of unlighted daybeacon #22A (just east of the charted WSTU radio tower). The entrance channel is outlined by unadorned pilings, and the cut carries about 5 feet of water at low tide. Mechanical repairs for gasoline and diesel engines are available and haul-outs are accomplished by a 30-ton travelift. The yard also maintains a very sparse ship's store. St. Lucie Marine has a few wet slips, but they are shallow, hard to enter, and reserved for the use of resident craft. No transient space is available.

Northside Marina (Standard Mile 6.5) (27 12.799 North/080 15.377 West)

The largest marina and pleasure-craft facility in Stuart guards the northerly banks, northwest of unlighted daybeacon #22A (a short hop west of St. Lucie Marine). Northside Marina features extensive transient and long-term dockage, plus on-site dining.

Northside's spacious docks consist of both sturdy, fixed, wooden and concrete-decked floating piers with 30- and 50-amp power hookups and water connections. Depths in the marked entrance channel run 7½ to 8 feet. Cruisers will find 7 to 8 feet of water in the outer slips, 7 feet in the middle berths, and 6 to 6½ feet at the innermost docks. A breakwater now encloses the entire harbor for protection from inclement weather. Gasoline and diesel fuel can be purchased at the outermost dock. Waste pump-out service is available dockside as well.

Shoreside you will find spotless, air-conditioned showers and a full Laundromat. A small

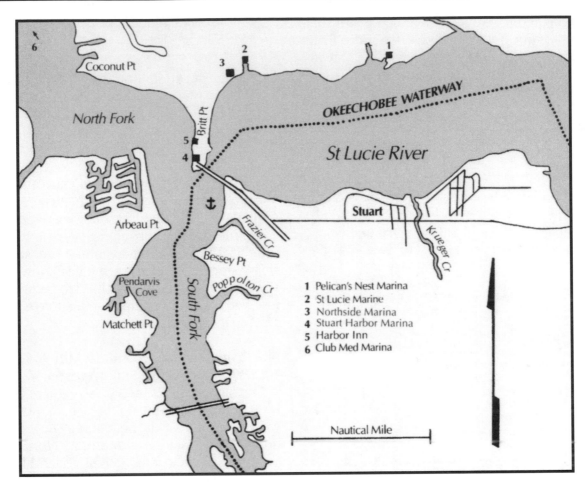

1 Pelican's Nest Marina
2 St Lucie Marine
3 Northside Marina
4 Stuart Harbor Marina
5 Harbor Inn
6 Club Med Marina

Nautical Mile

variety store is located in the dockmaster's office. A West Marine store is a short taxi ride north on U.S. 1.

Full engine repairs (gas and diesel) are afforded by Northside's full-service yard. Marine canvas and electronic repair service is also available. Haul-outs are accomplished by two travelifts (50 and 80 tons).

Wahoo's Restaurant (772-692-2333) is located immediately adjacent to the dockmaster's office. We were quite pleased with the grouper sandwiches here during our last visit. Wahoo's also features delightful fresh-air dining on a screened porch, overlooking both the

dockage basin and the St. Lucie River. The view is magnificent. Of course, a quick taxi ride can take you to the downtown restaurants described below (or a local supermarket). A convenience store is located within easy walking distance of the docks.

In a late-breaking development, just as this account is being tapped out on the keyboard, we have learned that Northside Marina has been sold, and that the new owners plan to build "condos." We have been told that the marina will continue to accept transients, but it is only to be expected that some changes in the character and services at Northside Marina

Northside Marina, Stuart

will come to pass as the new ownership moves along with its plans. Stay tuned to our free, on-line newsletter, the *Salty Southeast,* for more on Northside Marina.

Northside Marina (772) 692-4000

Approach depths—7½-8 feet
Dockside depths—6-8 feet
Accepts transients—yes
Transient dockage rate—average
Fixed wooden piers—yes
Floating concrete piers—yes
Dockside power connections—30 and 50 amps
Dockside water connections—yes
Showers—yes
Laundromat—yes
Waste pump-out—yes
Gasoline—yes
Diesel fuel—yes
Below-waterline repairs—yes
Mechanical repairs—yes
Ship's and variety store—small
Restaurant—on site and others nearby

Roosevelt Bridges

Anyone cruising the Okeechobee Waterway for the past several decades has probably had more than a few unhappy words to say about the Roosevelt twin bascule bridges and the adjacent railway span. These bridges lie southwest of flashing day-

beacon #23A, and have a scant closed vertical clearance of 7 feet (railway bridge) and 14 feet (bascule bridges). Couple this with train-dependent openings and more than a few mechanical problems and it's not too hard to understand why these spans have been an impediment to navigation.

For years there was talk about replacing the bascule spans with a high-rise structure. Happily, a most impressive high-rise now spans the river, but there is an unexpected twist. The old low-level Roosevelt bridges have been left in place, apparently at the heated request of some local businesses. On the plus side, the Roosevelt highway spans do open on demand if the poorly maintained railway bridge is open, and the latter is usually open unless a train is due.

North Fork Facilities and Anchorages (Standard Mile 8) (Various Lats/Lons—see below)

After passing under the twin Roosevelt bridges at Britt Point, the St. Lucie River splits into two branches. The northern arm is known appropriately enough as "North Fork." Transient dockage is now far harder to come

Old Roosevelt Bridges, Stuart

by on these waters than was true in years past. One small facility does offer a few berths, but most cruisers will need to look elsewhere for an overnight slip.

Several low-key marinas flank the eastern shores of Britt Point, north of unlighted daybeacon #2. Moving south to north, first up are the fixed, wooden docks of Stuart Harbor Marina (772-692-2261). This facility no longer offers much in the way of dockage or services for visitors.

The piers of Stuart Hatteras are found just past Stuart Harbor. This facility is in the business of yacht sales and service for their own boats. No transient services are available.

Next are the docks of Harbor Inn Boatel. This interesting facility features good waterside depths and dockage for transients. The adjacent motel is a good spot to take a break from the live-aboard life. The on-site restaurant known as "The Deck" features some good sandwiches and unlimited "liquid sunshine."

Club Med Marina, North Fork

Harbor Inn Boatel (772) 692-1200

Approach depths—10 feet
Dockside depths—6-7 feet
Accepts transients—yes
Transient dockage rate—average
Fixed wooden piers—yes
Dockside power connections—30 amps
Dockside water connections—yes
Restaurant—on site and others nearby

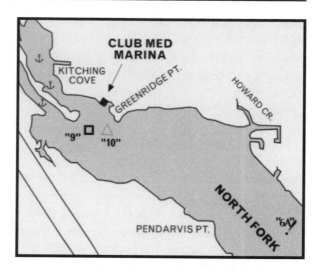

Finally, there are the Pier 1 Condo Docks, which are restricted to property owners and have no facilities for transients.

It's a long run of some 3.7 nautical miles up North Fork to Club Med Marina (772) 398-5006. This facility is located on the stream's northeastern shore, northwest of unlighted daybeacon #10, near 27 14.600 North/080 18.843 West. Overnight transients are no longer accepted at Club Med. That's really too bad, as this facility features two golf courses, a swimming pool, a host of tennis courts, and several restaurants. Oh well, at least they haven't built condos here yet.

Mariners who prefer the seclusion of an isolated anchorage have more than a little incentive to cruise the upstream waters of the

North Fork, St. Lucie River

St. Lucie's North Fork. Notice the charted body of water called Kitching Cove, northwest of Club Med Marina. This cove offers 6-foot minimum depths and near-perfect shelter from all winds.

A mooring field for local craft has been established just northwest of Club Med. During the winter months these waters are crowded, and swinging room would be at a premium. Instead, continue tracking your way northwest into the main body of Kitching Cove, near 27 14.941 North/080 19.341 West. Eventually you will spy a second mooring field ahead. Consider anchoring short of the second mooring field. Here you will find 6 to 8 feet of water, ample room for a 48 footer, and shelter for anything short of a full gale.

There is a second anchorage to consider as well, though room is a bit more limited. A whole series of markers leads visiting vessels into the deep waters northwest of unlighted daybeacon #9. This passage and the stream beyond hold minimum 6-foot depths with some soundings going up to 13 feet. Even with the narrower nature of these waters, captains piloting craft as large as 36 feet should find ample room to spend the night comfortably at anchor near 27 14.795 North/080 19.448 West. As you would expect, it would take hurricane-force winds and tidal surge to pose a problem in this haven. The surrounding shores are overlooked by a widely spaced collection of charming homes.

St. Lucie River—South Fork

The South Fork of the St. Lucie River leads Okeechobee-bound skippers south to St. LucieCanal via a well-marked, improved channel. Moderate to heavy residential development overlooks both shorelines, but these homes are quite attractive and make for interesting viewing while you cruise along. Between Britt Point and the canal's northern entrance, passing mariners will discover a popular anchorage and a single facility catering to cruising-size craft.

City of Stuart Mooring Field and South Point Anchorage Marina (Standard Mile 8) (Marina—27 11.997 North/080 15.602 West)

Big changes have already come, and more are on the way, to the South Fork waters, south of the Roosevelt Bridges. During past years, passing cruisers would have noted a host of anchored craft on the deep waters stretching out from the easterly shoreline south of the Roosevelt bridges (northwest of charted Frazier Creek—Standard Mile 8). Now, captains and crew will discover a large mooring field on these waters. Depths in the field run 8 to 12 feet, with good shelter from all but strong northwesterly winds.

There's good news and bad news concerning these big changes. Let's get the less-than-happy tale out of the way first. The city of Stuart has a management agreement with the state of Florida for the mooring field, and they claim to have leased the bottomland within their city limits from the state of Florida. As many of my readers already know, there is actually a Florida State statute that says quite clearly that no county nor municipality may regulate anchorage in Florida. That privilege is reserved solely for the state. Of course, this law has not prevented any number of communities in Florida from instituting local anchorage regulations by the simple expedient of simply ignoring the already-referred-to statute.

If Stuart, on the other hand, has really leased the bottomland from the state of Florida, they might well have a legal right to regulate anchorage on their local waters, at least as far as state law is concerned. Whether it was wise to antagonize the cruising community by taking such a course of action is, however, very much another question.

Nevertheless, that is just what has happened here. In 2003, all boats in the Stuart anchorage were required to pick up a mooring ball and to begin paying a monthly fee. This was the result of the city of Stuart passing a local regulation preventing anchorage anywhere within its city limits. We have been told that boat owners trying to anchor anywhere on the waters lying within the limits of Stuart have been given warnings, and in one instance, they have been ticketed. This writer has received dozens and dozens of angry e-mails from cruisers. I was also interviewed by both *Soundings* and *Cruising World* magazine concerning this issue. It is safe to say that the outcry of the cruising community was and is still being heard far and wide.

The good news, and there is some of this as well, is that the city of Stuart has built a nice dockmaster's building overlooking the mooring field and named it South Point Anchorage Marina (772-283-9225). Here, those paying for a mooring will find a dinghy dock, good showers, a Laundromat and a cruiser's lounge complete with paperback exchange library. The downtown historic district, with its many fine restaurants, reviewed below, can be accessed via a one- to four-block walk.

But wait, there's more. Plans are in the works to build a 100+-slip city marina on this site within the next two years. When complete, this facility will be a super addition to the Stuart cruising scene. Again, watch our free, on-line newsletter, the *Salty Southeast,* for upcoming details. Remember, all you need do to subscribe to the *Salty Southeast* is send an e-mail to opcom@cruisingguide.com containing the word "subscribe."

Downtown Stuart

Within the last several years, Stuart's historic "Old Town" district has been tastefully redeveloped around Osceola Street. Today, visitors will find a delightful collection of shops and restaurants. While some of our favorite dining spots have now faded into the fabric of the past, there are any number of other great places to slake a healthy appetite.

One of our personal favorites in Stuart is the Dos Amigos Mexican restaurant (300 S Federal Highway, 772-286-2546). It has the considerable advantage of being found less than two blocks from South Point Anchorage Marina. OK, no quibbling on this one. The fare that we have enjoyed on many occasions at Dos Amigos is simply the best Mexican-style cuisine that we have had anytime, anywhere. If you enjoy this style of dining, don't miss this one!

Anyone with a taste for French-style cuisine will certainly want to check out the Ashley restaurant (200 W Osceola Street, 772-221-9476). The veal served with port wine and the Pork Florentine are to die for.

Another great spot is elegant Flagler Grill (47 SW Flagler Avenue, 772-221-9517), featuring a full bar, a "gourmet menu," and simply delicious food. Reservations are highly recommended.

For fresh seafood, don't miss the Black Marlin (53 W Osceola Street, 772-286-3126). You won't find better fresh catch of the day anywhere.

And, for something a bit more informal, give the Riverwalk Café (201 SW St. Lucie, 772-221-1511) a look. The raw bar here is something of a modern-day legend in Stuart.

In addition to all these wonderful dining opportunities, there is also an eclectic selection of shops lining both sides of Osceola Street, ranging from fine jewelry stores to colorful antique dealers. Don't miss the restored Lyric Theater. A local company performs regularly at this architectural jewel.

As already mentioned, a three- to four-block walk will lead you to the Stuart Historic District from South Point Anchorage Marina. Cruisers docking in one of the more outlying marinas will need a taxi or rental car.

Numbers to know in Stuart:
Yellow Cab—772-334-1606
Dollar Car Rentals—772-283-2873
Enterprise Rent-A-Car—772-287-7260
West Marine—772-223-1515
Chamber of Commerce—772-287-1088

St. Lucie Canal Anchorage (Standard Mile 11.5) (27 08.905 North/080 15.555 West)

At flashing daybeacon #33 the Okeechobee Waterway enters St. Lucie Canal. The canal is well sheltered, adequately marked, and easily run. Initially, some heavy residential development lines the eastern shores, but soon you will see only an occasional home.

A branch of the South Fork, abandoned by

the Waterway, cuts off to the southeast at unlighted daybeacon #37. The initial stretch of this stream holds 7-foot depths and allows enough swinging room for a 34 footer. Be sure to set the hook short (northwest of) of the single private dock you will sight along the northeasterly banks. Upstream of this point, soundings decline markedly. You might want to employ a Bahamian-style mooring to minimize swinging room. The surrounding shores are virtually in their natural state. This anchorage features excellent protection from all winds. If you are looking to drop the hook between Stuart and Indiantown, this is "the" spot.

Upper South Fork Anchorage (Standard Mile 13) (27 07.786 North/080 15.891 West)

South of unlighted daybeacon #40, South Fork Creek makes into the Waterway's eastern shore. The lower reaches of this stream (the portion nearest to the Waterway) hold minimum 6-foot depths and feature excellent protection from all winds. Boats up to 32 feet should find sufficient swinging room to drop the hook here (possibly by employing a Bahamian mooring). Larger cruising craft will almost certainly want to anchor within 100 yards or so of the Okeechobee Waterway. Smaller vessels can continue upstream confidently. The South Fork's shoreline alternates between undeveloped patches and residential sections. For maximum privacy, consider anchoring in one of the undeveloped sections.

American Custom Yachts (Standard Mile 14) (27 07.093 North/080 16.310 West)

Between the high-rise, I-95 Twin Bridges and the Florida Turnpike span, a huge marina and boatyard graces the Waterway's southern banks near unlighted daybeacon #46. American Custom Yachts offers some of the most impressive repair facilities this side of Manatee Pocket. A huge work barn overlooks the docks facing the canal, and passing cruisers will undoubtedly observe many large, hauled-out boats being worked on or awaiting service. Practically every mechanical, below-waterline, topside, and marine carpentry repair or refinishing that you might ever require can be quickly undertaken by the impressive list of marine professionals at American Custom Yachts. The yard's travelift is rated at 150 tons. The firm also maintains a large parts department on the premises. There is even an on-site marine canvas dealer. In short, if it can't be fixed here, you may as well give up.

Fortunately for passing cruisers who happen not to be in need of repair, American Custom Yachts also accepts transients, on a strictly space-available basis, at their half-dozen fixed slips fronting the Waterway channel. Of course, should these berths be filled with service customers, you are out of luck. Depths alongside run 7 to 8 feet. American Custom Yachts' wet slips consist of wooden pilings set out from a concrete seawall. As you might expect, the latest power and water connections are readily available, as are showers, gasoline, and diesel fuel. Waste pump-out can be arranged.

American Custom Yachts (772) 286-2835
http://www.americancustomyachts.com

Approach depths—8-10 feet
Dockside depths—7-8 feet
Accepts transients—limited
  (when space is available)
Transient dockage rate—below average
Fixed wooden piers—yes
Dockside power connections—30
  and 50 amps
Dockside water connections—yes
Showers—yes
Waste pump-out—yes

Gasoline—yes
Diesel fuel—yes
Below-waterline repairs—yes (extensive)
Mechanical repairs—yes (extensive)
Part's store—yes

St. Lucie Lock (Standard Mile 15)

After cruising southwest for another nautical mile or so beyond the high-rise Thomas B. Manual/Florida Turnpike fixed bridge, you will encounter the St. Lucie Lock, the first of five locks on the Okeechobee Waterway. Be sure to read the navigation information below before attempting to enter this lock for the first time. Passage through the St. Lucie Lock can be a rough cruising experience.

Just southwest of the St. Lucie Lock, cruisers will sight a low-level, public (fixed, wooden) dock on the southeastern banks that can accommodate boats up to 36 feet. This ultra low key facility is associated with adjacent St. Lucie Lock Park. Overnight stays are allowed, but this isn't what one would call a polished marine facility. Minimum depths at the dock run 5 to 6 feet and some shoreside amenities such as showers and bathrooms are available.

St. Lucie Lock, Okeechobee Waterway

Indiantown and Indiantown Marina (Standard Mile 29.5) (27 00.512 North/080 28.082 West)

Indiantown offers the first formal marina facilities west of the St. Lucie Lock. After traveling for some 12 nautical miles with only intermittent houses along the canal, you will find Indiantown Marina a welcome sight.

As you approach Indiantown, watch the northern shores and you should soon see what will appear to be the corner of a stadium. This novel facility is the site of rodeo competitions held among central Florida's cowboys. If you are in town while a show is on, be sure to take the time to attend this novel event.

Continue watching the northern banks for a ranch high atop the banks. You may well spy the first of the Okeechobee region's many cows lazily watching your progress from the adjacent pasture. The entrance to Indiantown Marina will come abeam to the north shortly thereafter.

The present owners of Indiantown Marina took what was already a good facility and made it into one of the best and most unusual marinas in Florida. In addition to offering all the standard services, the marina encompasses an adjacent 20+-acre field where it provides extensive

American Custom Yachts

dry-stack storage on cradles and stand-offs. The yard's travelift is rated at 30 tons. During an earlier visit, it looked as if the field was growing sailcraft. There must have been several hundred sitting contentedly on dry land, some with work in progress, others just waiting out the summer (and hurricane) season.

Another unique service of Indiantown Marina is what one might term "artificial listing." Some others have termed this service "the Okeechobee Limbo." Just west of Indiantown, the Port Mayaca railroad, vertical lift bridge sets the height limit for the entire Okeechobee Waterway with its 49-foot vertical clearance. If you need just a few more feet to get your sailcraft through, the good folks at Indiantown Marina will install large water containers on one side of your boat, giving it an artificial list. With this novel plan in effect, boats with mast heights up to 53 feet can make it through. This service is also available for eastbound boats. With advance arrangements, the marina personnel will meet you west of the bridge, install the water jugs, and then bring you on through.

Wet-slip dockage at Indiantown Marina is first rate. Not only is the dockage basin well protected from all winds, but there is also no tide, due to the St. Lucie Lock to the east and the Port Mayaca Lock to the west. If I had to pick one spot to ride out Florida's heaviest weather, this would be it.

Depths in the dockage basin run 7 to 8 feet. All berths feature 20- and 50-amp power hookups and fresh-water connections. Good showers and a covered, but open to the weather, Laundromat are available. Gasoline and diesel fuel can be readily purchased dockside. In addition to the haul-out services described above, mechanical repairs can be arranged through independent contractors.

The marina maintains a ship's store on the premises, and daily runs are made to nearby marine-parts and equipment suppliers.

When it's time to feed an on-the-water appetite at Indiantown Marina, a whole array of choices is available. First of all, the marina provides a screened picnic and cookout room with kitchen facilities. Two supermarkets and a drugstore are within less than a mile of the docks (ask the friendly dockmasters for help with transportation). The local post office and a large citrus-fruit dealer are

Port Mayaca railway bridge, Okeechobee Waterway

located within a few blocks of the marina.

Are you up for something with a bit less preparation involved? Well then, consider having dinner (or lunch) at the nearby Seminole Country Inn (772-597-3777). Dating back to 1925, this venerable hostelry originally served as a hunting lodge and inn for passengers of the Seaboard Railroad. Extensively renovated, Seminole Country Inn is today clearly Indiantown's showplace. While the legendary Sunday buffet is no longer served, the food is still outstanding. Complimentary transportation to and from the docks is available to all guests at Indiantown Marina. If you are hankering for a pizza, Dee-Stefano's (772-597-5600) will deliver dockside.

We cannot leave Indiantown Marina without a word concerning the feeling of community at this notable facility. Potluck dinners and social gatherings among both the marina staff and cruisers are regular occurrences. This is just the sort of atmosphere that many mariners crave, and one that is so often absent in today's megamarinas.

If you have the feeling that this writer is high on Indiantown Marina, then you are on the right track. We suggest that you put a red circle around Indiantown on your chart, and be sure to stop and visit whenever your plans call for a cruise of the Okeechobee Waterway.

**Indiantown Marina (772) 597-2455
http://www.indiantownmarina.com**

**Approach depths—8-10 feet
Dockside depths—7-8 feet**

Indiantown Marina, Okeechobee Waterway

Accepts transients—yes
Transient dockage rate—below average
Fixed concrete piers—yes
Dockside power connections—20
  and 50 amps
Dockside water connections—yes
Showers—yes
Laundromat—yes
Gasoline—yes
Diesel fuel—yes
Below-waterline repairs—yes
Mechanical repairs—yes
  (independent contractors)
Ship's store—yes
Restaurant—nearby (complimentary
  transportation available)

Indiantown History   Indiantown is named for the few Indians who took shelter in this region following the last of the Seminole wars. Somehow, they managed to escape notice by the white soldiers and for many years subsisted by fishing and hunting along Okeechobee's eastern banks. In later times, when most of the surrounding swamp was drained and cleared, many took to raising cattle. Today, some of the most successful cattle farmers around Indiantown can proudly trace their ancestry to a Seminole great-great-grandfather.

On to Okeechobee

Some 7 nautical miles west of Indiantown Marina, you will spot a tall, rusty water tower off the southern banks. This is a signpost that you are approaching the Port Mayaca Lock (Standard Mile 39) and the entrance to Lake Okeechobee. Be sure to read the navigation data below before attempting to approach the lock. There is at least one hazardous spot on these waters.

Depending on the prevailing water levels, both gates of the Port Mayaca Lock are sometimes open to traffic. At most other times, the rise or fall on this lock is negligible. Even if the lock gates are open, approach at idle speed and be on the lookout.

Port Mayaca Lock

ST. LUCIE RIVER TO LAKE OKEECHOBEE NAVIGATION

Captains navigating the easternmost section of the Okeechoee Waterway should not encounter any unusual difficulty between Manatee Pocket and Lake Okeechobee. Simply hold to the marked channel, avoid the few trouble spots, and take care when entering and leaving the various locks. With these elementary precautions, you should be able to enjoy your cruise to Lake Okeechobee without misfortune.

St. Lucie Entrance   From a position south of unlighted daybeacon #6 and unlighted nun buoy #6A, abeam of Manatee Pocket's entrance, set course to pass between flashing daybeacon #7 and unlighted daybeacon #8. Be sure to stay south of #6, #6A, and #8. Shallows are found immediately north of these markers.

From #7 and #8, the channel turns to the northwest. Point to pass between flashing daybeacon #11 and unlighted daybeacon #10. Continue on the same course, pointing to pass between flashing daybeacon #13 and unlighted daybeacon #12, and come abeam of flashing daybeacon #13A to its fairly immediate easterly side. Between #12 and #13A, you will pass unlighted daybeacon #12A to its westerly side. Be sure to guard against any slippage to the east between #10 and #13A. Shoal water of 1 to 2 feet lies east of the channel along this stretch. By all accounts you must be sure to stay west of #12A. This aid to navigation warns of a new encroachment by the surrounding shoals.

From #13A, simply set course to pass flashing daybeacon #14 to its immediate westerly quarter and point to come abeam of flashing daybeacon #15 by at least 50 yards to its easterly quarter. Flashing daybeacon #15 sits hard by Hell Gate Point. A wide swath of deep water lies east of #15, while shallows are found between this marker and the point.

The entire stretch between flashing daybeacons #13 and #17 is known as Hell Gate. This name correctly implies the occasional presence of strong tidal currents. Be ready for this swiftly moving water as you cruise through.

Hell Gate Anchorage   From a position abeam of flashing daybeacon #15, cruise to the east-southeast. You can approach to within 50 yards of the easterly banks with good depths. Be wary of the correctly charted shallows to the south as you cruise between #15 and the eastern shoreline. For maximum swinging room, drop anchor north of these shoals.

St. Lucie River through Hell Gate   From a position abeam of flashing daybeacon #15, well to its easterly side, set course to come abeam of flashing daybeacon #17 to its easterly quarter. The current edition of chart 11428 shows the magenta line passing west of #17. This is incorrect. Shoals lie west of #17. Be sure to pass well east of #17.

Cruisers working their way upstream from #17 should set course to pass flashing daybeacon #19 to its northeasterly side. The track turns a bit to the northwest between #17 and #19. Note the charted finger of shoal water southwest of your track.

North of #19, the channel broadens and there are far fewer shoals to worry about. From #19, it is a straightforward run to the St. Lucie/Steele Point bascule bridge. This span, with a closed vertical clearance of 21 feet, has restrictive opening hours between December 1 and May 1. At this time of year, the bridge opens only on the hour and half-hour between 7:00 A.M. and 6:00 P.M. Weekends and federal holidays find the bridge opening on the hour, 20 minutes past, and 40 minutes past the hour from 8:00 A.M. till 6:00 P.M. At all other times of the day and year, the span opens on demand.

Once through the St. Lucie bridge, cruisers have a choice of two routes as the St. Lucie River cuts sharply to the west and heads for Stuart. The safer, but longer, passage is followed by rounding flashing daybeacon #21 to its easterly side and then cutting west on the midwidth of the river.

Captains piloting craft drawing less than 6 feet might consider cutting the corner at OK Woods Point. If you choose this route, keep well to the east of unlighted daybeacon #1 and north of unlighted daybeacon #3. Be sure to guard against the charted shoals surrounding OK Woods Point between #1 and #3.

Hoggs Cove Anchorage   Mariners planning to make use of the excellent anchorage in Hoggs Cove can begin working their way toward the northeastern shore once abeam of flashing daybeacon #21. Simply avoid the narrow 2-foot shoal at the cove's extreme northeastern tip, and you can cruise to within 50 yards of the shoreline with good depths.

Don't attempt to approach the waters around charted Pisgah Hill to the west. A long shoal strikes south from this promontory.

On to Stuart   West of flashing daybeacon #21, the river channel broadens and becomes relatively easy to follow. A wide band of shallows continues to stretch out from either shoreline, and these underwater obstructions must be respected.

Be sure to come abeam and pass flashing daybeacon #22 to its southerly side. A shoal lies north of #22. It is a long run between #21 (or unlighted daybeacon #3, depending on which of the alternate routes you follow past OK Woods Point) and #22. Have your binoculars handy to help pick out flashing daybeacon #22.

Before reaching #22, the channel to Pelican's Nest Marina will come up to the north. This cut consists of a series of unmarked pilings, denoting both sides of the channel. Simply cruise between the piles and the channel will eventually lead to the dockage basin. Just short of the piers, an alternate channel cuts off to port and heads toward a small-craft boatyard. Larger vessels should probably avoid this side channel.

From flashing daybeacon #22, set course to come abeam of unlighted daybeacon #22A to its fairly immediate southern side. The channels to both St. Lucie Marine and Northside Marina line the northerly banks, northwest of #22A. The passage to St. Lucie Marine will be discovered east of the Northside channel. The St. Lucie Marine cut is outlined by unadorned pilings. As you enter the small canal that services St. Lucie Marine, the yard's travelift will come abeam to port. Don't continue up the canal to the wet slips without specific instructions from the staff. A building shoal has all but cut off this passage.

Britt Point/Roosevelt Bridges   West of unlighted daybeacon #22A, point to come abeam of flashing daybeacon #23A well to its northerly side. Waters with only 2 feet of depth flank #23A to the south. Continue on course past #23A for 100 yards or so, then turn sharply south-southwest and pass #23A again, well to its westerly side, as you make your approach to the various Roosevelt spans.

Southwest of #23A, cruisers will discover the high-rise Roosevelt Bridge. With a full 65 feet of vertical clearance, this span is a welcome addition to the Stuart cruising scene. Unfortunately, we still have to deal with the old Roosevelt bridges and the intervening railway span.

A slow-speed zone is in effect in and around all the Roosevelt bridges. Be sure to proceed strictly at idle speed in these potentially congested waters.

The old Britt Point/Roosevelt bridges are a real cause for concern. Tidal currents run strongly through the surrounding waters, and these decrepit bridges break down on a more or less regular schedule. During an earlier cruise through this section of the Okeechobee, we saw divers attempting to ascertain the condition of the railway span's underpinnings. That is certainly an ominous sign, and you can quickly understand why this is a "maximum alert" portion of the Okeechobee Waterway.

For safety's sake, be sure the railroad and highway bridges are completely open before beginning your passage through the spans. With the many breakdowns these spans have suffered over the last several years, this is a very sensible precaution.

First up after the high-rise bridge is the railway span, with only 7 feet of closed vertical clearance. This bridge is usually open, but closes automatically as much as 30 minutes ahead of time when a train is due. A loud horn and flashing red lights warn of an imminent closing. Those who don't pay heed to these signals are in for a heap of trouble. Eastbound cruisers should also know that the highway bridges will not open when the railway span is closed.

After leaving the troublesome railway bridge in your wake, you are immediately confronted with the twin Roosevelt highway bascule bridges. Closed vertical clearance is set at 14 feet. Fortunately, these spans now open on demand, unless, of course, the opening mechanism has broken down. Good luck—you may need it!

Once through the old Roosevelt highway bridges, be sure to pass well east of unlighted daybeacon #2. This marker denotes a small shoal building south from Britt Point. Once abeam of #2, you can continue south on the Okeechobee Waterway along the waters of the St. Lucie River's South Fork, or round Britt Point and explore the river's North Fork.

North Fork   To enter North Fork, continue on the Okeechobee channel until you are well south of unlighted daybeacon #2. Then turn sharply back to the north and pass between unlighted daybeacon #1 to the west and #2 to the east. Soon the docks of Stuart Harbor Marina will come abeam to the east, followed by Stuart Hatteras and Harbor Inn Boatel.

Cruisers continuing upstream on North Fork should be sure to pass well northeast of unlighted daybeacons #3 and #5. These aids to navigation mark shoal waters building out from Dyer Point.

Once you pass unlighted daybeacon #5, good waters open out along a wide swath straddling the midwidth of North Fork. Simply stay southwest of widely spaced unlighted daybeacon #6 and flashing daybeacon #6A. Avoid both shorelines as they are shoal.

Northwest of #6A, the river begins a long slow turn to the west. Have your binoculars ready to help pick out the aids to navigation marking the upper fork's channels. You will first come upon charted, unlighted daybeacons #10 and #9. All boats should pass between these two aids to navigation. All too many cruisers have made the mistake of heading directly for the docks of Club Med Marina, flanking the northerly banks of lower Kitching Cove, before coming abeam of #10. This maneuver will land you in 4-foot depths.

Instead, come abeam and pass unlighted daybeacon #10 and only then turn north to the Club Med docks. Cruisers continuing upstream to the excellent anchorage on upper Kitching Cove need simply stick to the centerline as you work your way slowly through the mooring field adjacent to Club Med. Eventually the waters will narrow, and then swing a bit farther to the north. After making the turn, you will spy a second mooring field ahead. Consider anchoring just south of this second set of moorings. In really strong northerly blows, you might alternately continue following the midline

into the broad upper reaches of Kitching Cove. Minimum 6-foot depths run to within 200 yards of the northerly banks.

Don't attempt to enter the charted stream feeding into the northwestern corner of upper Kitching Cove. Depths finally drop off to some 4½ feet on this errant body of water.

A well-marked channel leads from a position between unlighted daybeacons #10 and #9 into the deep, charted stream southwest of Kitching Cove. Simply continue passing all red markers to your starboard side and take green beacons to port. Soon the channel leads into a sheltered stream where you can anchor most anywhere along the midwidth.

South to St. Lucie Canal Once through the old Britt Point bridges, set course to pass between unlighted daybeacons #24 and #23B. Favor #23B. Shallow water lies just west of #24. Between the bridges and #23B, you will pass the city of Stuart mooring field and South Point Anchorage Marina to the east.

Once #24 is in your wake, adjust course to the southwest a bit, and point to come abeam of and pass flashing daybeacon #25 to its fairly immediate westerly quarter. At #25, the passage turns to the south and follows an improved channel down the length of the South Fork to St. Lucie Canal. Depths outside of the marked cut deteriorate rapidly, falling off to the 2- and 3-foot levels south of flashing daybeacon #27. Be sure to stick strictly to the buoyed channel south of unlighted daybeacon #24.

South-southeast of unlighted can buoy #30, the channel passes under the fixed Palm City Bridge with 54 feet of vertical clearance. A long, restricted speed zone stretches south from this span to unlighted daybeacon #35 on St. Lucie Canal. Power captains can only grit their teeth and write their legislators.

St. Lucie Canal Entrance   South of the Palm City Bridge, it's a long run to the next aid to navigation, unlighted daybeacon #31. Shoal water flanks the channel to the east and west. Use your binoculars to pick out #31, and pass this aid fairly close to its westerly side. Continue on the same heading, pointing to pass between flashing daybeacon #33 and unlighted daybeacon #34. These two aids mark the entrance into St. Lucie Canal.

At #34, the canal begins a long, slow turn to the east, before resuming a more southerly course. Initially, you will spy a heavy concentration of mobile homes on the eastern banks, followed by some impressive private homes on the western shore farther upstream.

St. Lucie Canal Anchorage   An abandoned arm of the South Fork makes into the canal's southeastern banks at unlighted daybeacon #37. Enter this body of water on its centerline. Watch the port shore, and you will spy a private dock several hundred yards upstream. Be sure to cease your explorations and/or anchor northwest of (short of) this pier. Abeam and upstream of the dock, depths rise markedly.

On St. Lucie Canal   South of unlighted daybeacon #39, a minimum-wake zone restricts speed past several large private residences. Power craft should proceed through at idle speed.

South Fork Creek   Between unlighted daybeacons #39A and #40A, the St. Lucie Canal splits off from the South Fork, and the abandoned stream meanders to the southeast. If you cruise this creek seeking anchorage, favor the northern banks as you enter the stream. Cruise back to the mid-width after following the creek's first sharp turn to the south.

On the Canal   The twin, high-rise I-95 bridges span the Waterway just northeast of unlighted daybeacon #46. Overhead clearance is set at 56 feet. The docks and work buildings of American Custom Yachts will be spotted on the southern banks soon after you pass under this span.

Shortly after leaving the I-95 bridges behind, the canal passes under the Thomas B. Manual/Florida Turnpike Bridge southwest of unlighted daybeacon #46. This span has a vertical clearance of 55 feet. After leaving this second bridge in their wake, cruisers will soon encounter the St. Lucie Lock.

St. Lucie Lock   The St. Lucie Lock cuts the Waterway just southwest of unlighted daybeacon #49. As with all the locks on the Okeechobee Waterway, approach with caution. Sound your horn two long blasts followed by two short blasts and keep well back until the flashing traffic light turns green. You can also call the lockmaster on VHF channel 16 or 13.

Dolphins are provided for both the eastern and western approaches to the St. Lucie Lock, as they are on most of the Waterway locks. While these structures are primarily designed for commercial vessels, pleasure craft are welcome to moor to the pilings while waiting for the lock doors to open.

No-wake, idle speed restrictions are in

effect on both sides of the lock. This same rule holds true on all the other Okeechobee Waterway locks as well.

The St. Lucie lockmaster usually directs all traffic to the southern wall. Stand ready to catch the dock lines that the tender will hand down both front and aft.

The water levels in the Okeechobee Locks are adjusted by partially opening the gate on the outbound end of the lock. This unusual procedure can produce considerable turbulence, particularly when the water level in the lock is being raised. Put out plenty of fenders and have all hands stand by on the ropes, ready to fend off.

Additional turbulence can be expected when the lock gates are fully opened, though this seems to be more of a problem for vessels waiting to lock through in the opposite direction than those actually inside the cell. Remember to keep well back when another vessel is locking through as you approach the various gates.

St. Lucie Canal to Indiantown   Watch to port after exiting the St. Lucie Lock. The small dock associated with St. Lucie Lock Park will quickly come abeam.

Some 1.9 nautical miles southwest of the St. Lucie Lock's western entrance, the Waterway passes under the SSR 76A fixed bridge with a vertical clearance of 56 feet. An overhead power cable, also with 56 feet of clearance, is found just northeast of this span.

West (and southwest) of the St. Lucie Lock the canal continues along several arrow-straight stretches to the Indiantown twin bridges. It is a straightforward run to the spans, and you need only hold to the midwidth for good depths. Along the way you will spot a few isolated houses and several dams along the side of the canal which control drainage of the surrounding lands. Several more power lines cross this portion of the canal, the lowest having 56 feet of vertical clearance.

The Indiantown highway bridge crosses St. Lucie Canal some .4 nautical miles west of the charted "Micro-Tower" on the Waterway's southern banks. This fixed span has a vertical clearance of 55 feet.

Immediately beyond, the railroad span (with a closed vertical clearance of 7 feet) is usually open between 6:00 A.M. and 9:00 P.M., unless a train is due. There are sometimes long waits when a train is scheduled, but fortunately these are somewhat rare. Often, this bridge is closed during the evening and nighttime hours.

You will spot the entrance to Indiantown Marina on the northern shore some .4 nautical miles west of the railway span. Hold to the midwidth at the entrance. The fuel dock (with the harbormaster's office and ship's store just behind) will open out straight ahead while entry to the main dockage basin is found by swinging to starboard just short of the fuel pier.

On to Okeechobee   It is a run of some 7 nautical miles from Indiantown Marina to the Port Mayaca Lock. This stretch of St. Lucie Canal displays a marked similarity to the stream's eastern reaches. Again, except for one trouble spot just east of the Port Mayaca Lock, you need only hold to the center waters to protect props and keels. A host of power lines spans the canal between Indiantown and the Port Mayaca Lock.

Again, the lowest is set at an official clearance of 56 feet.

Soon after spotting the rusty water tank at Port Mayaca, you will encounter another railroad bridge. This pesky, vertical lift span has a vertical clearance of 49 feet when open (7 feet when closed). It sets the vertical clearance limit for the entire Okeechobee Waterway. If you need just a few more feet of clearance, contact Indiantown Marina about their artificial heeling service.

The Port Mayaca railway bridge is usually open unless a train is due. A flashing red light indicates that the bridge is about to close. Be sure to stay clear. Conversely, a flashing green light means that all is well to continue.

West of the railway span, slow down and pay closer attention to your navigation. Begin using inset 2 on chart 11428, which covers the approach to the Port Mayaca Lock and the eastern reaches of Lake Okeechobee. As the chart clearly shows, a large obstruction bisects the Waterway just east of the locks. This hazard is marked by unlighted daybeacon #52. Be sure to pass well to the south of #52 as you cruise toward the lock doors.

Between #52 and the Port Mayaca Lock, the Waterway is spanned by the Port Mayaca/Highway 98 fixed bridge with a vertical clearance of 55 feet. The westerly lock doors will be spied dead ahead immediately after you pass under this span.

Passage into Eastern Okeechobee Depending on the relative water levels in the lake and St. Lucie Canal, the doors at the Port Mayaca Lock often remain open. Even if the water level does need adjustment, you will most likely be raised or lowered only a short distance. Make your approach at idle speed and follow the lockmaster's mooring directions. The waters immediately adjacent to all the Okeechobee locks are no-wake zones.

The passage from the western mouth of the Port Mayaca Lock into Lake Okeechobee calls for caution, particularly for eastbound vessels. A narrow channel bordered by very shoal water leads from the lock doors to deeper waters west of flashing daybeacon #1.

Cruisers headed east on the Okeechobee Waterway during times of strong winds could quickly be set outside of this narrow cut while waiting for the lock to open. Captains of this ilk would do well to wait in the deeper waters west of #1 until the lock doors are completely open.

Westbound cruisers should set a careful course from the lock doors to pass between unlighted daybeacon #2 and flashing daybeacon #1. Favor the southern side of the channel a bit on this run, as #2 is closer to the northern shallows than is #1 to the southern shoals.

Lake Okeechobee

Isham Randolph, a noted engineer in the 1880s, once described Lake Okeechobee as "the great liquid heart of Florida." The Seminoles first dubbed this impressive water body Okeechobee, meaning big water. The lake is roughly circular, measuring some 32 nautical miles from north to south and 27 nautical miles from east to west. Its broad surface encompasses more than 730 square miles of often-restless waters. Depths range from as little as 6 to as much as 14 feet, though old-timers will hint at deeper holes where underground rivers flow into the lake. These consistently shallow depths can foster a steep chop in strong winds and visiting cruisers will find it prudent to wait for good weather before attempting either route across the great lake. In short, the operative word for Okeechobee is big, and those who have become used to the sheltered ICW on Florida's eastern seaboard are in for quite a shock.

Okeechobee History The story of the Okeechobee region begins long before the first Europeans sighted the shores of Florida. Almost two thousand years ago the Timucuan Indians began building a remarkable series of interconnecting mounds, roads, and canals on the shores of Lake Okeechobee. Some of these mounds were used for communal living and were obviously intended to lift the inhabitants up from the surrounding swamp. More interesting, however, are the many burial mounds that have been discovered on the southern and eastern banks of the great lake.

Perhaps the most impressive collection of mounds can still be seen by the adventurous explorer on Fisheating Creek, near Okeechobee's northwestern corner. Here a series of seven living mounds surrounds a large burial ground with what may have been a huge ceremonial mound to the east. In 1961 an expedition of the Florida Archaeological Society undertook an excavation of these ruins. The group found a large quantity of gold, silver, and copper ornaments, including a remarkably well preserved carving of a human hand. In the center of the hand was a replica of the human eye, wrought in twenty-four-karat gold. Perhaps the dig's most curious find, however, was a message etched on a clam shell, apparently by a Spanish captive. On one side was a map of the mound city's location with directions in Spanish. On the other were the word calos and more directions.

Archaeologists have been able to piece together a semblance of the true events from this remarkable clue. Early accounts of Spanish sailors captured by native Indians tell of a King Calos who led his people to the seashore and plundered Spanish wrecks. He would then return to his homeland well inland, where he had a council house that could accommodate 1,000 warriors. There is now good reason to believe that the mound city on Fisheating Creek was the legendary dwelling of King Calos.

Remarkably for a body of water its size, the existence of Lake Okeechobee remained a matter of legend for many years following Spanish settlement of Florida's east coast. Tales by Spanish captives spoke of a huge lake hidden in the province's impenetrable swamps, but since no gold was supposed to be there, the Spanish authorities never investigated.

In 1837 Lake Okeechobee was forcibly brought to the attention of Florida's populace. On Christmas Day, Col. Zachary Taylor stormed a strong party of Seminole warriors who, under the leadership of their great chief Coacoochee, had fortified a hammock near Okeechobee's northern shore. In spite of careful preparations by the Seminoles, Taylor ordered a frontal assault by his numerically superior forces. The Indians were overwhelmed, but not before exacting a severe price from their attackers.

An uncertain peace settled over the Okeechobee region after several more years of conflict, but this lukewarm truce was shattered in 1855. A party of army engineers maliciously destroyed the garden and orchard of Billy Bowlegs, probably the most influential Seminole chief of his time. This attack sparked the long, frustrating conflict known as the Third Seminole War. This time the federal government decided that rather than attempt to exterminate the Seminole population, it would encourage soldiers and private citizens to capture as many Indians as possible. The prisoners were to be deported to Oklahoma. As an inducement, a healthy bounty was offered for every living Seminole delivered to federal authorities.

This policy of capture and exportation was directly responsible for the formation of the so-called Lake Okeechobee boat companies. Squads of armed men would roam the lake and the surrounding countryside in search of their prey. Finally in 1858, Billy Bowlegs and 123 of his followers agreed to leave for the west. A few Seminoles continued to hide in the vast swamps and Everglades south of Lake Okeechobee, but for all practical purposes, this sad chapter in the lake's history was over.

In the few years remaining before the Civil War, a new industry was spawned on the shores of Lake Okeechobee that would one day grow into a vast enterprise. Until the mid-nineteenth century, large numbers of "scrub" cattle wandered Florida's open ranges and swamps. Enterprising individuals rounded up some of these strays and began herds, which eventually became an incredibly profitable business.

The War Between the States disrupted the cattle industry as Confederate and Union forces skirmished over the food supplies represented by central Florida's cattle. After peace was restored, however, the cattle industry flowered. Vast herds were driven west through the Okeechobee region to Fort Myers and ultimately to the port city of Punta Russa. From here the cows were put aboard ships bound for Cuba.

The Spanish purchasing agents paid well in gold coin, and many who had never known anything but poverty suddenly found themselves wealthy. This was the heyday of the Florida cracker. Though in later times the term "cracker" was used to describe rural residents of both Florida and Georgia, this expression originated with the central Florida cattle industry. The cowboys working the stock in the Okeechobee region used "strong whip(s), twelve to eighteen feet of braided buckskin fastened to a handle twelve to eighteen inches long." According to Alfred and Kathryn Hanna writing in their book, Lake Okeechobee, Wellspring of the Everglades, "An expert could curl the whip around the neck of the friskiest calf or lay open a strip on the side of the wildest steer. The pop or crack resulting in its use sounded like a rifle shot." Hence the name Florida cracker, and though the whips were little used following the screwworm epidemic of the 1930s, the name stuck and can still be heard from time to time on the shores of Lake Okeechobee.

Beginning in 1881, a remarkable visionary began a series of projects in the Okeechobee region that presaged a radical change for the lake and surrounding countryside. Hamilton Disston had already amassed a great fortune in Philadelphia when he visited the St. Johns River. Disston became fascinated with the agricultural potential of the vast swampland surrounding Lake Okeechobee. The principal snag was, of course, that the land had to be drained before it could be cultivated. Never one to let a little detail like several billion gallons of water stand in his way, he struck a deal with Governor Bloxham to drain the swamps in return for title to much of the reclaimed land.

Disston assembled a team of workmen and several dredgers to cut a series of canals connecting the upper Kissimmee River to Lake Okeechobee. Simultaneously, another project to join the lake to Caloosahatchee River was going forward. When both efforts were successfully completed, steamboats could make their way up the Caloosahatchee into Lake Okeechobee and continue up the Kissimmee River. While these impressive canals never really drained the surrounding lands as Disston had hoped, they did vastly improve transportation to and from the Okeechobee region.

Disston also encouraged settlement of the lands about Lake Okeechobee and was instrumental in the experimental agriculture of sugarcane and truck farming. If he had lived to a ripe old age, the future of Okeechobeeland might have been vastly different. As it was, he died at the relatively young age of fifty-five in 1893. His family, who had never believed in Disston's dreams, sold off his holdings to the highest bidder. His efforts were not in vain, however, for he did perhaps more than any other person to transform the Okeechobee region into one of the richest farming centers in all of Florida.

In 1905, one of the most dynamic governors in all of Florida's history took office in Tallahassee. Napoleon Broward had grown up in a rural environment on the St. Johns River. In 1895, Broward and his brother built the oceangoing tug *The Three Friends.* Shortly thereafter they began a lucrative and popular, though illegal, trading enterprise with the revolutionaries in Cuba. Though he was indicted for smuggling, the charges were dismissed and Napoleon found himself one of the best known figures in the state. In 1900 he was elected to the state legislature and assumed the governorship only five years later.

Napoleon Broward came to office as a "man of the people." Throughout his administration, he struggled for the rights of the common citizen against the interests of big business and the railroad companies. One of his pet ideas was to drain the lands about Lake Okeechobee. Broward saw this effort as a way to open up new lands for the people, free from any claims by the railroad companies.

Under his administration and those of his successors, a remarkable series of canals was built from Lake Okeechobee to the east coast. Eventually, narrow, man-made channels connected the lake to Fort Lauderdale, Palm Beach, and Miami. These were only marginally successful as a means of transportation, but they did begin the long and arduous task of land reclamation.

Broward also proposed a canal to connect Okeechobee to the St. Lucie River. This water link was not finished until 1937 after many other momentous events on the lake. This is the same route, improved a bit by the Corps of Engineers, that cruisers travel today on the Okeechobee Waterway.

As drainage projects went slowly forward under Broward's successors, unscrupulous land agents portrayed the "soon-to-be-drained" lands as a farmer's paradise. Countless thousands of acres were sold to unsuspecting settlers, who never dreamed they were buying "land by the gallon."

The ill-starred land boom was brought to a dramatic close by tragic events in 1926 and 1928. On Labor Day 1926, a hurricane piled the waters of Lake Okeechobee against the western banks, killing more than 300 people in the Moore Haven area. Two years later, in September 1928, a much stronger hurricane smashed into Palm Beach and then headed due west for the Okeechobee area. There was little warning in those days, and most residents were forced to take whatever shelter they could in their homes. Winds of 150 miles per hour or more forced more and more of the lake's waters against a weak earthen dike on the eastern and southeastern shores of the lake. This flimsy structure gave way and the pent-up waters floated many a home and building off its foundation, drowning the occupants.

The national attention focused on Lake Okeechobee in the aftermath of the 1928 hurricane led the federal government to undertake a massive program of flood control in the region. Strong earthen dikes were built around much of the lake, and efficient locks were installed and manned by well-trained personnel. Unquestionably, these impressive projects have prevented repetition of the 1928 tragedy, but they have also resulted in the overdraining of some Everglades land. Such problems as "muck fires," which can burn for years in the drained peat, continue to plague Okeechobeeland.

The Okeechobee story is not ended yet. In the 1960s the Army Corps of Engineers straightened the Kissimmee River channel leading to Lake Okeechobee. This project has proven to be a tragic mistake. The new course of the river has no purifying effect as did its former serpentine course, so that today the Kissimmee dumps vast quantities of fertilizer and agricultural chemicals washed off nearby farm lands into Lake Okeechobee. The great lake is showing signs of algae bloom and other effects of the washoff quite detrimental to its fish and other indigenous forms of life. There is a real danger that Okeechobee might become a dead lake, and that would be a great disaster indeed.

Okeechobee Today

In spite of Lake Okeechobee's impressive size, cruising destinations are limited. The flood-control dikes and locks constructed so painstakingly after the 1928 hurricane have cut off many canals and so-called dead rivers where small boats could once explore. Most of these locks are closed semipermanently, but even if they should chance to be open when you are passing, the waters beyond are mostly too treacherous and shallow for cruising craft.

Cruisers visiting Okeechobee today are pretty much limited to the two lake crossings associated with the Okeechobee Waterway. These alternate Waterway passages rejoin at the interesting village of Clewiston and continue north to the Moore Haven lock. Clewiston itself offers facilities for visiting cruisers and excellent dining. Only the Kissimmee River to the north offers any serious cruising possibilities off the Okeechobee Waterway, and these are severely limited.

Kissimmee River

As a result of the abortive Kissimmee River channel-straightening project of the 1960s, the so-called Kissimmee Waterway stretches north for many miles from Okeechobee to several large lakes. Unfortunately, there are three serious problems with this waterway for cruising craft. First, the controlling depth to Kissimmee Lake is only 3 feet; second, a fixed bridge not far from Lake Okeechobee sets the vertical clearance for the waterway at only 14 feet; and, finally, the route has never been charted by NOAA. For these reasons, cruising on the Kissimmee Waterway is pretty much limited to small craft, and the route north of Okeechobee is not recommended for visiting cruisers.

Lake Route—Okeechobee Waterway

The fastest, most direct transit across the great lake on the Okeechobee Waterway is the so-called lake or #1 route. This passage cuts across the southern portion of Lake Okeechobee for some 22 nautical miles before ducking behind a bank of protective islands at the village of Clewiston. The easterly portion of the channel cuts through deep water and in fair weather is easily run. Careful compass (and/or GPS) courses must be run between the widely spaced aids to navigation. Shoal water abuts the approach to Clewiston; you must take care to stay in the marked cut.

Breezes over 15 knots from any quarter, but particularly from the north and west, can set up a very healthy chop on the Lake Route. As a rule of thumb, if winds exceed 15 knots and are blowing from any direction other than the easterly quarter, the longer rim route (discussed below) should probably be your choice. Winds over 20 knots from any direction call for an extra day at the docks and a few more card games.

In fair weather, the Lake Route is probably the better choice if you are anxious to reach your destination or if you just want to see a bit of the lake's open waters. Plot your compass/GPS courses beforehand and keep a ready ear to the latest weather forecast.

Rim Route—Okeechobee Waterway

The Okeechobee Waterway Rim Route follows an unsheltered passage along the eastern and southern rim of the lake for some 13 nautical miles, before ducking behind a long chain of protective islands west and south of Pahokee. This passage is some 8 to 9 nautical miles longer than the Lake Route, but it is well sheltered from easterly, northeasterly, and southeasterly blows. It should, *however,* definitely be avoided in strong westerly and northwesterly breezes. Not only would cruising craft have to face a very healthy chop under these conditions, but the lee shore would also be uncomfortably close.

The Rim Route can boast two marinas not shared by the lake passage. Everglades Adventures RV & Sailing Resort at Pahokee (formerly Pahokee Marina and Campground) offers extensive, well-protected dockage for transients. Another small marina near Torry Island has a few slips and some services for visiting cruisers. If evening overtakes you or bad weather threatens, these havens can be most welcome.

North and east of the rim passage's protected section, the entire route is well outlined with *unlighted* daybeacons. While daylight navigation is a simple matter of passing each aid on its appropriate side, nighttime cruising would be a white-knuckle affair and is strictly not recommended.

Depths on the Rim Route run as shallow as 6 feet, though most soundings show depths of 8 to 10 feet. In the fall, lake levels are usually lowered in anticipation of the hurricane season. The 6-foot minimum is usually maintained during this period. In a severe drought, depths can (but usually don't) fall below charted levels. If drought conditions have persisted for some time before your cruise, it might be a good idea to check on the current Rim Route conditions at either the Port Mayaca or Moore Haven locks.

The Okeechobee Waterway Rim Route is recommended for those interested in a leisurely cruise. Skippers following the rim passage will be able to observe several drainage locks and some untouched natural scenery south of Bacom Point. Additionally, the village of Pahokee, which has escaped the eyesores of rampant commercial development, is definitely worth a visit. All in all, we usually prefer the Rim Route to its quicker sister passage, though of course you will have to assess the advantages and disadvantages of the two channels and decide which better fits your cruising plans.

An unfortunate visual aspect of the Rim Route is the acres and acres of dead Malaluka trees flanking the protected portion of the passage south of Clewiston. Each of these trees was purposely killed by a hand-intensive method known as girdling (removing a strip of bark around the entire circumference of the tree in question). This bizarre practice is part of Florida's effort to remove non-native trees from the state. The Malalukas were originally brought to Florida to help drain the Everglades and the lands about Lake Okeechobee. This was never really successful, but the trees have thrived to such an extent that it's feared they will soon crowd many native species into extinction.

Route South to Pahokee

Between the Port Mayaca Lock and Pahokee, the Rim Route is somewhat dull. The lake to the west stretches unbroken to the horizon, while observation of the mainland shore is limited to a view of the high dikes that protect the shoreline. Take heart; the best is yet to come.

Everglades Adventures RV & Sailing Resort (Standard Mile 50) (26 49.529 North/080 40.064 West)

The marina known as Everglades Adventures RV & Sailing Resort (formerly Pahokee Marina and Campground) comes up along the southeasterly banks of the Rim Route, at unlighted daybeacon #62. Where cruisers would once have found a newly minted, city-owned facility, visitors will now discover a privately leased operation. The marina itself has been augmented by rental cabins, pontoon boat rentals, guided fishing tours, airboat excursions, hiking trails, and guided fishing tours.

Cruisers will be more interested in the modern, well-protected, 50-slip harbor, virtually enclosed by a strong concrete breakwater. Transients are readily accepted at the floating concrete-decked piers. Minimum depths in the newly dredged harbor now run around 10 feet. Most slips have 30-amp power hookups (all have fresh water), but a few 50-amp connections are available as well. Hopefully, by the time you read this account, new showers and a Laundromat will have been constructed on the marina grounds. Currently, to wash away the day's grime and take care of those dirty duds, you must trek about a third of a mile to a shower and a Laundromat in the adjacent campground. Some mechanical repairs can be arranged through local contractors. Gasoline and diesel fuel can be purchased in the harbor. The on-site variety and fishing tackle store (with paperback exchange library) is OK for basic needs, but to restock your larder, a walk into town is required.

Speaking of downtown Pahokee, the local business district is only two blocks away, though you must hike up and then down the steep hill associated with the high earthen dike that separates Lake Okeechobee from Pahokee. Here you will find two supermarkets (an additional three-block walk away), a drugstore, Burger King, and Kentucky Fried Chicken. Ask the marina staff for directions, or call the local chamber of commerce at (561) 924-5579.

Everglades Adventures RV & Sailing Resort (561) 924-7832

Approach depths—6-12 feet
Dockside depths—10 feet
Accepts transients—yes
Transient dockage rate—below average
Floating concrete piers—yes
Dockside power connections—30

and (a few) 50 amps
Dockside water connections—yes
Showers—yes
Laundromat—nearby
Waste pump-out—yes
Gasoline—yes
Diesel fuel—yes
Mechanical repairs—limited
   (independent contractors)
Variety and tackle store—yes
Snack bar—yes
Restaurant—nearby

Pahokee

The village of Pahokee is one of those fascinating communities in the Okeechobee region that seem to be delightfully untouched by modern hustle and bustle. To be sure, Pahokee has all the modern conveniences, but the town has an easy-going nature and friendly inhabitants. You are more likely to find the conversation at the local breakfast spot turning to how the fish are biting rather than what's happening in Washington.

Pahokee's name recalls the ancient Indian term for the great Everglades to the south. Roughly translated, Pahokee means sea of grass.

Sugarcane is king in modern Pahokee and the United States Sugar Corporation maintains a huge processing plant just south of the town. On the outskirts of Pahokee, mammoth sugarcane fields stretch unbroken to the horizon and then seemingly fall off the earth.

Pahokee can claim at least one famous native son. Mel Tillis, noted country singer and performer, was born in this small village and still makes frequent visits to his homeplace. Ask any resident and he will be proud to tell you the story of Mr. Tillis's early years.

Slim's Fish Camp (Standard Mile 61) (26 42.290 North/080 42.827 West)

Near unlighted daybeacon #91, the Okeechobee Rim Route ducks behind a protective marsh barrier. The channel is reasonably well sheltered from this point to Clewiston, where it rejoins the Lake Route.

Some 3.2 nautical miles south of unlighted daybeacon #91, the Rim Route passes under the (still) hand-operated Torry/Kreamer Island swing bridge. Just south of the span, Slim's Fish Camp flanks the western shore. While this is mostly a small-craft fishing and pontoon-boat-oriented marina, some services for cruising craft are available as well. Most of Slim's wet slips are small, covered berths, designed for petite boats, but the long, outer face dock can accommodate vessels as large as 45 feet. Transients are accepted at this floating wooden pier. Depths run 5½ to 10 feet, and fresh-water connections and 30-amp power hookups are available as well. Mechanical repairs are offered for outboards only. Gasoline (no diesel fuel) is sold at Slim's, but the pump is on the shore, and larger craft will probably not be able to get close enough for a fill-up.

Torry/Kreamer Island bridge, Okeechobee Waterway

The adjacent variety and tackle store is fairly well supplied for a store of its type. Surprisingly, a goodly walk back over the bridge will lead you to a municipal golf course and a restaurant associated with this local attraction.

Slim's Fish Camp (561) 996-3844

Approach depths—6-12 feet
Dockside depths—5½-10 feet
Accepts transients—yes
Transient dockage rate—above average
Floating wooden pier—yes
Dockside power connections—30 amps
Dockside water connections—yes
Gasoline—yes
Mechanical repairs—limited
Variety and tackle store—yes
Restaurant—nearby

Rim Route Canal to Clewiston

South and west of the Torry/Kreamer Island bridge, the Rim Route continues to follow a deep, well-sheltered canal paralleling the southern and southwestern rim of Lake Okeechobee. Eventually the passage curves to the northwest and finally intersects the Lake Route at Clewiston, some 13 nautical miles from the Torry Island span.

If it weren't for the dead Malaluka trees (see above), this would be a lovely section of the Waterway. The lake shores still boast deep cypress swamps, interspersed here and there with little passages affording a quick view of the main lake. Occasionally, you can spot floating fish-camp houses nestled amid the cypress. Ospreys are often very much in evidence, and if you are careful you can sometimes watch these agile birds catch a fish and take off with their catch gripped firmly in their claws.

Clewiston (Standard Mile 65)

Some 2.3 nautical miles northwest of unlighted daybeacon #100, the Rim Route meets up with the Clewiston flood gate and intersects the Lake Route making in through a marked channel from Lake Okeechobee.

A hurricane lock separates the small creek serving the Clewiston waterfront from the Waterway. If water levels allow and bad weather is not in the offing, this lock is usually open. Otherwise, the gates operate from 5:30 A.M. to 9:00 P.M. from May 1 to October 31, and from 5:30 A.M. to 8:00 P.M. the rest of the year.

Hospitality seems to be an unvarying tradition in all the Okeechobee communities. Even so, we were impressed by the courteous, friendly aid given to strangers in Clewiston. This thriving village offers good dockage and excellent dining as well. If you are in the area and it's near the end of a long cruising day, Clewiston is well worth an overnight stop.

Clewiston boasts two marinas, one of which cruisers can use with confidence. The northernmost facility, Anglers Marina, lines the canal's western face, just a short hop south of

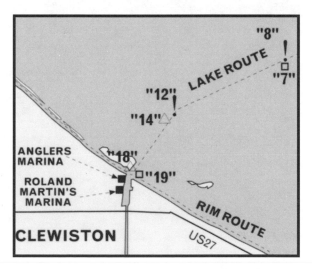

the hurricane gate. Anglers is pretty much limited to small craft, but it does offer a variety and tackle store plus an adjacent motel.

Cruising boats are welcome at Roland Martin's Marina on the Clewiston canal's western shore, about halfway between the hurricane gate and the low-level bridge barring further upstream cruising (near 26 45.508 North/080 55.123 West). Most transients are directed to the 700-foot, floating, wooden face dock, which features full power and water connections. Depths alongside typically run 6 feet, though occasionally, low-water levels drop soundings below this minimum. The management suggests that captains piloting deep-draft vessels call ahead to check on the latest depth situation.

Squeaky-clean showers and a full Laundromat are available shoreside. Gasoline and diesel fuel are on hand, and mechanical repairs are routinely arranged through local, independent contractors. The adjacent ship's, tackle, and variety store is quite large, and well supplied with all sorts of gear. If you need more extensive stores, the nearest supermarket is some 1½ miles away. If you aren't up for a walk of this duration, call R&K Transportation (863-983-8424). Many other shoreside merchants are only a five- to six-block walk from Roland's docks.

A restaurant serving breakfast and lunch is located in the marina ship's store. For the

Roland Martin's Marina, Clewiston

evening meal, read the review of the Clewiston Inn presented below. This outstanding dining facility is some two miles away—many will want to take a taxi to the inn's doors. For those who want to take a break from the live-aboard routine, Roland's maintains an adjacent motel with swimming pool. This pool is open to all visiting cruisers.

Roland Martin's Marina (863) 983-3151
http://www.rolandmartinmarina.com

Approach depths—6 feet
Dockside depths—6 feet
Accepts transients—yes
Transient dockage rate—above average
Floating wooden pier—yes
Dockside power connections—30
   and 50 amps
Dockside water connections—yes
Showers—yes
Laundromat—yes
Gasoline—yes
Diesel fuel—yes
Mechanical repairs—yes
   (independent contractors)
Ship's, variety, and tackle store—yes
   (extensive)
Restaurant—on site and others nearby

Clewiston's most prestigious dining and lodging establishment is the Clewiston Inn (863-983-8151 or 800-749-4466). Originally built in 1938 by the United States Sugar Corporation, the inn has been delighting patrons for many years with its Old South cooking and colonial atmosphere. The lobby is sheathed in cypress paneling with beamed ceilings and working fireplaces. Guest rooms recall a far more gracious era and can be accurately described as "simply charming."

Come mealtime, all attention becomes focused on the Colonial Dining Room. The luncheon buffets are justifiably popular, and the nighttime entrees are all that the famished could ask for.

While waiting for your table, consider having a cool drink in the lounge. This room's walls are adorned with several large murals depicting Everglades wildlife, painted by renowned outdoor artist Clinton Shepherd. Several years ago, the murals were appraised at $40,000, but their value has probably continued to grow since that date.

For those cruisers who wish to escape the live-aboard life for a time, the rooms at the inn are highly recommended. The Clewiston Inn prides itself on providing a "sense of almost-forgotten elegance." Judging from our short stay at the inn, this motto is certainly realized.

Numbers to know in Clewiston:
R&K Transportation—863-983-8424
Chamber of Commerce—863-983-7979

The Custard Apples of Clewiston

Any visitor to the western shores of Okeechobee is bound to hear a reference to the "custard apple forests" that once ringed the lake from Clewiston to Moore Haven. Though only a few specimens remain today, the lowly custard apple once held sway over more than thirty-two thousand acres in west Okeechobeeland.

Clewiston Inn

What is a custard apple? Dr. Lawrence Will, author of many books about the Okeechobee region, describes the tree as

> crooked, oh my gosh, its branching twisting trunk with outreaching buttress roots, writhed upward for twenty feet or more, their warped and shapeless branches covered with bright green and glossy leaves. . . . About the only pretty thing about the tree was its bright cream-colored blossoms, their thick outside petals surrounding narrow smaller ones, white on one side and blood red on the other. . . . The fruit didn't taste too bad, but golly Moses, you couldn't chew the thing for it was nothing but a mass of seeds in soft and pulpy meat. . . . People used to say the fruit was good for making custard . . . but who ever heard of a catfisherman's wife making custard.

What, you may ask, is the big deal about an ugly, twisted tree which produces a fruit that is barely fit to eat? Well, apparently, the custard apples possessed a unique beauty all their own. Dr. Will again comments:

> When these woods were in their prime, exploring their shadowy domain was an experience you'd not forget. Under leafy branches covered over with a solid blanket of white blossomed vines which made twilight at midday, you might walk for miles and scarcely glimpse the sky. . . . There was a peculiar fascination in walking through this murky forest, zigging and zagging between outreaching roots, dodging under crooked branches which tangled just beyond. . . . And so that was the custard apple wood, my friend, silent, peaceful, dark, mysterious and exotic in its shadowy coolness.

The custard apple trees were uprooted and burned by the thousands as the land about the western shores of Okeechobee was converted to vegetable farming. Today, there are only a few isolated remnants of the great forests, but the custard apple remains part and parcel of the Okeechobee tradition.

On to Moore Haven

The Okeechobee Waterway continues following a sheltered canal northwest from Clewiston to the Moore Haven lock. This is a very attractive section of the Waterway. The eastern banks alternate between marsh grass and deep, almost mysterious, cypress swamps. Those who enjoy natural scenery will find this portion of their voyage fascinating.

An older, charted channel intersects the Waterway near Liberty Point. While we sounded 8-foot depths in this cut, stumps and other obstructions have been reported, and this passage is strictly not recommended for cruising craft.

Moore Haven Anchorage (Standard Mile 77.5) (26 50.672 North/081 05.310 West)

At the Moore Haven lock, the Waterway cuts sharply to the south, but the sheltered canal continues northwest. The hyacinth fence that once blocked this upstream passage was removed years ago. Cruising craft as large as

Entrance to Moore Haven lock

48 feet will find plenty of swinging room amidst 8-foot depths after leaving one trouble spot behind. Check out the navigational discussion of this anchorage in the next section of this chapter before attempting first-time entry.

Otherwise, this haven affords excellent protection from foul weather, and a relatively undeveloped shoreline. There is some local water traffic, however, so be sure to show an anchor light.

OKEECHOBEE NAVIGATION

The two alternate routes on Lake Okeechobee require different navigational strategies. The Lake Route features some long runs between daybeacons, and the approach to Clewiston requires careful navigation of a narrow but well-marked channel. The Rim Route is the easiest to follow. Aids to navigation are numerous on the open portion of the run. Cruisers need only hold to the midline of the sheltered canal leading to Clewiston for safe passage along the westerly portion of the Rim Route.

Lake Route—Okeechobee Waterway Come abeam of flashing daybeacon #5 at the western end of the Port Mayaca Lock channel to its northerly side. Set a compass course for flashing daybeacon #6 to the southwest. Some 6.2 nautical miles separate #5 and #6. Along the way you will most likely sight the remains of a tall sunken barge, and several markers denoting this derelict's presence, north of your course. Keep well away from this hazard.

The run between #5 and #6 can seem to go on forever. If you are lucky enough to have a functioning GPS aboard, this is a good spot to make use of this electronic marvel.

Eastbound skippers may find flashing daybeacon #5 a bit hard to spot as they make their approach to the Port Mayaca Lock. Have your binoculars ready at hand to help pick out the channel markers.

You can pass flashing daybeacon #6 to either side. Continue on the same course, pointing eventually to come abeam of flashing daybeacon #7 by some .2 nautical miles to its northwest quarter. When approaching #7, observant skippers will spot the charted platforms (now in ruins) to the east. Don't mistake these old structures for the daybeacon.

Once abeam of #7, cut sharply to the south and set course to pass between unlighted daybeacons #9 and #12. Continue on the same track to come abeam of flashing daybeacon #14 to its easterly side. Between #12 and #14, you will sight unlighted daybeacon #13 well to the east. As chart 11428 shows, shoal water abuts both sides of the channel between #7 and #14. The 3- and 4-foot depths of Rocky Reef to the west are of particular concern. However, the channel is broad and prudent navigators who observe the various beacons should come through without too much difficulty.

From #14, the Lake Route turns sharply west. It is then a fairly straightforward run to unlighted daybeacon #1, which marks the northeastern entrance to the improved Clewiston approach channel. Northwest of unlighted daybeacon #2 a privately maintained, quick-flashing red "cylinder" daybeacon marks the first of the spoil banks created when the Clewiston channel was dredged. Keep away from this marker.

Continue following the ample markers into Clewiston. Stay strictly to the marked cut. Outside of the channel, depths quickly fall off to 3 feet or less.

At unlighted daybeacon #11, the Lake Route will begin to come under the lee of several marsh-grass islands. It is a straight shot in from this point between numerous pairs of daybeacons to the Clewiston lock. After you pass between unlighted daybeacons #19 and #20, the lock doors will appear dead ahead, preceded by the intersection with the Rim Route. From this point, cruising craft not bound for the facilities at Clewiston will cut northwest on the sheltered passage leading to the Moore Haven lock.

Rim Route—Okeechobee Waterway Use inset 2 on chart 11428 when navigating the waters between the western exit of the Port Mayaca Lock and the Okeechobee Waterway Rim Route's northerly entrance. Pay attention to business—depths outside of the marked channel rise quickly.

Come abeam of flashing daybeacon #1 to its northerly side. You should spot unlighted daybeacon #2 to the north, marking the northerly side of the channel. Continue on a westerly course for about 100 yards and then cut sharply to the south-southeast, pointing to pass between flashing daybeacon #2 and unlighted daybeacon #3. Along the way, unlighted daybeacon #1A will be passed well east of your course line.

Once you are between #2 and #3, the channel cuts sharply east toward the lake's easterly banks. Set course to come abeam of flashing daybeacon #4 to its northerly side. Continue past #4 for about 20 yards and then cut sharply, but not too quickly, to the south, pointing to pass unlighted daybeacon #4B to its easterly side.

From #4B, just follow the markers to Pahokee harbor. Westbound (southbound) navigators need only keep red daybeacons to their (the cruisers') starboard side and take green markers to port.

Between unlighted daybeacons #42 and #46, watch the eastern shore and you will spy the lock door blocking the Palm Beach Canal's entrance. This was one of the first canals dug in the Okeechobee region to drain the surrounding land.

You should sight a dun-colored water tower to the east shortly after passing the Palm Beach locks. This is your signal that Pahokee is just ahead.

Be sure to come abeam of unlighted daybeacon #62 to its southwesterly side. Shoal water lies north and northeast of #62.

Once you are abeam of #62, the entrance to Pahokee's concrete-breakwater-enclosed harbor will be obvious. Cruise into the basin, passing between unlighted daybeacons #1 and #2.

On to Torry Island Bridge South and west of Pahokee, the Rim Route remains straightforward, though daybeacons are spaced at wider intervals. South of unlighted daybeacon #72, itself north of Bacom Point, it might be best for navigators unfamiliar with the channel to run compass/GPS courses to the mouth of the sheltered canal leading to

Clewiston. You will enter this protected passage south of unlighted daybeacon #84.

A marked and charted side channel leading to deep water on Lake Okeechobee makes into the Rim Route south of Bacom Point, between unlighted daybeacons #76 and #80. Unfortunately, to continue cruising northwest safely into the main portion of the lake, you must pass between two charted but unmarked patches of shoal and rocky water. Strangers are advised against using this channel without specific local knowledge.

At unlighted daybeacon #84, the rim channel begins to pass behind a long finger of marsh, which shelters the route from the lake's often choppy waters. From this point, the Waterway remains well screened all the way to Moore Haven,

By the time you reach unlighted daybeacon #91, the Waterway will have passed into a well-defined canal. Soon after leaving #91 behind your stern, the channel takes a sharp jog to the southwest and hurries toward the Torry/Kreamer Island bridge.

The span crossing the Waterway from the mainland to Torry Island (with a closed vertical clearance of 11 feet) remains hand operated. Operation can be monumentally slow. We have had to wait for as long as fifteen minutes on occasion for the span to grind open. Theoretically, the bridge does open on demand (more or less) between 7:00 A.M. and 6:00 P.M. Monday through Thursday and from 7:00 A.M. to 7:00 P.M. Friday, Saturday, and Sunday. The span remains closed during the nighttime hours.

Just south-southwest of the Torry Island Bridge, the docks of Slim's Fish Camp will come up along the northwesterly shores. Power captains should cruise by at idle speed or otherwise risk injuring the many small fishing craft usually docked at Slim's.

Rim Route to Clewiston After putting the Torry/Kreamer span behind you, begin watching the eastern shore and you will soon catch sight of another lock. This usually closed structure marks the entrance of the old North New River and Hillsboro canals into Lake Okeechobee. Several miles farther along, passing cruisers will observe the lock to the Miami Canal on the south banks. These cuts were all part of the ambitious drainage plan initiated by Governor Broward.

Shortly after you pass the Miami Canal lock, the Waterway takes a bend to the northwest near unlighted daybeacon #92A, and heads for Clewiston. You will begin to pick up some markers along the northeastern banks that help to track your progress. Successful strategy for navigating the canal remains the usual holding to the centerline.

Clewiston Passing cruisers will encounter the Clewiston lock and the juncture with the Lake Route some 2.3 nautical miles northwest of unlighted daybeacon #100. Skippers making for Clewiston must cruise through the lock separating the Waterway and a small canal that serves the town's waterfront. The Clewiston lock is 50 feet wide and some 60 feet long. If the gates are closed (they often stand open), use the same procedure to request entry as you would on the Okeechobee Waterway locks.

South of the lock, a small cove will come abeam to starboard. This channel leads to

Anglers Marina and eventually to a popular launching area. Most cruising craft will want to continue straight ahead up the main Clewiston canal. Watch to port and you will catch sight of an Army Corps of Engineers work station. Several cranes may be present in the equipment yard.

Farther upstream, the long face dock of Roland Martin's Marina will come abeam to starboard. Before reaching this structure, visiting vessels will cruise by a small craft harbor where runabouts are docked under a shed roof.

The canal is eventually blocked by a low-level fixed bridge, barring farther upstream passage.

On to Moore Haven   Continue holding to the midwidth of the sheltered canal as you track your way northwest to the Moore Haven lock. No-wake, idle-speed restrictions are in place immediately northwest of the Waterway's intersection with the Clewiston lock. There is a similarly restricted stretch both northwest and southeast of charted Liberty Point.

Keep a sharp watch for the flotsam and jetsam that sometimes litter this section of the Waterway.

The eastern entrance to the Moore Haven lock will come abeam to port some 6 nautical miles past Liberty Point. Craft that must wait for a lock opening are free to tie to the assorted dolphins flanking the entrance.

Moore Haven Anchorage   To enter the convenient anchorage northwest of the lock entrance, continue northwest along the canal's centerline, past the main Waterway channel which cuts southwest to the Moore Haven lock. You will soon catch sight of a trailer park with its own dock flanking the southwesterly banks. Watch for a small, "No Wake" buoy along the northeasterly shores immediately after leaving the trailer park behind. A shoal has built out from the northeasterly banks along this stretch. Favor the southwesterly banks as you pass the "No Wake" buoy.

After leaving the buoy some 50 yards behind your stern, good depths once again open out almost from shore to shore for at least the next several hundred yards upstream. Choose any spot which strikes your fancy, set up a bright anchor light, and settle down for a restful evening.

Moore Haven Lock   The Moore Haven lock is similar to all the other Okeechobee locks, except that, for the first time, westbound vessels will now be lowered. Be sure to leave enough play in your mooring lines to allow for this drop in water level. Otherwise, you could be inquiring about cleat replacements at your next stop.

Moore Haven to Fort Myers

The Okeechobee Waterway passage from Moore Haven to Fort Myers is the most dynamic portion of the entire trans-Florida route. Moore Haven offers solid if low-key cruising facilities in a charming town that recalls the rough and ready days of the Florida crackers.

Farther to the west, cruising captains and crews pass down the Caloosahatchee Canal through an almost barren stretch of shoreline, broken occasionally by a marina or anchorage. Most of the surrounding countryside is screened off by the high dikes that shelter the canal. Nevertheless, your nose will most likely tell you that this is cattle country.

This rather forlorn stretch is followed by the rustic community of La Belle. If you are one of those travelers who enjoy small-town America, La Belle will surely merit your attention.

A bit farther to the west, the Waterway passes through its last lock and into the headwaters of Caloosahatchee River. Beginning as a small, rather sluggish stream, this river widens into an impressive body of water by the time it flows past Fort Myers. Along the way, several marinas and anchorages beckon cruisers to stop and rest awhile from their watery journey. This portion of the Okeechobee Waterway offers more anchorages than any other section between Stuart and Fort Myers.

The active, robust city of Fort Myers sits astride the wide Caloosahatchee River and offers extensive facilities for visiting cruisers. Whether you seek a quiet, secluded anchorage or a full-service marina, the passage from Moore Haven to Fort Myers is almost sure to satisfy.

Moore Haven (Standard Mile 78)

Moore Haven is another of the quiet, relaxed communities so typical of the Okeechobee region. With its roots in the cattle-raising era of the Florida cracker, the town is now the center of the region's sugarcane industry.

While acting as a mainstay for the local economy, the sugar trade can produce problems for visiting vessels. As part of the cane's cultivation, the fields are burnt off several times during the year. If the wind happens to be blowing toward the Moore Haven docks, your boat will most likely be covered with a black, almost oily residue that is decidedly difficult to clean. Fortunately, your chances of happening along during one of these burnings are rather slim.

The entire western shore of Lake Okeechobee, including Moore Haven, is also subject to another pest, with the curious local name of Chizzywinks. Often described as an overgrown mosquito, this less-than-welcome insect seems to hatch at unpredictable times and swarm among the pines along the lake shores. Cabin lights can attract them by the million. If you happen to be in the area during one of the hatchings, Ben Franklin's "early to bed" rule might be your best bet.

Both of Moore Haven's dockage facilities are within walking distance of the business district. The nearest grocery store is a healthy ten-block walk, but a hardware store is found less than two blocks away and the local library and post office sit within one block of the city docks. There is also a convenience store three blocks away.

Moore Haven Facilities (Various Lats/Lons—see below)

Southwest of the Moore Haven bascule

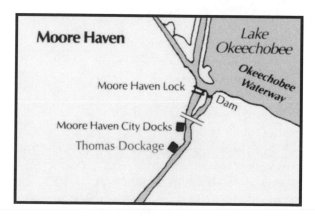

bridge, passing cruisers will soon catch sight of the Moore Haven City Docks along the northwestern banks, near 26 50.079 North/081 05.323 West. The small, municipal facility consists of an unattended, wooden face dock featuring full power and water connections. Depths alongside typically run 6½ to 7 feet. While most of this pier appeared to be in relatively good condition, we did find a few structural bolts sticking out from the pilings. Judicious use of fenders should solve this problem.

Once you are tied up, walk across the street to the small Moore Haven City Hall. After paying your overnight dockage fee, you will be presented with a key to the bathrooms (with showers), which are located in a small park immediately behind City Hall.

If you are looking for a spot to dine ashore, it is a two-block walk to the Moore Haven Restaurant (863-946-2929). This is pretty much the only game in town.

Moore Haven City Docks (863) 946-0711

Approach depths—8-12 feet
Dockside depths—6½-7 feet
Accepts transients—yes
Transient dockage rate—below average
Fixed wooden pier—yes
Dockside power connections—30
 and 50 amps
Dockside water connections—yes
Showers—yes
Restaurant—nearby

Moore Haven's second marina comes up immediately southwest of the city piers near 26 50.046 North/081 05.331 West. Thomas Dockage consists of two fixed, wooden face piers with fresh-water connections and 30- and 50-amp power hookups. Depths alongside the higher dock (where most transients are accommodated) range from 7 to 8 feet, with 5 to 6 feet of water at the lower pier.

Clean showers are available in the owner's residence across the street, though neither his large house nor the adjacent swimming pool is open to visitors. This handsome homeplace once served as an inn, but it is now a private residence. Dockage rates at Thomas Dockage match those of the city marina, so visiting cruisers can take their pick between the two without any worries about fee differentials. Fuel deliveries from tanker trucks can sometimes be arranged for boats that are ready to take on a large load of gasoline or diesel fuel. All the Moore Haven businesses described above are within virtually the same distance from Thomas Dockage as they are from the city docks.

Thomas Dockage (863) 946-1461

Approach depths—10-12 feet
Dockside depths—7-8 feet (larger dock)
 5-6 feet (smaller dock)
Accepts transients—yes
Transient dockage rate—below average
Fixed wooden piers—yes
Dockside power connections—30
 and 50 amps
Dockside water connections—yes
Showers—yes
Restaurant—nearby

Moore Haven History   Moore Haven was founded in the early twentieth century by James A. Moore, Jr., of Nova Scotia. As a West Coast entrepreneur, Moore had enjoyed success and then suffered financial failure. He came to Florida with the money he had salvaged with plans to organize the South Florida

Lands Company. He bought 100,000 acres of land, and Moore Haven was founded.

By 1916 Moore again found himself in financial difficulty and was forced to sell off his holdings at Moore Haven to several different investors. After a series of complicated financial maneuvers, much of the land about Moore Haven was acquired by John J. O'Brien, former editor of the *Philadelphia Public Ledger,* and George Q. Horwitz, a prominent attorney. Upon Horwitz's death, his widow, Marian, arrived to look after her interest.

No one knew it at the time, but Mrs. Horwitz was the harbinger of better days. In a few months, the town's new benefactor had built a general store, organized a bank, founded the DeSoto Stock Farms, formed a development corporation, and initiated a vegetable exchange. Marian married John O'Brien and the two continued to work for the betterment of the community. Eventually, she was elected mayor—even though the Nineteenth Amendment giving women the right to vote had yet to be passed, there was equal suffrage in Moore Haven.

In spite of all the O'Briens' good works, they were never totally accepted by the community. Their Roman Catholic faith, coupled with their obvious wealth and northern upbringing, was almost bound to be a source of friction with the fundamentalist Southern residents. Matters came to a head when African-Americans were imported to Moore Haven to help with the annual harvest. The town's white population was up in arms. The O'Briens supported the blacks' right to work and carried the day, but the seed of resentment had been sown.

Shortly thereafter, Moore Haven suffered a fire that consumed twenty-two houses and businesses. The 1926 hurricane wrought havoc in the small town. Even before these events, the O'Briens had become discouraged and turned their efforts elsewhere.

They attempted to found Lakeport, north of Moore Haven, by importing English and Belgian residents. This community failed, but the effort further alienated the O'Briens from the Okeechobee natives. The industrious couple then turned their attention to a colony of Japanese farmers south of Moore Haven at Sand Point. Here, much as at Moore Haven, the O'Briens almost single-handedly built the community into the city of Clewiston.

Resentment continued to grow, and one night when O'Brien was away, a shot was fired through a window of the couple's home and Marian received a nasty scalp wound. The assailant was never apprehended and shortly thereafter the O'Briens' home burned under mysterious circumstances.

The legacy of the O'Briens has lived on, however, and after Clewiston recovered from the twin hurricanes of 1926 and 1928, the town became the capital of the Everglades sugar industry. Marian O'Brien would have been very proud.

Lake Hicpochee (Standard Mile 82)

Shallow Lake Hicpochee intersects the Okeechobee Waterway some 3 nautical miles southwest of Moore Haven. While the lake's broad surface may look inviting, consistent 2- and 3-foot depths render this water body inaccessible to all but the smallest craft.

Hendry Isles Resort (Standard Mile 89)

Near Okeechobee Waterway Standard Mile 89, two facilities line the southerly banks. Chart 11428 notes the location of these firms with facility designation "56." First up is Hendry Isles Resort (863-983-8070). This development consists of a large camping ground, golf course, and motel. A small lagoon serving Hendry Isles cuts off from the southern banks.

In spite of reports we had received to the contrary, Hendry Isles has neglected their docks on the lagoon. There have not been any improvements, at least to our eyes, since 1987. Barring some future renovations, we do not recommend this facility for any cruising craft.

Glades Boat Storage (Standard Mile 89) (26 47.340 North/081 13.921 West)

Cruising captains in search of dry (on land) storage for larger craft, particularly sailing vessels, should give every consideration to Glades Boat Storage (863-983-3040). This firm has no wet slips, but you will sight a forest of masts from hauled sailcraft, and the yard's 40-ton travelift, just a short hop west of Hendry Isles (also on the southerly banks). Glades is a superfriendly, ultrahelpful operation that struck us as being first class in every regard. Once your vessel is hauled, whether for storage or do-it-yourself bottom work, you need buy nothing else from Glades. This practice is in marked contrast to other yards in eastern Florida. All repair work at Glades Boat Storage is strictly on a do-it-yourself basis.

Glades maintains a small ship's store, with paperback exchange library, and the cooperative management can help captains acquire most any marine equipment from nearby sources. There is also an on-site shower.

So, while there is no on-the-Waterway dockage offered, Glades Boat Storage is clearly one of the most popular repair yards between Stuart and Fort Myers.

Port La Belle Marina (Standard Mile 101) (26 45.975 North/081 24.287 West)

A large sign on the Waterway's southern shore some 1.8 nautical miles east of the La Belle Bridge heralds the entrance to popular Port La Belle Marina. Chart 11428 denotes the position of this marina with facility designation #56A.

Port La Belle features its own sheltered, naturally enclosed basin with floating metal-decked piers and full fueling facilities. Depths run 5 to 7 feet. Fresh-water hookups and 30-amp power connections are available.

Unfortunately, the floating docks at Port La Belle are somewhat limited in number, and they are often filled by resident craft. It would be best to call ahead for a dockage reservation rather than face disappointment at the end of a long cruising day. If you should find all the piers filled, the marina permits anchorage in the basin. You could then dinghy ashore to dine or play a round of golf.

Shoreside amenities include showers; a restaurant and lounge at the large, nearby clubhouse; and an eighteen-hole golf course. Horseback riding is also available. Many condominiums surround the yacht basin, and one comes away from Port La Belle with the idea that it is a success.

Several signs on the marina docks warn against feeding the alligators. This would not be a good place for Rover to take a swim!

Port La Belle Marina (863) 675-2261

Approach depths—5-6 feet
Dockside depths—6-7 feet
Accepts transients—yes
Transient dockage rate—below average
Floating metal-decked piers—yes
Dockside power connections—30 amps
Dockside water connections—yes
Showers—yes
Gasoline—yes
Diesel fuel—yes
Restaurant—on site

La Belle (Standard Mile 103) (Various Lats/Lons—see below)

West of the 28-foot bascule bridge, near Standard Mile 103, the charming, backwater community of La Belle lines both sides of the Waterway. While dockage facilities are somewhat limited, they are adequate for cruising visitors to make the acquaintance of this "other Florida" community.

During an earlier stay in La Belle, we were captivated at a local restaurant by an overheard conversation concerning the latest cattle breeding stock. Could this really be the same state that supports the condo caverns of Fort Lauderdale, Hollywood, and Hallandale?

We were equally taken with an underlying sense of enthusiasm pervading this entire community. La Belle is a town on the move. There is much new construction on the main highway and considerable evidence of recent expansion. Still, this is primarily a river and cattle town, and the bustle of southeastern Florida is noticeably absent.

For a small town, La Belle has a surprising number of shoreside attractions. The local library is located just behind the city docks (see below). And since La Belle is known for its honey production, be sure to check out Harold P. Curtis Honey Company (355 N Bridge Street, 863-675-2187), located less than a block south of the city docks on Highway 29. This firm maintains better than nine hundred working beehives. Samples of the many different types of honey are available for tasting before you make your purchase. An additional two-block walk will take you to a supermarket at the intersection of Highways 29 and 80. If you need tools, a local hardware store is found along this same stretch.

A public park lines the Waterway's southern shores, just east of the La Belle bascule bridge.

Every February the Swamp Cabbage Festival is held at this site. For those of you not in the know, Swamp Cabbage is the local term for "hearts of palm." The festival is a good old Southern celebration of arts, crafts, and, of course, food.

Dining in La Belle consists of what might be described as "solid" fare. Those seeking the latest quiche or casserole will probably be disappointed. The best (in our opinion) local restaurant is Flora and Ella's (550 Highway 80 N, 863-675-2891). A walk of almost two miles from the city piers is required to reach its doors. The effort may be worth it, however. The homemade pies, not to mention the fresh fried catfish, are legendary. Their breakfasts aren't anything to sneeze at either.

A bit closer, but still on Highway 80, visitors will find the Big V restaurant (863-675-2917) right beside the La Belle Motel (863-675-2971). Beef lovers will be more than pleased by the huge T-bones. There is also a nearby McDonald's for burger lovers.

The La Belle City Docks come up just west of the 28-foot bascule bridge on the southern banks, near 26 46.122 North/081 26.291 West. There is just enough room for two 35-footers to squeeze together at the fixed wooden pier. Depths alongside run 5 to 7 feet. A few low-key power and water connections are available. Free dockage is afforded for stays up to 72 hours; a fee is charged thereafter. Anchoring abeam of the docks, while leaving plenty of swinging room for moored craft, is permitted. You can then dinghy ashore to sample the town's charms.

La Belle City Docks (863) 675-2872

Approach depths—10-12 feet
Dockside depths—5-7 feet
Accepts transients—yes
Transient dockage rate—below average

Fixed wooden pier—yes
Dockside power connections—20 amps
Dockside water connections—yes
    (limited number)
Restaurant—several nearby

Visiting cruisers will be glad to learn that the River's Edge Motel Docks are available for overnight stops on the north side of the Waterway, just west of the La Belle bridge, near 26 46.161 North/081 26.347 West. This friendly facility features fixed, wooden piers with some power and water connections. Depths alongside again typically run 5 to 7 feet. If you rent a room at the adjacent motel, overnight dockage carries no additional charge. Transients (with or without a room) are welcome to make use of the swimming pool and shuffleboard court. A Laundromat, but no showers, is available for cruising, non-motel guests. You will need to walk back across the La Belle bascule bridge to reach the downtown district and its restaurants.

River's Edge Motel Docks (863) 675-6062

Approach depths—10-12 feet
Dockside depths—5-7 feet
Accepts transients—yes
Transient dockage rate—below average
Fixed wooden piers—yes
Dockside power connections—20 amps
Dockside water connections—yes
Laundromat—yes
Restaurant—several nearby

Caloosahatchee River

West of La Belle, the Okeechobee Waterway flows almost unnoticed into the headwaters of Caloosahatchee River. At first it's hard to tell that you have left the long canal behind and are finally in the river on the last stretch to Fort Myers. Eventually, though, you will see small loops and islands on both shores. Many of these are bends of the river left behind when the Army Corps of Engineers did some straightening of the stream's course in the 1930s. In spite of these channel improvements, the Caloosahatchee remains a lovely stream, alternating between extensive sections of natural shoreline and more developed areas.

Several of the Caloosahatchee's side loops are deep enough for overnight anchorage. Others are cheats and blinds that can quickly bring unwary navigators to grief. In the following section, you will find a review of the safer sidewaters, but remember, west of the W. P. Franklin lock, the waters again become tidal and bottom configurations are changeable. Feel your way into all sidewaters at idle speed and keep a weather eye on the sounder.

Rialto Harbor Docks (Standard Mile 119) (26 43.095 North/081 39.317 West)

One of the most unique marinas on the Okeechobee Waterway occupies the loop cutting into the main route's southerly banks near Standard Mile 119 (hard by chart 11428's notation "Subm Piles"). Rialto Harbor Docks consists of individual, one-boat (fixed wooden) piers flanking the loop's southerly

Old sternwheeler on Caloosahatchee River

shoreline. Each dock is graced by its own flower garden. Just behind the piers, the owner's large home and meticulously landscaped grounds overlook the water.

Entry into the loop is strictly by way of its western mouth. The eastside entrance is narrow and shoal. By making use of the western entrance, cruisers can expect minimum 6-foot approach depths and 6 to 11 feet of water at the individual piers. Transients are eagerly accepted at Rialto, though berths are somewhat limited, and it might be best to call ahead of time to check on availability. Freshwater hookups plus 30- and 50- (and a few 100-) amp power connections are provided. Showers and a cooling swimming pool are found shoreside. Visitors can also expect the novel service of daily newspaper delivery on their dock. A convenience store is located within a long walk of the dockage basin, but the harbormaster can often arrange for transportation to nearby grocery stores or the Fort Myers airport. There isn't a restaurant within walking distance, but a local pizza firm will deliver dockside.

All these dry statistics simply do not give an accurate impression of Rialto Harbor Docks' peaceful nature. If the idea of docking your boat in a secure harbor, nestled below tall trees with acres of landscaped grounds lying about your vessel, whets your appetite, then by all means make advance reservations and put Rialto Harbor in your cruising plans. Tell Milton that we sent you!

Rialto Harbor Docks (239) 728-3036
    http://www.rialtoharbor.com

Approach depths—6 feet
Dockside depths—6-11 feet
Accepts transients—yes
Transient dockage rate—above average
Fixed wooden piers—yes

Dockside power connections—30, 50, and (a few) 100 amps
Dockside water connections—yes
Showers—yes
Restaurant—pizza delivery

South Shore Anchorage (Standard Mile 120) (26 43.049 North/081 39.780 West)

Good overnight anchorage is afforded by the charted loop making into the Waterway's southern shore immediately east of charted Hickey Creek. Minimum 6-foot depths hold from the loop's westerly entrance into the rear portion of this stream. The easterly entrance is shoal and also plays host to a water-skiing course. Obviously you want to avoid this part of the loop like the proverbial plague.

Craft as large as 36 feet will find sufficient elbowroom and good protection from inclement weather on the waters lying about the rearward portion of the loop. The southerly shores exhibit light to moderate residential development, while the island to the north is completely in its natural state.

This is one of the best overnight stops on this portion of the Okeechobee Waterway for

Rialto Harbor Docks, Okeechobee Waterway

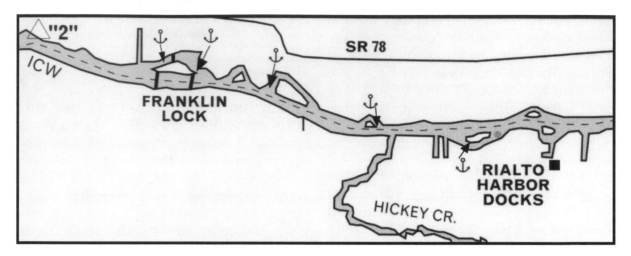

craft that can fit the size requirements outlined above. We recommend it highly.

North Shore Anchorage (Standard Mile 120.5) (26 43.156 North/081 40.338 West)

A stone's throw to the west of Hickey Creek, a small loop on the northern banks carries 6 to 7 feet of depth and features limited swinging room that would only be appropriate for boats as large as 32 feet (at the most). Protection is sufficient for use in all but the heaviest weather, and the holding ground seems to be thick mud. There is heavy residential development on the northern shores, but these homes are attractive and should enhance rather than detract from your stay.

Triple Loop Anchorages (Standard Mile 121) (Various Lats/Lons—see below)

Just west of Hickey Creek and the anchorage reviewed above, chart 11428 correctly identifies a triple loop bypass on the northern banks. The easternmost stream has shallow depths of 3 to 4 feet on its easterly reaches, but the western section holds 5 to 7 feet of water and is large enough for a 32-foot vessel to anchor safely near 26 43.324 North/081 40.984 West. Both shores are in their natural state. Be sure to read the navigation information on this creek before attempting entry.

The middle semicircle is shoal on both its entrances and should not be attempted by larger craft. Small boats that can stand some 3-foot depths will discover a wide, fairly deep lagoon on the rearward portion of this stream. This might be a great spot to break out the fishing pole or the lunch basket.

The westernmost of the three loops is actually quite different from the way it appears on chart 11428. This stream borders on the eastern face of the W. P. Franklin lock. Apparently, a man-made earthen dike has been built across the back of the one-time loop, so that the stream now appears as a deep cove in the northern banks.

This is perhaps the single best anchorage between Moore Haven and Fort Myers. While there is one unmarked shoal to avoid, most of the well-protected cove holds depths ranging from 7 to 9 feet. Craft up to 38 feet should be able to swing on the hook with plenty of elbow-room near 26 43.444 North/081 41.520 West. The entire cove is an official no-wake zone, so you will not be rudely awakened by the passage of a large power craft. This would be an excellent spot to swap stories while snugly anchored during foul weather. There is a launching ramp and a small park on the western banks, but otherwise the shoreline is in its natural state.

Similarly, the western portion of this cutoff loop is easily accessible to craft cruising east on the Okeechobee. This branch of the loop cuts off to the northeast, immediately west of the W. P. Franklin lock. Minimum depths of 6 feet with typical 7- to 8-foot soundings hold well in toward the rear of the cove. The initial portion of the loop (near 26 43.405 North/081 41.759 West) has enough swinging room for craft as large as 48 feet, while vessels up to 36 feet can fit snugly into the superprotected rear portion of the loop, near 26 43.422 North/081 41.689 West. As with the eastern side of this stream, much of the shoreline is guarded by a pleasant park. Clearly, this would be an excellent overnight stop, particularly for eastbound craft arriving a little too late in the day to clear the W. P. Franklin lock.

Daybeacon Anchorage (Standard Mile 122) (26 43.555 North/081 42.564 West)

West of unlighted daybeacon #2, yet another stream loops into the northern shoreline. While there are a few unmarked shallows to avoid, careful mariners piloting craft up to 40 feet should be able to enter safely and drop the hook securely. The waters with most swinging room will be discovered on the northern extreme of the loop. Most of the mainland banks support moderate residential development, while a horse farm occupies the western portion of the shoreline.

Do not attempt to enter the charted, tadpole-shaped offshoot to the north. Depths are too uncertain for cruising craft.

Olga Loop Anchorage (Standard Mile 123.5) (26 43.317 North/081 43.012 West)

The charted loop just northwest of the designation Olga on chart 11428 is certainly not the most easily entered of the Caloosahatchee River anchorages, but it can accommodate boats up to 36 feet, piloted by ultracautious skippers. The easterly entrance is too shallow for all but small craft, but the western inlet does feature a 6-foot channel. There is a large unmarked shoal to avoid, however. The best place to set the hook is on the stream's southernmost reaches. Be advised that this stream's mainland shores are now overlooked by heavy residential development. The island separating the loop from the main channel remains in its natural state. If you do enter this tricky sidewater, be sure to read the navigation information below before your first attempt.

Jack's Marine South (Standard Mile 124) (26 43.293 North/081 43.541 West)

Jack's Marine South flanks the southern banks of the Okeechobee Waterway at facility designation #59 on chart 11428. This ultrafriendly and accommodating, family-operated marina has a face dock fronting the main channel as well as some additional berths on a canal that strikes to the south. The canal carries some 4 to 5 feet of water, while the main dock has depths of 6 to 8 feet. Transients are gratefully accepted and are usually accommodated at the face pier fronting the Waterway. All berths feature 30-amp power hookups and fresh-water connections. Gasoline (no diesel fuel) is readily available. Good showers and a full Laundromat are a quick step from the docks. Notice the manicured grounds as you stroll by to wash off the day's grime. Mechanical repairs to gasoline power plants are offered, and smaller cruising craft can be hauled with a 10-ton travelift. The marina also maintains a ship's and variety store on the premises.

The dockmaster can usually arrange transportation to nearby restaurants (none are close enough for walking) and/or a supermarket and drugstore on Highway 80.

Without question Jack's Marine South offers one of the warmest welcomes of any facility between Stuart and Fort Myers. We recommend this firm unreservedly.

Jack's Marine South (239) 694-2708

Approach depths—10-12 feet
Dockside depths—6-8 feet (outer face dock)
 4-5 feet (canal docks)
Accepts transients—yes
Transient dockage rate—average
Fixed wooden piers—yes
Dockside power connections—30 amps
Dockside water connections—yes
Showers—yes
Laundromat—yes
Gasoline—yes
Below-waterline repairs—yes
Mechanical repairs—yes (gasoline only)
Ship's and variety store—yes
Restaurant—transportation usually available

Southern Shore Anchorage II (Standard Mile 124) (26 43.117 North/081 43.800 West)

Just west of Jack's Marine, another of the Caloosahatchee's many loops makes into the southern banks. As seems often to be the case, the eastern inlet is shoal and should not be attempted, while the western entrance has a broad channel with 6-foot depths. Swinging room at the back of the loop is sufficient for boats up to 36 feet, and the protection is excellent. For a bit more swinging room, ease into the rear-eastern portion of the loop just a bit, but, as noted above, don't attempt to cruise back to the main channel through the easterly entrance. The southern shores support moderate but attractive residential development. This is yet another good spot to ride out heavy weather.

Owl Creek Boat Works (Standard Mile 125) (26 43.607 North/081 45.053 West)

A 5½-7-foot channel marked by pairs of pilings strikes north into Owl Creek west of unlighted daybeacon #5. This cut eventually leads to Owl Creek Boat Works (239-543-2100), a complete repair and refit facility. Mechanical (gas and diesel), refinishing, carpentry, and fiberglass-repair services are all available. Haul-out capacity is extensive with three (count them, three) travelifts on site, rated at 30, 60, and 150 tons. Once your craft is hauled, you can perform your own bottom work or leave it to the yard's extensive team of professionals. Owl Creek is an obviously first rate operation that all cruising skippers can make use of with confidence.

Courtesy of our good friends at Royal Palm Yacht Club in Fort Myers, we have learned that Owl Creek and all its surrounding property have now been sold to a new developer. While the yard will remain in operation a few more years, eventually this entire region will

Owl Creek Boat Works

"go condo." When that happens, it seems likely that Owl Creek Boat Works will be only an Okeechobee Waterway veteran's memory.

Sweetwater Landing Marina (Standard Mile 126) (26 42.897 North/081 45.682 West)

Sometimes I'm truly amazed at how much things change in this business, and just how rapidly that change can occur. A good example of this rapidly altering reality can be found along the southern banks of the Caloosahatchee River, just west of the 27-foot, Wilson-Piggott bascule bridge, between unlighted daybeacons #6 and #8. Where once cruisers would have observed a rather skuzzy facility know as Marina 31, what will now appear is a huge residential and condo development with an attached marina. Fortunately for the cruising community, Sweetwater Landing Marina has chosen to accept transient craft for overnight or temporary dockage at their fixed wooden piers. Depths on the interior reaches of the harbor run about 5 feet at MLW, while several docks situated directly on the river carry a good 9 to 10 feet of water. Full 30- and 50-amp power hookups and freshwater connections are in the offing, as is waste pump-out service. There is even a well-supplied ship's and variety store on the premises.

Sweetwater Landing Marina was really just getting up and running as this account is being tapped out on the keyboard. While there is a low-key shower available currently, the management plans to add a whole array of climate-controlled showers and a Laundromat in the future. Similarly, gasoline can now be purchased, but hopefully diesel fuel will also be in the offing by 2005.

There is currently no restaurant within walking distance, though, again, one is planned in the adjacent development some time in the future. For the moment, be sure you arrive with a fully stocked galley.

It will be interesting over the next year or two to watch the continuing development of Sweetwater Landing. We'll try to keep you updated on developments in our *Salty Southeast* newsletter.

Sweetwater Landing Marina (239) 694-3850
http://www.sweetwaterlanding.net

Approach depths—6 feet
Dockside depths—5-10 feet MLW
Accepts transients—yes
Transient dockage rate—below average
Fixed wooden piers—yes
Dockside power connections—30
and 50 amps
Dockside water connections—yes
Showers—yes
Waste pump-out—yes
Gasoline—yes
Ship's and variety store—yes

Orange River (Standard Mile 129)

The entrance to Orange River comes up on the Waterway's southern shore at unlighted daybeacon #15, just east of the twin, Interstate 75, fixed bridges crossing the Caloosahatchee. We no longer recommend entry into this body of water by cruising-size craft. One of the former yards is out of business, and the river's bottom is littered with debris. Only small, shallow-draft craft should attempt to find their way to Coastal Marine Mart (239-694-4042), along the river's southerly reaches.

Fort Myers Yacht and Shipbuilding (Standard Mile 134) (26 39.268 North/081 51.311 West)

The marked channel cutting southeast to Fort Myers Yacht and Shipbuilding (239-332-7800) will come abeam to the southeast between flashing daybeacon #37 and unlighted daybeacon #39. This is a major repair yard offering every conceivable mechanical (gas and diesel), topside, and below-the-waterline repair service. The yard's travelift is rated at 30 tons. This is a yet another first-rate facility that can be trusted with even the most serious repair problem. Dockage is restricted to repair customers.

Fort Myers and Associated Facilities (Standard Mile 135) (Various Lats/Lons— see below)

Southwest of unlighted daybeacons #40 and #41, cruisers will sight three high-rise bridges crossing the Caloosahatchee River. These towering spans herald your arrival to the Fort Myers downtown waterfront. There are at least three marinas and one absolutely super yacht club to consider, not to mention all the many attractions in the downtown business district.

First up is Fort Myers Yacht Basin (26 38.870 North/081 52.180 West, Okeechobee Standard Mile 135), guarding the south-south-easterly banks between (moving east to west) the second and third bridges.

This first-class municipal marina actually encompasses two protected dockage basins enclosing 276 slips, as well as a long face dock fronting directly onto the river. While extensive space is always reserved for transients, advance reservations might be a wise course of action.

Visitors will find just about every type of dockage imaginable. Some slips are composed of wooden pilings set out from the concrete breakwater, while the eastern basin features a set of concrete floating docks reserved for smaller craft. All are absolutely first rate berths with 30-, 50-, and some 100-amp power hookups and water connections. While especially large pleasure craft sometimes have to be moored to the outer face dock, the two breakwater-enclosed basins pro-

Fort Myers Yacht Basin, Caloosahatchee River

vide better protection and are much to be preferred. Dockside depths in the east basin run about 7 feet, with soundings of 6 to 7 feet encountered in the west-side harbor. The outer face dock boasts at least 10 feet of water.

The marina ship's store, dockmaster's office, superb air-conditioned showers, clean bathrooms, and semi-open-air Laundromat occupy a good-sized building set between the two dockage basins. The ship's store at Fort Myers Yacht Basin (239-334-6446) is privately leased and well stocked with not only nautical but convenience-store-type food items as well.

Gasoline (both 89 and 93 octane grades available) and diesel fuel can be purchased at a fuel pier on the Caloosahatchee, immediately in front of the dockmaster's building (between the two dockage basins). Free waste pump-out is now offered at most every slip in the marina.

Visitors to Fort Myers Yacht Basin will find themselves a short step from the many attractions of downtown Fort Myers (see discussion below). A host of hotels, car rental agencies, and other shoreside businesses of all descriptions are a short stroll or taxi ride away.

Joe's Crab Shack (2024 W First Street, 312-332-1881) is also within walking distance, as is

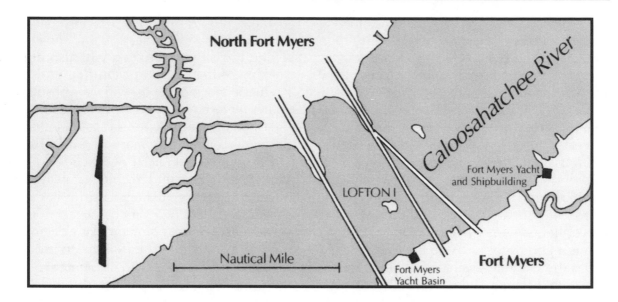

the French Connection (2288 First Street, 239-332-4443), both recommended by the local marina staff. Tucan Charlie's restaurant (2220 W First Street, 312-334-2727) is close by too. There is no longer a downtown grocery store accessible by foot, but you can easily take a taxi to and from one of the local supermarkets.

Fort Myers Yacht Basin (239) 334-8271

Approach depths—8-10 feet
Dockside depths—10 feet (fuel and face dock)
    7 feet (east basin)
    6-7 feet (west basin)
Accepts transients—yes
Transient dockage rate—below average
Fixed wooden and concrete docks—yes
Floating concrete docks—yes
Dockside power connections—up to 100 amps
Dockside water connections—yes
Waste pump-out—yes
Showers—yes
Laundromat—yes
Gasoline—yes
Diesel fuel—yes
Mechanical repairs—arranged through local independent contractors
Ship's and variety store—yes
Restaurant—several nearby

Several years ago the city of Fort Myers began sanctioning an official city anchorage behind charted Lofton Island (26 39.118 North/081 52.412 West, Okeechobee Standard Mile 135). This small body of land lies along the charted channel's northerly flank, opposite Fort Myers Yacht Basin. Since that time, the city has added a sailcraft-only, 25-buoy, fee-charging mooring field on these same waters. Fort Myers hopes to add another 25 mooring buoys in the future. A dinghy dock is available for those who pay for a mooring in the east basin of the Fort Myers city facility.

By the way, the city dockmaster has informed this writer that it was not Fort Myers' notion to restrict these moorings to sailing vessels. Rather, this was a requirement by the state of Florida. Fortunately, powercraft can still anchor on these waters with their own hook!

After traversing its unmarked entrance cut (see our navigational account of this anchorage below), cruising craft can curl around behind (north and northwest of) Lofton Island on the broad, correctly charted patch of 7- and

8-foot waters. Here you can pick up a mooring buoy or anchor. For maximum shelter, drop anchor as the body of Lofton Island comes abeam to the south, and be sure to leave plenty of swinging room between your vessel and any other pleasure craft that have picked up a mooring. Stay at least 50 yards off the isle's shoreline.

Protection is good from southerly blows, courtesy of the lee afforded by Lofton Island, and there is some shelter to the north from the mainland shores. This is most certainly, however, not a foul-weather hidey-hole. Nevertheless, when winds aren't too ornery, this is a good spot to spend the evening, and it has the distinct advantage of being within shouting distance of downtown Fort Myers.

The enclosed, well-protected dockage basin of Fort Myers' newest pleasure-craft facility guards the Caloosahatchee's southeasterly banks, west-southwest of the westernmost Fort Myers high-rise bridge, and southeast of flashing daybeacon #49. Centennial Harbour Marina (26 38.505 North/081 52.574 West, Okeechobee Standard Mile 135.5) has been completed since the last edition of this guide. When last we reported on this facility, only a portion of its dockage basin was in place. Now, the entire harbor is protected by a long breakwater, and there are many more wet slips.

The marina's scantily marked entrance channel carries 7 to 8 feet of water, while soundings of 6½ to 8 feet are typical in the breakwater-enclosed dockage basin. Transients are eagerly accepted, as well as large cruising groups. Full power and water connections are readily available dockside, as is waste pump-out service. Diesel fuel delivery can be arranged by way of a shoreside fuel truck for vessels requiring a goodly amount of petrol in the tank.

Nice, climate-controlled showers and an adjacent, air-conditioned Laundromat are located in the dockmaster's building just behind the basin. Here you will also find a welcome e-mail hookup. On-line cruisers, and that's now most of us, will be ever so glad of this feature. Joe's Crab Shack (239-332-1881), mentioned above, is located immediately adjacent to this marina, while Tucan Charlie's restaurant (2220 W First Street, 312-334-2727) is a scant two blocks away. The entire Fort Myers business district is easily accessible by foot or a very quick taxi ride.

There can be no argument that Centennial Harbour is a wonderful addition to the Fort Myers cruising scene. With its plentiful dockage (now breakwater protected) combined with the municipal marina's prodigious wet-slip space (see below), transient berth availability in and near downtown Fort Myers is quite impressive indeed.

Centennial Harbour Marina (239) 461-0775

Approach depths—7-8 feet
Dockside depths—6½-8 feet
Accepts transients—yes
Transient dockage rate—average
Floating concrete piers—yes
Dockside power connections—30
 and 50 amps
Dockside water connections—yes
Waste pump-out—yes
Showers—yes
Laundromat—yes
Variety store—small
Restaurant—next door and several nearby

The channel leading to the breakwater-enclosed harbor of Royal Palm Yacht Club (26 38.197 North/081 52.906 West, Okeechobee Standard Mile 135.5) cuts southeast between flashing daybeacon #54 and unlighted daybeacon #52. Good entrance depths of 7 to 8 feet lead to an occluded entrance marked by arrows painted on the breakwater. Inside the harbor, cruisers will find depths of 6 to 7 feet at fixed wooden slips (some set against the concrete breakwater). Members of other yacht clubs with reciprocal privileges are gladly accepted for guest dockage. The dockmaster is on duty from 8:00 A.M. to 4:00 P.M., Tuesday through Saturday, and from 8:00 A.M. to 3:00 P.M. Sundays. The club's slips feature both 30- and 50-amp power connections, as well as water connections. Shoreside, visitors will discover good showers in the clubhouse. Lunch and dinner are served in the club dining room Tuesday through Saturday. A convenience store is located two blocks to the north on McGregor Boulevard. Joe's Crab House restaurant (239-332-1881) can be reached by a three-block walk.

This writer gained the swift and sure impression that Royal Palm is an active club that is friendly to visiting cruisers from other clubs. If you are lucky enough to have the appropriate credentials, then by all means, give this facility your most serious consideration.

Royal Palm Yacht Club (239) 334-2176
http://www.rpyc.org

Approach depths—7-8 feet
Dockside depths—6-7 feet
Accepts transients—members of other yacht clubs with reciprocal privileges only
Fixed wooden piers—yes
Dockside power connections—30 and 50 amps
Dockside water connections—yes
Showers—yes
Restaurant—on site and nearby

Downtown Fort Myers

Numbers to know in Fort Myers include:
Bluebird Cab—239-275-8294
Preferred Taxi—239-334-0000
Yellow Cab of Fort Myers—239-332-1055
Avis Rental Cars—239-768-2022

Budget Rent A Car—239-768-1500
Hertz Rent A Car—239-768-3100
Boat/U.S. Marine Center—239-481-7447
West Marine—239-275-6077
Chamber of Commerce—239-332-3624

Within the last decade, Fort Myers has done a good job renovating its downtown waterfront. Where once old wharves and crumbling warehouses stood, cruising visitors will now find a lovely green park, an arts center, a convention complex, and the local chamber of commerce. All of these attractions are located within walking distance of the city marina on Edwards Drive. You might also take the time to stroll down First Street through the main downtown business district. It will soon be obvious that business is returning to this section of the city.

One cannot visit Fort Myers without getting the deep impression of a warm welcome and a general air of friendliness. It's no secret among my friends that Fort Myers is one of this writer's favorite cities in Western Florida. I hope you too will have the opportunity to make the acquaintance of this unique town that Thomas Edison adopted.

Fort Myers History   Fort Myers was established along the banks of the Caloosahatchee after the Seminole Indian wars in 1850. It was abandoned shortly thereafter, but again saw service during the Civil War. With the river serving as a ready source of transportation and commerce, the village of Fort Myers began growing about 1868, and the town was finally incorporated in 1911.

Beginning in the late 1800s Fort Myers played host to three giants of American science and industry. Thomas Alva Edison, perhaps America's greatest scientist, came south to the city by the Caloosahatchee searching for a healthful winter climate. He fell in love with Fort Myers and returned every winter for the rest of his days.

The energetic scientist soon bought a lot by the river and began to design his winter residence. The house was built in sections in Fairfield, Maine. The various components were then transported by two sailing schooners to Fort Myers, where they were assembled in 1886. This was one of the first prefabricated homes in the United States.

An extensive laboratory was added so that Edison could continue his scientific work while in residence. A swimming pool was built, braced with native bamboo rather than the usual steel rods. It was filled by an artesian well that was 1,100 feet deep.

Before long Edison managed to convince his friends Henry Ford and Harvey Firestone to share his winter quarters in Fort Myers. Ford eventually built a home next door to Edison, and the two remained fast friends until the great scientist's death.

While wintering in Fort Myers, Edison dreamed up the notion of manufacturing synthetic rubber from Florida's native goldenrod weed. With the financial backing of both Ford and Firestone, Edison managed to produce a new strain of the weed that grew to an astonishing 14 feet in height. History suggests that these experiments led to the modern-day production of synthetic rubber, without which automobile transportation would be impractical at best.

Thomas Edison loved tropical plants and was interested in the byproducts that might be derived from them. Over the years he established an elaborate botanical garden at his Fort Myers home, containing more than 1,000 plants from around the world. In one instance he planted a 2-inch (diameter) banyan tree that Harvey Firestone brought him from India. That same tree survives to this day, and the circumference of its trunk has increased to 400 feet.

Edison loved automobiles. Henry Ford presented a gift to his neighbor in 1907 of a prototype Model T Ford. For the next twenty years, Ford had his engineers add the latest updates to the car every twelve months. Edison refused to part with the original model for a newer version.

Today, both the Thomas Edison and Henry Ford homes (2350 McGregor Boulevard, 239-334-3614) have been preserved and are open to the public. The scientist's homeplace has been left just as it was upon Edison's death. The rooms are filled with memorabilia, including the phonographs, brass lamps, and carbon-filament light bulbs designed by Edison himself. The old laboratory is still intact and immensely impressive. A collection of antique cars is also on display, including Edison's 1908 Cadillac Opera Coupe, prototype Model T Ford, and a 1936 Brewster limousine.

All cruising and landlubber visitors to Fort Myers should make every effort to tour these two historic homes for themselves. They are open from 9:00 A.M. to 4:00 P.M. weekdays, and Sunday afternoons as well.

On to the Gulf of Mexico

This guide's coverage of the Okeechobee Waterway ends at Fort Myers. Farther to the west and southwest, the Caloosahatchee stretches for many facility-rich miles to the southern genesis of the western Florida ICW and the open waters of the Gulf. For a continuing review of these fascinating waters, please consult this writer's *Cruising Guide to Western Florida*.

Caloosahatchee River, Okeechobee Waterway

MOORE HAVEN TO FORT MYERS NAVIGATION

Successful navigation of the Okeechobee Waterway between Moore Haven and Fort Myers is about as simple as it gets. Most of the time you need only hold to the mid-width of the canal-like Waterway. As you approach Fort Myers, the Caloosahatchee River opens out into a wide body of water, but even here the channel is well outlined with aids to navigation. As always, you should nevertheless stay alert.

Moore Haven   South of the Moore Haven lock, cruisers will first encounter a railroad bridge with a closed vertical clearance of 5 feet. Fortunately, this span is usually open unless a train is due. Should you find it closed, be warned that this bridge is hand operated and opening can be a slow process. Be sure to use the easterly pass through. The Waterway is next spanned by twin fixed bridges with 55 feet of vertical clearance.

While passing the Moore Haven waterfront, you may spy a small creek cutting off to the west. In the past, some boats have attempted to anchor on these waters, but the stream is crossed by a power line with a scant 18 feet of vertical clearance. Add to that the presence of a small-craft, fishing-oriented marina on this creek, and it isn't hard to understand why we do not recommend stopping here.

Proceed at idle speed past the Moore Haven waterfront. You will pass the city dock on the western bank, followed by the twin face piers of Thomas Dockage. The eastern shore supports fairly heavy but attractive residential development. The homes on the eastern and southeastern banks continue lining the Waterway for a good distance upstream.

On the Waterway   After you leave Moore Haven, the Waterway's shores are low and marshy as far as Lake Hicpochee. Remember to hold strictly to the Waterway channel while passing through the lake. Outside of the improved cut, depths fall off immediately to grounding levels.

West of Lake Hicpochee, both shorelines soon rise to high earthen dikes. These hills provide excellent protection for the canal, and it takes a very hard blow indeed to raise an uncomfortable chop east of La Belle.

Hendry Isles Resort and Glades Boat Storage   The small stream cutting south to the dockage basin at Hendry Isles will come abeam to the south near Standard Mile 89. Cruising skippers are advised to bypass this facility entirely. Another quick hop to the west will bring up the haul-out facilities at Glades Boat Storage on the southern banks.

Ortona Lock   The Ortona lock blocks the Waterway some 1.3 nautical miles west of charted Long Hammock Creek. The change in water levels is usually not too drastic in this lock, and you should not experience any unusual difficulty. Boats should moor to the north wall unless otherwise instructed by the lockmaster.

On the Waterway   Just west of the Ortona lock, the charted railway span has now been removed. Hooray! One less bridge to worry about.

The Caloosahatchee Canal continues to take an easily followed, well-protected route (generally) west from Ortona lock. No anchorages or facilities are accessible short of Port La Belle Marina, near Standard Mile 101.

Port La Belle Marina   The entrance to Port La Belle will come up on the southern banks where chart 11428 pictures facility designation #56A. The channel to the marina is flanked by two unmarked pilings. Enter on the inlet's midwidth and head straight toward the docks. If the marina's berths are full and you choose to anchor in the basin, one of the best spots is between the docks and the western banks. Be sure to leave plenty of room for passing traffic.

La Belle   As you approach La Belle, watch the northern shores to catch a glimpse of several lovely homes atop the high earthen banks. These residences mark the easterly limits of the charming village of La Belle.

Large power vessels should cruise through La Belle's waters at idle speed. Many boat owners and those docked at the city pier will thank you.

The Highway 29 bascule bridge with 28 feet of vertical clearance crosses the Waterway in the heart of La Belle. This span opens on demand except from 10:00 P.M. to 6:00 A.M. During these late-night and early-morning hours, the bridge opens only with three hours' notice.

West of the Highway 29 bridge, the La Belle city docks will come abeam along the southern banks. The face piers belonging to River's Edge Motel line the northern shoreline on this same stretch.

On the Waterway   At the charted village of Denaud, cruisers will pass under a swing bridge with a closed vertical clearance of 9 feet. As usual for this section of the Waterway, this span opens on demand except during the nighttime hours. Unusually, passing craft are directed by a sign to one of the bridge's pass throughs or another, depending on their direction. Westbound vessels should take the northern leg, while eastbound boats are directed to the southern pass through.

It is a run of some 13 nautical miles from La Belle to the tiny village of Alva. Once a rough and ready carousing center for local cowboys, today Alva is so small that you could almost blink and miss it.

West of Alva, the Waterway begins its passage through the still locked upper reaches of Caloosahatchee River. The channel winds a bit one way and then the other along this stretch.

Between La Belle and Alva a number of loops appear on both banks. None of these is recommended for gunkholing or overnight anchorage. Most are shallow and choked with lily pads. If you are searching for a haven where you can drop the hook, hang on a bit longer. Several good anchorages appear at Alva and points west.

Eventually cruisers will meet up with the Alva bascule bridge, closed vertical clearance 23 feet. Again, expect the span to open on demand except at night.

The loop creek on the southern shore near the charted location of Owanita looks good, but it has consistent 3-foot depths. Only small craft drawing 2½ feet or less should attempt entry.

Rialto Harbor Docks Enter the southside loop east of Hickey Creek, home of Rialto Docks (easternmost of the two loop creeks adjoining the river's southerly banks, east of Hickey Creek). Strictly by way of its western inlet, slow down to minimum speed and carefully pick your way along the midwidth of the stream. Watch for a few low-key green can markers. Pass these to your port side. Soon, the first of Rialto's individual docks will come abeam to starboard. Don't attempt to cruise east past the last dock and reenter the main channel by way of the loop's easterly mouth. Depths of 4 feet or less are waiting to greet you on this passage.

South Shore Anchorage To make good your entry into the loop creek along the southerly banks closest to the eastern side of Hickey Creek, be sure to use the west-side inlet only. The eastern passage is shallow and foul. Cruise into the stream's centerline.

For best protection, continue cruising into the rear portion of the loop. Boats needing a bit more swinging room can squeeze into the eastern side of the loop's rearward section, but don't follow this passage very far. The eastern side of the loop is shoal and partially overgrown with lily pads.

Three-Loop Anchorages The easternmost of the three charted loop creeks, east of the W. P. Franklin lock (flanking the northern banks), has one entrance that is markedly deeper than the other. Cruising craft should use the westerly inlet and drop anchor before reaching the stream's first elbow turn to the southeast. Stick to the midwidth and you should find yourself in some 7 feet of water.

The middle creek has some deep water on its interior, but both entrances run to as little as 3-foot depths. This stream can only be entered safely by very small craft.

The sidewater just east of the Franklin lock is not as it appears on chart 11428. Because of changes made in the surrounding shoreline during lock construction, this water body is now a half-loop, baylike body of water that offers a wonderful haven.

Favor the port shore slightly as you enter the easterly reaches of this half-loop at idle speed. You should quickly catch sight of an orange and white no-wake buoy dead ahead. Pass this aid to its easterly side and continue into the wider section of the bay, still favoring the port banks slightly. The cove to the northeast and most of the starboard banks are shoal and should not be approached. Position your craft so that you will not swing into these shallows after setting the hook.

Similarly, the western side of this bisected loop can be used for convenient anchorage by boats cruising on the waters west of the W. P. Franklin lock. Simply enter this portion of the stream on its centerline, and drop anchor at a likely spot. The waters with the most swinging room are found near the entrance, while craft that can stand a touch less room will want to consider the most sheltered waters farther upstream.

W. P. Franklin Lock The W. P. Franklin lock is typical of locks on the Okeechobee Waterway. Small craft can signal to lock through via a chain pulley on the outer fender, but larger vessels should use the old, reliable two short followed by two long horn blasts. Moor to the southern lock walls unless otherwise instructed by the tender.

Daybeacon Anchorage Mariners can enter the semicircular creek on the northern shore just west of unlighted daybeacon #2 by either entrance. If you make use of the eastern inlet, favor the port shore slightly until you approach the rear of the loop. Cruise back to the midwidth and continue on the middle until the creek turns back to the south and heads for the Waterway.

Pleasure craft cruising the westerly portion of the stream should favor the western banks, as the eastern shore bordering the small island is shoal. Do not attempt to enter the charted tadpole-shaped offshoot to the north. It is much smaller than a casual study of chart 11428 would indicate.

Olga Anchorage The south shore loop just west of Olga must be entered via its westerly inlet. Favor the starboard shore heavily as you cruise into the creek. A large, charted shoal extends westward from the island shore into the entrance's midwidth. Once on the stream's interior, cruise back to the middle and select a likely spot at the rear of the loop to anchor.

On the Waterway Shortly after passing the above-described loop, you will catch sight of a cove that hooks back to the east along the southern banks. While there are several private docks on this sidewater, cruising craft should not attempt to enter as there are numerous unmarked 2-foot patches in and around this cove.

Southern Shore Anchorage II To enter the creek making into the southern banks of the Waterway near facility designation #59 on chart 11428, cruise into the centerline of the loop's western inlet. Maximum swinging room is found on the rear portion of the stream. The easterly gateway is quite shoal and should not be used.

On the Waterway West of Olga, residential development becomes increasingly evident on both shores of the Waterway. While most of these waters have no speed restrictions, large power cruisers would do well to cruise by at minimum speed. We have talked with several homeowners who have suffered through frequent monster wakes that throw salt water onto their lawns. Please be considerate!

Owl Creek Boat Works The well-marked entrance to Owl Creek Boat Works breaks off to the north between unlighted daybeacons #5 and #6. This channel does not present any problems if you keep to the marked cut.

On the Waterway Between unlighted daybeacons #6 and #8, a bascule bridge with a closed vertical clearance of 27 feet crosses the Waterway. For boats that can't clear this height, the span opens on demand, except between 10:00 P.M. and 6:00 A.M.

Just west of this span, the charted canal leading to newly minted Sweetwater Landing Marina will be spotted along the southerly banks. Enter on the midwidth. The dockage basin will soon open out dead ahead.

West of unlighted daybeacon #11, numerous signs restrict passing craft to idle speed. Manatees are quite numerous in these waters, and careful cruisers will proceed at minimal speed between #11 and flashing daybeacon #20. Mariners will note a skeletal metal sculpture of several manatees playing together on a small island east of unlighted daybeacon #15. Immediately past #15, the indifferently marked channel to Orange River will come abeam to the south.

Orange River   Remember, entry into Orange River is no longer recommended for any save small, shallow-draft power craft. As such, no navigational detail for this body of water will be presented here.

On the Waterway   West and southwest of flashing daybeacon #13, the waters begin to widen. Depths outside of the Waterway channel are quite skimpy. Be sure to observe all markers carefully and keep to the channel until deeper waters open out along the Caloosahatchee's track, southwest of Fort Myers.

West of unlighted daybeacon #15, the combined paths of the Okeechobee Waterway and Caloosahatchee River pass under the twin Interstate 75 high-rise fixed bridges. These spans sport a vertical clearance of 55 feet.

Farther to the west, a lift-type railway bridge with only 5 feet of closed vertical clearance crosses the river from north to south. When open, this span has a vertical gap of 55 feet. It is usually open unless a train is due.

Southwest of unlighted daybeacon #19,

the Caloosahatchee River opens out into a wide body of water that can produce a considerable chop in high winds. Depths remain skimpy outside of the marked cut. This is not the place to explore off the beaten path.

Northwest of unlighted daybeacon #36, a daybeacon-marked channel leads to Old Ferry Park. Unfortunately, depths of 3 to 4 feet are common in this cut. Cruising skippers are advised to bypass this side trip.

Between flashing daybeacon #37 and unlighted daybeacon #39, the easily followed channel to Fort Myers Yacht and Shipbuilding makes into the southeastern edge of the Caloosahatchee. Boats of almost any size and draft can enter without difficulty.

Fort Myers   Southwest of unlighted daybeacon #40, the channel is spanned by the first of two fixed high-rise bridges. Both these spans are part of the Highway 41 Bypass route, but they are also known as the Thomas Edison Bridge. These welcome structures replace an earlier low-level bascule bridge. They have a vertical clearance of 55 feet. A third (Highway 41 Business) fixed bridge with a 55-foot clearance crosses the Caloosahatchee about .8 of a nautical mile to the southwest.

No-wake restrictions are in effect along the Fort Myers waterfront between the bridges, and the Florida Marine Patrol is known for its strict enforcement on these waters. Captains who throw a wake will not only earn the ire of their fellow mariners, but they will most likely face a stiff fine as well.

As you cruise between the second and third bridges, the twin dockage basins of

Fort Myers Yacht Basin will soon come abeam on the southeastern banks. The dockmaster's office (and fuel dock) is located in the building separating the two harbors.

Lofton Island Anchorage and Mooring Field
For best depths, cruisers should depart the main river channel immediately west of the westerly span of the Edison bridge. Cruise to the north-northwest, keeping the bridge about 25 yards off your starboard side. Shallower water lies off Lofton Island's easterly shoreline, so best depths can be maintained by heavily favoring the bridge's westerly face. Similarly, soundings off the western shores of Lofton Island are quite thin.

Eventually, after tracking your way north-northwest just off the Edison bridge's westerly face, you will come abeam of the correctly charted, broad ribbon of deeper water that stretches to the southwest. Turn to port and follow these good depths to a point some 50 yards off Lofton Island's northerly banks. Here you will find room to anchor, or those captains who pilot a sailcraft can pick up one of the city-provided mooring buoys. Chances are that you will already find several fellow craft ensconced in this haven.

On to the Western Florida Coastline
Farther to the southwest, the Okeechobee Waterway and Caloosahatchee River pass under the third 55-foot span and leave the confines of this guide. For continuing coverage of Caloosahatchee River and all the other waters of Florida's fascinating Gulf Coast, please consult this writer's *Cruising Guide to Western Florida*.

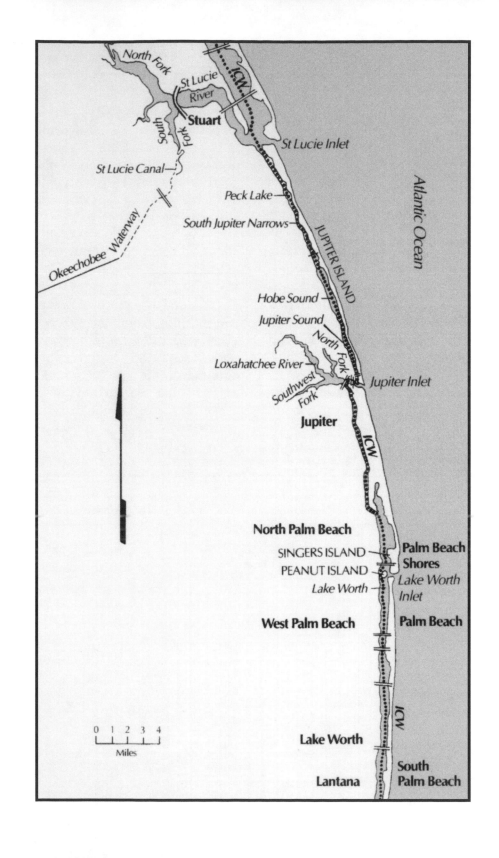

North Fork

St Lucie
River

South
Fork

Stuart

ICW

St Lucie Inlet

St Lucie Canal

Okeechobee Waterway

Peck Lake

South Jupiter Narrows

JUPITER ISLAND

Atlantic Ocean

Hobe Sound

Jupiter Sound

North Fork

Loxahatchee River

Southwest
Fork

Jupiter Inlet

Jupiter

ICW

North Palm Beach

SINGERS ISLAND

PEANUT ISLAND

Lake Worth

**Palm Beach
Shores**

Lake Worth
Inlet

West Palm Beach

Palm Beach

ICW

Lake Worth

0 1 2 3 4
Miles

Lantana

**South
Palm Beach**

St. Lucie Inlet to Palm Beach

The waters between St. Lucie Inlet and southern Palm Beach present a striking contrast. South of the inlet, the ICW follows a narrow, sheltered passage bordering on sparsely developed country. Then, as if by magic, passing cruisers will come upon the magnificent homes lining Hobe Sound. This development remains one of the most exclusive residential communities in all of Florida. After passing through Hobe Sound, you will cruise by Jupiter Inlet with its adjoining facilities and tall, red brick lighthouse. Farther south, the Waterway passes out into broad, shallow Lake Worth and meets up with the Palm Beaches.

Most people consider Palm Beach the northern limits of the "Gold Coast." Other people include the Hobe Sound complex, but this affluent, conservative mecca for the very rich is quite different from the boisterous Palm Beach communities. Personally, we think of the "Gold Coast" as stretching from North Palm Beach to Miami. This section of the coast is characterized by some of the most intense residential development that you will ever observe. High-rise condos dot the coast and private homes crowd each other. Many yards are so finely manicured that every blade of grass seems to have been individually clipped. Swimming pools by the dozen overlook the Waterway. Life is quick paced, and more people seem to be moving in constantly. The southeastern Florida "Gold Coast" is really without peer. Many find it exciting; others are glad to push on to the quieter waters of the Florida Keys. Only you can decide how the "Gold Coast" will fit into your cruising plans.

Charts Two NOAA charts are required to cover all the waters between St. Lucie Inlet and southern Palm Beach:
11472—details the ICW and all surrounding waters from St. Lucie Inlet to the Palm Beach Southern Boulevard Bridge
11467—provides coverage for the Waterway in the southernmost section of Palm Beach

Bridges
Highway 708/Hobe Sound Bridge—crosses ICW at Standard Mile 996, south of unlighted daybeacon #30—Bascule—21 feet (closed)—opens on demand
Highway 707 Bridge—crosses ICW at Standard Mile 1004, just north of Waterway's intersection with Loxahatchee River—Bascule—25 feet (closed)—opens on demand
Jupiter/U.S. 1 Federal Highway Bridge—crosses combined paths of ICW and Loxahatchee River at Standard Mile 1005, west of unlighted can buoy #3—Bascule—26 feet (closed)—opens on demand
Indiantown Road Bridge—crosses ICW at Standard Mile 1006, south of unlighted daybeacon #10—Bascule—35 feet (closed)—opens on demand
Donald Ross/Juno Beach Bridge—crosses ICW at Standard Mile 1009, well south of flashing daybeacon #25—Bascule—35 feet (closed)—opens on demand
PGA Boulevard Bridge—crosses ICW at

Standard Mile 1012.5—Bascule—24 feet (closed)—opens only on the quarter and three-quarter hour 7:00 A.M. to 9:00 A.M. and 4:00 P.M. to 7:00 P.M. weekdays; during weekends and holidays opens every 20 minutes 8:00 A.M. to 6:00 P.M. (November 1 to May 1 weekdays, 9:00 A.M. to 6:00 P.M.); at all other times opens on demand

North Palm Beach/Parker Bridge—crosses ICW and Lake Worth at Standard Mile 1014, southeast of intersection with North Palm Beach Waterway—Bascule—25 feet (closed)—year round opens only on the hour and half-hour 7:00 A.M. to 9:00 A.M. and 4:00 P.M. to 7:00 P.M. weekdays; November 1 to May 1, opens on the hour and every 20 minutes thereafter 9:00 A.M. to 4:00 P.M. (8:00 A.M. to 6:00 P.M. during weekends and holidays)

Riviera Beach Bridge—crosses ICW and Lake Worth at Standard Mile 1018, south of flashing daybeacon #36—Fixed—65 feet

Flagler Memorial Bridge—crosses ICW and Lake Worth at Standard Mile 1022, south of unlighted daybeacon #10—Bascule—17 feet (closed)—October 1 through May 31 will not open 7:30 A.M. to 9:30 A.M. and 4:00 P.M. to 5:45 P.M. weekdays, except opens at 8:30 A.M. and 4:45 P.M.; opens only on the hour and half-hour 9:30 A.M. to 4:00 P.M.; opens on demand during the evening and night

Royal Palm Bridge—crosses ICW at Standard Mile 1022.5, south of unlighted daybeacon #14—Bascule—14 feet (closed)—October 1 through May 31 will not open 7:45 A.M. to 9:45 A.M. and 3:30 P.M. to 5:45 P.M. weekdays, except opens at 8:45 A.M., 4:30 P.M., and 5:15 P.M.; opens only on the quarter and three-quarter hours 9:45 A.M. to 3:30 P.M.; opens on demand during the evening and night

Southern Boulevard Bridge—crosses ICW and southern Lake Worth at Standard Mile 1025, south of unlighted daybeacon #20—Bascule—14 feet (closed)—October 1 through May 31 will not open 7:30 A.M. to 9:15 A.M. and 4:30 P.M. to 6:30 P.M. weekdays, except opens at 8:15 A.M. and 5:30 P.M.

Chapter 8 Anchorage Summary (Note that anchorages are listed in geographic order, moving north to south.)

Peck Lake Anchorage—(Standard Mile 992)—located near 27 06.847 North/080 08.540 West, on the easterly waters of Peck Lake, east-southeast of flashing daybeacon #19—4-foot depths—reviewed on pages 410, 419

Lake Francis Anchorage—(Standard Mile 995)—located near 27 04.470 North/080 07.423 West, on the waters of the southern (of two) streams leading to charted Lake Francis, south of unlighted daybeacon #30—4-foot depths—reviewed on pages 410-11, 419

Harbor Island Anchorage—(Standard Mile 997.5)—located near 27 02.822 North/080 06.684 West, off the western shores of Harbor Island, north of unlighted daybeacon #35—5-foot depths—reviewed on pages 411, 420

Hobe Sound Anchorage—(Standard Mile 998.5)—located near 27 01.883 North/080 06.457 West, west of the ICW channel between unlighted daybeacons #38 and #40—6½-foot depths—reviewed on pages 411, 420

Conch Bar Anchorage—(Standard Mile 1001.5)—located near 26 59.358 North/080 05.508 West, to the west-northwest of unlighted daybeacon #49—8-foot depths—reviewed on pages 411, 420

Hell Gate Anchorage—(Standard Mile

1002.5)—located near 26 58.727 North/080 05.262 West, south-southeast of Blowing Rocks Marina and north of unlighted daybeacon #52—6-foot depths—reviewed on pages 412, 420
Jupiter Anchorage—(Standard Mile 1006.5)—located near 26 55.987 North/080 04.985 West, on the northern entrance of the loop creek that makes into the ICW's eastern flank, north of unlighted daybeacon #14—5½-foot depths—reviewed on pages 415, 421-22
North Palm Beach Waterway Anchorage—(Standard Mile 1013)—located near 26 49.734 North/080 04.165 West, on the waters of the first charted basin on the western banks of this alternate waterway that cuts off to the southwest of the ICW, northwest of the North Palm Beach/Parker Bridge—8-foot depths—reviewed on pages 425, 439

North Palm Beach Anchorage—(Standard Mile 1014)—located near 26 50.342 North/080 03.263 West, on the charted deep patch of water in the northern tip of Lake Worth—9-foot depths—reviewed on pages 427, 439-40
Peanut Island Anchorage—(Standard Mile 1018.5)—located near 26 46.476 North/080 02.494 West, in the charted patch of deep water east of Peanut Island and north-north-west of Lake Worth Inlet's flashing daybeacon #8—6-foot depths—reviewed on pages 429, 441
Lake Worth Inlet Anchorage—(Standard Mile 1018.5)—located near 26 46.085 North/080 02.637 West, anchor on the deep water south of the Lake Worth Inlet approach channel's flashing daybeacon #11—8-foot depths—reviewed on pages 432, 422

Chapter 8 Marina and Yacht-Club Summary
(Note that marinas and yacht clubs are listed in geographic order, moving north to south.)
Blowing Rocks Marina—(561) 746-3312—(Standard Mile 1002.5)—located near 26 58.756 North/080 05.311 West, flanking the Waterway's western banks north of unlighted daybeacon #52—transient dockage available—gasoline and diesel fuel available—4½-foot minimum depths—reviewed on pages 411-12, 420
Jib Yacht Club Marina—(561) 746-4300—(Standard Mile 1004)—located near 26 57.123 North/080 04.658 West, off the eastern banks of the ICW, south of unlighted daybeacon #60—transient dockage available—gasoline and diesel fuel available—6-foot minimum depths—reviewed on pages 412-15, 421
Jupiter Seasport Marina—(561) 575-0006—(Standard Mile 1005)—located near 26

56.804 North/080 05.031 West, perched on the southern banks of ICW—Loxahatchee River just east of the Jupiter/U.S. 1 bascule bridge—transient dockage available—gasoline and diesel fuel available—5-foot minimum depths, but typically 6 feet or better—reviewed on pages 414-15, 421
Jonathan's Landing Marina—(561) 747-8980—(Standard Mile 1007.5)—located near 26 55.111 North/080 04.849 West, north of unlighted daybeacon #18—transient dockage available—gasoline and diesel fuel available—6½-foot minimum depths—reviewed on pages 515, 422
Bluffs Marina—(561) 627-6688—(Standard Mile 1008.5)—located near 26 53.565 North/080 04.276 West, guarding the Waterway's eastern banks in a charted harbor south of flashing daybeacon #25—transient dockage available—6-foot minimum depths—reviewed on pages 415-16, 422

Frenchman's Creek Marina—(561) 627-6358—(Standard Mile 1009.5)—located near 26 52.827 North/080 04.410 West, in the charted harbor flanking the Waterway's western shores, just south of the Donald Ross bascule bridge (itself well south of flashing daybeacon #25)—transient dockage available—gasoline and diesel fuel available—7-foot minimum depths—reviewed on pages 416, 422

Seminole Boat Yard and Marine Center—(561) 622-7600—(Standard Mile 1012)—located near 26 50.808 North/080 04.034 West, off the western banks of the Waterway, just north of the PGA Boulevard Bridge—limited transient dockage available—reviewed on pages 417, 422-23

PGA Marina—(561) 626-0200—(Standard Mile 1012)—located near 26 50.709 North/080 04.014 West, off the western banks of the Waterway, just north of the PGA Boulevard Bridge—limited transient dockage sometimes available—gasoline and diesel fuel available—7-foot minimum depths—reviewed on pages 417-18, 423

North Palm Beach Marina—(561) 626-4919—(Standard Mile 1014)—located near 26 49.678 North/080 03.534 West, on the southwestern banks of the ICW shortly after you pass under the restricted North Palm Beach/Parker bridge—transient dockage available—gasoline and diesel fuel available—9-foot minimum depths—reviewed on pages 425-26, 439

Old Port Cove Marina—(561) 626-1760—(Standard Mile 1014)—located near 26 49.909 North/080 03.297 West, on the western shore of the northern Lake Worth channel, near unlighted daybeacon #7—transient dockage available—diesel fuel available—8-foot minimum depths—reviewed on pages 426, 439-40

Riviera Beach Municipal Marina—(561) 842-7806—(Standard Mile 1018)—located near 26 46.403 North/080 03.084 West, west of flashing daybeacon #42—transient dockage available—gasoline and diesel fuel available—6-foot minimum depths—reviewed on pages 428-29, 440

Sailfish Marina—(561) 844-1724—(Standard Mile 1018.5)—located near 26 46.626 North/080 02.430 West, on the western shores of Singers Island, north of Lake Worth Inlet—transient dockage available—gasoline and diesel fuel available—6-foot minimum depths—reviewed on pages 431, 441

Cannonsport Marina—(561) 848-7469—(Standard Mile 1018.5)—located near 26 46.824 North/080 02.422 West, on the western shores of Singers Island, north of Lake Worth Inlet—transient dockage available—gasoline and diesel fuel available—6-foot minimum depths—reviewed on pages 431-32, 441-42

Rybovich Spencer Marina & Boatyard—(561) 844-1800—(Standard Mile 1019.5)—located near 26 44.892 North/080 03.033 West, guarding Lake Worth's westerly banks south of unlighted daybeacon #4A—transient dockage available—gasoline and diesel fuel available—10-foot minimum depths—reviewed on pages 432-34, 442

Palm Beach Yacht Club & Marina—(561) 655-1944—(Standard Mile 1021)—located near 26 43.238 North/080 02.865 West, flanking the western banks between unlighted daybeacon #10 and the Flagler Memorial bascule bridge—transient dockage available—gasoline and diesel fuel available—6-foot minimum depths—reviewed on pages 434-35, 443

Palm Harbor Marina—(561) 655-4757—(Standard Mile 1021.5)—located near 26 42.995 North/080 02.929 West, occupying the charted harbor flanking Lake Worth's westerly banks between the Flagler Memorial bascule bridge and flashing daybeacon #12—transient dockage available—gasoline and diesel fuel available—7-foot minimum depths—reviewed on pages 435-36, 443

St. Lucie Inlet to Lake Worth

The run from St. Lucie Inlet to Lake Worth's northerly entrance is an enjoyable cruise as long as you're not in a hurry. Most of the route is quite sheltered and rough water is not a concern as long as winds are less than gale force. The adjoining shoreline offers a delightful contrast as undeveloped, subtropical banks alternate with the sumptuous homes of Hobe Sound. More modest but still handsome residences overlook the mainland shores here and there.

Facilities are found in greater and greater numbers as the Waterway tracks south to Lake Worth. Several marinas of particular note welcome visiting cruisers in Jupiter.

There are even some excellent anchorages along the way. One of the best offers access to a semideserted oceanside beach. Several of these overnight havens are well sheltered, while others are open to the wake of all passing vessels.

The cruise between St. Lucie Inlet and northern Palm Beach is interesting and visually appealing. With all the no-wake zones and low bridges, however, you should allow ampletime for your passage. Anyway, at a

Old Biltmore Hotel, Palm Beach

slower speed, you can fully enjoy the sights.

St. Lucie State Park (Standard Mile 989.5)

Southeast of flashing daybeacon #9, a large wooden pier associated with St. Lucie State Park juts out into the Waterway's eastern banks. Unlighted daybeacons #1 and #2 outline a small channel leading to this dock.

Most of the park dock is not really designed to accommodate pleasure craft. Of the two available slips, one is usually occupied by a Park Service pontoon boat. Depths alongside are a skinny 3 to 4 feet, too shallow for most larger vessels.

If you have a small outboard, the park is well worth visiting. The grounds include the undeveloped lands bordering the southern flank of St. Lucie Inlet. The dense vegetation must be seen to be fully appreciated. Picnic facilities are also available.

Peck Lake Anchorage (Standard Mile 992) (27 06.847 North/080 08.540 West)

The ICW intersects the wider waters of Peck Lake south-southeast of flashing daybeacon #15 and unlighted daybeacon #16. This body of water has been a popular anchorage for years with Waterway cruisers. Unfortunately, while boats drawing 4 feet or preferably less can still make use of this haven, depths have risen during the last several years, and more caution is now required than was necessary in the past.

Much of Peck Lake has always been shoal. The deep water stretches (more or less) from flashing daybeacon #19 toward the easterly banks. At the current time, best depths (such as they are) can be held by departing the Waterway immediately south-southeast of #19. Even by following this procedure we met up with a 4 to 4½-foot bar lying between the Waterway and the somewhat deeper water to the east. Once over this bar, depths of 6 to 7 feet seem to hold to within 75 yards of the easterly banks.

We strongly suggest that you now approach this anchorage with caution, particularly if your boat draws 4 or more feet. Feel your way along at idle speed with an eagle eye on the sounder.

If you are lucky enough to navigate your way safely into the deeper waters east of the bar, you will find an almost ideal place to drop the hook. This anchorage is well sheltered from virtually all wind directions, and the holding ground seems good.

After setting the anchor, consider breaking out the dinghy and ferrying over to the eastern shore. The ocean is just a short walk away. It's a great treat to take along a picnic and have one's noon meal while watching the restless ocean and semideserted beach. This is a very popular stopover on weekends and you will probably be joined by a large group of local cruisers. Otherwise, the surrounding shoreline is delightfully undeveloped, and you should not be disturbed during the night except perhaps by mosquitoes and the wake of a passing vessel.

Lake Francis Anchorage (Standard Mile 995) (27 04.470 North/080 07.423 West)

Two streams lead east to charted Lake Francis near unlighted daybeacon #30. While the lake itself is inaccessible to larger boats, the southerly stream can serve as a private and well-sheltered anchorage for vessels *under* 32 feet that draw less than 4 feet. Some 4- to 5-foot soundings at the stream's entrance make this anchorage a bit too risky for deeper-draft boats. The maximum swinging room is near the eastern extreme of the southerly creek, where the narrow offshoot tracks southeast to

Lake Francis. Here you can drop the hook in some 5 feet of water. The surrounding shoreline is in its natural state and is very pleasant. This is one of the most isolated and best protected anchorages north of Palm Beach, but the depth and swinging-room restrictions place it beyond the reach of many cruisers.

Hobe Sound (Standard Mile 996)

South of unlighted daybeacon #30, you will pass through the low-level Hobe Sound (Highway 708) bridge and enter a very secluded world. Only a select few other than cruisers are ever permitted to view the grand homes lining the sound's eastern banks. This is a colony of the very rich, who shun publicity and large crowds. Access to the community by land is tightly controlled, and it's practically impossible to gain admission without an invitation.

Passing mariners are more fortunate. No one restricts the Waterway, and many cruisers take the opportunity to glide idly by and ogle the sights. Have the camera ready and you might well take some photographs to remember.

Harbor Island Anchorage (Standard Mile 997.5) (27 02.822 North/080 06.684 West)

North of unlighted daybeacon #35, 5- to 7-foot depths are held between the Waterway and tiny Harbor Island adjoining the eastern banks. Craft under 40 feet drawing 4 feet or less can feel their way carefully to within 100 yards of the island's western shore and drop the hook in fairly protected waters. You will be exposed to the wake of all passing vessels, and speedboat traffic is very much in evidence on weekends. Otherwise, you should have a secure, comfortable night anchored next to the playground of the conservative rich.

Hobe Sound Anchorage (Standard Mile 998.5) (27 01.883 North/080 06.457 West

Good depths of 6½ to 8 feet stretch in well toward the westerly banks between unlighted daybeacons #38 and #40. Cruising craft can drop the hook within 75 yards of the banks with good protection to the west, southwest, and northwest. Strong northerly and southerly (southeasterly as well) winds could make for a bumpy evening. You may also be rocked by the wake of passing vessels. Be sure to show an anchor light.

Conch Bar Anchorage (Standard Mile 1001.5) (29 59.358 North/080 05.508 West)

The charted patch of deep water running along the Waterway's western side between Conch Bar and unlighted daybeacon #49 provides another good overnight anchorage. Boats as large as 45 feet will find ample swinging room and 8- to 10-foot depths to within 100 yards of the western shore. Protection is adequate for winds from most any direction under 25 knots, but the ICW channel is close by and passing power craft can sometimes send a wicked wake your way.

Blowing Rocks Marina (Standard Mile 1002.5) (26 58.756 North/080 05.311 West)

Blowing Rocks Marina flanks the Waterway's western banks north of unlighted daybeacon #52. The entrance channel cuts in near a large "No Wake" sign that fronts the Waterway. This cut is outlined by several floating markers. Blowing Rocks is a small facility that does accept transients and offers berths at floating, concrete piers with fresh-water hookups and 30- and 50-amp power connections. The piers are rather low and could use a bit of refurbishment. Low-water entrance depths in the marked channel run around 5½ to 6 feet, with at least 5½ feet of water in the outer slips and 4½-foot depths on the innermost berths. Gasoline, diesel fuel, and shoreside showers are all available. There is also a small ship's and variety store just behind the dockage basin. Some mechanical repairs to outboards and I/Os are offered, as well as light servicing for gas and diesel inboards. Dry-stack storage is on hand for smaller power craft. Panama Hattie's Restaurant (561-627-1545) is found within a long walk of Blowing Rocks.

Cruisers anchoring in the adjacent mooring field and anchorage (see below) can moor their dinghies at Blowing Rocks for a fee.

> **Blowing Rocks Marina (561) 746-3312**
>
> **Approach depths—5½-6 feet**
> **Dockside depths—4½-5½ feet**
> **Accepts transients—yes**
> **Transient dockage fee—average**
> **Floating concrete piers—yes**
> **Dockside power connections—30**
> ** and 50 amps**
> **Dockside water connections—yes**
> **Showers—yes**
> **Gasoline—yes**
> **Diesel fuel—yes**
> **Mechanical repairs—limited**
> **Ship's and variety store—yes (small)**
> **Restaurant—long walk**

Hell Gate Anchorage (Standard Mile 1002.5) (26 58.727 North/080 05.262 West)

South-southeast of Blowing Rocks Marina, passing mariners will note a number of anchored and moored craft. This anchorage and mooring field has been set up by local cruisers and is apparently, at least for the moment, without restriction. Minimum depths in the anchorage run around 6 to 6½ feet, but you cannot cut straight into the haven from the Waterway. See the navigational account below for entry instructions.

Shelter is good to the east and west, but minimal to the north. The adjoining western shoreline exhibits heavy development while the banks to the east are far more attractive. Cruisers spending an evening or two in this anchorage can moor their dinghies at nearby Blowing Rocks Marina (for a fee) while going ashore.

Jupiter Sound (Standard Mile 1002.5)

South of flashing daybeacon #53, the ICW enters the northern headwaters of Jupiter Sound. The luxurious homes to the north give way here to more modest residences that nonetheless look quite attractive from the water. The Waterway channel through the sound is noted for shoaling, and tidal currents are often very much in evidence.

Jib Yacht Club Marina (Standard Mile 1004) (26 57.123 North/080 04.658 West)

South of unlighted daybeacon #60, the Waterway passage narrows and begins its approach to Jupiter Inlet and Loxahatchee River. Before reaching these bodies of water, cruisers

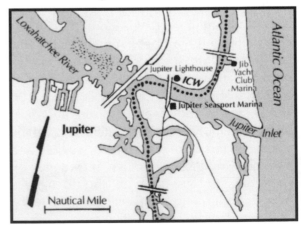

will pass under the Highway 707 bascule bridge. Immediately south of this span, the docks of Jib Yacht Club Marina will come abeam on the eastern banks. This friendly, well-appointed facility gladly accepts transients in its sheltered harbor when space is available. Call ahead of time to check on slip availability.

Dockage is at fixed piers with all power and water connections. Low-water depths alongside are an impressive 6 to 9 feet. Full fueling services are readily available and mechanical and dive service repairs can also be arranged. Showers and a small Laundromat are located on the premises. The dockmaster also maintains a small ship's store next to the docks.

Visiting cruisers are welcome to make use of the complex's on-site swimming pool. For those who enjoy a saltier bath, the public beach is within walking distance. When it's time to satisfy a hearty cruising appetite, ask the dockmaster for directions to the Jupiter Lighthouse Restaurant. It's a long walk (some will want to take a taxi), but this is a great spot for good old country cooking, and we recommend it highly. If you need taxi service in Jupiter, try calling Jupiter Taxi at (561) 743-7323.

Jib Yacht Club Marina (561) 746-4300
http://www.jibmarina.com

Approach depths—8-10 feet
Dockside depths—6-9 feet
**Accepts transients—yes (when space
 is available)**
Transient dockage rate—above average
Fixed wooden piers—yes
**Dockside power connections—30
 and 50 amps**
Dockside water connections—yes
Showers—yes
Laundromat—yes
Gasoline—yes
Diesel fuel—yes
**Mechanical repairs—yes
 (independent contractors)**

Ship's store—yes (small)
Restaurant—long walk

Jupiter Inlet and Loxahatchee River (Standard Mile 1004.5)

South of the Highway 707 Bridge, the ICW soon takes a sharp westerly turn into the foot of Loxahatchee River. Jupiter Inlet lies immediately to the east. Despite repeated dredging, this seaward cut remains in constant flux. On our last visit, we found the passage passable for all but deep-draft vessels. The situation could have changed by the time of your arrival. Check at one of the local marinas for the latest channel conditions before attempting this capricious cut.

The ICW tracks its way through lower Loxahatchee River for a short distance before turning south on Lake Worth Creek by way of

Cruising by Jupiter Lighthouse

an extraordinarily sharp, blind turn. Great care must be exercised in negotiating this passage.

The red brick Jupiter Lighthouse sits perched atop a high hill opposite unlighted can buoy #3. This old sentinel gazes to the east through its French lens, as it has since 1860. The lighthouse is surrounded by lush tropical vegetation and flanked by attractive, low-key homes. The lower Loxahatchee is one of the most visually appealing sections of the southern Florida ICW. Spend enough time to take in the sights, but don't become so taken with the view that you forget to watch the channel markers.

Jupiter Seasport Marina (Standard Mile 1005) (26 56.804 North/080 05.031 West)

Well-appointed Jupiter Seasport Marina sits perched on the southern banks of Loxahatchee River just east of the Jupiter/U.S. 1 bascule bridge. You can't miss it by virtue of its large, dry-stack storage building. Jupiter Seasport is a reliable operation and can be used with confidence by visiting cruisers.

Transients are readily accepted for overnight or temporary dockage at modern, fixed, concrete piers with full power and water connections. Depths on the outer slips run at least 8 feet while you can expect low-water soundings of 5 feet at the inner berths. As you might expect, considering this marina's location hard by Jupiter Inlet, a goodly amount of tidal current regularly sweeps through Jupiter Seasport's dockage basin. Be ready for these swiftly moving waters as you approach the piers.

Shoreside you will find good showers, a Laundromat, and an unusually large and well-supplied ship's and variety store. We particularly recommend this latter operation. The array of marine gear, not to mention nautically oriented clothing, is impressive. Gasoline and diesel fuel can be purchased dockside.

Mechanical repairs for gasoline engines are available on site, and independent technicians can be called in for diesel servicing.

Two restaurants are now located on the Jupiter Seasport grounds, immediately adjacent to the dockage basin. Both the Crab House Restaurant (561-744-1300) and Jettys Restaurant (561-461-1750) seem to be popular, but we have not had a chance to try either yet.

If you need taxi service in the Jupiter area, try calling Jupiter Taxi at (561) 743-7323.

Jupiter Seasport Marina (561) 575-0006

Approach depths—10-12 feet
Dockside depths—8 feet
   (minimum—outer docks)
   5 feet (minimum—inner docks)
Accepts transients—yes
Transient dockage rate—average
Fixed concrete piers—yes
Dockside power connections—30
   and 50 amps
Dockside water connections—yes
Showers—yes
Laundromat—yes
Gasoline—yes
Diesel fuel—yes
Mechanical repairs—yes (gasoline only;
   independent contractors for diesel)

Jupiter Seasport Marina

Ship's and variety store—yes
Restaurant—two on site

Jupiter Anchorage (Standard Mile 1006.5) (25 55.987 North/080 04.985 West)

After rounding the blind turn between flashing daybeacons #4 and #8, the ICW turns sharply south. Several loops intersect the Waterway's path between #8 and unlighted daybeacon #18. All are shallow with but one exception.

Boats up to 32 feet might consider anchoring in the northerly mouth of the small loop creek that makes into the eastern side of the Waterway immediately south of the Indiantown Road bascule bridge (north of unlighted daybeacon #14). Depths ranging from 5½ to 7 feet span the midwidth of the little stream's entrance. At all costs, don't get too close to the northerly entrance point.

For best depths and maximum swinging room, drop anchor just inside the stream's mouth. Here you will find surprisingly undeveloped shores and excellent protection from all winds.

This haven gives you the opportunity to restock your galley without needing to pay for overnight dockage. Once the hook is down, break out the dinghy. Look toward the southerly banks and you will spy a wooden pier. Depths alongside this dock run around 4 to 4½ feet at low tide. You can temporarily moor your dinghy to this structure and go ashore. After crossing a small field, you will spy a shopping center with a supermarket, drugstore, and McDonald's across the street.

Jonathan's Landing Marina (Standard Mile 1007.5) (26 55.111 North/080 04.849 West)

The extensive docks of Jonathan's Landing Marina lie to the west, north of unlighted daybeacon #18. This facility was, for many years, associated with the adjacent mammoth housing development. The marina is now privately owned and managed.

Transients are now eagerly accepted at Jonathan's Landing's fixed concrete piers featuring full power, fresh-water, and cable-television connections. Skippers staying over for the season can also arrange dockside telephone service. Depths in the protected harbor run 6½ to 8 feet. First-class showers, a full Laundromat, and a ship's store are all found shoreside. Gasoline and diesel fuel can be readily purchased at the fuel dock.

Visiting cruisers (and resident mariners) can now dine at the nearby Marina Club Cafe. This is a nice addition. Heretofore, a taxi ride was necessary for those who wanted to eat ashore.

Jonathan's Landing Marina (561) 747-8980
http://www.jlmclub.com

Approach depths—10-12 feet
Dockside depths—6½-8 feet
Accepts transients—yes
Transient dockage rate—above average
Fixed concrete piers—yes
Dockside power connections—30
    and 50 amps
Dockside water connections—yes
Showers—yes
Laundromat—yes
Gasoline—yes
Diesel fuel—yes
Ship's and variety store—yes
Restaurant—on-site

The Bluffs Marina (Standard Mile 1008.5) (26 53.565 North/080 04.276 West)

Wonderfully protected Bluffs Marina guards the Waterway's eastern banks in a charted harbor south of flashing daybeacon #25. Once inside the marina complex, visiting cruisers will agree that few facilities in southeastern

Florida afford this sort of protection from inclement weather. Except for the small entrance creek, the entire harbor is surrounded by land and tall condominiums. It would take a very strong blow indeed to raise a menacing wave in this basin. Minimum depths in the entrance canal run 6 feet, with 6 to 8 feet of water in the basin itself.

Delightfully, the management has chosen to accept transients for overnight or temporary dockage. The modern, fixed, concrete piers have all power and water connections. No fuel, repairs, or showers are available, however. A shopping center containing a restaurant is located within a long walk of the harbor. Ask any of the friendly dockmasters for directions.

The Bluffs Marina (561) 627-6688

Approach depths—6 feet (minimum)
Dockside depths—6-8 feet
Accepts transients—yes
Transient dockage rate—average
Fixed concrete piers—yes
Dockside power connections—30
 and 50 amps
Dockside water connections—yes
Restaurant—long walk

Frenchman's Creek Marina (Standard Mile 1009.5) (26 52.827 North/080 04.410 West)

The ultramodern docks of Frenchman's Creek Marina lie in the charted, well-protected harbor flanking the Waterway's western shores, just south of the Donald Ross bascule bridge (itself well south of flashing daybeacon #25). Transients are accepted at fixed, wooden piers offering full power, water, and telephone connections. Impressive depths of 7 to 8 feet lead through the entrance canal, followed by soundings of 8 to 10 feet dock-

side. Gasoline and diesel fuel are at hand, and mechanical repairs can be arranged. Showers, a ship's store, and a full Laundromat are convenient to the docks. There is even a waste pump-out service. As if all that weren't enough, a shopping center with several restaurants is within walking distance. To summarize, captains choosing to dock north of North Palm Beach could scarcely do better than to berth at this most accommodating facility.

Frenchman's Creek Marina (561) 627-6358
 http://www.frenchmansmarina.com/
 home.htm

Approach depths—7-8 feet
Dockside depths—8-10 feet
Accepts transients—yes
Transient dockage rate—average
Fixed wooden piers—yes
Dockside power connections—30
 and 50 amps
Dockside water connections—yes
Showers—yes
Laundromat—yes
Waste pump-out—yes
Gasoline—yes
Diesel fuel—yes
Mechanical repairs—yes
 (independent contractors)
Ship's and variety store—yes
Restaurant—several nearby

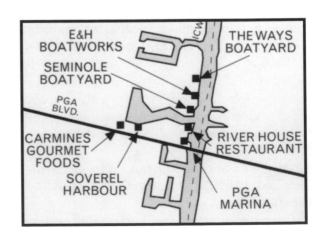

PGA Boulevard Bridge Facilities (Standard Mile 1012)

A host of marinas and boatyards lines the Waterway's western shore north of the PGA Boulevard Bridge. There is also the opportunity to visit the most fabulous gourmet store you will ever find!

The northernmost of the PGA Boulevard facilities is The Ways Boatyard (561-622-8582). This establishment offers both do-it-yourself and professional below-the-waterline repairs as well as mechanical servicing. The Ways' travelift is rated at 70 tons.

Immediately to the south is E & H Boatworks (561-622-8550). This facility offers professional haul-out services and full mechanical repairs for both gasoline- and diesel-powered motors. Haul-outs are accomplished by a marine railway rated at 70 tons.

A third service facility guards the Waterway's western banks just south of E & H. Seminole Boat Yard and Marine Center (near 26 50.808 North/080 04.034 West) features complete mechanical, topside, and below-waterline repairs. This facility specializes in hauling large power craft, though you will also spot a sailcraft on the ways from time to time. Their two travelifts are rated at 70 and 100 tons. The knowledgeable staff of Seminole can be counted upon to right almost any mechanical, electrical, or hull wrongs. Carpentry and yacht painting are also readily available. Do-it-yourself work is allowed. In short, if it can't be fixed or painted at Seminole Boat Yard, you may as well begin shopping for a new craft.

Seminole Boat Yard is one of the few operations of its type to offer transient dockage. A limited number of visitors can be accommodated at fixed, wooden piers with freshwater hookups and 30- and 50-amp power connections. There are even some shoreside showers. All the restaurants described below, clustered around the PGA Boulevard Bridge, are within easy walking distance.

Seminole Boat Yard and Marine Center (561) 622-7600

Approach depths—8-12 feet
Dockside depths—6 feet
Accepts transients—yes
Transient dockage rate—below average
Fixed wooden piers—yes
Dockside power connections—30 and 50 amps
Dockside water connections—yes
Showers—yes
Below-waterline repairs—yes (extensive)
Mechanical repairs—yes
Restaurant—several nearby

For many years Soverel Harbour (561-691-9554) maintained an extensive collection of slips on the charted offshoot leading west, south of Seminole Boat Yard. Now this firm has scaled back its operations and, while some slips in the sheltered basin are still under Soverel's control, many have been taken over by PGA Marina. This latter firm's headquarters fronts directly onto the ICW's western shoreline, south of River House Restaurant (see below) and immediately north of the PGA Boulevard Bridge, near 26 50.709 North/080 04.014 West. The marina's fuel docks (gas and diesel), ship's (and variety) store, and large, dry-stack storage operation are located at this southerly terminal.

PGA Marina's wet-slip dockage is found mostly in the protected basin, formerly the exclusive home of Soverel Harbour. Most of this wet-slip space is now leased out on a yearly basis, but transients are still occasionally accepted. The marina's fixed wooden and concrete piers are complemented by a full array of power and water connections.

Dockside depths run 7 to 11 feet. Showers are located in the old Soverel dockmaster's building. A Laundromat is found just across the street.

Both Carmines and River House restaurants, reviewed below, are within easy walking distance of the docks.

PGA Marina (561) 626-0200

Approach depths—10-12 feet
Dockside depths—7-11 feet
Accepts transients—limited
Transient dockage rate—average
Fixed concrete piers—yes (dockage basin)
Fixed wooden piers—yes (on ICW)
Dockside power connections—30
    and 50 amps
Dockside water connections—yes
Showers—yes
Gasoline—yes
Diesel fuel—yes
Ship's and variety store—yes
Restaurant—several nearby

Visiting cruisers with even a hint of interest in things culinary should spare no effort to check out the fabulous gourmet store just behind the PGA Marina-Soverel dockage basin. Carmines (561-775-0105) is quite simply one of the most impressive food stores, delicatessens, seafood bars, and butcher shops that this writer has ever visited. The prepared Italian-style foods including lasagna, manicotti, and baked ziti are always enough to make our mouths water. Throw in an unusually good collection of fine wines, a scrumptious on-site bakery, not to mention the adjacent Italian restaurant, and you have the recipe for one of the most exciting gastronomical finds in southeastern Florida. Take our word for this one—don't miss Carmines!

River House Restaurant (561-694-1188) fronts directly onto the western shores of the ICW between the PGA Marina dockage basin and its fuel dock. This fine dining spot features its own fixed wooden piers (6-foot depths) to which patrons are free to tie up while dining (no overnight stays allowed). We have not had the opportunity to sample the seafood delights of River House recently, but if past experience is any guide, the food should be excellent.

ST. LUCIE INLET TO LAKE WORTH NAVIGATION

Even though the entire passage from St. Lucie Inlet to Lake Worth is well sheltered, this run calls for caution and close attention to markers. Several shoals abut the Waterway channel. It's all too easy to stray just a bit off the path.

The waters lying about Jupiter Inlet call for a maximum alert. Strong tidal currents running from Loxahatchee River to and from the inlet can sweep unwary navigators into shallow water flanking both sides of the Waterway. Too many skippers have been enjoying the sights only to be brought up short with a hard grounding. Keep alert, be on guard against leeway, and keep a steady watch on the sounder.

No-wake zones begin to proliferate south of Jupiter. While most of these will be outlined in the following discussion, don't be surprised to find additional restrictions during your visit.

Passage South from St. Lucie Inlet to Peck Lake   Once between flashing daybeacon #4 and unlighted daybeacon #3A, where we left the ICW in chapter 6, the Waterway remains fairly well marked and relatively easy to follow into Great Pocket. As you pass unlighted daybeacon #7, look toward the eastern banks for a good view of a tall stand of Australian pines.

The small, charted channel running west between unlighted daybeacon #7 and flashing daybeacon #9 leads to some private docks. Passing cruisers are advised to keep clear.

Depths outside of the ICW in Great Pocket are quite shallow. We once helped pull a sailcraft off the bottom near unlighted daybeacon #12. The skipper thought he was on the correct course, but leeway had eased him onto the westside shoal. Keep a close watch aft to note quickly any lateral slippage.

South of flashing daybeacon #9 and unlighted daybeacon #10, the charted channel to St. Lucie State Park cuts off to the east. Remember, depths on this errant channel run as little as 3 feet. Larger cruising craft are advised to bypass this potential side trip.

A slow-speed zone begins at flashing daybeacon #14 and runs south to unlighted daybeacon #16. This is only a harbinger of things to come.

After passing between flashing daybeacon #15 and unlighted daybeacon #16, the Waterway passes out into the broader waters of Peck Lake.

Peck Lake Anchorage   The anchorage in Peck Lake has really shoaled over the last several years, and great care must now be exercised to stay off the bottom. Leave the ICW at idle speed and keep a sharp watch on the sounder. If your craft draws 4 feet or more, you may want to bypass this potential haven entirely.

Depart the Waterway immediately south-southeast of flashing daybeacon #19. Turn east and feel your way to within 200 yards of the eastern banks. After leaving the ICW, you will soon pass over a bar with (hopefully, but *no* guarantees) 4½-foot depths. Cruising farther to the east, depths improve to 6 and 7 feet. Once into this deeper water, drop the hook at any likely spot. If you aren't too tired after a long day of cruising, break out the dinghy and head for the beach.

On the Waterway   Minimum-wake restrictions are in effect south of unlighted daybeacon #21 to the Highway 708/Hobe Sound highway bridge. This is a long slow-speed section of the Waterway and power-craft skippers may find it quite boring.

Lake Francis Anchorage   Enter the southern creek leading to Lake Francis (south of unlighted daybeacon #30) on its midwidth. Depths at the entrance run from 4 to 5 feet, but readings deepen on the stream's interior. Craft requiring more swinging room should consider dropping the hook at the easternmost portion of the creek, near the small offshoot leading to Lake Francis. A Bahamian mooring might be a good idea in these relatively tight waters.

On the Waterway   Not far south of the Lake Francis creeks, passing cruisers will encounter the Highway 708/Hobe Sound bascule bridge. This span has a closed vertical clearance of 21 feet, and, thankfully, opens on demand.

The Waterway quickly passes into the headwaters of Hobe Sound south of the

Highway 708 bridge. Much of Hobe Sound is a minimum-wake zone. Official slow-speed restrictions are in effect between unlighted daybeacons #44 and #49. Even outside of this stretch, we have observed any number of manatees playing in the Waterway. Wise captains will proceed at minimal speed through the entire Hobe Sound region.

Harbor Island Anchorage To enter the anchorage near Harbor Island, leave the Waterway some 100 yards to the north of unlighted daybeacon #35. Work your way carefully toward the isle's north-south center point, keeping a weather eye on the sounder. If all goes well, you should be able to hold minimum 5-foot depths to within 100 yards of Harbor Island.

Hobe Sound Anchorage To make good your entry into the anchorage on the westerly shores of northern Hobe Sound, abandon the ICW's track about halfway between unlighted daybeacons #38 and #40. Turn west and feel your way to within 75 yards of the banks with your sounder. Be on guard against the correctly charted patch of 4-foot waters to the south.

Conch Bar Anchorage The anchorage south of the charted "Conch Bar" (north of flashing daybeacon #50) allows you to anchor farther from the ICW channel than you might expect from a casual study of chart 11472. Turn sharply west about 150 yards north of #50. Cruise into the cove's midwidth and drop the hook at any likely spot. Be sure to show an anchor light.

Blowing Rocks Marina and Hell Gate Anchorage Immediately north of unlighted daybeacon #52, the float-lined channel to Blowing Rocks Marina strikes off to the west. Captains bound for the marina need simply hold to midchannel between the markers.

Skippers making for the anchorage south-southeast of Blowing Rocks should not attempt to cruise into this haven directly from the Waterway. A shallow bar lies between the ICW and the anchorage. Instead, follow the Blowing Rocks entrance channel until the anchorage comes abeam to the south. Then, leave the marina cut, and cruise south into the basin. This series of maneuvers will assure maximum depths.

Jupiter Sound South of charted Hell Gate and flashing daybeacon #53, the ICW flows into Jupiter Sound. This body of water is noted for shoaling. In times past we have discovered 8-foot soundings directly on the Waterway channel. Proceed with caution.

South of unlighted daybeacon #60 the Waterway exchanges greetings with the Highway 707 Bridge. This span has a closed vertical clearance of 25 feet and opens on demand.

No-wake restrictions are in effect south of the Highway 707 Bridge all the way to the Indiantown Road Bridge. This means that the entire Jupiter Inlet-Loxahatchee River portion of the Waterway is a slow-speed zone. Slow down and divide your time among the sights, the channel markers, and your sounder.

A short hop south of the Highway 707 Bridge, the protected harbor of Jib Yacht

Club Marina will come abeam to the east. Cruise into the basin's centerline. The fuel dock and dockmaster's office will soon come abeam to starboard.

As you round the turn into Loxahatchee River, pass between flashing buoy #1 and unlighted nun buoy #2. Be prepared for strong currents. Once out into the midline of the Loxahatchee, all cruisers, except those planning to ply the questionable waters of Jupiter Inlet, should cut sharply west and point to pass unlighted can buoy #3 to its northern quarter. Once abeam of #3, you will have a good view of the Jupiter Lighthouse to the north and Jupiter Seaport Marina will lie to the south. Be ready for strong currents as you approach the docks of this facility.

From unlighted can buoy #3, point for the central pass through of the U.S. 1 bascule bridge. Fortunately this span (with closed vertical clearance of 26 feet) opens on demand.

West of the U.S. 1 bridge, the Waterway seems to head directly for the low-level bridges blocking the mouth of the upper Loxahatchee River. Between the two bridges, point to pass flashing daybeacon #4 to its southerly side and come abeam of unlighted daybeacon #7 to its northerly quarter.

The western reaches of the Loxahatchee are consistently shallow, and even if you could clear the low-level fixed spans, there is not enough depth for any but outboard craft. The Corps of Engineers has never established a definite channel in this river. Consequently, cruising craft are obliged to bypass this intriguing water body.

Past #7 the ICW rounds a hairpin turn leading south to Lake Worth Creek. **This is a maximum danger area and demands the greatest caution.** Northbound captains cannot see craft approaching from the inlet and vice versa. Curve around the turn at idle speed and be ready for a quick course change in case some hot dog happens to be approaching with the throttle open.

Don't mistake the offshoot west-southwest of flashing daybeacon #8 as the Waterway itself. Cruisers not used to the sharp turn away from the Loxahatchee into Lake Worth Creek could all too easily wander into these shoal waters. Depths of 3 to 4 feet are waiting to greet those who make this error.

Jupiter Inlet   As described earlier in this chapter, depths on Jupiter Inlet are highly questionable. If you do attempt the cut, be advised that at the current time the channel's only charted aids to navigation, unlighted daybeacons #1 and #2, are actually based on the twin stone jetties flanking either side of the inlet's passage out into the open sea. Obviously you don't want to approach either of these markers closely. Otherwise, the outside inlet channel is mostly unmarked, and shoals make their appearance all too often. It is highly advisable to check with one of the local marinas about current channel conditions before attempting this cut.

On the ICW   Moving farther south on the ICW and Lake Worth Creek, cruisers will come upon the Indiantown Road bascule bridge. Thankfully this 35-foot bascule span opens on demand. This is ever so welcome, particularly in light of the tidal currents which regularly scour these waters.

Jupiter Anchorage   The small anchorage along the easterly banks, north of unlighted daybeacon #14, should be entered on its midwidth. Stay away from the northside entrance point. A shoal seems to be building out from this promontory.

Be sure to set the hook immediately after coming inside the creek's mouth. Depths quickly drop off to 4 feet or less past the wide entrance. Using a Bahamian-style mooring would be helpful in preventing an accidental swing into the shoreline if the wind or current should shift during the night.

A wooden pier, suitable for dinghy docking, will be spotted along the southerly shoreline.

On the Waterway   South of the Indiantown Road bascule bridge, the long, slow-speed zone encompassing the ICW's passage through lower Loxahatchee River comes to an end. The Waterway now passes through an enclosed, canal-like passage as it wends its way down Lake Worth Creek to North Palm Beach. Again, virtually all the various loops and streams intersecting the ICW's track are shallow. Keep clear unless you have specific information to the contrary.

North of unlighted daybeacon #18, the entrance to Jonathan's Landing Marina will come abeam to the west. The channel is deep and obvious.

South of unlighted daybeacon #19, passing cruisers will spot a sign for Admiral's Cove Marina. This facility is now private and visitors are not encouraged.

Just south of unlighted daybeacon #23, Heron Kay Bed and Breakfast Inn (561-744-6315) overlooks the Waterway. This small inn has a tiny dock that is served by a loop creek. Unfortunately, we discovered that the stream's southerly reaches are quite shoal, and even its northern stretch has low-water

depths of 4 feet or slightly less. During an earlier visit, we found all available dockage consumed by one power craft.

South of flashing daybeacon #25, the canal-like entrance to the Bluffs Marina cuts off to the east. Stick to the canal's midline. The shores are protected with a rock covering. Soon the dockage basin will open out before you. The dockmaster's office is on the starboard point at the harbor's entrance. Check here for your slip assignment.

Another hop to the south past the Bluffs will bring the entrance to private Cypress Island Marina abeam to the west. No facilities for visitors are available.

Some .9 nautical miles south of flashing daybeacon #25 the Waterway passes under the Donald Ross/Juno Beach bascule bridge. This new span has a closed vertical clearance of 35 feet and opens on demand.

South of the Donald Ross span, the entrance to Frenchman's Creek Marina will come abeam to the west. A long canal leads from the Waterway to the protected dockage basin. As you make your approach to the basin, the fuel dock and dockmaster's headquarters will come abeam to starboard.

On to Lake Worth   It's a very straightforward, markerless run down Lake Worth Creek from the Donald Ross span to the PGA Boulevard Bridge. You will pick up a no-wake zone well north of the PGA span. Slow-speed restrictions are in effect until the waters south of the PGA bridge.

As you approach the PGA span, you will begin passing the wealth of facilities described earlier along the western banks. First comes The Ways Boatyard, followed by E & H Boatworks and Seminole Boat Yard and Marine Center. Next up is the entrance to Soverel Harbour and the PGA Marina docks. The entrance canal is deep and obvious.

Immediately south of the PGA Marina-Soverel Harbour entrance canal, River House Restaurant fronts the Waterway. Finally, the fuel dock and dry stack storage building of PGA Marina will appear along the western banks. Then, it's only a short hop to the PGA bridge itself.

The PGA Boulevard Bridge features a closed vertical clearance of 24 feet and a restricted opening schedule. On weekdays, the bridge opens only on the quarter and three-quarter hour between 7:00 A.M. and 9:00 A.M. and from 4:00 P.M. to 7:00 P.M. On weekends and holidays the span deigns to open every 20 minutes between the hours of 8:00 A.M. and 6:00 P.M. At all other times of the day and night, the span will open on demand. Weekdays November 1 to May 1, it opens on the hour and every 20 minutes thereafter from 9:00 A.M. to 6:00 P.M. How's that for a mind-boggling schedule?

The Waterway flows quickly south to several facilities associated with the community of North Palm Beach. Now, at last, the "Gold Coast" is truly in sight.

North Palm Beach to Lantana

Mariners cruising south from North Palm Beach soon find themselves face to face with Lake Worth. This shallow body of water has long been known as Palm Beach's mudhole. Perhaps that description is a bit too unkind. Nevertheless, the waters outside of the ICW channel are suspect, and apart from a few notable exceptions, pleasure craft would do well to stay on the Waterway.

Palm Beach—say that name anywhere in the United States and visions of the nation's most exclusive East Coast resort are sure to come to mind. That Palm Beach of fame is still very much a reality. A stroll down Worth Avenue will convince you that there are no more chic shops in Beverly Hills than here. A drive along the Palm Beach oceanfront bears mute testimony to the health and well-being of the affluent on these golden isles. Visit the famous Flagler estate, and you will learn how this once-tiny agricultural village was transformed almost single-handedly into the East Coast's winter playground. With the help of a taxi or rental car, cruisers have the opportunity to experience for themselves the fast-paced city that is Palm Beach.

These days there is more than one Palm Beach. On the mainland shore, West Palm Beach and North Palm Beach have become active cities in their own right, teeming with successful residents. Originally settled as a community for the workers and servants who built the resort colony across Lake Worth, West and North Palm Beach can now hold their own in any comparison of metropolitan centers in Florida.

You will find a host of services waiting to answer your every need in the greater Palm Beach region. Most are on the western shoreline, but Worth Avenue and the Palm Beach oceanfront are only a short taxi ride away. Several first-rate marinas stand ready to greet transients with friendly and courteous service. There are also several boatyards that can handle any mechanical, topside, or below-the-waterline repair.

Anchorages are, as you might imagine, rather crowded. The available havens are regularly stuffed with pleasure craft, even when the anchorage is in direct line with an inlet. This phenomenon simply goes to show how many cruisers have come to appreciate anchoring off.

Anchoring anywhere within Palm Beach County has become somewhat problematical. If you happen to drop your hook where no other pleasure craft are anchored, don't be too surprised if a local law-enforcement official either comes alongside to charge a fee or asks you to move on in a somewhat less-than-friendly manner.

The Palm Beaches can boast safe access to the open sea. Lake Worth Inlet is one of the most reliable seaward passages in all of eastern Florida. Large oceangoing freighters and cruise ships regularly make use of the cut. Consequently, it is kept well marked and carefully maintained. Strangers can use the channel with confidence, keeping in mind that the "easily run" inlet has yet to be invented.

Your first cruise through Lake Worth will be an unforgettable experience. Beginning with the high-rise condos lining the Waterway in North Palm Beach, the shoreside buildings reach truly mammoth proportions in the heart of the Palm Beach communities. Many cruisers spend the entire winter season in the Palm Beach area. While that may become a bit tedious for some, there is no denying the Palm Beach mystique. Stop for a day, a week, or a month; the memory of your time in this glittering resort will stay with you always.

Numbers to know in Palm Beach:
Yellow Cab—561-689-2222
Express Taxi—561-471-7777
Ace Taxi—561-832-2411
Budget Car Rental—561-683-2401
Avis Rent A Car—561-233-6400
West Marine—561-775-1434
Boat/U.S. Marine Center—561-684-4900
Chamber of Commerce—561-833-3711

The "Gold Coast"

Where did the name "Gold Coast" come from? Those visiting the region today may look at the massive condos and echo the old prospector, "There's gold in them there buildings." Actually, however, the name came from an event that took place several hundred years before the first condo rose in southeastern Florida.

In July 1715 a great treasure armada left Havana for Spain. In keeping with the navigational practices of the day, the fleet sailed north along the Gulf Stream current. A few days into the trip, shipboard barometers began a steady decline and seawise sailors predicted heavy weather ahead.

On July 30 a hurricane of tremendous force struck the hapless ships. Only one craft survived, captained by a Frenchman who disobeyed orders and sailed to the northeast, thereby missing the reefs that took his comrades. Official Spanish records show that more than $14 million in gold coins and jewels was lost. Even today, from time to time, scuba divers discover gold doubloons in the sands of southeastern Florida. So now when you hear Palm Beach and points south referred to as the "Gold Coast," you'll know the expression came from a great eighteenth-century sea disaster and not from a modern developer's dreams.

Harbour Point Marina(Standard Mile 1012.5)

Just north of the North Palm Beach Waterway (discussed below), a small but deep stream leads west to the sheltered dockage basin of Harbour Point Marina (561-622-6890). This facility is now a "brokerage marina," and no services are available for cruising craft.

North Palm Beach Waterway Anchorage (Standard Mile 1013) (26 49.734 North/080 04.165 West)

About midway between the PGA Boulevard and North Palm Beach/Parker bridges, the so-called North Palm Beach Waterway strikes to the southwest from the ICW's westerly banks. The northerly portion of this stream has minimum 8-foot depths. This passage is eventually blocked by a fixed bridge, but not before it leads to one of the best anchorages in the region.

The first charted basin on the western banks of this alternate waterway holds excellent

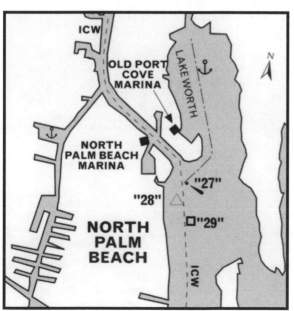

depths of 6 to 8 feet. Protection is more than adequate against the heaviest weather, and there is enough swinging room for any craft under 60 feet. Pleasant homes surround the southerly reaches of the basin, while the northern shore remains in its natural state. This is a very quiet anchorage and will certainly appeal to those who enjoy dropping the hook away from the hustle and bustle of shoreside life.

North Palm Beach Marina (Standard Mile 1014) 26 49.678 North/080 03.534 West

Impressive North Palm Beach Marina comes abeam on the southwestern banks of the ICW shortly after you pass under the restricted North Palm Beach bridge. North Palm Beach Marina is privately managed by the same first-rate firm that oversees Old Port Cove Marina (see below). For large, corporate operations, both these facilities exude a helpful and accommodating attitude that is all too absent in southeastern Florida. We recommend both marinas highly, particularly for power boats.

Transients are welcomed to fixed, concrete docks at North Palm Beach Marina in a large, enclosed harbor with superior protection from all winds. The dockage basin is surrounded by an impressive collection of low-rise condos, lending additional protection from the prevailing winds. Depths alongside run an impressive 9 feet or better. All slips boast full power and water connections. Clean showers and a semi-open-air Laundromat are found on the marina grounds, as are gasoline, diesel fuel, and waste pump-out service. There is even a ship's and variety store just behind the fuel pier. A convenience store and adjoining motel are within easy walking distance while a short taxi ride will take you to supermarkets and a host of restaurants.

North Palm Beach Marina (561) 626-4919
http://www.opch.com

Approach depths—10-14 feet
Dockside depths—9+ feet
Accepts transients—yes
Transient dockage rate—below average
Fixed concrete piers—yes
Dockside power connections—30 and 50 amps
Dockside water connections—yes
Showers—yes
Laundromat—yes
Waste pump-out—yes
Gasoline—yes
Diesel fuel—yes
Ship's and variety store—yes
Restaurant—several nearby

Old Port Cove Marina (Standard Mile 1014) (26 49.909 North/080 03.297 West)

Old Port Cove Marina perches on the western shore of the northern Lake Worth channel, near unlighted daybeacon #7. A deep, well-marked cut leaves the ICW at flashing daybeacon #27 and tracks its way north to this marina, and eventually farther north to a popular anchorage.

Old Port Cove, as mentioned above, is a superior marina complex in all aspects. We are continually amazed at the awesome collection of huge (80 percent power) yachts berthed at this facility. The harbor is enclosed by a concrete breakwater to the east and surrounded by mammoth condo complexes on the other three sides. Protection from inclement weather, as you might imagine, is excellent. Transient or seasonal dockers are accommodated at ultra-modern, fixed, concrete piers. Depths in the enclosed harbor run 8 to 11 feet, with at least 8 feet of water in the marked entrance channel. Fresh-water and 30-, 50-, and 100-amp power connections are available at all berths. Spotless showers, a full Laundromat, and a nice ship's

store are all located in the building overlooking the harbor's westerly shores. Diesel fuel, but no gasoline, can be purchased at a fuel dock that will be spied to port just as you enter the enclosed harbor.

Through a special arrangement with Old Port Cove, transients are welcome to make use of the adjacent country club facilities, which include heated swimming pool, dining room, tennis courts, and eighteen-hole golf course. There is even a yacht club on the premises with reciprocal arrangements for members of participating clubs. Cove Plaza, a shopping and professional center, and TGI Friday's restaurant are within walking distance.

Old Port Cove Marina (561) 626-1760
http://www.opch.com

Approach depths—8-14 feet
Dockside depths—8-11 feet
Accepts transients—yes
Transient dockage rate—below average
Fixed concrete piers—yes
Dockside power connections—30, 50, and 100 amps
Dockside water connections—yes
Showers—yes
Laundromat—yes
Diesel fuel—yes
Ship's and variety store—yes
Restaurant—nearby

Old Port Cove Marina, North Palm Beach

North Palm Beach Anchorage (Standard Mile 1014) (26 50.342 North/080 03.263 West)

The north Lake Worth channel continues north from Old Port Cove Marina to one of the best and most popular anchorages on the greater Palm Beach waters. Many pleasure craft regularly drop the hook in the wide, charted patch of deep water north of unlighted daybeacons #9 and #10. Protection is fair from all winds except southerly blows, which can be a real bear. This anchorage is not recommended when winds exceed 25 knots from any quarter or are over 20 knots from the south. Depths run between 9 and 11 feet. The surrounding shoreline is guarded by dense residential and commercial development. The lights at night look like a huge Christmas tree. Please do not trespass by landing your dinghy ashore on private property.

The charted channel leading north to Little Lake Worth is blocked by a low-level fixed bridge and cannot be used by larger boats.

Unfortunately, the city of North Palm Beach has instituted a half-baked (and in this writer's opinion, "illegal") scheme to charge cruising craft for the privilege of anchoring on the western half of this anchorage. This regulation is being challenged locally, and it may or may not be in place by the time of your arrival. Just don't be surprised if a local water cop pulls alongside and asks for a "community donation."

Lake Park Marina (Standard Mile 1016.5) (26 47.596 North/080 03.102 West)

South of the intersection between the ICW and the north Lake Worth channel, at flashing daybeacon #27, the Waterway begins to track its way through a mostly shallow section of Lake Worth. The docks of Lake Park Marina (561-881-3345) sit behind a concrete breakwater, west of flashing daybeacon #34. This low-key municipal facility, strangely enough, does not allow visitors to spend the evening and nighttime hours aboard. As a consequence, Lake Park Marina has little interest to visiting cruisers. No fuel, repairs, or showers are available either.

Lake Worth Inlet (Standard Mile 1018.5)

South of the fixed, high-rise Riviera Beach highway bridge (south of unlighted daybeacon #37), the Waterway flows around the western shore of mostly undeveloped Peanut Island and through the Palm Beach commercial turning basin. Many marinas and boatyards line the mainland shore in the Riviera Beach area, while the channel serving Lake Worth Inlet flows due east. There are additional facilities on the western shore of Singers Island, accessible by way of an alternate channel leading north from the inlet.

Lake Worth Inlet itself is deep and well marked. Twin stone jetties line the cut's juncture with the open sea. In fair weather, this just may be one of the most painless inlets to run that you ever encounter. Many aids to navigation in the channel are charted, a sure sign of a stable channel.

New Port Cove Marine Center (Standard Mile 1017.5)

Yet another facility under the Old Port Cove management team, New Port Cove Marina & Boat Yard (561-844-2504), graces Lake Worth's western shoreline immediately south of the Riviera Beach high-rise bridge. The marina part of this operation is a dry stack storage operation for smaller power craft, and no services other than gasoline are available for cruising craft.

The boatyard is more interesting. Here boats

are hauled out by a 60-ton travelift and bottom work is performed either professionally or on a do-it-yourself basis. Full mechanical servicing for both gasoline and diesel power plants is available as well.

Riviera Beach Municipal Marina (Standard Mile 1018) 26 46.403 North/080 03.084 West

The breakwater-enclosed harbor of Riviera Beach (Municipal) Marina will be spied west of flashing daybeacon #42. Once known as one of the seediest marinas in eastern Florida, this facility has been vastly improved.

Riviera Marina is now eager to attract transient visitors and features sheltered overnight berths almost within sight of Lake Worth Inlet, at (mostly) fixed concrete piers. The entrance to the dockage basin actually sits well north of the fuel dock and the marina's dry-stack storage building. Depth in the marked entry channel runs 6 to 7 feet, with at least 6 feet of water dockside.

Riviera Beach Municipal Marina

All berths feature power (30 and 50 amps), fresh-water, cable-television, and telephone connections. Gasoline and diesel fuel are readily available, as are full mechanical repairs and waste pump-out. Air-conditioned showers and a semi-open-air Laundromat are found on the premises. There is also a tiny ship's store associated with the on-site Club Nautico boat-rental operation.

An on-site restaurant known as the Tiki Waterfront Sea Grill offers open-air dining and seems very popular with the local party crowd on weekends. One of the large oceangoing gambling ships that now seem to be popping up here, there, and yonder in Florida makes its home at Riviera Beach Municipal Marina as well. Neither this writer nor the marina staff suggests venturing outside of the locked gates during the evening hours except by taxi. There is all-night security at this marina, and the guards will be glad to let cruisers in and out of the gates.

Riviera Beach Municipal Marina
  (561) 842-7806
  http://www.rivierabch.com/marina

Approach depths—6-7 feet
Dockside depths—6 feet (minimum)
Accepts transients—yes
Transient dockage rate—below average
Fixed concrete piers—yes
**Dockside power connections—30
  and 50 amps**
Dockside water connections—yes
Showers—yes
Laundromat—yes
Waste pump-out—yes
Gasoline—yes
Diesel fuel—yes
Mechanical repairs—yes
Ship's store—small
Restaurant—on site

Cracker Boy Boat Works (561-845-0357), not to be confused with the facility of the same name in Fort Pierce, is found just south of Riviera Beach Marina. This yard specializes in extensive below-the-waterline repairs. Do-it-yourself work is allowed on hauled craft. For those who want it done professionally, Cracker Boy's trained staff can take on most any hull repair or repainting task. The on-site travelift is rated at 70 tons.

Peanut Island Anchorage (Standard Mile 1018.5) 26 46.476 North/080 02.494 West

South of unlighted daybeacon #43, the ICW intersects the eastward-running channel leading to Lake Worth Inlet. Not only does this cut lead to the open sea, but cruisers can cut to the north, just east of flashing daybeacon #8, and visit a popular anchorage as well as three marinas lining the westerly shores of Singers Island.

We have always been somewhat amazed at the host of pleasure boats continually anchored in the charted patch of deep water east of Peanut Island. Entry into this haven calls for a tricky cruise between unmarked shoals, and the anchorage is open to rough water and strong tides from the nearby inlet. Nevertheless, many pleasure craft seem to be willing to put up with these inconveniences to anchor close by reliable Lake Worth Inlet.

Once past the tricky entrance, cruisers should find 6 to 7 feet of water in the Peanut Island anchorage. Swinging room is sufficient for boats up to 45 feet. Protection would seem to be inadequate in winds exceeding 20, or possibly 15, knots. Be sure to read the navigation information on this anchorage below before attempting entry.

Singers Island Facilities (Standard Mile 1018.5) (Various Lats/Lons—see below)

Two marinas welcome cruising visitors on

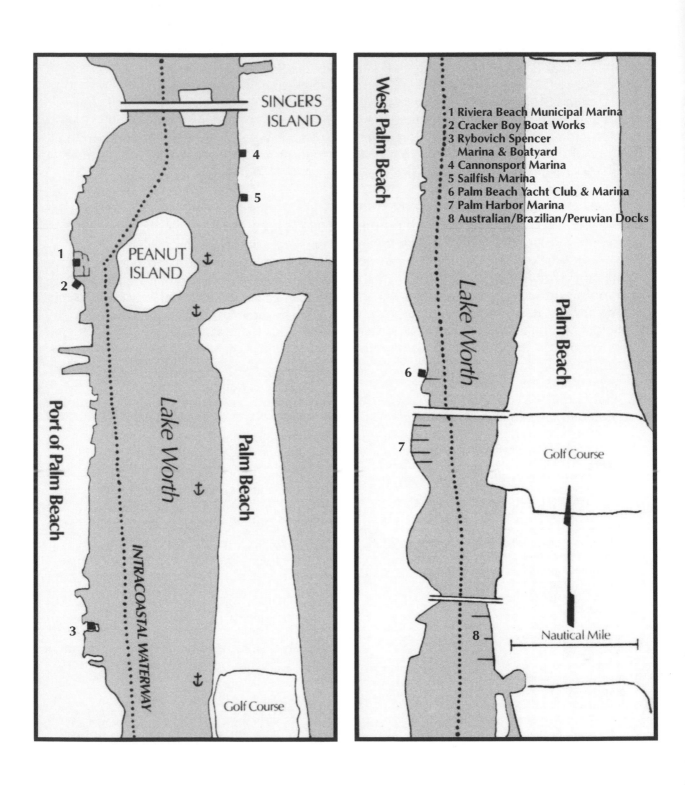

SINGERS
ISLAND

PEANUT
ISLAND

Port of Palm Beach

Lake Worth

Palm Beach

INTRACOASTAL WATERWAY

Golf Course

1
2
4
5
3

West Palm Beach

1 Riviera Beach Municipal Marina
2 Cracker Boy Boat Works
3 Rybovich Spencer
  Marina & Boatyard
4 Cannonsport Marina
5 Sailfish Marina
6 Palm Beach Yacht Club & Marina
7 Palm Harbor Marina
8 Australian/Brazilian/Peruvian Docks

Lake Worth

Palm Beach

Golf Course

Golf Course

Nautical Mile

6
7
8

the western shores of Singers Island, north of Lake Worth Inlet. These facilities are accessible via the charted tongue of deep water leading north from the inlet approach channel; do not attempt the charted cut flowing east from the ICW, immediately south of the A1A bridge. While local captains may use this latter passage successfully, it is narrow, unmarked, and borders on very shallow waters.

The southernmost of the three facilities is Sailfish Marina (not to be confused with Sailfish Marina of Stuart, 26 46.626 North/080 02.430 West). This is a sprawling facility that seems to draw large crowds to its waterfront bar on weekends. Transient and seasonal craft are accepted at concrete and wooden fixed piers with every power and water connection. Depths alongside run from 6 to as much as 11 feet. Gasoline and diesel fuel are available at an inner fuel dock for smaller craft, while larger boats are serviced at an outer pier. Good showers and a full Laundromat, not to mention a welcome swimming pool, are located in the complex. There is also a ship's and variety store (plus clothing) on hand. Mechanical repairs can sometimes be arranged through local, independent technicians. An on-site restaurant and huge open-air bar are quite popular with local patrons, and there is even an adjoining motel for those who wish to rest ashore. Considering this facility's popularity, it might be best to call ahead for reservations, particularly during the transient seasons.

Sailfish Marina (561) 844-1724
   http://www.sailfishmarina.com

Approach depths—6-10 feet
Dockside depths—6-11 feet
Accepts transients—yes
Transient dockage rate—above average
Fixed wooden and concrete piers—yes
Dockside power connections—30
   and 50 amps
Dockside water connections—yes
Showers—yes
Laundromat—yes
Gasoline—yes
Diesel fuel—yes
Mechanical repairs—limited
   (independent contractors)
Ship's and variety store—yes
Restaurant—on site

Next up is Cannonsport Marina (26 46.824 North/080 02.422 West), one of the last privately owned, "mom and pop" marinas in southeastern Florida. We were very pleased to find Cannonsport prospering during our latest visit.

Passing cruisers can be assured of receiving a very warm welcome at Cannonsport. Dockage is at fixed wooden piers with 30-, 50-, and 100-amp power, telephone, fresh-water, and cable-television connections. Cannonsport also offers high-speed Internet access. Impressive depths alongside of 10 to as much as 14 feet should be adequate for even the longest-legged vessels. Excellent showers and a full Laundromat are available. Both gasoline and diesel fuel are ready at hand, and mechanical repairs can often be arranged through local, independent contractors. The on-site ship's store contains a quality assortment of marine and convenience-store-type items. Several restaurants are within easy walking distance, including Portofinos (561-844-2162). Of course, you could always take a short taxi ride to any of the dozens and dozens of dining spots in nearby West Palm or Palm Beach.

If you, like this writer, sometimes find the high-speed hustle and bustle of southeastern Florida to be just a bit too much, let me suggest tying up at Cannonsport. The homey atmosphere has marvelous recuperative powers. Oh yes, if you have any problems, just ask for "Teddy Bear," the marina pooch. He's the one really in charge.

> **Cannonsport Marina (561) 848-7469**
> **http://www.cannonsport.com**
>
> **Approach depths—6-10 feet**
> **Dockside depths—10-14 feet**
> **Accepts transients—yes**
> **Transient dockage rate—above average**
> **Fixed wooden piers—yes**
> **Dockside power connections—30,**
>   **50, and 100 amps**
> **Dockside water connections—yes**
> **Showers—yes**
> **Laundromat—yes**
> **Gasoline—yes**
> **Diesel fuel—yes**
> **Mechanical repairs—yes**
>   **(independent contractors)**
> **Ship's and variety store—yes**
> **Restaurant—several nearby**

Lake Worth Inlet Anchorage (Standard Mile 1018.5) (26 46.085 North/080 02.637 West)

Passing cruisers sometimes anchor in the deep water south of the Lake Worth Inlet approach channel's flashing daybeacon #11 (west of unlighted daybeacon #2). This spot is somewhat sheltered from easterly winds by the southern side of the inlet and from northerly blows by Peanut Island. Strong southerly breezes would make for a decidedly uncomfortable night, however. Depths run from 8 to 15 feet and there is ample room for a 50 footer. The Peanut Island shores to the north are delightfully natural, except for the picturesque Coast Guard base, while the banks to the east are overlooked by heavy residential development.

Alternate Palm Beach Channel

A quick study of insets 2 and 3 on chart 11472 reveals that a partially marked, deepwater channel continues south along the western banks of Palm Beach from the Lake Worth Inlet channel. We have always held minimum 5-foot depths, with much of the route showing deeper soundings, all the way to a point just north of unlighted daybeacon #8 (found well to the west on the ICW). We were then able to make our way back to the Waterway between the charted spoil areas, holding minimum 6-foot depths.

Cruising along this alternate passage is very pleasurable indeed. Many modest but attractive homes overlook the water, and the channel is delightfully void of other traffic most of the time. If you enjoy getting off the beaten track, this channel could be your ticket to an enjoyable journey. Be sure to read the navigation information below on this channel before making a first-time attempt.

Rybovich Spencer Marina & Boatyard (Standard Mile 1019.5) (26 44.892 North/080 03.033 West)

The largest single marina and yard facility in the Palm Beaches guards Lake Worth's westerly banks south of unlighted daybeacon #4A. There are actually three marked entry channels. The northerly cut leads to a few small-craft services while the center channel escorts cruisers to the old Rybovich (before its merger with Spencer Boat Company) harbor. The southerly passage escorts cruisers to the marina dockage basin.

The massive Rybovich Spencer complex covers 22 acres and provides every conceivable service for pleasure craft and their crews. The dockage harbor is located less than 1 mile from Lake Worth Inlet, with no intervening bridges. The marina portion of this operation readily accepts transients at first-class, floating, concrete-decked docks. Impressive dockside depths run 10 feet or better. Fresh-water and 30-, 50-, and 100-amp power connections are provided. Some slips also have telephone hookups. Shoreside you will find clean showers and a Laundromat. Gasoline and diesel fuel can be purchased dockside, and waste pump-out service is also available. The basin is partially breakwater enclosed and well sheltered from all but unusually strong easterly winds.

When it comes time for the evening meal, visiting cruisers will again want to call a taxi. This is not the area to go wandering around on foot after dark. The Rybovich Spencer complex has good nighttime security, and the gates are locked after dark. The accommodating security guards will be glad to open up and see you to your taxi, and readmit you upon your return.

Cruisers coming to Rybovich Spencer in need of repair work must have a lucky star shining over their journey. Either it can be fixed here, or you'd better get down to your nearest broker and look into the purchase of a new craft. Mechanical repairs for diesel engines, fiberglass, paint, metal, custom woodworking, and electrical (plus generator) services are all available. Service work on gasoline engines can be arranged. Wow—how's that for a lineup of repair capabilities?

Haul-out capacities are also extensive, with a 77-ton travelift on site, supplemented by both a 125-ton and 1,000-ton marine railway.

Rybovich Spencer Marina & Boatyard

Wonder if they're planning on hauling any aircraft carriers? Even with all these features, the management of Rybovich Spencer has informed this writer that the yard is engaged in a "10-year upgrade." Maybe by the time this program is finished, they'll have the ability to airlift your boat!

We cannot leave the Rybovich Spencer facility without noting another of its outstanding offerings. One of the largest independent ship's stores in the southeastern U.S. is an integral part of this complex. The store fronts the highway, but is within an easy step of the dockage basin. Any true cruiser will want to set aside a bit of time simply to wander the aisles, ogling at all the nautical gear. Careful; all this hardware looks so good it could be damaging to your wallet!

Finally, it should be noted that in addition to Rybovich Spencer's many services and facilities, the staff and management seem to exude that friendliness and "can-do" attitude that is usually far more prevalent among smaller operations. Obviously, the Rybovich Spencer folks have not forgotten how they got where they are, and are determined to keep going in the same direction. This entire operation receives our highest endorsement.

> **Rybovich Spencer Marina & Boatyard**
>   **(561) 844-1800**
>   **http://www.rybovich.com**
>
> **Approach depths—10-12 feet**
> **Dockside depths—10+ feet**
> **Accepts transients—yes**
> **Transient dockage rate—below average**
> **Floating concrete piers—yes**
> **Dockside power connections—30,**
>   **50, and 100 amps**
> **Dockside water connections—yes**
> **Showers—yes**
> **Laundromat—yes**
> **Gasoline—yes**
> **Diesel fuel—yes**

> **Waste pump-out—yes**
> **Below-waterline repairs—yes (extensive)**
> **Mechanical repairs—yes (extensive)**
> **Ship's store—yes (extensive)**
> **Restaurant—taxi ride necessary**

Palm Beach Yacht Club & Marina (Standard Mile 1021) 26 43.238 North/080 02.865 West

Palm Beach Yacht Club & Marina (formerly Flagler Marina) flanks the western banks between unlighted daybeacon #10 and the Flagler Memorial bascule bridge. This facility is a private club that has, fortunately, chosen to accept Waterway transients (without the need for any yacht club reciprocal arrangements). Berths are available at modern, fixed, concrete docks with metal-decked finger piers. Fresh-water and 30-, 50-, and 100-amp power connections are on hand. Depths run 6 to 7 feet at most slips. The harbor is partially breakwater enclosed, but still a bit open to easterly blows. Cruisers should also be ready for strong tidal currents as they approach their slip in this basin. We were surprised to find the waters moving this swiftly here, but they do, so put that in your pipe and smoke it.

Fair showers and a partially open-air Laundromat are found in the yacht club building located on the docks. Gasoline and diesel fuel are offered and some mechanical repairs can be arranged through independent contractors. The dockmaster's office doubles as a ship's and nautical-clothing store. The yacht club dining room, upstairs over the ship's store and accessible by elevator, is open to transient (not landlubber) visitors. A Publix supermarket is found on the eastern side of Flagler Memorial Bridge. Those not up for a hike may want to take a taxi.

Palm Beach Yacht Club & Marina
(561) 655-1944
http://www.pbyachtclub.com

Approach depths—9-12 feet
Dockside depths—6-7 feet (minimum)
Accepts transients—yes
Transient dockage rate—above average
Fixed concrete piers—yes
Dockside power connections—30,
**   50, and 100 amps**
Dockside water connections—yes
Showers—yes
Laundromat—yes
Gasoline—yes
Diesel fuel—yes
Mechanical repairs—limited
**   (independent contractors)**

Ship's and variety store—yes
Restaurant—on site

Palm Harbor Marina (Standard Mile 1021.5) (26 42. 995 North/080 02.929 West)

Palm Harbor Marina has the largest dockage basin in West Palm Beach. This facility occupies the charted harbor flanking Lake Worth's westerly banks between the Flagler Memorial bascule bridge and flashing daybeacon #12.

Palm Harbor accepts transients at its fixed, concrete piers and features full power and water connections. Depths in the (partially) breakwater-enclosed harbor run from 7 to 10

Palm Beach Yacht Club & Marina

feet at low water. Protection is pretty good from all but really heavy weather, and there seems to be somewhat less tidal current here than is found at Palm Beach Yacht Club & Marina, just to the north. Several large condo towers and a huge parking garage overlook the dockage complex and serve as an impressive backdrop. Nighttime security is very much in evidence.

This facility's shoreside showers are partially climate controlled, and the adjacent Laundromat is first rate. Gasoline and diesel fuel are ready for pumping and there is a ship's and variety store just behind the docks with a good assortment of convenience-store-type food items. Some mechanical repairs can be arranged through independent locals. Several restaurants are found some two blocks away on popular Clematis Street. Ask the marina staff for directions and recommendations. A Publix supermarket is found on the eastern side of Flagler Memorial Bridge. Those not up for a hike may want to take a taxi to this facility.

Visitors will also be pleased to learn that Palm Harbor Marina has a working relationship with the awesome Breakers Hotel across the water in Palm Beach proper. Marina visitors have access to the Breakers' golf, tennis, and beach club facilities. Transportation is provided.

Still not enough for you? Well, consider a stroll or a quick taxi ride across the Flagler Memorial Bridge to the Flagler Museum (1 Whitehall Way, 561-655-2833). This attraction is well worth your while.

Palm Harbor Marina (561) 655-4757

Approach depths—10-12 feet
Dockside depths—7-10 feet (minimum)
Accepts transients—yes
Transient dockage rate—above average
Fixed concrete piers—yes
Dockside power connections—30
   and 50 amps
Dockside water connections—yes
Showers—yes
Laundromat—yes
Gasoline—yes
Diesel fuel—yes
Mechanical repairs—limited
   (independent contractors)
Ship's and variety store—yes
Restaurant—several nearby

The Amazing Mr. Flagler

Immediately south of the Southern Boulevard Bridge (itself south of unlighted daybeacon #20), look to the east. Between the trees you should be able to see the rear portion of the partially restored historic site known as Whitehall. This proud structure was once the home of Henry Flagler, a man who almost single-handedly developed the eastern coast of Florida into a tourist mecca.

Henry Morrison Flagler was born on January 2, 1830, in Hopewell, New York, the son of a Presbyterian minister. At the age of fourteen, Flagler left home with nine cents to make his fortune. He traveled to Ohio, where he took a job as a store clerk earning five dollars a month plus room and board. He worked his way through the ranks to become manager of the store and soon thereafter accepted an important post with the Harkness Grain and Distillery Company. By 1853, Flagler had become a partner of the company. He married the owner's daughter, Mary, in November of the same year.

Next, Flagler invested heavily in the salt industry, which was turning a nice profit at the time. The end of the Civil War saw the salt market collapse and Flagler bankrupt. He moved to Cleveland and once again made a fortune, this time in the grain business.

While Flagler was involved in making his second fortune, another young businessman in Cleveland saw a bright future for the oil industry. John D. Rockefeller began to seek additional sources of capital to expand his small oil company. Flagler and Rockefeller struck a deal, and along with a third English partner, these two future giants of American industry formed the Standard Oil Company in 1870. Flagler became one of the wealthiest men in the nation.

Flagler moved to New York in 1877, and his wife, Mary, died soon thereafter. Flagler withdrew from the active management of the oil giant he had helped to create. In June 1883 he married Ida Alice Shrouds, a nurse who had tended his first wife. The newly married couple honeymooned in St. Augustine, where Flagler was swept up by the city's old-world charm.

The first step in the Flagler development of Florida's east coast was the construction of the Ponce de Leon and Alcazar hotels in St. Augustine. Both resorts, along with a third hostelry, the Cordova, which Flagler bought and remodeled, were successful.

Flagler accurately foresaw that a strong tourist economy could not develop without superior transportation facilities. By 1890 he had bought most of the existing rail facilities in eastern Florida. He then connected the various lines with his own track, thereby forming the first comprehensive rail system in Florida's history. Now passengers could ride from New York to St. Augustine without ever changing trains.

It was on the shores of Lake Worth that Flagler chose to build his ultimate resort community. As late as 1878, the Lake Worth settlement consisted of only twenty-five families. Flagler lost no time in building the great Royal Poiciana Hotel, which opened in 1894. In only a short time this fabulous hostelry became "the country's most fashionable winter gathering place" for the nation's rich. Flagler also built the Breakers on the ocean shore. Destroyed by fire in 1903 and 1925, it was rebuilt after each conflagration.

The glitter of Palm Beach's tinsel has not faded since Flagler's day. Even after the great developer's death, more and more successful Americans built incredibly lush "ocean cottages" in Palm Beach, and in later years, palm-lined Worth Avenue developed as a world-famous avenue.

Flagler built his own home, Whitehall, in Palm Beach as a wedding present to his new bride, Mary Lily Kenan of North Carolina. (Flagler's second wife had become mentally unbalanced, and she was eventually committed to an asylum.) Following Flagler's death, Whitehall was sold and for a time was used as a hotel. In 1959, Henry Flagler's granddaughter, Jean Flagler Matthews, and a group of dedicated visionaries bought the old homeplace and partially restored Whitehall to its former glory. Visitors are now welcome to this important shrine of Floridian history. If you stop in the Palm Beach area, you should take advantage of this opportunity.

Most men would have been more than satisfied after developing Florida's east coast from St. Augustine to Palm Beach and linking the region to the northern states with a modern railway. Henry Flagler, however, was not an ordinary man. In December 1894 and again in 1895 the coldest weather on record struck Florida. Vegetables, orange groves, and coconut trees were laid waste. Many residents were suddenly devoid of income.

Flagler extended credit without interest and distributed free seed and cuttings for replanting to many who had been ruined during the great freeze. He was always generous with his hard-won wealth. He gave widely to charities and founded many an organization to minister to the needs of those less fortunate than himself.

In the midst of the replanting effort a spray of fresh orange blossoms arrived from Julia D. Tuttle, a widow who lived in a remote settlement far to the south. Fort Dallas had been founded during the Seminole wars but had remained only a small outpost amidst a vast wilderness. Now Mrs. Tuttle was showing the great developer that the struggling community had attributes that could not be matched to the north.

Flagler was quite impressed and set off for Fort Dallas. As the miles of virgin swamp rolled by, he was somehow able to divine the vast potential of this seemingly trackless wilderness. By 1896 Flagler's crews had completed a railway to Fort Dallas, and the city's first hotel, The Royal Palm, was opened for business. So popular was Henry Flagler with the citizens of the region that many wanted to call the city Flagler. Flagler himself objected, suggesting the Indianderived name Miami.

Before his death, Flagler stretched his tracks all the way to Key West, where he hoped to found a great overseas shipping port. The first train rolled into Key West on January 22, 1912. Now eighty-two years old, Flagler himself was aboard. Facing the assembled crowd of jubilant onlookers, the great developer told all who could hear,

"Now I can die happy; my dream is fulfilled."

Henry Morrison Flagler never lived to see his Key West railway become one of his only failures. He died less than eighteen months later, on May 20, 1913. One of his contemporaries, George W. Perkins, perhaps best summed up his vision: "That any man could have the genius to see of what this wilderness of waterless sand and underbrush was capable, and then have the nerve to build a railroad here, is more marvelous than similar development anywhere else in the world."

Australian-Brazilian-Peruvian Docks (26 42.195 North/080 02.700 West)

Southernmost of the Palm Beach facilities is the Australian-Brazilian-Peruvian Docks (561-838-5463). You will undoubtedly see many large yachts docked here. All of the berths at this facility are rented out by the season. The dockmaster has informed me that if a resident craft happens to be absent for an extended period, he will occasionally accept transients who make arrangements ahead of time. No fueling or repair services are available

NORTH PALM BEACH TO LANTANA NAVIGATION

Safe navigation of the Lake Worth-ICW channel is not a matter to be taken lightly. Much of the lake is quite shallow and shoal water abuts the Waterway along much of its passage. It's often a long run between aids to navigation, and tidal currents, courtesy of nearby Lake Worth Inlet, can ease unobservant navigators out of the channel all too quickly. Be sure to watch your stern carefully for any excessive leeway. Keep alert, have chart 11472 at hand, and maintain a steady watch on the sounder.

Except for the side trips documented below, Lake Worth is not the place to cruise off the beaten path. Depths on chart 11472 are not always to be trusted outside of the ICW. Some of these soundings are based on older surveys and shoaling is now very much in evidence. Be sure to read the navigational information below and plan your cruise accordingly. With these elementary precautions, mariners can enjoy their visit to the Palm Beaches instead of giving the local boatyards some extra repair business.

North Palm Beach Waterway The North Palm Beach Waterway cuts off to the southwest about halfway between the PGA Boulevard and North Palm Beach/Parker bridges. Enter the approach canal on its midwidth and continue upstream along the centerline at idle speed. Watch to port and you will sight a golf course bordering the shoreline. This recreational facility is followed by a group of private homes and docks, also on the port banks. Soon the large, square cove that serves as a superior anchorage will come up to starboard. Drop the hook at any likely place near the midline and settle down for an undisturbed evening. Don't approach any of the surrounding shorelines too closely.

On the Waterway South of its intersection with the North Palm Beach Waterway, the ICW soon passes under the restricted, North Palm Beach/Parker Bridge. This span, with a closed vertical clearance of 25 feet, has a very complicated schedule. Year round, it opens only on the hour and half-hour, Monday through Friday, between the hours of 7:00 A.M. and 9:00 A.M. and again between 4:00 P.M. and 7:00 P.M. From November 1 to May 1, between 9:00 A.M. and 4:00 P.M., as well as during weekends and holidays (8:00 A.M. to 6:00 P.M.), the bridge opens on the hour and every 20 minutes thereafter.

A no-wake zone extends from the Parker Bridge all the way into Lake Worth. Don't ask me about this one, folks; we could not see any on-the-water justification for such a rule.

Once through the Parker Bridge, watch to the northeast for some very high rise condos bordering the Waterway. These impressive structures have beautifully manicured grounds and make pleasant viewing from the water.

The entrance to North Palm Beach Marina comes up off the southwestern banks along this stretch. Cruise into the canal serving the marina on its midwidth. Soon, the fuel dock and ship's store will come abeam to starboard.

The Waterway soon flows into the northern headwaters of Lake Worth. After the sheltered passage from St. Lucie Inlet, it may take a minute to adjust your perspective to the wider range of vision. The north Lake Worth channel intersects the Waterway near flashing daybeacon #27.

Slow down as you enter Lake Worth and sort out all the markers. The aids to navigation outlining the southerly portion of the north Lake Worth channel can easily be confused with the Waterway markers. Cruisers continuing south on the ICW should come abeam and pass flashing daybeacon #27 to its westerly side and take unlighted daybeacon #28 to its easterly quarter.

North Lake Worth Channel If you choose to cruise the north Lake Worth channel, either to visit Old Port Cove Marina or to anchor in the deep water to the north, break off to the east-northeast at flashing daybeacon #27 and cruise between the southernmost markers on the north Lake Worth channel, unlighted daybeacons #1 and #2. Pass between the next two pairs of unlighted daybeacons and continue on the same course for about 25 yards past #5 and #6. From this point, the channel curves to the north. Follow the bend in the cut by curving lazily around to the north, pointing to come between unlighted daybeacons #7 and #8. The entrance to Old Port Cove will come abeam to the west, north of unlighted daybeacon #7.

North of #7 and #8, the channel is straight and obvious. After passing between unlighted daybeacons #9 and #10, you will be in the heart of the Lake Worth anchorage. Drop your hook at any likely spot with enough room between you and your neighbors. Be sure to cease your explorations well before reaching the charted shallows abutting the northern shore.

On the Waterway The ICW channel running through the northern portion of Lake Worth borders on consistently shallow water, with depths of 3 to 4 feet being the norm outside of the Waterway. The initial run south from flashing daybeacon #27 is a straight shot. As usual, pass all red, even-numbered aids to navigation to their easterly sides, and take green markers to their westerly quarter.

Markers are spaced a bit far apart on this run through the northern Lake Worth-ICW section. Have your binoculars and chart 11472 at hand to quickly resolve any confusion.

After passing between flashing daybeacon #30A and unlighted daybeacon #31, the channel bends slightly to the south. Set course to next cruise between unlighted daybeacons #33 and #32. Continue on the same track, pointing to come abeam and pass flashing daybeacon #34 to its easterly side. Immediately south of #34, the marked channel to Lake Park Marina cuts off to the west.

From flashing daybeacon #34, it is an almost straight run to the Riviera Beach fixed bridge. Along the way you will pass to the east side of flashing daybeacon #36.

The Riviera Beach high-rise span has a vertical clearance of 65 feet and presents no problem. South of the bridge, switch to inset 2 of chart 11472. This blowup connects with inset 3 and should be used for all navigation of the ICW and Lake Worth south past the Royal Palm bascule bridge.

Chart 11472 (inset 2) depicts a narrow channel leading east immediately south of the Riviera Beach high-rise bridge. We specifically do not recommend this passage as an alternate route to reach the facilities at Singers Island. The channel borders on very shoal water. While local captains frequently make use of this cut, visitors would do well to leave this route to those with specific local knowledge.

The ICW continues south on the same heading for some .2 nautical miles past the Riviera Beach Bridge. At flashing daybeacon #39, the Waterway channel bends to the southwest and soon borders the undeveloped shores of Peanut Island to the east. This passage is strewn with markers courtesy of the several marinas flanking these waters. Slow down and sort out the various beacons. The Waterway, by and large, runs hard by the western shores of Peanut Island. Be sure to pass unlighted daybeacon #41 to its westerly side and come abeam of flashing daybeacon #42 to its easterly quarter. This entire run is part of a no-wake zone. Power captains should proceed at idle speed and use the extra time to sort out the confusing markers.

The marked channel to Riviera Beach Municipal Marina will be spotted near flashing daybeacon #42.

South of #42, the Waterway again resumes its southerly track. After passing unlighted daybeacon #43 to its westerly side, the ICW soon leads through the heart of the Port of Palm Beach commercial turning basin. As the shores of Peanut Island begin to fall away, the Lake Worth Inlet approach channel will come abeam to the east.

Lake Worth Inlet Navigation of Lake Worth Inlet is an elementary matter of following the various aids that are clearly charted on inset 2 of chart 11472. As you are now headed toward the open sea, pass all red, even-numbered aids to navigation to your port side and take green markers to starboard.

Cruisers entering Lake Worth Inlet from the open sea can take advantage of a correctly charted pair of range markers on the eastern shores of Peanut Island. During the day, you will most likely not need to use these navigational aids, but at night, they can be most instructive.

Look to the north as you approach flashing daybeacon #11. You will quickly spy the classic design of the old Peanut Island Coast Guard station, which now houses a fascinating museum.

Surprisingly enough, the shoreline adjacent to the old Coast Guard station is very popular with weekend outboarders. Be on the lookout for swimmers and small boats when you run the channel, particularly on weekends.

Eventually, cruisers should come abeam of flashing daybeacon #8 by about 25 yards or so to its southerly side. You can then continue through the inlet channel straight out to sea, or cut north to visit the Peanut Island anchorage or the Singers Island facilities.

Peanut Island Anchorage Entering the finger of deep water east of Peanut Island is a far-from-simple proposition. To reach the anchorage safely, navigators must cruise between very shallow water to the east and another shoal to the west.

If you make the attempt, set a careful course from flashing daybeacon #8 to pass between the triangle of shallow water striking east from Peanut Island and the large shoal lining the western side of the Singers Island channel. In fair weather, the two shoals are quite visible at low tide. This greatly simplifies your task. In low light or foul weather, cruisers have only their sounders and the already-anchored boats in the haven to guide them. Proceed at idle speed and keep a constant watch on the sounder. Good luck!

Singers Island Channel The cut leading north from Lake Worth Inlet, flanking the western shores of Singers Island, allows access to the two marinas on this isle. Unfortunately, the charted shoal lying west of this passage, separating the channel from the anchorage described above, has built out farther to the east than is shown on the current edition of chart 11472. While passage to and from the various marinas is still quite practical, this run now requires a bit more caution.

To enter the Singers Island channel, continue cruising past flashing daybeacon #8 on the Lake Worth Inlet cut as if you were putting out to sea. Some 100 yards east of #8, cut 90 degrees to the north and enter the Singers Island channel by favoring the easterly shoreline slightly. As you continue to track your way north, pass hard by the westerly tips of the various marina piers. Those who deviate even slightly to the west will find that shoal water is waiting to greet their keels.

Captains cruising north on the Singers Island passage will first discover Sailfish Marina, followed by Cannonsport Marina. Discontinue your cruise once abeam of Cannonsport. Farther passage north is not recommended for strangers. Remember also, we do not recommend the channel running west back to the ICW, just south of the Riviera Beach Bridge, for any but local cruisers.

Lake Worth Inlet Anchorage and Alternate Palm Beach Channel

To anchor on the charted patch of deep water south of the Lake Worth Inlet approach channel, depart the seaward cut immediately east of flashing daybeacon #11. Turn sharply south, staying at least 25 yards west of unlighted daybeacon #2. Drop anchor well short of the charted shallows to the south, abutting unlighted daybeacon #4.

Cruisers bent on exploring the pleasant channel running along the eastern shores of Lake Worth, south of Lake Worth Inlet, may continue south from the anchorage by pointing to come abeam of unlighted daybeacon #4 by some 15 yards to its easterly quarter. Be on guard against the charted shoal bordering the western side of the channel between #2 and #4. Continue on the same course, pointing to come abeam of unlighted daybeacon #6, also to its easterly side.

South of #6, minimum 5-foot depths (with most soundings being much deeper) spread out in a broad swath for some 1.5 nautical miles. While in the past some cruisers have attempted to follow this channel as far south as Flagler Memorial Bridge, we do not recommend such a passage. Unmarked shoals become too abundant near the bridge for a safe return to the Waterway.

Far safer is the passage between unlighted daybeacon #8 on the ICW and the alternate channel. Simply continue following the easterly shoreline until #8 comes abeam well to the west. You can then turn directly toward the daybeacon and rejoin the Waterway at #8.

South on the ICW from the Turning Basin

Take a moment as you cruise past the Port of Palm Beach turning basin to observe the large oceangoing freighters and luxury cruise liners often docked at the nearby wharves.

South of the turning basin, the ICW borders on some deepwater sections, but as chart 11472 clearly indicates, there are still plenty of 2- to 4-foot shoals on both sides of the Waterway.

As you approach unlighted daybeacon #4A, take a moment to sort out the various daybeacons. Three marked cuts strike west to Rybovich Spencer Marina & Boatyard between #4A and unlighted daybeacon #6. South of #4A, the ICW eventually passes between flashing daybeacon #5 and unlighted daybeacon #6. Daybeacon #6 sits hard by the westerly banks and it can be hard to pick out.

From #5 and #6, the Waterway once again works its way farther from shore. Point to pass unlighted daybeacon #7 to its fairly immediate westerly side.

After passing between flashing daybeacon #9 and unlighted daybeacon #10 the Flagler Memorial bascule bridge will be sighted dead ahead. Short of this span, the enclosed harbor of Palm Beach Yacht Club & Marina will come abeam to the west.

The Flagler Memorial span has a closed vertical clearance of 17 feet and a restrictive opening schedule on weekdays. From October 1 through May 31 the bridge will not open between 7:30 A.M. and 9:30 A.M. and between 4:00 P.M. and 5:45 P.M., except for scheduled openings at 8:30 A.M. and 4:45 P.M. From 9:30 A.M. to 4:00 P.M. the span opens only on the hour and half-hour. The bridge opens on demand during the evening and night.

On the Waterway South of Flagler Memorial Bridge, the extensive docks of Palm Harbor Marina will be spotted to the west. The entrance into the breakwater-enclosed harbor lies almost midway along the basin's north-to-south axis.

It's a fairly straightforward run from the Flagler Memorial span south to the Royal Palm bascule span. Watch out for the charted 2-foot shoal bordering the Waterway's western flank south of unlighted daybeacon #14. Favor the eastern side of the channel between #14 and the bridge.

The Royal Palm bascule bridge (closed vertical clearance, 14 feet) also has complicated opening restrictions. From October 1 through May 31 the span is closed on weekdays from 7:45 A.M. to 9:45 A.M. and from 3:30 P.M. to 5:45 P.M. except that it opens at 8:45 A.M., 4:30 P.M., and 5:15 P.M. From 9:45 A.M. to 3:30 P.M. the bridge opens on the quarter and three-quarter hours. Like Flagler Memorial, it opens on demand during the night.

Once through the Royal Palm Bridge, switch back to the main section of chart 11472 for navigation south to the Southern Boulevard Bridge. Again, stick strictly to the marked cut.

Just in case you haven't quite had your fill of restrictive schedules, the Southern Boulevard Bridge (closed vertical clearance, 14 feet) remains closed on weekdays between October 1 and May 31 from 7:30 A.M. to 9:15 A.M. and from 4:30 P.M. to 6:30 P.M., excepting openings at 8:15 A.M. and 5:30 P.M. Take along a good book to read while waiting for these three bridges.

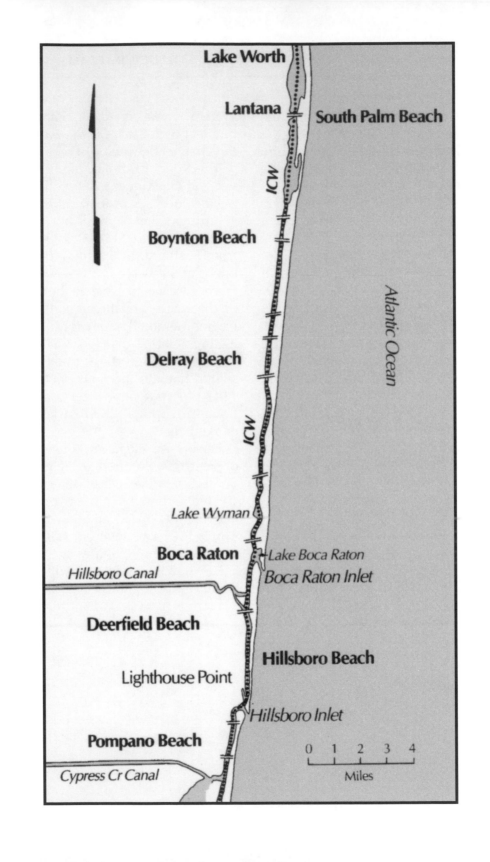

Lake Worth to Pompano

The eastern Florida ICW follows lower Lake Worth from West Palm Beach's southern boundary to Boynton Beach. The Waterway then ducks into a sheltered passage running south to the yachting capital of Fort Lauderdale. This is another run with a great variety of cruising conditions.

South of Palm Beach, coastal communities on both shores rub elbows with their fellows. Without the city limit signs, it would be hard to tell when you leave one town and pass into the next. The land south of Lantana has been developed into a solid mass of private homes, huge condo complexes, and commercial shopping centers.

The Waterway's run through southern Lake Worth is similar to the northern Palm Beach passage. However, the lake is even shallower outside of the ICW channel in this region. You must take great care not to stray from the marked cut, or a hard grounding could easily be the unfortunate result.

South of Boynton Beach, the Waterway passes through a mostly man-made canal running between an almost continuous line of concrete seawalls. Passage through these seemingly protected waters is no picnic. This writer and his first mate have dubbed this portion of the ICW "hot-dog capital of the world." On any day, but particularly on Saturday and Sunday, passing cruisers can expect to meet a host of speedboats operated by pilots who don't seem to have the least understanding of the rules of the road or of common courtesy. Be on guard against these hot dogs as you work your way south to Fort Lauderdale.

Even without the speed demons, there are problems enough with the Waterway south of Boynton Beach. Official no-wake zones litter the ICW in greater and greater numbers north of Miami. The Florida Marine Patrol and local law-enforcement officials are especially vigilant south of Boynton Beach, and violators of speed restrictions are often ticketed. Captains are also legally responsible for any damage caused by their wake, even when speeds are not regulated. Back off the throttles and take your time while cruising this populated portion of the Waterway.

As if the no-wake zones do not cause sufficient delay, skippers must also contend with a host of low-level bridges with restrictive opening schedules. Between South Palm Beach and Miami mariners must now face nearly two dozen spans with scheduled opening hours. Build extra time in your cruising itinerary for the passage south from Palm Beach. At least the more leisurely pace will allow a better view of the surroundings.

The scenery throughout the southerly portion of Lake Worth is less than spectacular. Heavy residential development overlooks both banks, with some of the homes and buildings lacking the care and grooming so evident farther south. To be sure, there are many exceptions to this rule. The waterside communities of Lake Worth and Lantana present a mostly attractive face to Waterway travelers.

Captains and crew cruising the canal-like portion of the ICW south of Boynton Beach will observe many beautiful homes with carefully manicured yards. Many of these lavish residences have their own swimming pools and private docks. When passing a boat berthed directly on the Waterway, please slow down and reduce your wake. The last thing the cruising community needs is more no-wake zones!

It is difficult to overstate the problem caused in this restricted portion of the Waterway by residual wake bouncing off the concrete seawalls. During weekends when motorboat traffic is heavy, the many wakes smashing back and forth into each other from the seawalls can create swells that make a 20-knot blow on Indian River seem like a picnic. Take your time and strap down all movable objects on board.

Anchoring is a strictly regulated activity in this entire region. New regulations are being enacted constantly, and we cannot guarantee that the legal anchorage today will not become a ticketing spot for the county sheriff's department tomorrow.

Facilities south of Palm Beach to Pompano are adequate but rather low key. Transient dockage is at a premium. With a few notable exceptions, the area marinas are smaller; a few are perhaps on their last legs.

Waterside restaurants with their own dockage crowd the Waterway shores in ever-increasing numbers as you move south to Fort Lauderdale. It would take a cruising guide devoted exclusively to dining in order to even begin listing all these waterside facilities. Be assured, however, that a goodly selection of these restaurants is reviewed below.

Our best suggestion concerning the passage between Palm Beach and Fort Lauderdale is to sit back, watch out for the hot dogs, laugh at the restrictive bridges, and enjoy the scenery. Have a good cruise!

Charts A single NOAA chart provides complete navigational coverage of the Waterway and its auxiliary waters from Lantana to Fort Lauderdale:

11467—follows the ICW from southern Palm Beach to Fort Lauderdale

Bridges
Lake Worth/Lake Avenue Bridge—crosses ICW at Standard Mile 1029, south of unlighted daybeacon #33—Bascule—35 feet (closed)—opens on demand

Lantana Avenue Bridge—crosses ICW at Standard Mile 1032, south of unlighted daybeacon #38—Bascule—13 feet (closed)—December 1 through April 30 opens only on the hour and every 15 minutes thereafter 7:00 A.M. to 6:00 P.M. weekdays (10:00 A.M. to 6:00 P.M. during weekends and holidays); at all other times opens on demand

Boynton Beach Inlet/Highway A1A Bridge—crosses approach to Boynton Beach Inlet east of ICW—Fixed—18 feet

Ocean Avenue/Boynton Beach Bridge—crosses ICW at Standard Mile 1035, south of flashing daybeacon #52—Bascule—21 feet (closed)—opens on demand

Briny Breezes/SE 15th Street Bridge—crosses ICW at Standard Mile 1036—Bascule—25 feet (closed)—opens on demand

George Bush/NE 8th Street Bridge—crosses ICW at Standard Mile 1039, south of unlighted daybeacon #52A—Bascule—9 feet (closed)—opens on demand weekdays; during weekends November 1 through May 31 opens only on the hour and every 15 minutes thereafter 11:00 A.M. to 6:00 P.M.

Atlantic Avenue Bridge—crosses ICW at Standard Mile 1039.5—Bascule—12 feet (closed)—November 1 through May 31 opens only on the hour and half-hour 10:00 A.M. to 6:00 P.M. weekdays; at all other times of the day and year, opens on demand

Linton Boulevard Bridges—crosses ICW at Standard Mile 1041—Bascule—30 feet (closed)—opens on demand

Spanish River Boulevard (twin) Bridge—crosses ICW at Standard Mile 1045—Bascule—25 feet (closed)—opens on demand (flashing green light means it's OK to proceed; red light warns of an imminent closing)

Palmetto Park Road Bridge—crosses ICW at Standard Mile 1047.5—Bascule—19 feet (closed)—opens on demand—watch out for extremely strong tidal currents!

Boca Raton Inlet/Highway A1A Bridge—crosses approach to Boca Raton Inlet near the southeasterly corner of Lake Boca Raton—Bascule—23 feet (closed)—opens on demand

East Camino Real Bridge—crosses ICW at Standard Mile 1048, south of flashing daybeacon #67—Bascule—9 feet (closed)—opens on the hour and every 15 minutes thereafter 7:00 A.M. to 6:00 P.M.

J. D. Butler/S. R. 810 Bridge—crosses ICW at Standard Mile 1050, south of unlighted daybeacon #2—Bascule—21 feet (closed)—October 1 through May 31, Monday through Thursday, opens on the hour and every 20 minutes thereafter 7:00 A.M. to 6:00 P.M.; October 1 through May 31, Friday through Sunday, opens on the hour and half-hour 7:00 A.M. to 6:00 P.M.; at all other times of the day and year, opens on demand

Hillsboro Inlet/Highway A1A Bridge—crosses Hillsboro Inlet southeast of flashing daybeacon #71—Bascule—13 feet (closed)—opens only on the hour and every 15 minutes thereafter 7:00 A.M. to 6:00 P.M.; at all other times, opens on demand

Pompano Beach/NE 14th Street Bridge—crosses ICW at Standard Mile 1055, south of flashing daybeacon #73—Bascule—15 feet (closed)—opens only on the quarter and three-quarter hour 7:00 A.M. to 6:00 P.M.; at all other times, opens on demand

Atlantic Boulevard Bridge—crosses ICW at Standard Mile 1056, north of unlighted daybeacon #74—Bascule—15 feet (closed)—opens only on the hour and half-hour 7:00 A.M. to 6:00 P.M.; at all other times, opens on demand

---

Chapter 9 Anchorage Summary (Note that anchorages are arranged in geographic order, moving north to south.)

Lantana Anchorage—(Standard Mile 1031)—located near 26 34.988 North/080 02.781 West, just west of the ICW channel, south of the Lantana bascule bridge—6-foot depths—reviewed on pages 449, 460

Bel Marra Anchorage—(Standard Mile 1042)—located near 26 25.429 North/080 04.036 West, on the charted, lakelike body of water abutting the ICW's westerly flank, north of the charted position of Bel Marra—6-foot minimum

depths—reviewed on pages 452, 461

Lake Boca Raton Anchorage—(Standard Mile 1048)—located near 26 20.776 North/080 04.352 West, on the northeastern section of Lake Boca Raton—6-foot minimum depths, but entrance channel can be tricky—reviewed on pages 454, 462

Lettuce Lake Anchorage—(Standard Mile 1057)—located 26 13.292 North/080 05.705 West, on the covelike body of water along the Waterway's eastern banks between unlighted daybeacon #74 and flashing daybeacon #76—7-foot minimum

depths—reviewed on pages 458, 464
Lake Santa Barbara Anchorage—(Standard Mile 1057)—located near 26 13.374 North/080

05.827 West, opposite the Lettuce Lake anchorage reviewed above—6-foot depths—reviewed on pages 458, 464-65

Chapter 9 Marina and Yacht-Club Summary

(Note that marinas and yacht clubs are arranged in geographic order, moving north to south.)
Murrelle Marine—(561) 582-3213—(Standard Mile 1030.5)—located near 26 35.495 North/080 02.919 West, guarding the Waterway's western banks, west of unlighted daybeacon #38—transient dockage available—5-foot minimum depths—reviewed on pages 448-49, 459
Delray Beach Yacht Club—(561) 272-2700—(Standard Mile 1039.5)—located near 26 27.540 North/080 03.810 West, along the Waterway's eastern banks, south of the Atlantic Avenue Bridge—transient dockage available—6-foot minimum depths—reviewed on pages 451, 461
Delray Harbor Club Marina—(561) 276-0376—(Standard Mile 1041)—located near 26 26.753 North/080 03.939 West, lying along the ICW's westerly banks, west of the charted bubble of 7- to 9-foot water near facility designation #16 on chart 11467—transient dockage available—gasoline and diesel fuel available—6-foot minimum depths—reviewed on pages 451-52, 461
Boca Raton Resort & Club Marina—(561) 395-3000—(Standard Mile 1048)—located near 26 20.611 North/080 04.632 West, flanking the western banks of the combined Lake Boca

Raton and ICW passage, north of unlighted daybeacon #66—transient dockage available for larger cruising craft—gasoline and diesel fuel available—reviewed on pages 452-53, 462
Royal Palm Yacht & Country Club—(561) 395-2100—(Standard Mile 1050)—located near 26 19.525 North/080 05.299 West, on the charted Hillsboro Drainage Canal, cutting off from the western banks of the ICW well south of flashing daybeacon #67—transient dockage available for members of yacht clubs with appropriate reciprocal privileges—gasoline and diesel fuel available for members and accredited guests only—6-foot minimum depths—reviewed on pages 454-55, 463
Lighthouse Point Yacht Club—(954) 942-6688—(Standard Mile 1052)—located near 26 17.073 North/080 05.011 West, south of unlighted daybeacon #68 on the large canal making into the western shores of the Waterway—transient dockage available—gasoline and diesel fuel available—7-foot minimum depths—reviewed on pages 455-56
Lighthouse Point Marina—(954) 942-8118—(Standard Mile 1054)—located near 26 15.994 North/080 04.982 West, in the charted harbor north of unlighted daybeacon #70—transient dockage available—gasoline and diesel fuel available—minimum 6-foot depths—reviewed on pages 456-57, 464

Murrelle Marine (Standard Mile 1030.5) (26 35.495 North/080 02.919 West)

The first marine facility south of the Southern Boulevard Bridge guards the Waterway's western banks, west of unlighted

daybeacon #38. Murrelle Marine is a small, somewhat funky boatyard that offers the unusual feature (for a repair facility) of overnight dockage. Transients are accepted, when space is available, at either a single fixed wooden or a single fixed concrete dock. Low-water depths run around 5 to 5½ feet. Most slips offer fresh water and 30-amp power hookups, though two 50-amp connections are available at selected locations. Fair showers are on hand and a Laundromat is within walking distance. There is a small, meagerly stocked ship's store adjoining the yard office. Considering Murrelle Marine's limited dockage, it would be a wise practice to call ahead of time and check on slip availability before committing to an overnight stay.

Several restaurants are within walking distance. These dining spots are grouped around the nearby causeway leading to the Lantana Avenue Bridge. Chief among these choices is the Old Key Lime House (302 E Ocean Avenue, 561-533-5220). A taxi ride will be necessary to reach the nearest local supermarket.

Repair services are fairly extensive at Murrelle Marine. A collection of on-site, independent repair firms can provide just about any mechanical (gas and diesel), welding, fiberglass, marine carpentry, and underwater hardware services that might ever be required. The yard's travelift is rated at 35 tons.

Murrelle Marine (561) 582-3213

Approach depths—5-6 feet
Dockside depths—5-5½ feet (minimum)
Accepts transients—yes
Transient dockage fee—below average
Fixed wooden and concrete pier—yes
Dockside power connections—mostly
   30 amps, two 50 amps
Dockside water connections—yes
Showers—yes
Below-waterline repairs—yes
Mechanical repairs—yes
Ship's store—yes (small)
Restaurant—several nearby

Lantana Anchorage (Standard Mile 1031) (26 34.988 North/080 02.781 West)

South of the Lantana bascule bridge, minimum 6-foot depths extend west from the Waterway to a series of charter-craft docks. West of these piers, the bottom quickly shelves upward. Boats as large as 40 feet should be able to find enough elbowroom to swing comfortably on the hook. Protection is good for winds blowing from the north, northwest, west, or southwest. Southern or southeastern blows call for a cruise down the ICW to the next available anchorage. The adjoining shoreline is heavily developed. Automobile noise and headlights can be more than a little problem at night for those trying to get their rest.

Boynton Beach Marinas (Standard Mile 1032.5)

The harbor and large dry stack storage building of Palm Beach Yacht Center (26 33.615 North/080 03.039 West, 561-588-9911) will be spied on the ICW's western shoreline, just south of unlighted daybeacon #43. This impressive complex offers gasoline, diesel fuel, mechanical, and below-waterline repairs. All on-the-water dockage is apparently taken up by resident craft, and the management has clearly informed this writer that transients are not accepted. Visitors will readily come to appreciate this facility's emphasis on new power-boat sales. The yard's travelift is rated at 75 tons.

Next up is Gateway Marina (26 33.253 North/080 03.124, West 561-588-1211), located to the west of flashing daybeacon #44. This is primarily a boat-sales dealership and no facilities for cruisers, outside of gasoline, are available.

Boynton Beach Inlet (Standard Mile 1033)

The marked but mostly uncharted passage

to Boynton Beach Inlet cuts to the east near unlighted daybeacon #46. Actually, there are two channels; the more prolifically marked of the two leads to a small county dock and launching ramp. The northerly cut is actually the so-called channel leading to the inlet.

Visiting cruisers are strictly advised against using Boynton Beach Inlet. While visiting these waters, we once watched a large, local head boat as the captain attempted to enter the cut. A huge swell picked up the boat like a tooth-pick and almost deposited it on the flanking rock jetty. This incident is typical of Boynton inlet. Strong tidal currents, large swells, and a constricted channel all combine to make this seaward passage one of the most treacherous in southeastern Florida. We don't even advise putting to sea in the wake of a local boat. If your plans call for offshore cruising, Lake Worth Inlet to the north or Hillsboro Inlet to the south would far better serve your purpose.

Boynton Beach Waterside Restaurants (Standard Mile 1034.5)

Hungry cruisers will be delighted with the two restaurants guarding the Waterway's western banks, immediately north of the Ocean Avenue/Boynton Beach Bridge (south of flashing daybeacon #52). The northernmost of the pair is Two Georges Restaurant (561-736-2717). This spot features outdoor dining with fresh seafood as the obvious forte.

The southernmost of the two is the Banana Boat Restaurant (561-732-9400). This popular dining spot and bar offers simply wonderful seafood. We were more than taken with our fried grouper sandwiches during a previous visit. The burgers also looked yummy. This is a restaurant with a relaxed, fun atmosphere and, judging from its prodigious population of diners during our time here, the Banana Boat is more than appreciated.

Delray Beach

Amidst the fast-paced life of southeastern Florida, Delray Beach is an island of quaint, old-Florida customs. Two yacht clubs welcome transient cruisers. Pause for a moment in your travels to stroll the quiet reaches of Atlantic Avenue just north of the municipal marina. This intriguing lane is chock-full of quaint shops and fine restaurants. Mostly, though, just take some time to enjoy this small sample of old Florida before plunging south.

Delray Beach History Delray Beach was the setting for an unusual community of farmers early in the twentieth century. A dedicated group of Japanese immigrants came to Delray in 1906 looking for a better life. They began industriously planting on a large tract of land between Delray and Boca Raton. At first pineapples were the principal crop, but later the colony's cultivation

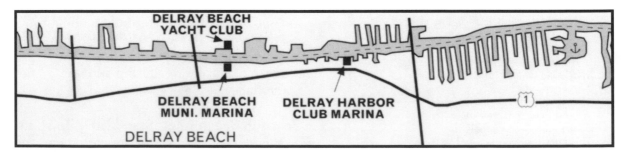

included many types of winter vegetables.

This unique enterprise became known as the Yamato Colony. It continued to flourish until the beginning of World War II, when national prejudice against Japanese immigrants brought the farming efforts to an abrupt halt.

Today the courage and perseverance of the Yamato farmers is remembered by the Morikami Museum of Japanese Culture. The exhibits feature beautifully landscaped gardens and a tribute to Sukeji Morikami, one of the first Yamato immigrants. Inquire at either of the local yacht clubs to arrange transportation to this unusual attraction.

Delray Beach Facilities

Delray Beach features two yacht clubs that cater to cruising visitors. Additionally, there is another marina that offers little in the way of services for nonresident craft. This latter facility, known as Delray Beach Municipal Marina, flanks the Waterway's western shoreline. It no longer accepts boats for overnight dockage and no other transient services are available.

The docks of friendly Delray Beach Yacht Club (Standard Mile 1039.5) come abeam on the eastern banks, south of the Atlantic Avenue Bridge, near 26 27.540 North/080 03.810 West. This delightful club gladly accepts transients for overnight dockage at its well-protected, fixed, wooden piers featuring full power and water connections. Showers and a Laundromat are available to transients in the clubhouse. Unfortunately, the club dining room and swimming pool are reserved for the use of members. Several restaurants on nearby Atlantic Avenue are within a 5- to 10-minute walk.

Delray Beach Yacht Club (561) 272-2700

Approach depths—7 feet
Dockside depths—6-7 feet (minimum)

Accepts transients—yes
Transient dockage rate—average
Fixed wooden piers—yes
Dockside power connections—30
   and 50 amps
Dockside water connections—yes
Showers—yes
Laundromat—yes
Restaurant—several nearby

Southernmost of the city's facilities is the Delray Harbor Club Marina (Standard Mile 1041), lying along the ICW's westerly banks, west of the charted bubble of 7- to 9-foot water near facility designation #16 on chart 11467 (near 26 26.753 North/080 03.939 West). This marina is associated with a large condo complex. Its sheltered dockage basin sits just below this impressive structure. Transients are accepted at the club's fixed concrete piers with 30- and 50-amp power connections and fresh-water hookups. Low-water soundings in the harbor run around 6 feet. Showers are available in the clubhouse and a Laundromat is found within walking distance. There is even a refreshing swimming pool at which visitors are welcome. Gas and diesel fuel are available and there is a ship's store fronting directly onto the Waterway, just behind the fuel pier. Several restaurants are within walking distance. Ask the helpful staff for recommendations.

Delray Harbor Club Marina (561) 276-0376
http://www.delrayharborclub.com

Approach depths—8-10 feet
Dockside depths—6 feet (minimum)
Accepts transients—yes
Transient dockage rate—above average
Fixed concrete piers—yes
Dockside power connections—30
   and 50 amps
Dockside water connections—yes
Showers—yes
Laundromat—walking distance

Gasoline—yes
Diesel fuel—yes
Ship's store—yes
Restaurant—several nearby

Bel Marra Anchorage (Standard Mile 1042) (26 25.429 North/080 04.036 West)

Study chart 11467 for a moment and notice the round, lakelike body of water abutting the ICW's westerly flank, north of the charted position of Bel Marra. Three charted streams come off the northern shore of this lake.

Cruisers in search of good anchorage between Delray Beach and Boca Raton need look no further. This body of water boasts excellent protection from all winds, 6-foot minimum depths, and enough swinging room for any pleasure craft smaller than an aircraft carrier. Surprise, surprise, the surrounding shores are occupied by heavy residential and condo development. While it's not exactly the equal of a remote stream on the St. Johns River, this is about as good as anchorage gets in southeastern Florida.

Boca Raton (Standard Mile 1048)

South of the Palmetto Park Road Bridge, the Waterway quickly flows through a current-strewn passage into Lake Boca Raton. This wide, partially deep body of water serves the city of the same name.

Since the mid-1980s, Boca Raton has made a serious bid to become one of the leading resorts in southeastern Florida. With the waterside Boca Raton Club now serving as a hotel and convention center, many worldwide organizations gather regularly in this bustling community. A vast collection of shopping centers, hotels, motels, and restaurants graces Boca Raton's busy streets. If this rate of expansion continues, Palm Beach had better watch out!

Cruising visitors (whose craft are of sufficient size) may berth at the fabulous club and hotel described below, or they might choose to anchor in Lake Boca Raton. Either way, a visit to this unique community is sure to provide some lasting memories.

Boca Raton Resort & Club Marina (Standard Mile 1048) (26 20.611 North/080 04.632 West)

The docks of famous Boca Raton Resort & Club flank the western banks of the combined Lake Boca Raton and ICW passage, north of unlighted daybeacon #66. Upon entering Lake Boca Raton, cruisers who have not lost their powers of sight will quickly spy the high-rise tower associated with the club.

This posh marina offers limited transient dockage for boats 50 feet and larger at a single, fixed, concrete pier. Full power and water connections, as well as shoreside showers, are available. Of course, most power craft docking at this facility are fully self-contained. Valet service for laundry and dry cleaning is also offered. We have always found the one available pier to be filled with several massive power craft during the winter season. Fueling service and access to the hotel's many facilities, including its swimming pool, beach club, golf course, and world-renowned dining rooms, are also available. Be sure to call ahead of time for reservations.

Boca Raton Resort & Club Marina (561) 447-3474

Approach depths—8-12 feet
Dockside depths—6-8 feet
Accepts transients—yes
  (minimum size—50 feet)
Transient dockage fee—above average
Fixed concrete pier—yes
Dockside power connections—30

and 50 amps (one 100 amps)
Dockside water connections—yes
Showers—yes
Gasoline—yes
Diesel fuel—yes
Restaurant—on site

Boca Raton Club and the Famous Mr. Mizner

Addison Cairns Mizner was born in 1872 in Sacramento, California. Mizner came to Florida in the early part of the century as an architect and developer. He is credited with building some of the grandest homes for some of the wealthiest clients in Palm Beach. During the Florida land boom of the early 1920s, Mizner was considered one of America's leading architects.

In April 1925, Mizner and his brother, Wilson, organized a joint venture with such notables of the day as Harold Vanderbilt, Irving Berlin, Coleman du Pont, Elizabeth Arden, and Clarence H. Geist. They purchased over 16,000 acres at the Boca Raton Inlet, including two miles of beachfront. By June, Mizner's company owned two-thirds of Boca Raton.

Contemporaries credit Mizner with visions of developing an entire city of Spanish and Mediterranean architecture, which he believed perfect for Florida's climate and landscape.

In May 1925, Mizner announced plans to build a 100-room inn on the west side of Lake Boca Raton. Inspired by the art of Spain and Italy, he incorporated his own dreams in the design and development of what would eventually be known as the Cloister Inn. Mizner painted, carved wood, worked with various metals, and did much of the detail work himself while the inn was being built. He even opened his own terra-cotta factory where molds were made for the tiles being used in the hotel. He imported some of his building materials from the old University of Seville building in Spain.

The Cloister formally opened on February 26, 1926. It was to be Mizner's swan song. Before many months passed, the great 1926 hurricane struck, and the second great Florida land boom was at a tragic end. Mizner was ruined. The great architect was forced to leave Florida a broken man.

Ultimately, Clarence Geist, one of the original partners, took over the remaining assets of the development company and reopened the

Boca Raton Club tower, Lake Boca Raton

Cloisters as the Boca Raton Club. The grandeur of Mizner's architecture still lives in this elegant reminder of Florida's first boom days.

Lake Boca Raton Anchorage (Standard Mile 1048) (26 20.776 North/080 04.352 West)

Cruisers on a somewhat more limited budget than those who are able to sample the dockside delights of the Boca Raton Club may anchor within sight of the hotel's tower on the northerly reaches of Lake Boca Raton. There are several unmarked shoals to avoid, but with care you should be able to drop the hook in 6 to 7½ feet of water with fair protection from all winds save strong southerly blows. After traversing the tricky entrance near flashing daybeacon #65, captains will find maximum swinging room on the waters bordering the lake's easterly shoreline. While there is plenty of space for almost any size vessel, boats larger than 45 feet or those drawing more than 5 feet might be a bit unwieldy for the passage circumventing the shallows. The lake is surrounded by heavy residential and commercial development. Nighttime brings out a galaxy of shoreside lights. An evening vigil in the cockpit is more than worthwhile. Be sure to read the navigational information below before attempting to use this anchorage.

Boca Raton Inlet (Standard Mile 1048.5)

The shoal-lined channel leading to Boca Raton Inlet breaks off to the east near flashing daybeacon #67. This most unreliable seaward cut can be a bear when wind and tide oppose. We have observed large breakers at the easterly end of the entrance jetties on more than one occasion. Tidal currents run very quickly through the inner portion of the channel, and just to make matters a bit more complicated,

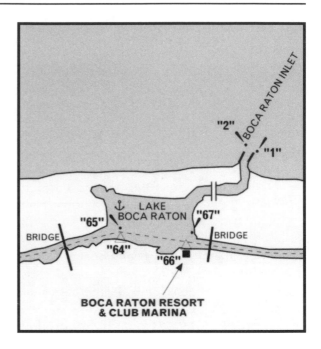

a bascule bridge with a vertical clearance of 23 feet crosses the approach cut. Sailcraft are obliged to contend with the strong currents while waiting for the bridge to open.

While it is barely possible for strangers to use Boca Raton Inlet, most cruisers would be better served by Lake Worth Inlet to the north or the Port Everglades seaward passage in Fort Lauderdale. If you choose to make the attempt anyway, watch for a local craft putting out to sea and follow in its wake.

Deerfield Beach and Associated Facilities (Standard Mile 1050)

South of Boca Raton, the ICW briefly follows the headwaters of Hillsboro River. Without the chart, you could barely detect the change in the concrete-lined passage. West of unlighted daybeacon #2, the dredged Hillsboro Drainage Canal meanders to the northwest and offers access to a first-rate yacht club.

Follow the canal's midwidth upstream past Deerfield Island Park's beautifully natural shores (to starboard) as the stream flows through a lazy bend to the north. Eventually, the waters will open out into a wide basin and the docks of Royal Palm Yacht & Country Club will be spotted dead ahead, on the harbor's northerly banks, near 26 19.525 North/080 05.299 West.

Royal Palm accepts cruising visitors who are members of other yacht clubs with appropriate reciprocal agreements. Slip reservations must be made at least 24 hours in advance. The club dockmaster is on duty 8:00 A.M. to 4:00 P.M., seven days a week. Dockage is afforded at fixed, concrete piers with fresh water and 30- and 50-amp power connections. Depths alongside run around 6 feet. Showers (but no laundry service) are available in the pool house. Gasoline and diesel fuel can be purchased dockside by members and accredited guests only.

Royal Palm also features a large swimming pool and multiple tennis courts, all open to cruising visitors. The two on-site dining rooms are open Tuesday through Saturday for lunch and dinner. One of the dining rooms is closed during the summer. Jackets are required for "gentlemen" after 6:00 P.M. Royal Palm Plaza shopping center is one mile away. Several restaurants, including the Cove (see below), are even closer.

Royal Palm Yacht & Country Club
  (561) 395-2100
  http://www.rpycc.org

Approach depths—6+ feet
Dockside depths—6+ feet
Accepts transients—members of other
  yacht clubs with appropriate
  reciprocal arrangements
Fixed concrete piers—yes

Dockside power connections—30
  and 50 amps
Dockside water connections—yes
Showers—yes
Gasoline—members and
  accredited guests only
Diesel fuel—members and
  accredited guests only
Restaurant—two on site and others nearby

South of the Hillsboro Drainage Canal, the Waterway passes under the J. D. Butler/Hillsboro bascule bridge. A notable restaurant lines the western banks immediately south of this span, and this establishment offers complimentary dockage for their patrons.

Near Standard Mile 1050.5, the docks of Cove Marina and Restaurant (954-427-9747) will come abeam. This facility does not usually accept transients. Most of the available slips are occupied by local craft. The Cove is, however, happy to provide temporary dockage while you dine at its restaurant. Please check with the dockmaster before leaving your boat. Low-tide depths run around 5 feet. No other marine services besides gasoline are available for visitors.

Cove Restaurant overlooks the rear portion of Cove Marina. We highly recommend this waterside cafe. It features open-air dining and attractive, tasty dishes, served with an out-island flair. This is a great casual dining spot for either lunch or dinner.

Lighthouse Point Yacht Club (Standard Mile 1052) 26 17.073 North/080 05.011 West

South of unlighted daybeacon #68, a large canal makes into the western shores of the Waterway. This stream leads to Lighthouse Point Yacht Club. Transients are accepted at this modern, well-sheltered facility, though the dockmaster has informed this writer that most overnighters are members of other accredited yacht clubs. This is not a requirement, however. Some five slips are kept open during the winter season for this purpose.

Transient and resident vessels are accommodated at fixed, wooden piers with fresh water and 30- and 50-amp power connections. Depths run around 7 to 8 feet dockside, as they do in the approach canal. Complete fueling facilities are also available.

Visiting cruisers who are lucky enough to be members of other clubs with appropriate reciprocal agreements are afforded full clubhouse privileges. This rich array of amenities includes an Olympic-size swimming pool, tennis courts, racquetball court, health spa, and full dining room. Visitors lacking the necessary yacht-club affiliations will probably need to take a taxi in order to find their way to a restaurant.

Lighthouse Point Yacht Club (954) 942-6688
http://www.lpryc.com

Approach depths—7-8 feet
Dockside depths—7-8 feet
Accepts transients—yes
Transient dockage rate—above average
Fixed wooden piers—yes
Dockside power connections—30
  and 50 amps
Dockside water connections—yes
Gasoline—yes
Diesel fuel—yes
Restaurant—on site (for yacht-club
  members only)

Lighthouse Point Marina (Standard Mile 1054) (26 15.994 North/080 04.982 West)

South of unlighted daybeacon #68B, the waterway begins its passage through a long no-wake zone that runs past the Hillsboro Inlet channel. Lighthouse Point Marina, the only full-service marine facility of its type between Lantana and Fort Lauderdale, guards the ICW's western flank, just a stone's throw north of the Waterway's intersection with the inlet.

Lighthouse Point Marina is located in the charted harbor north of unlighted daybeacon #70. This facility is obviously well managed and boasts ultramodern, fixed, wooden piers set amidst scrupulously kept grounds. Transients are readily accommodated, and all slips feature full power and water connections. Minimum low-water dockside depths run around 6 feet with typical low-tide soundings of 6½ to 7 feet. Excellent showers and a full Laundromat are also close at hand. Gasoline and diesel fuel can be pumped pierside, and a nice ship's and variety store is perched on the outer dock.

Lighthouse Point features its own dining spot, the Galley Grill (954-788-4745). According to local cruisers, it serves the freshest seafood as well as several beef and sandwich dishes.

There is still another dining choice available for fortunate patrons of this marina. Within walking distance of the docks, a small ferry carries hungry customers across the water to Cap's Place (954-941-0418). This venerable dining spot is located on the easterly banks of the same offshoot that hosts Lighthouse Point Marina. Cap's has been serving wonderful seafood for many years now, and its reputation is almost legend.

Lighthouse Point Marina (954) 942-8118

Approach depths—7-8 feet
Dockside depths—6-7 feet (minimum)
Accepts transients—yes
Transient dockage rate—above average
Fixed wooden piers—yes
Dockside power connections—30

and 50 amps
Dockside water connections—yes
Showers—yes
Laundromat—yes
Gasoline—yes
Diesel fuel—yes
Below-waterline repairs—yes
Mechanical repairs—yes
Ship's and variety store—yes
Restaurant—on site and another nearby

After passing Hillsboro Inlet, the ICW turns briefly to the west. Several small marinas line the southern banks between the seaward passage and flashing daybeacon #73. Pretty much all the available dockage is occupied by local craft, particularly charter fishing boats. While it might be possible to buy some fuel here, Lighthouse Point Marina would probably better serve your purposes.

Hillsboro Inlet (Standard Mile 1054)

Hillsboro Inlet is certainly more reliable than either the Boynton Beach or Boca Raton seaward cuts, but it's no walk in the shade, either. Strong tidal currents regularly sweep the channel, and markers must be shifted frequently to follow the ever-changing sands. Nevertheless, the Coast Guard is known for its vigilance in keeping up with the latest changes, and captains can usually rely on the inlet's aids to navigation. Twin stone jetties flank the inlet's seaward passage, lending additional stability to the cut. In August 2004, minimum depths seemed to be 7 to 10 feet, but, remember, the bottom could easily have shifted by the time you read this account.

During fair-weather days, strangers should be able to put to sea in relative safety through the Hillsboro passage. Of course, as always, if you can spot a local running the inlet, it would be best to follow in his wake.

The inner portion of the inlet channel is spanned by a restricted bascule bridge with

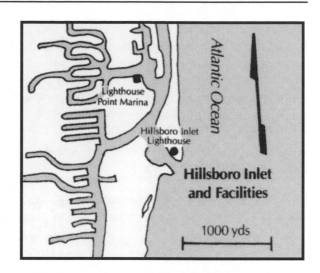

Hillsboro Inlet and Facilities

1000 yds

only 13 feet of closed vertical clearance. Cruisers must be careful to allow for tidal currents while waiting for this span to open.

The 136-foot, skeletal steel Hillsboro Lighthouse calmly overlooks the inlet's northern shores. Boasting one of the most powerful lights on the entire eastern seaboard, this old sentinel has been guiding ships to safety for many years.

Merritt's Boat and Engine Works (Standard Mile 1055) (26 15.136 North/080 05.418 West)

A large canal on the Waterway's western banks, just north of Standard Mile 1055, is home to Merritt's Boat and Engine Works (954-941-5207). This yard and boat fabricator flanks the stream's northern shore near its intersection with the ICW. Merritt's is a full-service repair yard that boasts both a 60-ton travelift and a 100-ton travelift. Complete mechanical (gas and diesel), electrical, and fiberglass repairs are readily available and, believe me, this firm has the quality mechanics and technicians to do the job right the first time.

Merritt's also manufactures custom, cold-molded wooden-hulled power craft. During our last visit, we were treated to an in-depth tour of a 55 footer under construction. We were most impressed with the quality craftsmanship and meticulous attention to detail. If you happen to be in the market for a new sportsfisherman over 50 feet, give the good folks at Merritt's a call.

Pompano Beach Facilities and Anchorages (Standard Mile 1056)

The piers associated with Sands Harbor Resort (954-942-9100) and Taha Marine (954-785-4737) come up on the eastern banks just north of the Atlantic Boulevard bascule bridge, near 26 13.984 North/080 05.566 West. This position is identified by facility notations #27 and #29 on chart 11467.

It has been our experience that most of the fixed, wooden slips here (7-foot low-water depths) are usually occupied by resident craft. The berths are under the control of Sands Harbor. If you are desperate for an overnight stop, call ahead to check on slip availability. Visiting cruisers who successfully find a place to moor are welcome to make use of the adjacent swimming pool. The hotel is, of course, on hand for those who would like to spend a few nights off the water.

Gasoline, diesel fuel, and a dockside ship's and variety store are under the auspices of Taha Marine. Their pier fronts directly onto the Waterway.

Two anchorages are available to cruising skippers in Pompano Beach. Lettuce Lake (26 13.292 North/080 05.705 West, Standard Mile 1057) is really a covelike indention on the Waterway's eastern banks between unlighted daybeacon #74 and flashing daybeacon #76. The "lake" has minimum 7-foot depths, but it is wide open to the wake of all passing vessels. Otherwise, protection is sufficient in anything short of a full gale. The surrounding shores sport a close-packed collection of private homes. There should be enough swinging room for boats up to 45 feet. This isn't a quiet, isolated anchorage, but it is one of the few havens available north of the Fort Lauderdale official anchorage.

It is also possible to drop the hook in Lake Santa Barbara to the west, near 26 13.374 North/080 05.827 West. Reports indicate that, from time to time, local police ask mariners anchored on this body of water to move on their way. Apparently, in years past some cruising "mavericks" abused their anchoring privileges by landing their dinghies on private property and staying for months on end. If you do use this anchorage, keep the dinghy on board and limit your stay to forty-eight hours.

Minimum depths in Lake Santa Barbara run around 6 feet and the waters are better sheltered from wake than Lettuce Lake across the way. However, Santa Barbara is much larger than Lettuce Lake, and in really nasty weather, it could foster a bit of a chop—probably not enough to be really dangerous, just a bit uncomfortable. Boats of almost any size should be to able drop the hook with plenty of elbow-room. Be sure to anchor near the midwidth to leave ample space for any passing traffic.

LAKE WORTH TO POMPANO BEACH NAVIGATION

Successful navigation of the ICW south   of Palm Beach to Fort Lauderdale is not a matter to be taken lightly. Swift tidal currents scour this stretch of the Waterway, courtesy of the three inlets along the way. These swiftly moving waters are more than enough to set slow-moving trawlers and sailcraft outside of the marked cut. Even in the protected canal south of Boynton Beach, more than one low-powered boat has been shoved rudely into the pilings of a bridge while waiting for the span to open.

Watch your stern carefully for leeway while you are on the waters of southern Lake Worth. Be ready to make quick course corrections. Stay well back from the various bridges in the protected portion of the Waterway to the south. If you must wait for a span to open, keep well clear of all other craft and both shorelines. Have all hands stand by for fending off in tight places if the current is strong. Waiting for a bridge to open can be anything but an idle pastime.

The ICW south of Palm Beach is peppered with no-wake zones. Be prepared to find even more restricted waters than those that existed at the time of this writing.

Again, be warned against the rough conditions created by residual wake on the protected canal-like passage south of Boynton Beach. You simply will have to see the Waterway on a weekend to believe how choppy this portion of the ICW can become.

Keep alert, watch over your stern, and strap down movable objects. Cruisers taking these elementary precautions should come through to Fort Lauderdale with nothing worse than a few well-bounced eyeballs.

South Lake Worth   The ICW knifes through the shallow reaches of southern Lake Worth for about 8.5 nautical miles between the Southern Boulevard Bridge and Boynton Beach. This section of the lake is even shallower than its northern counterpart. Stick strictly to the marked cut and take every precaution against lateral leeway easing you out of the channel.

On the Waterway   After passing through the Southern Boulevard Bridge, say goodbye to chart 11472 and break out 11467 for continued navigation to the south. If you're like this writer, you will feel as if you have been using 11472 forever!

The Waterway passes the eastern mouth of the West Palm Beach Canal, west of unlighted daybeacon #26. This old cut was one of the original canals leading to Lake Okeechobee. For many years it provided transportation to that remote region and helped to drain the intervening lands. Now the canal is blocked by several low-level fixed bridges. For all its rich history, this stream is probably best bypassed.

The Lake Worth-Lake Avenue bascule bridge crosses the Waterway about .5 nautical miles south of unlighted daybeacon #33. It has a closed vertical clearance of 35 feet and opens on demand for sailcraft needing more clearance.

South of unlighted daybeacon #38, cruisers will spot a sign for Murrelle Marine along the ICW's westerly edge. The channel leading to the marina is unmarked. Our best advice is simply to cruise from the sign directly into the dockage basin to the west. By using this strategy, we were able to hold minimum 5-foot depths.

The Waterway is next spanned by the Lantana Avenue bascule bridge (closed vertical clearance 13 feet) between unlighted daybeacons #38 and #40. From December 1 through April 30, on weekdays, this span opens only on the hour and the quarter, half, and three-quarter hours between 7:00 A.M. and 6:00 P.M. On weekends and holidays, the same restrictions apply between 10:00 A.M. and 6:00 P.M. At all other times the bridge opens on demand.

Lantana Anchorage   To enter the small deepwater patch south of the Lantana bridge (west of the ICW), continue on the Waterway channel until you are some 100 yards south of the westside causeway. Then turn 90 degrees to the west and, proceeding at idle speed, feel your way along with the sounder for some 75 to 100 yards. Be sure to stop before cruising past the charter-craft docks along the northerly banks.

On the ICW   The entrance cut to Palm Beach Yacht Center will come abeam to the west near flashing daybeacon #44. The marina channel is indifferently marked by unadorned pilings. Simply cruise between the various piles into the dockage basin.

South of flashing daybeacon #44 and unlighted daybeacon #45, the ICW quickly flows toward its intersection with forgettable Boynton Beach Inlet.

Boynton Beach Inlet   The Boynton Beach Inlet channels, such as they are, come up east of unlighted daybeacon #46. These twin routes are very confusing, not the least of which reason is that there are two channels. The northern of the two is actually the direct inlet channel, and it has by far the more meager markings. Nevertheless, the

channel is fairly straightforward into the canal-like passage that eventually leads to the open sea. The tidal current that rips through this canal has to be seen to be believed. The channel is also spanned by a fixed bridge with only 18 feet of vertical clearance. If you can't clear this height don't even think about entering the inlet. Once between the breakwaters with the ocean in sight, you're on your own.

The southern, well-marked channel actually cuts east to a small county park with four docks and launching ramps. No services for cruisers are to be found at this facility.

On the Waterway   Flashing daybeacon #52 marks the northerly entrance into the sheltered portion of the ICW leading to Fort Lauderdale. If you happen to arrive when Waterway traffic is light, running the canal should be a pleasant experience. If you enter on the weekend, watch out!

Once into the canal, you will soon approach the Ocean Avenue/Boynton Beach Bridge. No-wake restrictions are in effect above and below this span. Just north of the bridge, Two Georges and Banana Boat restaurants line the westerly shoreline.

The Ocean Avenue bascule span has a closed vertical clearance of 21 feet and it opens on demand.

Some .75 nautical miles south of the Boynton Beach span the Briny Breezes/SE 15th Street Bridge crosses the Waterway. Again, no-wake speeds are in effect north and south of the span. This bridge has a closed vertical clearance of 25 feet, and it also opens on demand.

Chart 11467 correctly identifies a small shoal abutting the western shore marked by unlighted daybeacon #52A. Be sure to pass #52A well to its easterly side.

As you are passing #52A, check out the eastern banks. Those who can observe the shoreline from a fly-bridge will sight an extensive golf course flanking the Waterway for quite some distance.

Just south of unlighted daybeacon #52A, passing cruisers will encounter the George Bush/NE 8th Street bascule bridge. This low-level span has a closed clearance of only 9 feet and a restricted schedule of opening. The bridge still opens on demand during weekdays, but on weekends the span opens only on the hour and every fifteen minutes thereafter from 11:00 A.M. to 6:00 P.M., between November 1 and May 31. Southbound boats waiting for the bridge must take care to avoid the charted shoal abutting the eastern bank. We once stirred a lot of mud when we accidentally drifted onto these shallows while waiting for the bridge to open. Idle-speed restrictions cover the Waterway for the entire passage south through Delray Beach.

Adding insult to injury, the Atlantic Avenue Bridge crosses the Waterway .7 of a mile south of the 8th Street span. A closed vertical clearance of 12 feet combines with scheduled openings to create yet another delay. The bridge opens only on the hour and half-hour between 10:00 A.M. and 6:00 P.M., Monday through Friday, from November 1 to May 31. At all other times of the day and year the span opens on demand.

South of the Atlantic Avenue span, Delray Beach Municipal Marina will be spied along the western banks, with the docks of Delray Beach Yacht Club to the east.

Don't attempt to anchor in the square-shaped cove, east of the Waterway, immediately south of the Delray Beach Yacht Club. Depths have risen to 3 feet at low water.

Delray's southernmost facility, Delray Harbor Club Marina, is easily spotted along the westerly banks. The dockage basin is overlooked by a tall condo building. The harbor's entrance lies on the north side of the complex.

Finally, Delray Beach's third bridge (the Linton Boulevard Bridge) is a bascule structure with 30 feet of closed vertical clearance. Sailcraft skippers who cannot clear the 30-foot height will be relieved to learn that this bridge does open on demand.

Bel Marra Anchorage   To enter the circular lake anchorage flanking the western banks, north of Bel Marra, cruise from the Waterway into the entry stream's midwidth. Continue into the middle of the almost perfectly circular lake beyond. Be sure to drop the anchor well away from any of the canals that lead off the lake to private homes and docks.

On the Waterway   After a mercifully bridgeless section, the ICW flows under the twin Spanish River Boulevard bascule bridges near Standard Mile 1045. Thankfully, these spans have a closed vertical clearance of 25 feet and they open on demand. Flashing green lights signal that both bridges are safely open. Do not proceed through on a red light.

Flashing daybeacon #56 introduces southbound Waterway cruisers to shallow Lake Wyman. Depths outside of the Waterway are more than suspect in the lake and some 1- and 2-foot shoals flank portions of the channel. Watch for leeway and stay strictly to the Waterway channel while passing through Lake Wyman.

Lake Boca Raton   The northern entrance into Lake Boca Raton may just be one of the most treacherous sections of the entire eastern Florida ICW. It is hard to overstate how swiftly tidal currents boil under the Palmetto Park Road Bridge, spanning the lake's narrow northerly entrance. We once watched amazed as the 31-foot cabin cruiser on which we were passengers, equipped with twin 225-hp. Chrysler inboards, barely made any headway against the current while turning 1,800 RPMs. Trawlers and sailcraft (not to mention a few cabin cruisers as well) can be, and sometimes are, slammed into the bridge's pilings with disastrous results. The greatest possible caution must be practiced by all captains when approaching this span.

The Palmetto Park Road Bridge has a closed vertical clearance of 19 feet, so many power craft can clear the span without the need to worry about an opening. For those of us who must signal for an opening, at least the span does open on demand. Be aware that the bridge tender has been known to be a bit slow on the trigger.

Once through the lake's northern entrance, slow down. No-wake regulations are in force throughout Lake Boca Raton. Watch dead ahead and you should spy the tall tower of the Boca Raton Resort & Club Marina. An overnight anchorage soon comes abeam to the east.

The overnight haven in Lake Boca Raton is complicated by the presence of a 3- to 4-foot shoal running across a good portion of the lake's midsection, fronting the Waterway's eastern flank. To bypass this hazard, cut sharply to the east just north of flashing daybeacon #65. Pass #65 to starboard and proceed into the lake by continuing to favor the northern banks heavily. Once the midwidth of the lake comes abeam to starboard, you can begin to feel your way carefully south with the sounder for a bit more swinging room. If soundings start to rise, reverse your course back to the north and cruise a bit farther east before attempting to make a cut to the south. Don't attempt to reach the Boca Raton Inlet channel from the lake anchorage, Depths are much too uncertain. To reach the inlet, cruise back to the Waterway and enter the channel on the southern shores of the lake.

Favor the western side of the Waterway channel a bit as you cruise south through Lake Boca Raton. As chart 11467 correctly indicates, a 3- and 4-foot shoal abuts the eastern face of the ICW channel.

Boca Raton Inlet   Remember that the Boca Raton Inlet is a capricious cut that most certainly requires local knowledge for successful navigation. Hillsboro Inlet, to the south, or, even better, Port Everglades inlet in Fort Lauderdale will better serve most cruising craft.

To enter the Boca Raton Inlet channel from the ICW, leave the Waterway immediately north of flashing daybeacon #67. Shoaling has occurred on the northern side of the channel along this stretch. Those who stray too far from #67 will find themselves in 3- and 4-foot waters.

No-wake restrictions remain in effect as far as the 23-foot bascule span. Even past this structure, wise captains will continue on at slow speed to better follow the difficult channel.

Favor the southern shore as you cruise east on the inlet approach channel toward the passage's southerly bend. As you round this turn, cruise quickly back to the midwidth and pass under the central section of the 23-foot bascule bridge spanning the inlet. Normally, this bridge opens on demand.

Be on guard against swift currents while waiting for the inlet bridge. East of the span the channel becomes less certain. Flashing daybeacons #1 and #2 mark the easterly extremes of the twin rock and concrete jetties flanking the inlet's passage out into the open sea. Both #1 and #2 are founded on the jetties—stay well clear of both aids.

East of #1 and #2, all markers cease. Those without specific and timely local knowledge can be in a world of trouble.

On the ICW   The Waterway's southern exit from Lake Boca Raton is spanned by the low-level East Camino Real bascule bridge (with a closed vertical clearance of 9 feet). All but small power craft will have to contend with the bridge's restrictive opening schedule. Currently, the span opens on the hour and every fifteen minutes thereafter from 7:00 A.M. to 6:00 P.M., year round.

Again, be on guard against swift currents when passing through this bridge. Fortunately, the waters do not seem to move quite as fast here as those on the lake's northern entrance.

Hillsboro Drainage Canal   Enter the canal by passing unlighted daybeacon #2 to your starboard side. Cruisers need only hold to the canal's midline for good depths upstream to Royal Palm Yacht & Country Club.

On the Waterway   The ICW passes through the J. D. Butler/S. R. 810 Bridge just south of the Hillsboro Canal. No-wake restrictions are strictly in force for a good distance south of the span, and we have observed several boats being ticketed for creating a minor wake. Be sure to proceed at idle speed only in this section.

The J. D. Butler/S. R. 810 Bridge has a closed vertical clearance of 21 feet and follows—guess what—restricted opening times that can only be described as complicated. From October 1 to May 31, the bridge opens on the hour and every twenty minutes thereafter, Monday through Thursday, between 7:00 A.M. and 6:00 P.M. From Friday through Sunday, October 1 to May 31, the bridge opens only on the hour and half hour. At all other times of the day and year, the bridge opens on demand.

Cove Marina and Restaurant comes abeam along the western banks, immediately south of the S. R. 810 bridge.

South of unlighted daybeacon #68B, the entrance canal leading to Lighthouse Point Yacht Club makes into the western banks. Enter the canal on its midline. After cruising west for some 200 yards, you will see the dockage basin opening out to the south.

At #68B, the Waterway begins its approach to Hillsboro Inlet. Again, no-wake regulations are rigidly enforced south to flashing daybeacon #73. Be on guard against strong currents as you pass the mouth of the Hillsboro Inlet channel. Happily, tidal currents do not seem to be as swift here as those to the north at Boca Raton.

Captains will discover the entrance to Lighthouse Point Marina north of unlighted daybeacon #70. Favor the southern banks slightly as you cruise from the Waterway to Lighthouse Point's docks. Shoal water abuts the northern side of the approach canal.

Don't attempt to explore the waters north of Lighthouse Point Marina. Depths quickly rise to 4-foot levels and nighttime anchorage is no longer allowed on these waters.

Hillsboro Inlet   Most aids to navigation on Hillsboro Inlet remain uncharted. Nevertheless, the channel appears to be adequate for strangers to run during the daylight hours in fair weather. The entire seaward passage out to the easterly tips of the twin, protecting stone jetties is an official no-wake zone. Be sure to cruise along at slow speed.

The inlet is spanned by a bascule bridge with 13 feet of closed vertical clearance. This pesky span has restrictive opening hours. From 7:00 A.M. to 6:00 P.M. the bridge opens only on the hour and every fifteen minutes thereafter, year round. If you are caught by this restrictive schedule, and have to wait for a scheduled opening, be on maximum alert for the strong tidal currents that regularly scour this passage. Cruisers approaching from the seaward side should be especially cautious!

On the ICW   The looong no-wake zone stretching south past Hillsboro Inlet finally comes to an end at flashing daybeacon #73. Most power captains will be cheering lustily at this point. Soon, the easterly mouth of charted Hillsboro Canal will come abeam to the west.

Hillsboro Drainage Canal   Enter the Hillsboro Canal on its midwidth. Merritt's Boat and Engine Works will be sighted to starboard.

On the Waterway   The Pompano Beach/NE 14th Street Bridge at Standard Mile 1055 has a closed vertical clearance of 15 feet, and it too has regulated opening hours. From 7:00 A.M. to 6:00 P.M. the span opens on the quarter and three-quarter hours year round. Try not to say too many unhappy things while waiting for yet another bridge to open.

Another run of 1.1 nautical miles will lead southbound cruisers to the northerly face of the Atlantic Boulevard bascule bridge (with closed vertical clearance of 15 feet) and another set of regulated opening times. The bridge opens on the hour and half-hour from 7:00 A.M. to 6:00 P.M. year round.

North of the bridge, the docks of Sands Harbor Hotel and Marina and Taha Marine abut the Waterway's easterly shoreline. Entry is obvious.

Lettuce Lake   Cruisers who decide on anchoring in Lettuce Lake should enter this body of water on the midline of its north-to-south axis. Work your way to within 100 yards of the eastern banks for best protection before dropping the hook. Remember, you will be exposed to the wake of all passing vessels.

Lake Santa Barbara   This lake should also be entered on its midwidth. Avoid both shorelines and pick out any likely spot to drop the hook. Be sure to anchor so as not to obstruct passage from any of the surrounding canals and offshoots.

On the Waterway As you move south from Lettuce and Santa Barbara lakes, the Waterway quickly flows to meet the Commercial Boulevard Bridge. This span is the northern gateway to the city of Fort Lauderdale, famous among mariners for many a year. Continuing coverage of the ICW and the fascinating waters of Fort Lauderdale will be presented in the next chapter.

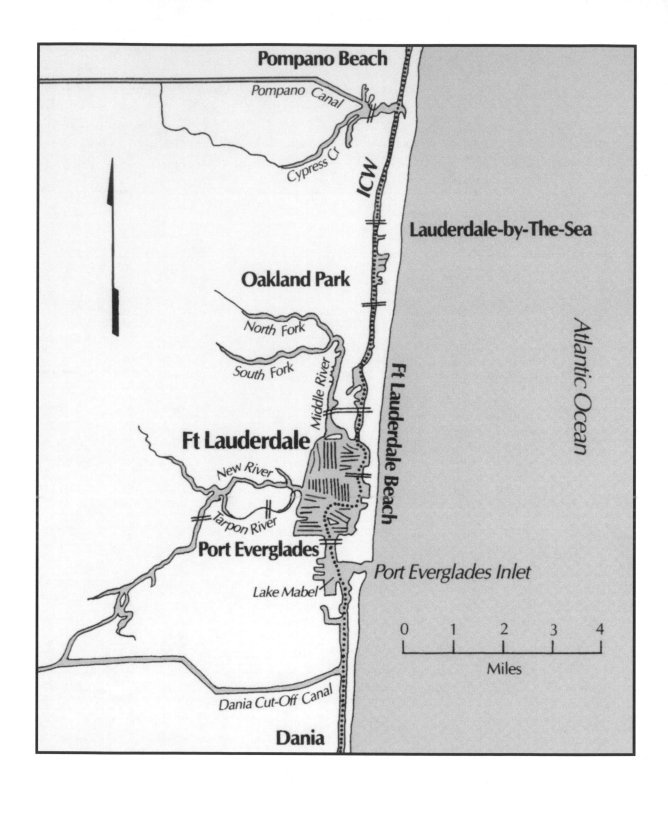

Fort Lauderdale

What would you call a city that has more than 17,000 resident pleasure craft, hordes of waterborne transient visitors, and more miles of canals and waterways than you can count? How about the Venice of America or the yachting capital of Florida? These titles have been applied to the city of Fort Lauderdale from time to time, and while they tell the story to some extent, both fall short of the mark.

Those who have never visited this heavily developed community before will be amazed by the interconnecting canals that honeycomb the region. Even more astoundingly, practically all these byways are lined with a steady flow of large, or rather huge, pleasure boats.

Many cruisers visit Fort Lauderdale year after year to ride out the cold winter to the north. More so-called snowbirds set their course for this water-oriented city than any other in all of eastern (or western) Florida. Because of this popularity, it's almost mandatory to have docking reservations during the transient season (September to May). Otherwise, you may just find yourself completely out of luck. When we arrived one November day and found our supposedly reserved dock already filled with two other craft, there was barely another slip left in the whole city.

Fort Lauderdale is very different now from the easygoing city this writer knew as a boy in the 1950s. In those days my family spent many a happy day exploring the city's canals in small outboard skiffs and fishing off Port Everglades Inlet. Today, Fort Lauderdale is one of the most heavily developed communities in Florida. An incredible string of highrise condos, dense residential developments, and innumerable shopping centers rings the town's waterways. Landside traffic has increased so that it's often impossible to recognize the Fort Lauderdale of yesterday. Cruisers visiting the city's waters for the first time will discover what the term "condo caverns" really means.

All this development is not necessarily bad news for mariners, however. There are without a doubt more waterside restaurants and service centers than in any other city from Maine to Miami. As you might expect, there is also an awesome collection of marinas and boatyards eager to serve transient cruisers. Bahia Mar, one of the largest marinas in the world, fronts onto the ICW in the heart of Fort Lauderdale. Pier 66 is another famous haven for yachtsmen. In addition to these mammoth facilities, there are also many smaller marinas, including the Fort Lauderdale city docks, which offer temporary berths. Captains needing service work will find boatyards and service dealerships offering every imaginable repair. If you can't have it fixed or replaced in Fort Lauderdale, you may as well give up.

On the other hand, it is only fair to observe that with all the influx of people and development has come a serious crime problem. We have never felt as threatened here as in Miami, but the crime rate, particularly in western Fort Lauderdale, is most certainly an unhappy mark on this city's image.

Anchorage in Fort Lauderdale is restricted to one official (thoroughly inadequate) haven just south of the Las Olas bridge. Mariners should probably not attempt to anchor overnight anywhere else within the city limits. Should you try, a local law-enforcement official may come along and ask you to move.

This writer cannot think of Fort Lauderdale without the warming light of my early memories boating and cruising in this city by the sea. My father, to whose memory this book is dedicated, used to love Fort Lauderdale and its offshore angling. Year after year he and my mother piloted a succession of boats down the Waterway from North Carolina to this modern-day Venice. As his son, I seem to be following in his path. We hope you will find as much pleasure as we have taken in the watery byways of this unique community. If you come away with only half of the good memories that this writer and his first-rate first mate enjoy, then your trip will have been more than justified.

Numbers to know in Fort Lauderdale:
Yellow Cab—954-777-7777
Enterprise Rent-A-Car—954-764-3144
Budget Car Rental—954-359-4700
Avis Rent A Car—954-345-5860
Hertz Rent A Car—954-764-1199
West Marine (1201 Federal Highway) —954-564-6767
West Marine (2300 Federal Highway) —954-527-5540
Boat/US Marine Center—954-523-7993
Fort Lauderdale Municipal Marina at Las Olas Bridge—954-828-7200
Fort Lauderdale Municipal Marina New River Docks—954-828-5423
Fort Lauderdale Municipal Marina at Cooley's Landing—954-828-4626
Fort Lauderdale Visitors Center—954-765-4466

Charts The same NOAA chart that provided coverage of the Waterway south from Lantana also details all of Fort Lauderdale's waters, including New River and Port Everglades Inlet: **11467**—gives excellent navigation detail of all Fort Lauderdale's waters

Bridges

Commercial Boulevard Bridge—crosses ICW at Standard Mile 1059—Bascule—15 feet (closed)— November 1 through May 15 opens only on the hour and every 15 minutes thereafter 8:00 A.M. to 6:00 P.M. weekdays, daily; the rest of the year, apparently opens on demand

Oakland Park Bridge—crosses ICW at Standard Mile 1060.5—Bascule—22 feet (closed)—November 15 through May 15 opens only on the hour and every 20 minutes thereafter 7:00 A.M. to 10:00 P.M. weekdays; during weekends, opens only on the hour and every 15 minutes thereafter 10:00 A.M. to 10:00 P.M.; the rest of the year, opens on demand

Sunrise Boulevard (twin) Bridge—crosses ICW at Standard Mile 1062.5—Bascule—25 feet (closed)—November 15 through May 15 opens only on the hour and every 15 minutes thereafter 10:00 A.M. to 6:00 p.m.; the rest of the year, opens on demand

Las Olas Boulevard Bridge—crosses ICW at Standard Mile 1064, south of flashing daybeacon #8—Bascule—31 feet (closed)—opens on demand

SE 17th Street/Brooks Memorial Bridge—crosses ICW at Standard Mile 1066.5—Bascule—55 feet (closed)—year round, opens only on the hour and half-hour, seven days a week from 7:00 A.M. to 7:00 P.M.—at all other times it opens on demand

Third Avenue Bridge—crosses New River upstream of charted location of U.S. 1—Bascule—16 feet (closed)—will not open 7:30 A.M. to 8:30 A.M. and 4:30 P.M. to 5:30 P.M. weekdays—at all other times opens on demand

Andrews Avenue Bridge—crosses New River immediately upstream of Third Avenue Bridge—Bascule—21 feet (closed)—opens on demand (but will not open when the railway bridge, just to the west, is closed)

FEC Railway Bridge—crosses New River upstream of Andrews Avenue Bridge—Bascule—4 feet (closed)—usually open unless a train is due (and has been known to remain closed long after and sometimes even before a train has passed)

William H. Marshall Bridge—crosses New River near facility designation #47F on chart 11467, New River Extension—Bascule—20 feet (closed)—opens on demand

12th Street/Davie Boulevard Bridge—crosses New River at charted location of Highway 736—Bascule—21 feet (closed)—will not open 7:30 A.M. to 8:30 A.M. and 4:30 P.M. to 5:30 P.M. weekdays; at all other times opens on demand

I-95 Twin Bridges—cross New River upstream of facility designation #52A on chart 11467, New River Extension—Fixed—55 feet

"SCL" Railway Bridge—crosses New River just upstream of I-95 fixed bridges—Bascule—2 feet (closed)—usually open, but watch out for strong currents

State Road 84 Bridge—crosses New River upstream of its second split near facility designation #56 on chart 11467, New River Extension—Bascule—21 feet (closed)—opens only with 24 hours' notice, and even then you'd better have a good reason for making the request

---

Chapter 10 Anchorage Summary (Note that anchorages are listed in geographic order, moving north to south.)

Fort Lauderdale Official Anchorage—(Standard Mile 1064)—located near 26 07.160 North/080 06.631 West, in the charted cove indenting the westerly banks south of the Las Olas bascule bridge—6½-foot depths—reviewed on pages 476, 485

Chapter 10 Marina and Yacht-Club Summary (Note that marinas and yacht clubs along the patch of the ICW are listed in geographic order, moving north to south. Marinas and yacht clubs located along the New River are listed at the end of this section in geographic order, moving east to west.)

Coral Ridge Yacht Club—(954) 566-7886—(Standard Mile 1062.5)—located near 26 08.429 North/080 06.502 West, along the Waterway's western shoreline, immediately north of the Sunrise Boulevard Bridge—transient dockage available for members of other yacht clubs with appropriate reciprocal privileges—7+-foot minimum depths—reviewed on pages 473-74

Fort Lauderdale Municipal Marina at Las Olas Bridge—(954) 759-5200—(Standard Mile 1064)—located near 26 07.191 North/080 06.496 West, off the ICW's eastern shoreline, immediately north and south (mostly on the north side) of the Las Olas bascule bridge—transient dockage available—6-foot minimum depths—reviewed on pages 474-75, 485

Hall of Fame Marina—(954) 764-3975—(Standard Mile 1064)—located near 26 07.016 North/080 06.450 West, along the Waterway's eastern banks, just south of the Las Olas City Marina—transient dockage available for craft 40 feet and larger—7½-foot minimum depths—reviewed on pages 476, 485

Bahia Mar Yachting Center—(954) 764-2233—(Standard Mile 1064.5)—located near 26 06.808 North/080 06.505 West, along the Waterway's easterly flank, south of the Las Olas Boulevard Bridge—transient dockage available for craft 40 feet and larger—gasoline and diesel fuel available—10+-foot minimum depths—reviewed on pages 476-78, 485

Lauderdale Yacht Club—(954) 524-5500—(Standard Mile 1066)—located near 26 06.487 North/080 07.396 West, entrance channel runs west-northwest from the Waterway, south of flashing daybeacon #24—transient dockage available for members of other yacht clubs with appropriate reciprocal privileges—6-foot minimum depths—reviewed on pages 478-79, 486

Pier 66 Yacht Harbor—(954) 525-6666—(Standard Mile 1066.5)—located near 26 06.129 North/080 07.076 West, lying along the Waterway's eastern shore, just north of the SE 17th Street bridge—transient dockage available—gasoline and diesel fuel available—10+-foot minimum depths—reviewed on pages 479-80, 486

Marriott Portside Marina—(954) 527-6781—(Standard Mile 1066.5)—located near 26 06.103 North/080 07.283 West, opposite Pier 66 along the ICW's western flank, just north of the SE 17th Street bridge—transient dockage available—11-foot minimum depths—reviewed on pages 482, 486

Marina Inn and Yacht Harbor—(954) 525-3484—(Standard Mile 1066.5)—located near 26 05.993 North/080 07.037 West, fronting the Waterway's eastern banks, immediately south of the SE 17th Street bridge—transient dockage available—10-foot minimum depths—reviewed on pages 482-83, 486

Fort Lauderdale New River/Downtown Municipal Docks—(954) 828-5423—located near 26 07.036 North/080 08.505 West, on both banks of the New River, between the Third Avenue and Andrews Avenue bridges—transient dockage available—7-foot minimum depths—reviewed on pages 489-90

Cooley's Landing, City of Fort Lauderdale Municipal Docks—(954) 828-4626—located near 26 07.031 North/080 08.939 West, gracing New River's northwesterly banks immediately upstream (southwest) of the William H. Marshall Bridge—transient dockage available—7-foot minimum depths—reviewed on pages 494-95

Summerfield Boat Works—(954) 525-4726—located near 26 05.973 North/080 09.661 West, along the northern shore of New River just as this stream takes a bend to the west, near facility designation #50 on the New River inset of chart 11467—limited transient dockage available—7-foot minimum depths—reviewed on page 495

Jackson Marine Center—(954) 792-4900—located near 26 05.821 North/080 10.186 West, on the north shores of New River, immediately upstream of the charted "SCL" railway span—transient dockage available—7-foot minimum depths—reviewed on page 496

Marina Bay Hotel Resort and Marina—(954) 791-7600—located near 26 05.548 North/080 10.257 West, found in the large charted cove indenting New River's southern banks at facility designation #53 on the New River inset of chart 11467—transient dockage available—8-foot minimum depths—reviewed on pages 496-97

Fort Lauderdale History   As early as 1793 the Lewis family is known to have been living on the banks of New River near the present location of Fort Lauderdale. By 1821 when Florida became part of the United States, Mr. Lewis had died, but his widow, Frankee Lewis, was still on the land. In 1824 she petitioned for and received 600 acres from the federal government. Richard Fitzpatrick bought the Lewis claim in 1830, and Mrs. Lewis moved to Miami (then known as Fort Dallas).

By the mid-1830s, Fitzpatrick and a partner, William Cooley, were reported to be growing arrowroot along the river. At least two other families had joined the tiny settlement. A mill had been built to convert this interesting plant to starch.

In December 1835 tragedy struck. In defiance of efforts to remove their tribe to western lands, the Seminole nation took to battle. Maj. Francis Dade and 100 soldiers under his command were surprised and slaughtered near the Withlacoochee River.

Ignorant of the impending conflict, the few citizens living by New River went about their business. They had always been on good terms with the Indians. On January 6, however, a war party descended on the Cooley home and killed Mrs. Cooley, her three children, and the family's tutor. William Cooley happened to be away at the time. This tragic event is today commemorated by a quiet park and one of Fort Lauderdale's dockage complexes, both on the banks of New River and dedicated to the memory of those brave pioneers.

The Second Seminole War was under way. Former president Andrew Jackson suggested to his good friend Joel R. Poinsett, secretary of war, that one of his faithful officers from the War of 1812 be dispatched to southern Florida. Maj. William Lauderdale was thereby sought out, and he promised to raise a considerable company of volunteers to help.

Major Lauderdale and his five companies reached the banks of New River in January 1838. They lost no time in constructing a small wooden fort within sight of the water. By April, Lauderdale's tour of service had expired, and he began the journey home to Tennessee by way of the Mississippi River. He was never to complete his voyage. On May 10, 1838 the officer for whom the yachting capital of southeastern Florida would one day be named died of natural causes at Baton Rouge.

Other officers manned the fort until the end of the war and a second post was eventually established near the beach. The two forts were abandoned in February 1842. They were reoccupied briefly during the Third Seminole War in 1856 but were permanently deserted thereafter.

There followed what has been called the "dark age" of the entire region that is now Fort Lauderdale. Throughout the Civil War and into the early stages of Reconstruction, there was no settlement or activity along New River.

Finally in 1876 the federal government built twenty-five "Houses of Refuge" on the coast of eastern Florida for the succor of shipwrecked mariners. The beach near the future city was chosen as one site.

By 1891, settlement was at last returning to the region. A post office was established that year and was originally known as Vreeland's Island. Progress was further stirred by the establishment of a regular stage route from Jupiter to North Miami. The stage used to cross New River near modern Tarpon Bend. On January 31, 1893, Frank Stranahan took over the operation of a ferry at this point. We shall hear more about Stranahan and his determined wife later in this chapter.

In 1887 Fort Lauderdale had its first, albeit rather small, real-estate boom. Arthur T.

Williams of Fernandina attempted to sell lots near the beach for ten dollars each. He didn't have any takers, and the project died on the vine. How surprised Williams would be to know that you could not buy a square inch of land on the beach for ten dollars today!

True progress finally came to Fort Lauderdale when Henry Flagler extended his railway through the small settlement in 1896. Not only did this new artery of transportation bring visitors to the village, it finally provided local farmers a ready outlet for their produce. Without a doubt, the rise of the great city we know of today as Fort Lauderdale began with the completion of Flagler's remarkable railroad.

In 1899 an epidemic of yellow fever struck Fort Lauderdale, but by 1900, the city had begun to grow in earnest. Residents and visitors alike walked and boated several miles to the nearby beach, and large yachts began visiting the town by way of old New River Inlet.

In 1907, the citizens of Fort Lauderdale were eagerly looking forward to the opening of New River Canal leading to Lake Okeechobee. They believed that the Everglades would drain soon thereafter, opening up the largest tract of super-fertile farmland in America. That dream, as we have already seen, was never realized. The real-estate speculation brought on by the drainage project eventually collapsed completely. Fort Lauderdale finally abandoned the dream of a "superfarm" to the west and slowly turned its collective attention to attracting the tourist trade.

Finally in 1911, Fort Lauderdale was officially incorporated. The new town could boast over 5,000 residents and more seemed to be pouring in daily. This happy era of progress was temporarily halted by a great fire in June 1912. Almost the entire business district burned to the ground. Only the frame structure of the old Osceola Inn was saved.

By 1913 there was great agitation to construct a deepwater harbor. People still had faith in the Everglades drainage project and the town's citizens confidently looked forward to the day when vast quantities of produce would leave the city's waterfront. Though that dream of abundance would be frustrated until very recent times, the seed of an idea was planted that would one day flower into the modern, deep-water harbor we know today as Port Everglades.

In January 1915 an independent company was formed to build Las Olas Boulevard as an easily traveled route to the beach. After many private and public efforts, the road was at last opened in 1917. Now visitors could follow a well-defined route across two bridges to the beach. As the years passed, more and more shops were built along Las Olas. Swampland was filled in and extensive residential development was undertaken north of the road. Today, Las Olas has returned as one of the most fashionable avenues in Fort Lauderdale for shopping and dining.

Fort Lauderdale by Water

Fort Lauderdale's impressive waterside facilities and attractions can be basically divided into two categories, those marinas, boatyards, and restaurants lining the ICW and their counterparts on New River. The facilities on the Waterway will be reviewed first, followed by those on the river.

Oakland Park Boulevard Restaurants (Standard Mile 1060.5)

Cruisers approaching the north face of the Commercial Boulevard Bridge will sight a sign that reads, "Welcome to Fort Lauderdale, the Yachting Capital of the World." Now, you know that the "Venice of America" is just beyond.

Moving south, cruisers will next encounter

the Oakland Park Bridge. North of this span the docks of Yesterdays Restaurant (954-561-4400) will come abeam on the western banks. This fine eatery is noted for its wide menu and reasonable prices. It is very popular with "baby boomers" and is usually crowded on weekends.

Yesterdays' docks hold minimum 7-foot depths and should be sufficient for any but the largest pleasure yachts. Berths are limited to dining patrons.

South of the Oakland Park Bridge, Marine Mar Boat Storage comes abeam to the east. This is a small craft, dry dock storage business. No facilities except gasoline are available for cruising craft.

South of Marine Mar, two restaurants, each with its own docks, line the ICW's easterly banks. Minimum depths on both these piers are 7 feet. First up is Shooters Restaurant (954-566-2855), followed by another branch of Charley's Crab (954-561-4800). Both establishments feature waterfront dining and/or bar service. There are even more bars behind these two dining spots. This writer's cousin, Robbie Byrd, a Fort Lauderdale native, has dubbed this pair "the Bermuda Triangle." When asked the derivation of this appellation, Robbie replied that "you can go in there on a Saturday night and never be heard from again." Of course, the reason you won't be heard from again is that patrons are too busy eating and drinking to ever again pay heed to the outside world.

Hugh Taylor Birch State Park

Between the Oakland Park and Sunrise Boulevard spans, the ICW borders on the wonderfully undeveloped shores of Hugh Taylor Birch State Park to the east. This is one of the last significant undeveloped properties in Fort Lauderdale. Unfortunately, there is no water access to the park, but those who find their way to the front gates via motorized land transportation will discover a multitude of biking and nature trails amidst the magnificent foliage. The park's main entrance makes into the northerly side of Sunrise Boulevard's easterly tip, near Atlantic Boulevard.

Coral Ridge Yacht Club (Standard Mile 1062.5) (26 08.429 North/080 06.502 West)

Elegant Coral Ridge Yacht Club gazes benignly out from the Waterway's western shoreline immediately north of the Sunrise Boulevard Bridge. This club offers guest dockage to members of other yacht clubs with appropriate reciprocal privileges. Guests *must* reserve dockage at least 24 hours in advance of their arrival.

All berths are at fixed wooden piers with 7+-foot soundings. There are actually two sets of berths. One long face dock fronts directly onto the ICW. A second set of slips occupies the banks just south of the yacht club. Coral Ridge does not employ a regular dockmaster.

Full power and water connections are available dockside. Guests are also extended privileges at the club's large swimming pool and tennis courts. The on-site dining room is open for lunch and dinner seven days a week, but the club is closed on Mondays. The huge Galleria Mall is within easy walking distance. Here you will find a host of sophisticated retail operations and several restaurants. Cruisers in need of galley supplies will probably want to take a taxi.

Coral Ridge Yacht Club (954) 566-7886
http://www.coralridgeyachtclub.com

Approach depths—10-12 feet
Dockside depths—7+ feet (minimum)
Accepts transients—members of other
**   yacht clubs with appropriate**
**   reciprocal arrangements**
Fixed wooden piers—yes

Coral Ridge Yacht Club, Fort Lauderdale

**Dockside power connections—30
   and 50 amps
Dockside water connections—yes
Restaurant—on site and others nearby**

Middle River (Standard Mile 1063.5)

Middle River breaks off to the west, south of the Sunrise Boulevard Bridge, near flashing daybeacon #3. This wide, deep stream eventually takes a turn to the north and is blocked by a very low fixed bridge. While depths are typically in the 6- to 12-foot range, boats need enter only for sightseeing. The surrounding shoreline is mostly lined by dense but pleasant residential development. While this might be a good spot to drop the hook for lunch, there are no facilities catering to transients on the stream and overnight anchorage is not permitted.

Fort Lauderdale Municipal Marina at Las Olas Bridge (Standard Mile 1064) (26 07.191 North/080 06.496 West)

The city of Fort Lauderdale maintains three facilities for visiting cruisers on the town's waterways. The Fort Lauderdale Municipal Marina at Las Olas Bridge guards the Waterway's eastern shoreline immediately north and south (mostly on the north side) of the Las Olas bascule bridge. This is the latest offering from the "Venice of America," and the services plus the

many amenities are impressive indeed.

Transient cruisers are gladly accepted at ultramodern, concrete, fixed piers and fiberglass-decked floating docks, featuring fresh water; 30-, 50-, and 100-amp power; cable-television; and telephone connections. Depths alongside are 6 feet or better. A waste pump-out hookup is available at every single slip in the marina. This is one of only a handful of marinas in the entire southeastern U.S. that offers this most welcome service. While, as with most city marinas, there is nothing in the way of on-site repair services, the friendly dockmasters will be glad to recommend independent contractors for light mechanical repairs.

Dockage reservations are not accepted at any of the Fort Lauderdale city marina facilities. They operate on a strictly first-come, first-served arrangement. The dockmasters have informed this writer that they welcome advance calls from cruisers to check whether any slips are available. You should call pretty close to your arrival time, however, or that open slip might be filled by the time of your arrival.

Shoreside, cruisers will discover that the entire complex is overlooked by a municipal parking lot set amidst pleasing landscaping. There is also a large dockmaster's building featuring absolutely first rate, fully climate-controlled showers and Laundromat. The marina also boasts 24-hour security, which is not an inconsequential advantage in this region.

For galley restocking, or to visit the many shops and restaurants on western Las Olas Boulevard (see the New River section below), bus #11 will take you right down Las Olas. A bus stop is located just behind the marina, directly in front of the Monster Deli. What could be more convenient?

It should be noted too that mariners docked at the Las Olas city marina are within walking distance of Fort Lauderdale's famous beaches. It is also a mere two-block walk to Atlantic Boulevard and the public beach. Many restaurants, hotels, and condos line the western flank of Atlantic Boulevard. Cruisers docking at the Las Olas slips have the opportunity to sample this eclectic mix for themselves.

Fort Lauderdale Municipal Marina at Las Olas Bridge (954) 828-7200 http://www.ci.fortlauderdale.fl.us /marinas/lasolas.htm

Approach depths—8-12 feet
Dockside depths—6 feet (minimum)
Accepts transients—yes
Transient dockage rate—average
Fixed concrete piers—yes
Floating fiberglass piers—yes
Dockside power connections—30, 50, and 100 amps
Dockside water connections—yes
Waste pump-out—yes (hookup at every slip)
Showers—yes
Laundromat—yes
Mechanical repairs—yes (independent contractors)
Restaurant—several nearby

Fort Lauderdale Municipal Marina at Las Olas Bridge

Hall of Fame Marina (Standard Mile 1064) (26 07.016 North/080 06.450 West)

Hall of Fame Marina lies along the Waterway's eastern banks, just south of the Las Olas city marina reviewed above. The marina is located adjacent to the famed Fort Lauderdale Olympic pool and "Swimming Hall of Fame." While dockage slips are located both north and south of the swimming complex, the dockmaster's office is found at the eastern end of the northern rank of piers.

Owned and managed by the exemplary Westrec Corporation, Hall of Fame offers visiting cruisers a warm greeting. Transients piloting vessels 40 feet and larger are welcome, and dockage is afforded at ultramodern, fixed, concrete piers featuring all power, water, cable-television, and telephone connections. Spotless showers and a full Laundromat are available shoreside.

Hall of Fame Marina is located within walking distance of the beachside business district, discussed above. There is also a convenience store next door, and it is only a quick walk to the specialty food store at Bahia Mar (see below).

> **Hall of Fame Marina (954) 764-3975**
> **http://www.halloffamemarina.com**
>
> Approach depths—10-12 feet
> Dockside depths—7½-8 feet (minimum)
> Accepts transients—yes
>   (40-foot size minimum)
> Transient dockage rate—above average
> Fixed concrete piers—yes
> Dockside power connections—30
>   and 50 amps
> Dockside water connections—yes
> Showers—yes
> Laundromat—yes
> Restaurant—several nearby

Fort Lauderdale Official Anchorage (Standard Mile 1064) (26 07.160 North/080 06.631 West)

The only officially sanctioned anchorage in the entire Fort Lauderdale region is located in the charted cove indenting the westerly banks south of the Las Olas bascule bridge. This haven is often crowded with pleasure boats of all sizes and descriptions, but there is usually room for one more. Depths range from 6½ to as much as 9 feet. Protection is excellent from northern and westerly blows, but a strong easterly breeze could raise an unwelcome chop.

Anchorage for the first 24 hours in this basin is without charge. Thereafter, visiting cruisers will be assigned a mooring buoy and assessed a fee of $10.00 per day. In return, the city maintains a convenient dinghy dock and trash disposal station on the bay's northern shore. From this pier, cruisers on foot will probably want to cross the Las Olas bridge. Here you will find convenience stores and restaurants. A short taxi or bus (take bus #11) ride west on Las Olas will bring you to the notable downtown business district (see below).

Bahia Mar Yachting Center (Standard Mile 1064.5) (26 06.808 North/080 06.505 West)

What marina has the largest collection of huge Hatteras, Bertram, and Feadship yachts on the entire eastern seaboard? If you didn't guess Bahia Mar, do not pass "Go" or collect your $200.

There is no more impressive marina in the world than Bahia Mar, in our opinion. Boasting 330 slips, this mammoth facility is home to the most awesome fleet of huge pleasure craft we have ever seen. As you might imagine, the marina boasts every imaginable service. Its location will be more than obvious along the Waterway's easterly flank, south of the Las Olas Boulevard Bridge.

As with most marinas in Fort Lauderdale,

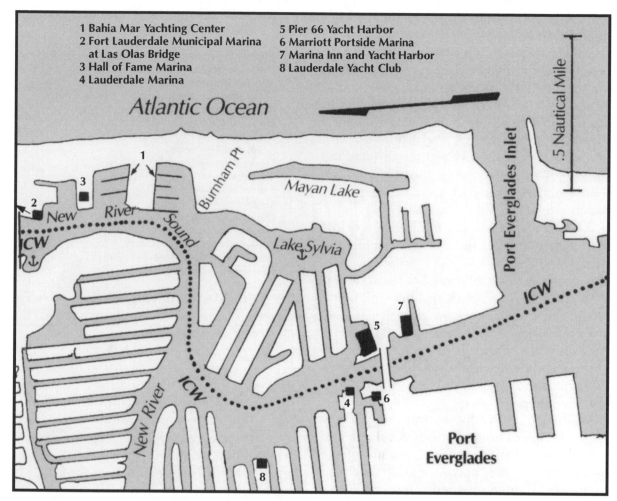

1 Bahia Mar Yachting Center
2 Fort Lauderdale Municipal Marina
   at Las Olas Bridge
3 Hall of Fame Marina
4 Lauderdale Marina
5 Pier 66 Yacht Harbor
6 Marriott Portside Marina
7 Marina Inn and Yacht Harbor
8 Lauderdale Yacht Club

Atlantic Ocean

Mayan Lake

Lake Sylvia

Burnham Pt

New River Sound

ICW

New River

ICW

Port Everglades Inlet

ICW

Port
Everglades

.5 Nautical Mile

it is almost mandatory to make dockage reservations well in advance of your arrival. Bahia Mar has a toll-free number, (800) 327-8154, which cruisers can call to make arrangements.

Bahia Mar boasts two dockage basins, to the north and south, separated by a huge parking lot, high-rise hotel, and shopping complex. The fuel dock (gasoline and diesel fuel), harbormaster's office, and downsized ship's store sit just behind a long, wooden face dock that runs between the two harbors. Transients piloting vessels 40 feet or larger are gladly accommodated in either basin (or the face dock) at both fixed wooden and concrete piers. Depths at all slips are 10 feet or better. Anyone got a keel deeper than that? Of course, power connections are restricted to 30 amps—just kidding! As you might imagine when considering a marina of this ilk, fresh-water, cable-television, telephone, and 30-, 50-, and 100-amp power connections are available. Extensive showers and a full Laundromat are found near the heated swimming pool (open to cruising visitors) between the two dockage harbors. Mechanical repairs can often be arranged through local, independent contractors.

Speaking of swimming pools, Bahia Mar boasts an impressive collection of unusual amenities. Full "room service" is available dockside. The adjacent 300-room Radisson Hotel is luxurious and highly recommended for those who want to spend a little time off the water (assuming your wallet can stand the strain). Visitors also have the use of four on-site tennis courts. The Fort Lauderdale public beach is just across the road.

A small variety-ship's is now found just behind the fuel pier. There is also a small food market and deli in the adjacent retail complex. This business fronts Atlantic Boulevard and is a bit of a step from the docks, but well worth the effort.

Besides the market and deli, Bahia Mar hosts a wide selection of retail businesses grouped around the Radisson Hotel. An extensive collection of yacht brokerages and a full-line dive shop are among these firms.

When it comes time to satisfy a healthy appetite, your choices are many. Taxis can quickly ferry visiting cruisers to any of the restaurants reviewed above, or those described below. For something a little closer to home, consider the main dining room at the Radisson. This is one of those spots where you will want to dig out your last clean shirt—you know, the one stuffed under the forward V-berth.

Of course, Bahia Mar is famous for something else besides its size and list of services. The marina served as the fictional home of author John MacDonald's offbeat detective hero, Travis McGee. Avid readers of the McGee novels will certainly want to visit famed Slip-F18. Here visitors will be pleased to find a mockup of McGee's trusty boat and waterside home, *The Busted Flush*.

Bahia Mar Yachting Center (954) 764-2233
http://www.bahiamar.net/marina.html

Approach depths—10-12 feet
Dockside depths—10+ feet
Accepts transients—yes
  (40 foot size minimum)
Transient dockage rate—above average
Fixed wooden and concrete piers—yes
Dockside power connections—30,
  50, and 100 amps
Dockside water connections—yes
Showers—yes
Laundromat—yes
Gasoline—yes
Diesel fuel—yes
Mechanical repairs—yes
  (independent contractors)
Ship's and variety store—yes (small)
Restaurant—several nearby

The Split (Standard Mile 1065)

West of flashing daybeacon #16, the Waterway channel forks. The ICW curves to the south and flows quickly toward the 17th Street Bridge. New River strikes to the west and leads to numerous marinas, boatyards, and waterside restaurants, not to mention Fort Lauderdale's most important historic site. For now, we will turn our attention to those facilities lining the Waterway. The passage up New River will be covered later in this chapter.

Lauderdale Yacht Club (Standard Mile 1066) (26 06.487 North/080 07.396 West)

West of unlighted daybeacon #26, a charted channel leads to the docks of Lauderdale Yacht Club. The large clubhouse and adjacent swimming pool are readily visible from the Waterway. Guest dockage privileges are extended to members of other yacht clubs with appropriate reciprocal privileges. Dockage is at smaller, fixed, wooden piers with 6- to 7-foot soundings at low tide. The entrance channel carries at least 7 feet of depth at low water, but a mistake at the sparsely marked entrance (from the ICW) could land cruisers in considerably less depth. Full power and water connections are offered. Showers are available in the clubhouse. The on-site swimming pool (open from June through Labor Day only) and tennis courts are also open to visitors.

The Lauderdale Yacht Club employs a dockmaster seven days a week from 8:30 A.M. to 5:30 P.M. Due to limited slip space for visitors, reservations must be made in advance.

The club dining room is open Tuesday through Sunday for both lunch and dinner. A varied collection of other restaurants is fairly close by, but most visitors will want to take a taxi to these dining spots.

> **Lauderdale Yacht Club (954) 524-5500**
> **http://www.lyc.org**
>
> **Approach depths—7 feet (minimum)**
> **Dockside depths—6-7 feet (minimum)**
> **Accepts transients—members of other**
> **yacht clubs with appropriate**
> **reciprocal arrangements**
> **Fixed wooden piers—yes**
> **Dockside power connections—30**
> **and 50 amps**
> **Dockside water connections—yes**
> **Showers—yes**
> **Restaurant—on site**

Pier 66 Yacht Harbor (Standard Mile 1066.5) (26 06.129 North/080 07.076 West)

The extensive docks of Pier 66 Yacht Harbor grace the Waterway's eastern shore just north of the SE 17th Street Bridge. This is one of the best-known marinas in southern Florida. Many cruisers make Pier 66 a yearly stop to ride out the winter months. Those lucky enough to berth

Lauderdale Yacht Club, Fort Lauderdale

at this impressive facility will find truly world class amenities and a very friendly welcome.

In the 1990s the entire Pier 66 complex came under the Hyatt umbrella. The new management did much to restore the marina, adjacent hotel, and its six restaurants to their former status as a world-class resort. With these improvements, we once again heartily recommend a stop at Pier 66, particularly for larger power craft. Of course, dockage here could not be described as "inexpensive."

This writer cannot pass without a word of nostalgia about Pier 66. It was here that, as a boy, I spent many a happy winter with my family living aboard my father's classic, Harkers Island 48-foot wooden-hulled sportsfisherman. Of course, both Fort Lauderdale and Pier 66 were a bit simpler and less crowded during those times. When I think back on those happy days, it's not too difficult to understand why I developed a lifelong love for the water and those who go cruising upon its breadth.

Pier 66 dockage consists of 142 ultramodern, fixed, concrete slips with every imaginable power, water, cable-television, and telephone connection. Low-water depths alongside are 10 feet or better. Transients are gladly accepted when there are open slips. Call well in advance of your arrival for dockage reservations.

Pier 66 features a ship's and variety store guarding the dockage basin's northwesterly point, adjacent to the fuel dock. The fuel pier itself faces directly onto the eastern flank of the ICW and offers both gasoline and diesel fuel. Spotless showers and a full Laundromat are found off the main harbor's southerly banks. Dry-cleaning valet service is also available. Mechanical repairs can often be arranged through local, independent technicians.

Associated with the marina is the Pier 66 Hyatt Hotel, six restaurants, and the world-famous revolving cocktail lounge. This large hostelry boats 388 rooms and is known throughout Fort Lauderdale for its beautiful grounds, fine dining, and spectacular views of the city. Hotel room service is available dockside and a marina concierge will gladly handle any personal needs, including rental cars, laundry, and local entertainment. There is even a health and beauty spa in the complex. Marina guests are also entitled to the use of the hotel's swimming pool (and poolside bar), putting green, tennis courts, and other outdoor activities.

Hungry cruisers or hotel patrons are not forgotten at Pier 66 Yacht Harbor. There are six restaurants to choose from. Of course, the main dining room in the Hyatt Hotel is nothing if not elegant. Gee whiz, you might even want to don a coat and tie for this one.

Grill 66 Bar (954-728-3500) sits perched on Pier 66 harbor's southwesterly corner. The food here is superb, if a bit pricey.

For something a bit more down to earth, try the Pelican Bar for lunch or a cooling afternoon drink. This open-air grill and bar is perched atop the ship's store and commands a wonderful view of the busy ICW section north of the 17th Street Bridge. There are few more relaxing ways to end a cruising day than by sipping a cool drink in the Pelican while watching the Waterway traffic.

A long walk west across the 17th Street Bridge will bring cruisers to a Publix Supermarket shopping center on the north side of the road. Those not up to this hike will want to take a taxi or a rental car. In addition to the supermarket, be sure to check out fabulous Bluewater Books and Charts (see below), in this same shopping center.

One of Pier 66's most popular attractions is its revolving lounge and bar, which perches atop the hotel. Some of our most memorable evenings in Fort Lauderdale have been spent sitting at a comfortable table, sipping drinks some twelve stories above the parking lot while watching the light fade from the surrounding land and waters. As the city lights begin to wink, you may come to the conclusion that this is what the cruising life is really all about. Compared to a beautifully isolated anchorage on St. Johns River? Well, you will have to decide for yourself, but both are unforgettable experiences.

**Pier 66 Yacht Harbor (954) 525-6666
    (800) 327-3796**

**Approach depths—10-12 feet
Dockside depths—10+ feet
Accepts transients—yes
Transient dockage rate—above average
Fixed concrete piers—yes
Dockside power connections—30,
    50, and 100 amps
Dockside water connections—yes
Showers—yes
Laundromat—yes
Gasoline—yes
Diesel fuel—yes
Mechanical repairs—yes
    (independent contractors)
Ship's and variety store—yes (extensive)
Restaurant—six on site**

Pier 66 Yacht Harbor, Fort Lauderdale

Other 17th Street Facilities (Standard Mile 1066.5) (Various Lats/Lons—see below)

Lauderdale Marina (26 06.202 North/080 07.185 West, 954-523-8507) flanks the ICW's westerly banks, opposite Pier 66. This facility occupies the point of land sandwiched between the two charted canals due west of flashing daybeacon #27.

Lauderdale Marina has been servicing cruising craft since 1948. This Waterway stop is well known for its reasonable fuel prices. The fixed, concrete fuel pier fronts directly onto the ICW, and depths alongside run 15 feet or better! Many Waterway veterans make it a point to top their tanks off here, year after year.

The marina also features not one but two stores. The unit overlooking the fuel dock is a combination variety, fishing tackle, and dive shop. Convenience-store-type food items are available. Behind the piers, and next to Fifteenth Street Fisheries restaurant, cruisers will find a full-line ship's store and gift shop. Here mariners can browse through a noteworthy collection of marine hardware and nautical clothing.

Captains can also tie temporarily to the piers of Lauderdale Marina while patronizing the adjacent Fifteenth Street Fisheries restaurant

(954-763-2777). This fabulous dining spot is one of the most respected seafood restaurants in Fort Lauderdale, a reputation it well deserves. Many tables look out on the Waterway through huge plate-glass windows. The interior features wooden walls and ceilings set off with a decidedly nautical decor. The broiled seafood is wonderful (give the salmon a try), but be warned, an evening meal with cocktails could very well eat up a $50.00 bill.

Though it's a good step away from Lauderdale Marina's docks, cruisers can hike west on 17th Street to the Publix Supermarket shopping center, where they will find one of the finest nautical bookstores in all of America. Bluewater Books and Charts (1481 SE 17th Street, 954-763-6533 or 800-942-2583) carries a mind-boggling array of nautical books, charts, videos, computer programs, and other printed and electronic nautical material. The staff is ultrafriendly and thoroughly knowledgeable.

Just south of Lauderdale Marina, a small canal strikes off to the west and leads to several additional low-key facilities. None of these firms offers anything in the way of transient dockage.

Cable Marine Inc. (954-462-2822) will come abeam on the port banks, near 26 06.139 North/080 07.532 West. This modern boatyard offers extensive mechanical (gas and diesel), topside, and below-the-waterline repairs. Cable Marine exudes good management. A visiting skipper will only need to take a single look at the yard facilities to know he or she has come to the right place for service work. The yard's travelift is rated at 40 tons. Cable Marine also owns a second repair yard on upper New River, which will be reviewed later in this chapter.

A little farther on, Intracoastal Marine Service, Inc. flanks the southern banks. This facility dry-docks vast numbers of small craft in an adjacent metal storage building. Again, no facilities are available for transients.

Southport Raw Bar Restaurant (954-525-2526) lines the canal's westerly tip. This wateringhole features its own docks with enough room for one or two 30 footers. Depths alongside run around 6 feet at low water. Dining patrons are welcome to tie up while visiting Southport Raw Bar. We found the servings here rather small for what we paid, but the raw bar is popular and has been around for many years. It's also a much quicker walk from these piers to Bluewater Books and Charts (see above) and the Publix Supermarket. Try buying a beer or another cool drink, and then walk over to check out the bookstore.

One last facility occupies the Waterway's western banks, immediately north of the 17th Street Bridge. Marriott Portside Marina has one long, fixed face pier, fronting directly onto the ICW, and additional slips on the canal just north of the hotel (near 26 06.103 North/080 07.283 West). Portside is privately managed, and only nominally associated with the huge, adjacent Marina Marriott hotel.

Transients and seasonal dockers are welcomed at modern, fixed, concrete piers with every power, water, and cable-television connection. Showers and laundry service are available shoreside.

The high-rise Marriott Hotel looks out confidently over the marina docks. Patrons of the marina are welcome to use the hotel's health club, sauna, tennis courts, and swimming pool. There are three restaurants in the complex to choose from, ranging from an informal grill to a formally sumptuous dining extravaganza. The Publix Supermarket shopping center (home to Bluewater Books and Charts) is a long, but do-able walk from the Portside docks north on 17th Street.

As you might expect, advance reservations are almost a necessity at this most well-appointed marina. Call well ahead of time and get ready for a decidedly affluent cruising experience.

Marriott Portside Marina (954) 527-6781

Approach depths—13-14 feet
Dockside depths—11-13 feet
Accepts transients—yes
Transient dockage rate—above average
Fixed concrete piers—yes
Dockside power connections—30,
   50, and 100 amps
Dockside water connections—yes
Showers—yes
Laundry service—yes
Restaurant—three on site

An additional marina borders the Waterway channel's eastern banks south of the 17th Street Bridge. Marina Inn and Yacht Harbor (26 05.993 North/080 07.037 West) features a concrete breakwater-enclosed harbor with some additional berths located on a canal running to the east. There is also some truly deep-water dockage at a face pier fronting the ICW.

The outer dock has unusually deep soundings, ranging up to 25 feet, but ships docked here are subject to considerable chop. The inner slips (fixed, wooden docks) are more sheltered and have at least 10 feet of water, but maneuvering room is at a premium in the enclosed harbor.

Marina Inn gladly accepts transients, though you should call ahead for dockage reservations. Fresh water and 30- and 50-amp power connections are at hand. There is a Laundromat on the premises.

The adjacent Best Western Marina Inn is convenient for those wanting to spend a night or two ashore. This complex includes two restaurants and two lounges. Visiting cruisers may also make use of the inn's heated swimming pool and Jacuzzi. An adjacent strip shopping center has fifteen shops, including a drugstore and meat market. For a full supermarket, you will still need to hike to the Publix shopping center, described above.

Marina Inn and Yacht Harbor (954) 525-3484

Approach depths—12-20 feet
Dockside depths—20-25 feet
    (outer face dock)
    10+ feet (harbor docks)
Accepts transients—yes
Transient dockage rate—above average
Fixed wooden piers—yes
Dockside power connections—30
    and 50 amps
Dockside water connections—yes
Laundromat—yes
Restaurant—two on site

Port Everglades

South of the 17th Street Bridge, the Waterway flows quickly into the Port Everglades turning basin. Since it boasts one of the deepest harbors on the eastern seaboard, an impressive array of freighters, tankers, and luxurious cruise ships makes regular stops at this commercial harbor. Passing mariners are welcome to inspect the docked vessels. Simply cruise slowly to the port's various wharves and avoid any tugs or commercial traffic. It can be a little humbling to take your 30 footer next to a huge ocean liner, but it's a fascinating experience, nevertheless.

Port Everglades Inlet (Standard Mile 1067)

Port Everglades Inlet is one of the most stable and clearly marked channels of any seaward cut in Florida. This passage is heavily used by commercial freighters, cruise liners, and innumerable sportsfishermen. In fair weather, strangers can cruise the inlet with as much confidence as one can ever have when crossing that often unstable barrier between inland waters and the wide blue sea.

The inlet is even attractive. While huge condo complexes overlook the northern banks, the southern shore is delightfully in its natural state. Twin stone jetties flank the intersection with the open sea. In the last decade, the shifting sand has buried some of the old jetty stones, though a few can still be seen along the way.

For those who enjoy angling, here's a special hint from this writer's early days in Fort Lauderdale. Try buying some live shrimp and hooking them just behind the head, using clear monofilament line. Go to the far sea buoy of the Port Everglades Inlet and carefully drop your bait over the side. Pull out the line by hand (as opposed to casting it from your boat) and allow your craft to drift with the current. Use a wire leader but no weight. Replace the shrimp whenever you suspect it has died. My father and I used to catch mackerel, blues, and jack by using this method, while all the traditional fishermen came back with empty pails.

ICW NAVIGATION FROM COMMERCIAL BOULEVARD TO PORT EVERGLADES

Successful navigation of the Waterway through Fort Lauderdale is an elementary lesson in coastal piloting, complicated by a few restricted bridges and some swift tidal currents. South of the Las Olas bascule bridge, virtually all the city's waters are under slow-speed, no-wake restrictions. Probably the best plan of attack in cruising the city's waterways is to proceed along exclusively at idle speed.

As part of Broward County's (Fort Lauderdale) Noise Abatement Regulation, all area bridges have been outfitted with VHF radios monitoring channels 13 and 16. Cruisers are encouraged to contact the various span operators by radio rather than the traditional method of blowing the horn.

On the ICW The Commercial Boulevard Bridge introduces captains to Fort Lauderdale's restricted-opening spans. This bridge opens every fifteen minutes from 8:00 A.M. to 6:00 P.M. (beginning at the top of the hour), daily (November 1 to May 15). With the span's closed vertical clearance of 15 feet, most cruising craft will be obliged to wait.

It's a straightforward run down the ICW from Commercial Boulevard to the Oakland Park Bridge. Just north of this latter span, the fixed wooden face dock of Yesterdays Restaurant will be passed along the western shoreline.

The Oakland Park Bridge (closed vertical clearance, 22 feet) also has regulated opening hours. On weekdays from November 15 to May 15, the span opens at the top of the hour and every twenty minutes thereafter from 7:00 A.M. to 10:00 P.M. On Saturday and Sunday from November 15 to May 15 it opens every fifteen minutes (beginning at the top of the hour) from 10:00 A.M. to 10:00 P.M.

South of the Oakland Park Beach Boulevard bridge, no-wake restrictions are in effect as you cruise past Marine Mar Boat Storage and the several restaurants bordering the eastern banks. Be sure to continue along at idle speed until spotting the "Resume Normal Safe Operation" sign.

No-wake restrictions resume north of the Sunrise Boulevard Bridge and continue for some distance south of the span. As you enter this slow-speed zone, Coral Ridge Yacht Club will come up to the west.

The delightfully natural shores of Hugh Taylor Birch State Park line the Waterway's eastern banks above and below the Sunrise Boulevard Bridge. Be sure to pause in your travels for a moment to appreciate this last bit of natural Florida within the Fort Lauderdale city limits.

The Sunrise Boulevard Bridge has a closed vertical clearance of 25 feet and a restricted opening schedule between November 15 and May 15. During this time of the year, the span opens only on the hour and every fifteen minutes thereafter between 10:00 A.M. and 6:00 P.M., seven days a week.

Avoid the charted cove indenting the eastern banks south of Sunrise Boulevard. Depths are more than questionable in this sidewater. Favor the western side of the channel when passing.

The no-wake zone ends a short hop south of the Sunrise span, but begins anew north of the Las Olas span. Power captains should enjoy this run. It is the last unrestricted stretch of the Waterway north of Port Everglades.

Middle River Flashing daybeacon #3 marks the juncture of the ICW and Middle River. If you enter this sidewater, continue cruising on the Waterway until you are some 50 yards south of #3. You can then turn sharply to the west and enter the mid-width of the river's mouth.

On the Waterway South of flashing daybeacon #3, a patch of shoal water abuts the eastern side of the channel. On many occasions, we have sounded depths of less than 3 feet in this cove. Come abeam of and pass flashing daybeacon #5 to its westerly side and immediately set a new course to pass unlighted daybeacon #7 to its westerly side. Come abeam of flashing daybeacon #8 to its easterly quarter. Favor the western side of the channel on this entire run.

South of #8, switch to inset 1 of chart 11467 for continued navigation in the Fort Lauderdale region. This blowup details all the channels and aids to navigation on the ICW and approaches to New River. The inset covers the Waterway and its auxiliary waters south through the Port Everglades turning basin. It also includes a detailed account of Port Everglades Inlet's interior reaches.

By the time you reach flashing daybeacon #8, the Las Olas bascule bridge will be spotted dead ahead. Watch for the no-wake sign. These regulations now remain in effect all the way to Port Everglades. To make life simple, you can just think of the entire Fort Lauderdale section of the ICW, as well as the New River channel, as one big, no-wake zone.

The Las Olas span has a closed vertical clearance of 31 feet, and surprisingly it opens on demand. The waters north and south of this bridge are often more than a little congested. The Fort Lauderdale Harbor Police are especially vigilant in ticketing

any hot dogs who go speeding through.

Cruisers passing through the Las Olas bridge will spot the new Fort Lauderdale Municipal Marina at Las Olas Bridge city docks to the east and the official anchorage basin to the west. A bit farther along, Hall of Fame Marina and Bahia Mar Yachting Center will come up to the east like small cities of their own.

Flashing daybeacon #13 and unlighted daybeacon #14 signal a sharp westward turn in the ICW. Be sure to pass between #13 and #14 and then set course to come abeam of flashing daybeacon #16 to its southerly side.

The Big Split Unlighted junction daybeacon #A marks the "big split" in Fort Lauderdale's waterways. The ICW curls around to the south and hurries on to Pier 66, the 17th Street Bridge, and eventually Port Everglades and its inlet. A straight shot west leads to downtown Fort Lauderdale and the impressive collection of restaurants, marinas, and boatyards lining New River. This account will now go on to detail the passage south to Port Everglades. The New River alternative will be covered in the next section of this chapter.

To continue south on the ICW, pass #A to its southerly side and continue on course, coming abeam of flashing daybeacon #17 to is fairly immediate northerly side. Don't let the New River aids to navigation, west of #A, be a cause for confusion, These markers come into play only when cruising upstream on New River (see below).

Flashing daybeacon #17 marks the northerly beginning of a long, slow turn to the south for the ICW channel. Observe all markers carefully along this stretch. Shallow water lies along both sides of the Waterway passage.

North of flashing daybeacon #20, an alternate channel allows ready access to New River for northbound craft. This passage will be covered in the New River section below.

On to the 17th Street Bridge   South of unlighted daybeacon #24A, the channel to Lauderdale Yacht Club cuts back to the west-northwest. Stay on the ICW until you are just north of unlighted daybeacon #26. Then turn to the west-northwest, passing #26 to your port side, and cruise between the various unadorned pilings (outlining the channel) to the club's docks.

South of flashing daybeacon #27, captains will enter one of the most populated stretches of the eastern Florida ICW. At any time, but particularly on weekends, a small army of boats may be cruising both north and south of the SE 17th Street/Brooks Memorial Bridge. Add to this traffic the boats entering and leaving Pier 66 Yacht Harbor to the east and Lauderdale Marina and Marriott Portside Marina to the west, and it doesn't require too much imagination to discern that this is a maximum-alert area for all cruising skippers.

Just to make life a bit more interesting, strong tidal currents rip under the 17th Street span. Trawlers and sailcraft should be particularly alert for these swiftly moving waters. At times, this entire situation can seem like one giant, nautical free-for-all. Our best advice is to remain alert to your entire on-the-water situation, and take action at the first hint of a developing problem.

On the plus side, deep water stretches almost from shore to shore immediately north and south of the 17th Street Bridge. This wide channel at least gives you a little room to play with.

One of the happiest developments on the Fort Lauderdale section of the Florida ICW during the last several years has been the arrival of a new 55-foot version (closed vertical clearance) of the 17th Street bascule bridge. With this sort of clearance, all but large sailcraft will be able to saunter on under this span with nary a problem. Sailors who do need the 17th bridge to open will have to contend with, you guessed it, a restricted opening schedule. Year round, this span opens only on the hour and half-hour, seven days a week, from 7:00 A.M. to 7:00 P.M.

Once the 17th Street span is in your wake, the enclosed dockage basin of Marina Inn and Yacht Harbor will come abeam to the east. Farther to the south, the waters broaden out into the Port Everglades turning basin.

Port Everglades Turning Basin   The Waterway channel tracking south through the Port Everglades turning basin is well marked, consistently deep, and thoroughly charted. There are really only two spots with which to be at all concerned. As shown on inset 1 of chart 11467, some very shallow water flanks the ICW north and east of flashing daybeacon #29. Favor the westerly side of the channel between the 17th Street Bridge and #29.

Chart 11467 (inset 1) also correctly identifies a large shoal abutting the eastern portion of the Waterway channel south of the ICW's intersection with the inlet. To avoid these shallows, simply favor the westerly banks as you pass charted "Pier 7."

Port Everglades Inlet   Port Everglades Inlet boasts a wide, deep, and clearly defined channel. Most aids to navigation are clearly charted. Stay clear of the correctly charted shallows along the extreme northerly banks, and observe any uncharted markers you might discover along this stretch. When entering from the ICW, be sure to avoid the charted shoal striking out from the southern point of the inlet channel's westerly flank.

Many cruisers regularly use Port Everglades Inlet to begin an offshore run to the north or south, bypassing the heavily regulated section of the Waterway between Palm Beach and Miami. Southbound craft can abandon the inlet channel several hundred yards east of flashing daybeacon #5.

Cruisers headed for points north have to contend with a long, partially submerged jetty and spoil bank flanking the northern side of the inlet's passage out into the open sea. For best depths, continue following the inlet channel for a least 400 yards east of flashing buoys #2 and #3. You can then cut to the north without having to worry about any underwater obstructions.

New River (Standard Mile 1065)

According to tradition, New River was named by two Indians who fell into a deep sleep one night while on a fishing expedition to the coast. Both dreamed of a majestic river newly sprung from the earth, flowing beside rich green shores and teeming with succulent fish. When the two awoke, they found, much to their astonishment, that their dream had come true. A fresh stream had seemingly leapt from the earth near their campsite. They named the water body New River and departed to tell their fellows farther inland about this miraculous occurrence. How surprised those two Native Americans would be today to see what has become of their "new" river.

New River cuts a meandering path through the heart of downtown Fort Lauderdale. Eventually the stream curls around to the south and leaves the trappings of civilization behind. While this uppermost section of the river is not recommended for cruising craft, the stream eventually joins the western reaches of Dania Cut-Off Canal, which, in turn, leads back to the ICW.

Between the ICW intersection and the wilderness portion of the river, there are many miles of incredibly heavy urban, residential, and commercial development lining both shores. Some houses along the way are quite attractive with carefully groomed yards, freshly painted walls, and private docks. Others are not in such good shape. The downtown business district is readily visible from the water and makes for interesting viewing indeed. Fort Lauderdale is, in many ways, a new city and nowhere is this newness more apparent than in its tall, immaculately clean office buildings.

On the other hand, there are also many old buildings along New River. Perhaps the single

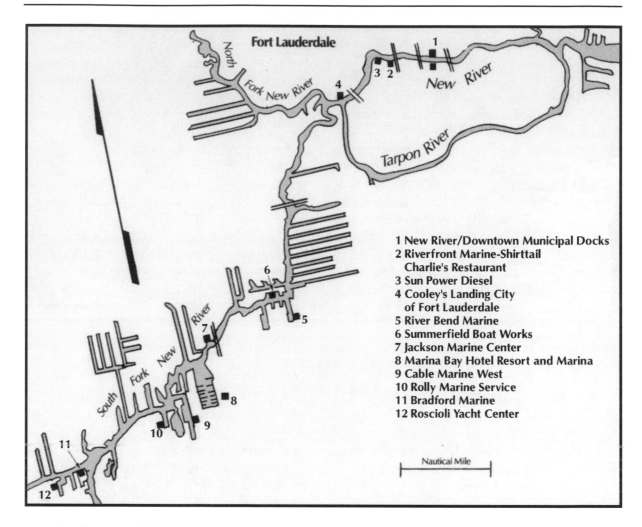

1 New River/Downtown Municipal Docks
2 Riverfront Marine-Shirttail
   Charlie's Restaurant
3 Sun Power Diesel
4 Cooley's Landing City
   of Fort Lauderdale
5 River Bend Marine
6 Summerfield Boat Works
7 Jackson Marine Center
8 Marina Bay Hotel Resort and Marina
9 Cable Marine West
10 Rolly Marine Service
11 Bradford Marine
12 Roscioli Yacht Center

Nautical Mile

most handsome public structure on the entire passage is the recently expanded Riverside Hotel. This venerable hostelry looks out over its immaculate grounds to the river, as it has for many a year. Like a fine wine, the Riverside seems only to have improved with age.

One of the outstanding features along New River's course is Fort Lauderdale's "Riverwalk Park." This crowning achievement of downtown redevelopment lines both shores of New River between historic Stranahan House and the city docks at Cooley's Landing. It's a genuine delight to pace up and down the long brick walkways shaded by tall trees and subtropical foliage. The many museums and exhibition centers adjacent to the Riverwalk add immeasurably to this attraction's charms.

While captains seeking service work have always been able to find what they needed on New River, visiting cruisers can now expect a much improved transient dockage situation as well. In addition to the long-used city docks on New River, Fort Lauderdale has a third dockage complex along the river's northwesterly banks, southwest of the William H. Marshall Bridge. A few private firms offer some transient dockage as well, but most of these nonmunicipal slips are reserved for seasonal dockage.

There is really no practical anchorage on New River. The stream's track is too narrow to drop the hook without obstructing traffic. Besides, as you will remember, anchorage is only permitted in the official basin near the Las Olas bridge.

A cruise up New River is a must for any first-time visitor to Fort Lauderdale. It's not going too far to say that those who have not seen the New River passage have not seen the city.

Tarpon River

Shallow Tarpon River makes into New River's southerly shoreline at unlighted daybeacon #12. Local outboard craft regularly ply this errant stream on their way to and from the ICW, but consistent depths of 3 to 4 feet render it inaccessible to most cruising craft.

Eastern New River

The easternmost section of New River between the ICW and Third Avenue Bridge is without facilities, but it is a most attractive section of the stream. Beautiful homes overlook the waterway, and many a passing cruiser has looked down from his flybridge with envy at the cool swimming pools in the passing backyards.

About midway between the river's mouth and its first bridge, Cooley Park calmly overlooks the northern shore. This quiet, secluded corner commemorates the savage deaths of the Cooley family at the beginning of the Second Seminole Indian War. Today the park is used from time to time for open-air concerts and craft shows.

Riverside Hotel

Cruisers approaching the Third Avenue Bridge will spy the single fixed, wooden face dock of elegant Riverside Hotel (954-467-0671) along the northern banks. The hotel's piers are rented by the season, but the hotel itself with its wonderful restaurants is well within walking distance of the municipal slips farther upstream on New River.

Riverside Hotel is located on the far side of an immaculately manicured swath of the greenest grass you will ever see. This establishment is one of the oldest surviving hostelries in the city, and it has recently undergone a serious expansion. Both its restaurants are outstanding!

Fort Lauderdale New River/Downtown Municipal Docks (26 07.036 North/080 08.505 West)

The city of Fort Lauderdale maintains extensive dockage on both banks of the river, between the Third Avenue and Andrews Avenue bridges. Many of these fortunate slips front directly onto Riverwalk Park. The shops and restaurants on Las Olas Boulevard (see below) are only a short walk away. These are some of the most prized slips in Fort Lauderdale, and the demand for this dockage space is high.

The New River/Downtown berths consist of face docks composed of pilings set against a concrete seawall. Full power, fresh-water, cable-television, and telephone hookups are provided, as is waste pump-out services. The many shops and restaurants on Las Olas Boulevard are only a few blocks away.

As with all Fort Lauderdale municipal dockage, slip space on the New River/Downtown docks is at a premium. Call the city dockmaster's office at (954) 828-5423 or (800) 385-3625 for slip availability.

New River/Downtown Municipal Docks
(954) 828-5423
http://www.ci.fortlauderdale.fl.us/marinas/
newriver.htm

Approach depths—8 feet (minimum)
Dockside depths—7 feet (minimum)
Accepts transients—yes
Transient dockage rate—below average
Fixed concrete piers—yes
Dockside power connections—30 and 50
amps
Dockside water connections—yes
Waste pump-out—yes
Restaurant—several nearby

Riverwalk Park and New River, Fort Lauderdale

Riverwalk Park

It's nice to know that tax money can be well spent sometimes. Fort Lauderdale's Riverwalk Park cuts a colorful path along both banks of New River between historic Stranahan House and the Cooley's Landing dockage complex. There is a small detour around the William H. Marshall Bridge, but otherwise the park is complete. Walking the shade-lined, bricked paths is a sure cure for those who have seen one too many waves.

A host of attractions lines Riverwalk Park along its northern flank. Among these are the Broward Center for the Performing Arts, Museum of Discovery and Science, historic Bryan Homes, Fort Lauderdale Historical Society Headquarters and Museum, Fort Lauderdale Public Library, Museum of Art, and Esplanade Park. By all accounts, don't miss the IMAX Theater in the Discovery Center. Here "breathtaking" films are presented on a five-story screen.

A wide collection of festivals is held at the Riverwalk and nearby Las Olas Boulevard throughout the year. During one of our previous visits, a fascinating exhibit of old cars was in progress. Check with the city dockmaster to see which events are scheduled during your time in Fort Lauderdale.

The Riverwalk is a wonderful achievement and adds immeasurably to the appeal of docking in downtown Fort Lauderdale. The park borders both on the Cooley's Landing municipal dockage complex (see below) as well as the New River/Downtown slips. No matter which location you choose (or are lucky enough to find space), tying up amidst the Riverwalk is one of the best cruising experiences in Florida.

Las Olas Boulevard Shopping and Dining District

As a boy spending his early winter months in Fort Lauderdale, this writer remembers downtown Las Olas Boulevard as "the" center of the city's business district. As with virtually all communities in the U.S., this district fell on hard times through the 1970s and 1980s. Now, we are happy to report that, once again, both sides of Las Olas are teeming with exclusive shops and restaurants.

The Las Olas business district is within an easy step of the New River/Downtown docks. Similarly, cruisers berthing at Cooley's Landing (see below) need only wend their way by foot to the eastern end of the Riverwalk. Here, hard

Las Olas Boulevard, Fort Lauderdale

by historic Stranahan House and the underground U.S. 1 tunnel, Las Olas begins its easterly path.

The remainder of Las Olas, running east, is lined with a fascinating collection of shops and restaurants for five or six blocks. Connoisseurs of French cuisine will definitely want to check out Cafe La Bonne Crepe (815 E Las Olas, 954-761-1515). The quiches are wonderful, and the crepes will not soon be forgotten. Try to get one of the outside tables so you can enjoy the fine food while watching the Las Olas traffic drift on by.

The Cafe Europa (726 E Las Olas, 954-763-6600) features an extensive dessert bar, gourmet pizza, and wonderful sandwiches. Don't miss this one. Again, the outside tables are the best spot!

The expanded version of the venerable Riverside Hotel (620 E Las Olas, 954-467-0671) features two restaurants. Both Cafe Indigo and the Golden Lyon Restaurant are superb, and both feature optional open-air dining.

Are you beginning to get the idea? The downtown Las Olas business district is one of those places where you could spend hours and hours, and still not exhaust all the neat shops and interesting places to dine. We suggest that you include a visit to Las Olas Boulevard in your travel plans no matter where you find dockage space in the "Venice of America."

Historic Stranahan House

Mariners cruising between the Third Avenue and Andrews Avenue bridges will

The Cafe Europa, Las Olas Boulevard

undoubtedly take note of a particularly handsome home on the northern shore between the two spans. This house might seem to be a bit out of place amidst the modern development of Las Olas Boulevard. As a matter of fact, it most definitely belongs to a far-removed era of Fort Lauderdale history.

In a city that has systematically destroyed almost every vestige of its past, it is indeed fortunate that the Stranahan home has survived. There is perhaps no more historic site in all of southeastern Florida.

In 1892 a camp and ferry were established on the banks of New River, and a young Ohioan, Frank Stranahan, was hired to take charge. The Seminole Indians camped nearby were natural trading partners for the energetic Stranahan, exchanging such items as otter pelts, egret plumes, and alligator hides for foodstuffs and such trinkets as they wanted.

Affluent sportsmen of the day began visiting the young settlement on New River. Among the distinguished guests were Adm. George Dewey and Henry Morrison Flagler. Flagler's East Coast Railway reached Fort Lauderdale

in 1896 and ushered in an unprecedented era of development and progress.

By 1899 the village had fostered a small crop of boys and girls, and the Dade County School Board assigned eighteen-year-old Ivy Julia Cromartie to the post of schoolteacher.

At the time of Ivy's arrival, Frank Stranahan was serving as postmaster, in addition to his trading duties. Tradition tells us that the two met in the small post office. It must have been love at first sight. They were married on August 16, 1900, in Lemon City (now North Miami).

The happy couple soon returned to Fort Lauderdale and took up residence in a small home near the Stranahan store. Mrs. Stranahan soon became interested in the welfare of the Seminole children living about the village and spent countless unpaid hours teaching the young Indians to read and write. Throughout her long life, Ivy Stranahan was noted for her selfless service to Native Americans.

By 1901, Frank began construction of a new store that would ultimately become the couple's home. The building was constructed of Dade County pine, known for its resistance to termites and dampness. The Stranahans decided to build broad, sweeping verandas on three sides of the house. These impressive additions both gave the house an elegant appearance and served as a sleeping place for the Seminoles who came to trade.

The second story could originally be reached only by an exterior staircase. Town meetings, dances, and other community events were often held there.

Frank Stranahan's business ventures grew apace with his standing in the community. In 1910, he was instrumental in the organization of the Fort Lauderdale State Bank. He also founded the Stranahan Building Company. By 1920 the Stranahan house had become one of the most notable landmarks in Fort Lauderdale. It was used as a setting for a silent movie, and appeared on several old postcards.

The collapse of the second Florida land boom in the late 1920s dealt a fatal blow to Frank Stranahan's favorite project, the Fort Lauderdale Bank. In failing health and racked with guilt, he drowned himself in New River.

The courage associated with the Stranahan house was not at an end, however. Mrs. Stranahan struggled to hold on to the historic homeplace. As the Great Depression deepened, she rented the ground floor as a tea room and inn. In 1939 the E. J. Blackwells leased the home on a long-term basis and opened the Pioneer House Restaurant. I can just remember my parents taking me to the Pioneer House as a young boy in the 1950s— I recall looking out over the river's restless waters and thinking that I'd like to be out there on a boat.

Many years later this writer's aunt was working with a law firm in Fort Lauderdale. As a legal secretary, she was called to the Stranahan house to witness "Mrs. Ivy's" last will and testament. According to my aunt, Mrs. Stranahan was still sharp and very much in control. A few years later, in August 1971, Ivy Stranahan died. Her death was mourned by the whole city.

Following Mrs. Stranahan's death a dedicated group of volunteers acquired the house and eventually returned the exterior to its original appearance. The interior has also been lovingly restored. Visitors are enthusiastically received on Wednesdays and Fridays from 10:00 A.M. to 4:00 P.M. and on Sundays from 1:00 to 4:00 P.M. There is no dockage for cruising visitors, but Stranahan House is within walking distance of either municipal dockage complex on New River.

Other Facilities and Attractions on New River

Moving west of Andrews Avenue bascule bridge on New River, the Hatteras-Allied Marine docks will come abeam on the southern shore. Passing cruisers will most likely note several new Hatteras yachts waiting at the docks for prospective owners.

Immediately after passing under the railway bridge that spans New River just west of the Andrews span, cruisers will note Riverfront Marina (954-527-1829) on the southern shore. This facility dry-docks small craft but no overnight or seasonal dockage is available. Gasoline and diesel fuel can be purchased at a fuel dock fronting the river. There is also a full-line ship's store between the marina and Shirttail Charlie's Restaurant.

Next door to Riverfront Marina, the memorable dining establishment known as Shirttail Charlie's Restaurant (954-463-3474) is named for a simple-minded Seminole who, according to legend, was condemned always to wear his shirttail out because of some minor tribal infraction. He is supposed to have caused quite a stir in the young town of Fort Lauderdale by taking the only bath of his life near this very spot.

Charlie's is one of the most popular purveyors of fresh seafood on New River. The restaurant has a distinct double character. Downstairs, patrons can take their ease at waterside tables while overlooking New River. The food served here can only be described as quite good.

On the other hand, the cuisine prepared upstairs is also consistently tasty and demands any serious seafood lover's attention. Recently, this writer and his mate enjoyed Charlie's superb fried shrimp and broiled mackerel. The attractive upstairs dining room is set off with a decidedly nautical decor and features air conditioning. An unusual round bar sits just behind the dining room. Most upstairs tables afford a good view of the water through multiple windows. You can look down at the patrons below with the sure knowledge that everyone is having a good meal.

Shirttail Charlie's maintains its own fixed, wooden riverside docks, to which patrons are free to tie while dining. With minimum 7-foot depths, even a 45 footer can berth alongside.

A bit farther upstream on the opposite shore are the historic Bryan Homes. The twin home-places are some of the oldest houses left standing in Fort Lauderdale. They were originally built by Perry Bryan's two sons, Tom and Reid, in the early twentieth century. After going through some rough times, these two venerable homes have been restored. One house is currently in use by the nearby Museum of Discovery and Science. The other has been converted into a member of the redoubtable Chart House Restaurant (954-523-0177) chain. As with all Chart House restaurants, the food here is far above average. The Chart House maintains its own piers on the river, and boats up to 50 feet can berth at the docks in 6½- to 7-foot minimum depths.

Across New River from the Chart House dock, Sun Power Diesel Service (954-522-4775)

Shirttail Charlie's Restaurant, New River

offers extensive mechanical (gas and diesel) repairs and fueling service. Wet-slip dockage is for service customers only.

Upstream of Sun Power Diesel, New River bends sharply to the southwest. Soon the narrowing stream begins its approach to the William H. Marshall Bridge.

Cooley's Landing, City of Fort Lauderdale Municipal Docks (26 07.031 North/080 08.939 West)

The city of Fort Lauderdale's third dockage complex graces New River's northwesterly banks immediately upstream (southwest) of the William H. Marshall Bridge. Cooley's Landing accommodates visiting cruisers at first-rate, fixed, concrete piers (with wooden pilings). Depths alongside are 7 feet or better. A full array of power, water, cable-television, and telephone connections is on hand at each slip. Shoreside, cruising visitors will find excellent showers, a full Laundromat, and a small paperback exchange library in a modern building, just behind the docks. Waste pump-out connections are available at each slip!

The adjoining grounds are beautifully landscaped, with a large parking lot and several launching ramps for small craft. With a quick detour over the bridge, and around Mango Marine, visiting cruisers can stroll down the charming Riverwalk to all its many attractions as well as the shops and restaurants of the Las Olas business district. It's a bit of a walk, but during fair weather, the journey is ever so pleasant.

You don't have to be a rocket scientist to discern that, with its fine services and superb dockage, Cooley's Landing is on the top of many a cruiser's list. Be sure to give the dockmaster a call ahead of time to check on berth availability.

**Cooley's Landing, City of Fort Lauderdale
Municipal Docks (954) 828-4626
http://www.ci.fort-lauderdale.fl.us/
marinas/cooleys.htm**

Approach depths—10-12 feet
Dockside depths—7-10 feet
Accepts transients—yes
Transient dockage rate—below average
Fixed concrete piers—yes
Dockside power connections—30
    and 50 amps
Dockside water connections—yes
Showers—yes
Laundromat—yes
Waste pump-out—yes
Restaurant—several within a fairly long walk

North Fork, New River

New River splits into northern and southern branches less than 1 mile upstream from the Marshall Bridge. The northerly fork borders on some beautiful private homes with their own docks, but you must first pass through the 11th Avenue swing bridge, which is soon followed by a low-level fixed span. There are no facilities or anchorages on this portion of the river.

Summerfield Boat Works (26 05.973 North/080 09.661 West)

Summerfield Boat Works appears on the northern shore just as New River takes a bend to the west, near facility designation #50 on the New River inset of chart 11467. This full-service repair yard offers extensive mechanical (gas and diesel), marine carpentry, welding and below-waterline, haul-out repairs for both power and sailcraft. Summerfield's travelift is rated at 70 tons, and they also boast a 25-ton mobile crane. Do-it-yourself work is allowed on hauled boats, or you can leave the job to the yard's professionals.

Summerfield also maintains extensive wet-slip dockage. The firm's covered slips are usually rented out on a seasonal basis, but transients are occasionally accepted at the open piers when space is available. Depths alongside run 7 to 8 feet, and fresh water and 30- and 50-amp power connections are available. There are also some shoreside showers, as well as a small ship's store on the premises.

Summerfield is yet another in the series of friendly yards and marinas on New River that are very much concerned with meeting their customer's needs. Visiting cruisers and service customers alike can moor to the docks of this yard and marina with confidence.

**Summerfield Boat Works (954) 525-4726
http://www.summerfieldboat.com/**

Approach depths—8-10 feet
Dockside depths—7-8 feet
Accepts transients—yes
    (when space is available)
Transient dockage rate—below average
Fixed wooden piers—yes
Dockside power connections—30
    and 50 amps
Dockside water connections—yes
Showers—yes
Below-waterline repairs—yes (extensive)
Mechanical repairs—yes (extensive)
Ship's store—yes (small)

River Bend Marine (26 05.842 North/080 09.671 West)

Directly across the river from Summerfield, River Bend Marine (954-523-1832) occupies the charted offshoot striking south. River Bend is a full-service repair yard that can usually perform any mechanical (gas and diesel) and below-the-waterline repair you need. Haul-outs are accomplished by a 75-ton travelift. Marine carpentry service is available, and this facility also specializes in long-term storage of sailcraft. No overnight dockage is to be had, though seasonal slips are available at River Bend's extensive piers.

Broward Yachts

Broward Yachts (954-925-8118) is located in the next upstream offshoot on the southern banks. This establishment manufactures the magnificent Broward yacht, surely one of the most impressive cruising boats on the water today. The yard will also perform repairs on other boats if time permits. Be sure to make arrangements ahead of time so the busy yard can fit you into its schedule. No dockage, fuel, or other transient services are available.

Jackson Marine Center 26 05.821 North/080 10.186 West

Cruisers working their way up New River will quickly spot the extensive docks associated with Jackson Marine Center to the northwest, immediately after passing through the charted "SCL" railway span. This friendly, family owned facility accepts transients for an overnight (or short-term) stay, though most of the marine center's berths are given over to seasonal dockage by the month. Dockage is at fixed, wooden piers featuring fresh water and 30- and 50-amp power connections. Depths alongside run 7 feet or better. The vast majority of Jackson's slips are covered, so berths are pretty much limited to power craft and sailcraft with unstepped masts. However, be advised that Jackson can accommodate very large power craft. Dry storage for power craft up to 41 feet is also available.

Extensive mechanical (gas and diesel) and below-waterline, haul-out repairs are readily available. Jackson's travelift is rated at 70 tons. There is also a marine carpenter on staff and a complete bottom and topside painting shop. Skippers in need of a new bimini top will be glad to learn that a marine canvas shop is also located in the complex. An extensive ship's and parts store just behind the dockage area can supply almost any hardware a cruiser might ever require.

Whether you are seeking overnight or seasonal dockage, service work, or just a warm welcome from a bunch of friendly nautical professionals, Jackson Marine Center can fill the bill. Tell them that we sent you.

**Jackson Marine Center (954) 792-4900
http://www.jacksonmarine.com**

**Approach depths—8-10 feet
Dockside depths—7-10 feet
Accepts transients—yes
Transient dockage rate—below average
Fixed wooden piers—yes (mostly covered)
Dockside power connections—30
   and 50 amps
Dockside water connections—yes
Below-waterline repairs—yes (extensive)
Mechanical repairs—yes (extensive)
Ship's store—yes**

Marina Bay Hotel Resort and Marina (26 05.548 North/080 10.257 West)

The Marina Bay collection of floating docks is found in the large charted cove indenting New River's southern banks at facility designation #53 on the New River inset of chart 11467. The marina is now backed by a recently expanded and updated condo complex, which is quite impressive indeed.

Marina Bay is a large operation with 180 wet slips. Transients are eagerly accepted for overnight dockage or a longer stay at floating, fiberglass-decked piers complemented by 50-amp power hookups and water and cable-television connections. Dockside soundings run around 8 to 10 feet. Showers and a Laundromat are available shoreside.

The adjacent Ramada Inn is also quite

extensive and is obviously convenient for lodging ashore. Visiting cruisers are welcome at the complex's swimming pool, tennis courts, and golf driving range. The on-site Marina Bay Waterfront Restaurant seems to be a popular restaurant, with plenty of customers, even during the summer months.

Marina Bay Hotel Resort and Marina
(954) 791-7600
http://matinabayyachtclubandresort.com

Approach depths—8-10 feet
Dockside depths—8-10 feet
Accepts transients—yes
Transient dockage rate—average
Floating fiberglass piers—yes
Dockside power connections—50 amps
Dockside water connections—yes
Showers—yes
Laundromat—yes
Restaurant—on site

Cable Marine West (26 05.458 North/080 10.403 West)

Cable Marine West (954-587-4000) is the first of two facilities located in the triple side-by-side artificial coves at facility designation #53B on chart 11467. Cable Marine West maintains an extensive collection of unusually large covered slips in its harbor. This dockage is rented out on a seasonal or day-to-day basis, though the management has informed this writer that Cable Marine is not a transient facility. Extensive mechanical (gas and diesel), topside, and below-the-waterline service work is also offered. The on-site travelift is rated at 80 tons.

Rolly Marine Service (26 05.458 North/080 10.533 West)

Rolly Marine Service (954-583-5300) occupies the westernmost of the three coves near facility designation #53B. Some of the marina's slips are covered, while others are out in the open. Again, dockage is pretty much limited to seasonal clients. Extensive mechanical (gas and diesel), below-waterline (120-ton travelift), and topside repair services are available.

Bradford Marine (26 05.228 North/080 11.162 West)

New River eventually divides for a second time southwest of the cove that plays host to Rolly Marine Center. Bradford Marine (954-791-3800) maintains an extensive collection of covered slips on the northern branch of New River near facility designation #56 on chart 11467.

Bradford Marine boasts what may be the largest repair and repainting facility for (mostly huge) power craft in southeastern Florida. Many of the most prestigious power yachts in America make their way to Bradford's year after year for a new Imron or Awlgrip coating. Captains cruising this upstream portion of New River should take a few moments to cruise by the various slips at Bradford. You will most likely see one of the most awesome collections of mammoth power yachts imaginable. Obviously, Bradford offers everything in the way of mechanical, haul-out, and topside repairs. All wet-slip storage is set aside for seasonal storage of larger power craft.

In addition to all the painting and fiberglass repairs, Bradford Marine hauls out large power craft via a 250-ton marine railway. Full mechanical repairs for both gasoline and diesel power plants are also available.

Roscioli Yacht Center (26 05.217 North/080 11.243 West)

Roscioli Yacht Center (954-581-9200) is located just upstream from Bradford Marine. This large and impressive facility provides seasonal storage for power boats at ultramodern covered slips. Full mechanical (gas and diesel) and below-the-waterline repairs can also be had. Roscioli hauls craft via a 100-ton marine railway.

South New River Canal

Upstream from Bradford Marine, the south fork of New River soon leaves all development behind. This stream eventually leads to Dania Cut-Off Canal, but the passage is not recommend for visitors. The river is quickly blocked by the State Road 84 Bridge with a closed vertical clearance of 21 feet. This span requires twenty-four hours' notice to open.

Even if you could get past the bridge, our bent prop attests to the presence of underwater stumps in the canal. It is by far the wisest course of action to discontinue your explorations of

NEW RIVER NAVIGATION

New River south of the State Road 84 span.

All skippers cruising New River should proceed strictly at idle speed and keep to the midwidth. By following these simple rules, you should have no difficulty in navigating the developed portion of New River. The route need not be further detailed here except to outline the river's entrance and mention the several bridges with regulated schedules.

No-wake regulations are in effect over the entire course of New River. Please observe these restrictions for everyone's safety and peace of mind.

New River Entry   Cruisers working their way south down the ICW should depart the Waterway at unlighted daybeacon #A. Pass #A to its immediate northerly side and continue on to the west, pointing to pass between the first two aids to navigation on the New River channel, unlighted daybeacons #1 and #2.

The same track will lead you between unlighted daybeacons #3 and #4, and soon thereafter between flashing daybeacon #6 and unlighted daybeacon #5. Shallow water lies south of #1 and #3. Be sure to stay north of these markers.

Between #3 and #5, an alternate channel comes into the main New River cut from the south. This route is a useful shortcut for northbound Waterway cruisers.

Chart 11467 correctly identifies a marked cut running almost due north from unlighted daybeacon #23. Cruisers using this cut should depart from the Waterway at #23 and set a course to pass flashing daybeacon #20 to its westerly side. A large shoal abuts the cut to the east. Even at high tide, you can sometimes see old limbs and stumps protruding above the water's surface.

Once abeam of flashing daybeacon #20, continue straight ahead into the main New River channel, favoring the western banks. You will soon encounter unlighted daybeacon #2, marking the eastern edge of the alternate channel. Be sure to stay west of #2.

Continue north past #2 until the gap between New River's flashing daybeacon #6 and unlighted daybeacon #5 comes abeam to the west. You can then swing 90 degrees to the west and follow the markers upstream.

New River Bridges   The first span as you move upstream on New River is the Third

Avenue Bridge. It has a closed vertical clearance of 16 feet. The bridge is shut from 7:30 A.M. to 8:30 A.M. and between 4:30 P.M. and 5:30 P.M. Monday through Friday. At all other times the bridge opens on demand.

The Andrews Avenue Bridge is next, with, a closed vertical clearance of 21 feet. Surprisingly enough, this span currently opens on demand, except that it will not open when the railway bridge, just to the west, is closed.

The railroad bridge spanning New River just upstream from Andrews Avenue is usually open unless a train is due. Unfortunately, the bridge operator has been known to leave the bridge closed long after a train has passed, and sometimes even before a train is due. I was once caught behind the span for a good ten minutes after the clatter of a passing train had died away. Repeated horn blowing and calls on the VHF were all to no avail.

The William H. Marshall Bridge comes up after the river's first sharp bend to the south. This span has a closed vertical clearance of 20 feet and opens on demand.

Next up is the 12th Street/Davie Boulevard bascule bridge, with a closed vertical clearance of 21 feet. Yes, friends, this one is regulated. The bridge does not open weekdays between 7:30 A.M. and 8:30 A.M. and again from 4:30 P.M. to 5:30 P.M.

Farther to the west, New River passes under the I-95 twin spans. These bridges have a vertical clearance of approximately 55 feet and could be a problem for particularly tall sailcraft. Shortly thereafter, a second railway bridge, with a closed vertical clearance of 2 feet, spans the stream. Rail traffic is not as heavy at this bridge as that found on its easterly sister, and cruisers will usually find the bridge standing open. Be on guard against strong currents at this span if it should happen to be closed. Sailcraft and trawlers should wait well back from the bridge.

Upstream Limits West of the charted position of Rolly Marine Service (at facility designation #53B), the river splits for a second time. The southern fork leads to South New River Canal, but the stream is spanned by the State Road 84 Bridge with a vertical clearance of 21 feet. Twenty-four hours' notice is required to open this span, and, even then, you'd better have a good reason for making the request.

The South Canal is a wilderness stream that is delightfully undeveloped. Unfortunately, it also has several underwater stumps waiting to damage your props and rudders. Obviously, this channel is not recommended for cruising craft.

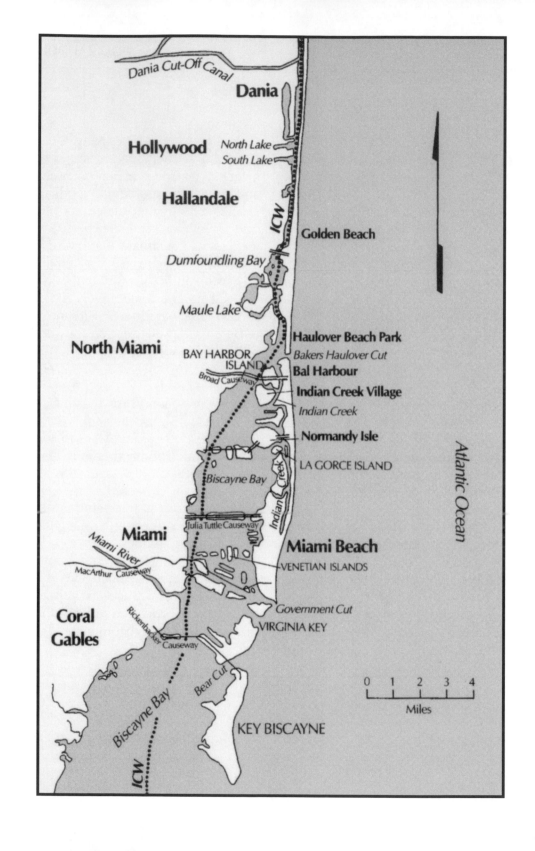

Dania to Miami

The southernmost waters of eastern Florida present a mixed bag of cruising opportunities for visiting mariners. Quite honestly, many captains regularly choose to avoid the ICW passage from Port Everglades to Miami by cruising south offshore. Over the last decade, the number of no-wake zones on the ICW between Port Everglades and North Miami, not to mention the restricted bridges, has proliferated to such an extent that, unless foul weather is in the offing or there is a particular port of call in Dania, Hollywood, or Hallandale that you want to visit, it might be better to give a nod to the offshore route.

Power-craft skippers will be very frustrated by the slow-speed zones. With only a very few exceptions, the entire run south from Port Everglades to North Miami is under speed restrictions. Sailors will be equally exasperated with the restricted bridges. It can seemingly take forever for either type of craft to make this relatively short run. Just to make life a bit more interesting, there is also a navigationally difficult section of the Waterway with plenty of attendant shoaling to contend with. In a word or two, this part of the Waterway can really try the patience of any cruiser, whether traveling under power or sail.

The outside run from Port Everglades Inlet to Government Cut Inlet in Miami is straightforward. With fair weather in the offing, navigators can simply follow the beach south (keeping well offshore) to the buoyed passage striking west on Government Cut.

For those who do choose to travel the southernmost section of the eastern Florida ICW, the run from Dania to Miami can be roughly divided into two very different regions. To the north, the Waterway borders on the teeming communities of Dania, Hollywood, Hallandale, and Golden Beach. Farther to the south, the ICW flows through the broad waters of Biscayne Bay to Miami and Miami Beach.

Sailors should be aware of a significant height limitation on this section of the ICW. Vertical clearance for the run between Fort Lauderdale and Miami is set at 56 feet by the fixed Julia Tuttle Causeway Bridge. Tall sailcraft that need more clearance **must** make the outside run to Government Cut Inlet in order to reach Miami.

Two inlets serve extreme southeastern Florida. Bakers Haulover Inlet is a fairly low key seaward cut with swift tidal currents and a 32-foot fixed bridge. It is used regularly by small power craft, but this passage is not for the faint-hearted. Government Cut is the principal Miami inlet. This well-marked, stable channel is used extensively by large oceangoing craft.

Facilities from Port Everglades to Miami run the gamut from clean, well-managed marina operations to truly seedy boatyards that feature a multitude of sunken vessels. These are waters where you should exercise considerable discretion when choosing a service yard or a place to berth.

Surprisingly, anchorage in Miami waters is mostly unrestricted. Many deep passages run between the various causeway islands and bridges spanning the bay between Miami and the beach. Several of these backwaters can make excellent temporary havens.

A cruise up Miami River does lead to at least one excellent boatyard. Otherwise, the shores of upper Miami River are overlooked by one of the most motley collections of old buildings and worn-out structures that this writer has ever seen.

Charts Our old friend chart 11467 continues its coverage south from Fort Lauderdale to Key Biscayne:

11467—covers all waters between Fort Lauderdale and Key Biscayne, including Bakers Haulover Inlet, the approaches to Miami Beach, Government Cut Inlet, and Miami River

Bridges

Dania/Beach Boulevard Bridge—crosses ICW at Standard Mile 1069.5, south of intersection with Dania Cut-Off Canal—Bascule—22 feet (closed)—opens on demand

Sheridan Street/Hollywood Bridge—crosses ICW at Standard Mile 1071, south of flashing daybeacon #39A—Bascule—22 feet (closed)—opens on demand

Hollywood Boulevard Bridge—crosses ICW at Standard Mile 1072, south of flashing daybeacon #40—Bascule—25 feet (closed)—November 15 through May 15 opens only on the hour and half-hour 10:00 A.M. to 6:00 P.M. (9:00 A.M. to 7:00 P.M. during weekends and holidays the rest of the year)

Hallandale Beach/State Road 824—crosses ICW at Standard Mile 1074, well south of unlighted daybeacon #42—Bascule—22 feet (closed)—opens only on the quarter and three-quarter hour 7:15 A.M. to 6:15 P.M.

Golden Beach/Dumfoundling Bay Bridge—crosses ICW at Standard Mile 1076.5, south of Turnberry Isle Marina—Fixed—65 feet

Sunny Isles Causeway Bridge—crosses ICW at Standard Mile 1078, south of unlighted daybeacon #57—Bascule—30 feet (closed)—opens only on the quarter and three-quarter hour 7:00 A.M. to 6:00 P.M. weekdays (10:00 A.M. to 6:00 P.M. during weekends and holidays)

Broad Causeway Bridge—crosses ICW at Standard Mile 1081.5, south of unlighted daybeacon #13—Bascule—32 feet (closed)—opens only on the quarter and three-quarter hour 8:00 A.M. to 6:00 P.M.

79th Street Causeway easternmost span—crosses Miami Beach Channel south of unlighted daybeacon #8—Bascule—25 feet (closed)—opens on demand

Allison Island Bridge—crosses Indian Creek east of Allison Island—Bascule—11 feet (closed)—opens on demand

Julia Tuttle Causeway easternmost span—crosses Miami Beach Channel south of unlighted daybeacon #25—Fixed—35 feet

Venetian Causeway Bridge span between Belle Isle and Rivo Alto Island—crosses Miami Beach Channel south of unlighted daybeacon #15—Bascule—9 feet (closed)—November 1 through April 30 will not open 7:15 A.M. to 8:45 A.M. and 4:45 P.M. to 6:15 P.M. weekdays, except opens at 7:45 A.M., 8:15 A.M., 5:15 P.M., and 5:45 P.M.; at all other times opens on demand

MacArthur Causeway easternmost span—crosses Miami Beach Channel southeast of Star Island—Fixed—35 feet

79th Street Causeway Bridge—crosses ICW at Standard Mile 1085, south of flashing daybeacon #26—Bascule—25 feet (closed)—opens on demand

Julia Tuttle Causeway Bridge—crosses ICW at Standard Mile 1087, south of unlighted daybeacon #39—Fixed—56 feet (sets the height limit for the ICW between Fort Lauderdale and Miami)
Venetian Causeway Bridge—crosses ICW at Standard Mile 1088.5—Bascule—8 feet (closed)—November 30 through April 30 opens only on the hour and half-hour 7:00 A.M. to 9:00 A.M. and 4:30 P.M. to 6:30 P.M. weekdays; at all other times opens on demand
MacArthur Causeway Bridge—crosses ICW at Standard Mile 1089, a short hop south of the Venetian Causeway Bridge—Fixed—65 feet
Dodge Island Highway Bridge—crosses ICW at Standard Mile 1089.5, south of flashing daybeacon #50—Fixed—65 feet
Dodge Island Railway Bridge—crosses ICW at Standard Mile 1089.5, south of flashing daybeacon #50—Bascule—22 feet (closed)—usually open unless a train is due
Miami River bridges—Bascule—16-21 feet (closed)—usually will not open 7:30 A.M. to 9:00 A.M. and 4:30 P.M. and 6:00 P.M.

Chapter 11 Anchorage Summary (Note that anchorages are listed in geographic order, moving north to south.)
Dumfoundling Bay Anchorage—(Standard Mile 1077)—located near 25 56.919 North/080 07.527 West, on the charted bubble of deep water just opposite the charted westward-flowing channel, north of flashing daybeacon #49—5-foot depths—reviewed on pages 511, 516
Maule Lake Anchorage—(Standard Mile 1077.5)—located near 25 56.053 North/080 08.690 West, on the center section of Maule Lake—6-foot depths—reviewed on pages 512-13, 516
Biscayne Point Anchorage (Miami Beach Channel)—located near 25 51.955 North/080 08.258 West, on the charted finger of deep water north of Biscayne Point—7-foot depths—reviewed on pages 520-21, 528
Monument Island Anchorage (Miami Beach Channel)—located near 25 47.186 North/080 09.102 West, northeast of the island with a charted "Monument," south-southeast of Rivo Alto Island—7-foot depths—reviewed on pages 523, 530
Star Island Anchorage (Miami Beach Channel)—located near 25 46.601 North/080 09.269 West, between the eastern tip of Palm Island and the western shores of Star Island—6-foot depths—reviewed on pages 523, 531
Palm Island Anchorage (Miami Beach Channel)—located near 25 46.618 North/080 09.571 West, on the waters lying between the southern shores of Palm Island and MacArthur Causeway—6-foot depths—reviewed on pages 523, 531

Chapter 11 Marina and Yacht-Club Summary (Note that marinas and yacht clubs are listed in geographic order, moving north to south. These facilities are further divided in the Miami region, with the marinas and clubs on the Miami Beach side of Biscayne Bay listed first, followed by those along the path of the ICW.)

Harbour Towne Marina—(954) 926-0300—(Standard Mile 1068.5)—located near 26 03.571 North/080 07.830 West, astride the first charted 5-foot harbor on the southern banks on the Dania Cut-Off Canal—transient dockage available—gasoline and diesel fuel available—8-foot minimum

depths—reviewed on pages 505-6, 514
Royale Palm Yacht Basin—(954) 923-5900—(Standard Mile 1068.5)—located near 26 03.527 North/080 07.974 West, guarding Dania Canal's southern shores in the charted 7-foot cove west of Harbour Towne—transient dockage available—8-foot minimum depths—reviewed on pages 506-7, 514
Hollywood Marina—(954) 921-3035—(Standard Mile 1071.5)—located near 26 00.883 North/080 07.129 West, south of flashing daybeacon #40, on the southern shores of North Lake—transient dockage available—gasoline and diesel fuel available—6½-foot minimum depths—reviewed on pages 508, 515
Waterways Marina—(305) 935-4295—(Standard Mile 1075)—located near 25 58.189 North/080 07.764 West, in the charted harbor just south of Standard Mile 1075, along the ICW's western shore—transient dockage available—10-foot minimum depths—reviewed on pages 509-10, 516
Turnberry Isle Marina—(305) 933-6934—(Standard Mile 1076)—located near 25 57.527 North/080 07.642 West, in the charted harbor intersecting the Waterway's western banks, about .3 of a nautical mile north of the 65-foot Golden Beach fixed bridge—transient dockage available for boats 40 feet and larger—10-foot minimum depths—reviewed on pages 510-11, 516
Maule Lake Marina—(305) 945-0808—(Standard Mile 1077.5)—located near 25 56.106 North/080 08.953 West, on Maule Lake's western shoreline—transient dockage available—gasoline and diesel fuel available—7-foot min. depths—reviewed on pages 511-12, 516
Grand View Palace Marina—(305) 861-5343—(Miami Beach Channel)—located near 25 50.895 North/080 08.667 West, on the eastern shores of Treasure Island, just south of the bridge spanning the gap between Treasure Island and Normandy Isle—transient dockage available—gasoline and diesel fuel available—6-foot minimum depths—reviewed on pages 521, 529
Sunset Harbor Yacht Club—(305) 673-0044—(Miami Beach Channel)—located near 25 47.716 North/080 08.729 West, along the alternate Miami Beach Channel's westerly banks between the Julia Tuttle and Venetian Causeway—marina was finishing up a major rebuilding at the time of this writing, but most likely transient dockage will be available by the time this account finds its way into your hands—reviewed on pages 522-23, 530
Miami Beach Marina—(305) 673-6000—(Miami Beach Channel)—located near 25 46.244 North/080 08.383 West, on the southwesternmost shores of Miami Beach, just west of the Government Cut Inlet—transient dockage available—gasoline and diesel fuel available—10-foot min. depths—reviewed on pages 524-25, 531
Keystone Point Marina—(305) 940-6236—(Standard Mile 1081)—located near 25 53.833 North/080 09.528 West, reached by a cruise down the marked channel leading west from unlighted daybeacon #12—transient dockage available—gasoline and diesel fuel available—5-foot min. depths—reviewed on page 525
Sealine Marina—(305) 377-3625—(Standard Mile 1089)—located near 25 47.454 North/080 11.070 West, at the western foot of the westward-flowing channel south of flashing daybeacon #48—transient dockage available—gasoline and diesel fuel available—6-foot min. depths—reviewed on pages 525-26
Dupont Plaza Hotel and Marina—(305) 358-2541—(Standard Mile 1090)—located near 25 46.204 North/080 11.332 West, on the northern banks, just inside the mouth of Miami River, west-southwest of the Waterway's unlighted daybeacon #57—transient dockage available—10-foot min. depths—reviewed on pages 534-35

Dania to Bakers Haulover Inlet

The northern stretch of the ICW leading from Dania to Miami presents a variety of striking contrasts. The northerly portion of this run borders low-key residential and commercial development. Conversely, at Hollywood and Hallandale, Waterway visitors will discover anew the meaning of the term "condo caverns." Here, the ICW is seemingly enclosed by mammoth concrete and steel towers.

This stretch of the Waterway is quite sheltered and cruisers need not concern themselves about adverse weather conditions short of a gale. Eventually the passage leads to wide Biscayne Bay, where water conditions are very different.

A reasonably good selection of marinas is available along the run from Dania to Bakers Haulover. Beginning with the two facilities on Dania Cut-Off Canal, visiting cruisers will also find reliable services in Hollywood and Maule Lake.

Anchorage is practically nonexistent north of Biscayne Bay. With a very few exceptions, skippers preferring to anchor off will either have to stop in Fort Lauderdale or continue south to the Miami area.

John Q. Loyd Park (Standard Mile 1067.5)

Just south of the ICW-Port Everglades Inlet intersection, a small channel leads east to a dock and launching ramp associated with John Q. Loyd State Park. This pleasant recreation area takes in the undeveloped beach bordering the southern side of Port Everglades Inlet. The surrounding countryside is a beautiful blend of tall cedar trees and dense tropical foliage.

Unfortunately, the small harbor holds only 4-foot depths, and a sign warns that dockage is available only for those launching at the park ramps. If you are able to acquire land transportation, this would still be a wonderful place to visit.

Dania Cut-Off Canal Facilities (Standard Mile 1068.5) (Various Lats/Lons—see below)

Dania Cut-Off Canal strikes west at flashing daybeacon #35. This artificial waterway is consistently deep over the first several miles of its course, and boats of almost any size can enter the channel with confidence. Several facilities line the cut, ranging from a full-service marina offering transient dockage to a most impressive boatyard.

The canal's shoreline presents a great variety of conditions. Some portions are completely in their natural state and seem almost out of place in this highly developed region. Attractive residential communities border the cut in some places while homes that can only be described as seedy overlook the channel in still other locations. Cruising the Dania Canal should not be boring.

As you move from east to west, Harbour Towne Marina is the first in a group of four adjacent facilities on the canal. The marina is located astride the first charted 5-foot harbor on the southern banks (actual depths are far more impressive) near 26 03.571 North/080 07.830 West. Managed by the Westrec Corporation, Harbour Towne can be considered one of the very best places to dock or have your boat serviced between Fort Lauderdale and Miami.

Harbour Towne boasts two dockage basins carved in the canal's southerly banks. Transients are readily accepted for overnight or temporary dockage at both fixed wooden and concrete piers. The twin harbors are very well sheltered and should be a good spot to ride out heavy weather. Depths alongside run around 8 feet at low water in the two dockage basins, with 11 to 12 feet of water at the fuel dock. Full power and water connections are available, as is waste pump-out service. The on-site showers and full Laundromat are extra nice. There is also a ship's and variety store just behind the fuel dock. Harbour Towne's huge dry-dock storage building, accommodating smaller power craft, is prominent from the water.

Gasoline and diesel fuel can be purchased at the fuel pier, and mechanical repair services are offered for both gasoline and diesel engines by way of an on-site, independent service firm. Haul-outs are accomplished with a 60-ton travelift.

The old site of Tugboat Annie's restaurant, located between Harbour Towne's two dockage basins, is empty at this time, and no restaurant is available on site. This situation may very well have changed for the better by the time of your arrival, but then again, maybe not. To be on the safe side, plan to arrive with a stocked galley.

Harbour Towne Marina is a decidedly superior facility, and we recommend it to our fellow cruisers without reservation. Tell the dockmasters and staff that we sent you.

Harbour Towne Marina (954) 926-0300
http://www.westrec.com/
harbourtowne.html

Approach depths—9-13 feet
Dockside depths—8 feet
  (minimum—dockage basins)
  11-12 feet (minimum—fuel
  dock and restaurant docks)
Accepts transients—yes
Transient dockage rate—average
Fixed wooden piers—yes

Fixed concrete piers—yes
Dockside power connections—30
  and 50 amps
Dockside water connections—yes
Showers—yes
Laundromat—yes
Waste pump-out—yes
Gasoline—yes
Diesel fuel—yes
Below-waterline repairs—yes
Mechanical repairs—yes
Ship's and variety store—yes

Almost directly across the canal from Harbour Towne, Playboy Marine Center (26 03.645 North/080 07.850 West, 954-920-0533) occupies the northerly banks of the deep cove on the northern banks. This small yard has an 88-ton travelift and offers do-it-yourself, below-the-waterline repairs.

Royale Palm Yacht Basin guards Dania Canal's southern shores in the charted 7-foot cove west of Harbour Towne, near 26 03.527 North/080 07.974 West. This is another of the friendly facilities on the canal that gladly welcomes transients. Overnight berths are at fixed, wooden piers with full power, water, and cable-television connections. The harbor is protected from all winds and boasts low-water soundings of 8 to 9 feet. Showers and a Laundromat are on hand, and a small ship's store is located on the premises. Cruisers journeying through the Florida summer will be happy to learn that Royale Palm features a swimming pool open to visitors. Mechanical (gas and diesel) servicing and haul-outs via a 50-ton travelift are available.

Royale Palm Yacht Basin (954) 923-5900
http://www.royalepalm.com

Approach depths—9-13 feet
Dockside depths—8-9 feet
Accepts transients—yes
Transient dockage rate—above average
Fixed wooden piers—yes

Dockside power connections—30
 and 50 amps
Dockside water connections—yes
Showers—yes
Laundromat—yes
Below-waterline repairs—yes
Mechanical repairs—yes
Ship's store—yes (small)
Restaurant—one nearby

Derecktor-Gunnell Boat Yard (954-920-5756) is the westernmost of the four facilities. This large yard flanks the northern banks west of unlighted nun buoy #2, near 26 03.612 North/080 08.056 West. Derecktor-Gunnell just may be the finest repair facility between Fort Lauderdale and Miami. Featuring full mechanical (gas and diesel), below-the-waterline, electrical, fiberglass, and marine carpentry servicing, Derecktor assures a job done right the first time. Its two travelifts are rated at 60 and 160 tons. All wet-slip dockage is reserved for service customers.

West of Derecktor-Gunnell Boat Yard, Dania Cut-Off Canal continues deep for several miles to the west. Eventually this stream joins the South Fork of New River. Several decidedly low key marine facilities line the canal between Derecktor and the intersection with New River. To reach these various establishments, you must cruise under several low-level pipelines. The reputation of the facilities on the upper portion of Dania Cut-Off Canal is not exactly sterling, and these establishments will not be further covered in this guide.

Seafare Marina (Standard Mile 1069)

Less than .1 nautical miles north of the Dania bascule bridge (south of flashing daybeacon #35), another facility will come abeam on the eastern shore. Seafare used to be a combination marina, restaurant, and shopping complex. Within the last decade, this complex has obviously fallen on hard times. The large, on-site restaurant has closed, and only a few of the retail operations remain. The marina is still in business, but you must be able to clear an 18-foot fixed bridge to enter the harbor. Most cruising craft would be better served by the marinas on Dania Cut-Off Canal, or the Hollywood municipal marina, not far to the south.

Dania Waterway Restaurants and Shoreside Facilities (Standard Mile 1069.5)

The downtown Dania business district sits astride U.S. Highway 1. It is too far from the water for walking, but a quick taxi ride will get you there. Here visitors will find a supermarket, drugstore, and several restaurants.

South of the Dania bascule bridge (north of flashing daybeacon #36), several restaurants and shoreside stores with their own docks are available to cruisers on the eastern banks. First up is Martha's Restaurant (954-923-5444). This popular dining attraction offers some of the finest seafood to be found anywhere. For those who prefer a taste of salt air with their meals, Martha's also features open-air dining overlooking the ICW.

Martha's Restaurant maintains extensive docks to which all customers are free to tie. Depths are in the 8- to 9-foot range. There should be plenty of room for even mammoth Hatteras and Bertram yachts to berth comfortably.

Numbers to know in Dania:
Yellow Cab—954-565-5400
Friendly Checker Cab—954-923-9999
Budget Car Rental—954-359-4747
Hertz Rent A Car—954-764-1199
Chamber of Commerce—954-926-2323

Hollywood Facilities (Standard Mile 1071.5) (Various Lats/Lons—see below)

South of the Sheridan Street bascule bridge (itself south of flashing daybeacon #39A), cruisers will begin their approach to the side-by-side cities of Hollywood and Hallandale. The concrete and steel condo towers overlooking the Waterway along this stretch are nothing short of awesome. Of all the places we have visited in eastern Florida, Hollywood and Hallandale are the most representative of the heavy development so common south of Palm Beach.

The one and only municipal facility available to transient cruisers between Fort Lauderdale and Miami is found south of flashing daybeacon #40, on the southern shores of North Lake, near 26 00.883 North/080 07.129 West. Hollywood Marina (maintained by the city of Hollywood) features modern, fixed, concrete piers and depths alongside of 6½ feet or better. Several shoals and rocks lie just north of the marina's entrance from the ICW. Be sure to review the navigational account of this facility presented below.

Berths on Hollywood Marina's "A" dock have both 30- and 50-amp power connections, while slips on the "B," "C," and "D" piers have 30-amp hookups. All have freshwater outlets. Showers, but no Laundromat, are offered in the dockmaster's building, perched on the harbor's southeastern point. Gasoline and diesel fuel are readily available at a pump dock fronting the Waterway. Some mechanical repairs can be arranged through independent contractors.

There are no restaurants within walking distance of Hollywood Marina, but you can easily call Yellow Cab at (954) 565-5400 or Friendly Checker Cab at (954) 923-9999. Both can quickly ferry you into the Hollywood business district, where visitors will not only find a host of restaurant choices, but a Publix Supermarket and a Walgreen Drug Store.

Hollywood Marina (954) 921-3035

Approach depths—6-10 feet
Dockside depths—6½-8 feet (minimum)
Accepts transients—yes
Transient dockage rate—below average
Fixed concrete piers—yes
Dockside power connections—30
 & 50 amp ("A" dock)
 30 amp ("B," "C," and "D" docks)
Dockside water connections—yes
Showers—yes
Gasoline—yes
Diesel fuel—yes
Mechanical repairs—limited
 (independent contractors)
Restaurant—taxi ride necessary

South Lake (Standard Mile 1072)

Navigators studying chart 11467 will quickly note "North Lake" and "South Lake" flanking the Waterway's western edge in Hollywood. Of course, North Lake is the home of Hollywood Marina (see above). South Lake, on the other hand, can serve as a good anchorage. In spite of the 4- and 5-foot soundings noted on chart 11467, we discovered a broad patch of 20+-foot waters along the lake's midline. Anchorage here would be a practical possibility for any size pleasure craft as long as you have at least 150 feet of anchor rode aboard. The surrounding shores are populated by intense residential development.

The only problem with this haven is its relative lack of shelter during foul weather. South Lake is considerably larger than a casual study of 11467 might lead you to believe. Winds over 25 knots have more than enough fetch to create an uncomfortable chop.

Cruising craft that can stand some low-water soundings of 5½ feet might alternately choose to anchor on South Lake's westerly tip. There

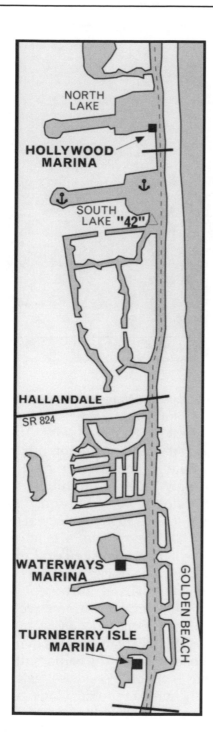

is one unmarked shoal to avoid, but with proper precautions, it's easily bypassed. The westerly waters of South Lake boast enough room for a 48 footer and superior shelter from all but easterly winds. The shoreline is composed of green grass set up from a concrete seawall. A street runs hard by the lake's shores, and nighttime traffic could conceivably be a problem, but was not during our time here.

Hallandale

As you cruise south on the ICW, the next community to come along is Hallandale. If it weren't for the chart designation or city limit signs, it would be hard to tell the difference.

Waterways Marina (Standard Mile 1075) 25 58.189 North/080 07.764 West

Waterways Marina graces the ICW's western shore in the charted harbor just south of Standard Mile 1075. A charted canal leads from the ICW into the dockage basin. Waterways Marina is associated with a huge retail, restaurant, and townhouse complex. While the management has informed this writer that transient craft are accepted for overnight or temporary dockage, we suggest advance arrangements. On two different occasions, we have arrived at or near midday, only to find the piers unattended. Waterways' harbor is well sheltered from all winds and features ultramodern, fixed, concrete slips fronting a beautifully landscaped waterfront. Impressive entrance and dockside depths of 10 feet should be enough for even the longest-legged vessels. Full power, water, telephone, and cable-television connections are on hand at every slip. Showers and a Laundromat are found just behind the dockmaster's office.

The adjacent shopping complex is within

Waterways Marina

an easy step of the docks. Here, among a wide assortment of retail businesses, visiting cruisers will discover several restaurants.

Waterways Marina (305) 935-4295
http://waterwaysmarina.com/home.htm

Approach depths—10 feet
Dockside depths—10 feet
Accepts transients—yes
Transient dockage rate—above average
Fixed concrete piers—yes
Dockside power connections—30
    and 50 amps
Dockside water connections—yes
Showers—yes
Laundromat—yes
Restaurant—several on site

Turnberry Isle Marina (Standard Mile 1076) (25 57.527 North/080 07.642 West)

The extensive docks of Turnberry Isle Marina are discovered in the charted harbor intersecting the Waterway's western banks, about .3 of a nautical mile north of the 65-foot Golden Beach fixed bridge. This facility is associated with a mammoth high-rise condo-hotel and country-club project. Surprisingly (and delightfully), transients piloting boats 40 feet and larger are accepted for overnight dockage. During our visits to Turnberry Isle, we have always found the harbor populated exclusively with power craft. The dockmaster has informed this writer that sailcraft are accepted as well, if they fit the minimum 40-foot requirement.

While there is one wooden-decked, floating dock, most larger craft are accommodated at fixed, concrete piers. The harbor's shelter from all winds is about as good as it gets. It would take truly hurricane-force winds to be a real problem at Turnberry Isle.

All slips feature 30- and 50-amp power

hookups and fresh-water connections. Many berths are also equipped with 100-amp hookups. Shoreside, visitors will find showers at two locations and a full Laundromat. There is also a welcome crew lounge with color television, pool table, and dartboard. During the winter season, drinks are sold at this location as well.

Visitors to the marina have the same privileges as motel guests. Cruisers can take advantage of the tennis courts, health spa, beach club, and four swimming pools. There are 11 (count them, 11) bars and restaurants in the Turnberry Isle complex. Tram service is provided to the main country club and a nearby shopping center. Wow—has anyone got more full service than that?

Over and above all these vital statistics, we would be remiss if we did not mention the caring attitude expressed by the staff and dockmaster at Turnberry Isle. Every boat is met and newspapers are delivered to your cockpit each morning. With all these world-class amenities, we can only conclude that Turnberry's popularity will continue to grow. Be sure to call for dockage reservations well in advance of your arrival.

Turnberry Isle Marina (305) 933-6934

800-327-7028
www.turnberryisle.com

Approach depths—10 feet
Dockside depths—10 feet
Accepts transients—yes
    (minimum size—40 feet)
Transient dockage rate—above average
Floating wooden pier—yes
Fixed concrete piers—yes
Dockside power connections—30,
    50, and (a few) 100 amps
Dockside water connections—yes
Showers—yes

Turnberry Isle Marina

Laundromat—yes
Ship's store—yes
Restaurant—several on site

Dumfoundling Bay Anchorage (Standard Mile 1077) (25 56.919 North/080 07.527 West)

An anchorage of questionable usefulness lies in Dumfoundling Bay, south of Hallandale. Chart 11467 correctly identifies a bubble of deep water just opposite the charted westward-flowing channel, north of flashing daybeacon #49. Minimum 5- to 6-foot depths are held for at least 200 yards to the east. Protection is good from northerly blows, but this anchorage could be a real bear in strong southerly winds. There should be enough swinging room for a 38 footer, but boats drawing more than 4½ feet should probably not attempt to access this potential haven.

Williams Island Marinas

The colossal Williams Island development flanks the Waterway's western banks south of the 65-foot Golden Beach bridge. This complex maintains two marinas, but both are private.

Maule Lake Facilities (Standard Mile 1077.5) (Various Lats/Lons—see below)

An enigmatic channel cuts west from

unlighted daybeacon #54 through the northernmost of the charted canals leading to Maule Lake. Maule Lake Marina, boasting 175 slips, guards the lake's western shoreline near 25 56.106 North/080 08.953 West and offers services to resident and visiting cruisers alike.

Maule Lake Marina has clearly been rejuvenated over the last several years. The on-site restaurant has been remodeled and reopened. The docks are once again teeming with boats, and no fewer than four on-site, independent service firms stand ready to assist cruisers in need of repairs. We once again recommend Maule Lake Marina to all cruising captains of both the power and sail variety.

Transients are readily accepted at Maule Lake Marina. Overnight berths are found at fixed concrete piers with all power and water connections. Approach depths through the canal and across the lake run 8 feet or better, with at least 7-foot soundings in the dockage basin. Two sets of showers and a Laundromat are located in the complex. Gasoline and diesel fuel can be purchased, and below-waterline repairs are available directly through Maule Lake Marina (travelift rated at 68 tons).

Additionally, fiberglass repairs are available through Marine Fiberglass and Refinishing, Inc. (305-947-1312). These service firms are located on the harbor's southerly banks.

The on-site Tuna's Waterfront Grill (305-945-2567) is quite good. We have enjoyed wonderful seafood sandwiches here. Visiting cruisers can be assured of a good meal here during their stay.

Maule Lake Marina (305) 945-0808

Approach depths—8-10 feet
Dockside depths—7-15 feet

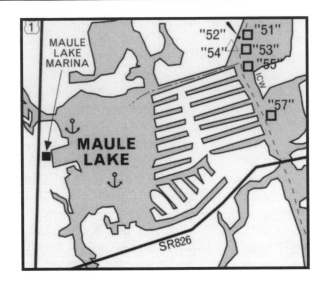

Accepts transients—yes
Transient dockage rate—below average
Fixed concrete piers—yes
Dockside power connections—30 and 50 amps
Dockside water connections—yes
Showers—yes
Laundromat—yes
Gasoline—yes
Diesel fuel—yes
Below-waterline repairs—yes
Mechanical repairs—yes
Restaurant—on site

On several occasions, we have observed sailcraft anchored on Maule Lake, near 25 56.053 North/080 08.690 West, well away from any marina traffic. This would be an excellent spot to drop the hook in some 6 to 11 feet of water, provided that future restrictions do not prohibit anchoring in the lake. No regulations are in force at the time of writing, but it might be best to check at Maule Lake Marina before you set the hook.

With strong winds in the forecast, it would be a good idea to anchor within 100 yards of the lee shore. Maule Lake is mostly surrounded by surprisingly light development, and a stay on this usually tranquil body of water can be a true delight.

Shooters Complex (Standard Mile 1078)

A large shopping and dining complex with its own docks lines the ICW's western banks south of unlighted daybeacon #57 (just north of the Sunny Isles bascule bridge). While there are many shops to see and explore, the star attraction is obviously Shooters Restaurant. This popular dining spot is under the same ownership as the Shooters in Fort Lauderdale. The food is just as good and the open-air dining and drinking within sight of the Waterway is at least as pleasant.

We might also add that the restaurant's popularity is very much in evidence. A large and convivial crowd can be expected during the afternoons and evenings on Saturdays and Sundays. If you enjoy a party atmosphere, then by all means set your course for this enjoyable Waterway stop.

Shooters' docks are first-rate, wooden face-type piers. Depths are an impressive 7 to 12 feet. Vessels as large as 45 feet, with almost any draft, should be able to berth at Shooters without difficulty. Patrons of either the restaurant or the shopping complex are welcome at the docks while visiting the complex. However, no overnight dockage is allowed.

Oleta River (Standard Mile 1078.5)

South of the Highway 826 (Sunny Isles) bascule bridge, the ICW meets up with Oleta River along its western banks. This surprisingly undeveloped stream runs back to Maule Lake and makes for a delightful cruise, but only for small craft. Depths of 3 to 4 feet render this body of water too risky for larger boats.

The ICW and Bakers Haulover Inlet (Standard Mile 1080)

As the ICW approaches Bakers Haulover Inlet, tidal currents pick up markedly and shoaling on the Waterway channel becomes virtually commonplace. A mammoth shoal occupies the wide patch of water between the inlet and the Waterway. These shifting sands, as well as some shallow water to the west, seem to be continually sifting into the channel. The cut is periodically dredged, but between channel maintenance, depths can rise to 8 feet (or worse) right in the middle of the Waterway. Be sure to read the navigational detail below before attempting to cruise south of the inlet.

Bakers Haulover Inlet is noted for its strong tidal currents and an unmarked channel. The cut is crossed by a fixed bridge with a vertical clearance of 32 feet. Obviously, sailcraft should avoid this seaward passage like a good case of the black plague.

All captains piloting craft larger than 22 feet should probably avoid Bakers Haulover Inlet unless you are lucky enough to follow a local vessel through the cut. Even then, be on guard against leeway caused by strong currents and keep a weather eye on the sounder.

A correctly charted, alternate channel runs south from flashing daybeacon #5 to Bakers Haulover Inlet. This cut currently maintains minimum 8-foot depths. As you cruise from #5 towards the inlet, Haulover Beach Park will come abeam to the east.

A bit farther to the south, a public fuel dock will come up to the east. Here you can purchase both gasoline and diesel fuel. This facility is heavily used by smaller power craft on weekends.

DANIA TO BAKERS HAVLOVER INLET NAVIGATION

Successful navigation of the Waterway from Dania to Bakers Haulover Inlet could be reduced to the old saw of sticking to the well-marked channel. This is not the place to explore the waters off the ICW. Outside of the channel, depths quickly rise to grounding levels.

Tidal currents can run quickly along this stretch, particularly near Port Everglades and Bakers Haulover inlets. Keep a sharp watch aft as well as ahead to note quickly any lateral slippage.

The no-wake zones along this stretch have grown to such an extent that you may as well expect to cruise along at idle speed virtually the entire time. There are only one or two brief respites from these speed restrictions.

The presence of many regulated bridges will also be a cause of delay and frustration for sailors. Again, our best advice is to build plenty of extra time in your cruising itinerary.

Except for the side trips documented below, keep to the Waterway, watch for leeway, and maintain a steady watch on the sounder. With these elementary precautions in mind, you should sight the problem stretch of the Waterway adjacent to Bakers Haulover without any unexpected problems.

On the Waterway   Chart 11467 correctly notes a long shoal building out from the southern flank of Port Everglades Inlet's western entrance. When passing the inlet on the Waterway, favor the ICW's western banks heavily. Do not approach unlighted daybeacon #1 to the east. Cruise back to the midwidth of the Waterway south of the charted Pier 9 dry dock on the western shoreline.

North of flashing daybeacon #35, Waterway cruisers will pass a containerized-ship loading facility on the western banks. Watch out for any large ships that may be entering or putting out to sea.

Along this same stretch, a sign along the eastern side of the ICW warns of underwater rocks stretching out from the easterly banks. Favor the western banks slightly to avoid these hazards.

Dania Cut-Off Canal   The easterly mouth of Dania Cut-Off Canal makes into the Waterway's western flank at flashing daybeacon #35. Be sure to use the Dania Cut-Off Canal extension on chart 11467 when navigating this stream. Its greater detail gives a good picture of the water's general layout.

Enter the canal on its midwidth (don't cut either corner) and continue cruising west on the centerline. After you pass through an undeveloped section, the docks of Harbour Towne Marina will come abeam to the south, followed by Royale Palm Yacht Basin on the same shore. Playboy Marine Center and Derecktor-Gunnell Boat Yard line the northerly banks.

One shoal on the canal does call for extra caution. Unlighted nun buoy #2 should be passed strictly on its southerly side.

Further passage west on Dania Cut-Off Canal is no longer recommended by this writer for any but small power craft. The overhanging pipelines are too low for most larger vessels.

On the Waterway Farther to the south, the Waterway meets up with the Dania/Beach Boulevard bascule bridge. It has a closed vertical clearance of 22 feet and opens on demand.

South of the Dania span, the surrounding waters open out to the west. Stick strictly to the Waterway channel. As shown on chart 11467, 3- and 4-foot water lies west of the channel.

South of flashing daybeacon #39A the ICW soon ducks under the Sheridan Street/Hollywood Bridge. This span has a closed vertical clearance of 22 feet, and, thankfully, it opens on demand.

We no longer recommend anchorage in the charted coves north and south of the Sheridan bridge's easterly causeway. Depths have risen on both these false havens, and the southside cove is flanked by private docks.

Hollywood Marina Hollywood Marina will be spotted on the southern shores of North Lake, south of flashing daybeacon #40. Entry into Hollywood Marina is complicated by the presence of shoals and underwater "boulders" just north of the docks. Cruisers are strongly advised to stop at the outer fuel dock first, and get entrance instructions from the dockmaster.

Should the dockmaster not be on duty, enter the marina by continuing on the Waterway until you come abeam of the northerly tip of the fuel dock. Then cut 90 degrees to the west and point to pass the northern end of the fuel dock by some 15 yards (no farther) to your port side. As you

continue into the marina, hug the northerly tip of the docks. Stay as close to the piers as practical, without risk of collision.

South Lake Anchorage Enter South Lake anywhere within shouting distance of its centerline for good depths. In fair weather, you need only select any likely spot to drop the hook.

Cruisers bound for South Lake's sheltered westerly reaches should begin favoring the southern banks as they enter the narrower tongue of water extending west to the round basin anchorage. An uncharted shoal makes out from the northerly shoreline along this stretch. If depths start to rise, give way slightly to the south and see if soundings improve.

On the Waterway The Hollywood Boulevard Bridge spans the Waterway between North Lake and South Lake. This structure has a closed vertical clearance of 25 feet. Boats that cannot clear this height must contend with restricted opening times. This bridge opens only on the hour and half-hour from 10:00 A.M. to 6:00 P.M. between November 15 and May 15. During the rest of the year, the bridge is restricted only on weekends and holidays. During these times the hours between 9:00 A.M. and 7:00 P.M. see openings on the hour and half-hour, as well. Strong tidal currents have been noted near the span. Low-powered craft should wait well back from the bridge and away from other vessels.

The ICW channel south of the Hollywood Boulevard Bridge is perhaps the best example of "condo caverns" on the whole run from Fort Lauderdale to North

Miami. Towering developments overlook this entire section. At times it feels as if you are cruising between walls of concrete, glass, and steel.

The Hallandale Beach/State Road 824 span crosses the Waterway well south of unlighted daybeacon #42. This bridge has a closed vertical clearance of 22 feet and opens only on the quarter and three-quarter hour from 7:15 A.M. to 6:15 P.M. year round, seven days a week.

South of the State Road 824 bridge the entrances to Waterways Marina then Turnberry Isle Marina will come abeam along the western shoreline. Enter the Waterways connecting canal on its mid-width. Cruise west at idle speed. Eventually, the dockage complex will be sighted dead ahead, marked by an imitation lighthouse.

Turnberry Isle's entrance canal should also be entered by way of its midwidth. Eventually the stream turns to the south. The dockage basin will then open out to the east.

The Golden Beach/Dumfoundling Bay high-rise, fixed span crosses the ICW north of Dumfoundling Bay. Featuring a vertical clearance of 65 feet, this bridge need not concern Waterway cruisers. Don't you wish all the bridges between Fort Lauderdale and Miami were like this structure?

Dumfoundling Bay Anchorage   Except for the anchorage on Dumfoundling Bay discussed below, depths outside of the Waterway quickly give way to 3- and 4-foot readings. Watch for leeway and stay to the ICW channel north of unlighted daybeacon #55.

To reach the anchorage on Dumfoundling Bay, depart the Waterway once abeam of the charted channel leading west, well north of flashing daybeacon #49. Cruise east at idle speed, favoring the northern shore. Be sure to set the hook before reaching the charted shoal water at the rear of the cove.

Maule Lake Entrance   During times past, many a skipper has attempted to enter Maule Lake by cruising past (still) charted, unlighted daybeacon #2 (north of unlighted daybeacon #54) and then turning south into the northernmost canal leading to Maule Lake. Those following this errant procedure landed in 3-foot waters. Daybeacon #2 has now been replaced by a "Shoal" sign. Don't go anywhere near this marker.

Instead, leave the ICW south of #54 and cruise into the midwidth of the charted, northernmost canal cutting west to Maule Lake. Proceed strictly at idle speed! The passage parallels a large apartment complex on the southern shore, and numerous signs warn against throwing any wake.

As you enter Maule Lake itself, continue straight out into the wider water. Avoid the southern point at the end of the canal. A rocky shoal abuts this promontory.

Maule Lake is mostly deep, with the exception of some shoal water abutting the northern banks. Cruise southwest into the lake's midwaters before cutting west to the harbor. This procedure will avoid the charted finger of shallower water that stretches south from the northerly banks.

On the Waterway   The Sunny Isles Causeway Bridge lies south of unlighted daybeacon #57 and just north of the Oleta River intersection. This span has a closed vertical clearance of 30 feet. While most power craft can clear this bridge, sailors must still contend with a restricted opening schedule. Year round, the bridge opens on the quarter and three-quarter hour from 7:00 A.M. to 6:00 P.M. on weekdays. On weekends and holidays, the restricted hours are 10:00 A.M. to 6:00 P.M.

Approaching Bakers Haulover Inlet Southsoutheast of flashing daybeacon #60, switch to inset 2 of chart 11467. It is very important for navigators to use the greater detail of this blowup while cruising these difficult waters.

It's hard to overemphasize just how fast tidal currents can flow near Bakers Haulover. Be on maximum alert for leeway and expect to find different markings from those shown on the chart. This stretch has chronic shoaling problems, and markers on both the Waterway and the inlet approach channel are frequently shifted. There are no

more tricky waters than those adjacent to Haulover Inlet on the entire run from Fort Lauderdale to Miami.

After passing between flashing daybeacon #5 and unlighted daybeacon #4A, the Waterway cuts to the southwest. Southbound cruisers should pass all subsequent green, odd-numbered aids to navigation to their (the cruisers') port sides and take red markers to starboard. Very shallow water is found east of the channel between unlighted daybeacon #6A and unlighted daybeacon #11. Observe all markers scrupulously between #6A and #11.

Mariners bound for the Bakers Haulover Inlet should leave the Waterway abeam of flashing daybeacon #5. Follow the charted deep water along the eastern banks to the inlet's seaward passage. Stay about 50 yards from shore and you should have no difficulty short of the inlet. After that, you're on your own.

North Miami to Miami River

The southernmost waters of the eastern Florida ICW can make for an interesting cruise. The tall towers of downtown Miami and the once opulent hotels of Miami Beach are quite a sight from the water. If indeed the greater Miami region is not what it once was, it is also better than it used to be.

The waters of extreme southeasterly Florida also undergo a radical transformation from their northern counterparts. Gone are the sheltered passages from Palm Beach to North Miami. South of Bakers Haulover, the Waterway meets the headwaters of broad

Biscayne Bay. As the eastern Florida ICW runs on to its southerly path to Rickenbacker Causeway, the bay's waters become ever wider. South of Miami River, you can almost smell the cruising possibilities of the Keys beyond.

The Waterway channel is not the only route to explore in Miami. An alternate passage runs along Miami Beach's westerly shoreline. This well-defined channel can be safely followed to Government Cut Inlet. Along the way, visiting cruisers may choose to berth at one of the several hotel docks that serve the community of Miami Beach. It's quite an experience to stop for a night or two in this old resort. The grandeur of the past may have faded, but the name Miami Beach still conjures up an image of sun and fun from coast to coast. Three first-rate commercial marinas also provide considerable transient dockage and a whole range of other services for cruising craft on the alternate Miami Beach channel.

Miami River tracks its well-worn path inland from downtown Miami. While this cut is still far from prime cruising grounds, it can claim several repair facilities. This water body will be examined separately at the end of this chapter.

So-called Government Cut Inlet is one of the most reliable seaward passages in southeastern Florida. The channel is used regularly by large and not-so-large commercial freighters and cruise ships. Consequently, it is carefully maintained and well marked.

During the last decade, transient dockage has improved measurably in the greater Miami area. Several new marinas have combined with existing facilities to swell the ranks of transient slips. Security is very much a concern in this area, and visiting cruisers will want to be sure the marina they pick has a secure perimeter.

Miami teems with boatyards of all descriptions. Some are modern, reliable establishments that the visiting cruiser can use with confidence. Others are located at the other end of the proverbial stick.

Contrary to expectations, several anchorages are available near Miami and Miami Beach. The alternate channel leading to the beach lends access to any number of sheltered havens amid the small islands and causeways that line Biscayne Bay's midwidth. As yet, there seem to be no anchorage restrictions on these waters except those dictated by common sense and courtesy.

The waters of greater Miami undoubtedly comprise a real treat for first-time visitors to the Sunshine State. If you have never visited the city by water before, get ready for a totally different experience. Have the camera ready!

Miami

Miami is one of the largest cities in Florida. It is still the business center of southeastern Florida, but its prospects for the future are clouded by a crime problem that seems to go on unchecked. There was a day when Miami and its sister community, Miami Beach, were undoubtedly the leading cities in all of the Sunshine State. That time, however, now belongs to the past.

After its heyday, Miami suffered a period of urban blight, as did many cities in the United States. The name Miami was no longer synonymous with a pleasure resort. A rising crime rate and other problems caused tourists to abandon the city.

Happily, the story has now changed somewhat. Determined efforts by Miami's leaders fostered major changes in the 1980s and 1990s. New, ultramodern skyscrapers and hotels now look out over the city's waterfront. The waters of Biscayne Bay and Miami River are now vastly cleaner than they were only a few years ago. There is much evidence of a city getting back on its feet. While it still has a long way to go in regaining its glorious past, this great city is working to rekindle the dreams that once made the likes of Henry Flagler and Julia Tuttle quiver with anticipation.

Numbers to know in Miami:
Central Cab—305-532-5555
Metro Cab—305-888-8888

Budget Car Rental—305-871-2722
Alamo Rent A Car—305-633-4132
Premiere Car Rentals—305-254-2544
West Marine (8687 Coral Way)—
305-263-7465
West Marine (19407 S Dixie
Highway)—305-232-0811
West Marine (16215 Biscayne
Boulevard)—305-947-6333
Boat/US Marine Center—305-895-1870
Chamber of Commerce—305-350-7700

Miami History   For a city of its size and importance, it's strange to realize how recent a phenomenon is the rise of Miami. It really was not until the late nineteenth century when Flagler's marvelous railway arrived that Miami began to come into its own.

Ponce de Leon is credited with visiting the mangrove swamp that would one day become Miami in 1513. No other recorded instance of European exploration exists until 1565 when Menendez visited the region briefly while pursuing the French refugees from Fort Caroline.

In 1808 two brothers, John and James Egan, acquired a Spanish land grant along the northern banks of Miami River. Soon afterward the family of Jonathan and Polly Lewis settled south of the river.

All these private holdings were purchased by Richard Fitzpatrick of Key West in 1827. Until the Seminole wars, he grew cotton and sugarcane on the surrounding land. He also planted many guavas and tropical fruit trees.

By 1837 the Seminole wars had brought Fitzpatrick's small empire to an end. As part of the attempt to rout the Seminoles from their Everglades hideaways, the federal government built Fort Dallas on the shores of Miami River. Many of Fitzpatrick's prize fruit trees were cut down to afford a better view of any enemy approaching from the surrounding countryside.

In 1843 William F. English arrived at Fort Dallas to take over the Fitzpatrick holdings. We know he erected slave quarters in 1846, and it seems likely that English engaged in agricultural pursuits for at least three years thereafter. The Civil War ruined English and brought all development to an end.

As late as 1886 a "Florida directory gives the population of Miami as one hundred and fifty." It was not until the great freeze of 1895 that the determination of one settler was to start Miami on its rise to prominence.

Julia Tuttle emigrated to Fort Dallas sometime after 1890. Learning of Flagler's plans to extend his railroad to Palm Beach, the widow was tireless in her efforts to convince the great developer to extend the line to Florida's southernmost reaches. She was not successful until 1895 when all the orange trees around Palm Beach and points north were destroyed by a great freeze. Mrs. Tuttle sent Flagler a spray of fresh orange blossoms and induced the developer to visit Fort Dallas.

Julia Tuttle was a smart businesswoman. She donated much of her property to Flagler to help with the railway expansion. However, she craftily divided up the land in such a way that for Flagler to develop his share, he must first build roads and bridges through her holdings. It is fitting that the courage and resilience of this remarkable character are remembered today in the causeway across Biscayne Bay that bears her name.

The first train pulled into Miami on April 15, 1896. The city was finally incorporated as "Miami" later that year. The name was derived from an almost-forgotten local Indian tribe, and tradition asserts that it was suggested by Henry Flagler himself.

Seemingly, Miami has never looked back since those great events at the turn of the century. The city was the center of the great 1920s real-estate boom. The phenomenal development of Miami Beach across Biscayne Bay as an exclusive resort community was but one of the success stories of that happy era. Though many shared in this mammoth undertaking, George E. Merrick is perhaps best remembered for changing this once-desolate mangrove swamp into the teeming community we know today.

Indian Creek (Standard Mile 1080.5)

A narrow channel makes off to the south from Bakers Haulover Inlet into the northern portion of Indian Creek. If it were not for shoaling problems and several low, fixed bridges, this passage could serve as a means to reach the Miami Beach alternate channel. As it is, northern Indian Creek can only be traversed by small craft.

The main branch of Indian Creek serves as the principal Miami Beach waterfront. This body of water can be reached via an alternate channel paralleling the beach, detailed below.

Miami Beach Channel, Anchorages, and Facilities (Standard Mile 1082) (Various Lats/Lons—see below)

South of Broad Causeway bascule bridge, pleasure boats that can clear two 35-foot fixed bridges may follow an alternate channel southeast and then south from unlighted daybeacon #16 to the Miami Beach waterfront and eventually to Government Cut Inlet. Even if you can't clear the fixed bridges, there are several anchorages and marinas, north of the spans, that are accessible to any cruising craft drawing 5½ feet or less. The entire Miami Beach Channel is fairly well marked and offers several anchorages along the way. Minimum depths are 5½ to 6 feet, with most of the route sounding in the 7- to 10-foot range. This passage provides a closeup view of the heavy residential and commercial development along the western shores of Miami Beach.

The first available anchorage will be found

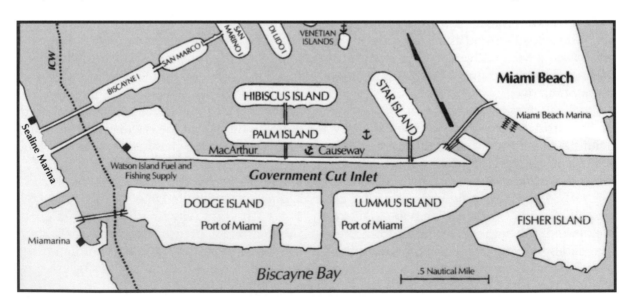

on the charted finger of deep water north of Biscayne Point, near 25 51.955 North/080 08.258 West. Boats up to 45 feet can drop the hook here with excellent protection from southern and easterly winds. Hard blows from the north or west could make for a very bumpy evening. The anchorage is surrounded by heavy residential development. While it's far from isolated, this is a good spot to ride out the night, provided the fickle wind chooses to cooperate.

After passing through the shoal-plagued stretch of the Miami Beach Channel between unlighted daybeacon #8 and the 25-foot bascule span of the 79th Street Causeway, cruisers will come upon Grand View Palace Marina on the eastern shores of Treasure Island, just south of the bridge near 25 50.895 North/080 08.667 West. This location is noted as facility designation #90 on chart 11467. It can also be reached by boats cruising north on the Miami Beach Channel from Government Cut Inlet. Of course, this southerly approach demands that captains pass under the MacArthur and Julia Tuttle 35-foot fixed bridges spanning the channel between Government Cut and Treasure Island.

Transients are accepted at the harbor's fixed, concrete piers. Depths alongside run 6 feet or better. The harbor is somewhat open to strong southerly winds, but it is protected to the east, west, and north. Full power, water, cable-television, and telephone connections are on hand, as are showers and a full Laundromat. Gasoline and diesel fuel can be purchased. The marina features 24-hour security, a feature now very important for Miami-area facilities.

Grand View's dockage basin is overlooked by a huge, high-rise condo. A small arcade shopping center is found on the ground floor of this structure, featuring a dry cleaner, video-rental dealership, and delicatessen.

Cruising visitors are welcomed at the complex's heated swimming pool, Jacuzzi, and fitness center. You will probably want to take a taxi to visit any of the many Miami or Miami Beach restaurants.

Grand View Palace Marina (305) 861-5343

Approach depths—7-8 feet
Dockside depths—6 feet (minimum)
Accepts transients—yes
Transient dockage rate—average
Fixed concrete piers—yes
Dockside power connections—30 and 50 amps
Dockside water connections—yes
Showers—yes
Laundromat—yes
Gasoline—yes
Diesel fuel—yes
Restaurant—taxi ride necessary

Miami Beach Waterfront

South of the 79th Street Causeway Bridge, the Miami Beach Channel turns to the east.

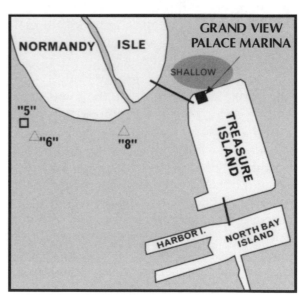

By departing the main cut at La Gorce Island, and then tracking your way first east and then south on Indian Creek, you will discover the older downtown Miami Beach facilities along this stream's easterly banks.

What can one say about Miami Beach today? To be sure, the community still has an active tourist and convention industry. But undeniably modern Miami Beach has certainly lost something of those days in the 1920s and again in the 1950s when it vied with Palm Beach as the most prestigious seaside resort in Florida.

Reminders do remain of those glorious days. The Fontainbleau Hotel still looks proudly over the ocean, and chic shops continue to crowd the various boulevards. Still, there is no denying that the prestige of past times is now wanting. Visitors today will find a much less exuberant community than the Miami Beach of the past several decades.

For cruisers, the Miami Beach waterfront facilities are low-key indeed. In fact, they consist of mostly unattended docks. These berths can be reserved through the various hotels. The piers are in only fair condition. No fueling or repair services are available anywhere on the principal waterfront.

As you move from north to south, beginning at the intersection with the small canal leading to Surprise Lake, you will find the Wyndham Resort docks, followed by those of Eden Roc, the Fontainbleau, and finally the Best Western Beach Resort. The Best Western docks are the smallest of the lot and no longer accept any transients. All these piers are located side by side, and it's often difficult to tell one from the other. If you wish to berth at any of these facilities, be sure to call ahead and make reservations with the hotel of your choice.

Wyndham Resort Docks (786) 234-0184

Approach depths—7-10 feet
Dockside depths—7 feet
Accepts transients—hotel patrons only
Transient dockage rate—above average
Fixed piers—yes
Dockside power connections—30
    and 50 amps
Dockside water connections—yes

Eden Roc Docks (305) 531-0000

Approach depths—7-10 feet
Dockside depths—7 feet
Transient dockage rate—above average
Accepts transients—hotel patrons only
Fixed piers—yes
Dockside power connections—30
    and 50 amps
Dockside water connections—yes

Fontainbleau Docks (305) 538-2000

Approach depths—7-10 feet
Dockside depths—7-8 feet
Accepts transients—yes
Transient dockage rate—above average
Fixed piers—yes
Dockside power connections—30
    and 50 amps
Dockside water connections—yes

Miami Beach Channel to Government Cut (Various Lats/Lons—see below)

The alternate Miami Beach passage continues south past the Julia Tuttle and Venetian causeways via a mostly well marked channel. Vertical clearance is set by the 35-foot fixed bridge spanning the eastern end of Julia Tuttle Causeway.

Sunset Harbour Yacht Club (formerly Sunset Harbor Marina) is located between the Julia Tuttle and Venetian Causeway spans, near 25 47.716 North/080 08.729 West. This facility is just finishing up a major rebuilding and expansion as this account is being written.

Without a doubt, what was already a first-class pleasure-craft facility will soon become a world-class marina. Unfortunately, no one has been able to give us any definite information about services and rates at this time. So, in light of our long-standing policy of not reporting on marinas until we can see them for ourselves, we will have nothing further to say about Sunset Harbour in this edition. However, we strongly suggest that those seeking dockage in the Miami region call (305) 673-0044 and check on the latest guest-slip availability at this facility. It's virtually certain that long before the next edition of this guidebook finds its way to the newsstands, Sunset Harbour will once again be offering the very best that the cruising community can expect. We also suggest you subscribe to our on-line newsletter the *Salty Southeast* (subscription instructions are in the introduction of this guidebook), for updates on the evolving situation at Sunset Harbour.

South of the Venetian Causeway Bridge, several anchorages are available for cruising craft. Boats can anchor northeast of the small island marked "Monument," south-southeast of Rivo Alto Island, near 25 47.186 North/080 09.102 West. BE SURE to set the hook well east of the marked cable area and north of the shoal water abutting the island's eastern banks. Depths run around 7 feet, and there should be enough swinging room for craft up to 35 feet. Protection is good in southerly winds but inadequate in strong northern or westerly breezes. The island itself is undeveloped, except for a series of curious concrete statues that have been much vandalized.

It is also quite possible for boats of almost any size to anchor between the eastern tip of Palm Island and the western shores of Star Island in some 6 to 7 feet of water near 25

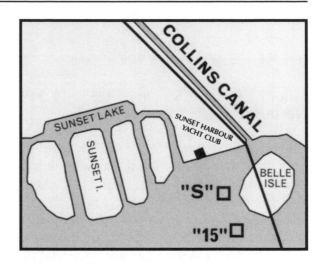

46.601 North/080 09.269 West. This spot is well sheltered from all winds save northerly blows. Palm Island to the west is heavily developed with private homes.

Probably the most sheltered haven in this area is found on the charted deep water between MacArthur Causeway and Palm Island, near 25 46.618 North/080 09.571 West. The waters east-southeast of the charted, low-level fixed bridge afford depths of 6 to 9 feet. Craft up to 40 feet should have enough elbowroom, and protection should be sufficient to ride out any foul weather short of a full gale. The causeway presents treelined shores to the south, while houses lie side by side on Palm Island to the north.

Cruising craft of most any size drawing 6 feet or less can cruise west from the Miami Beach Channel, on both sides of the Venetian Causeway, and rejoin the Waterway route bordering the principal Miami waterfront. These marinas will be covered along with the city waterfront later in this chapter.

South of MacArthur Causeway Bridge, the alternate Miami Beach Channel rushes to join Government Cut. After cruisers pass under the

35-foot fixed MacArthur Causeway span, one of the finest marinas in the greater Miami region comes abeam to the northeast.

Miami Beach Marina (25 46.244 North/080 08.383 West

Miami Beach Marina is a world-class pleasure-craft facility that features 400 wet slips plus 1,000 feet of floating docks specifically intended for smaller craft. Skippers of these fleet vessels are encouraged to stop for a day, or even an hour or two while dining at Monty's Restaurant or shopping at the marina stores.

Miami Beach Marina has always been in a most advantageous location hard by the entrance to Government Cut Inlet. Cruisers putting to sea through the inlet, or those entering from the briny blue, can prepare for or rest from their journeys at Miami Beach Marina's breakwater-enclosed harbor, without having to worry about any bridges or even the ICW channel.

Transients are eagerly accepted at Miami Beach Marina's fixed, concrete piers and concrete-decked, floating docks (for smaller craft). The harbor's breakwater effectively shelters the slips from foul weather and a majority of the swift tidal currents that regularly sweep in and out of Government Cut. Skippers should still be on guard against these swiftly moving waters as they approach the harbor.

All slips feature 30- and 50-amp power (plus fresh-water) connections and a few berths have 100-amp hookups as well. Cable-television and telephone connections are also on hand. Miami Beach Marina now features wireless Internet service. Air-conditioned showers and open-air Laundromats are available at three locations throughout the complex. Security, particularly at night, is carefully maintained. Gasoline and diesel can

be purchased at the fuel pier. While the marina does not directly employ any technicians, mechanical repairs can usually be arranged through independent contractors. Visiting cruisers are welcome at the on-site, heated swimming pool.

Hungry cruisers berthed at Miami Beach Marina are in luck. The on-site Monty's Restaurant (305-858-1431) seems to serve excellent cuisine.

The shopping complex behind the basin's center section is filled with interesting stores. Scuba divers will discover a full-service dive shop in the complex. Mariners will certainly want to check out the Hopkins Carter Marine store (305-534-0300). This shop's vast selection of nautical hardware, publications, and charts is the envy of any other ship's store in Miami.

By all accounts, don't miss Neam's Market (305-538-3500). This combination delicatessen, gourmet food store, bakery, and wine shop is enough to put a shine in any true cook's eyes. Don't miss the seafood and butcher bars—the selections during our last visit were outstanding and made for a memorable evening meal later in our galley.

We are reminded of that old television commercial that with adjustment might say, "If you can find a better marina, stay there." Certainly, there are few other marinas in the greater Miami region that can lay claim to so many positive attributes.

Miami Beach Marina (305) 673-6000
   http://www.miamibeachmarina.com/

Approach depths—5½ to
   6 feet (minimum via northerly approach)
   15+ feet (via Government Cut Inlet)
Dockside depths—10-17 feet
Accepts transients—yes
Transient dockage rate—above average

Floating concrete piers—yes
  (for smaller vessels)
Fixed concrete piers—yes
Dockside power connections—30,
  50, and (a few) 100 amps
Dockside water connections—yes
Showers—yes
Laundromat—yes
Gasoline—yes
Diesel fuel—yes
Mechanical repairs—yes
  (independent contractors)
Ship' store—yes (in shopping complex)
Restaurant—on site

Miami's Causeways

Cruisers studying the various channels south of Broad Causeway will quickly note five causeways crossing the bay between the mainland and the eastern islands. Three of these remarkable spans are partially comprised of a series of heavily developed, artificial islands. It's easy to see from the chart that these landmasses are unnatural, but from the water they appear as small islands that have every right to be there. Actually, these isles are some of the most valued real-estate property in greater Miami. As chart 11467 indicates, deep water surrounds most of the various land bodies, and careful mariners are free to take a closer inspection. Please don't abuse the privilege by trespassing!

Miami ICW Route and Facilities (Various Lats/Lons—see below)

The well-marked ICW passage continues south through the ever-widening waters of Biscayne Bay, past the Miami waterfront. From the 79th Street Causeway to Rickenbacker Causeway, the Waterway hugs the mainland shore and affords a good view of downtown Miami. Along the way, several facilities are available to cruising craft.

Small Keystone Point Marina (25 53.833 North/080 09.528 West, Standard Mile 1081) is reached by a long cruise down the marked channel leading west from unlighted daybeacon #12. Just before encountering the mainland shore, the cut turns north and leads to New Arch Creek. A mile cruise down this arrow-straight stream is still necessary to reach the marina.

Keystone accepts transients (but not liveaboards) at fixed, wooden piers. Depths in the harbor are an impressive 8 feet or better, but some 5-foot approach depths in New Arch Creek may be a bit skimpy for particularly long legged vessels. Fresh water and 30- and 50-amp power connections are available, and both gasoline and diesel fuel can be purchased dockside. Mechanical repairs (gas and diesel) are offered and boats can be hauled with a 70-ton travelift.

Keystone Point Marina (305) 940-6236

Approach depths—5-10 feet
Dockside depths—8-20 feet
Accepts transients—yes
Transient dockage rate—below average
Fixed wooden piers—yes
**Dockside power connections—30
  and 50 amps**
Dockside water connections—yes
Gasoline—yes
Diesel fuel—yes
Below-waterline repairs—yes
Mechanical repairs—yes

Miami Facilities (Various Lats/Lons—see below)

South of flashing daybeacon #48, a charted, pile-marked channel making off to the west leads to our favorite facility in mainland Miami, near 25 47.454 North/080 11.070 West. Sealine Marina, located just east of the mammoth Biscayne Marriott Hotel (305-374-3900), is an absolutely first-rate facility. The harbor is enclosed by a concrete breakwater for superior protection. Transients are accepted at the Sealine's fixed concrete piers (with fixed wooden finger piers). Low-tide soundings in the approach channel run 6 to 9 feet, with 8 feet or more of water in the dockage basin. Fresh water and 30- and 50-amp power connections are on hand. Spotless showers and a Laundromat are available on the docks, saving nautical visitors a hike up to the hotel. Gasoline and diesel fuel are once again available. A ship's and variety store is perched out on the docks. Twenty-four-hour security is also provided.

Should you have the yearning to spend a night or two ashore, and your wallet can stand the pressure, the adjacent Marriott Hotel is luxurious. Here you will also find three restaurants and a shopping arcade on the ground floor. Cruisers in search of galley supplies will be glad to learn that a nice deli and gourmet grocery store is located among these firms.

> **Sealine Marina (305) 377-3625**
> **http://www.sealinemarina.com**
>
> **Approach depths—6-9 feet**
> **Dockside depths—8-10 feet**
> **Accepts transients—yes**
> **Transient dockage rate—above average**
> **Fixed concrete piers—yes**
> **Dockside power connections—30**
> ** and 50 amps**
> **Dockside water connections—yes**
> **Showers—yes**
> **Laundromat—yes**
> **Gasoline—yes**
> **Diesel fuel—yes**
> **Ship's and variety store—yes**
> **Restaurant—three on site**

A deep passage strikes east between the Venetian Causeway and MacArthur Causeway bridges. Initially, the passage borders on the shores of Watson Island to the south. As the shores drop away, passing cruisers will note the small piers of Miami Yacht Club on the isle's shoreline. To quote one member, this is a "workingman's yacht club." Even though we found the members to be unfailingly friendly, there are no transient services available.

The southern terminus of this cove is occupied by Miami Outboard Club. The organization maintains docks near the charted "MKR" on the western end of MacArthur Causeway. Again, cruising skippers will not find any facilities at this club.

The old Miami city marina, rebuilt and renamed a few years ago as Miamarina (25 46.740 North/080 11.107 West, Standard Mile 1089.5), is located in the charted, dredged harbor on the mainland shore, south of the Dodge Island bridges (west of flashing daybeacon #53). Entrance and interior depths run from 9 to 11 feet. Quite frankly, we only advise stopping here while shopping or dining at the adjacent Bayside shopping complex.

Government Cut Inlet (Standard Mile 1089)

Three channels converge east of Lummus Island at Government Cut Inlet. The first is the Miami Beach route already considered earlier in this chapter. The second is the principal Government Cut passage, north of Lummus and Dodge islands, while the third is a wide, marked channel flanking Dodge and Lummus islands to the south. While the northside ("second") channel is still probably the easiest to follow, the route south of Lummus and Dodge islands can also be used with confidence by visiting cruisers.

Be advised that following the September 2001 atrocities, pleasure-craft traffic on the second (middle) channel has been sometimes restricted. This stricture has created a burden for pleasure craft, as this is the most direct route to Government Cut Inlet. It's very unclear at the time of this writing whether some or none of these restrictions will be in place by the time of your arrival. Watch for warning signs, and check at one of the local marinas for the latest.

Government Cut Inlet itself is one of the most reliable seaward passages on Florida's east coast. The channel is used daily by large and medium-sized oceangoing freighters, not to mention more than a few huge cruise ships.

BAKERS HAULOVER TO GOVERNMENT CUT INLET NAVIGATION

Successful navigation of eastern Florida's southernmost waters is certainly no walk in the park. Strong tidal currents regularly scour the regional channels and can play havoc with slow-moving trawlers and sailcraft under auxiliary power. Shoaling is a constant problem along some stretches of the ICW, and shallow water flanks a good portion of the Waterway passage. All captains should be on guard against being swept into the various bridges across the channel.

Speaking of bridges, most (though not all) of the spans crossing the various passages in greater Miami have restricted opening schedules. Again, it would be better to allow extra time in your cruising plans rather than become frustrated at the delays.

Remember also that the fixed Julia Tuttle Causeway Bridge, with a vertical clearance of 56 feet, sets the height clearance for the inland run from Fort Lauderdale to Miami. Sailcraft that need more clearance will have to make the offshore run from Port Everglades Inlet to Government Cut.

No-wake zones are also a very frequent companion on the run south. The alternate Miami Beach cut is particularly plagued with speed regulations. A good rule of thumb is to slow down and proceed at idle speed whenever you see craft docked within the reach of your wake, even if you don't see a "No-Wake" sign. Remember, you are legally responsible for any damage caused by your wake, whether or not you are in a regulated speed zone.

Northern Indian Creek   Chart 11467 shows a small, unmarked channel leading south from Bakers Haulover into the northern reaches of Indian Creek. This cut carries minimum 5-foot depths but the northerly section of Indian Creek, to which it leads, is blocked by a low-level (12 feet), fixed bridge.

Another channel cuts northwest from the northern mouth of Indian Creek and rejoins the ICW between flashing daybeacon #9 and unlighted daybeacon #11. While local cruisers use this channel regularly, it is unmarked and borders on a large shoal to the north. Visiting mariners would be better served by following the Waterway.

On the Waterway   Moving south from Bakers Haulover Inlet, captains are immediately treated to yet another problem-plagued stretch. Between flashing daybeacon #5 and Broad Causeway, shoaling along the Waterway is a constant problem. Tidal currents run very swiftly through these waters, and it is a constant challenge to stay in the channel. This entire run has been designated a no-wake zone, possibly in an effort to help preserve the precarious channel. Proceed at idle speed, keep a weather eye on the sounder, and maintain a supersharp watch for leeway.

Because of the bottom strata's changeable nature along this portion of the ICW, you can expect to find any number of new markers not shown on chart 11467. We usually find several additional daybeacons during our cruises through this stretch, but these markers will undoubtedly be changed by the time you read this account. Our best advice is to observe the usual ICW color scheme of aids to navigation, with southbound craft passing green aids to their (the cruisers') port sides and taking red beacons to starboard.

New Arch Creek   The channel cutting west to New Arch Creek leaves the ICW at unlighted daybeacon #12. This route runs first west, and then turns north-northeast, paralleling the westerly banks. North of unlighted daybeacon #16, you will again turn to the west while passing through the mouth of New Arch Creek. Most of this route is straightforward and easily run for boats drawing less than 4½ feet. When rounding the point into the creek, don't slip to the north or east. Shallow water lies in the broad waters outside of the channel.

On the ICW   South-southwest of unlighted daybeacon #13, the ICW exchanges greetings with the Broad Causeway Bridge. This span opens on the quarter and three-quarter hour from 8:00 A.M. to 6:00 P.M. year round, seven days a week. With the bridge's closed vertical clearance of 32 feet, most powercraft will not have to worry with an opening.

West of unlighted daybeacon #16, a charted, well-defined channel leads in to a yacht club on the mainland shore. There are no services available for visitors, and most cruising craft should probably keep clear.

Alternate Miami Beach Passage   Let us depart for a moment from our discussion of the Miami ICW to review the alternate Miami Beach Channel. Coverage of the Waterway will resume following our review of the beach route.

From unlighted daybeacon #16, navigators can follow the large, charted bubble of deep water southeast to Biscayne Point. Be sure to avoid the finger of shallow water marked by flashing daybeacon #2. Come abeam and pass #2 to its easterly side.

Cruisers bound for the anchorage north of Biscayne Point should work their way east along the finger of land leading to the point, keeping the point's northerly shoreline about 75 yards to starboard. As correctly shown on chart 11467, very shallow water lies to the north.

To continue on toward Miami Beach, cruise through the marked and dredged cut leading to Normandy Isle. Pass unlighted daybeacons #4 and #6 to their easterly sides and take unlighted daybeacons #3 and #5 to their westerly quarters.

Once abeam of Normandy Isle's northwestern corner, continue cruising south around the shoreline. Be sure to pass east of unlighted daybeacon #8. From #8, begin a slow turn to the southeast, pointing eventually for the pass through in the 79th Street Causeway's easterly, bascule span.

The channel between Normandy Isle and the 79th Street bascule bridge is one of the most shoal-plagued portions of this alternate route. If your craft draws more than 4½ feet, you would do well to wait for high or at least midtide before transiting this part of the cut.

Cruisers studying chart 11467 may notice a charted channel striking east from the northern shores of Normandy Isle. Avoid this cut. Several large, unmarked shoals render this so-called channel much too tricky for larger boats.

The 79th Street Causeway's eastern bascule span has a closed vertical clearance of 25 feet and, wonder of wonders, it opens on demand. Cruisers attempting to call this bridge via their VHF radios should be sure to specify the *eastern* 79th Street Causeway bridge. A westerly portion of this causeway crosses the ICW, and the similarities in names can be confusing.

Just beyond the bridge, Grand View Palace Marina will come abeam to the southwest. Enter the marina by way of its entrance through the protecting breakwater. Don't slip to the south. Shallow water lies off the basin's southeastern tip.

The main channel continues to curve around Normandy Isle. Stay about 100 yards south of the Normandy Isle shoreline in this section. Unlike the passage farther north, some shallow water does abut this shoreline. Pass between flashing daybeacon #11 and unlighted daybeacon #10, as the channel curves again to the south. Stay away from #10 and the next southerly aid to navigation, unlighted daybeacon #12. Both these aids to navigation are founded in shoal water. Pass well northeast of #10 and well east of #12.

Once abeam of unlighted daybeacon #10, you must decide whether to continue straight ahead into Indian Creek, which provides access to the Miami Beach waterfront, or turn south towards Government Cut Inlet. The channel leading to the inlet has a vertical clearance limit of 35 feet set by two fixed bridges. One spans the gap on the easterly end of Julia Tuttle Causeway, while the other connects MacArthur Causeway and Miami Beach.

Indian Creek and Miami Beach Favor the LaGorce Island shore heavily as you cruise into Indian Creek to avoid the charted patch of 4-foot water. East of this trouble spot, good depths open out almost from the shore to shore.

Use the easterly passage while cruising past Allison Island. The westerly cut is blocked by a low-level fixed span. The east-side channel is also crossed by a bridge, this one a bascule span (11-foot closed vertical clearance) that opens on demand.

As you come abeam of Allison Island's northern tip, begin favoring the eastern shoreline. Chart 11467 correctly identifies several shallow patches along the western banks.

Soon the various hotel face docks will come up along the easterly shoreline. Hopefully you will have made advance arrangements as these piers are mostly unattended.

Cruisers leaving the Miami Beach waterfront will be obliged to retrace their steps by the route just described. The small channel running west by way of Surprise Lake and shallow Collins Canal are both blocked by low-level, fixed bridges with only enough clearance for small outboards.

South to Government Cut by the Miami Beach Channel   Navigation of the Miami Beach Channel south to Julia Tuttle Causeway is fairly simple. A series of unlighted but well-placed daybeacons marks shallower water to the west.

Between unlighted daybeacons #22 and #24, the channel cuts briefly to the west-southwest before ducking south into a marked, improved channel flowing through the fixed bridge associated with Julia Tuttle Causeway. Pass unlighted daybeacon #25 to your immediate port side as you enter the bridge channel.

The Julia Tuttle-Miami Beach Channel fixed span has a vertical clearance of 35 feet and sets the overhead height clearance for the passage to Government Cut Inlet. Don't attempt the charted channel paralleling the northern side of Julia Tuttle Causeway and eventually running west to the ICW! This passage is unmarked, shoal in places, and borders on very shallow water.

Once through the Julia Tuttle bridge, point to come abeam and pass unlighted daybeacon #26 to its fairly immediate easterly side. South of #26, good depths again spread out in a far broader band. Shallow water still lies to the west, however.

The broadening channel escorts cruisers south to the northern shores of Belle Isle. Along the way, the enclosed dockage basin of Sunset Harbour Yacht Club will be sighted south of unlighted daybeacon #28. You may alternately reach this facility by way of the marked channel running along the northerly flank of Venetian Causeway. This route will be covered in the next section of this chapter.

A low-level fixed span (vertical clearance, 6 feet) crosses from Belle Isle to Miami Beach, but a bascule bridge spans the gap between Belle and Rivo Alto isles. Two unlighted daybeacons lead to this latter span. Come abeam of unlighted daybeacon #30 to its easterly side and continue on course for some 25 yards. Then, turn sharply west and point to pass unlighted daybeacon #15 to its southerly quarter. Soon the Venetian Causeway Bridge will come abeam to the south. Turn 90 degrees to the south and point for the bridge's central pass through.

The Miami Beach Channel/Venetian Causeway bascule bridge has a closed vertical clearance of 9 feet and a restricted opening schedule. Monday through Friday, from November 1 to April 30, the span is closed from 7:15 A.M. to 8.45 A.M. and again from 4:45 P.M. to 6:15 P.M., except for openings at 7:45 A.M., 8:15 A.M., 5:15 P.M. and 5:45 P.M. Otherwise, this bridge opens on demand.

Miami Beach Anchorages   South of Venetian Causeway, a wide swath of good depths spreads out over most of the waters north of MacArthur Causeway. Cruising craft bound for the small anchorage northeast of "Monument Island" should be careful to avoid the charted shoal east and south of this landmass. Stay well north of unlighted daybeacon #2. Work your way around to the northeastern tip of Monument Island, staying some 50 yards off the island's shores. Drop anchor well east of the charted cable area.

Two other anchorages near Palm Island are accessible by turning west off the main Miami Beach Channel and passing some 50 yards north of Monument Island.

Continue on the same track for some 100 yards west of this landmass. Then, turn sharply to the south, and follow the deep water to a point some 75 to 100 yards east of Palm Island's easterly tip. Long-legged craft should be on guard against the small, correctly charted patch of 5-foot waters off the isle's northeastern shores. In all but stormy weather, you can drop anchor off Palm Island's easterly reaches. For even more shelter, track your way south between Palm Island and MacArthur Causeway. Drop your hook east of the low-level fixed bridge.

On to Government Cut Cruisers bound for Miami Beach Marina or Government Cut Inlet should simply cruise under the MacArthur Causeway 35-foot fixed bridge. Watch to the southwest immediately after leaving the bridge behind and you will quickly spot the Causeway Island Coast Guard Base. Miami Beach Marina's lengthy concrete breakwater will quickly come abeam to the northeast.

Cruisers entering Miami Beach Marina should be ready for swift tidal currents as they approach the breakwater entrance. Once inside the basin, the water movement is lessened by the concrete barriers.

Southeast of the marina, a broad, deep passage soon leads to Government Cut Inlet. It should be noted that skippers cruising on the ICW can alternately make their way to Miami Beach Marina by way of the Government Cut approach channel.

We will now turn our attention to the Miami ICW. The Government Cut approach channel will be reviewed in this section.

ICW to Miami Moving south on the eastern Florida ICW, where we left the Waterway at unlighted daybeacon #16 (to begin our coverage of the Miami Beach Channel), the channel is narrow but well marked and mostly straightforward to the 79th Street Causeway Bridge.

Observe all markers carefully along the way, and don't become confused by the private daybeacons marking several side channels. One of these private passages cuts west from unlighted daybeacon #16, and another is found west of the gap between unlighted daybeacons #20 and #21.

At flashing daybeacon #26, the Waterway takes a sharp turn to the south and soon approaches the 79th Street Causeway bascule bridge. This span has a closed vertical clearance of 25 feet, but it opens on demand.

Between the 79th Street and Julia Tuttle causeway bridges, the Waterway borders on 2- and 3-foot waters for much of its length. Stick to the marked cut and keep a sharp watch for leeway.

The charted channel at unlighted daybeacon #29 allows access to a private yacht club on the mainland shore. There are no services available for transients. Don't confuse this cut's marking with the Waterway's daybeacons.

The bridge spanning the gap between the mainland and Julia Tuttle Causeway is a fixed span with a 56-foot vertical clearance. As noted earlier, this bridge sets the height limit for the Waterway channel between Fort Lauderdale and Miami.

Don't attempt to cruise east on the charted channel north of Julia Tuttle Causeway to the Miami Beach Channel.

This cut is unmarked and has shoaled severely in several places.

South of the Julia Tuttle bridge, the ICW continues to cut a path through shoal water to Venetian Causeway. Switch to inset 3 of chart 11467 for navigating the waters between Venetian Causeway and Claughton Island.

Just north of the Venetian Causeway Bridge, mariners can pick their way east through a broad, marked swath of deep water, all the way to the Miami Beach Channel. Eastbound craft on this cut should pass all red, even-numbered aids to navigation to their (the markers') northerly sides, and take green beacons to their southerly quarters. Be sure to avoid any northerly slippage while traversing this channel. The waters to the north are shoal and pocked with old pilings. The route intersects the Miami Beach passage at unlighted daybeacon #30. At this point, you may cut north to Sunset Harbour Yacht Club (north of unlighted daybeacon #28), or turn south and follow the Miami Beach Channel to Miami Beach Marina and/or Government Cut Inlet, as described above.

Back on the main ICW channel, the Venetian Causeway Bridge crosses the ICW south of flashing daybeacon #49. Would you believe that it has a restricted opening schedule? Just kidding! From Monday to Friday, November 1 through April 30, this bridge opens only on the hour and half-hour 7:00 A.M. to 9:00 A.M. and again from 4:30 P.M. to 6:30 P.M. The span has a closed vertical clearance of a mere 8 feet, so most cruising-size craft will have to contend with these limiting hours. To avoid long delays, plan your cruise around this schedule.

Captains should be on maximum alert for strong tidal currents while waiting for the Venetian Causeway Bridge. Low-powered craft may have a difficult time staying in the channel and avoiding other boats.

The fixed high-rise MacArthur Causeway Bridge spans the ICW just a stone's throw south of the Venetian span.

Government Cut Inlet   The principal channel leading to Government Cut Inlet cuts a bold path to the east, south of MacArthur Causeway. This channel is wide and easily followed, though it usually features some swift currents. Watch to the south as you traverse the cut's length and you will have a good view of the Miami commercial port facilities. Continue on the well-marked passage between the charted jetties out to sea. As you are now headed toward the open sea, all red markers should be passed to your port side and green aids taken to starboard.

Please remember that some security regulations might or might not be in effect on the channel described above at the time of your arrival. Watch carefully for warning signs, and just to be sure, check at one of the local marinas about current regulations.

Cruisers continuing south on the ICW should come abeam of flashing daybeacon #50 to its easterly side. The channel now turns to the south-southwest and quickly approaches the twin Dodge Island highway and railway bridges. The highway span is a fixed structure with 65 feet of vertical clearance. The railway bridge (22 feet closed vertical clearance) is usually open unless a train is due. South of the Dodge Island bridges, the entrance to Miamarina will come abeam to the west.

Continuing south on the Waterway, point to pass flashing daybeacon #53 to its westerly quarter. Set course to pass well west of unlighted daybeacon #53A and flashing daybeacon #55. Stay away from #53A. This aid is founded in shoal water.

South-southeast of #55, use your binoculars to identify the next ICW aid to navigation, unlighted daybeacon #57. The markers cutting west-southwest to Miami River, and those striking east-northeast to Government Cut Inlet, can cause confusion.

A second inlet approach channel runs east on the southern flanks of Dodge and Lummus islands. Navigators who carefully study chart 11467 (inset 3) should be able to reach Government Cut by way of this route with a good measure of confidence.

To reach the alternate inlet approach channel, leave the ICW just north of unlighted daybeacon #57. Cut to the east-northeast pointing to come abeam of flashing daybeacon #17 to its northerly side, while passing flashing daybeacon #18 and unlighted daybeacon #16 to their southerly side.

From a position north of #17, the broad channel cuts to the east-southeast. Point to come abeam of flashing daybeacon #15 well to its northerly side. Continued navigation to the east falls under the category of remembering our old red-right-returning rule. As you are now headed toward the sea, pass all red markers to your port side and take all green aids to starboard. Eventually, the alternate channel joins up with the main Government Cut Inlet passage at the eastern tip of Lummus Island.

West-southwest of unlighted daybeacon #57, the Miami River channel makes into the ICW's westerly flank.

Miami River (Standard Mile 1090)

First the good news: Miami River is today considerably cleaner than it was just a few years ago. Most of the sunken derelicts that once lined the channel have been removed, and passing cruisers will see little evidence of the unmentionable boat junkyards that once lined this sad stream. Today, a collection of boatyards and service facilities of all descriptions lines both banks of the river. Some are found as much as 4 miles upstream from the ICW intersection. Many are fine, well-managed facilities that mariners can use with full confidence. Others are not so reliable.

Minimum depths of 10 feet can be expected on the river itself. The stream's two major auxiliary waters, South Fork and Tamiami Canal, hold depths in the 6- to 8-foot region.

The other side of the coin must also be acknowledged. In spite of the recent improvements, most skippers and their galley slaves will find a cruise on the waters of Miami River less than visually appealing. Certain portions of the river still border on shores where you fervently hope that your boat does not break down.

All in all, a visit to Miami River, particularly the easterly section of the stream, is a good idea for those who need service work. There is even one facility at the river's mouth that offers transient dockage. Call ahead of time and have arrangements made with the yard of your choice for the particular repairs you need.

The following account does not pretend to present an exhaustive list of the various service establishments on Miami River. That task would just about require a book of its own. Rather, we will present brief accounts of those facilities that struck this writer as worthy of mention. Don't be surprised when you visit to find many boatyards and marinas in addition to those discussed below.

The face-style docks of Dupont Plaza Hotel and Marina flank the river's northern shore just inside the river's easterly entrance, near 25 46.204 North/080 11.332 West. These piers are located under the watchful glance of the ultramodern, high-rise Dupont Hotel. The Dupont accepts transients and offers berths at fixed, concrete piers with fresh water and 30-50-amp power connections. The adjacent hotel features a full dining room with Continental and American food.

Swift tidal currents plague the easterly section of Miami River, and docking at the height of the ebb and flood can be tricky indeed. Take care as you approach the docks, and be ready for the strong tidal flow.

Dupont Plaza Hotel and Marina
(305) 358-2541

Approach depths—10-12 feet
Dockside depths—10-11 feet
Accepts transients—yes
Transient dockage rate—above average
Fixed concrete piers—yes
Dockside power connections—30
and 50 amps
Dockside water connections—yes
Restaurant—on site

Norseman Shipbuilding Corporation (305-545-6815) will come abeam on the southern banks west of the Northwest 5th Street Bridge. This facility specializes in building boats of its own, but some topside and below-the-waterline repairs are available.

Crowded between a host of other small yards, Merrill-Stevens Dry Dock (305-324-5211) will come abeam on the northern (and southern) shore just west of the Northwest 12th Avenue Bridge. This facility is the most prestigious repair firm in the greater Miami region. To be succinct, they can do it all. Services include mechanical (gas and diesel), paint, carpentry, fiberglass, electrical, canvas, and marine air-conditioning repairs. How's that for an impressive lineup? Boats are hauled either by a 70-ton travel lift or a 500-ton marine railway.

Austral International Marina (305-325-0177) is found on the river's northern banks a bit farther to the west. Below-the-waterline repairs are available here. The yard uses a crane for haul-outs. Power craft up to 37 feet, and sailcraft as large as 33 feet, can be hauled.

Tamiami Canal splits off from Miami River west of the Northwest 17th Avenue Bridge. This cut holds 5- to 7-foot depths and leads to a few facilities. Eventually the passage is blocked by a low-level fixed bridge.

Bojean Boatyard (305-633-8919) is located on the southern shore not far from the canal's intersection with Miami River. Haul-out (30 ton travelift), below-waterline repairs are available.

Jones Boat Yard (305-635-0891) flanks the southern shores of Tamiami Canal. For a facility so far removed, Jones Boat Yard seems to be a topnotch operation. Again, full mechanical (gas and diesel) and below-the-waterline repairs are available. The yard's travel lift is rated at 60 tons.

A bit farther upstream, Miami River is blocked by a dam. To us it seemed like a long, long way from the ICW intersection.

MIAMI RIVER NAVIGATION

Very little information need be presented here about navigating Miami River except the old saw about holding to the midwidth. Tidal currents do run swiftly on the river, particularly along the easterly portion of the stream. Low-powered craft should be on guard against this rapid water lest they have an untimely meeting with the heavy traffic that is sometimes encountered on the passage.

Except for the entrance east of the SE 2nd Avenue Bridge, the entire river is a no-wake zone. Courteous captains will also cruise along at idle speed past the Dupont Plaza Hotel and Marina docks.

To make good your entrance into Miami River from the ICW, depart the Waterway just north of unlighted daybeacon #57. Cut to the west-southwest and pass unlighted daybeacons #1 and #3 to their northerly sides as you cruise into the river's mouth. The docks of Dupont Plaza will come abeam to the north soon after you enter the stream.

Visiting and resident mariners must contend with a battery of bascule bridges crossing Miami River. These spans have closed vertical clearances ranging from 16 to 21 feet. Usually all the river spans are closed from 7:30 A.M. to 9:00 A.M. and again between 4:30 P.M. and 6:00 P.M.

And Finally

Well, we made it! I hope you have enjoyed our exploration of the remarkably diverse waters of eastern Florida as much as we have. Perhaps you will agree that no other coastline anywhere else in the world has so many different faces to show visiting cruisers.

For continuing coverage of the waters of southern Miami, Coconut Grove, Key Biscayne, and moving still farther south and west to the fabled Florida Keys, please consult *Cruising the Florida Keys,* penned by this writer and his illustrious friend Morgan Stinemetz. Keep the teak oiled and the fiberglass shined and have a great trip. Good luck and good cruising!

GOOD CRUISING!

Bibliography

Bartram, John. *Diary of a Journey Through the Carolinas, Georgia and Florida from July 1, 1765 to April 10, 1942*. Philadelphia: American Philosophical Society, 1952.

Bartram, William. *Travels*. Edited, with commentary and annotated index by Francis Harper. Naturalists ed. New Haven: Yale University Press, 1958.

Cabell, James Branch, and Hanna, Alfred J. *The St. Johns—A Parade of Diversities*. New York: Farrar & Rinehart, 1943.

Cash, William T. *The Story of Florida*. 4 vols. New York: The American Historical Society, Inc., 1938.

Hanna, Alfred J., and Hanna, Kathryn A. *Lake Okeechobee, Wellspring of the Everglades*. Indianapolis: Bobbs-Merrill, 1948.

Lamme, Vernon. *Florida Lore Not Found in the History Books*. Boynton Beach, Florida: Star Publishing Company, 1973.

Lamme, Vernon. *More Florida Lore Not Found in History Books*. Boynton Beach, Florida: Star Publishing Company, 1978.

Panagopoulos, E. P. *New Smyrna: An Eighteenth Century Greek Odyssey*. Gainesville: University of Florida Press, 1966.

Strickland, Alice. *The Valiant Pioneers: A History of Ormond Beach, Volusia County, Florida*. Coral Gables, Fla.: University of Miami Press, 1963.

Tebeau, Charlton W. *A History of Florida*. Coral Gables, Fla.: University of Miami Press, 1971.

Weilding, Philip, and Burghard, August. *Checkered Sunshine: The Story of Fort Lauderdale, 1793-1955*. Gainesville: University of Florida Press, 1966.

Will, Lawrence E. *A Cracker History of Lake Okeechobee*. St. Petersburg, Fla.: Great Outdoors Publishing Co., 1964.

Will, Lawrence E. *Okeechobee Boats and Skippers*. St. Petersburg, Fla.: Great Outdoors Publishing Co., 1965.

Will, Lawrence E. *Okeechobee Hurricane and the Hoover Dike*. St. Petersburg, Fla.: Great Outdoors Publishing Co., 1961.

Will, Lawrence E. *A Dredgeman of Cape Sable*. St. Petersburg, Fla.: Great Outdoors Publishing Co., 1967.

Will, Lawrence E. *Okeechobee Catfishing*. St. Petersburg, Fla.: Great Outdoors Publishing Co., 1965.

Index

Claiborne Young publishes an on-line newsletter known as *The Salty Southeast*. This *free* publication presents all sorts of nautical information and happenings, plus recent changes to the waters and pleasure-craft facilities in the southeastern U.S. You can read *The Salty Southeast* on Claiborne's Web site at http://www.CruisingGuide.com or subscribe directly.

If you would prefer that future issues be sent directly to your e-mail address, send e-mail to majordomo@netpath.net. Leave the subject line blank, and in the body of the e-mail type the words "subscribe saltyse" (without the quotation marks). These two words *must* appear in your e-mail or your subscription won't be successfully added. If your subscription is successful, you will be automatically informed by e-mail, courtesy of the majordomo software package. If you have trouble subscribing, send us e-mail to that effect at opcom@netpath.net.

Let us emphasize, there is *no* charge for this service. It is our privilege to make this information available to our fellow cruisers!